MW00332127

Guidelines
for Office Microsoft® 2010

Nancy Muir | Anita Verno

Paradigm
PUBLISHING
St. Paul • Indianapolis

Managing Editor	Sonja Brown
Developmental Editors	Christine Hurney, Brenda Palo
Contributing Writers	Lisa A. Bucki, Jan Marrelli
Production Editor	Bob Dreas
Cover and Text Designer	Leslie Anderson
Production Specialists	Jaana Bykonich, Ryan Hamner, Julie Johnston
Copy Editors	Susan Capecchi, Amanda Tristano
Proofreader	Molly McBeath
Tester	Lindsay Ryan
Indexer	Schroeder Indexing Services
Illustrator	Cohographics

Acknowledgements: The authors, editors, and publisher thank the following instructors for their helpful suggestions during the planning and development of this textbook: **Julia Basham**, Southern State Community College, Wilmington, OH; **Linda Bettinger**, Southeast Community College, Lincoln, NE; **Lee Ann Boyer**, Mountainland Applied Technical College, Orem, UT; **Lynn Byrd**, Delta State University, Cleveland, MS; **Sally Chumbley**, Evergreen Valley College, San Jose, CA; **Diva Conrad**, City College of San Francisco, San Francisco, CA; **Diane Cornilsen**, Ashford University, Clinton, IA; **Billy Cunningham**, Malcolm X College, Chicago, IL; **Jan Davidson**, Lambton College, Sarnia, Ontario; **Shawna DePlonty**, Sault College of Applied Arts and Technology, Sault Ste. Marie, Ontario; **Mark Doran**, Jackson State Community College, Jackson, TN; **Beverly Forsberg**, Metropolitan Community College, Omaha, NE; **Brian Fuschetto**, Bergen Community College, Paramus, NJ; **Madlyn Huber**, Bridgerland Applied Technology College, Logan, UT; **Jennifer Ingram**, Pulaski Technical College, North Little Rock, AR; **Robertt Neilly**, Seneca College, Newnham Campus, Toronto, Ontario; **Lisa Parsons**, Butler Community College, El Dorado, KS; **Joanne S. Patti**, Community College of Philadelphia, Philadelphia, PA; **Karen Smith**, Technical College of the Lowcountry, Beaufort, SC; **Kathy Tamerlano**, Cuyahoga Community College, Cleveland, OH; **Janine Tiffany**, Reading Area Community College, Reading, PA; **George Ann Woodward**, South Florida Community College, Avon Park, FL

Photo Credits: Page 543 IPhone, Courtesy of Apple Inc.; Page 561 chocolate dessert, © Lachlan Hardy; Page 581 Lee Petty, ISC Archives via Getty Images

Care has been taken to verify the accuracy of information presented in this book. However, the authors, editors, and publisher cannot accept responsibility for Web, e-mail, newsgroup, or chat room subject matter or content, or for consequences from application of the information in this book, and make no warranty, expressed or implied, with respect to its content.

Trademarks: Some of the product names and company names included in this book have been used for identification purposes only and may be trademarks or registered trade names of their respective manufacturers and sellers. For example, Access, Excel, Internet Explorer, Microsoft, Outlook, OneNote, PowerPoint, and Windows are trademarks or registered trademarks of Microsoft Corporation in the United States and/or other countries. The authors, editors, and publisher disclaim any affiliation, association, or connection with, or sponsorship or endorsement by, such owners.

We have made every effort to trace the ownership of all copyrighted material and to secure permission from copyright holders. In the event of any question arising as to the use of any material, we will be pleased to make the necessary corrections in future printings. Thanks are due to the aforementioned authors, publishers, and agents for permission to use the materials indicated.

ISBN 978-0-76384-212-3 (text)
ISBN 978-0-76384-260-4 (text, CD)

CONTENTS

Preface

Learning how to use software should be a simple, straightforward, and engaging experience—right? We think so too, and that's why we wrote *Guidelines for Microsoft Office 2010*.

The publishers of this book listened to what students and instructors were saying about how they wanted to learn the Office suite of programs. What they heard time and again was that people wanted an easy-to-understand book about Office basics that they could use without feeling overwhelmed.

This book is the result. We have taken a step-by-step visual approach to teaching the key features of the Office programs, building knowledge in a logical and easy-to-follow way. We have incorporated end-of-chapter and end-of-module activities that help reinforce learning and assess whether you can apply your new skills in realistic work and school situations. As a bonus, we offer videos on the Student Resources CD for those who want to see each step of each skill demonstrated on screen. See the *Guidelines for Getting Started* section (pages 2-3) for more information about using the CD packaged with this book and for computer system requirements.

Clear and Simple Instruction

Guidelines for Microsoft Office 2010 offers a simple path to mastering Office basics. This path is designed with you in mind and created in a number of ways. First, we prepare you for succeeding in the course by teaching you how to use Outlook to manage your schedules, OneNote to take notes, and the PrintScreen and Windows Snipping Tool to take screen captures. Then you learn some essential computer hardware and software concepts, Windows and Internet basics, and some important features that work in much the same way across the major Office programs.

In the Word, Excel, Access, and PowerPoint modules, you focus on completing tasks using the Office Ribbon, which is a set of graphical tools and commands organized by common tasks. In addition, we provide keystroke combinations and shortcut menus as alternative ways for getting things done. By the time you complete this book, you will be familiar with all the basic tools the Office Ribbon offers and know the advantages of several shortcut methods.

Clear objectives at the beginning of each chapter help you understand what you will accomplish. You are also told which files you need from the Student Resources CD and you're shown the final document or file you produce by completing the chapter skills.

Each skill is presented in a two- or four-page layout with steps always on the left page and screenshots always on the right page. Callouts showing you where to click are numbered to match the steps. By reading the steps and studying the screenshots, you can easily follow every task covered in this book.

In order to keep your learning on track from skill to skill, we provide completed skill images so you can see where you should end up after you complete the steps in each skill.

Interesting Step-by-Step Projects

The modules of this book that address the main Office programs (Word, Excel, Access, and PowerPoint) follow an engaging scenario involving the business of running a chocolate museum that offers exhibits, manages fund-raising efforts, and maintains a gift shop.

Each file you create has a goal—to communicate, educate, manage the business, or entertain the public. When you finish a chapter, you will have created useful materials and learned Office features and skills along the way.

Additional Courseware

Book-specific Website   Go to the Internet Resource Center at www.emcp.net/guidelines to find additional learning tools and reference materials. You can access the same data files that are on the Student Resources CD along with study aids, web links, and tips for using computers effectively in academic and workplace settings.

SNAP Training and Assessment   SNAP is a Web-based program offering an interactive venue for learning Microsoft Office 2010. Along with a learning management system, *SNAP for Guidelines 2010* provides the Skills Videos, hands-on skill tests live in the Office programs, document-based assessments, a concepts test bank, and an online grade book.

Web-based eBook   If you don't want to carry around a textbook, you can travel light by accessing the entire book's contents through the eBook. The *Guidelines* eBook includes hyperlinks to the Skills Videos and dynamic navigation tools to bookmark, highlight, take notes, and jump to specific pages.

Instructor Resources

Print, DVD, and Internet Tools   Instructor resources are available in the printed Instructor's Guide, on DVD, and at the password-protected instructor area of the Internet Resource Center at www.emcp.net/guidelines. These materials include:

- Syllabus suggestions and course planning resources
- Lesson plans with teaching hints and lecture tips
- Model answers and rubrics for evaluating student work
- **EXAM**VIEW® software and test banks (on DVD only)
- PowerPoint® presentations with lecture notes and audio support

Blackboard Cartridge   This set of files allows instructors to create a personalized Blackboard website for their course and provides course content, tests, and the mechanisms for establishing e-discussions and online group conferences. Available content includes a syllabus, test banks, PowerPoint presentations with audio support, and supplementary course materials. Upon request, the files can be available within 24–48 hours. Hosting the site is the responsibility of the educational institution.

Wishing you success with *Guidelines for Microsoft Office 2010*—Nancy Muir and Anita Verno

INTRODUCTION

Your Digital Toolkit

In this book, you learn to use several computer application programs that combine to make an application *suite*. This suite of programs is called Microsoft Office 2010. The programs you learn to use, also referred to as *software*, work with your operating system to enable you to perform various types of tasks. The programs in the suite include Word, a word processing program; Excel, a spreadsheet program; Access, a database program; OneNote, an electronic notebook program; Outlook, a personal information manager; and PowerPoint, a presentation program. You also learn the basic features of the Windows 7 operating system and the Web browsers Internet Explorer 8.0 and Mozilla Firefox.

The Guidelines Book Package
Your book comes with a Student Resources CD that contains 1) files required for completing the activities and 2) Skills Videos that, step by step, demonstrate each skill in the book. You also need access to a computer that has an Internet connection and the Windows 7 operating system with Microsoft Office 2010 software installed. The data files, along with additional references and resources, are also available at the book's website at www.emcp.net/guidelines.

Hardware and Software Requirements
Your book is designed for a computer running a standard installation of the Microsoft Office Standard 2010 or Professional 2010 Edition and the Microsoft Windows 7 (Home Premium, Business, or Ultimate) operating system. To run this suite and operating system effectively, your computer should have the following capabilities:

- 1 gigahertz (GHz) processor or higher; 1 gigabyte (GB) RAM (32-bit) or 2 GB RAM (64-bit)
- CD/DVD drive, USB port, and USB drive or other removable storage medium
- 16 GB available hard-disk space (32-bit) or 20 GB (64-bit)
- DirectX 9 graphics device with WDD7 1.0 or higher

- 1024 by 768 monitor resolution *Note: Screen captures in this book were created using a resolution of 1280 by 800; screens set at a higher resolution may have slightly different proportions.*
- Computer mouse or other pointing device

Start-Up and Shut-Down Procedures
You need to know how to turn the computer on and off and how to insert a CD or DVD and flash drive (if you store your course work on one).

- **To turn on the computer:** Press the power button ⏻ on the front of the CPU, which loads the Windows 7 operating system and prepares the computer for input from you. You may need to log in using assigned user name and password.
- **To insert a CD or DVD:** Press the Open button on the front panel of the CD or DVD drive and the tray opens. Place the disc in the tray with the disc label facing up. Press the Open button again to close the tray.
- **To insert a flash drive:** Insert your flash drive into a USB port. Note that there is only one way to insert the flash drive, so you may have to flip it over so that it fits. Do not force the flash drive into the port. If you need help ejecting the flash drive, check with your instructor.
- **To turn off the computer:** When you are finished working with your computer, click the Windows Start 🪟 button and then click the Shut down option.

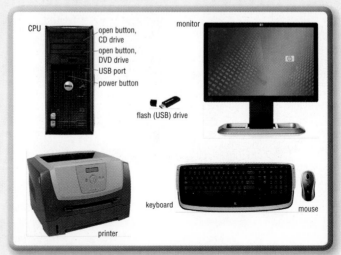

Started

Using the Student Resources CD

Video L_C1_S01

The Student Resources CD that comes with your book contains videos that demonstrate the steps for each skill in the book. You can use the videos to preview the skills before you start working or to clarify how to perform the steps if you have difficulty completing a skill. To run the skills video, your computer needs to have a web browser and the Adobe Flash Player plugin installed. Flash Player is available free of charge from Adobe online at get.adobe.com/flashplayer.

The Student Resources CD also contains typed documents and files you need to complete the module or chapter skills, chapter assessments, and module assessments. Module 2, Chapter 2 teaches you how to copy each module's folder of files from the CD to your flash drive (or other storage medium). Note that you don't need any files for the Introduction, Module 1 and Module 3.

Starting an Office 2010 Application Program

The first module in your book uses the Outlook and OneNote programs. To start Outlook or another program in the Office suite, follow these steps:

1 Click the ⊞ Start button.

2 Click *All Programs*.

3 Click *Microsoft Office*.

4 Click the name of the program you want to start.

Chapter 1

Managing Your Time with Microsoft® Outlook 2010

Developing good organizational and time management skills can help you succeed in both school and your career. Personal information management software, such as Outlook, can simplify the organization of personal and business activities and help you stay on top of things. Outlook contains tools for organizing appointments, managing email, and keeping track of contacts.

One aspect of managing time involves keeping an organized schedule. Calendar is an Outlook scheduling tool that you can use to keep track of appointments, create reminders about events, and schedule meetings.

Knowing where to quickly find email addresses or phone numbers for personal and business contacts is also an essential organizational and time management skill. Contacts is an Outlook tool for creating an electronic address book that stores contact information for the people you communicate with. Because Contacts is linked to your Outlook email address book and the Outlook Social Connector, you can stay up-to-date on your social networks without leaving Outlook.

Skills You Learn

1 Open Outlook and display the Calendar
2 Schedule an appointment in Outlook Calendar
3 Schedule a meeting
4 Add a contact
5 Search for contacts and appointments

Files You Need
In this chapter, you do not need any student data files.

What You Create
In this chapter, you learn how to use Outlook to organize your personal, school, and career life. You schedule an appointment and a meeting in Outlook's digital Calendar. You then send an electronic invitation to others, inviting them to attend a scheduled meeting. You also add your personal and business contacts to Outlook's Contacts list and you learn how to always have schedule and contact information at your fingertips.

Scheduled Appointment

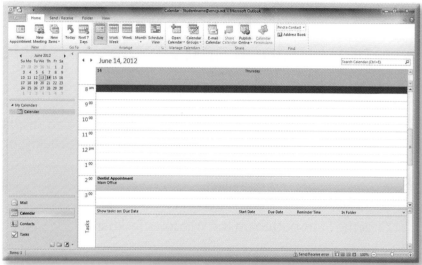

Completed Skill 2

Scheduled Meeting

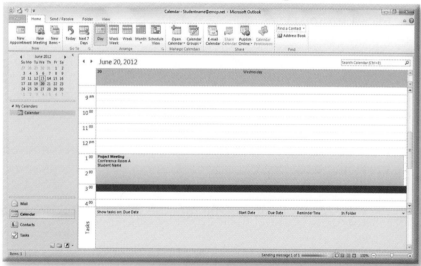

Completed Skill 3

New Contact

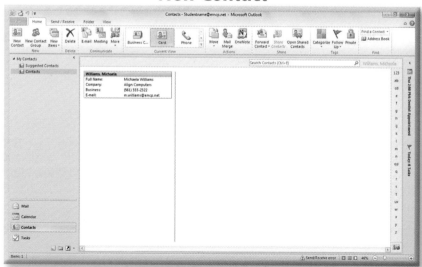

Completed Skill 4

Introduction

Skill 1   Open Outlook and Display the Calendar

Video   I_C1_S01

Outlook contains four main tools—*Mail*, *Calendar*, *Contacts*, and *Tasks*. When you start Outlook, the Mail tool displays by default. Use the Navigation pane at the left of the screen to switch to the Calendar tool. You can display the calendar in a daily, weekly, or monthly view.

Steps

1 *Another Way*
If you have used Microsoft Outlook recently, the program name appears in the recently used programs list along the left side of the Start menu. Simply click on it there to open it.

1 Click the Start button on the Windows Taskbar.

2 Click *All Programs*. You may also simply hover the mouse pointer over *All Programs* and all the program names display.

3 Click *Microsoft Office*.

4 Click *Microsoft Outlook 2010* on the list of applications in the menu.

5 *Shortcut*
Display Calendar
Ctrl + 2

5 Click the Calendar button in the Navigation pane.

6 If the Day view is not active, click the Day button in the Arrange group on the Home tab.

▶**Tip** To move forward or backward a day in Day view, or to move to the next or previous month in Month view, you can use the Forward and Back navigation buttons.

7 Click the Month button in the Arrange group on the Home tab.

8 Click the Next 7 Days button in the Go To group on the Home tab.

▶**Tip** The current date will display or be highlighted, depending on the view.

9 Click tomorrow's date in the Date Navigator at the top of the Navigation pane.

10 Click the Today button in the Go To group to display your calendar for today.

Taking It Further

Customizing the Look of Your Calendar   The View tab contains many options for customizing the look of your calendar. To change the background color, click the Color button in the Color group and then click a background color. You can also change the time intervals shown in the Calendar by clicking the Time Scale button in the Arrangement group and selecting an interval in the drop-down list. You can also use the Time Scale button to change the time zone.

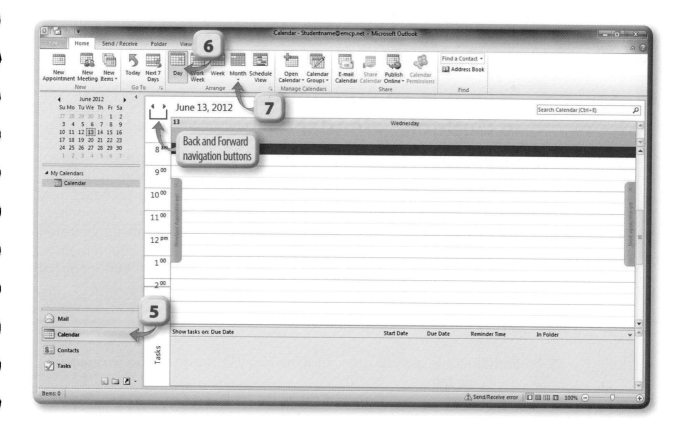

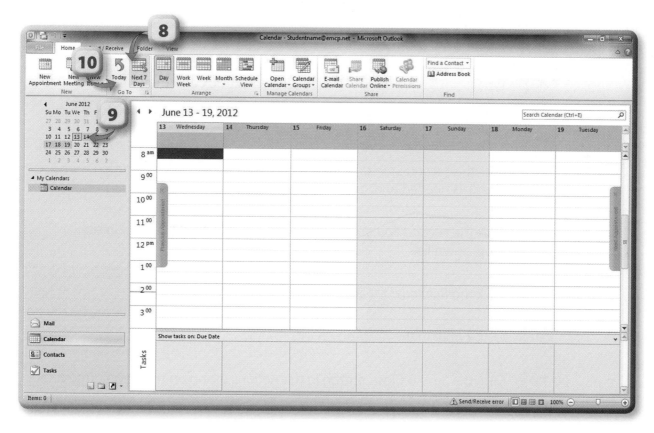

Introduction

Introduction

Skill 2

Schedule an Appointment in Outlook Calendar

Video I_C1_S02

Calendar can help keep you organized when you use it to schedule appointments. An appointment is any activity that you schedule in your calendar with a starting time and an ending time. You can schedule homework assignments and exams as appointments. If you specify an appointment location, it is shown in parentheses next to the appointment information. You can also set an appointment reminder to help you remember the appointment. You can add appointments in any view.

Steps

1 With Outlook Calendar open, click the Today button in the Go To group on the Home tab.

2 Click tomorrow's date in the Date Navigator at the top of the Navigation pane.

3 Click the New Appointment button in the New group on the Home tab.

3 Shortcut
Create New Appointment
Ctrl + N

4 Type Dentist Appointment in the *Subject* text box and then press the Tab key.

5 Type Main Office in the *Location* text box.

6 Click the second *Start time* list arrow and click *2:00 PM* in the drop-down list. (Scroll as needed to display *2:00 PM* in the list.)

▶**Tip** Click the *All day event* check box if the activity lasts the entire day and does not have a start or end time, such as a vacation day.

7 Click the second *End time* list arrow and click *3:00 PM (1 hour)* in the drop-down list.

▶**Tip** Choose another date for *End time* in order to schedule a multiple-day appointment, such as a vacation or conference.

8 Click the *Reminder* list arrow in the Options group on the Appointment tab.

9 Click *1 hour* in the drop-down list.

▶**Tip** In the Options group, use the Recurrence button to enter an appointment that occurs on a regular basis, such as daily, weekly, monthly, or yearly.

10 Click the Save & Close button in the Actions group on the Appointment tab.

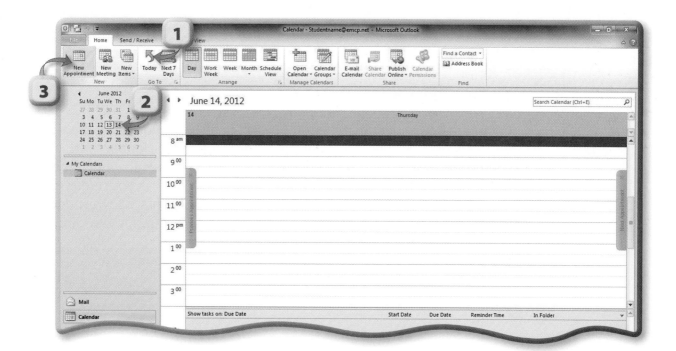

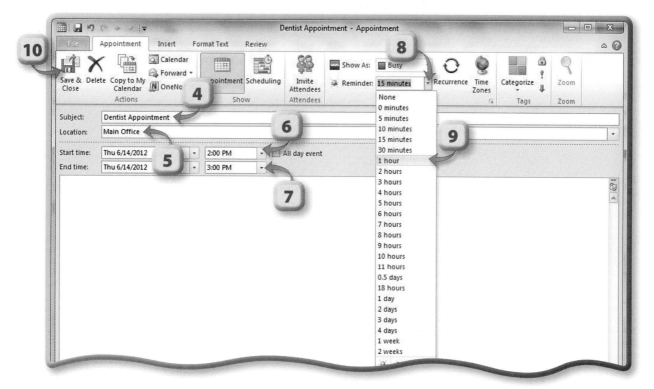

Taking It Further

Organizing Your Calendar To help organize your school schedule, you can create appointments for project due dates and homework assignments. You may want to add a reminder to these appointments to help you get your work finished on time. You can also plan your course work by creating a multi-day appointment with the subject "Chapter 1" to show which days you plan to work on this chapter.

Introduction

Skill 3 — Schedule a Meeting

Video I_C1_S03

If you need to schedule a meeting, you can use Outlook Calendar to send out a meeting request. A meeting request is an appointment that is sent to other people and can include the meeting location and other important information about the meeting, such as its topic and goals. Sending a meeting request is one way you can integrate the Outlook Calendar and eMail tools. Responses to your meeting requests appear in your email Inbox folder. Recipients can respond to a meeting request by adding the meeting to their Outlook Calendars or declining the request.

Steps

1 With Outlook Calendar open, click the Day button in the Arrange group on the Home tab.

2 Click the New Meeting button in the New group.

3 Type Project Meeting in the *Subject* text box and then press the Tab key.

4 Type Conference Room A in the *Location* text box.

5 Click the first *Start time* list arrow and click the date that is one week from today in the drop-down list. The date displayed for the *End time* also changes.

6 Click the second *Start time* list arrow and click *1:00 PM* in the drop-down list.

7 Click the second *End time* list arrow and click *3:00 PM (2 hours)* in the drop-down list.

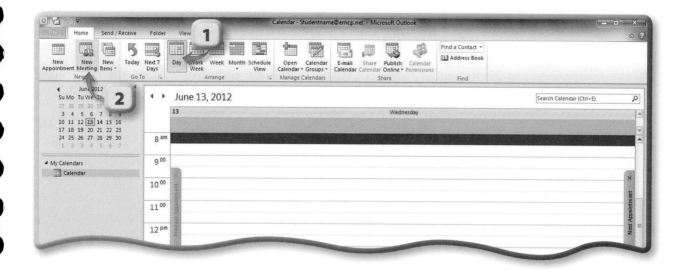

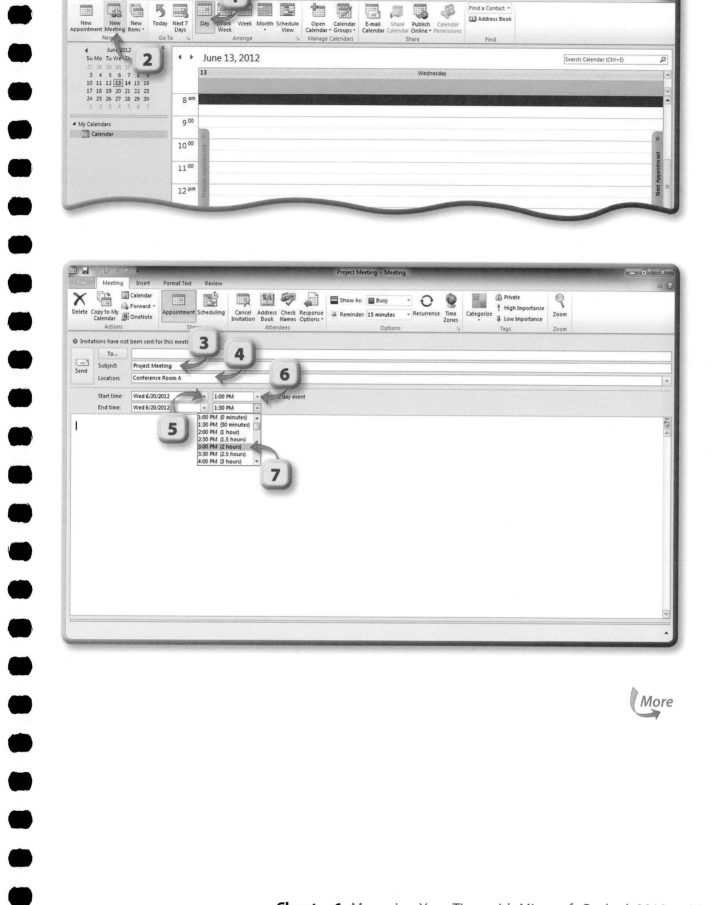

More

8 Type *Please bring your research notes* in the body of the meeting request.

Tip You can also click the To button to select email addresses from your Address Book.

Tip If you are working on a computer that has Outlook configured for your personal use, you will be able to complete Steps 10–14.

Tip Separate email addresses with a comma (,) or semi-colon (;) if you are inviting more than one person to the meeting.

9 Exchange email addresses with a classmate and type the classmate's email address in the *To* text box.

10 Click the Send button.

11 Click the Mail button in the Navigation pane to check your email.

12 Double-click the new email you received from your classmate.

13 Click the Accept button.

14 In the drop-down list, click *Send the Response Now* to respond to the meeting request.

Taking It Further

Configuring Outlook Outlook needs to be set up or configured for a specific user. If you are using Outlook on a shared computer, you will need to log in to Outlook before you can use it. However, for security purposes most schools do not permit students to configure Outlook.

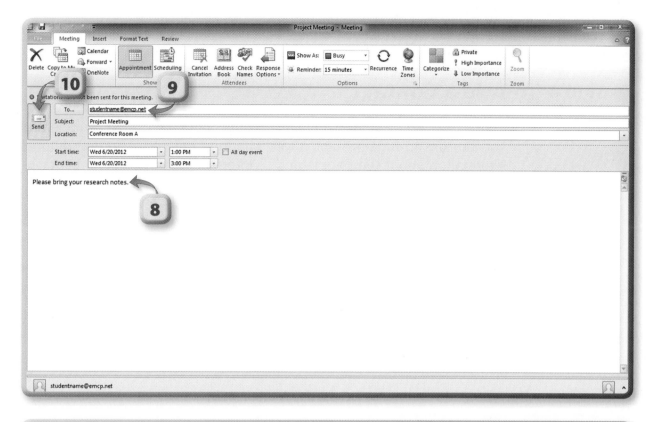

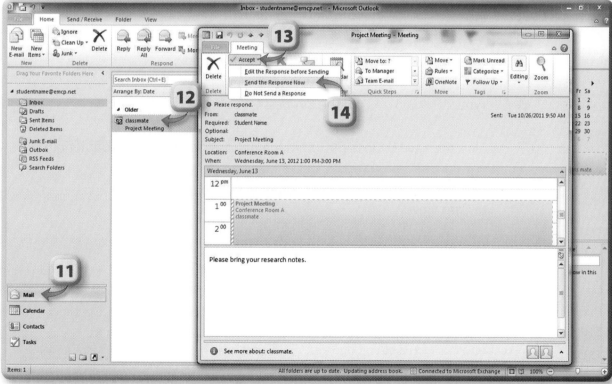

Introduction

Introduction

Chapter 1

Skill 4

Add a Contact

Video I_C1_S04

Contacts is an Outlook tool that you can use to organize and save information about the people and businesses that you communicate with. The information you enter about a contact can include just the contact's name and email address, or it can include additional information, such as the contact's street address, cell phone number, picture, birthday, and so forth.

Steps

1 Shortcut
Display Contacts
Ctrl + 3

Tip The *File as* text box is completed automatically after you enter the full name. This entry is used to organize the Contacts list in alphabetical order.

Tip The *Display as* text box is completed automatically after you enter the email address.

Tip If, after typing in the phone number, a Location Information dialog box appears, click Cancel to close the dialog box. If another warning message appears, click OK to close the dialog box.

1 With Outlook open, click the Contacts button in the Navigation pane.

2 Click the New Contact button in the New group on the Home tab.

3 Type Michaela Williams in the *Full Name* text box.

4 Type Align Computers in the *Company* text box.

5 Type m.williams@emcp.net in the *E-mail* text box.

6 Type (561) 555-2322 in the *Business* text box.

7 Click the Save & Close button in the Actions group on the Contact tab.

8 Click the Card button in the Current View group on the Home tab to change to Card view.

Taking It Further

Adding Contact Pictures You can add a picture to a contact form to help you quickly connect a face to a name or a logo to a business contact. If both the sender and the recipient use Microsoft Outlook 2010 or Microsoft Office Outlook 2007, the contact's picture will appear in the email message header. To add a picture, click the Picture button in the Options group on the Contact tab and then click *Add Picture*. Browse to locate the picture that you want to add, and then double-click the file name.

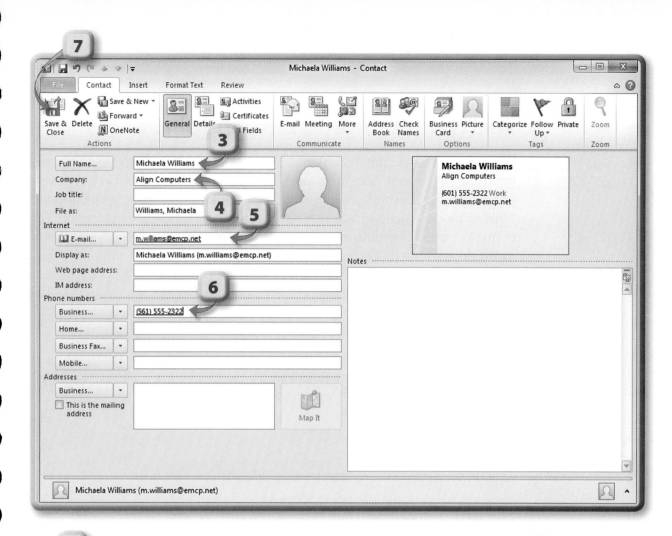

Introduction

Introduction

Skill 5

Search for Contacts and Appointments

Video I_C1_S05

Being organized means having information at your fingertips and knowing how best to manage it. With Outlook, you can easily find contacts and appointments by using the *Search Contacts* and *Search Calendar* text boxes. You only need to type in the information you are looking for—and you can even search using partial information. For example, you can type part of a business name or phone number.

Steps

1 With Outlook open, click the Calendar button in the Navigation pane.

2 Click in the *Search Calendar* text box and type Dentist Appointment. Outlook displays the appointment you created in Skill 2.

3 Double-click the appointment.

4 Change the appointment start time to *2:30 PM*.

5 Change the appointment end time to *3:30 PM*.

6 Click the Save & Close button in the Actions group.

7 Click the Contacts button in the Navigation pane.

8 Click in the *Search Contacts* text box and type (561. Outlook displays the Michaela Williams contact.

9 Click the Close Search button in the Close group on the Search Tools Search tab.

10 Click Close to close Outlook.

2 *Shortcut*
Open *Search Calendar* Text Box
Ctrl + E

▶ *Tip* You can refine your search by using the buttons on the Search Tools Search tab

8 *Shortcut*
Open *Search Contacts* Text Box
Ctrl + E

Taking It Further

Exploring the Search Tools Search Tab
When you click the Search Contacts or Search Calendar text box, the Search Tools Search tab appears, enabling you to refine your search. Commands in the Scope group specify which Outlook folders are included in your search. Use commands in the Refine group to narrow your search. Commands in the Options group allow you to reuse previous searches, saving you time and effort retyping search criteria. For example, click the Recent Searches button and you find your recent search for *Dentist Appointment* in the drop-down list.

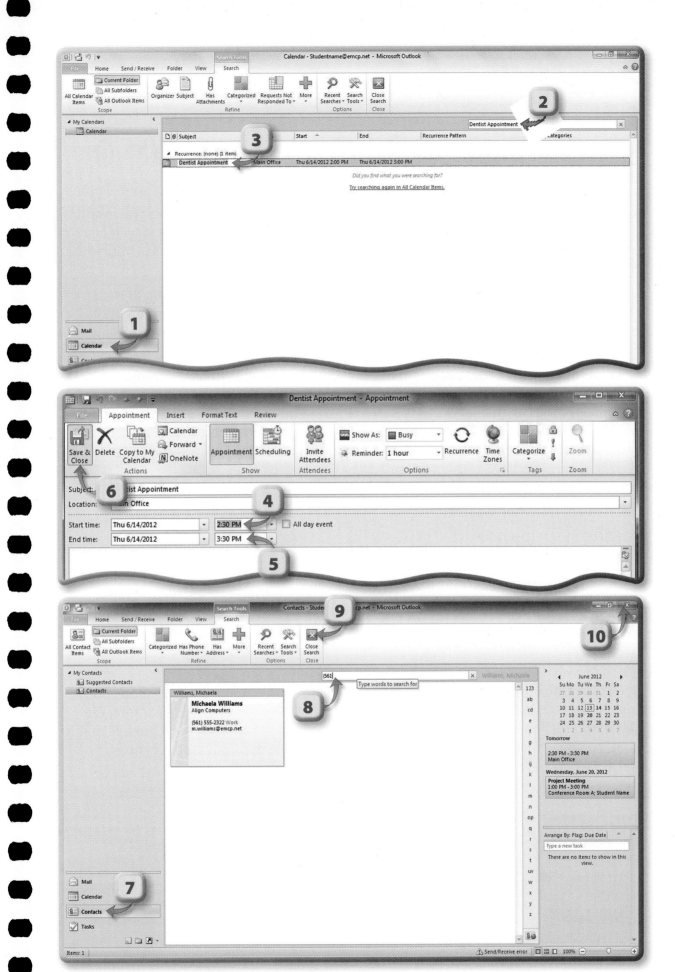

Chapter 2

Using Microsoft® OneNote 2010

Do you ever take notes and then lose the piece of paper you wrote them on? Do you ever find a great website and then have to spend time searching for it when you want to view it again? One way to avoid these problems is to use OneNote as a digital notebook for all of your ideas and important information.

As a student, you probably have used a binder or notebook with subject dividers to keep your course notes organized. OneNote builds on the same idea, but stores your notebook electronically, on the computer, and organizes it into sections. Each section can represent a different subject and contain one or more pages.

OneNote has many advantages over a paper notebook. You are able to type information or copy from a website or other document. You are also able to easily delete, move, and update the information. You can use keywords to search the notebook, which helps you to quickly find what you need. Plus, OneNote automatically saves your information, including source Web addresses, so you don't have to worry about losing your notes.

Skills You Learn

1   Create a notebook with sections
2   Add content to a page
3   Tag notes
4   Insert a link to online content

Files You Need
In this chapter, you do not need any student data files.

What You Create
In this chapter, you create a digital notebook and organize the notebook into sections. You add and fill pages, flag important notes with tags, and include links to outside content. We suggest that once you know how to use OneNote, you make a section for each module in this textbook. As you work through the textbook, use the pages in each notebook section for your assignments and study notes.

Digital Notebook

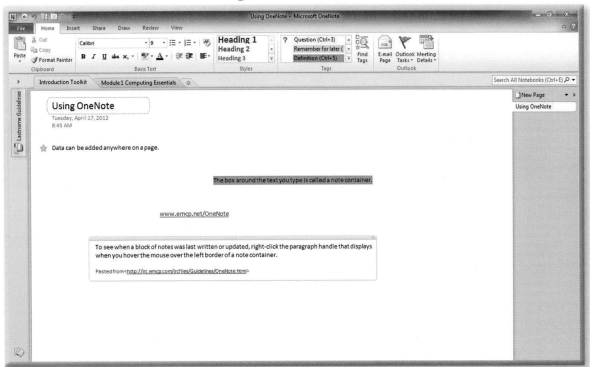

Introduction

Skill 1

Create a Notebook with Sections

 I_C2_S01

In OneNote, you can create a digital notebook to collect all of your notes and information in one place. You can then search for information quickly and easily. Each new notebook you create consists of one section and one page. By default, the page contains a title box. Below the title box, OneNote lists the date and time that you created the page.

Steps

1 *Another Way*
If you have used Microsoft OneNote recently, the program name appears in the recently used programs list along the left side of the Start menu. Simply click on it there to open it.

1 Click the Start button on the Windows taskbar.

2 Click *All Programs*.

3 Click *Microsoft Office*.

4 Click *Microsoft OneNote 2010* on the list of applications that appears in the menu.

5 Click the File tab.

6 Click New.

7 Click *My Computer*.

8 Type Lastname Guidelines in the *Name* text box, but replace *Lastname* with your last name.

9 Click Browse and save the notebook on your storage medium.

10 Click Create Notebook.

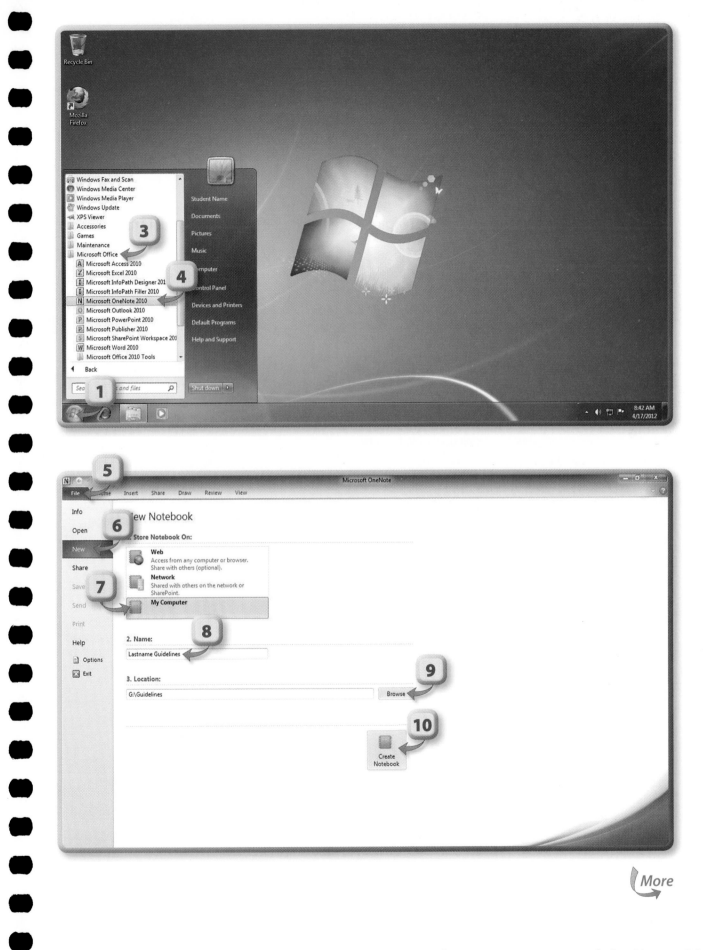

More

11 Right-click the New Section 1 tab and click *Rename*.

12 Type Introduction Toolkit and press Enter. Use this OneNote section for your notes from the Introduction section of this textbook.

13 Click the Create a New Section tab, type Module 1 Computing Essentials, and then press Enter. Use this section for your notes from Module 1 of this textbook.

14 If you are not continuing on to the next skill, click the Close button.

▶ **Tip** Color code your section tabs to better organize the sections containing similar material. To do this, right-click the tab, click *Section Color*, and then choose a color from the list.

▶ **Tip** OneNote automatically and continuously saves your work so there is no need for you to save it manually.

Taking It Further

Storing a Notebook on the Web   When you create a new notebook, you can choose to store it on the Web rather than on your computer as you did in Step 7 of Skill 1. If the notebook is stored on the Web, you will then be able to access your notebook from any computer or any web browser. To store your notebook on the Web, you will need a location, such as a SkyDrive account. SkyDrive is a free online storage service. You can sign in to your SkyDrive account when you select the option to store your notebook on the Web. If you don't have a SkyDrive account, you can click the Sign up for Windows Live SkyDrive link.

Completed Skill 1

Introduction

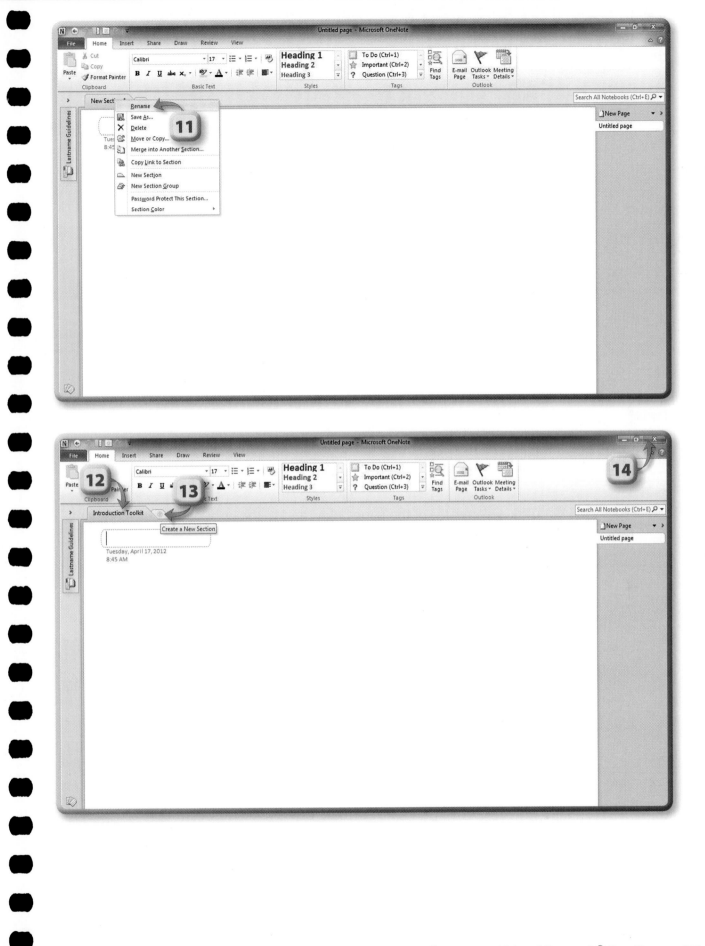

Introduction

Skill 2

Add Content to a Page

 Video ▶ I_C2_S02

You can add data anywhere on a notebook page. To type your notes, click the spot on the page where you want the note to appear and then start typing. OneNote creates a box called a *note container* around each block of text that you type.

The content in a note container is not limited to text—you can also add pictures, tables, equations, files, screenshots, audio, video, and original drawings. You can also move and size note containers.

Steps

1 With your Guidelines OneNote notebook open, click the Introduction Toolkit tab, if it is not already selected.

▶ **Tip** Each page title also appears on its corresponding page tab in the right-hand pane. If you leave the title box blank, the text in the first line of your notes automatically becomes the title of the page.

2 Type Using OneNote in the title box to change the name of the page.

3 Click a blank area of the page below the current time and type Data can be added anywhere on a page. You have added a self-help tip on your notebook page.

4 Click a blank area of the page below and to the right of the note container you created in Step 3 and type The box around the text you type is called a note container.

▶ **Tip** You can move note containers by hovering your mouse pointer over the top bar until the mouse pointer turns into four arrows. You can then drag the container to move it to another location on the page.

5 If you are not continuing on to the next skill, click the Close button.

Taking It Further

Creating and Naming New Pages

Typically, a notebook section in a paper notebook consists of more than one page. To add a new page to the current section of your OneNote notebook, click the New Page tab drop-down arrow in the right-hand pane and then click *New Page*. You can navigate among pages by clicking a page tab in the right-hand pane. When naming a page, keep in mind that page names should be meaningful and reflect the page content. You can change the page name by typing text in the title box.

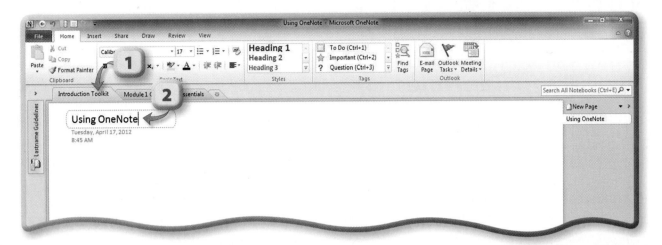

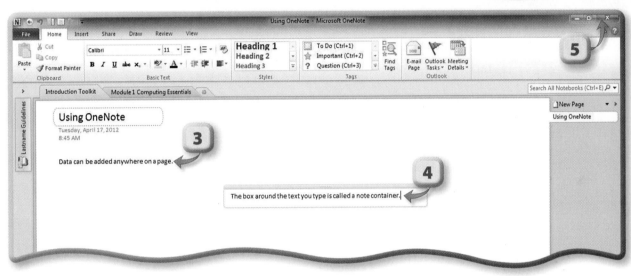

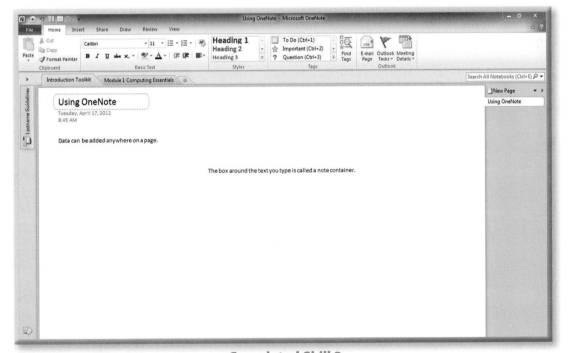

Completed Skill 2

Introduction

Skill 3

Video ▶ I_C2_S03

Tag Notes

When you are taking a lot of notes, it is useful to be able to flag important notes so you can go back to them quickly. OneNote makes this easy by providing several predefined note tags, such as *Important* and *To Do*. Use these predefined note tags to organize your notes. You can also create your own custom note tags and create a summary of tagged items.

Steps

1. With your Guidelines OneNote notebook open, click the Introduction Toolkit tab, if it is not already selected.

2. Click the note container containing the text *Data can be added anywhere on a page.*

3. Click the Home tab.

4. Click the More button next to the Tags gallery in the Tags group.

▶Tip Click *Customize Tags* in the Tags gallery to create your own custom note tag.

5. Click *Important*.

6. Click the note container containing the text *The box around the text you type is called a note container.*

7 **Another Way**
Right-click a note container and click *Tag*.

7. Click the More button next to the Tags gallery in the Tags group on the Home tab.

8. Click *Definition*.

▶Tip The Tags Summary pane shows all tagged items. Use the *Group tags by* and *Search* drop-down arrows to filter the tags.

9. Click Find Tags in the Tags group on the Home tab to display the Tags Summary pane.

10. Click the Close button on the Tags Summary pane to close it.

11. Click the Close button if you are not continuing on to the next skill.

Completed Skill 3

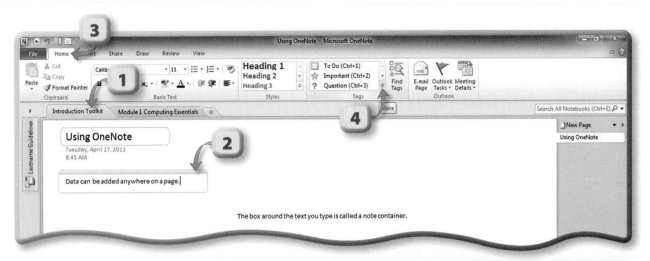

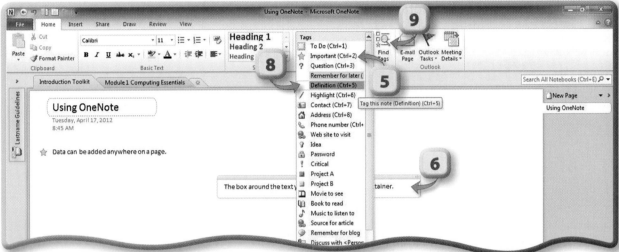

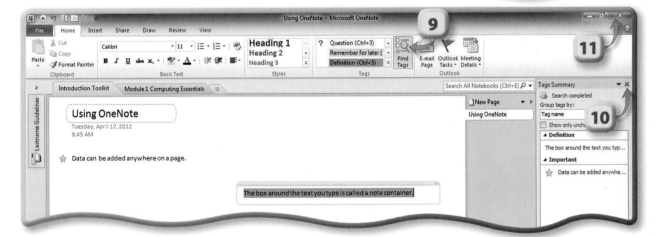

Taking It Further

Creating and Using a To-Do List If you need to create a task or to-do list, use the *To Do* tag. This tag adds a check box to the left of the content in a note container. You can then create a To Do list on a separate page by clicking the Find Tags button and then clicking the Create Summary Page button at the bottom of the Tags Summary task pane. Once you create this list, you can use it to keep track of which tasks are completed and which remain. To indicate that you have done a task, click the *To Do* check box next to the item, which places a check mark in the box.

Introduction

Skill 4

Insert a Link to Online Content

Video   I_C2_S04

When researching on the Web, you can copy useful information from a web page to a OneNote page. OneNote creates a note container for the pasted information. A great feature of OneNote is that when you paste that information into the OneNote page, it automatically places the website's location (URL) in the note container. Having the URL with your research notes ensures that you know where the information came from and saves you time in documenting your research sources. Plus, you can easily go back to the website by clicking the link on the OneNote page.

Steps

1 With your Guidelines OneNote notebook open, click the Introduction Toolkit tab, if it is not already selected.

2 Click a blank area of the page below the existing note containers and type www.emcp.net/OneNote.

3 Click the link www.emcp.net/OneNote to display the web page in your browser window.

4 On the displayed web page, triple-click the text below *OneNote Tip* to select it.

5 Press Ctrl + C to copy the selected information to your Clipboard.

6 Close the browser window.

▶ *Tip* Create a list of the websites in your notebook pages by tagging them as *Web sites to visit*. Later, you can create a Tags Summary list of all such websites. If you add links, click the Refresh Results button to update the list.

7 Click a blank area of the *Using OneNote* page and press Ctrl + V to paste the copied information. The information is pasted along with the URL that records where the information was pasted from.

8 Click the Close button to close OneNote.

Taking It Further

Linking within a Notebook You can also create links to locations within your notebook. These links allow you to navigate your notes quickly. Right-click any text paragraph, page tab, or section tab and click *Copy Link to* (the word that follows to will change depending on what is right-clicked). Next, place the insertion point where you want to insert the link and then press Ctrl + V. When you click the link, it will jump to the paragraph, page, or section whose destination link you copied.

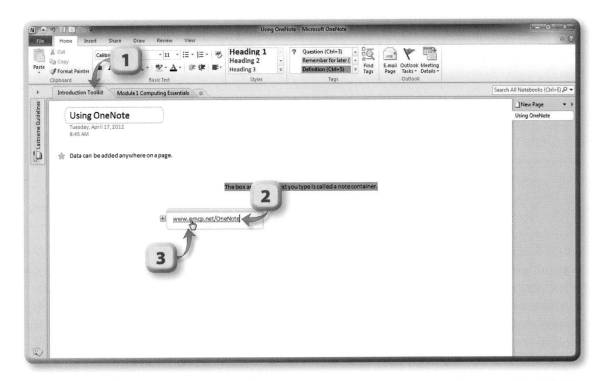

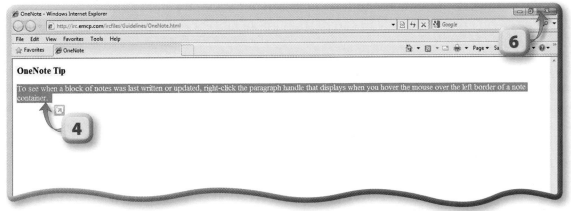

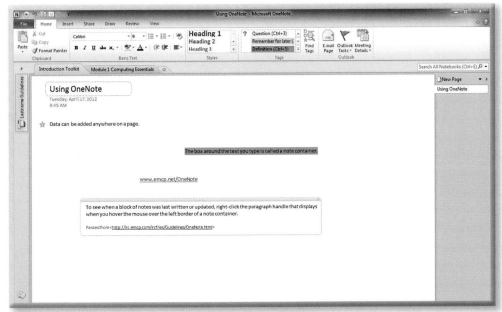

Completed Skill 4

Chapter 3

Taking Screenshots

A screenshot captures a picture of your computer monitor screen. You can use screenshots to create a simple instruction manual by inserting the screenshots in a document and adding callouts or labels to point out specific items in the pictures. You can also attach a screenshot to an email message.

As you work through this textbook, if you have difficulty or encounter an error message, you can take a screenshot and send it to your instructor. After reviewing the screenshot, your instructor can then help you to learn what went wrong or explain how to fix the error. Your instructor may also want you to take a screenshot to confirm that you have completed some of the skills or assessments in this textbook.

You can capture a screenshot of the entire desktop by using the Print Screen key. The Print Screen key copies the screenshot to the Clipboard. A temporary storage area, the Clipboard holds the screen image so that you can paste it into a file. For example, you could paste it into a WordPad document.

On occasion, you may need to capture only a portion of the screen. You can then use the Snipping Tool program instead of the Print Screen key. This program is a Windows 7 utility. With Snipping Tool, you can capture a portion of the screen, copy it to the Clipboard, and then paste it in a document. You can also save the screen snipping in various graphic file formats.

Skills You Learn

1 Take a screenshot
2 Use the Snipping Tool

Files You Need
In this chapter, you do not need any student data files.

What You Create
In this chapter, you capture an image of your entire desktop and paste it in a WordPad document. You also capture an image of the Taskbar on your desktop and add it to your study notes in OneNote.

Desktop Screenshot

Taskbar Screenshot Pasted into OneNote

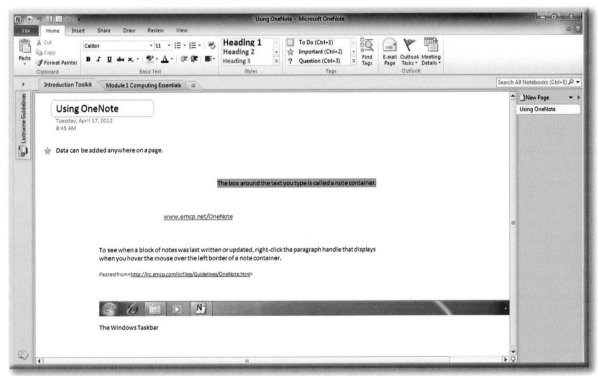

Introduction

Skill 1

Video I_C3_S01

Take a Screenshot

You can use the Print Screen key to take a screenshot of your entire screen, such as the desktop, including the Taskbar and all open windows. This key is located at the top-right area of your keyboard. When you press the Print Screen key, the image of your current screen is copied to a temporary storage area called the Clipboard. You can then paste the screenshot into a document. In this skill, you paste a screenshot into WordPad. WordPad is a utility that is installed with Windows 7.

Steps

▶ **Tip** On a laptop computer, you often need to press the Fn Key while you press the Print Screen key.

▶ **Tip** The Windows Clipboard will store only the most recent image captured.

1 Close any open windows to clear your desktop.

2 Press the Print Screen key to copy a screenshot, or image, of the desktop.

3 Click the Start button.

4 Click *All Programs*.

5 Click *Accessories*.

6 Click *WordPad* to open the program.

7 Click the WordPad tab.

8 Click *Page setup*.

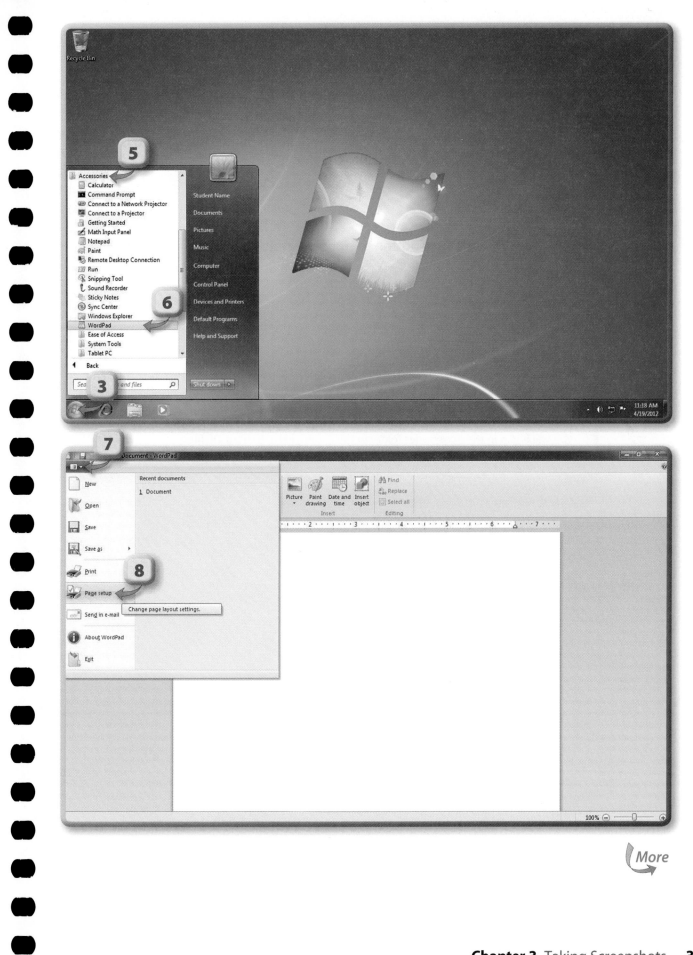

More

▶ Tip Landscape orientation makes the width of the page longer than the height and is a better fit for most screenshots.

▶ Tip You have several options for sharing a screenshot. You can print it and share the hard copy. In addition, you can save the document you pasted it into and then send it as an email attachment.

9 Click the *Landscape* option in the *Orientation* section of the Page Setup dialog box.

10 Click OK to close the Page Setup dialog box.

11 Click the Paste button in the Clipboard group of the Home tab to paste the screenshot of your desktop into the document.

12 Close the document.

13 Click the Don't Save button to close the WordPad window without saving the file.

Taking It Further

Using the Paint Program If you want to edit a screenshot, you can paste the screenshot in an image editing program, such as the Paint program. The Paint program is another Windows 7 utility and you will find it in the Accessories folder in the Start menu. You can use the tools in the Paint program to add callouts, erase or crop part of the screenshot, rotate the screenshot, and resize the screenshot. You can also add and edit the screenshot colors. You can choose to save the screenshot from within Paint as a JPG, PNG, BMP, or TIF file.

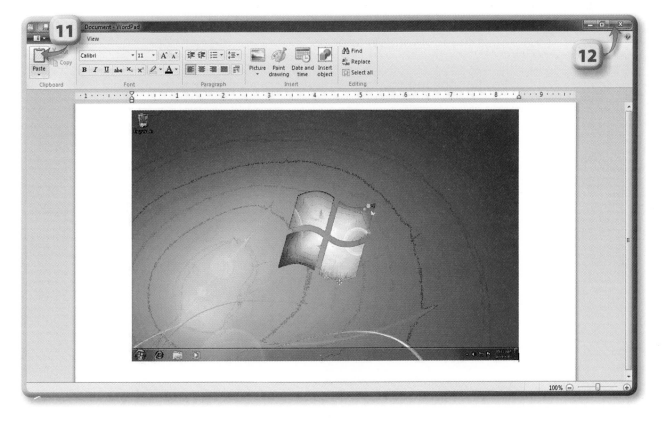

Introduction

Introduction

Skill 2

Video   I_C3_S02

Use the Snipping Tool

In Skill 1, you learned to take a screenshot of the entire desktop by pressing the Print Screen key. If you want to capture only a portion of the screen, instead of the entire desktop, you can use the Snipping Tool. Snipping Tool is a Windows 7 utility. After you take a screenshot with the Snipping Tool, you can copy it to the Clipboard and then paste it into a document. You can also save the file and insert it into a document or send it as an email attachment.

Steps

1 Click the Start button.

2 Click *All Programs*.

3 Click *Accessories*.

4 Click *Snipping Tool* in the list of applications. The screen dims and the Snipping Tool window appears.

5 Position the mouse pointer on the top-left corner of the Taskbar.

6 Press and hold the left mouse button and then drag your mouse to the lower-right corner of the Taskbar. The selected area is surrounded by a red border.

7 Release the left mouse button to display the screenshot in the Snipping Tool window.

8 Click the Copy button to copy the screenshot to the Clipboard.

9 Click the Start button.

10 Click *WordPad*.

▶**Tip** If you want to capture the entire screen, simply click in one corner and drag to the corner diagonal to it.

▶**Tip** If you are not happy with the capture, click the New button to start over.

▶**Tip** If *WordPad* does not appear in the list of frequently used programs above *All Programs*, follow Steps 4-6 in Skill 1.

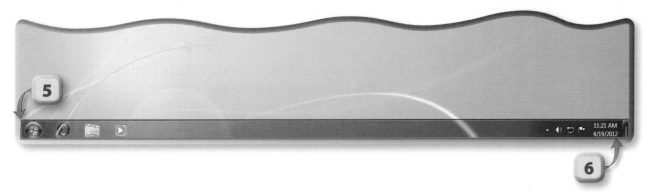

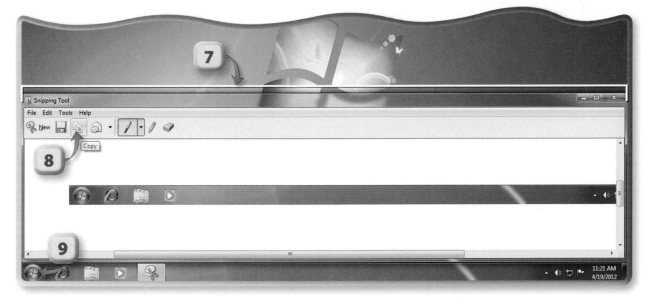

 More

Introduction

11 **Another Way**
As an alternative to copying and pasting the screenshot, you can save the screenshot and then insert it in a document.

▶**Tip** You have several options for sharing a snipped screen. You can print it and share the hard copy. If you want to share an electronic copy, you can save the image as a graphic file from within the Snipping Tool, and then share the graphic file as an email attachment or upload it to a web page.

▶**Tip** You do not need to save the snipped image to WordPad before saving it to OneNote.

11 Click the Paste button in the Clipboard group on the Home tab to paste the Taskbar screenshot into the document.

12 Press the Enter key and then type, This screenshot of the Taskbar was created using the Snipping Tool.

13 Close the WordPad document.

14 Click the Don't Save button to close the WordPad window without saving the document.

15 Click the Close button in the upper-right corner of the Snipping Tool window.

16 In the warning box asking if you want to save changes to the snip, click No.

17 Start OneNote.

18 Click the Introduction Toolkit tab.

19 Click a blank area of the page and then click the Paste button in the Clipboard group on the Home tab to paste the screenshot of the Taskbar on the OneNote page.

20 Type The Windows Taskbar.

21 Close OneNote.

Taking It Further

Learning More about the Snipping Tool When you capture screenshots with the Snipping Tool, you can save them in a variety of common graphic file formats, including JPG, PNG, and GIF. If you save your screenshot, you will be able to use it again later. You can also annotate screenshots in the Snipping Tool by clicking the Pen button on the toolbar and then writing on or around the screenshot. If you make a mistake, click the Eraser button and erase your mistake.

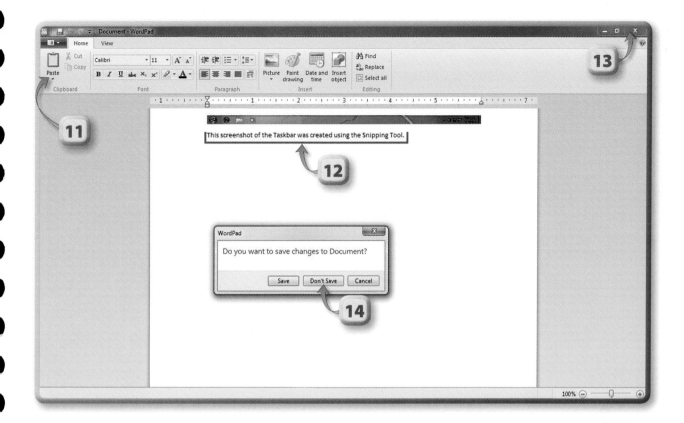

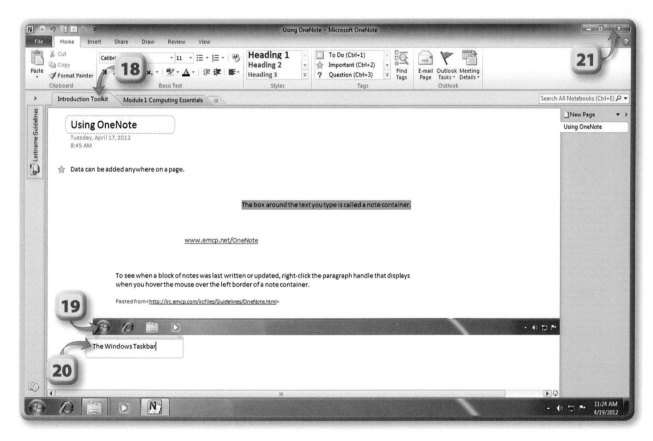

Introduction

MODULE 1

Computing Essentials

What Is a Computer System and How Does It Work?

How Do Operating Systems Software and Applications Software Differ?

This module provides a brief overview of fundamental computing concepts, including the components of a computer system, the methods computers use to process data, the elements of a computer network, and the two major types of software for personal computer systems.

Step-by-step activities are not included with these concepts. Instead, you are encouraged to explore your own computer system to identify the hardware and software components described in this module. Doing so will help you understand the amazing capabilities of the computing devices you work with every day.

What Is a Computer System

A personal computer system is made up of a central processing unit (CPU) and any attached equipment, or hardware. The hardware and software in a computer system work together to turn data into information through a process called the *information processing cycle*. Every personal computing device—from a smartphone to a laptop or desktop computer—uses a basic information processing cycle, which follows these steps:

1 The user enters data using an input device such as a keyboard or touch screen.

2 The CPU processes the data into information and stores it in the internal memory.

3 Information is sent to the computer's screen or another output device such as a printer.

4 Information is stored on a flash drive or other storage medium for future use.

Computer System Hardware

The illustration below shows a typical desktop computer system with the hardware responsible for carrying out the four parts of the information processing cycle.

Input devices. These hardware items, such as a mouse or keyboard, allow you to enter commands and data into your computer.

Processing component. The CPU performs the mathematical operations and coordinates the functions of the computer system. In a personal computer, the CPU is typically a microprocessor. It is located on the motherboard, the main circuit board of the computer. The physical location of the motherboard varies, depending on the type of computer. For example, in a laptop, the CPU may be in the lower half. In a desktop computer, the CPU may be in a tower.

Output devices. The job of output devices is to display information from your computer in a variety of forms, including in print, as sound, or as images.

Storage devices. You use storage devices for saving data that you want to use again. Storage media, ranging from your computer hard drive to removable storage such as a DVD or flash drive, vary in the amount of data they can store. Flash drives are popular because they are small, highly portable, inexpensive, and can hold a large amount of data.

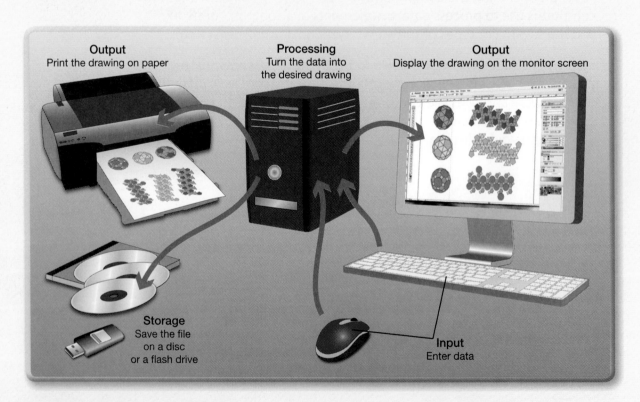

Output
Print the drawing on paper

Processing
Turn the data into the desired drawing

Output
Display the drawing on the monitor screen

Storage
Save the file on a disc or a flash drive

Input
Enter data

and How Does It Work?

The Motherboard

The main circuit board in a computer is called the motherboard and its importance in the system deserves special attention. The motherboard is a thin sheet of fiberglass or other material with electrical pathways that connect these key components of the information processing cycle:

- microprocessor/CPU
- memory chips
- expansion slots for holding expansion cards

The illustration below shows these motherboard components, along with other necessary elements, including a power supply and ports for "plugging in" external hardware, such as a keyboard, mouse, and printer.

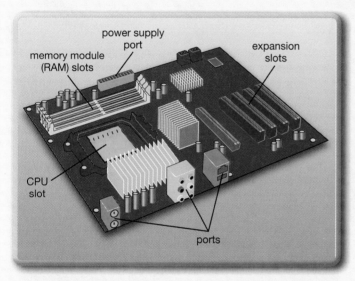

Microprocessor. The CPU of your computer is a microprocessor (also called *processor*) located on the motherboard. It is a thin wafer or chip containing an integrated circuit that processes your requests. Some computers have two or more processors.

Memory. Two kinds of memory are part of your computer, and they are provided on tiny silicon chips etched with electrical circuits: (1) permanent memory, called read-only memory, or ROM, which contains start-up instructions and other permanent instructions; (2) temporary memory, called random access memory, or RAM, which holds data while your computer is on. When you turn off your computer, the RAM content is erased.

Expansion slots. You can add expansion cards to your motherboard to add capabilities such as increased processing power and enhanced video and audio.

A Computer Network

Computers linked together in a network offer a way to share information and resources. A *network* is a combination of hardware, software, and communication media. Two key types of networks are local area networks (LANs), which connect nearby computers within a home or business, and wide area networks (WANs), which connect distant computers, such as those among a company's branch offices around the country. The Internet is the largest of all WANs. The illustration below shows examples of the devices that make up a basic network.

Individual computing devices. You can connect various computing devices to each other and to the Internet via a network. Networks require a communications medium, such as a wireless signal or a cable. With a network, you can share files and resources, such as a printer or scanner.

Modem. A modem is the hardware that sends and receives data to or from a transmission source, such as a phone or cable line. Types of modems typically used in homes and small offices include dial-up, cable, DSL, and satellite.

Network adapter. A network adapter enables your computer to connect to a wired or wireless network. Wired computers typically support Ethernet standards while wireless computers support Wi-Fi standards. A network interface card (NIC) is one type of network adapter your computer can contain.

Wireless access point. Wireless access points and routers relay data among devices on a network.

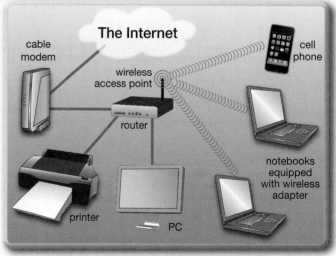

Software is the set of instructions that tells your computer what to do. Personal computer users work with two basic types of software: operating systems and applications. Microsoft Windows, Apple Computer's

MacOS, and Linux are examples of operating systems. Word, Excel, and the other programs in the Microsoft Office Suite are examples of applications.

Operating Systems Software

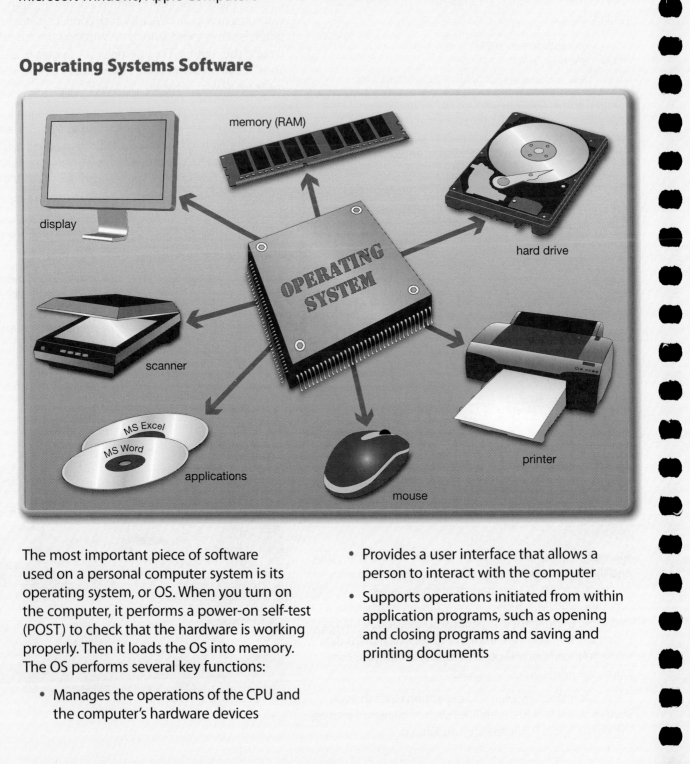

The most important piece of software used on a personal computer system is its operating system, or OS. When you turn on the computer, it performs a power-on self-test (POST) to check that the hardware is working properly. Then it loads the OS into memory. The OS performs several key functions:

- Manages the operations of the CPU and the computer's hardware devices

- Provides a user interface that allows a person to interact with the computer

- Supports operations initiated from within application programs, such as opening and closing programs and saving and printing documents

and Applications Software Differ?

Applications Software

Applications software is the name for the group of programs you use to get your computer-based projects done. Applications include spreadsheets that perform numeric calculations, word processors that create text-based documents, presentation software that creates slide shows, and database software that sorts and manages huge amounts of data. But there are many more, including games, tax preparation, Web design, desktop publishing, and audio and video programs. All of these applications enhance your experience using the computer and provide many tools for completing personal, academic, and work projects.

Some applications may be configured for use on a particular computing device—for example, on a tablet device such as the iPad, on a cell phone, or on a gaming device. Whatever use you might imagine for a computer is likely to have an application available, and new programs are created almost daily. Consider, for example, how many small applications, called *apps*, already are available for mobile phones such as the iPhone.

MODULE 2

Microsoft® Windows 7

Chapter 2, Skill 2 of this module teaches you how to copy the module's folder of files to your flash drive or other storage medium. No files are required for Chapter 1.

Guidelines for Using the

Windows 7 is an operating system. Your computer must have an operating system installed before it can function and before you can install other application programs, such as Microsoft Word.

The operating system performs basic tasks, including recognizing input from the keyboard and the mouse, sending output to the monitor, keeping track of saved files and folders, and controlling disk drives and printers.

Understanding how Windows Interacts with Applications

An application program, such as Microsoft Word, interacts with the operating system to execute many of its commands, including opening and saving a file. Even when you click your mouse to select a command in Word, the operating system is what recognizes the input from the mouse and communicates that information to the application. Similarly, when you print a document, the application program interacts with the operating system in order to communicate with the printer.

The drawing below illustrates the relationships among the user, the application programs, the operating system, and the computer hardware.

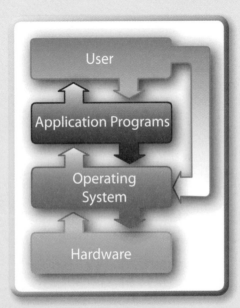

Getting Started with Windows

Have you ever wondered how Windows got its name? Microsoft chose the term *windows* to describe the graphical user interface (GUI) that it developed for use on personal computers. Earlier operating systems had used word-based commands. With Windows (as with Apple's Mac OS that came before it), users worked within a window-like frame that included pull-down menus, icons, and dialog boxes. All of these features were designed to create a simple way for users to interact with computers.

Managing Files and Folders

Much of the work you do on a computer involves creating a document or some other kind of file that you want to save for reference or for later use. Your computer's operating system provides the tools for organizing files into folders and for copying, moving, or deleting files and folders. Learning how to manage files and folders is a critical skill in using computers successfully.

As you progress through this textbook, you will use Windows 7 commands to copy module folders from the Student Resources CD to your storage medium. The first page of each module displays information about the files needed along with a reminder to copy that module's folder of files (if required). As you work on a module, you save your files to that same folder on your storage medium so you can find them easily.

Files are named to indicate the module, the chapter (when chapters are present), and the skill. For example, the file C2-S8-RecycleBin.docx is a file that is created or opened in Module 2, Chapter 2, Skill 8. And the file M4-S2-Sales.xlsx is a file that is created or opened in Module 4, Skill 2. Note that because Module 4 does not contain separate chapters, its file names do not include a chapter number.

Power of Windows

The screen capture at the right shows how the folders copied to a flash drive (identified as *Removable Disk* in the Address Bar) might be displayed.

Changing Settings and Using Accessories

Windows 7 offers a Control Panel component where you can add or remove printers and other hardware devices. You can also change the screen resolution, change the date and time settings, and uninstall programs. If you have any visual or hearing impairments, you can request that Windows suggest the best settings choices. You simply answer a few questions and Windows makes recommendations. The screen image at the right shows some of the settings choices offered on the Appearance and Personalization screen of the Control Panel.

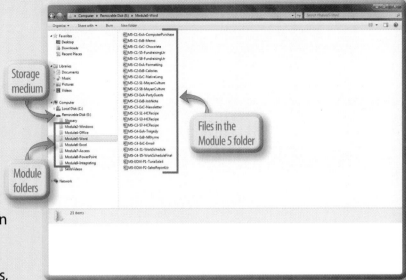

Storage medium

Module folders

Files in the Module 5 folder

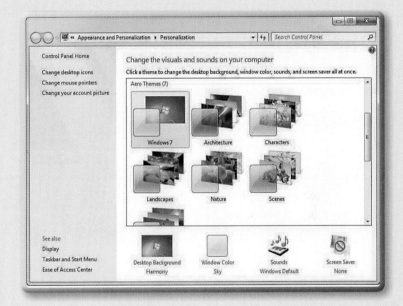

With a Windows 7 installation, several handy utility programs are installed and stored in the Accessories folder, as shown in the screen image at the left. Notepad and WordPad, for example, perform basic word processing functions. With the Snipping Tool, you can create screen captures (images) of parts of a screen. Windows Explorer offers file and folder management features.

Chapter 1

Navigating around Windows

Windows 7 is the latest Windows operating system. Operating system software is run automatically when the computer is turned on. It is used to control processing and peripherals, run application software, and control input and output, among other tasks. Every computer must have an operating system installed in order to function.

When you purchase a computer, it usually comes with an operating system already installed on it. Once you begin using your computer, most of the work of the operating system occurs "behind the scenes," so most users are unaware of its role. However, understanding what an operating system does and learning to use some of the Windows 7 tools and features will help you to become a more productive and efficient computer user.

Skills You Learn

1   Start and log on to Windows 7
2   Work with a pointing device
3   Work with tools on the Taskbar
4   Open and close programs
5   Manipulate windows
6   Move among open windows
7   Work with menus and toolbars
8   Use keyboard shortcuts
9   Make selections in dialog boxes
10   Shut down or put Windows to sleep

Files You Need
In this chapter, you do not need any student data files.

What You Create
In this chapter, you gain an understanding of what an operating system does and learn how to use some of the Windows 7 tools and features. You learn what to do when you are finished working on your computer for the day. You also become familiar with the applications, such as Internet Explorer and Notepad, that come with the Windows 7 operating system.

Windows

Skill 1

Video M2_C1_S01

Start and Log on to Windows 7

When you turn on a Windows-based computer, the operating system starts up automatically. If you have set up separate users for the computer, an introductory screen displays where you can click an icon to log on, entering a password if required. If your computer is connected to a network, you may also be asked to enter a network password. If only one user is set up on the computer and that user has no password, the desktop displays when the user turns on the computer.

Once the windows desktop displays, you can access all your files and applications from the desktop. The desktop also contains icons for tools and features similar to what you might find on a typical work desk, such as a clock and a calendar. You become familiar with the desktop interface as you complete the steps below.

Steps

1 Turn on your computer. The Windows introductory screen displays. (If the desktop displays immediately, skip to Step 5.)

2 Click the appropriate user icon (if user icons display).

▶**Tip** Passwords in Windows 7 are case-sensitive, meaning that the computer "sees" an uppercase *A* and a lowercase *a* as different characters.

3 Type your user name and password in the text boxes (if required).

4 Press Enter or click the arrow button to the right of the text box. The desktop displays. ***Note:*** *Check with your instructor if you have problems logging in.*

5 Click the Start button in the lower-left corner of your screen. The Start menu appears, displaying a list of applications you can launch by clicking on the appropriate icon. Click a blank area of the desktop to close the Start menu.

6 Move your mouse to the bottom of the screen, just to the right of the Start button. This horizontal band is called the Taskbar, containing program icons you can click to open programs.

7 Move your mouse over the far right area of the Taskbar. This is the notification area, containing button icons and showing the status of certain system functions, such as speakers, network connections, and battery power for a laptop. Leave your desktop displayed. You will continue exploring the desktop and using the mouse in the next skill.

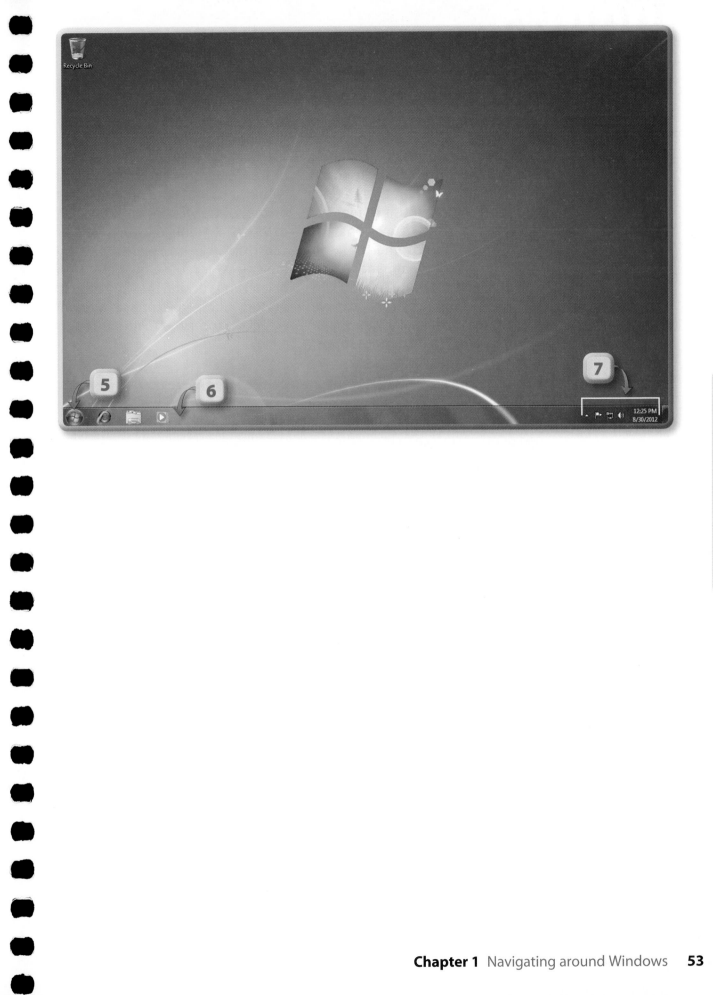

Windows

Windows

Skill 2

Video ▶ M2_C1_S02

Work with a Pointing Device

The mouse is a type of input device typically referred to as a pointing device. *Input devices* are used to communicate with an application. You can use the mouse to identify the names and functions of buttons, icons, and other desktop locations; select commands, text, and objects; and respond to application prompts. The mouse pointer commonly takes the shape of an arrow ▷ but it changes shape, depending on the task.

Usually, you click the left mouse button once to select a command within a menu. For some features or tools, you double-click an icon to open a menu or window. You can display a short-cut menu by moving your mouse over a button or icon and clicking the right mouse button. Some mice have a scroll wheel on top for scrolling through a file.

Steps

▶ Tip Laptop computers include a touchpad, which can be used instead of a mouse. Drag your finger on the touchpad to move the mouse pointer.

▶ Tip ScreenTips provide the name of the item and sometimes include a brief description of what the item does.

1 With the desktop displayed, move the mouse around on top of the mouse pad or other surface to move the pointer around the screen.

2 Move the pointer over the current time and date in the notification area of the Taskbar. The current date displays in a ScreenTip.

3 Move the mouse pointer to the Recycle Bin icon to highlight and display a ScreenTip explaining the function of the icon.

4 Right-click (press the right mouse button) the Recycle Bin icon to display a short-cut menu.

5 Click in a blank area of the desktop to close the menu.

▶ Tip Permanently delete the contents of the Recycle Bin by clicking *Empty Recycle Bin* in the Recycle Bin shortcut menu.

6 Double-click the Recycle Bin icon. A window opens, displaying a list of files and folders you have deleted. You can still retrieve files or folders if you need to use them, because they remain in the bin until you permanently delete them.

7 Click the Close button (red X) in the top-right corner of the Recycle Bin window to close it.

Taking It Further

Reviewing Mouse Technology You'll find many types of mouse devices. A traditional mouse has a trackball that you roll on a flat smooth surface to move the mouse pointer. This type of mouse works best with a mouse pad. Newer mouse types use technologies such as optical sensors, infrared light, radio signals, and Bluetooth to eliminate the need for trackballs, cords, and mouse pads.

Contains the files and folders that you have deleted.

Open
Empty Recycle Bin

Create shortcut
Rename

Properties

Recycle Bin

Recycle Bin

Organize ▾

☆ Favorites
    Desktop
    Downloads
    Recent Places

Libraries
    Documents
    Music
    Pictures
    Videos

Computer
    Local Disk (C:)
    Removable Disk

Search Recycle Bin

0 items

Windows

Windows

Chapter 1

Skill 3

Video M2_C1_S03

Work with Tools on the Taskbar

The Taskbar along the bottom of the desktop contains the Start button. Just to the right of the Start button are program icons that are *pinned* to the Taskbar. A pinned icon is always displayed on the Taskbar, and you can open the associated program by clicking on such icons. Open applications also display an icon on the Taskbar. Another Taskbar area is the notification area, at the far right. Icons here show the status of certain system functions, such as the Action Center. The Action Center is a single area that displays important messages about security and maintenance settings.

Steps

1 With the desktop displayed, click the Start button to open the Start menu.

2 Click a blank area of the desktop to close the Start menu.

▶**Tip** To pin a program to the Taskbar, right-click an open program icon on the Taskbar and select *Pin this program to taskbar*.

3 Click the pinned Windows Explorer button in the task buttons area on the Taskbar to open the Windows Explorer window and view your Libraries. (Libraries are discussed in Chapter 2.)

4 Click the Close button in the Libraries window.

5 Click the Speaker button in the notification area on the Taskbar to display the Speaker volume controls.

6 Press the left mouse button and drag the speaker volume control lever to the mid-point mark on the bar (*50*), releasing the mouse button to set the level there.

7 Click the Action Center button (shaped like a small pennant) in the notification area on the Taskbar.

8 Review the information in the Action Center by clicking the Open Action Center link.

9 Close the Action Center window by clicking the Close button.

▶**Tip** To change the date and time, you would click the Change Date and Time Settings link.

10 Click the current time and date in the Taskbar to display a calendar and clock.

11 Click the Show desktop button, a vertical bar at the right side of the Taskbar. Click this button to display the desktop at any time.

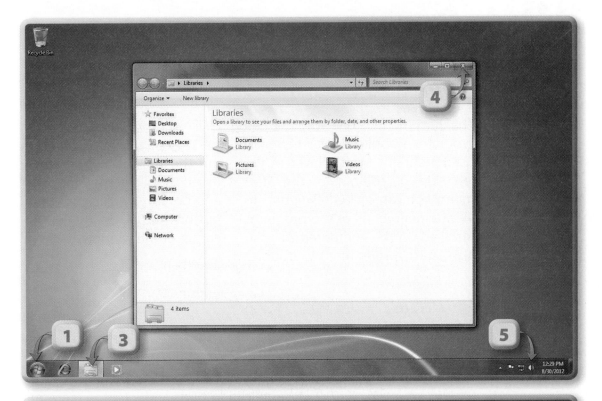

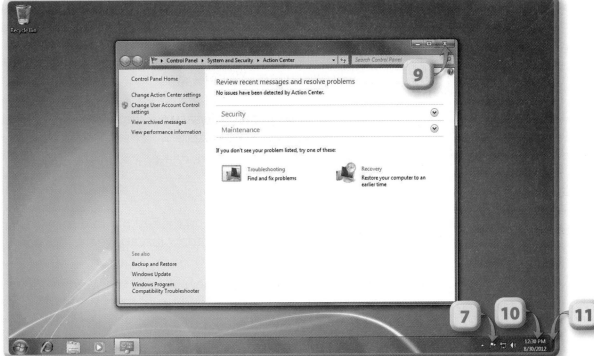

Taking It Further

Changing Notification Area Icons   You can add as many icons as you like to the notification area of the Taskbar. To avoid clutter, display only those icons you want visible at all times. Keep the rest of the icons in the overflow area, which you can display by clicking the Show Hidden Icons button.

Windows

Skill 4

Open and Close Programs

Video M2_C1_S04

The Start menu is one way to open programs or applications. Frequently used programs are displayed at the left side, or column, of the Start menu. You can click *All Programs* to view a menu of all of the programs installed on the computer. You can also start programs by double-clicking a program icon on the desktop or clicking a program icon on the Taskbar. Programs open in an application window. Close a program by clicking the Close button (red X) in the upper-right corner of the window.

Steps

1 Shortcut
Display Start Menu
Ctrl + Esc

▶**Tip** If *Microsoft Word 2010* is not displayed in the list of frequently used programs on the left side of the menu, click *All Programs*, click *Microsoft Office*, and then click *Microsoft Word 2010*.

1 Click the Start button to display the Start menu.

2 Click *Microsoft Word 2010*. The application starts and a button representing the open Word program appears on the Taskbar.

3 Click the Internet Explorer button on the Taskbar. Internet Explorer starts and the home page displays.

4 Click the Show desktop button on the Taskbar to display the desktop.

5 Double-click the Recycle Bin button on the desktop to open the Recycle Bin window.

▶**Tip** The Live Preview feature enables you to take a quick look at other open windows without clicking away from the window you are currently working in.

6 Move the pointer over the Word button on the Taskbar to display a Live Preview thumbnail of the open Word window just above the Taskbar.

7 Click Document1 in the thumbnail preview to open the Word window.

8 Click the Close button to close Microsoft Word 2010.

9 Move the mouse back to the Recycle Bin window and click the Close button.

10 Hover the mouse pointer over the Internet Explorer button on the Taskbar to open the Live Preview thumbnail, hover the mouse pointer over the thumbnail until the Close button displays in the top-right corner, and then click the Close button. The Internet Explorer window closes.

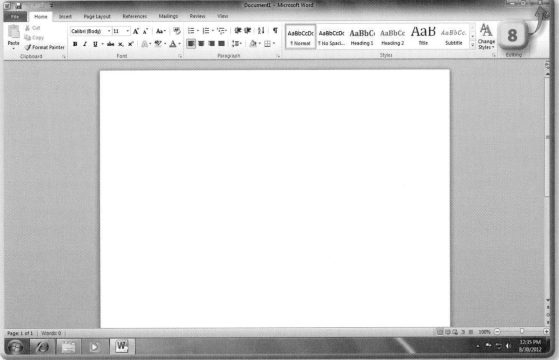

Taking It Further

Using Jump Lists   Jump Lists are a new Windows 7 feature. They display recent documents, tasks, or commands for a particular application. You can open a Jump List from the Taskbar or from the Start menu. For example, on the Taskbar, right-click the Internet Explorer button to display a list of frequently visited websites. Or right-click the Outlook button on the Taskbar to display a list of Outlook Tasks, such as *New Contact*. You then open items in a Jump List by clicking them. In the Start menu, click the arrow to the right of the program's name to view the Jump List.

Windows

Windows

Skill 5

Manipulate Windows

Video M2_C1_S05

In the previous skill, you learned to open and close program windows. In this skill, you learn techniques for manipulating windows, including minimizing, maximizing, restoring, resizing, and moving windows. You will find these techniques useful when working with more than one window. For example, when you minimize a window, it is reduced to a button on the Taskbar. You can then work on other tasks without having to close the first program or file. Maximizing a window increases the window to full-screen size so you can focus on that file or program. You can size and move windows that are not maximized so you can view other open windows at the same time.

Steps

▶**Tip** The home page in a browser can be set by the user, so the home page that displays in Step 1 will vary.

1 Click the Internet Explorer button on the Taskbar. The Internet Explorer window opens and the home page displays.

2 Click the Minimize button to reduce the window to a button on the Taskbar.

▶**Tip** If more than one Internet Explorer window is open, clicking the Internet Explorer button will provide a Live Preview of the choices. Hover the mouse over the thumbnail for the window you wish to maximize and then click.

3 Click the Internet Explorer button on the Taskbar to redisplay the window.

4 If the window does not currently fill the entire screen, click the Maximize button to enlarge the window size. The Maximize button turns into a Restore Down button when the window fills the entire screen.

5 Click the Restore Down button to reduce the size of the window.

6 Move the window slightly to the right by pressing the mouse button on the Title bar and dragging to the right.

▶**Tip** Any window that is not maximized can be moved.

7 Place your mouse pointer on the right window border and the pointer changes to a two-headed arrow. Resize the window to be smaller by pressing the mouse button on the window border and dragging to the left.

8 Place your mouse pointer on the bottom border of the window and the pointer changes to a two-headed arrow. Resize the window to be smaller by pressing the mouse button on the window border and dragging upward.

9 Click the Maximize button to increase the window size so it fills the screen.

10 Click the Close button to close the window.

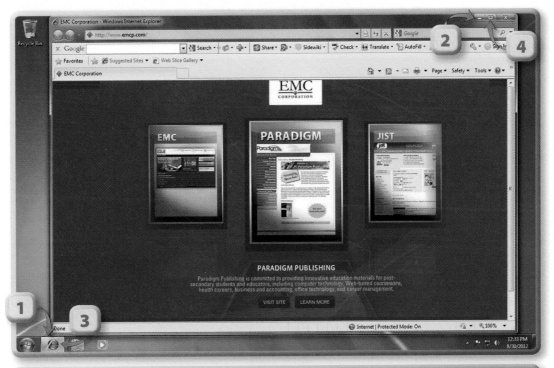

Taking It Further

Previewing Windows When you minimize a window, it is reduced to a Taskbar button or icon. The Taskbar button represents the minimized application. However, if you have two Word documents open and you minimize both of them, only one Word icon appears on the Taskbar. If you move your mouse over the Word button on the Taskbar, thumbnails of each minimized Word document appear. This new Windows 7 feature is called Live Preview. Click the thumbnail of the document you want to redisplay to open it. You can also close a document from the Live Preview feature by clicking the Close button (red X) that appears on a thumbnail in Live Preview.

Windows

Skill 6

Video M2_C1_S06

Move among Open Windows

You have probably noticed that Windows 7 lets you have more than one window open at a time and move among them. This flexibility is referred to as multitasking. Knowing the techniques available to move among open windows can help you to manage your workload more efficiently.

Steps

Tip The home page in a browser can be set by the user, so the home page that displays in Step 1 will vary.

1 Click the Internet Explorer button on the Taskbar. The Internet Explorer window opens and the home page displays. If the window does not fill the entire screen, click the Maximize button to enlarge it.

2 Click the Windows Explorer button on the Taskbar, to display your Libraries.

3 Right-click a blank area of the Taskbar to display the shortcut menu.

Tip The cascade arrangement only works with windows that are not minimized.

4 Click *Cascade windows* to display the Internet Explorer and Libraries windows in a cascade arrangement.

5 Right-click a blank area of the Taskbar to display the shortcut menu.

Tip Press Alt + Tab and then continue holding down Alt while repeatedly pressing Tab to move from window to window. Release the Alt key when the window you want to move to is highlighted.

6 Click *Show windows side by side* to display the windows in a side-by-side arrangement.

7 Click the Maximize button in the Internet Explorer window.

8 Right-click the Windows Explorer button on the Taskbar.

9 Click *Close window* to close the Libraries window.

10 Click the Close button to close the Internet Explorer window.

Taking It Further

Shaking Windows Windows 7 includes some new features for manipulating windows. One such feature is called *Shake*. To experiment with Shake, open at least three windows and use the Restore Down button to reduce the size of all three windows. Pick one of the windows and then press and drag that window side to side quickly. All of the open windows minimize except the one you are "shaking." This feature provides a quick way to minimize multiple windows.

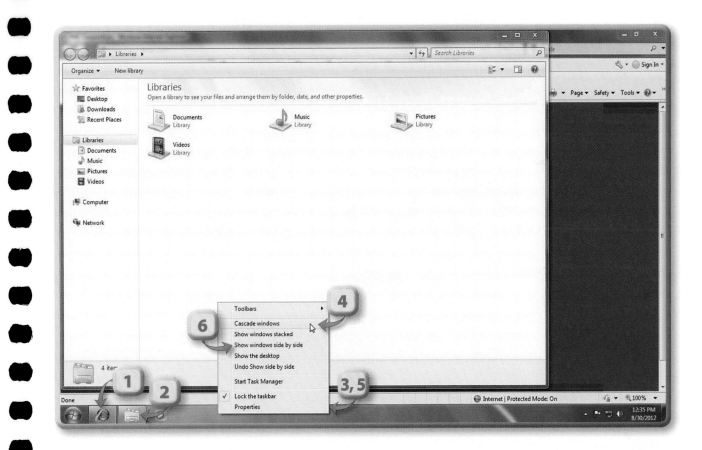

Windows

Windows

Video ▶ M2_C1_S07

Work with Menus and Toolbars

In Windows 7 and other applications, you work with a variety of menus and toolbars. You can display shortcut menus by right-clicking an item on the screen. You can display other menus by using the keyboard. Still others display when you click a drop-down list or toolbar button. Toolbars contain a variety of command buttons for an application and are typically found near the top of an application window.

Steps

1 Click the Windows Explorer button on the Taskbar.

2 Click the Organize button to display a menu.

3 Point to *Layout* to display a submenu.

▶**Tip** When you point to a menu option that also contains a small arrow, a submenu appears.

4 Click the Close button to close the Libraries window.

5 Click the Start button in the Taskbar.

6 Click in the *Search programs and files* box and type Notepad. Notepad appears in the *Programs* list.

▶**Tip** Notepad is a text editing program that comes with the Windows operating system.

▶**Tip** Skill 9 of this chapter introduces dialog boxes.

7 Click *Notepad* to display the Notepad window.

8 Click the File button at the top of the Notepad screen. Some of the options in the displayed menu have an ellipsis (…) after them. Ellipses signify that a dialog box displays when the option is selected.

9 Point to the Format button to display the menu.

10 **Shortcut**
Close an Open Menu
Esc

10 If there is not a check mark next to *Word Wrap*, click the *Word Wrap* option. The menu closes. (If there is a check mark, indicating that the feature is active, click in the Notepad window to close the menu.)

▶**Tip** A check mark indicates that the feature toggles on and off when you click it.

11 Click the Format button. *Word Wrap* has a check mark beside it, indicating that the option has been turned on.

12 Click the Close button to close the Notepad window.

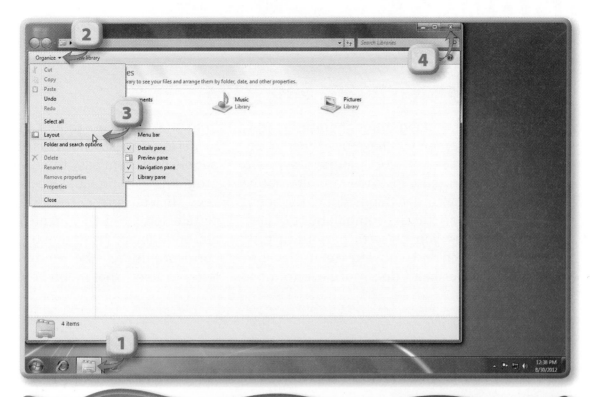

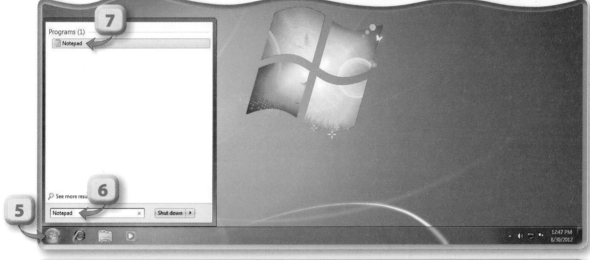

Taking It Further

Using Toolbars   Toolbars are found in many Windows applications, including Internet Explorer. Typically, certain toolbars are turned on by default and others can be turned on by the user. Right-click a toolbar to see the other available toolbars you can display. Toolbars with a check mark beside them are turned on and displayed.

Windows

Windows

Use Keyboard Shortcuts

Video M2_C1_S08

In working through tasks in this chapter, you have used the mouse to select commands. Keyboard shortcuts provide an alternative way to get things done. Keyboard shortcuts are combinations of keys that you press to perform a task, such as copying text. Because your hand does not have to move from the keyboard to the mouse to perform these shortcuts, some people find them easy to use. Most programs also provide accelerator keys. If you press the Alt key, certain letters in the menu items are underlined. Press the key that corresponds to the underlined letter to select that menu item.

Steps

1. Click the Windows Explorer button on the Taskbar to open the window in Library view.

2. Press the Alt key to activate the menu bar. Each menu item contains an underlined letter.

3. Press the *F* key to display the File menu or press another accelerator key, such as *V,* to display a different menu.

4. Press Alt + F4 to close the Windows Explorer window.

5. From the desktop, press F1 to display the Windows Help and Support window.

6. Press the Tab key two times. A different command or link in the Help window is highlighted each time you press Tab.

7. Press Alt + F4 to close the Windows Help and Support window.

8. Press Ctrl + Esc to display the Start menu.

9. Press the Up Arrow key several times. A different menu item is highlighted each time you press the key.

10. Press Esc to close the Start menu.

Tip Many keyboard shortcuts, such as Alt + F4, perform the same function in all Office applications. For example, Alt + F4 will close a Word window and it will also close an Internet Explorer window.

Tip The F1 key is used in most programs to display the Help menu.

Tip Press Enter to select a highlighted command, link, or menu item.

Taking It Further

Memorizing Your Favorite Keyboard Shortcuts   Memorizing common keyboard shortcuts can save you time and increase your productivity. For example, many Office users prefer using Ctrl + C and Ctrl + V to copy and paste information rather than selecting commands from a shortcut menu or from the ribbon. To learn more, display the Windows Help window and type *keyboard shortcuts* in the Search Help box. After pressing Enter, click one of the result links and then research keyboard shortcuts that could help you become more efficient.

Windows

Skill 9

Video M2_C1_S09

Make Selections in Dialog Boxes

You can interact with Windows and other applications by using settings in dialog boxes. Dialog boxes allow you to specify details for a setting or to make choices about how an application performs a procedure. For example, you can interact with the Print dialog box to select a printer, designate which pages to print, and choose the number of copies to print. In this skill, you become familiar with common dialog box features by using the Notepad application that is built into Windows. Common dialog box features include check boxes, option buttons, list boxes, and boxes where you can select a value, such as the number of copies to print.

Steps

1. Click the Start button on the Taskbar to display the Start Menu.

▶ **Tip** If Notepad is not in the recently used programs list in the Start Menu, click *All Programs* and then click *Accessories*.

2. Click *Notepad* to start the Notepad program.

3. Type your first name.

4. Click Format to display the Format menu.

▶ **Tip** In other Office programs, font formatting is applied only to selected text.

5. Click *Font* to display the Font dialog box.

6. Click *18* in the *Size* list box.

7. Click *Bold* in the *Font style* list box.

8. Click OK. Your first name is now displayed in a larger font size and in bold text. Everything you type will be larger and also bold until you reset these settings in the Format menu. Every new or old text file opened in Notepad will display using these settings. The settings are not stored with the file.

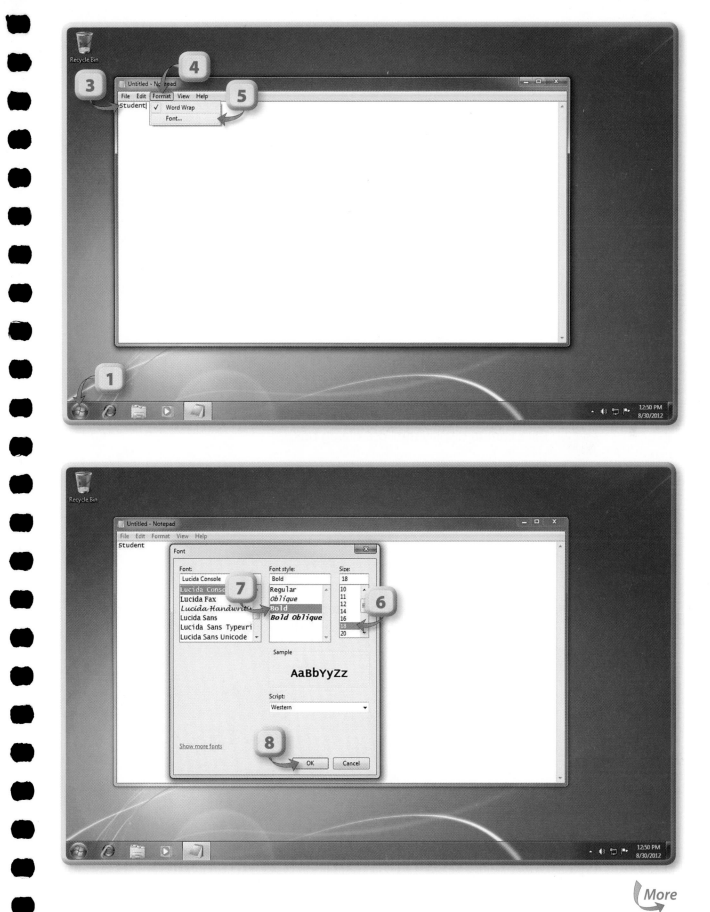

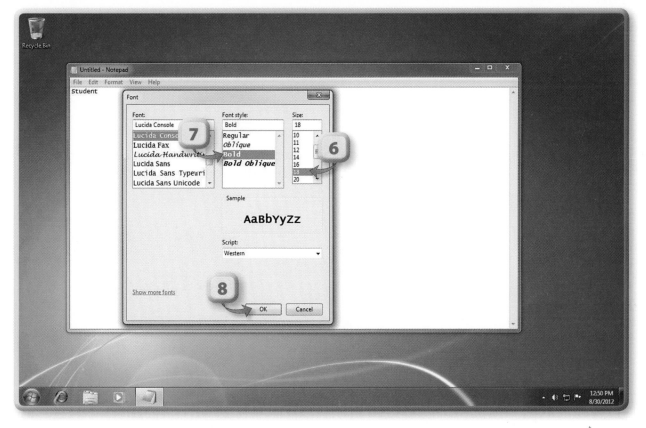

More

9 Click File to display the File menu.

10 Click *Print* to display the Print dialog box.

11 Click the *Print to file* check box to insert a check mark.

12 Click the up arrow next to the *Number of copies* box to increase the number of copies. The number increases with each click.

13 Click the down arrow next to the *Number of copies* box to decrease the number of copies. The number decreases with each click.

14 Double-click the number in the *Number of copies* box to select it and then type 5.

15 Click the Cancel button to close the dialog box without printing.

16 Click Format to display the Format menu.

17 Click *Font* to display the Font dialog box.

18 Click *Regular* in the *Font style* list box.

19 Click *11* in the *Size* list box.

20 Click OK.

21 Click the Close button on the Notepad window and when a warning box asks if you want to save changes, click the Don't Save button.

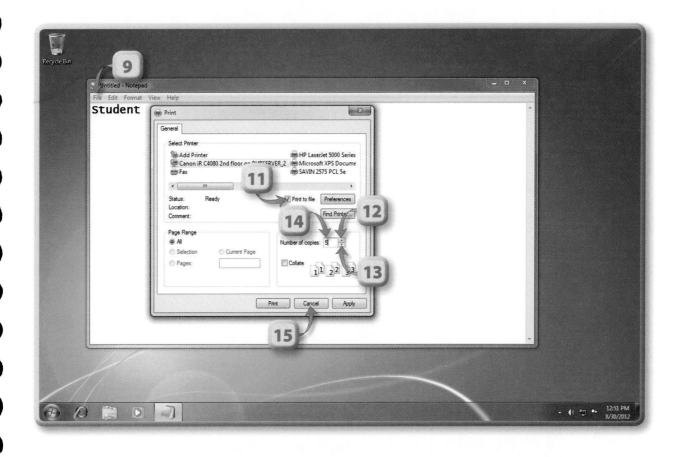

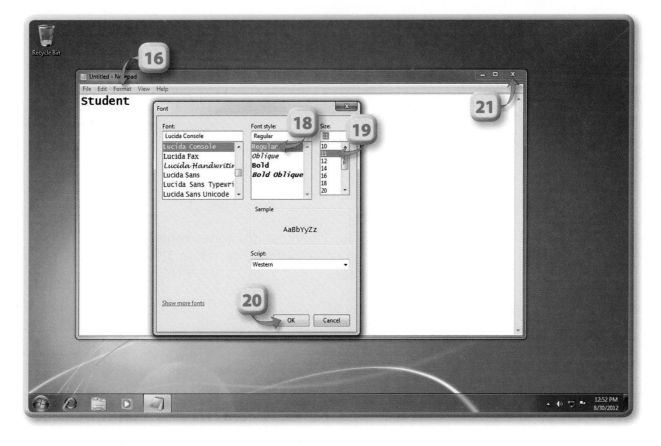

Windows

Skill 10

Shut Down or Put Windows to Sleep

 Video M2_C1_S10

When you are finished working on your computer, you have a variety of settings to choose from. You can put your computer to sleep, which saves power without your having to close all of your files and shut down your system. You can lock your computer, which hides the desktop and requires you to enter a password to unlock the computer if your account is password protected. You can also log off or switch users if more than one user has an account on your computer. Or, if you prefer, you can shut the computer down completely.

Steps

1 *Shortcut*
Open the Start Menu
Ctrl + Esc

1   Click the Start button.

2   Click the Shut down button arrow.

3   Click *Lock*. The Windows 7 log on screen displays with your user account and the word *Locked*.

▶**Tip** If your computer is on a network, you may have to press Ctrl + Alt + Delete and then enter your username and password to unlock your computer.

4   Click the icon for your user account.

5   Type your password in the *Password* text box and press Enter. This action unlocks the system and displays the desktop.

▶**Tip** If you are working in a computer lab, be sure to close all open files and remove your storage medium before leaving the lab.

6   Click the Start button to display the Start menu.

7   Click the Shut down button arrow.

8   Click *Sleep*. Sleep places the computer in a power-conservation state that allows you to resume work quickly when you return. This setting is useful if you are working on a laptop.

Taking It Further

Restarting Sometimes your computer stops working or freezes up and you need to restart it. You can restart the computer by pressing Ctrl + Alt + Delete or by selecting *Restart* in the Shut down menu. When you have finished working on your computer for a time, you can shut it down. You shut down the computer by clicking the Shut down button in the Start menu. Be sure you have saved and closed all files prior to shutting down the computer.

Chapter 2

Managing Files and Folders

A *file* is a collection of data that is stored on a hard drive or other storage medium. Everything that a computer does is based on data stored in files. Files can be stored on any storage medium, including a hard drive, a removable USB flash drive, a server, or a CD/DVD.

File names have two parts: a descriptive name you assign, such as *Resume*, and a file extension automatically assigned by the application when you save the file. For example, Excel workbook files have an .xlsx extension, PowerPoint presentation files have a .pptx extension, Access database files have an .accdb extension, and Word documents have a .docx extension. An extension indicates the file type and is used by the operating system to recognize which application to use to open the file.

Using the Windows Explorer window, you can copy, rename, organize, delete, and search for files. Deleted files are sent to the Recycle Bin where they are held for a time, permanently deleted, or restored to their original location on the computer. Files can also be compressed to reduce the file size, making it easier to email the files or transfer them to another computer. Files from various folders can be placed together into a Library, a logical grouping that helps you work with related sets of files. By default, Windows contains four libraries: Documents, Music, Pictures, and Videos.

Skills You Learn

1 Use Windows Explorer
2 Copy a folder from the Student Resources CD
3 Create a folder
4 Rename files and folders
5 Compress and extract files
6 Search for files
7 Delete files and folders
8 Use the Recycle Bin

Files You Need
In this chapter, you need the following student data file.

M2-C2-S8-RecycleBin.docx

What You Create
In this chapter, you learn to manage the files and folders on your computer. You start to create a folder structure on your removable USB flash drive that reflects the modules in this textbook by copying a folder from the Student Resources CD. As you work through this module and the other modules in the textbook, you will use this folder structure to organize your files.

Windows

Skill 1

Use Windows Explorer

Video M2_C2_S01

Windows Explorer is the file management interface in Windows 7. A Windows Explorer window lets you view the folders and files in a selected storage location, such as your hard drive, DVD drive, server, or removable USB drive. Features of a Windows Explorer window include a Navigation pane, an Address bar, a toolbar, a Search box, and a Details pane.

Steps

▶ **Tip** Libraries are a structure for organizing and managing your files in Windows 7. They are similar to folders, but different in that a library gathers together files that may be stored in several locations on your computer.

▶ **Tip** The Pictures library on your computer will contain different files from those shown.

1. With the desktop displayed, right-click the Start button.

2. Click *Open Windows Explorer* to open the Windows Explorer window.

3. Double-click *Pictures* in the *Libraries* section of the Navigation pane.

4. The path in the Address bar changes to show that you are viewing the Pictures library.

5. The Details pane shows how many items are in the Pictures library.

6. Click the View button arrow on the toolbar.

7. Click *Details* to display details about each file, including its size and date last modified, in the Windows Explorer window.

8. Click the View button and return your computer to its original setting if you made a change to the setting in Step 7.

9. Click *Desktop* in the *Favorites* section in the Navigation pane to display desktop files and folders.

10. Click the Back button to redisplay the Pictures library.

11. Close the Windows Explorer window.

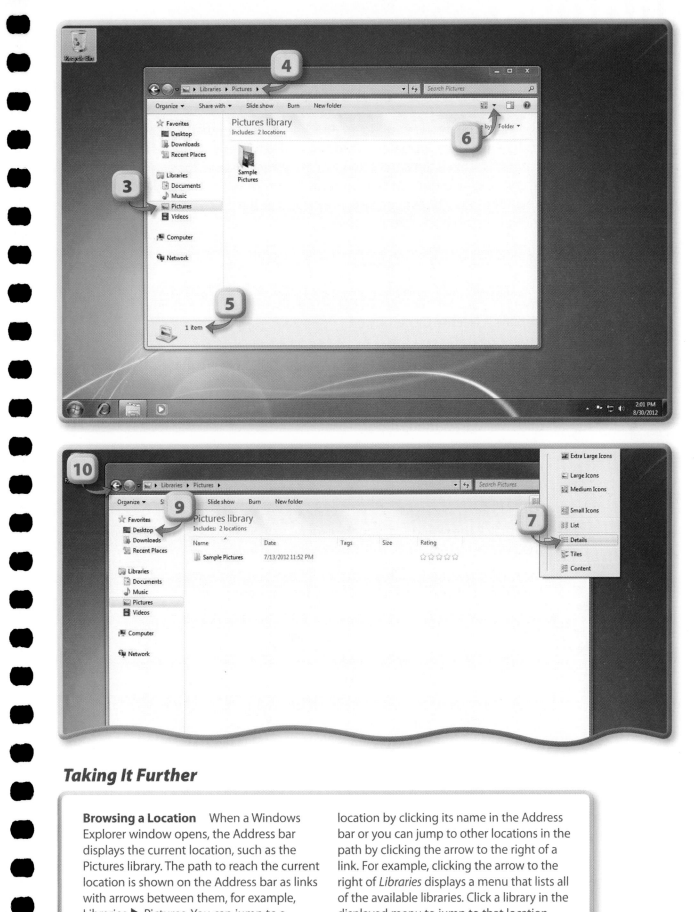

Taking It Further

Browsing a Location When a Windows Explorer window opens, the Address bar displays the current location, such as the Pictures library. The path to reach the current location is shown on the Address bar as links with arrows between them, for example, Libraries ▶ Pictures. You can jump to a location by clicking its name in the Address bar or you can jump to other locations in the path by clicking the arrow to the right of a link. For example, clicking the arrow to the right of *Libraries* displays a menu that lists all of the available libraries. Click a library in the displayed menu to jump to that location.

Windows

Skill 2

Video M2_C2_S02

Copy a Folder from the Student Resources CD

Some of the work you do in this course involves opening student data files. These files are organized by module in folders on the Student Resources CD. The first page of each module in this book, provides (when necessary) instructions for copying the folder you need from the CD to your storage medium. In this skill, you practice this procedure using a USB flash drive.

Steps

1 Insert the Student Resources CD in the disc drive. If an AutoPlay window displays, click the Close button.

▶ **Tip** If you are not using a USB flash drive and are working in a computer lab, ask your instructor where you should save your files.

2 Insert your USB flash drive in an available USB port. If an AutoPlay window displays, click the Close button.

3 Click the Start button.

4 Click *Computer* to display the Windows Explorer window. This window displays all of the storage locations on your computer.

5 Right-click the disk drive, which displays as *Guidelines-Student-Resources*, in the Content pane and select *Open in a new window*.

6 Click the *Module2-Windows* folder in the Content pane.

7 Click the Organize button on the toolbar.

8 Click *Copy* in the drop-down list.

9 Click the Back button.

▶ **Tip** Your computer may display the removable disk storage location with the name *Removable Disk, USB Disk,* or *External Disk*. Or, if you've renamed your disk, it will display that name.

10 Double-click the removable disk drive that corresponds to your USB flash drive in the Content pane.

11 Click the Organize button on the toolbar.

12 Click *Paste* in the drop-down list.

13 Close the Windows Explorer window.

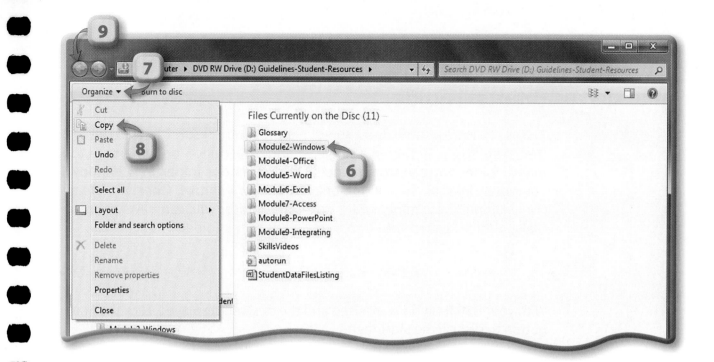

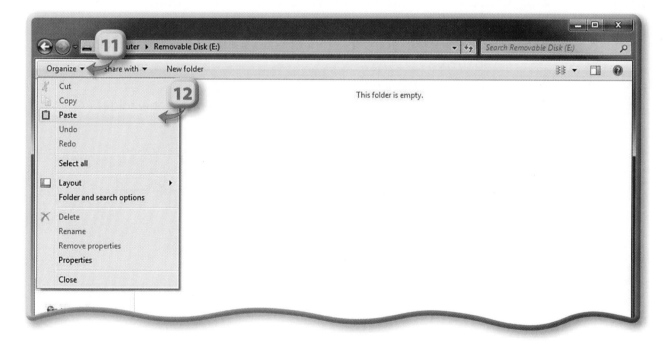

Taking It Further

Copying Folders Another Way Folders can also be moved and copied by using the drag-and-drop method. One easy way to do this is to open two Windows Explorer windows and arrange them so that both are visible on the screen. You can then drag a folder from one window to the other. This method will either copy or move the folder, depending on the destination location. If you drag the folder to a different disk location, the folder will be copied. If the new folder location is on the same disk, the folder will be moved.

Windows

Skill 3

Video   M2_C2_S03

Create a Folder

Just as you store printed documents that relate to each other in a single manila folder, you can store related computer files in virtual folders. For example, you might want to make a folder called *Job Search* to store your resume, cover letters, and portfolio documents. You can create a folder in a Windows Explorer window. Once you create the folder, you can save or move files to the folder.

Steps

1 With your USB flash drive inserted and the desktop displayed, click the Start button to display the Start menu.

2 Click *Computer* to display the Windows Explorer window.

3 Double-click the removable disk drive to see the list of files or folders saved there.

4 Click the New folder button on the toolbar to create a new folder.

5 Type Module2-Skill3 and press Enter.

6 Double-click the *Module2-Skill3* folder, which is currently empty.

7 Click the Back button.

8 Close the Windows Explorer window.

Taking It Further

Creating a New Library   By default, Windows has four pre-defined libraries (Music, Pictures, Documents, and Video). You can create additional libraries from the Windows Explorer window by clicking the New Library button. A new library appears with its name open for editing. Type a unique name for your library. Remember, a library is different from a folder in that it is a place to compile like types of files. To set the library type, right-click the new library and in the dialog box that appears, click *Optimize This Library for* and choose a type from the list. For example, if you want to use the new library for podcasts, *Music* would be a good fit because it would include audio files. Use the Include a Folder button and choose the folders and files you want to include in the new library and click OK to save your changes.

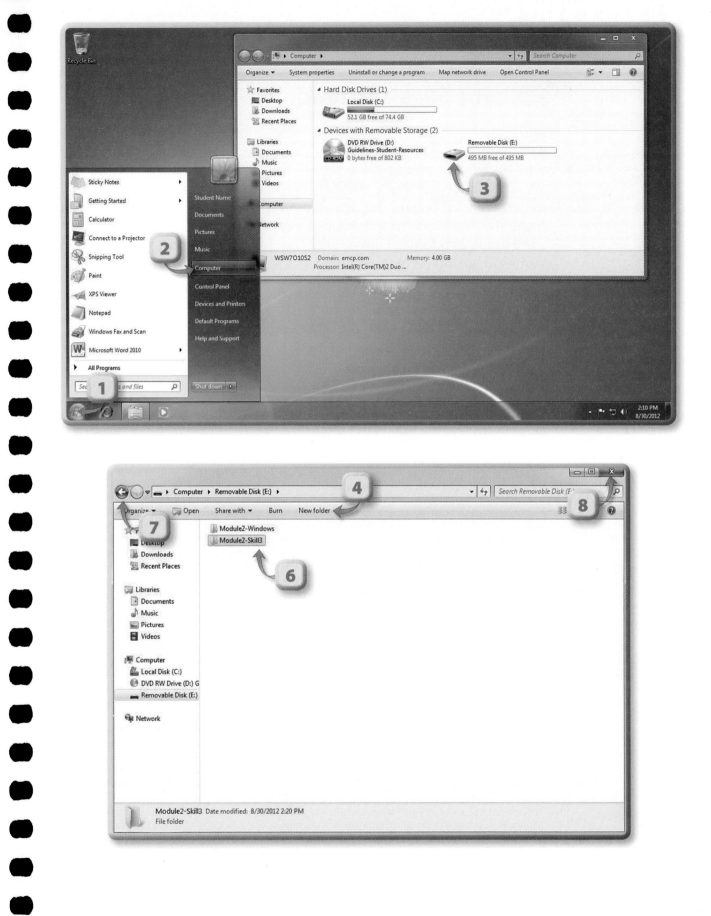

Windows

Skill 4

Video M2_C2_S04

Rename Files and Folders

You may need to rename a file or folder after you create it. File and folder names can be up to 255 characters in length and can include spaces. Certain characters, including \ / : * ? " < > |, cannot be used in file and folder names. File names have an extension, such as .docx, which the computer program adds automatically when the file is saved. You should not change the file extension when you rename a file because the extension tells the computer which application to use to open the file.

Steps

1. With your USB flash drive inserted and the desktop displayed, click the Start button and then click *Computer*.

2. Double-click the removable disk drive to see the list of files or folders already saved to your USB flash drive.

3. Right-click the *Module2-Skill3* folder to display the Shortcut menu.

4 *Shortcut*
Rename
F2

4. Click *Rename*. At this point the folder name becomes available for editing.

5. Type Module2-Practice and press Enter. The *Module2-Skill3* folder is renamed *Module2-Practice.*

6. Make sure that Module2-Practice is selected and then click the Organize button on the toolbar to display the menu.

7. Click *Rename* to make the folder name available for editing.

8. Type Module2-CompletedSkills and press Enter. The *Module2-Practice* folder is renamed *Module2-CompletedSkills*.

9. Close the Windows Explorer window.

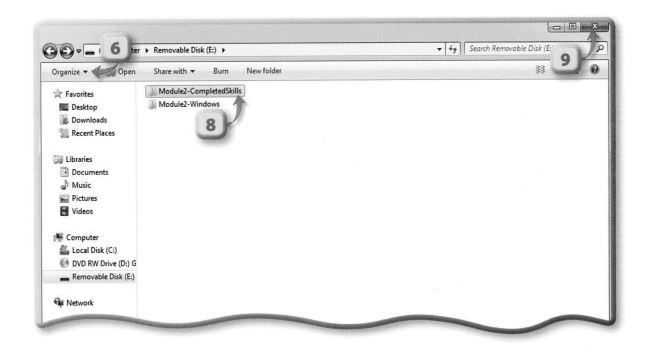

Taking It Further

Renaming Multiple Files If you want to rename a series of files, such as photo files (.jpg) from a digital camera, you can do so quickly if you use a specific prefix to name each of the files. For example, you could use the prefix *photo* to rename a batch of files *photo(1).jpg, photo(2).jpg, photo(3). jpg, photo(4).jpg*, and so forth. To do so, in a Windows Explorer window, hold down the Ctrl key and click each file you want to rename. Then press the F2 key, type the prefix you will use to rename the files, and then press Enter. The computer automatically adds the parenthetical numbers after your prefix to differentiate the files.

Windows

Windows

Skill 5

Compress and Extract Files

Video M2_C2_S05

If you have large files that you need to email or transfer to another computer, you may want to first compress, or zip, the files. Compressed, or zipped, files take up less storage space and can be transferred to other computers more quickly than uncompressed files. Folders can also be compressed. Compressing a folder combines all of the files in the folder into a single compressed file, which is smaller in size than the total of the individual file sizes. In order to edit a compressed file, you must first extract the files. Extracting essentially means to reverse the process, or to uncompress or unzip the file once you are ready to use it.

Steps

1 With your USB flash drive inserted, click the Start button and then click *Computer*.

2 Double-click the removable disk drive to see the list of files or folders already saved there.

3 Right-click the *Module2-Windows* folder to display a shortcut menu.

▶**Tip** Be aware that you will probably hear both terms, *compressed* and *zipped* used to describe such files.

4 Point to *Send to* and click *Compressed (zipped) folder*. The zipped folder appears with a folder icon with a zipper image on it.

5 Double-click the zipped *Module2-Windows* folder.

▶**Tip** Many compressed files have a .zip extension. Others have an .rar extension or other special extension, depending on the compression application used.

6 Click the Extract all files button on the toolbar to open the Extract Compressed (Zipped) Folders dialog box.

7 Click the Browse button.

8 Browse to the *Module2-CompletedSkills* folder on your USB flash drive and click it.

9 Click OK.

10 Click the Extract button. When the Module2-CompletedSkills folder window opens, the compressed folder has been extracted and is located within the Module2-CompletedSkills folder.

11 Close the two open windows.

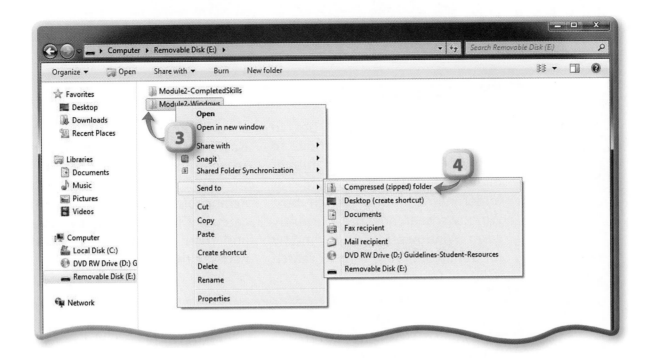

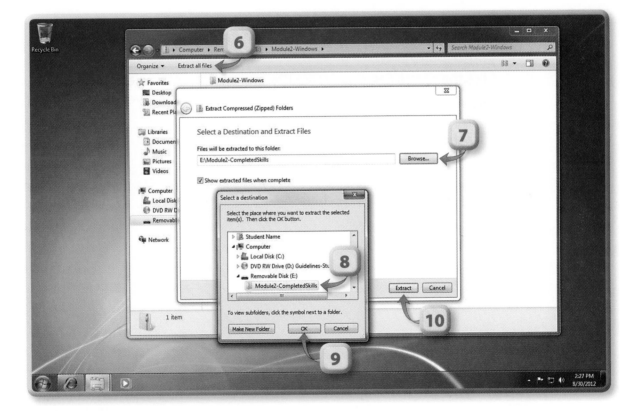

Taking It Further

Displaying File Extensions In a default Windows Explorer window, file extensions are not displayed. However, some users prefer to have Windows display file extensions. To turn on the display of file extensions, click the Organize button in a Windows Explorer window and select *Folder and search options*. Click the View tab and then click the check mark in the *Hide extensions for known file types* check box to display extensions.

Windows

Windows

Video ▶ M2_C2_S06

Search for Files

You can use the Search box in a Windows Explorer window to quickly locate a specific file or folder. When you type a file or folder name in the Search box, Windows searches the currently open Windows Explorer window for a match. If you want to search a different location, use the Navigation pane to change the search location. For example, to search your USB drive, click *Removable Disk* in the *Computer* category in the Navigation pane and then enter the file or folder name in the Search box.

Steps

1 With your USB flash drive inserted and the desktop displayed, click the Start button and then click *Computer*.

2 Double-click the removable disk drive name in the Navigation pane.

3 Click the *Search Removable Disk* box and type Module2. Search results display in the window, indicating there are four occurrences of *Module2*.

4 Click the Clear button next to the Search box.

▶**Tip** The * is a wildcard that can be used to specify any combination of characters. In this case, you are searching for all files with a .zip file extension because * tells the computer to retrieve files with any name appearing to the left of the .zip extension.

5 In the Search Removable Disk box, type *.zip. The Search feature finds one zipped file, which is listed in the search results.

6 Click the Clear button next to the Search box.

7 Close the Windows Explorer window.

Taking It Further

Repeating a Search and Using Search Filters   When you click in a Search box in a Windows Explorer window, previous searches are displayed in a drop-down list. Click a previous search to repeat it. The drop-down list also contains filter categories, such as *Date modified*, that you can use to refine your search. For example, if you know that you updated a particular file last Tuesday or Wednesday, you can click the *Date modified* filter category and then click a date or date range to narrow the search for files or folders that were saved on a specific date or within a specific date range.

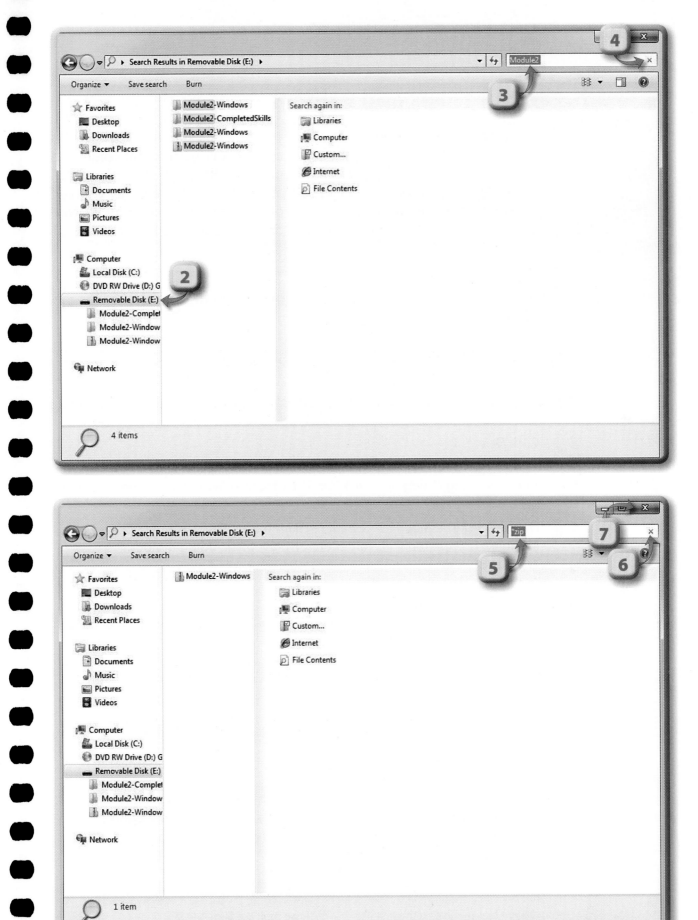

Windows

Windows

Skill 7

Delete Files and Folders

Video M2_C2_S07

If you have files that you no longer need on your computer, you should delete them. Regularly deleting such files will help keep your files organized and free up disk space. You can also delete a folder. When you delete a folder, all of the files and folders within that folder are deleted. Be sure to look within all subfolders to remind yourself of the complete contents before deleting the outer folder.

Steps

1 With your USB flash drive inserted, click the Start button and then click *Computer*.

2 Double-click the removable disk drive name in the Navigation bar.

3 *Another Way*
Click the file and then press the Delete key on your keyboard.

3 Right-click the zipped *Module2-Windows* folder to display a shortcut menu.

4 Click *Delete*.

5 At the warning dialog box, click Yes. The Module2-Windows.zip file is deleted.

6 Double-click the *Module2-CompletedSkills* folder. The contents of the Module2-CompletedSkills folder are displayed, including a Module2-Windows folder.

7 Right-click the *Module2-Windows* folder.

8 Click *Delete*.

9 Click Yes, to delete the folder.

10 Close the Windows Explorer window.

Taking It Further

Deleting Multiple Files You can delete multiple files by first selecting them. If you want to delete a series of files listed one after the other, select those adjacent files by clicking the first file and then holding down the Shift key while clicking the last file. Select nonadjacent files by clicking the first file and then holding down the Ctrl key while clicking the other files. Once you've selected several files, click the Organize button and then select *Delete* in the drop-down menu. Alternatively, once you have selected the files, you can press the Delete key to delete those multiple files.

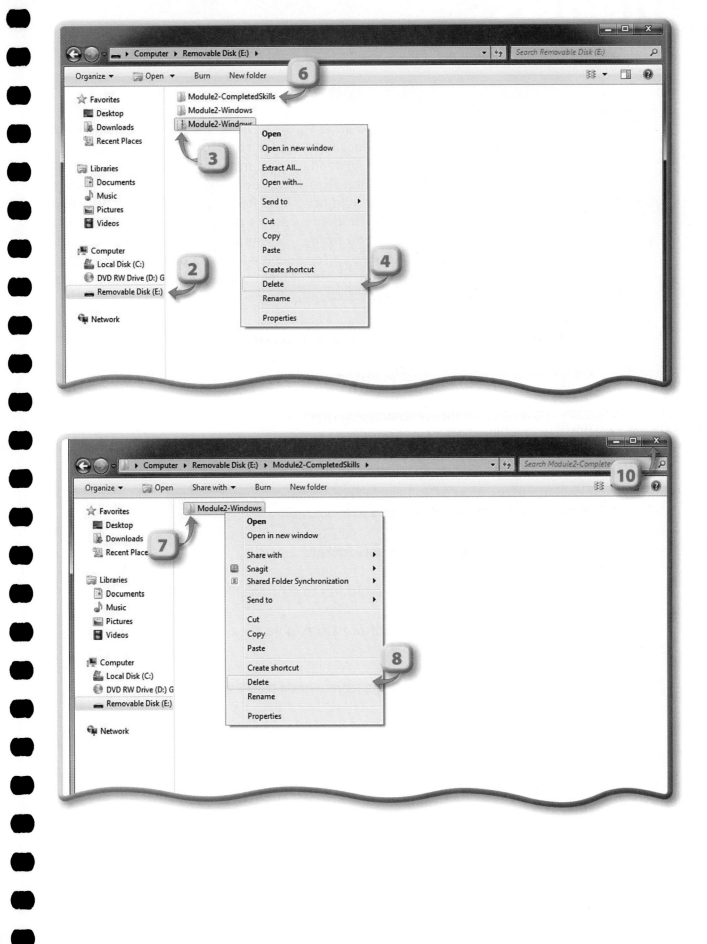

Windows

Skill 8

Use the Recycle Bin

Video M2_C2_S08

In Windows 7, when you delete a file from the hard drive, it does not, in fact, get deleted. It is instead moved to the Recycle Bin. The Recycle Bin is a temporary holding area for deleted files and folders. The Recycle Bin protects you from accidental loss of files because, if you change your mind about deleting the file that was stored on your hard drive, you can restore it back to its original location. When you are absolutely sure the file is no longer needed, you can empty the Recycle Bin. The Recycle Bin stores deleted files until it runs out of storage space. Then it will start deleting files, beginning with the files that have been in the bin the longest.

Steps

1 With your USB flash drive inserted, click the Start button and then *Computer*.

2 Double-click the removable disk drive.

3 Double-click the *Module2-Windows* folder in the Content pane.

4 Drag the **M2-C2-S8-RecycleBin.docx** file onto your desktop.

5 Right-click the **M2-C2-S8-RecycleBin.docx** file on the desktop and click *Delete*. A warning dialog box displays.

6 At the warning dialog box, click Yes to send the file to the Recycle Bin.

7 Click the Show desktop button, which looks like a vertical bar on the right-hand side of the Taskbar.

8 Double-click the Recycle Bin icon to open the Recycle Bin window.

9 Locate and then click **M2-C2-RecycleBin.docx** in the Recycle Bin window.

10 Click the Restore this item button on the toolbar. Notice that the file is restored to its previous location on your desktop.

11 Close the Recycle Bin window.

12 Repeat Steps 5 and 6 to delete the file from the desktop.

13 Eject the Student Resources CD and your USB flash drive from the computer.

▶**Tip** Dragging a file from a folder onto the desktop copies the file; the file is not removed from the folder.

▶**Tip** When you delete a file or folder that is saved on a removable disk, it is not sent to the Recycle Bin. It is permanently deleted.

▶**Tip** The Recycle Bin displays on the desktop by default. If the icon is not on your desktop, right-click the desktop, click *Personalize*, click *Change desktop icons*, and then click the *Recycle Bin* check box. You may not be able to personalize the desktop in a public lab.

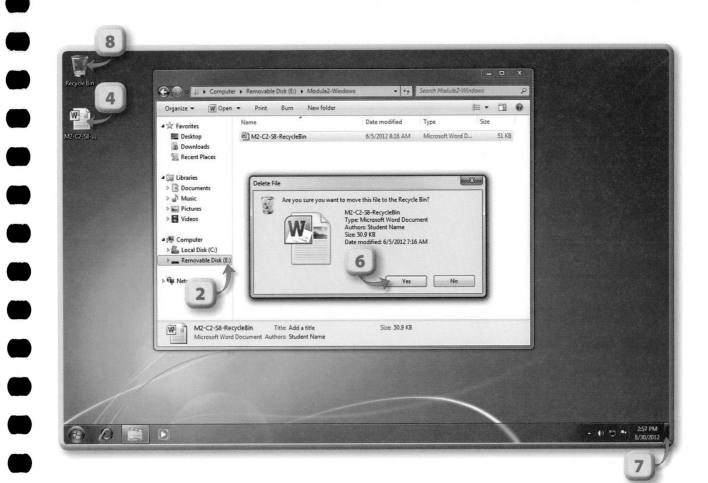

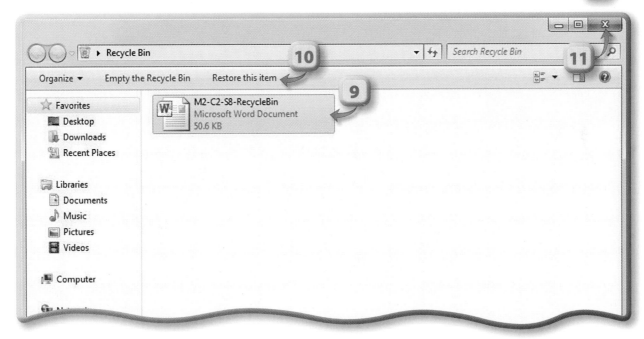

Taking It Further

Adjusting the Recycle Bin Properties   The maximum storage size of the Recycle Bin can be adjusted by right-clicking the *Recycle Bin* icon, clicking *Properties*, then entering a different number in the *Maximum size* box. You can also turn the Recycle Bin off (although doing so is not recommended) by selecting the option *Don't move files to the Recycle Bin. Remove files immediately when deleted*.

Chapter 3

Working with Windows Settings, Gadgets, and Accessories

Typically, when you purchase a computer, Windows has already been installed for you. Therefore, many of the Windows settings on your computer are the default settings applied during the installation process. You can, however, change many of the Windows 7 settings in order to personalize your computer. You can access and adjust most system settings for your computer through the Control Panel.

The Control Panel settings are organized into categories. Some of the tasks you can perform in the Control Panel include reviewing your computer's status, adding a hardware device, uninstalling a program, adding a user account, adjusting the screen resolution, and changing the time zone that the computer clock uses.

Along with exploring the Control Panel, you learn in this chapter about the gadgets that you can add to your desktop. You also become familiar with some handy programs that are located in the Accessories folder. These programs come with Windows 7.

Skills You Learn

1 Explore the Control Panel
2 Set the date and time
3 Modify the appearance of Windows
4 Change the Windows theme
5 Use Windows Accessories
6 Review firewall settings
7 Manage Windows Update settings
8 Use Windows Help
9 Use Gadgets

Files You Need
In this chapter, you do not need any student data files.

What You Create
Because you may not be allowed to review or make certain changes to your school computers, you explore many of the system settings but do not change them. Also, depending on the configuration of your school's computer lab, you may not be able to access some of the settings covered in this chapter. However, you can use the knowledge in this chapter to change the settings on your home or business computer at a later date.

Windows

Skill 1

Explore the Control Panel

Video M2_C3_S01

The Control Panel is organized into categories and subcategories. Click a category link, such as <u>Appearance and Personalization</u>, to display additional subcategories and tasks. Follow the links to display and modify settings for your computer.

Steps

1 Shortcut
Display the Start menu
Ctrl + Esc

▶ **Tip** *Category* should be selected in the *View by* list at the upper-right corner of the window. If *Large icons* or *Small icons* are displayed instead, click the drop-down arrow and select *Category*.

4 Another Way
Click the <u>Control Panel Home</u> link in the left-hand pane.

1 Click the Start button on the Taskbar.

2 Click *Control Panel* to display the Control Panel window and view the Control Panel categories.

3 Click the <u>Review your computer's status</u> link under the <u>System and Security</u> category link and review the displayed information.

4 Click the Back button to redisplay the Control Panel category links.

5 Click the <u>Adjust screen resolution</u> link under the <u>Appearance and Personalization</u> category link. The computer's current screen resolution settings display.

6 Click the Back button.

7 Click the <u>Hardware and Sound</u> category link to display the subcategories and tasks.

8 Click the Back button.

9 Click the Close button to close the Control Panel.

Taking It Further

Exploring Ease of Access The Control Panel's <u>Ease of Access</u> category link displays links to accessibility tools and options. One of the tools found in the <u>Optimize visual display</u> link is the Magnifier. This tool displays a magnified version of the screen above the regular screen to help users with vision challenges. Another tool replaces sounds with visual cues. You can also change how your mouse and keyboard work. Changes made in the Ease of Access Center will apply automatically each time you log on to your computer.

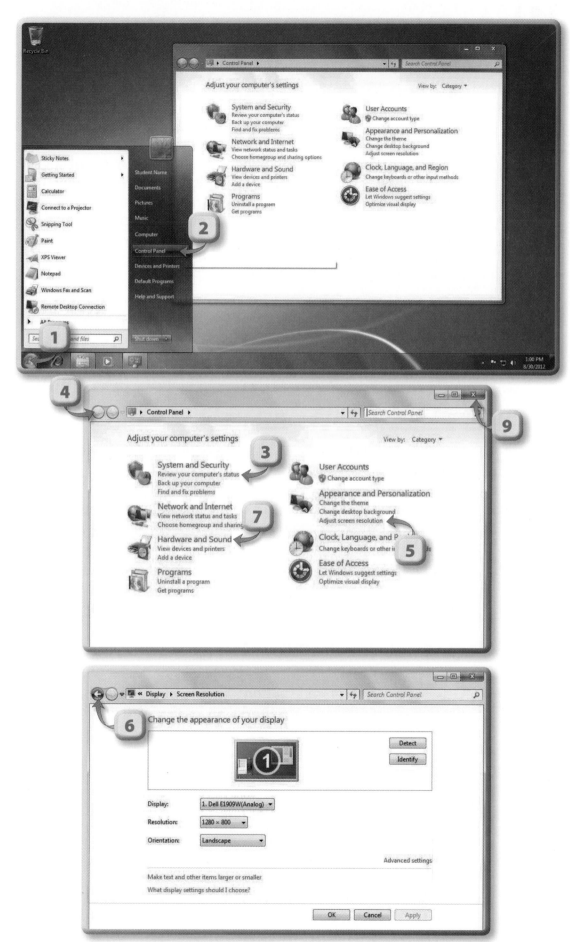

Windows

Windows

Skill 2

Video M2_C3_S02

Set the Date and Time

You use the <u>Clock, Language, and Region</u> category link in the Control Panel to set the computer's date, time, and time zone. The date and time must be set correctly because your computer includes those settings in a time stamp that it adds to your email messages and to the files you save. You may also rely on the clock that displays in the notification area of the Taskbar to show you the correct local time. Also, if you bring your computer when you travel to different time zones, you should know how to change the various date and time settings.

Steps

1 Click the Start button on the Taskbar.

2 Click *Control Panel*.

3 Click the <u>Clock, Language, and Region</u> category link to display tasks in that category.

4 Click the <u>Set the time and date</u> link under the <u>Date and Time</u> subcategory link to display the Date and Time dialog box.

5 Click the Change date and time button. You can change the date by clicking a different date on the calendar and change the time by typing or selecting a new time.

6 Click Cancel to close the Date and Time Settings dialog box.

7 Click the Change time zone button. The current time zone is selected in the *Time zone* option box and the *Automatically adjust the clock for Daylight Saving Time* option is also selected.

8 Click Cancel to close the Time Zone Settings dialog box.

9 Click Cancel to close the Date and Time dialog box.

10 Click the Close button to close the Control Panel window.

> **Tip** Be sure that *Category* is selected in the *View by* list. To do so, click the arrow next to the *View by* list and click *Category*.

> **3** *Another Way*
> You can also change the date, time, and time zone by right-clicking the clock in the notification area on the Taskbar and clicking *Adjust date/time*.

> **Tip** Because the date and time are probably set correctly on your computer, you do not change them in this skill.

> **Tip** A check mark placed in the box before the option *Automatically adjust clock for Daylight Saving Time* means the option is turned on.

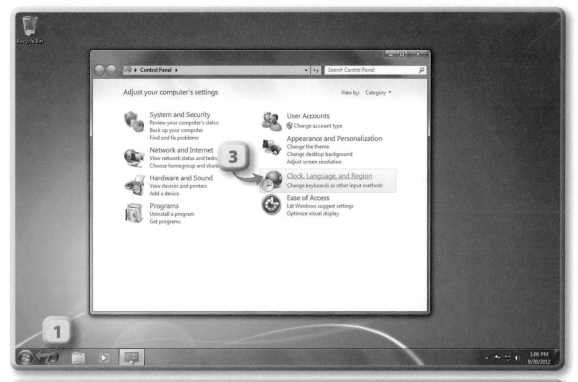

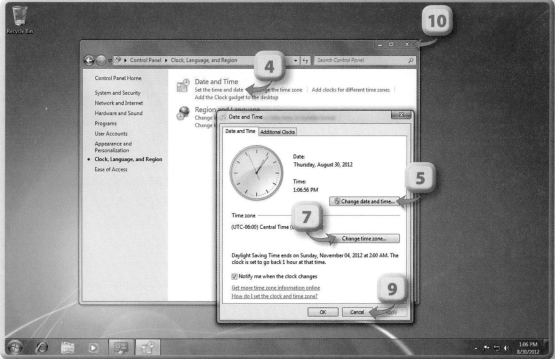

Taking It Further

Adding Clocks for Different Time Zones You can add one or two additional clocks to the Windows 7 Taskbar. You may want these clocks in view if you are corresponding with family or business contacts in different time zones and need to be aware of their time schedules. To add an additional clock, click the Clock, Language, and Region category link in the Control Panel and then click the Set the time and date link. Next, click the Additional Clocks tab. Click the *Show this clock* option and then select a time zone for the new clock.

Windows

Skill 3

Modify the Appearance of Windows

Video   M2_C3_S03

Windows 7 has a default appearance and uses a default color scheme. It applies a specific color, not only to the window borders, but also to the Start menu and Taskbar. The transparent setting, which is referred to as *glass*, is designed to help you focus on the content of your open windows. You can choose a different color for these elements and enable or disable transparency.

Steps

1 Right-click the desktop to display a shortcut menu.

2 Click *Personalize*.

3 Click the <u>Window Color</u> link in the bottom of the window.

4 Click *Lime* (the fifth option in the top row).

5 Click the *Enable transparency* option to remove the check mark.

6 Drag the Color intensity bar slightly to the right.

7 Click the arrow button next to Show color mixer.

8 Drag the *Brightness* bar slightly to the left.

9 Click the Cancel button.

10 Click the Close button to close the Control Panel window.

▶**Tip** If you are working at your personal computer and you wish to save the changes made to the appearance of Windows, click the Save changes button.

Taking It Further

Changing Screen Savers   A screen saver is a moving picture or pattern that displays automatically when the computer has been idle for a specified period of time. Screen savers were originally intended for saving CRT monitors from screen burn-in, but now are frequently used to personalize a computer. You can also use a screen saver to hide your work when you're away from your computer, or use one with a password to enhance your computer's security. To change your screen saver and specify when it should be displayed, right-click the desktop, click *Personalize*, and then click *Screen Saver*. The Screen Saver Setting dialog box displays for you to specify settings for your screen saver.

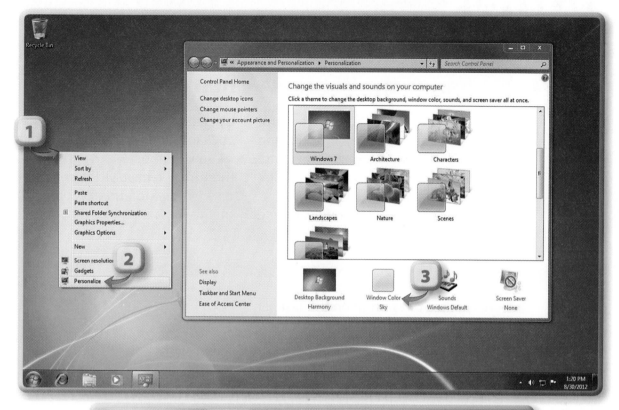

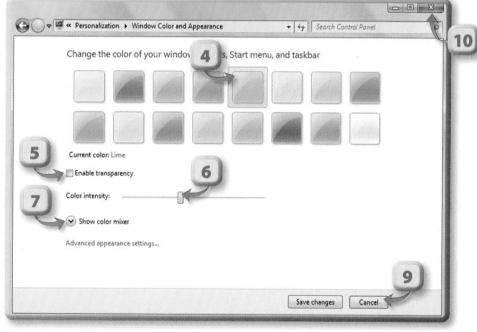

Windows

Windows

Skill 4

Video ▶ M2_C3_S04

Change the Windows Theme

Windows comes with several predesigned themes. A theme includes a desktop background, screen saver, window border color, and sound scheme. Windows applies the *Aero Windows 7* theme by default, but you can change it. You can choose an another installed theme, choose a high-contrast theme if you have vision challenges, or even create and save your own theme.

Steps

1. Click the Start button on the Taskbar.

2. Click *Control Panel* to display the Control Panel window.

▶**Tip** Turn on your computer's sound to hear the sounds associated with the different themes. If necessary, first plug your speakers or headphones into the output jack.

3. Click the <u>Change the theme</u> link under the <u>Appearance and Personalization</u> category link.

4. Scroll to view the themes in the *Aero Themes* section and then click *Nature*.

5. Click the Minimize button to see the Nature background.

5 *Another Way*
Click the Show desktop button on the Taskbar.

6. Click the Control Panel button on the Taskbar to redisplay the Control Panel window.

▶**Tip** When a theme is selected, the theme settings are displayed at the bottom of the window. For example, the High Contrast Black theme summary indicates the desktop background is a *Solid Color*, the window color is *High Contrast*, the sounds are *Windows Default*, and there is no screen saver.

7. Scroll to view the themes in the *Basic and High Contrast Themes* section and then click *High Contrast Black*.

8. Scroll to view the themes in the *Aero Themes* section and then click *Windows 7* to restore the default Windows theme or click the default theme for your computer.

9. Click the Close button to close the Control Panel window.

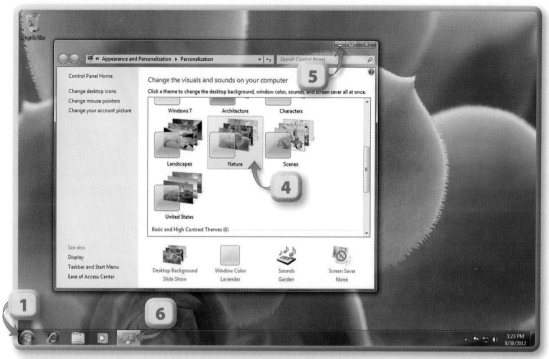

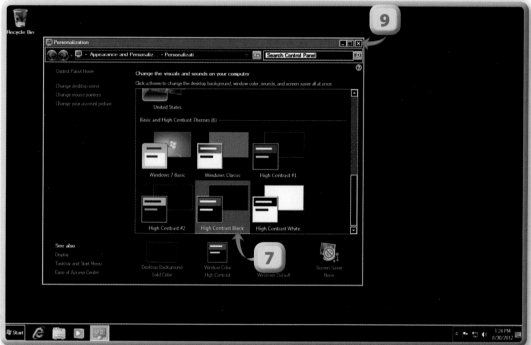

Taking It Further

Creating a Customized Theme   Once you select a theme, you can customize it by changing the theme's background, window color, sounds, and screen saver. Click the Change the theme link under the Appearance and Personalization category link in the Control Panel. Click any theme to apply it to your desktop. Then click the links at the bottom of the window (Desktop Background, Window Color, Sounds, and Screen Saver) to display options for those settings. Review your preferences within each category, select what you like, and when each option looks just the way you want it to, click Save Changes or Apply. Your new theme then appears under *My Themes* as an Unsaved Theme. Save the theme and give it a name by clicking the Save theme link.

Windows

Skill 5

Video ▶ M2_C3_S05

Use Windows Accessories

Windows 7 comes with some handy extra utility programs that are located in the Accessories folder. These programs include the *Snipping Tool*, which you can use to capture information on the screen; *Sticky Notes*, which lets you create electronic "sticky notes;" *Connect to Projector*, which helps you hook up your computer to a projector; *Sync Center*, which lets you sync any folder in your computer with a folder in an external drive; *Paint*, which is image editor software; *Calculator*, which you can use to perform calculations; the text editor *NotePad*; and *WordPad*, a simple word processor.

Steps

1 Click the Start button on the Taskbar.

2 Click *All Programs*.

3 Click *Accessories* to display the Accessories menu.

▶ *Tip* The Calculator view can be changed to Scientific to provide access to mathematical functions like *sin* and *cos*.

4 Click *Calculator* and the Calculator program starts. Try a calculation: For example, divide your total textbook costs of $475 by 5 to find the average cost per book.

5 Click the Close button to close the Calculator window.

6 Click the Start button on the Taskbar.

7 Type sticky in the *Search programs and files* box. Notice that *Sticky Notes* is highlighted under the *Programs* section of the Start Menu.

8 Press Enter to start the Sticky Notes program.

9 Type Meeting at 2 p.m.

10 Right-click the text you typed in the sticky note to display a shortcut menu.

11 Click *Pink* and the sticky note's color changes.

12 Click the Close button on the sticky note.

13 Click Yes to delete the sticky note.

Taking It Further

Trying the Paint Program   You can use the Paint program to draw, color, and edit pictures. The Paint program contains a toolbox with a variety of drawing tools, such as the Line tool and the Pencil tool, which can be used to create lines and curves. You can change the effect of the drawing tools.

For example, you can make the lines you draw using the Line tool thicker or thinner. You can also change the color of the tool. Images you edit or create in Paint can be saved in a variety of graphic formats, including GIF, JPG, TIF, and PNG.

Windows

Skill 6

Video ▶ M2_C3_S06

Review Firewall Settings

A firewall is software or hardware that checks information coming to your computer from a network such as the Internet. The firewall then either blocks the information or allows it to pass through to your computer, depending on your firewall settings. The Windows Firewall is enabled by default. You can check your Windows Firewall status and settings in the Control Panel.

Steps

1 Click the Start button on the Taskbar.

2 Click *Control Panel*.

3 Click the <u>System and Security</u> category link.

4 Click the <u>Check firewall status</u> link under the <u>Windows Firewall</u> subcategory link to review your firewall status.

5 In the left pane, click the <u>Turn Windows Firewall on or off</u> link.

6 Review the firewall settings but do not make changes. Your settings may look different from the settings shown.

7 Click Cancel.

8 Click the Close button to close the Control Panel window.

▶**Tip** You may need special user permissions to see the firewall settings.

▶**Tip** In Windows 7, you can have separate firewall settings for public and private networks. Also, the firewall may be turned off because another firewall program is installed on the computer or because the computer is connected to a network with another firewall program installed.

Taking It Further

Keeping Spyware Under Control Spyware is a type of program that can be installed on your computer, without your knowledge, to collect information about you and your online activities. Spyware may be downloaded when you click a link or go to an untrusted site. Keylogging spyware is one of the most dangerous types, as it allows its creator to track your keystrokes, for example as you enter passwords or account numbers. It's important that you use a spyware detection program to detect and remove spyware. Run a computer scan on a regular basis (for example, every few days or once a week) because spyware may be downloaded to your computer frequently as you browse the Internet. Other precautions to avoid various types of malware include using features such as Windows Defender, built into the Windows operating system; turning on Windows Firewall to prevent access to your computer; and installing antivirus software on your computer and updating it frequently.

Windows

Windows

Skill 7 — Manage Windows Update Settings

Video M2_C3_S07

Microsoft has a feature called Windows Update that allows you to download the latest updates to Windows 7 and other Microsoft products. Windows Update is set to run automatically by default. It downloads updates for you as these items become available. To check your Windows Update settings and review which updates have been installed, you can click the <u>System and Security</u> category link in the Control Panel.

Steps

1 Click the Start button on the Taskbar.

2 Click *Control Panel*.

> **Tip** Be sure that *Category* is selected in the *View by* list.

3 Click the <u>System and Security</u> category link.

4 Click the <u>Windows Update</u> subcategory link and review the Windows Update information.

> **Tip** You can double-click an update in the list to display additional details.

5 Click the <u>View update history</u> link in the left pane and review the update history information.

6 Click the Back button.

> **Tip** The update settings may be different on your computer.

7 Click the <u>Change settings</u> link in the left pane and review the settings.

8 Click Cancel to close the dialog box without saving changes.

9 Click the Close button to close the Control Panel window.

> **Tip** The *Optional updates* section targets elements of Windows 7 that you may or may not use, such as specific drivers or foreign language packs.

Taking It Further

Understanding Windows Update Settings   It is useful to understand some of the Windows update options so you can make informed choices about which updates to install. Depending on your current update needs, you may see different types of suggested updates. The *Important updates* section provide updates that affect your computer's security, privacy, and reliability. The *Recommended updates* section offers updates that improve your computer's performance but do not address fundamental issues with your computer or with the Windows 7 software. You must run all of these types of updates manually.

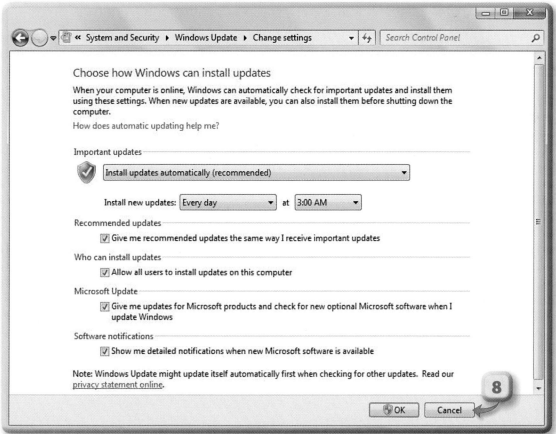

Windows

Skill 8

Video M2_C3_S08

Use Windows Help

Windows has many more features, tools, and accessories than this textbook covers. However, the Windows Help and Support system can help you troubleshoot and explore other features and settings. The Windows Help and Support system uses both the help files that are stored on your computer and online help to find answers to your questions. You can either browse through help topics or search for help on a particular topic.

Steps

1 Click the Start button on the Taskbar to display the Start menu.

2 Shortcut
Windows Help and Support
F1

2 Click *Help and Support*.

▶**Tip** If you have an Internet connection, make sure Online Help is selected and appears on the button at the bottom right corner of the Windows Help and Support window.

3 Click the <u>Learn about Windows Basics</u> link.

4 Scroll down and click the <u>Learn about Windows games</u> link in the *Pictures and games* section. Review the information about Windows games.

5 Click in the Search Help box.

6 Type install fonts and press Enter to display the search results.

7 Click the <u>Install or delete fonts</u> link and review the information.

8 Click the Help and Support home button.

9 Click the Close button to close the Windows Help and Support window.

Taking It Further

Seeking More Support If you cannot find the answer you are looking for, click the More support options button at the lower left corner of the Windows Help and Support window. Clicking this button displays links and resources that you can use to access additional support. For example, you will find information about using Windows Remote Assistance to let a friend access your computer over the Internet and help you fix a problem. You will also find a link to the Microsoft Answers website, which is an online community of experts who may be able to help you.

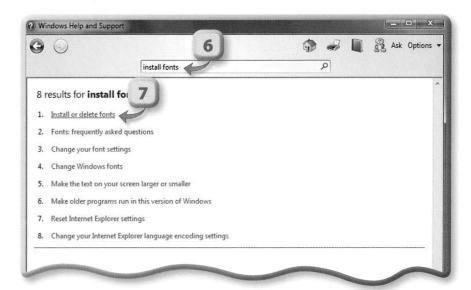

Windows

Skill 9

Use Gadgets

Video M2_C3_S09

Windows 7 includes mini-programs called *gadgets* that you can add to your desktop. Once placed on the desktop, these gadgets display information, such as the time or date, current weather, or breaking news headlines, which you can monitor while working in other programs. You can even set up a slide show of your favorite photos.

Steps

1 With the desktop displayed, right-click the desktop to display the shortcut menu.

2 Click *Gadgets*.

3 *Another Way*
Drag the gadget from the Gadgets window to the desktop.

3 Double-click *Clock* to add the Clock gadget to your desktop.

4 Move the mouse pointer over the Clock gadget to display the toolbar to the right of the gadget.

5 Click the Options button to display the Options for the Clocks gadget.

6 Scroll through the Clock options.

7 Click Cancel.

8 Double-click *Calendar* to add the Calendar gadget to your desktop.

9 Click the Larger size button to increase the size of the Calendar gadget.

10 Click the Close button in the Calendar toolbar to remove the gadget from the desktop.

11 Click the Close button to close the Gadgets window.

Taking It Further

Trying More Gadgets You can use the standard gadgets or you can download additional gadgets online. To view the available gadgets, right-click the desktop and then click *Gadgets* in the shortcut menu. In the Gadgets window, click the Get more gadgets online link. This link takes you to a Microsoft Windows website where you can view and download additional gadgets. At this site you will find a variety of gadgets, including those that monitor traffic, translate foreign languages, convert measurements, and search the Internet.

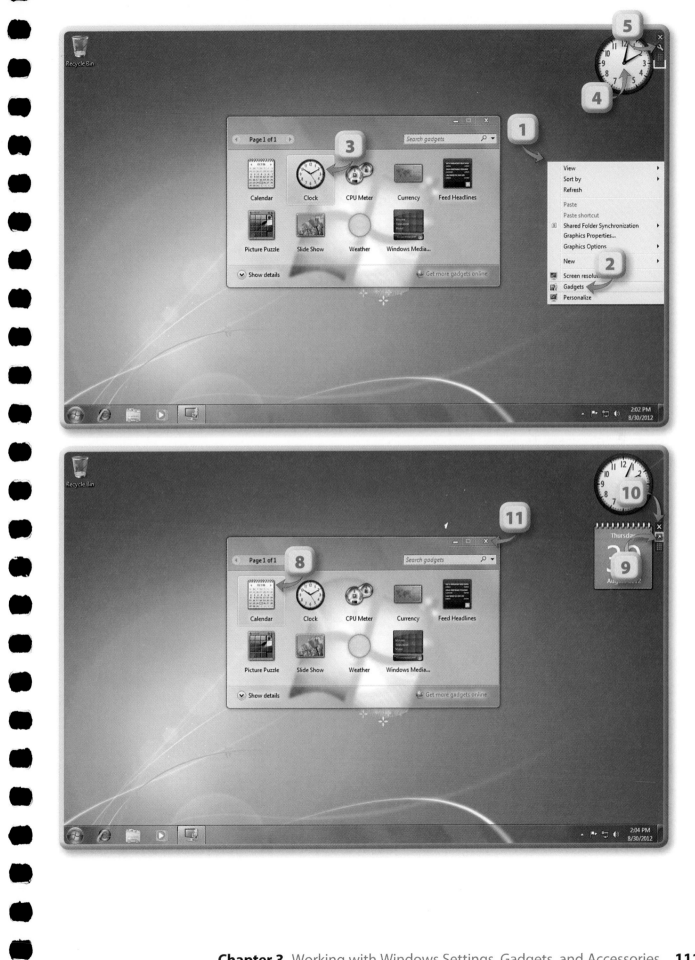

MODULE 3

Internet Basics

Skills You Learn

1. Explore the Microsoft Internet Explorer 8.0 Interface
2. Explore the Mozilla Firefox Interface
3. Navigate among web pages
4. Use tabbed browsing
5. Set up a home page
6. Follow links and history
7. Save sites as Favorites/Bookmark
8. Download files
9. Print a Web page
10. Use search engines

Files You Need

In this module, you do not need any student data files.

What You Create

In this module, you learn to use two of the most popular web browsers, Microsoft Internet Explorer and Mozilla Firefox, to quickly navigate among web pages and become familiar with tabbed browsing. You can designate a home page that displays every time you start your browser and you save or bookmark sites that you would like to return to at a later date. You learn to download files and print a web page. You also learn tips for specifying search criteria in order to find the information you are looking for on the Internet.

Guidelines for Using

The Internet is the largest computer network in the world. You can use the Internet to communicate and share data with others all over the world.

In order to access and connect to the Internet, you need the following:

- a computer
- a hotspot that provides free Internet access or an account with an Internet service provider (ISP) and related communications hardware such as a DSL modem, cable modem, or dial-up modem
- a wireless network card or an Ethernet card in your computer to support connectivity
- a Web browser

Internet Service Provider

An Internet service provider (ISP) is a company that provides access to the Internet through one or more servers, which are large, powerful computers. ISPs usually charge a monthly fee. The ISP provides connection instructions and, depending on the type of Internet connection you have, may provide you with necessary equipment, such as a cable modem or router. The ISP may also provide email accounts and other information services. If you use a school computer or connect to the school's network, you will use the school's ISP and should ask your instructor how to connect to the Internet. You can find hotspots at many colleges and some retail locations that offer wireless Internet connection, often without a fee.

Connection Options

The way you connect to the Internet varies according to the kind of Internet connection you have. The illustration below shows types of connections and the essential equipment required for each type.

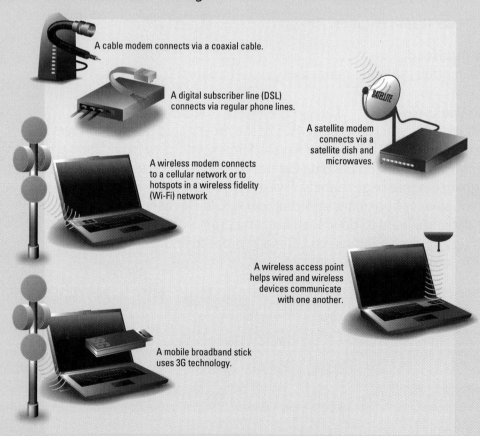

A cable modem connects via a coaxial cable.

A digital subscriber line (DSL) connects via regular phone lines.

A satellite modem connects via a satellite dish and microwaves.

A wireless modem connects to a cellular network or to hotspots in a wireless fidelity (Wi-Fi) network

A wireless access point helps wired and wireless devices communicate with one another.

A mobile broadband stick uses 3G technology.

the Internet

Web Browsers

A web browser is a software program that allows you to locate and view web pages. The term *web page* refers to a single page or document, whereas *website* refers to all of the web pages that make up a site.

Most browsers have similar interfaces and features, so browser choice is usually a matter of individual preference. Browser usage statistics vary, depending on the information source, but a recent estimate states that Internet Explorer has approximately 45% of the market and Firefox, approximately 30%. Other popular browsers include Safari, Chrome, and Opera. Portable devices, such as your cell phone, use mobile browsers designed to work on smaller devices. Shown below are screen captures of the National Park Service's website, accessed using Mozilla Firefox and Internet Explorer. Notice the similar features, including the Address/Location bars (where you type the address of a website), the Search boxes, and the Command/Menu bar options.

Mozilla Firefox Browser

Internet Explorer Browser

Internet Basics

Skill 1

Video M3_C1_S01

Explore the Microsoft Internet Explorer 8.0 Interface

Internet Explorer is a web browser developed by Microsoft and included with the Windows operating system. Internet Explorer's interface has several toolbars, including the Menu bar and the Command bar. Additional toolbars are the Address bar, where you can type a web address, and the Status bar, which is located along the bottom of the Internet Explorer window and displays messages such as the download progress of a web page. In this skill, you become familiar with Internet Explorer's user interface. You also display and locate information on a web page, use the Command bar to access commands and settings, browse Internet Explorer Help, and display the Menu bar.

Steps

▶ **Tip** Depending on your system configuration, the steps to start Internet Explorer may vary.

1 Click the Internet Explorer button, located on the Windows Taskbar, to start Internet Explorer.

2 *Another Way*
Type *google* and press
Ctrl + Enter

2 Select the text in the Address bar, type www.google.com, and then press Enter to display the home page for Google.

▶ **Tip** Use the Command bar to access Internet Explorer commands and settings.

3 Click the Page button on the Command bar.

4 Click *Text Size*.

▶ **Tip** Clicking Larger changes web page text size, unless the web page creator explicitly set the size.

5 Click *Larger* to increase the text size on the web page.

6 Click the Help button on the Command bar.

7 *Shortcut*
Internet Explorer Help
F1

7 Click *Internet Explorer Help* to display the Windows Help and Support window.

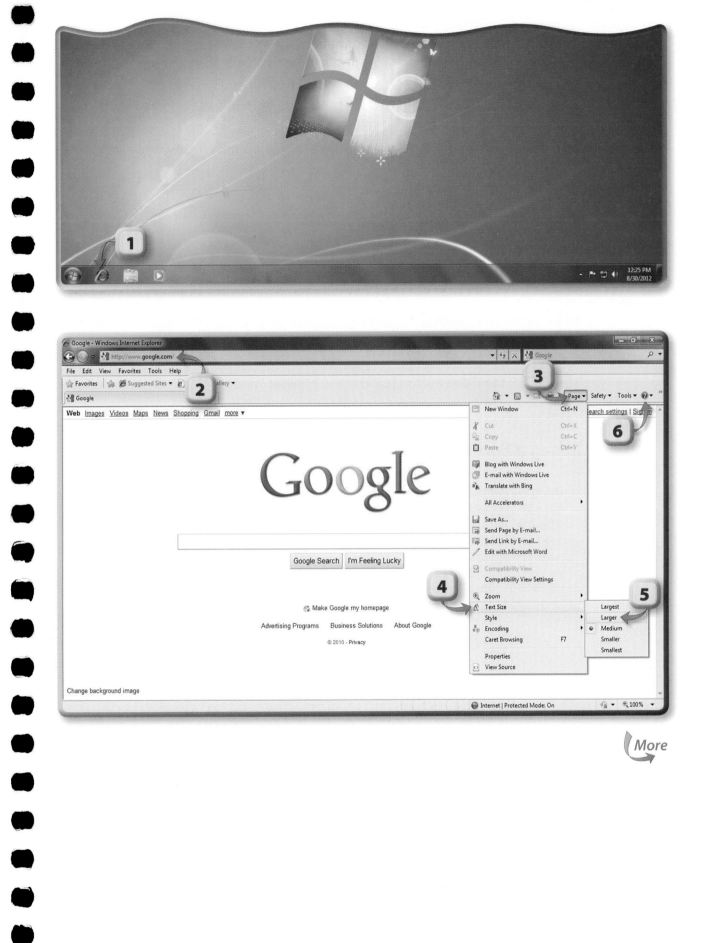

More

Internet Basics

8 Scroll to browse the help information. The Search Help box, where you type keywords to find help on a specific topic, is also available in this window.

9 Click the Close button to close the Windows Help and Support window.

10 Press the Alt key to display the Menu bar, if it is not already displayed.

11 Click Edit on the Menu bar.

12 *Shortcut*
Open Search Box
Ctrl + F

12 Click *Find on this Page*.

13 Type Advanced Search in the *Find* text box.

14 *Advanced Search* is highlighted on the web page and that the Find toolbar indicates one match.

15 Click the Close button to close the browser window.

Taking It Further

Using the Refresh and Stop Buttons
Many websites, such as newspaper websites, refresh or update their site content on a regular basis. Some websites do so automatically, but others require action on your part. To refresh website content, click the Refresh button, located to the right of the Address bar. Or you can simply press the F5 key. If you start to load a website and change your mind, or if the website is taking a long time to load, you can stop the loading process by clicking the Stop button. The Stop button is located next to the Refresh button.

Internet Basics

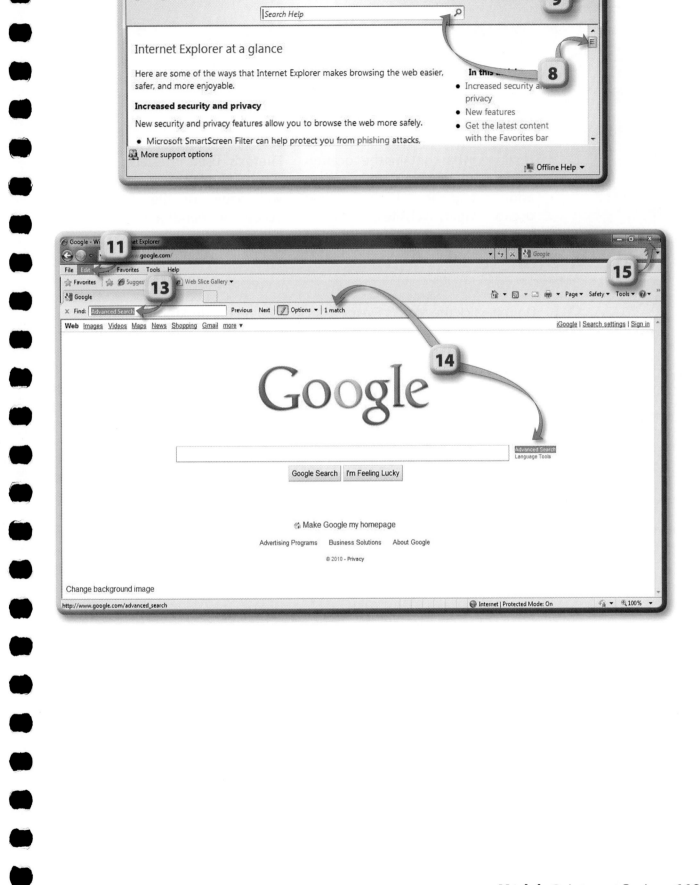

Internet Basics

Internet Basics

Skill 2 — Explore the Mozilla Firefox Interface

Video M3_C1_S02

Firefox is a web browser developed by Mozilla. A free download of Firefox is available from www.mozilla.com. Firefox's interface includes the Menu bar and the Navigation bar. The Navigation bar contains the Location bar, where you can type a web address, and the buttons that you use to navigate websites. The Status bar is located along the bottom of the Firefox window and displays messages that alert you to current activities, such as progress in opening a new web page. In this skill, you become familiar with Firefox's user interface. You also display and locate information on a web page, use the Menu bar to access commands and settings, and browse Firefox Help.

Steps

1 Double-click the *Mozilla Firefox* icon, located on the desktop, to start Firefox.

② Shortcut
Select the URL in the Location bar
Ctrl + L

2 Select the text in the Location bar, type www.google.com, and then press Enter to display the home page for Google.

▶ **Tip** Use the Menu bar to access Firefox commands and settings.

3 Click View on the Menu bar.

4 Click *Zoom* and then click *Zoom In* to increase the text size.

⑤ Shortcut
Decrease Font Size
Ctrl + -
Increase Font Size
Ctrl + +

5 Press Ctrl and then - to decrease the text size.

6 Click Help on the Menu bar.

⑦ Shortcut
Firefox Help
F1

7 Click *Firefox Help*. The Firefox Help web page displays in a new tab in the Firefox window.

8 Scroll to browse the help information. The Search box, where you type keywords to find help on a specific topic, is also available on this page.

▶ **Tip** Tabs are discussed further in Skill 4.

9 Click the Close Tab button to close the Firefox Help tab.

▶ **Tip** Use the down arrow key, the wheel on your mouse, or the vertical scroll bar to scroll down the Firefox Help window.

10 Click Edit on the Menu bar.

11 Click *Find*. The Find bar is displayed at the bottom of the window.

▶ **Tip** Click the Next button in the Find bar to find the next occurrence of the search text.

12 Type Advanced Search in the *Find* text box. The Advanced Search hyperlink is highlighted on the web page.

13 Click the Close button to close the browser window.

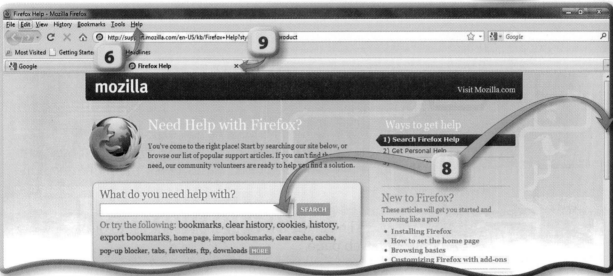

Internet Basics

Module 3

Skill 3

Video M3_C1_S03

Navigate among Web Pages

You can go to a particular web page by typing a Uniform Resource Location (URL), such as http://www.emcp.com in the Address or Location bar of a web browser. The URL specifies the address of a web page on the Internet. Web pages contain links. Each link displays another web page when you click it. Links are usually underlined but may also take other forms, including buttons. You can click the Back and Forward buttons on the browser's interface to navigate through web pages you have already visited. Click the Home button to display the Home page, which is the page displayed when you start the web browser.

Steps

1 Start Internet Explorer.

2 Select the URL in the Address bar, type www.usda.gov, and then press Enter to display the home page for the United States Department of Agriculture (USDA).

3 Click the Agriculture link in the *Browse by Subject* link list to display the USDA Agriculture web page.

4 Scroll down and view the content on the USDA Agriculture web page.

5 Click the Crop Explorer link in the *Spotlights* section to open a new browser window containing the USDA Foreign Agricultural Service Crop Explorer home page.

6 Click a location, such as *West Africa,* on the world map graphic.

7 Click the Back button to return to the USDA Foreign Agricultural Service Crop Explorer home page.

8 Click the Close button to close the browser window containing the Crop Explorer home page.

9 At the USDA Agriculture web page, click the Back button to return to the USDA home page.

10 Click the Close button to close the browser window.

▶**Tip** When you enter the upper-level URL for a site (www.emcp.com), the page that appears is that website's home page.

▶**Tip** Hyperlinks or links display in a variety of ways on web pages, including as buttons, images, icons or underlined text.

▶**Tip** Use the down arrow key, the wheel on your mouse, or the vertical scroll bar to scroll down the web page.

▶**Tip** You can click the Back button and the Forward button to navigate back and forth through locations you have already visited.

Taking It Further

Browsing on a Mac The Safari browser is provided with the Mac operating system, although anybody can download it and use it on any computer. Safari provides a slightly different browsing experience from the more PC-centric browsers like Internet Explorer. There is no menu bar, only a row of icons at the top of the browser. The first two are forward and backward buttons; the third button sends you to a page of thumbnail representations of recently visited sites; the fourth displays a Bookmark menu where you can access your browsing history or sites you have bookmarked; and the last displays a short menu for adding a bookmark. This less-cluttered interface is preferred by some and is in line with Apple's tendency to produce well-designed, graphical interfaces.

Internet Basics

Skill 4

Video   M3_C1_S04

Use Tabbed Browsing

Tabbed browsing is a browser feature that allows you to open more than one website in a single browser window. You can switch between websites by clicking the tab you want to view. When a new tab is opened in Internet Explorer, you can type a web address in the Address bar to open another site.

Steps

1   Start Internet Explorer.

2   Type www.emcp.com in the Address bar and press Enter.

3   Click the New Tab button.

3 *Shortcut*
New Tab (both IE and Firefox)
Ctrl + T

4   Type www.google.com in the Address bar and press Enter to display the Google home page in the new tab.

5   Click the EMC Corporation tab to display it.

6   Click the Quick Tabs button to display a thumbnail view of all your open tabs.

7   Click the EMC Corporation thumbnail.

8   Click the Close Tab button to close the EMC Corporation tab.

9 *Another Way*
To open a new tab from a link on a web page, right-click the link and click *Open in New Tab* (IE) or *Open Link in New Tab* (Firefox).

9   Click the New Tab button.

10   In the *Reopen closed tabs* section of the window, click the <u>EMC Corporation</u> link.

▶ **Tip** When you close Firefox, a prompt asks if you want to save your tabs for the next time you start Firefox. Click Save and Quit to save them or click Quit to close without saving them.

11   Click the Close button and then click the Close all tabs button to close the browser window.

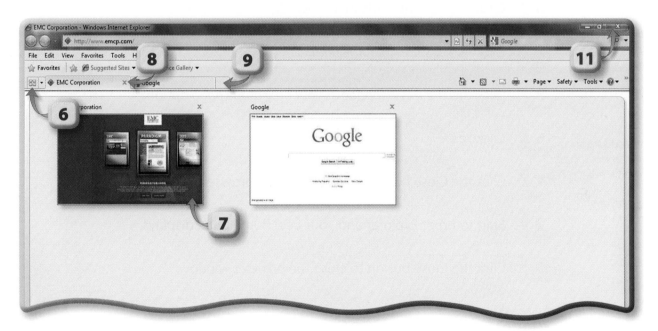

Taking It Further

Exploring New Tab Options   When you open a new tab in Internet Explorer, notice the two sections *Use an Accelerator* and *Browse with InPrivate*. Accelerators allow you to select text on a web page and then use that text to complete additional tasks, such as opening a street address in a mapping website or looking up the dictionary definition of a word. InPrivate browsing automatically clears your website history when you close the browser window, thus enabling you to surf the Web without leaving a history trail. Private browsing is also available in Firefox by clicking Tools on the Menu bar and then clicking *Start Private Browsing*.

Internet Basics

Skill 5 Set Up a Home Page

Video M3_C1_S05

When you start your web browser, the page you see is called the browser's home page. This page also displays when you click the Home button in your web browser. Therefore, you probably want your home page to be a web page that you visit often. For example, your home page might be your company's website or one of your favorite news and information sites. In this skill, you set the home page for your browser.

Steps

1 Start Internet Explorer.

2 Type www.emcp.com in the Address bar and press Enter.

3 Click to the Home button arrow.

4 Click *Add or Change Home Page*.

5 Click the *Use this webpage as your only home page* option.

6 Click Yes.

7 Click the Close button to close the web browser.

8 Start Internet Explorer and your new home page displays.

9 Click the Close button to close the browser window.

▶**Tip** If you are using this skill to change the home page on your personal or home computer, rather than entering www.emcp.com, navigate to the web page that you plan to use as your home page.

▶**Tip** To set up a home page in Firefox, display the website you want as your home page, press the web page icon that displays at the left of the web address in the Location bar, and then drag it to the Home button. Click Yes in the Set Home Page window.

7 *Shortcut*
Close Browser
Alt + F4

Taking It Further

Choosing Multiple Home Pages Do you find it impossible to decide on just one home page? You may maintain more than one home page by having a set of two or more tabs display when you start your browser. To create a set of tabs in Internet Explorer, navigate to the selected web page, click the arrow next to the Home button, and then click *Add or Change Home Page*. Next, click the *Add this webpage to your home page tabs* option. Repeat these steps for each page you want to add to your home page tab set.

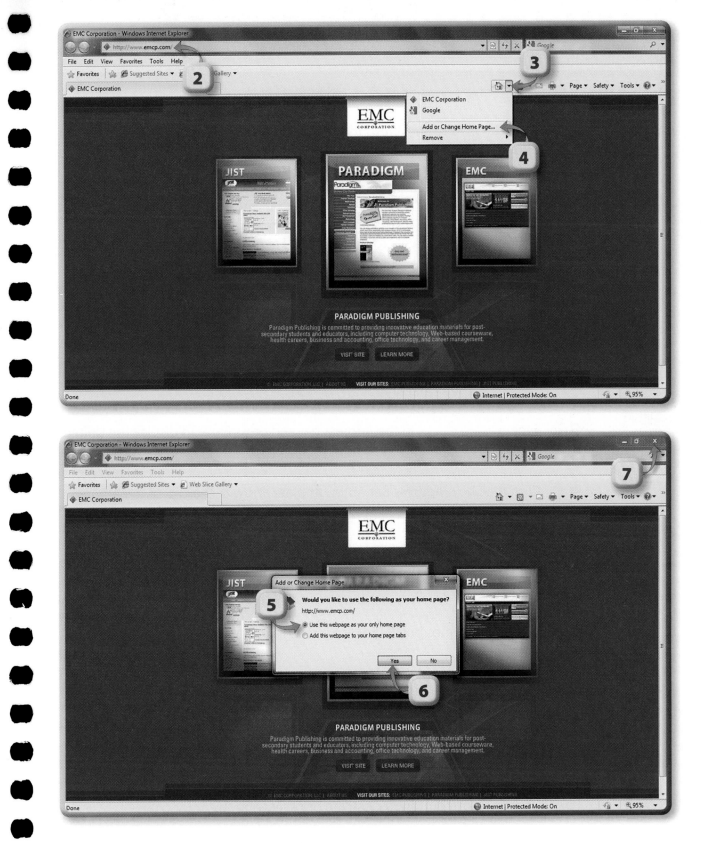

Internet Basics

Skill 6

Video ▶ M3_C1_S06

Follow Links and History

As you browse the Web, Internet Explorer stores information about the websites you visit. Having this information stored on your computer can be helpful. It can improve your web browsing speed and also can help you to find sites you have already visited, without requiring you to remember and type their URLs. Previously visited sites are displayed in the Address bar and you can also access them through the History tab in the Favorites Center.

Steps

1 Start Internet Explorer.

2 Type www.nps.gov in the Address bar and press Enter to display the National Park Service website.

3 Type www.usda.gov in the Address bar and press Enter to display the United States Department of Agriculture home page.

4 Click the Show Address Bar AutoComplete arrow at the end of the Address bar to display a list of web addresses that you have previously typed into the Address bar.

5 Click *http://www.nps.gov/*. The National Park Service website displays without your having to retype the web address.

6 Click the Favorites button to display the Favorites Center.

7 Click the History tab.

8 Click *Today* to display the websites you visited today.

9 Click the usda (www.usda.gov) link to redisplay the USDA home page.

10 Click the Close button to close the browser window.

▶**Tip** When you type the first few letters of a web address in the Address bar, Internet Explorer displays a list of previously entered web addresses that begin with those letters. Click one and press Enter to go to it.

▶**Tip** In Firefox, you can type keywords in the Location bar and it will make suggestions based not only on your previously visited URLs, but also on similar web page titles and on the tags in your bookmarks and history. Mozilla refers to this feature as the "Awesome Bar."

Taking It Further

Changing History Duration By default, Internet Explorer keeps a 20-day history of the web pages you have visited. After 20 days, it automatically deletes those history entries. To change the number of days that Internet Explorer keeps your web page history, click Tools in the Menu bar and then click *Internet Options*. In the Internet Options dialog box, click the General tab and then click the Settings button in the *Browsing history* section. In the *History* section of the Temporary Internet Files and History Settings dialog box, specify the number of days you prefer. If you do not want a web page history kept, set the number of days to *0*. Click OK to close the Temporary Internet Files and History Settings window. Click OK to close the Internet Options window.

Internet Basics

Internet Basics

Skill 7

Save Sites as Favorites/Bookmarks

Internet Explorer *favorites* are links that you save to websites you visit frequently. Firefox has a similar feature, but refers to these favorite sites as *bookmarks*. In Internet Explorer, when you add a website to your Favorites bar, you can then go to that site by simply clicking its name, instead of having to type its web address. If you add a large number of sites to favorites/bookmarks, you can organize them within folders to easily find the site you are looking for.

Steps

1 Start Internet Explorer.

2 Type www.nws.noaa.gov in the Address bar and press Enter to display the website for the National Weather Service.

3 Click the Favorites button to display the Favorites Center.

4 Click the Add to Favorites button and a dialog box displays.

5 Click the Add button to add this site to your Favorites list.

6 Type www.nps.gov in the Address bar and press Enter to display the website for the U.S. National Park Service.

7 Click the Favorites button to display the Favorites Center.

8 Click the Favorites tab.

9 Click the <u>NOAA's National Weather Service</u> link in the Favorites list to redisplay the National Weather Service page.

10 Click the Close button to close the browser window.

4 *Shortcut*
Add a Favorite
Ctrl + D

▶**Tip** Click the New Folder button to create a new folder within your Favorites folder. You can create new folders, as needed, to organize your favorites.

▶**Tip** In Firefox, click Bookmarks and then click *Bookmark This Page* to add a bookmark. Click the Done button.

▶**Tip** To view suggestions for other websites based on the web page you are currently viewing, click the <u>See Suggested Sites</u> link at the bottom of the Favorites bar. You may need to click <u>Turn on Suggested Sites</u> first.

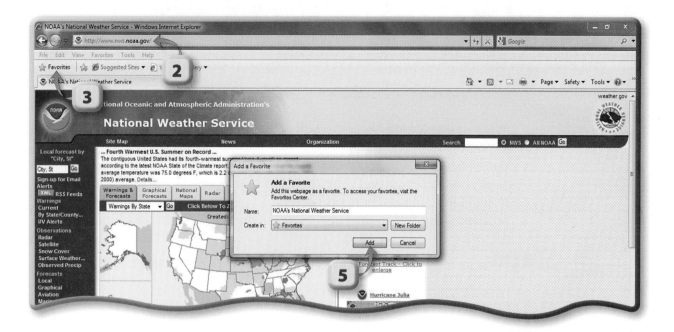

Taking It Further

Cleaning Out Your Favorites   After a while your favorites or bookmarks list can get kind of long, making it hard to find what you need. (A long list defeats the whole purpose of easy-to-find favorites!)

Periodically review and delete listed sites that you no longer visit very often. To do so in Internet Explorer, click Favorites to display the Favorites Center, right-click an item, and then click *Delete* from the shortcut menu.

Internet Basics

Module 3

Skill 8

Download Files

Video M3_C1_S08

When you download a file, you transfer it from the Internet to your computer or another digital device, such as an MP3 player. Commonly downloaded files include programs, software updates, images, and music files. In contrast, when you upload a file, you transfer it from your computer or other device to a site on the Internet. In this skill, you download an image and a PDF document from a web page.

Steps

Tip When you download a file, you take a risk that the file will contain a virus or a program that can damage your computer or your stored information. Be sure to install and use an antivirus program and only download files from sites you trust.

Tip The Pictures library is usually the default location for saving images.

Tip Copyright laws protect much of the information on the Internet. Before using files you have downloaded from the Internet, check the source site for restrictions.

1 Start Internet Explorer.

2 Type www.emcp.net/guidelines/M3S8 in the Address bar and press Enter.

3 Position the arrow pointer on the large textbook cover image and then right-click to display a menu.

4 Click *Save Picture As* to display the Save Picture dialog box.

5 Click Save to save the image to your Pictures library.

6 Click the View Contents Listing (PDF) link to open the page. Whether the page opens in a browser window or in Adobe Reader depends on your Adobe Reader settings. The page will not open if Adobe Reader is not installed on your computer.

7 Click the Close button to close the window containing the PDF.

8 Click the Close button to close the browser window.

Taking It Further

Installing Adobe Reader Adobe Reader is a useful program for people who share files frequently. The program is free and is installed with the Windows Operating System. No matter the originating program, if a file is saved in PDF format, Reader allows you to view it. If you enable comments in the PDF using Adobe Acrobat, people with Adobe Reader can provide input on a PDF file, making it a great tool for group reviews of files. To get and install Adobe Reader, go to http://get.adobe.com/reader/ and click the Download Now button. If you have certain security settings in place, you may first have to agree to install an ActiveX Control on your computer or give Windows permission to download the software. Once you have cleared those security hurdles, a dialog box appears with an Install or Don't Install button. Click the Install button and Adobe Reader installs on your computer.

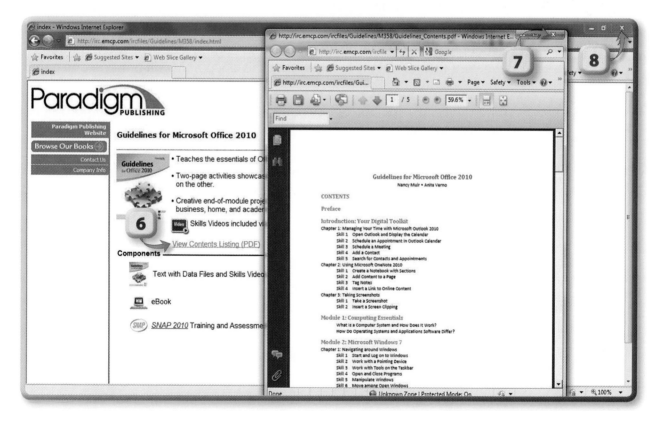

Internet Basics

Skill 9

Video M3_C1_S09

Print a Web Page

You may want to print the information you find on a web page. Keep in mind that web pages are not typically designed to fit on a printed page. So it is usually a good idea to preview the document before you print it. Previewing will show you exactly what the printed document will look like and how many pages are required for the printout. You can then adjust the page orientation, scaling, and margins, if necessary, in the Print Preview window before you click Print.

Steps

1 Start Internet Explorer.

2 Type www.onguardonline.gov in the Address bar and press Enter.

3 Click the Print button arrow.

4 Click *Print Preview* to display how the web page will appear when printed. The Print Preview window shows that this document will print on one page.

5 Click the Landscape button to change the page orientation from portrait to landscape format.

6 Drag the top vertical Adjust margin marker (it looks like a horizontal line with up- and down-pointing arrows) up slightly to set the top margin closer to the top of the page.

7 Click the Print Document button.

8 In the Print dialog box, either click Print or click Cancel if you do not want to print the page.

9 Click the Close button to close the browser window.

4 *Another Way*
Press the Alt key to display the menu bar, click the File tab, and then click *Print Preview*.

▶ *Tip* In Firefox, click File and then click Print Preview to display the Print Preview window.

▶ *Tip* By default, the Print Size is set to *Shrink To Fit*. Stretch or shrink the page size by clicking the Print Size drop-down arrow and selecting a percentage.

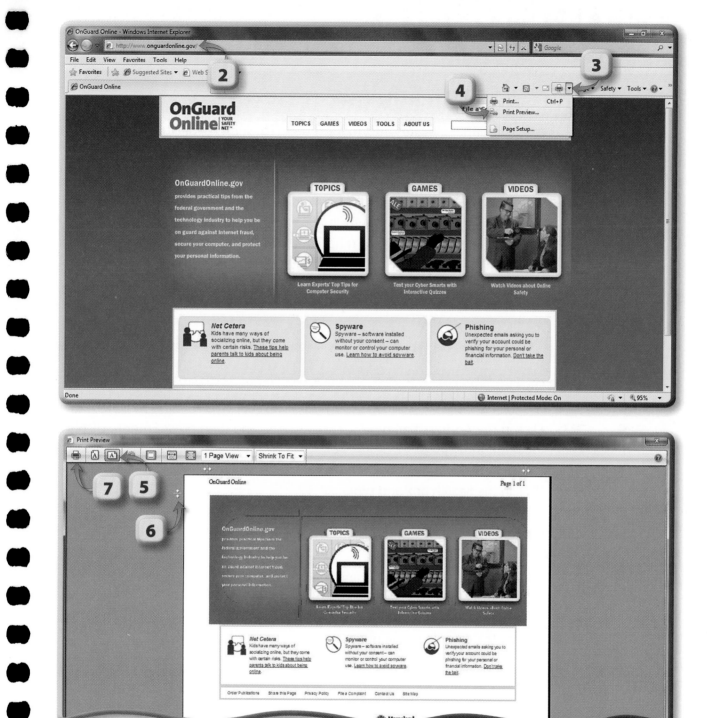

Taking It Further

Adding Headers and Footers to Printed Web Pages   Place additional information at the top and bottom of your web page printouts by using headers and footers. For example, add the current date or time, page numbers, the window title, or the web page address in a header or footer. To add a header and footer in Internet Explorer, click the Print button arrow. Then click *Page Setup* to display the Page Setup dialog box. Click the buttons in the *Headers and Footers* section and then click the items you want to print in the header and footer areas of the page. In Firefox, click *Page Setup* in the File menu and in the Page Setup dialog box, select the Margins & Header/Footer tab.

Internet Basics

Module 3

Skill 10

Video M3_C1_S10

Use Search Engines

A search engine locates information on the Web. Search engines look through web pages for words or phrases you specify and then return a list of matches. A variety of search engines is available, including Google (www.google.com), Yahoo! (www.yahoo.com), Bing (www.bing.com), and Ask (www.ask.com).

To search for information in a search engine, type your search criteria in the Search box and then press the Enter key or click the Search button. Most search engines include tools to help you specify search criteria in order to narrow your search.

Steps

1 Start Internet Explorer.

2 Click in the Address bar, type www.bing.com, and then press Enter to display the Bing home page.

3 Click in the Search box and type new york city attractions.

4 Click the Search button to display the search results.

5 Click a link that interests you and read the information at that site.

6 Click in the Address bar, type www.google.com, and then press Enter to display the Google home page.

7 Click the Images link.

8 Click in the Search Images box and type red roses.

9 Click the Search Images button. The search results display web pages that contain images of red roses.

10 Click the Close button to close the browser window.

▶**Tip** Internet Explorer displays suggestions as you type words into the Search box. Click a suggestion to start the search without having to type the rest of the word or phrase.

▶**Tip** In both Internet Explorer 8.0 and Firefox, search engines are accessible from the Search box at the right of the Address bar or Location bar. You can change the default search engine listed in this box by clicking the arrow at the right of the Search box and then choosing your preferred search engine.

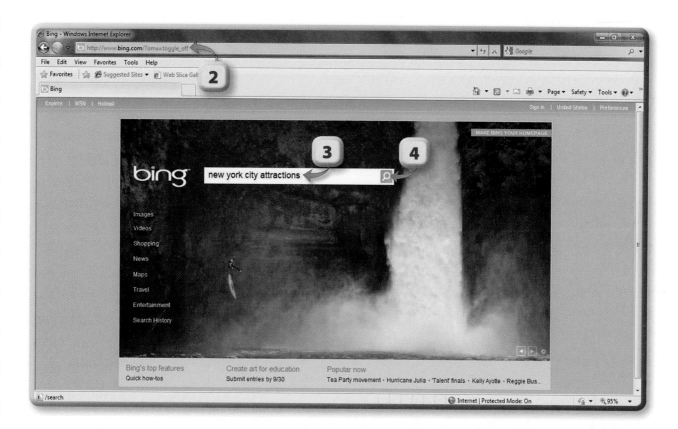

Taking It Further

Using Advanced Search Because the Internet contains such a large quantity of information, you may sometimes have difficulty finding exactly what you want. To help you search more successfully, most search engines offer an Advanced Search link with options for narrowing your search. In Google, click the Advanced Search link to display options such as "...*don't show pages that have any of these unwanted words*." Advanced Search empowers you with many options, including specifying that your search take place within a particular site or domain, such as at the site youtube.com or at sites ending with the domain destination .gov.

MODULE 4

Microsoft® Office 2010 Suite Overview

Skills You Learn

1 Create a file and display Backstage view
2 Open and save a file
3 Understand the ribbon
4 Navigate within a file
5 Use Find and Replace
6 Use Undo and Redo
7 Change views and zoom percentage
8 Check spelling and grammar
9 Use formatting tools
10 Print a file
11 Use Help
12 Use Microsoft Office 2010 Web Apps

Files You Need

In this module, you need the following student data files.

S2-Sales.xlsx

S3-TravelDeals.docx

What You Create

In this module, you edit a travel agency flyer by using features common across several applications. When learning to open and save files, you work with an Excel Sales workbook. You also learn to add images and illustrations to a document, giving it a professional look.

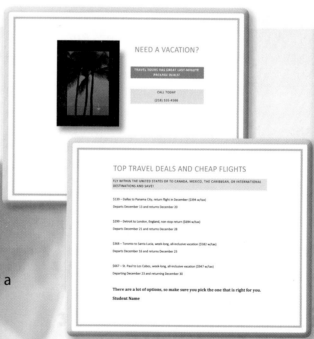

NEED A VACATION?

TRAVEL TOURS HAS GREAT LAST-MINUTE PACKAGE DEALS!

CALL TODAY
(218) 555-4566

TOP TRAVEL DEALS AND CHEAP FLIGHTS

FLY WITHIN THE UNITED STATES OR TO CANADA, MEXICO, THE CARIBBEAN, OR INTERNATIONAL DESTINATIONS AND SAVE!

$139 – Dallas to Panama City, return flight in December ($394 w/tax)
Departs December 13 and returns December 20

$299 – Detroit to London, England, non-stop return ($694 w/tax)
Departs December 21 and returns December 28

$368 – Toronto to Santa Lucia, week-long, all-inclusive vacation ($582 w/tax)
Departs December 16 and returns December 23

$667 – St. Paul to Los Cabos, week-long, all-inclusive vacation ($947 w/tax)
Departing December 23 and returning December 30

There are a lot of options, so make sure you pick the one that is right for you.
Student Name

Travel Deals Flyer

Before beginning the module skills, copy the Module4-Office folder from the Student Resources CD to your storage medium. The copied folder will become the working folder for this module.

Guidelines for Understanding

The Microsoft Office 2010 suite is made up of several applications. Earlier in this book, you learned to use Outlook to manage your schedule and contacts list and OneNote to create a digital notebook. Other applications in the Office suite include:

- **Access 2010** Use this database application to store and organize large amounts of data. For example, all the bits of information a company gathers about its customers and suppliers can be stored in a database. You can query a database to find specific information, such as all customers who live in a certain city. You can also produce reports from the data.

- **Excel 2010** This spreadsheet application to enter numbers or other data into a grid of rows and columns. Once data is entered, Excel can perform automatic calculations, such as adding numbers to get a total. Excel can also create graphs from the data. Organizations and individuals use spreadsheets to track inventory, manage budgets, balance checkbooks, and create income statements.

- **PowerPoint 2010** Use this presentation application to create slides that support an oral presentation. The slides help the audience follow and understand the key points of the presentation. Photos and charts in the slides can add visual interest.

- **Word 2010** With this word processor application, you can produce professional-looking documents, including letters, resumes, reports, and much more.

Even though each application in the Office suite is designed to perform a specific task, all applications have some common interface elements and commands. Learning about the shared features of the applications—their common "look and feel"—reduces the time you need to master the entire Office suite.

Shared Interface Elements

Each Office application interface includes the Quick Access Toolbar and the ribbon. The Quick Access Toolbar allows you to add icons for the actions you use often, such as undoing a change and saving a file. You can place your own choices on this toolbar for most-often-used commands. The ribbon is the main interface feature. The File tab on the ribbon displays the Backstage view, which includes file management options, such as opening, printing, and saving. The ribbon offers other tabs and groups of commands that are related to each other—for example, the Page Layout tab contains a Page Setup group and a Themes group. Some of the common interface elements are shown in the image below:

Office Suite Basics

Shared Commands

In the Print tab Backstage view, many of the commands are the same for Excel, Word, and PowerPoint. Compare the screens below for similarities.

Becoming familiar with common interface elements and commands now, before starting the skills in the Word, Excel, Access, and PowerPoint modules, will speed up your learning in each application.

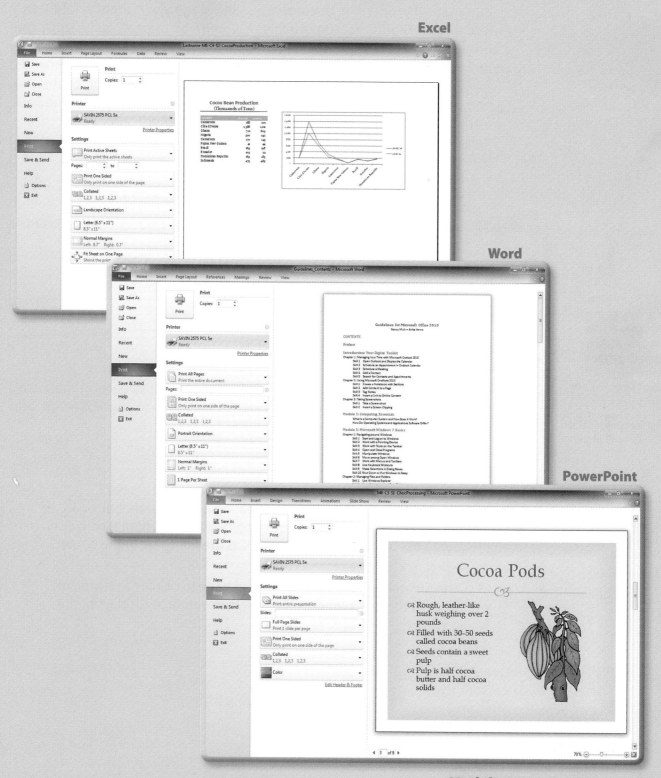

Microsoft Office

Skill 1 — Create a File and Display Backstage View

Video M4_C0_S01

When you open Excel, the program automatically opens a blank workbook. Similarly, Word automatically opens a document, and PowerPoint automatically opens a presentation. Access starts in Backstage view. You will move to Backstage view in Word, Excel, and PowerPoint, and see it again in Access, when you work with files, send data to the printer, and use Help. In all of the programs, the Backstage view contains a set of commands that allows you to manage your files and perform file tasks, such as saving or printing. Backstage view contains four Quick Command buttons at the top left—Save, Save As, Open, and Close. Just below these Quick Commands, the Backstage view presents six tabs—Info, Recent, New, Print, Save & Send, and Help. Two buttons display below the Help tab—Options and Exit.

Steps

1 Click the Start button on the Windows Taskbar.

2 Click *All Programs*.

2 Another Way
If you have used Microsoft Excel recently, the program name will appear in the recently used programs list along the left side of the Start menu above *All Programs*. Simply click it in the list to open it.

▶**Tip** The Title bar displays the file and program name.

3 Scroll down the program list and click *Microsoft Office*.

4 Click *Microsoft Excel 2010* in the list of applications that appears in the menu. Excel starts a blank workbook and *Book1 - Microsoft Excel* displays in the Title bar.

5 Click the File tab.

6 Shortcut
Open New Document, Workbook, or Presentation
Ctrl + N

▶**Tip** Each application in the Office suite has a different colored Backstage view. Excel's color is green.

6 Click the New tab to see options for creating a blank workbook or a workbook based on a template. The *Blank workbook* option is active and a preview of the blank workbook displays at the right side of the screen.

7 Click the Create button in the right-hand pane to display a new blank workbook in the Excel window. *Book2 - Microsoft Excel* displays in the Title bar.

More

Microsoft Office

8 Click the File tab.

9 Click the Help tab to view the Help options that are displayed in Backstage view.

10 Click the File tab to display the blank Book2 Excel file and to make the Home tab active.

11 Click the Close window button below the red Close button to close the unsaved Book2 blank file while keeping Excel open. Unsaved Book 2 closes and Book 1 displays.

12 Click the Close window button again to close the unsaved Book1 blank file while keeping Excel open. You continue to work in Excel in the next skill.

Taking It Further

Customizing the Quick Access Toolbar   The applications in the Office suite have a Quick Access toolbar in the top left corner of the window. The standard buttons include Save, Undo, and Redo. You can customize the toolbar by clicking the Customize Quick Access Toolbar button and selecting from the options on the drop-down list. If you want more commands organized by the tab of the ribbon on which they reside, click *More Commands* to see a dizzying number of additional options. Customizing the Quick Access toolbar is just one example of the many ways you can customize the Office applications to help you do your work more efficiently.

Microsoft Office

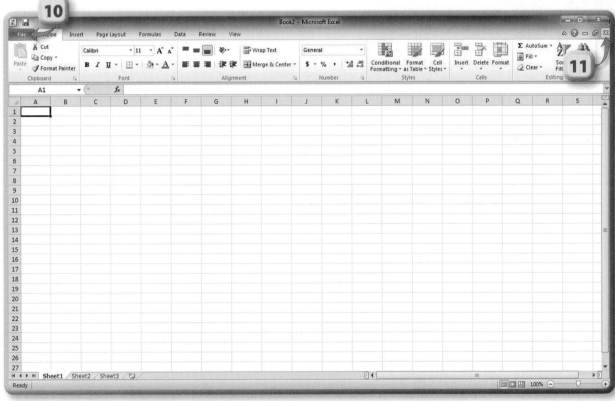

Microsoft Office

Skill 2

 Video M4_C0_S02

Open and Save a File

As you saw in the previous skill, files can be created by selecting a blank workbook or from a template available in Backstage view. You can also find the commands for opening an existing file in the Backstage view. When you save a file, you can save it to a folder on the computer's hard disk; on a CD, DVD, or flash drive; on the desktop; or on a network drive. You can also save the file in any one of a variety of file formats.

Steps

▶**Tip** If Excel is not already open, start Excel and close the Book1 window.

2 *Shortcut*
Open a Document, Workbook, or Presentation
Ctrl + O

▶**Tip** Module 3, Chapter 2 provides instruction in file management.

6 *Shortcut*
Save As
F12

1 With the Excel window active, click the File tab.

2 Click the Open button.

3 Navigate to the student data file named **M4-S2-Sales.xlsx** in your Module 4 working folder.

4 With the **M4-S2-Sales.xlsx file** selected in the *File name* text box in the Open dialog box, click the Open button. The selected file appears in your Excel window.

5 Click the File tab.

6 Click the Save As button.

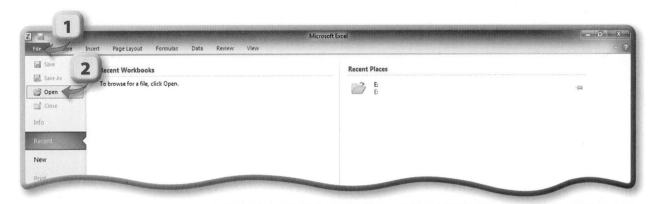

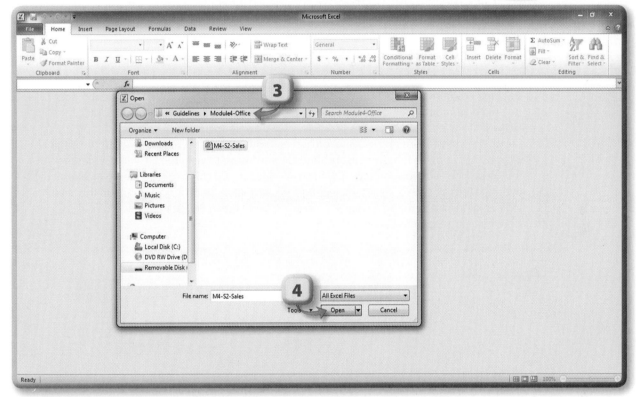

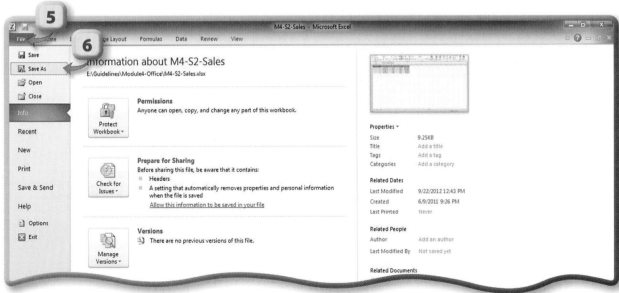

More

Tip File names should be descriptive of the file's contents so you can find them easily. A valid file name cannot contain certain characters. Colons (:), asterisks (*), or question marks (?) are examples of these characters.

7 In the *File name* text box, type Lastname-M4-S2-Sales, but replace *Lastname* with your last name. Be sure to save the file to your Module 4 working folder on your storage medium.

8 Click the Save button.

9 Click the File tab.

10 Click the Exit button to close the file and Excel.

Taking It Further

Saving Files in Alternate Formats By default, documents, workbooks, presentations, and databases are saved as files in their native format: .docx in Word, .xlsx in Excel, .pptx in PowerPoint, and .accdb in Access. However, you can save files in an alternate format, such as PDF, by selecting a different format in the *Save as type* drop-down list in the Save As dialog box. PDF is the format used by a document reader program called Adobe Reader. You can download the free Adobe Reader program, which allows you those without the original software to view the file with formatting intact. You can also save files in an alternative format by selecting an option in the Save & Send tab in Backstage view.

Microsoft Office

Microsoft Office

Microsoft Office

Understand the Ribbon

Video M4_C0_S03

The ribbon is an interface element that is displayed in the application window. It is designed to help you quickly find the commands that you need to complete a task. The ribbon is organized into a series of tabs. Each tab relates to a type of activity, such as inserting objects or formatting the visual or text elements on a page. In a tab, commands are organized in logical groups. For example, the Bold, Italic, and Font Color buttons are in the Font group on the Home tab. In order to reduce screen clutter, some tabs, known as contextual tabs, are shown when you select certain types of objects such as tables or pictures. The Picture Tools Format tab is an example of a contextual tab.

Steps

1 Open the Word student data file named **M4-S3-TravelDeals.docx** and, if you have not already done so, save the file to your Module 4 working folder on your storage medium.

▶**Tip** When a Word, Excel, or PowerPoint file opens, the Home tab is active.

2 Click the Insert tab on the ribbon.

3 Click the picture in the document. The Picture Tools Format tab is added to the ribbon when the picture is selected.

5 *Shortcut*

Minimize the Ribbon
Ctrl + F1

4 Click the Picture Tools Format tab to view the four groups that contain the picture editing commands: Adjust, Picture Styles, Arrange, and Size.

▶**Tip** When the ribbon is minimized, you can still access commands by clicking a tab. The ribbon automatically minimizes after the command is selected.

5 Click the Minimize the Ribbon button to minimize the ribbon and display only the ribbon's tabs.

6 Click the Expand the Ribbon button to redisplay the entire ribbon.

7 *Shortcut*

Close the Application
Alt + F4

7 If you are not continuing on to the next skill, close the document and Word by clicking the Close button.

Taking It Further

Using the Keyboard with Ribbon Tabs   Office 2010 provides keyboard access keys for the ribbon so you can quickly perform tasks without using the mouse. When you press the Alt key in any of the Office 2010 applications, letters—called KeyTips—are displayed on each tab. Depending on which letter you press, you may be shown additional KeyTips. For example, if the Home tab is the active tab and you press N, the Insert tab displays along with the KeyTips for the groups on that tab. Press the letter of the task you want to complete. To cancel the action that you are taking and hide the KeyTips, press the Alt key.

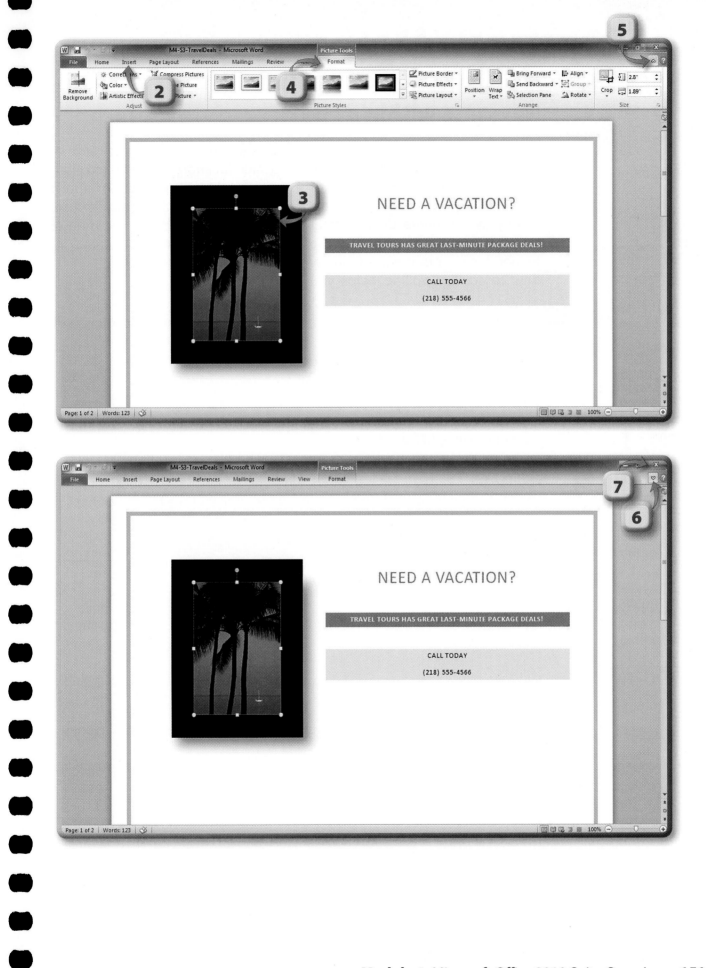

Microsoft Office

Microsoft Office

Video M4_C0_S04

Navigate within a File

Many files you create in each of the Office applications will be more than one page long. Your monitor is a fixed size and may not be able to display the entire document at once. To navigate around these longer documents, it helps to know how to scroll. Scrolling helps you quickly find information or reach a specific location in the file so that you can then make edits or apply additional formatting. You can use both the keyboard and the mouse to navigate to specific locations in a file.

Steps

1 If it is not already open, open the student data file named **M4-S3-TravelDeals.docx**, the file used in Skill 3.

2 Move the insertion point to the beginning of the document, immediately in front of the title, *NEED A VACATION?*

3 Position the mouse pointer on the down scroll arrow on the vertical scroll bar. Click the left mouse button several times, until you see the top of the second page of the document.

4 Press the Page Down key on the keyboard. The insertion point moves within the title *TOP TRAVEL DEALS AND CHEAP FLIGHTS* on page 2.

5 Press the Home key. The insertion point moves to the start of the title line on page 2.

6 Press the End key. The insertion point moves to the end of the title line.

7 Press the Down Arrow key twice. The insertion point moves down two lines.

8 Drag the scroll bar to the top of page 1. The insertion point remains on page 2.

2 Shortcut
Move Insertion Point to Top of File
Ctrl + Home

▶**Tip** When you open a Word document, the insertion point is automatically at the beginning of the document.

▶**Tip** Scrolling does not move the insertion point.

▶**Tip** Your keyboard may not look exactly the same as the keyboard shown. Certain keys may be in different locations.

▶**Tip** If your mouse has a scroll wheel, you can roll the wheel to scroll through the document.

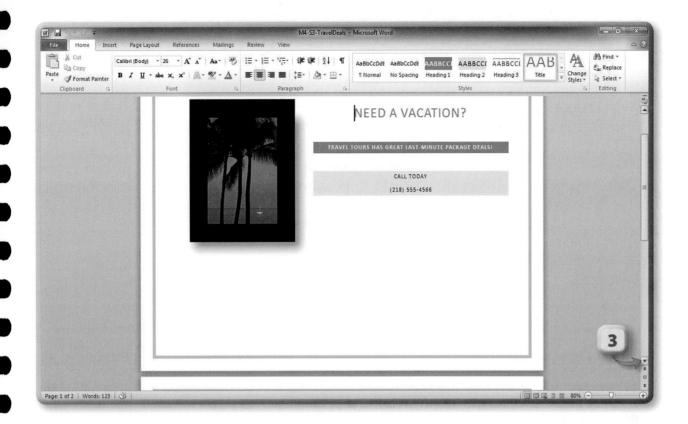

Taking It Further

Navigating with Keyboard Shortcuts
You can use key combinations to move the insertion point to a specific location in a file. Press Ctrl + Home to move to the start of a document in Word. In Excel, press Ctrl + Home to move to the first cell in the worksheet. Press Ctrl + End to move to the end of a document in Word or to the last cell

in the worksheet in Excel. Press the F5 key in Word to display the Find and Replace dialog box with the Go To tab selected. Pressing F5 in Excel will open the Go To dialog box. In Word, you can type a page number to move the insertion point to a specific page, and in Excel, you can type a cell address to move quickly to that cell.

Microsoft Office

Skill 5

Video ▶ M4_CO_S05

Use Find and Replace

The Find feature enables you to search for specific characters or formatting. When the Find feature locates items that match your search terms, the results are displayed in the Navigation pane.

Similarly, the Find and Replace feature allows you to search for specific characters or formatting and replace them with other characters or formatting.

Steps

1 If it is not already open, open the student data file named **M4-S3-TravelDeals.docx** and save the file as **S5-TravelDeals**. Be sure to save the file to your Module 4 working folder on your storage medium.

2 *Shortcut*
Find
Ctrl + F

2 Click the Find button in the Editing group on the Home tab.

3 Type September in the Navigation pane Search box. Search text matches are highlighted in the document and listed in the Navigation pane.

4 Click the Close button in the upper right corner of the Navigation pane.

5 *Shortcut*
Move to Top of Document
Ctrl + Home

5 Scroll to the top of the document and click at the beginning of the line, *NEED A VACATION*. You decide to update the flyer by replacing all occurrences of *September* with *December*.

6 Click the Replace button in the Editing group. This opens the Find and Replace dialog box and *September* is in the *Find what* text box.

7 Type December in the *Replace with* text box.

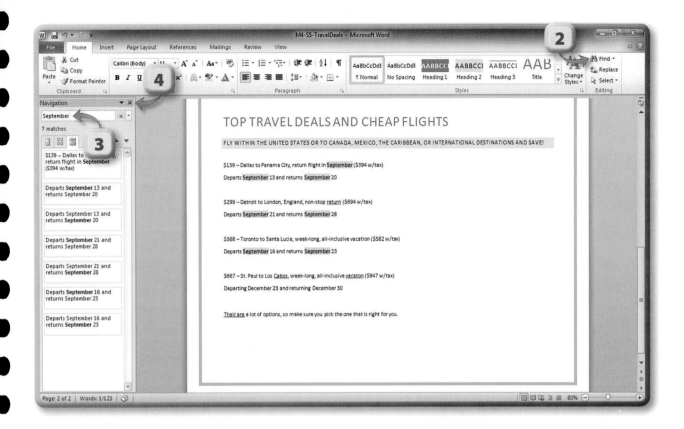

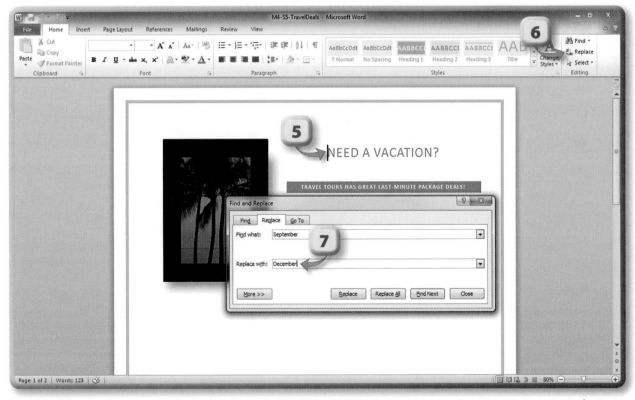

More

8 Click the Replace All button.

9 In the dialog box saying that seven replacements have been made, click OK.

10 Click the Close button to close the Find and Replace dialog box.

11 Save the file by clicking the Save button on the Quick Access toolbar.

NEED A VACATION?

TRAVEL TOURS HAS GREAT LAST-MINUTE PACKAGE DEALS!

CALL TODAY
(218) 555-4566

TOP TRAVEL DEALS AND CHEAP FLIGHTS

FLY WITHIN THE UNITED STATES OR TO CANADA, MEXICO, THE CARIBBEAN, OR INTERNATIONAL DESTINATIONS AND SAVE!

$139 – Dallas to Panama City, return flight in December ($394 w/tax)
Departs December 13 and returns December 20

$299 – Detroit to London, England, non-stop return ($694 w/tax)
Departs December 21 and returns December 28

$368 – Toronto to Santa Lucia, week-long, all-inclusive vacation ($582 w/tax)
Departs December 16 and returns December 23

$667 – St. Paul to Los Cabos, week-long, all-inclusive vacaton ($947 w/tax)
Departing December 23 and returning December 30

Their are a lot of options, so make sure you pick the one that is right for you.

Completed Skill 5

Microsoft Office

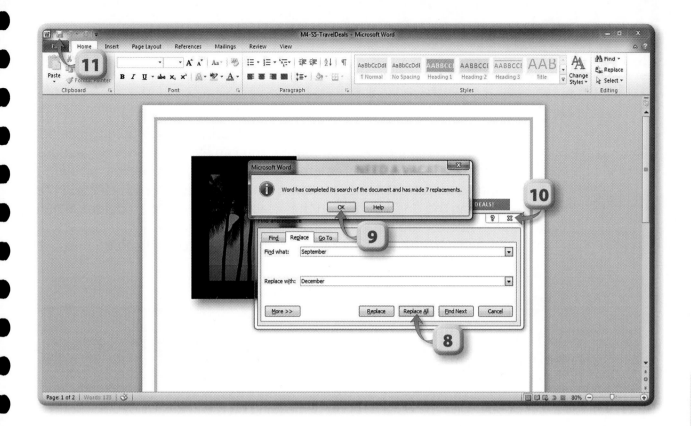

Taking It Further

Finding with Narrower Limits   Click the More button in the Find and Replace dialog box to display additional search options. Select the *Match case* option to locate text with the same capitalization as that of the search text. For example, a search for *January* will not find *JANUARY*. Select *Find* *whole words only* to locate text that entirely matches the search text. For example, a search for *every* will not find *everyone*. Use the Format button in the Find and Replace dialog box to search for formatting, such as a specific font.

Microsoft Office

Skill 6

Video M4_C0_S06

Use Undo and Redo

Have you ever deleted text and then changed your mind? Fortunately, you can restore the text you deleted during your current work session by clicking the Undo button on the Quick Access toolbar. The Undo button reverses the last action you performed, including formatting, deletions, insertions, and so on. You can even undo several actions at a time by clicking the arrow on the Undo button and selecting the actions you want to delete. When you want to repeat the last action performed, click the Redo button.

Steps

1 If it is not already open, open **M4-S5-TravelDeals.docx**, the file you saved in the previous skill. Save the file as **M4-S6-TravelDeals**.

▶**Tip** Double-click to select an entire word. Triple-click to select an entire paragraph.

2 Double-click the word *Need* in the heading on the first page of the document.

3 Click the Cut button in the Clipboard group on the Home tab. This removes the word *Need*.

4 *Shortcut*
Undo
Ctrl + Z

4 Click the Undo button in the Quick Access toolbar. The last action is reversed so that *Need* appears in the heading of the document.

5 Press the End key.

6 Type ?. (Do not type the period.)

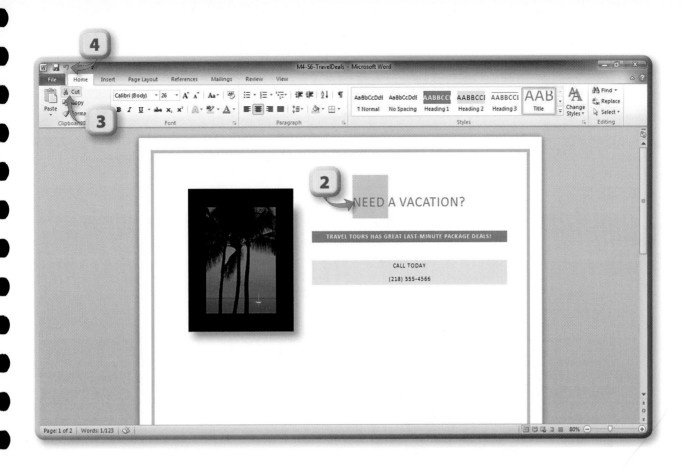

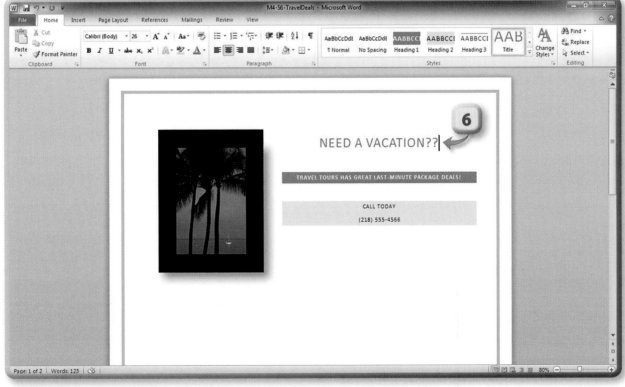

More

7 *Shortcut*
Redo
Ctrl + Y

▶**Tip** You can undo two actions at once by selecting the second item on the Undo list, three actions by selecting the third, and so on.

▶**Tip** The default number of available undos varies in each Office application and can be changed if needed.

7 Click the Redo button in the Quick Access toolbar.

8 Click the Undo button arrow.

9 In the drop-down list click the second action, *Typing "?"*. This leaves just one *?* in the document.

10 Save the file by clicking the Save button on the Quick Access toolbar.

NEED A VACATION?

TRAVEL TOURS HAS GREAT LAST-MINUTE PACKAGE DEALS!

CALL TODAY
(218) 555-4566

TOP TRAVEL DEALS AND CHEAP FLIGHTS

FLY WITHIN THE UNITED STATES OR TO CANADA, MEXICO, THE CARIBBEAN, OR INTERNATIONAL DESTINATIONS AND SAVE!

$139 – Dallas to Panama City, return flight in December ($394 w/tax)
Departs December 13 and returns December 20

$299 – Detroit to London, England, non-stop return ($694 w/tax)
Departs December 21 and returns December 28

$368 – Toronto to Santa Lucia, week-long, all-inclusive vacation ($582 w/tax)
Departs December 16 and returns December 23

$667 – St. Paul to Los Cabos, week-long, all-inclusive vacaton ($947 w/tax)
Departing December 23 and returning December 30

Their are a lot of options, so make sure you pick the one that is right for you.

Completed Skill 6

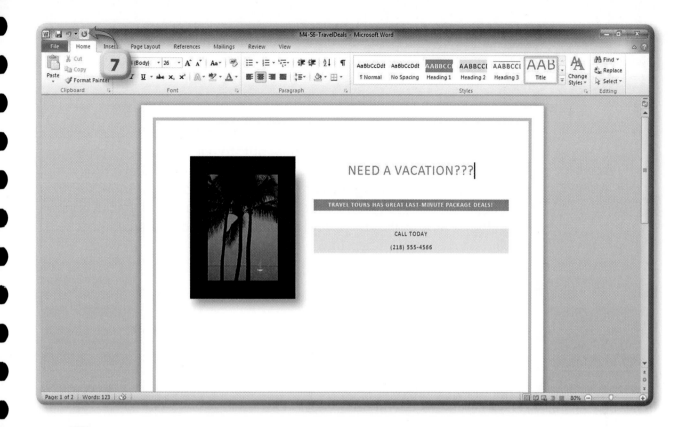

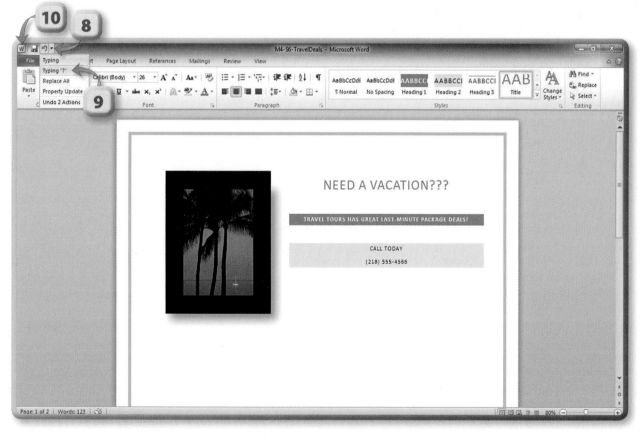

Microsoft Office

Microsoft Office

Skill 7 | ## Change Views and Zoom Percentage

Video | M4_C0_S07

The View tab in Excel, PowerPoint, and Word contains buttons for changing the view. You will also find buttons for changing the zoom percentage while you are viewing a file. By default, a file is viewed at 100% of its normal size. However, you may want to zoom in or zoom out to view different parts of a document. Excel, PowerPoint, and Word also contain a Zoom slider bar on the Status bar that allows you to adjust the zoom percentage.

Steps

1. If it is not already open, open **M4-S6-TravelDeals.docx**, the file you saved in the previous skill. Save the file as **M4-S7-TravelDeals**.

2. Click the View tab.

3. Click the Two Pages button in the Zoom group.

4. Click the One Page button in the Zoom group.

5. Click the Zoom button in the Zoom group to open the Zoom dialog box.

6. Click the *75%* option in the *Zoom to* section of the dialog box.

7. Click OK.

8. Drag the Zoom slider bar on the Status bar to *100%*.

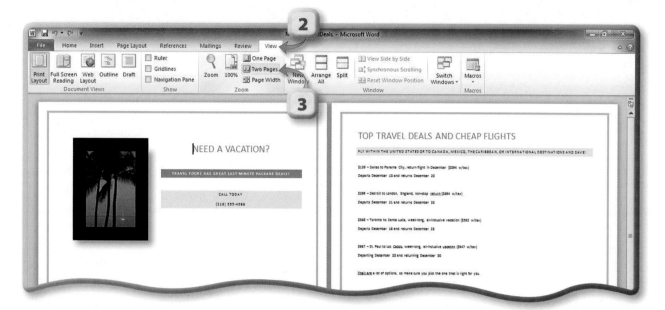

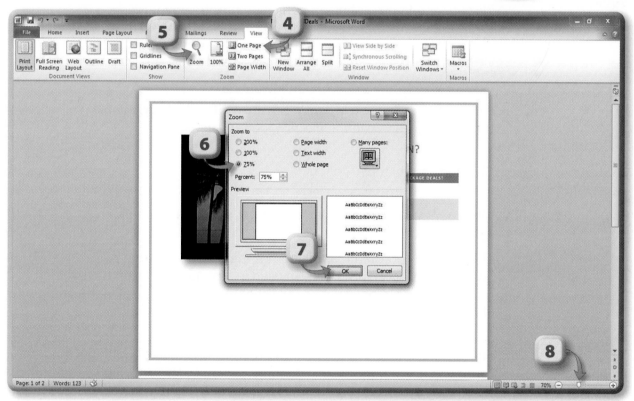

Taking It Further

Experimenting with Views Additional information about views is presented later in the book, but you can experiment now with the different views by clicking the various view options. For example, in Word, click the Web Layout button in the Document Views group of the View tab to view the document as a web page. In Word, you can also click the Full Screen Reading button to view the document in a full screen, which maximizes the screen space available and makes a document easier to read. In Excel, click the Page Layout button in the Workbook Views group on the View tab to view the worksheet as a printed page. In PowerPoint, click the Notes Page button in the Presentation Views group on the View tab to view and edit the speaker notes.

Microsoft Office

Skill 8

Check Spelling and Grammar

Video ▶ M4_CO_S08

The Office applications include a spelling checker that verifies that words are correctly spelled by comparing them to a built-in dictionary. In Word and PowerPoint, if a word is spelled incorrectly or is not in the dictionary file, a red wavy line appears below it. In Excel and Access, the spelling check is not automatic but you can start it by clicking the Spelling button, which is on the Review tab in Excel and on the Home tab in Access. Grammar is also checked during this process. A green wavy line indicates a possible grammatical error. The spelling checker also looks for contextual errors, such as the use of *there* instead of *their*, and flags possible problems with a wavy blue line. Because of the limitations of the spelling checker, always carefully proofread your files.

Steps

1 If it is not already open, open **M4-S7-TravelDeals.docx**, the file you saved in the previous skill. Save the file as **M4-S8-TravelDeals**.

2 Click the Review tab.

3 Click the Spelling & Grammar button in the Proofing group.

3 *Shortcut*
Spelling & Grammar
F7

4 The Spelling and Grammar dialog box identifies a possible subject-verb agreement error. *Return* is a term used in a particular way in the travel industry, where it indicates a return flight. Click the Ignore Once button so a change is not made.

5 The spelling checker indicates that *Cabos* is misspelled. Los Cabos is a proper name but is not in the dictionary file, so Word's spelling checker flags it as an error. Click the Ignore Once button so a change is not made.

6 *Another Way*
Right-click a word with a red, green, or blue wavy line and select the correct replacement from the popup menu.

6 At the screen showing the misspelled word *vacaton*, click the Change button to correct the error.

▶ *Tip* When the spelling checker presents several suggestions, select the correct choice before clicking Change.

7 When the spelling checker identifies the possible contextual error of using *Their are* rather than *There are*, click the Change button to correct the problem.

8 Click OK when prompted that the spelling and grammar check is complete.

9 Save the file by clicking the Save button on the Quick Access toolbar.

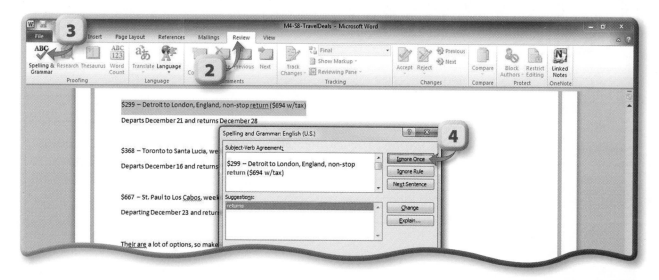

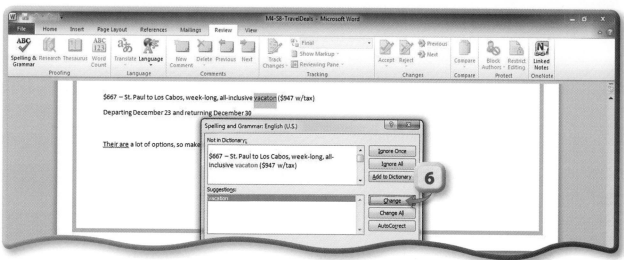

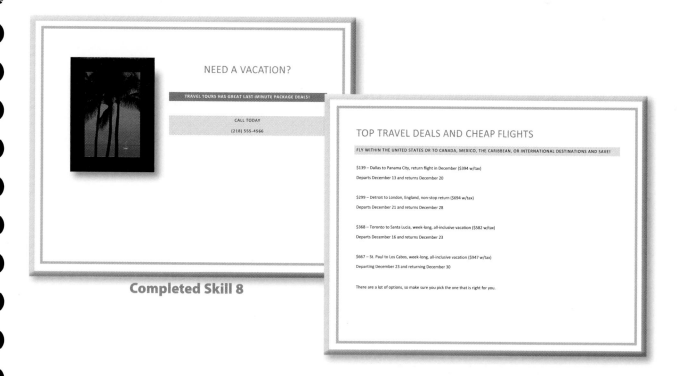

Completed Skill 8

Microsoft Office

Skill 9

Use Formatting Tools

Video M4_CO_S09

The way text appears on a page is called its *format*. The Home tab Font group in Excel, PowerPoint, and Word and the Text Formatting group in Access contain many of the same formatting buttons, such as Bold, Italic, Underline, Font, and Font Size. These buttons can all be used to apply character formatting. You need to select text before applying character formatting.

Steps

1 If is not already open, open **M4-S8-TravelDeals.docx**, the file you saved in the previous skill. Save the file as **M4-S9-TravelDeals**.

2 At the bottom of page 2, triple-click the last line of text that begins *There are a lot of options....*

3 Click the Home tab.

4 Click the *Font* text box arrow in the Font group.

5 Click *Cambria* in the drop-down gallery.

6 Click the Bold button in the Font group on the Home tab.

7 Click the *Font Size* text box arrow.

8 Click *14* in the drop-down list.

9 Click at the end of the last line of text, press Enter, and type your name on a new line.

10 Save the file.

▶**Tip** Triple-clicking selects a whole paragraph of text.

▶**Tip** The default font used by all of the Office applications is Calibri.

▶**Tip** Fonts in the *All Fonts* section of the gallery are listed in alphabetical order.

6 *Shortcut*
Apply Bold Formatting
Ctrl + B

Taking It Further

Using Other Formatting Buttons   Other Font group buttons are available, such as the Grow Font and Shrink Font buttons. You can quickly increase or decrease the text size with these buttons. You can change the color of your text with the Font Color button. The Italic button applies italic formatting and the Underline button applies underlining to the selected text. If you apply formatting and then decide you would like to remove it, just click the Clear Formatting button.

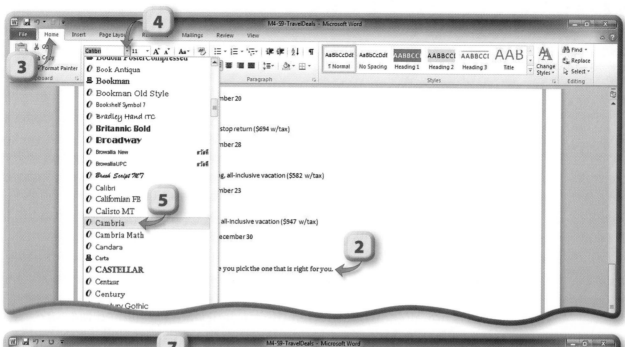

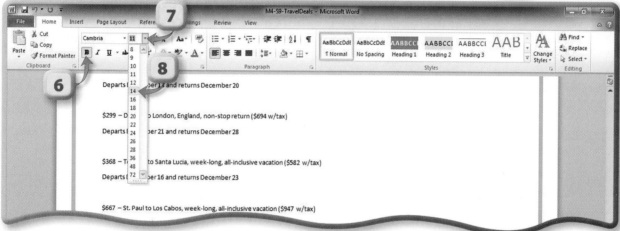

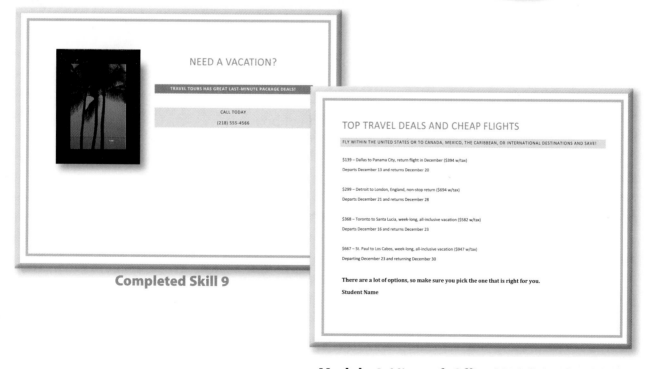

Completed Skill 9

Microsoft Office

Microsoft Office

Print a File

Video M4_C0_S10

Print settings are on the Print tab in Backstage view. The Print tab displays a preview of what your printed file will look like and also lets you make print settings, such as the number of copies to print, the page orientation, page size, and page margins. You can also zoom in on the preview image to make sure all settings are correct prior to printing a copy. Previewing your document carefully and printing only the final copy saves you time, money, and paper.

Steps

1 If it is not already open, open the student data file named **M4-S9-TravelDeals.docx**, the file you saved in the previous skill. Save the file as **Lastname-M4-S10-TravelDeals**, but replace *Lastname* with your last name. Be sure to save the file to your Module 4 working folder on your storage medium.

2 Place the insertion point at the beginning of the document.

3 Click the File tab.

4 *Shortcut*
Print
Ctrl + P

4 Click the Print tab. A preview of the first page of the document appears in the preview area.

▶**Tip** To go back to your file and make changes before you print it, click any tab.

5 Click the Next Page button on the bottom of the window to preview page 2 of the document.

6 Click the *Copies* measurement box up arrow. The number of copies to be printed changes from *1* to *2*.

7 Type 1 in the *Copies* measurement box.

More

Microsoft Office

8 Click *Normal Margins* in the Settings category.

▶ *Tip* The preview may change when you change the print settings.

9 Click *Wide* in the option list.

10 Verify that your instructor would like you to submit a printed copy of the document. Click the Print button if you need a printout.

11 Click the Close button.

12 At the warning box asking if you want to save changes, click Save.

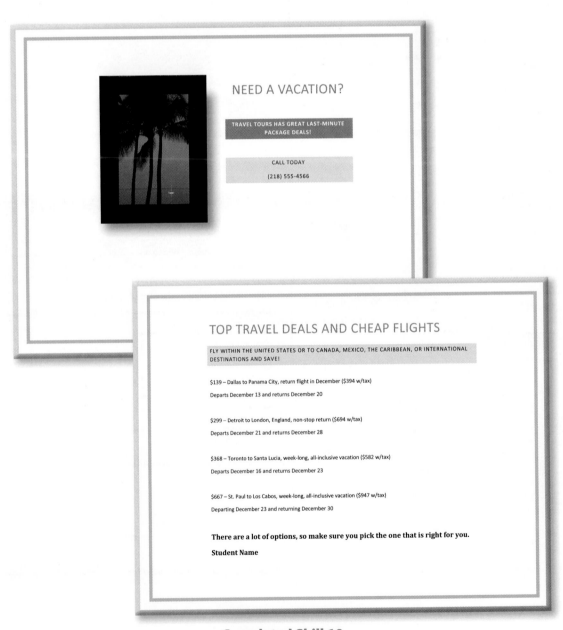

Completed Skill 10

Microsoft Office

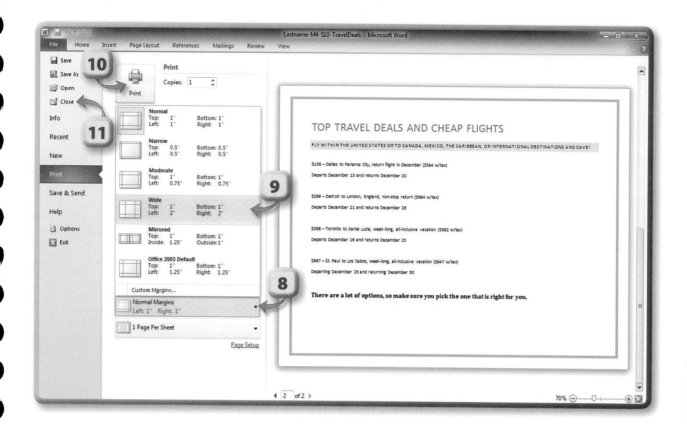

Taking It Further

Experimenting with Print Settings When you change a print setting in Backstage view, the preview adjusts to show you what impact the change you have chosen will have on the printed file. Try changing the paper size, the page orientation (e.g., portrait versus landscape), and the margins. You can also click the Printer Properties link to display printer options, such as the type of paper (e.g., plain paper or photo paper), print quality (e.g., draft or high), and color options (e.g., sepia or grayscale).

Microsoft Office

Skill 11   Use Help

Video   M4_C0_S11

Each Microsoft Office application has its own Help window. The Help window functions similarly to a web browser. You can click links to view Help topics and use Navigation buttons to move among previously visited pages. You can also search for specific keywords.

Steps

1   Start Excel.

2 Shortcut
Help
F1

2   Click the Microsoft Excel Help button to display the Excel Help window.

3   Click the Charts hyperlink in the *Browse Excel 2010 support* section.

4   Click the Creating charts hyperlink.

5   Click the Available chart types hyperlink and then read about the *Available chart types*.

6   Click the Back button to return to the previous page.

7   Click the Home button to go to the initial Help window.

8   Type conditional formatting in the *Search* box near the top of the window and then press Enter.

9   Click a link to read information about conditional formatting.

▶**Tip** You can print Help topics by clicking the Print button on the Help window toolbar.

10   Click the Close button to close the Help window.

11   Close Excel.

Taking It Further

Taking Advantage of the Office.com Website If you have an Internet connection, the Help window provides links to the Office.com website. You can click the images link to connect to the Office.com site and download images to enhance your documents, workbooks, and presentations. You can click the templates link to connect to the Office.com site and download templates for creating documents, worksheets, and presentations. The downloads link takes you to a page in the Office.com site where you are able to access additional downloads to complement the applications in the Office suite.

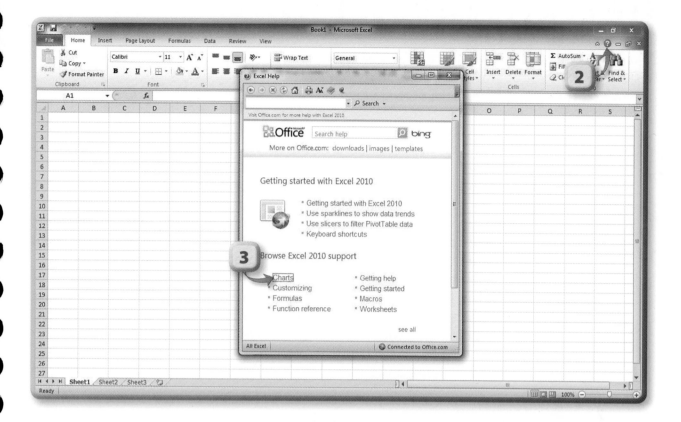

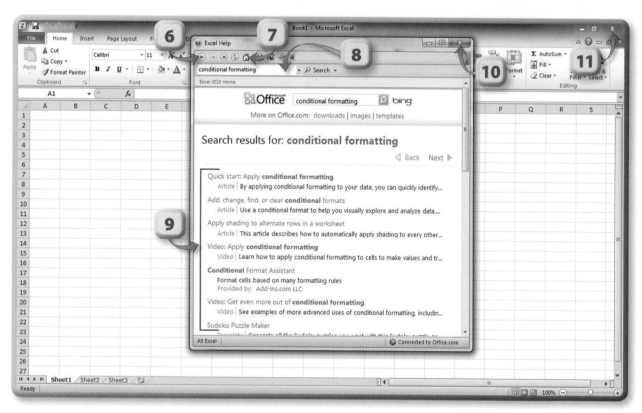

Microsoft Office

Microsoft Office

Skill 12

Use Microsoft Office 2010 Web Apps

Video M4_C0_S12

The Microsoft Office 2010 Web Apps are cloud-based versions of Word, Excel, PowerPoint, and OneNote, which means you can access them online. The Web Apps allow you to work on your PC, laptop, or mobile device from anywhere that provides you with an Internet connection. You do not have to install or download any extra software and the Web Apps are compatible with most major web browsers, including Internet Explorer, Firefox, and Safari.

In order to use the Web Apps, you will need to first create a Windows Live ID. Once you have set up a Windows Live ID, you can save your Office documents from your computer to your SkyDrive account. This account is handy if you want to access your files on a different computer. Note that you do not have to have Office installed on a computer in order to use the Office Web Apps.

Steps

▶ *Tip* You get 25 GB of free personal storage with your SkyDrive account.

1 Start your web browser and, if you do not already have one, create a Windows Live ID at skydrive.live.com. Once you have your SkyDrive account, log in.

2 Click *New*.

3 Click *Word document* from the drop-down list.

▶ *Tip* The first step when creating a Web App document is to name it.

4 Type M4-S12-WebApps in the *Name* text box.

5 Click the Save button to create a new Word Web App document and simultaneously save it on your SkyDrive.

6 Click the Insert tab. The Word Web App is a "light" version of Word and not all ribbon tabs and buttons are available.

7 Click the File tab.

8 Click *Close*.

9 Click the Close button to close the browser window.

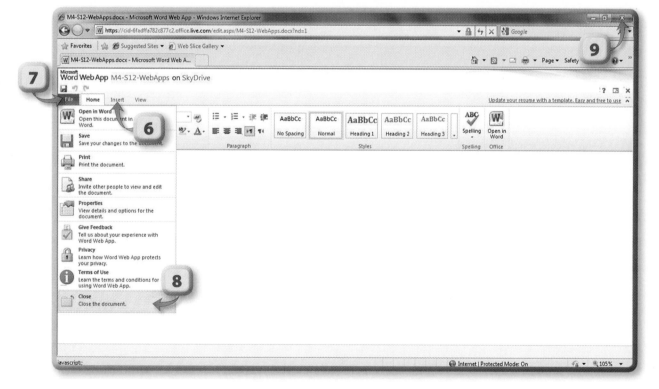

Taking It Further

Saving to the Web To save a document that already exists on your hard drive to your SkyDrive account, click File, click Save & Send, and then click *Save to Web*. You can then select your SkyDrive account and the appropriate folder.

MODULE 5

Microsoft® Word 2010

 Before beginning the module skills, copy the Module5–Word folder from the Student Resources CD to your storage medium. The copied folder will become the working folder for this module.

Guidelines for Planning and

U sing Word, you can create a variety of documents, such as business letters, reports, and recipe cards, as shown in these examples.

Report

Business Letter

Origins of Chocolate in Mayan Culture

Report from The Chocolate Museum, Posted February 24, 2012

Introduction
Key Points

- Cacao was an important crop and cultural influence in the Mayan culture
- The Mayan culture began cultivating cocoa over 2,500 years ago
- Chocolate became a major force in Mayan society
- In the heyday of Mayan society cacao beans were an important commodity

Cacao was an important crop and cultural influence in the Mayan culture, a Central American society with a rich heritage of early written language, art, architecture, and astronomical systems. This culture is thought to have peaked between 250 AD and 900 AD. Its demise was largely brought about by the arrival of Spanish explorers in the seventeenth century.

Cacao's popularity followed this timeline:

1. Traces of chocolate found in Mayan pots dating from 600 BC.
2. Cacao and hot water brewed by Mayans and Aztecs in Pre-Columbian era.
3. Cortez brings hot chocolate back to Spain in 1527.
4. European courts develop passion for chocolate drinks in seventeenth and eighteenth centuries.
5. 1825 Van Houten of Holland discovers how to degrease chocolate, spreading its popularity.

Cacao Varieties
The Mayan culture began cultivating cocoa over 2,500 years ago. Criollo cacao came from Central America, and evolved separately from the cacao in the Amazon River basin that belong to the Forastero variety. Criollo cacao trees are still found in the Lacandonia rainforest.[1]

Criollo cacao is a wild variety that is genetically distinct from the other varieties of cacao found throughout Central and South America.

---
[1] The Lacandonia rainforest is located in the eastern part of the state of Chiapas, Mexico.

Chocolate through History
One of the Mayan myths of creation tells of a woman who stroked a head impaled on a cacao tree and then magically became impregnated. She escaped to earth to avoid her father's wrath and gave birth to twins, the ancestors of the Mayan culture.

Chocolate was a major force in Mayan society. Pottery cups unearthed in the nineteenth century are called *chocolateros* by local Indians and were possibly used in ceremonial events. These cups include hollow handles, which were used to blow into a chocolate drink to create foam, a practice especially associated with Mayans (*see Figure 1-1*).

Figure 1.1: A Mayan pottery cup known as a "chocolatero."

Traces of chocolate drinks found on Mayan pottery were analyzed and the contents suggest that Mayans also added honey and pepper to their drinks. (Trivedi)

Chocolate and the Mayan Economy
In the heyday of Mayan society, cacao beans were an important commodity used in trade among the Mayans and with other societies. For example, a record from 1530 notes the purchase of a rabbit and some turkey eggs for 10 cacao beans. However, the value of cacao declined over the years, according to the Museum of San Cristobal. In 1535, 200 beans were worth one real (a unit of currency). By 1720, according to Robert Miller, "one real would be worth only 15 beans." (Miller)

Works Cited
Miller, Robert J. The Mayan Empire. New York: Cultural Exchange, 1998.

Trivedi, Bijal P. "Ancient Chocolate Found in a Mayan Teapot." National Geographic Today (2009): 24-30.

March 26, 2012

Helen Starkey
The Chocolate Museum
2541 Jardine Street
Boston, MA 02115

Mr. Arthur Renfrew
98 Elm Street
Brookline, MA 02116

Dear Mr. Renfrew:

Thank you for your recent contribution to the museum of $500 and your ongoing support of our mission. Your contribution will help us to continue programs that educate, entertain, and help the chocolate industry to improve its products and practices.

For example, did you know that growers of cacao beans who subscribe to fair trade practices guarantee not only the quality of their products, but also that they do not support child labor or slavery in their businesses? Also, many chocolate manufacturers use additives such as wax in making their chocolate, reducing the amount of valuable anti-oxidants that their products provide. Educating the public about issues such as these helps to make the chocolate industry a thriving and responsible part of our world.

According to "A Taste of Slavery," by Sudarsan Raghavan and Sumana Chatterjee, Knight Ridder Newspapers, June 24, 2001:

There may be a hidden ingredient in the chocolate cake you baked, the candy bars your children sold for their school fundraiser, or that fudge ripple ice cream cone you enjoyed on Saturday afternoon.

Forty-three percent of the world's cocoa beans, the raw material in chocolate, come from small, scattered farms in this poor West African country. And on some of the farms, the hot, hard work of clearing the fields and harvesting the fruit is done by boys who were sold or tricked into slavery. Most of them are between the ages of 12 and 16. Some are as young as 9.

In addition to helping us educate the public and support a responsible industry, you are helping to support some fun and entertaining exhibits. This year we are introducing three new exhibits to our museum: Chocolate and the Aztec Culture; Chocolate in Art, Movies, and Music; and Chocolate Tasting Parties: Hosting Your Own Chocolate Fest!

MEXICAN HOT CHOCOLATE
Mexico has a long history of chocolate growing and chocolate consumption. Try this delicious authentic recipe for Mexican hot chocolate to discover how flavors such as chili pepper and cinnamon can enhance this popular drink.

Ingredients

Quantity	Ingredient
2 cups	Boiling water
1 pepper	Chili pepper, cut in half, seeds removed
5 cups	Light cream
1 bean	Vanilla bean, split lengthwise
1 to 2 sticks	Cinnamon sticks
8 ounces	Mexican chocolate, coarsely chopped
2 tablespoons, or to taste	Honey
1 tablespoon	Ground almonds or hazelnuts
Dollop	Whipped cream

Recipe Card

Y ou can also use pre-designed documents called templates to create common marketing and business documents such as agendas, brochures, expense reports, and flyers.

Office.com Templates

Agendas · Award certificates · Brochures · Budgets

Envelopes · Expense reports · Faxes · Flyers

Creating Word Documents

Whatever type of document you create, taking the time to plan your message will help ensure clear and effective communication. Planning involves deciding on a purpose, identifying your audience, selecting the topic, and choosing a format.

Your purpose, or reason for writing, might be to make a point, to inform, to convince others to believe as you do, or to entertain. Making sure you know your goal helps you decide what to say as you begin to write.

"Audience" is the person or group of people you expect to read what you write. The more you know about your audience, the better you can target your message.

Often, the type of document you are creating and the features available in Word help shape your decisions about how much to write and how to present it. For example, if you are writing a memo to a group of museum volunteers about an exhibit work schedule, you are likely to keep the memo short and visually attractive while making sure the information can be read quickly and easily. Word offers features to help you achieve that goal, as shown below.

Insert graphics to add visual interest to Word documents.

Format and align text to get your message across.

Use features, such as tables and bulleted or numbered lists, to organize data.

MEMORANDUM

To: Chocolate in the Media Volunteers:
Randy, Sarah, Troy, Carol, Heather, Rob, Ty, Annie

From: Helen Starkey

Date: October 25, 2012

Re: Opening Weekend Work Schedule

Here's the final work schedule for the opening of this exhibit on the weekend of November 17.

Volunteer Name	Assignment	Day	Hours
Randy O'Hara	TV show viewing room	Saturday	10-5
		Sunday	10-2
Sarah Marchand	Music station	Saturday	10-2
Troy Butler	TV show viewing room	Sunday	2-5
Carol Wang	Movie viewing room	Saturday & Sunday	10-2
Heather Menendez	Music station	Sunday	10-2
Rob Clifford	Music station	Saturday & Sunday	2-5
Ty Parks	Movie viewing room	Saturday & Sunday	2-5
Annie Suddahara	Backup for all areas	Saturday & Sunday	2-5

Thanks for your help with the exhibit!

Chapter 1

Creating Documents

In Word, you can start from scratch with a blank document, open existing documents, or open documents based on templates (pre-designed documents). In this chapter you practice a combination of these three methods.

With a document open, the next logical step is to enter and edit text. (These actions are the digital equivalent of scribbling text on a piece of paper, crossing out what you do not like, and adding more words as needed.) Word offers tools that help you enter text, select text and make changes to it, and move or copy text from one place to another in that document.

If you are not a spelling expert, you will appreciate the Spell Check feature, which can spell *Mississippi* even if you can't. You can also change various properties of your document pages, such as the margins (these determine the width of the white space bordering your text) and where breaks occur between one page and another, such as between the title page and the first page of a report.

Skills You Learn

1. Enter and edit text
2. Use cut, copy, and paste
3. Perform a spell check
4. Create a document based on a template
5. Indent and add tabs using the Ruler
6. Set margins
7. Insert a page break
8. Add headers and footers

Files You Need
In this chapter, you need the following student data files.

M5-C1-S5-FundraisingLtr.docx

M5-C1-S8-FundraisingLtr.docx

What You Create

You work for The Chocolate Museum, a nonprofit organization that provides educational exhibits and information on the history of chocolate and its role in world cultures. The Museum contains a small gift shop and various exhibits and is supported by paid memberships and donations. Through this and the next several modules of this book, you create and edit a variety of files that can help the Museum raise funds, launch exhibits, track exhibit and gift store costs, organize membership lists, and educate visitors.

In this chapter, you create a simple fundraising letter acknowledging a contribution that has been made to the Museum as part of its 2012 fund drive.

Fundraising Letter

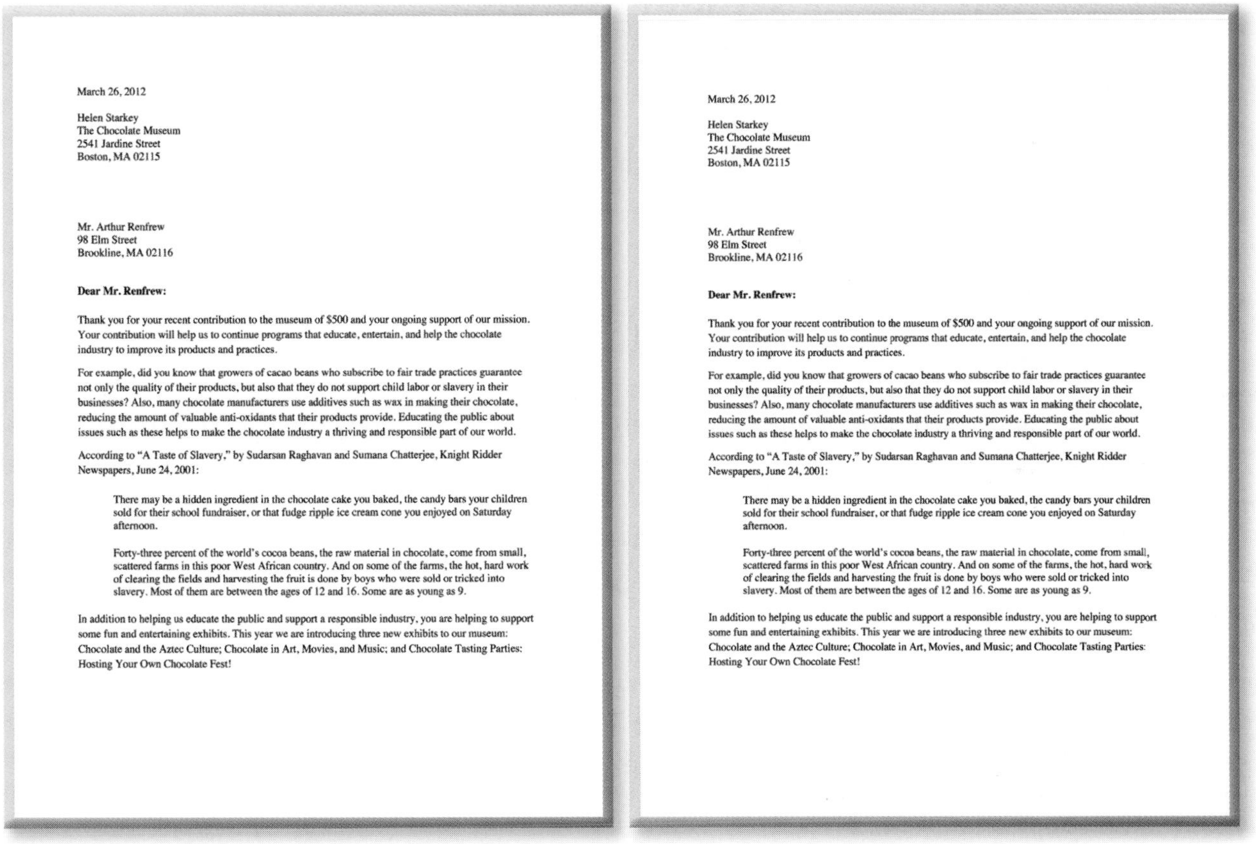

March 26, 2012

Helen Starkey
The Chocolate Museum
2541 Jardine Street
Boston, MA 02115

Mr. Arthur Renfrew
98 Elm Street
Brookline, MA 02116

Dear Mr. Renfrew:

Thank you for your recent contribution to the museum of $500 and your ongoing support of our mission. Your contribution will help us to continue programs that educate, entertain, and help the chocolate industry to improve its products and practices.

For example, did you know that growers of cacao beans who subscribe to fair trade practices guarantee not only the quality of their products, but also that they do not support child labor or slavery in their businesses? Also, many chocolate manufacturers use additives such as wax in making their chocolate, reducing the amount of valuable anti-oxidants that their products provide. Educating the public about issues such as these helps to make the chocolate industry a thriving and responsible part of our world.

According to "A Taste of Slavery," by Sudarsan Raghavan and Sumana Chatterjee, Knight Ridder Newspapers, June 24, 2001:

> There may be a hidden ingredient in the chocolate cake you baked, the candy bars your children sold for their school fundraiser, or that fudge ripple ice cream cone you enjoyed on Saturday afternoon.
>
> Forty-three percent of the world's cocoa beans, the raw material in chocolate, come from small, scattered farms in this poor West African country. And on some of the farms, the hot, hard work of clearing the fields and harvesting the fruit is done by boys who were sold or tricked into slavery. Most of them are between the ages of 12 and 16. Some are as young as 9.

In addition to helping us educate the public and support a responsible industry, you are helping to support some fun and entertaining exhibits. This year we are introducing three new exhibits to our museum: Chocolate and the Aztec Culture; Chocolate in Art, Movies, and Music; and Chocolate Tasting Parties: Hosting Your Own Chocolate Fest!

March 26, 2012

Helen Starkey
The Chocolate Museum
2541 Jardine Street
Boston, MA 02115

Mr. Arthur Renfrew
98 Elm Street
Brookline, MA 02116

Dear Mr. Renfrew:

Thank you for your recent contribution to the museum of $500 and your ongoing support of our mission. Your contribution will help us to continue programs that educate, entertain, and help the chocolate industry to improve its products and practices.

For example, did you know that growers of cacao beans who subscribe to fair trade practices guarantee not only the quality of their products, but also that they do not support child labor or slavery in their businesses? Also, many chocolate manufacturers use additives such as wax in making their chocolate, reducing the amount of valuable anti-oxidants that their products provide. Educating the public about issues such as these helps to make the chocolate industry a thriving and responsible part of our world.

According to "A Taste of Slavery," by Sudarsan Raghavan and Sumana Chatterjee, Knight Ridder Newspapers, June 24, 2001:

> There may be a hidden ingredient in the chocolate cake you baked, the candy bars your children sold for their school fundraiser, or that fudge ripple ice cream cone you enjoyed on Saturday afternoon.
>
> Forty-three percent of the world's cocoa beans, the raw material in chocolate, come from small, scattered farms in this poor West African country. And on some of the farms, the hot, hard work of clearing the fields and harvesting the fruit is done by boys who were sold or tricked into slavery. Most of them are between the ages of 12 and 16. Some are as young as 9.

In addition to helping us educate the public and support a responsible industry, you are helping to support some fun and entertaining exhibits. This year we are introducing three new exhibits to our museum: Chocolate and the Aztec Culture; Chocolate in Art, Movies, and Music; and Chocolate Tasting Parties: Hosting Your Own Chocolate Fest!

Word

Video M5_C1_S01

Enter and Edit Text

You learned in Module 4 how to create and save new documents in any Office application. In this skill, you practice those skills as you begin to type text into a new Word document. Once you enter text, you can then perform basic edits to it, such as adding new text, deleting text you no longer need, and correcting errors.

Steps

▶ **Tip** If you have used Microsoft Word recently, the program name will appear in the recently used programs list along the left side of the Start menu. Simply click on it there to open it.

1 Open Word, which displays a new, blank document.

2 Click the File tab and click Save.

3 In the Save As dialog box, locate the Module 5 working folder you created on your storage medium, and type the file name M5-C1-S1-FundraisingLtr.

4 Click the Save button.

5 *Another Way*
Note that Word suggests the current date as you type and when it does, you can press Enter to accept it, rather than typing the entire date.

5 Type the current date and press Enter twice.

▶ **Tip** Pressing Shift + Enter inserts a soft return, which prevents Word from creating a new paragraph and keeps the line spacing that would appear within a paragraph.

6 Type your name, press Shift + Enter, and then type the following text:

The Chocolate Museum [**Press Shift + Enter.**]

2551 Jardine Drive [**Press Shift + Enter.**]

Boston, MA 02115 [**Press Shift + Enter.**]

(617) 555-9890

▶ **Tip** Note that you only press the Enter key at the end of a paragraph or after an entry in a list, for example. Within paragraphs, Word wraps your text to a new line automatically.

7 Press the Enter key twice and then type the text provided for you at the top of the next page. (Type it exactly as written—if there are mistakes, you will correct them later!)

8 Click in the second line of the first address, to the right of the word *Drive*. A blinking cursor appears, indicating the insertion point (the place where you are currently working in the document).

Mrs. Agatha Kimbell [Press Shift + Enter.]

22 Oak Lane [Press Shift + Enter.]

Watertown, MA 02118 [Press Enter twice.]

Dear Mrs. Kimbell: [Press Enter.]

Thank you for your recent contribution to the museum of $500 and your ongoing support of our mission. [Press Enter.]

For example, did you know that growers of cacao beans who subscribe to fair trade practices guarantee not only the quality of their products, but also that they do not support child labor or slavery in their businesses? Also, many chocolate manufacturers use additives such as wax in making their chocolate, reducing the amount of valuable anti oxidants that their products provide. Educating the public about issues such as these helps to make the chocolate industry a thriving and responsible part of our world. [Press Enter.]

Your contribution will help us to continue programs that educate, entertain, and help the chocolate industry to improve it's products and practices. [Press Enter.]

Sincerely yours, [Press Enter 2 times.]

[Your name] [Press Shift + Enter.]

Development Director

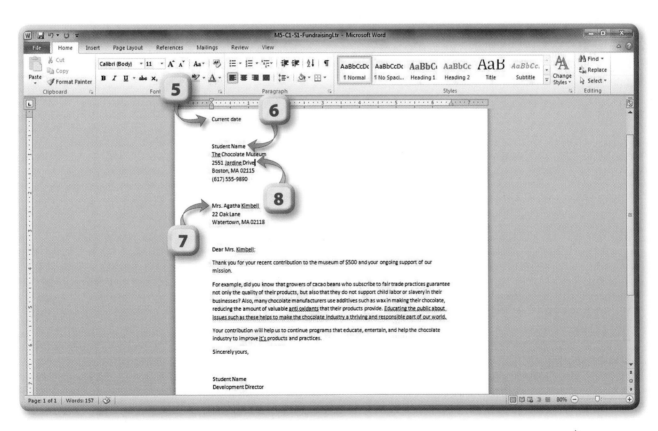

More

Tip The Delete key deletes the character to the right of the insertion point. The Backspace key deletes the character to the left of the insertion point.

9 Press the Backspace key five times noticing that the letters to the left of the cursor are being deleted, one at a time.

10 Type the word Street.

11 You made a mistake in the street number (*2551*), so click between the two 5s in that number and then type 4. Press the Delete key to delete the number 5 to the right of the insertion point. The address should now read *2541*.

Tip It is a good idea to save your files frequently so you do not lose valuable work. For more detailed steps for saving a file, see Module 4, Skill 4.

12 Save the file.

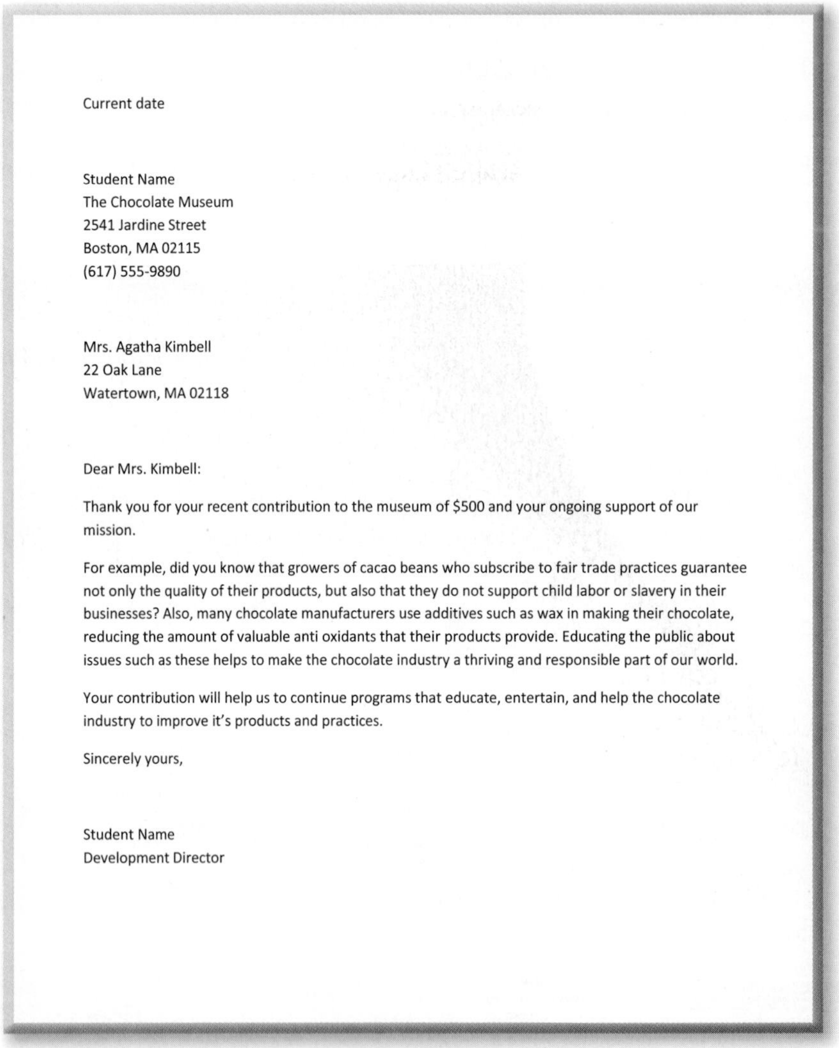

Current date

Student Name
The Chocolate Museum
2541 Jardine Street
Boston, MA 02115
(617) 555-9890

Mrs. Agatha Kimbell
22 Oak Lane
Watertown, MA 02118

Dear Mrs. Kimbell:

Thank you for your recent contribution to the museum of $500 and your ongoing support of our mission.

For example, did you know that growers of cacao beans who subscribe to fair trade practices guarantee not only the quality of their products, but also that they do not support child labor or slavery in their businesses? Also, many chocolate manufacturers use additives such as wax in making their chocolate, reducing the amount of valuable anti oxidants that their products provide. Educating the public about issues such as these helps to make the chocolate industry a thriving and responsible part of our world.

Your contribution will help us to continue programs that educate, entertain, and help the chocolate industry to improve it's products and practices.

Sincerely yours,

Student Name
Development Director

Completed Skill 1

Word

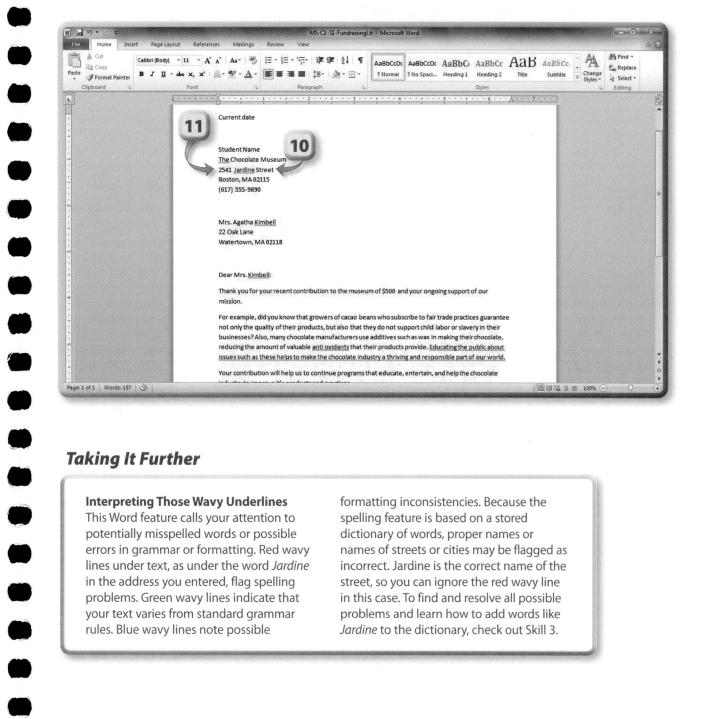

Taking It Further

Interpreting Those Wavy Underlines
This Word feature calls your attention to potentially misspelled words or possible errors in grammar or formatting. Red wavy lines under text, as under the word *Jardine* in the address you entered, flag spelling problems. Green wavy lines indicate that your text varies from standard grammar rules. Blue wavy lines note possible formatting inconsistencies. Because the spelling feature is based on a stored dictionary of words, proper names or names of streets or cities may be flagged as incorrect. Jardine is the correct name of the street, so you can ignore the red wavy line in this case. To find and resolve all possible problems and learn how to add words like *Jardine* to the dictionary, check out Skill 3.

Word

Skill 2

Use Cut, Copy, and Paste

Video M5_C1_S02

Beyond simple text editing such as deleting and adding text, you might also need to take a sentence or block of text from one place in a document and move it or place a copy of it in another location. For example, you might decide that a paragraph on the first page of a letter really works better on the second page. Or you could copy the opening sentence of the letter, place the copy at the end, and edit it slightly to summarize the letter's purpose. To perform these tasks, you start by selecting the text and then you perform an action using either the cut or copy tool along with the paste tool. These tools are located on the Home tab of the Word ribbon.

Steps

1 If it is not already open, open **M5-C1-S1-FundraisingLtr.docx**, the file you saved in the previous skill, and save the file as **M5-C1-S2-FundraisingLtr**. Be sure to save the file in your Module 5 working folder on your storage medium.

2 Place your mouse pointer in the margin to the left of the second paragraph, which begins with the words *For example*…. The cursor changes from a line to an arrow shape.

▶ ***Tip*** Single-clicking in the selection area at the left of a Word document selects a single line of text, double-clicking in the same area selects the whole paragraph, and triple-clicking selects all of the text in the entire document.

3 Double-click to select the entire paragraph.

4 Click the Home tab and then click the Cut button in the Clipboard group. The text is cut from the document.

5 Click just to the left of the *S* in the word *Sincerely* in the signature block at the end of the document (but do not select the word).

6 Click the Paste button in the Clipboard group on the Home tab. The paragraph now appears at the indicated location.

More

11 *Shortcut*
Save or Resave a
Document
Ctrl + S

Word

7 Select the first sentence of the document, which begins with the words *Thank you for your....*

8 Click the Copy button in the Clipboard group on the Home tab.

9 Click to the left of the word *Sincerely* and then click the Paste button. A copy of the sentence now appears at the new location.

10 Using any of the editing methods from the previous skill, edit the copied sentence to read *Thank you again for your ongoing support of our mission.*

11 Save the file.

Current date

Student Name
The Chocolate Museum
2541 Jardine Street
Boston, MA 02115
(617) 555-9890

Mrs. Agatha Kimbell
22 Oak Lane
Watertown, MA 02118

Dear Mrs. Kimbell:

Thank you for your recent contribution to the museum of $500 and your ongoing support of our mission.

Your contribution will help us to continue programs that educate, entertain, and help the chocolate industry to improve it's products and practices.

For example, did you know that growers of cacao beans who subscribe to fair trade practices guarantee not only the quality of their products, but also that they do not support child labor or slavery in their businesses? Also, many chocolate manufacturers use additives such as wax in making their chocolate, reducing the amount of valuable anti oxidants that their products provide. Educating the public about issues such as these helps to make the chocolate industry a thriving and responsible part of our world.

Thank you again for your ongoing support of our mission.

Sincerely yours,

Student Name
Development Director

Completed Skill 2

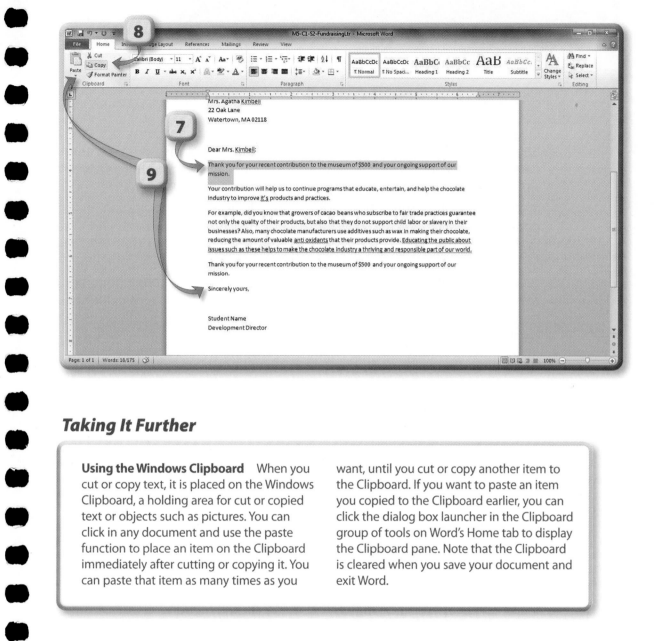

Taking It Further

Using the Windows Clipboard   When you cut or copy text, it is placed on the Windows Clipboard, a holding area for cut or copied text or objects such as pictures. You can click in any document and use the paste function to place an item on the Clipboard immediately after cutting or copying it. You can paste that item as many times as you want, until you cut or copy another item to the Clipboard. If you want to paste an item you copied to the Clipboard earlier, you can click the dialog box launcher in the Clipboard group of tools on Word's Home tab to display the Clipboard pane. Note that the Clipboard is cleared when you save your document and exit Word.

Word

Video M5_C1_S03

Perform a Spell Check

Even if you are a good speller, the Spell Check feature can help you to catch typos or other spelling-based mistakes. Knowing how to use this important tool ensures that your documents are correct and polished to create the best impression. Spell Check also checks common grammar mistakes. You can choose to make the suggested corrections or ignore them. For example, the spell checker might flag a product name, such as iPad, as incorrect, and the grammar checker might flag a bullet point phrase as a sentence fragment even though it reads just as you want it to. But remember that this feature isn't foolproof. It will not flag mistakes with sound-alike words, such as using the word *fair* when you mean *fare*, so you should also proofread your document carefully after you run Spell Check. In this skill, you learn how to use the Spell Check feature and make appropriate choices for changes.

Steps

1 If it is not already open, open **M5-C1-S2-FundraisingLtr.docx**, the file you saved in the previous skill, and save the file as **M5-C1-S3-FundraisingLtr**.

2 Click the Review tab.

▶ Tip What's the difference between Ignore Once and Ignore All? If you use a term, such as a company's name, several times in a document, choose Ignore All. If there is only one instance of a misspelling or misuse—say you are quoting someone who said *ain't*, but you do not want that word anywhere else in your document—choose Ignore Once.

3 Click the Spelling & Grammar button in the Proofing group. This opens the Spelling and Grammar dialog box. If the dialog box suggests a change in the spelling of your name in the document, click the Ignore All button.

4 The checker identifies *Jardine* as a misspelled word. Since *Jardine* is spelled correctly, click the Ignore All button.

5 The checker highlights the return address block and suggests that the *The* in *The Chocolate Museum* should not be capitalized. Since it is correct as typed, click the Ignore Once button.

6 The spelling of *Kimbell* is also correct, so click the Ignore All button.

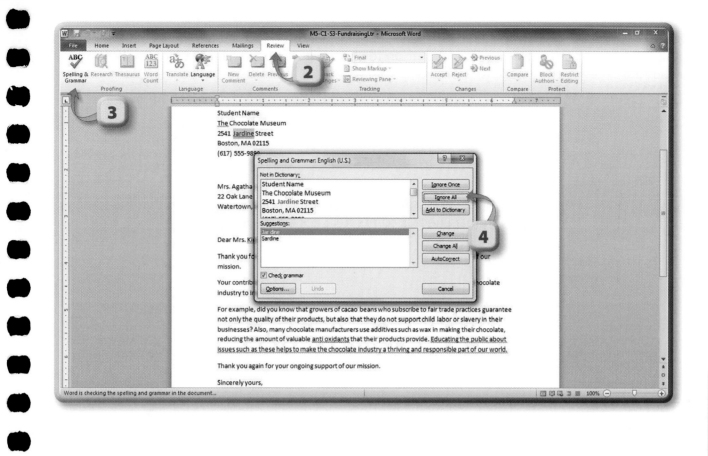

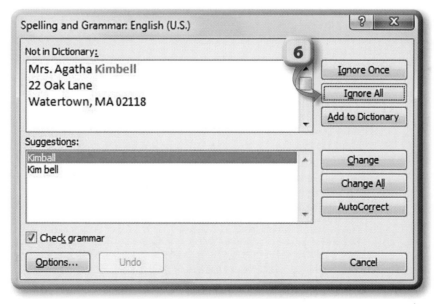

More

Word

7 The next flagged word is a grammar error: you entered *it's* instead of *its*. Click the Change button to change *it's* to the suggested form of the word.

8 Click the Change button again to change *anti oxidants* to *anti-oxidants*.

9 The checker highlights the sentence that begins *Educating the public* as a fragment. However, it is correct as is. Click Ignore Once.

10 When the checker is finished, a dialog box appears, stating that the spelling and grammar check is complete. Click OK to close it.

11 Save the file.

12 Print a hard copy or submit the file as directed by your instructor.

13 Close the file.

Current date

Student Name
The Chocolate Museum
2541 Jardine Street
Boston, MA 02115
(617) 555-9890

Mrs. Agatha Kimbell
22 Oak Lane
Watertown, MA 02118

Dear Mrs. Kimbell:

Thank you for your recent contribution to the museum of $500 and your ongoing support of our mission.

Your contribution will help us to continue programs that educate, entertain, and help the chocolate industry to improve its products and practices.

For example, did you know that growers of cacao beans who subscribe to fair trade practices guarantee not only the quality of their products, but also that they do not support child labor or slavery in their businesses? Also, many chocolate manufacturers use additives such as wax in making their chocolate, reducing the amount of valuable anti-oxidants that their products provide. Educating the public about issues such as these helps to make the chocolate industry a thriving and responsible part of our world.

Thank you again for your ongoing support of our mission.

Sincerely yours,

Student Name
Development Director

Completed Skill 3

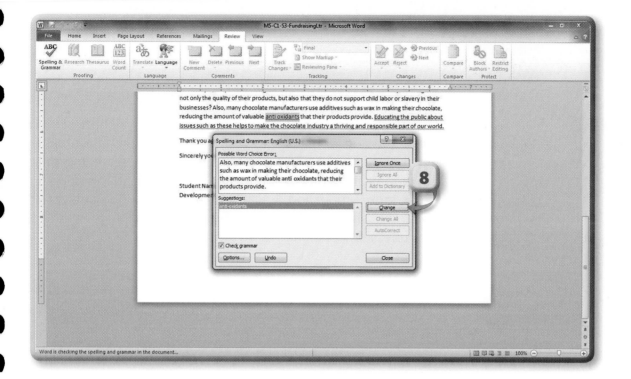

Taking It Further

Adding a Word to Your Dictionary   While performing a spell check, you may encounter a word you know to be correct, but that keeps getting flagged by Word because it is not in the built-in dictionary. In that situation, you can save yourself the time spent checking the word again and again in each spell check by adding it to your dictionary. For example, let's say your company's name is SweetShoppe. While performing a spell check, simply click the Add to Dictionary button when the word is challenged and you will never have to verify it again.

Word

Chapter 1

Skill 4

Video   M5_C1_S04

Create a Document Based on a Template

You can begin a document such as your fundraising letter in a blank document and then apply formatting and add graphical elements to make it look more appealing. However, a handy shortcut to achieve a more professional-looking document is to open a pre-designed document based on a template. Several such templates come built into Office 2010, and in this skill, you learn how to locate one and use it for a fundraising letter.

Steps

1   With Word open, click New on the File tab.

2   In the Available Templates category, click the Sample templates button.

3   Click the *Equity Letter* option.

4   Click the Create button.

5   Click *[Pick the date]* and click the down arrow on the field that appears.

6   Select the current date on the drop-down calendar.

7   Make sure the name on the next line is your name. (Word takes this from the computer user's name. If it is not correct, you can change it.)

8   Click *[Type the sender company name]* and type The Chocolate Museum.

9   Click *[Type the sender company address]* and type 2541 Jardine Street, and then press Shift + Enter, and type Boston, MA 02115.

▶**Tip** Note that the template includes text formatting such as a specific font, font formatting such as bold, and font size, as well as graphical elements. Choose a template that provides a look that matches your company's style or the tone of your content.

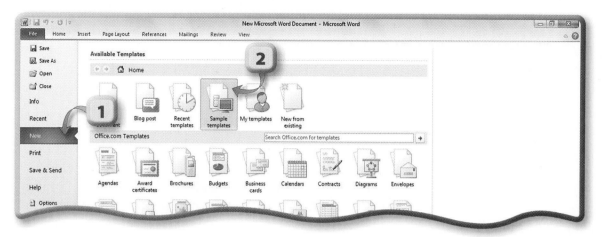

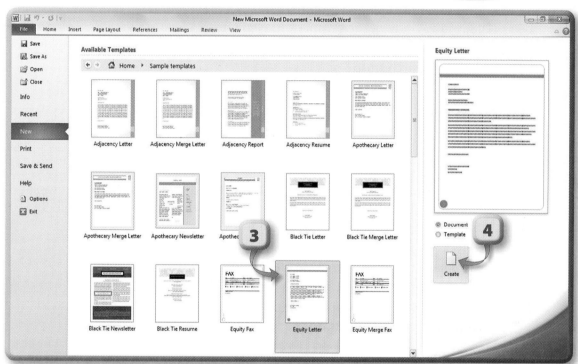

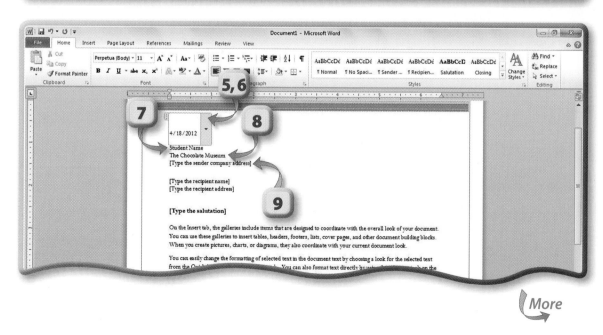

More

Word

10 Click *[Type the recipient name]* and type Mr. Arthur Renfrew.

11 Click *[Type the recipient address]* and type 98 Elm Street, and then press Shift + Enter, and type Brookline, MA 02116.

12 Type Dear Mr. Renfrew: in the *[Type the salutation]* line.

13 Open **M5-C1-S3-FundraisingLtr.docx**, the file you saved in the previous skill. Select the body of the letter, beginning with *Thank you* and continuing down to the closing block that ends with *Development Director*, and then click the Copy button.

▶**Tip** Text can be entered directly into the body of the template-based letter.

14 Click in the body of the template-based letter.

15 Press the Paste button.

16 Select the closing block placeholders and all text below the pasted text.

17 Press the Delete key to delete them.

18 Save the file as **Lastname-M5-C1-S4-TemplateFundraisingLtr**, but replace *Lastname* with your last name. Be sure to save the file in your Module 5 working folder on your storage medium.

19 Print a hard copy or submit the file as directed by your instructor.

20 Close **M5-C1-S3-FundraisingLtr.docx** and **Lastname-M5-C1-S4-TemplateFundraisingLtr.docx**.

Completed Skill 4

Word

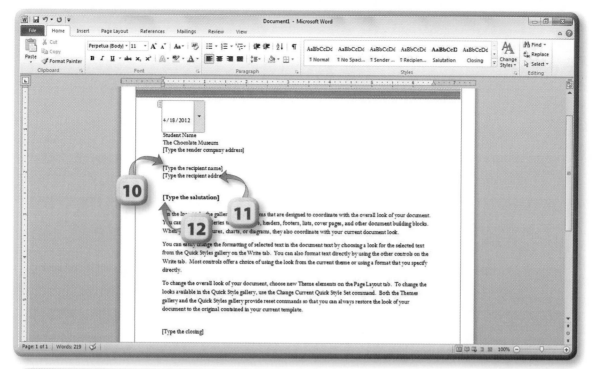

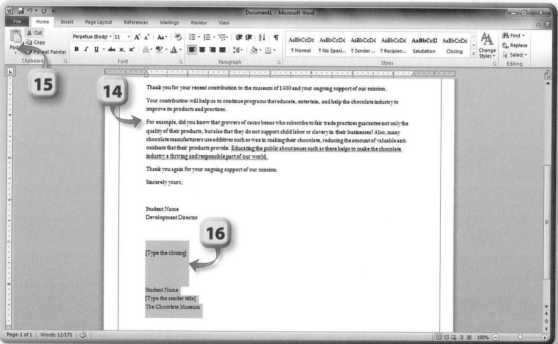

Taking It Further

Creating Your Own Template   If you have created a document that you consider a good starting point for other documents of the same type, why not create your own template? You can do so by saving your original file using *Word Template* as the *Save as Type* option in the Save As dialog box. Then, when starting a new document, click File, New, and choose the *New from Existing* option. Locate your template file and click Create. A new file opens, based on the template layout, ready for your changes. The file can be saved in the same manner as any other Word document. Using this method, you can reuse the text, formatting, and graphics that you applied to the first file. You will also save time and add consistency to your documents.

Word

Skill 5

Video ▶ M5_C1_S05

Indent and Add Tabs Using the Ruler

In certain situations, you may want to indent a block of text in a document. For example, according to standard document formats, a long quote should always be indented. Or you might want to set off a block of text, such as a product guarantee in a flyer, to call attention to it. You can use the Ruler in Word to indent text, set margins (discussed in Skill 6), and set tabs. Tabs allow you to align text using a specific spot on the Ruler. Tabs are set by default at every half inch, but you can set additional tabs and set new tabs to replace preset tabs.

In this skill, you first display the Ruler and indent two paragraphs of text, and then add a left tab and decimal tab to create two short lists of data.

Steps

Indent Paragraphs of Text

1 Open the student data file named **M5-C1-S5-FundraisingLtr.docx** and, if you have not already done so, save the file in your Module 5 working folder on your storage medium.

2 If the Ruler is not already displayed, click the View tab.

3 Click the *Ruler* check box to insert a check mark.

4 Select the fourth and fifth paragraphs of the body of the letter beginning with *There may be a hidden ingredient…* and ending with *…as young as 9.*

5 On the Ruler, drag the Left Indent indicator one-half inch to the right so that it rests at the one-half-inch mark on the Ruler and then release the mouse button.

6 Click at the end of the next paragraph, after the words *Chocolate Fest!*, and press Enter.

Set a Left Tab and a Decimal Tab

7 **Type the text** Here is a summary of our donations for the last three years showing how our support is growing: **and press Enter.**

▶**Tip** To see how items on your page line up, you can display gridlines on your page, which is like graph paper applying to your document. Click the View tab and then click the *Gridlines* check box to insert a check mark.

▶**Tip** To drag an item successfully, you must press the left mouse button and hold it down while you move the mouse along. When you release the mouse button, you end the drag.

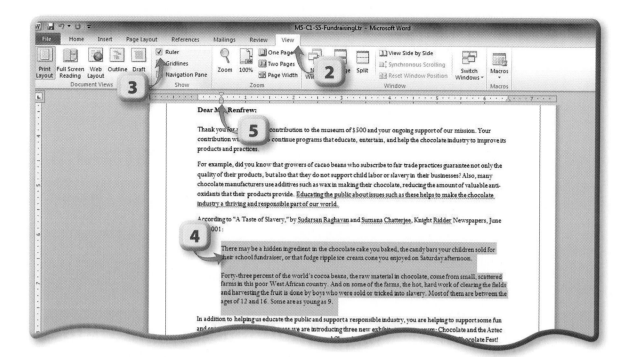

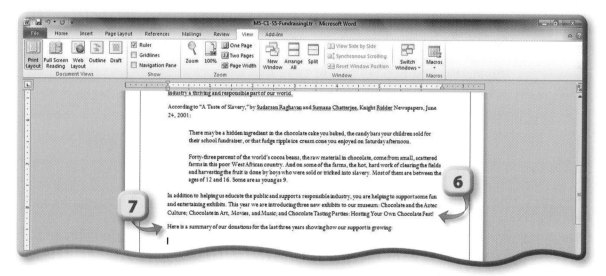

More

Taking It Further

Indenting Text in Paragraphs In the letter example used in this chapter, you use a block style, which does not require the first word of each paragraph to be indented. Other document formats may require you to indent the first word in each paragraph. To do so, open the Paragraph dialog box by clicking the dialog launcher button in the Paragraph group on the Home tab. Adjust the measurement for the left indentation, choose *First Line* from the *Special* drop-down list, and then click OK to save the changes. Note that you can also adjust indentation from the right side of the page by using a right indentation setting.

8 Click the 2-inch mark and the 3.5-inch mark on the Ruler. These actions place two left tabs, removing any default tabs to the left of them on the Ruler for the currently selected line.

9 Press the Tab key and type Year.

10 Press Tab again, type Total Donations, and then press Enter.

11 Remove the left tab symbol at the 3.5-inch mark by dragging it down and off the Ruler.

▶Tip Left, right, and center tabs place the left edge, right edge, or center of the text you enter at the tab location. Decimal tab is used for columns of numbers and it places the decimal point at the specified tab location, thereby lining up those numbers vertically.

12 Click the tab selector on the left side of the Ruler three times until the ScreenTip reads *Decimal Tab* when you hover your mouse over the tab selector.

13 Click the 4-inch mark on the Ruler, which places a decimal tab on the Ruler.

14 Type the following three additional lines, pressing Tab once before typing each year, pressing Tab once before adding each dollar amount, and pressing Enter after typing the first two dollar amounts. Do not press Enter after typing the last dollar amount.

2011 $100,789.00

2010 $97,988.00

2009 $89,322.00

15 Save the file.

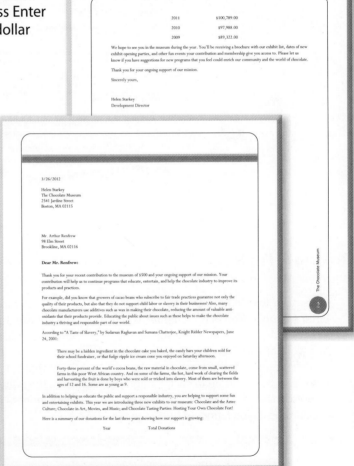

Completed Skill 5

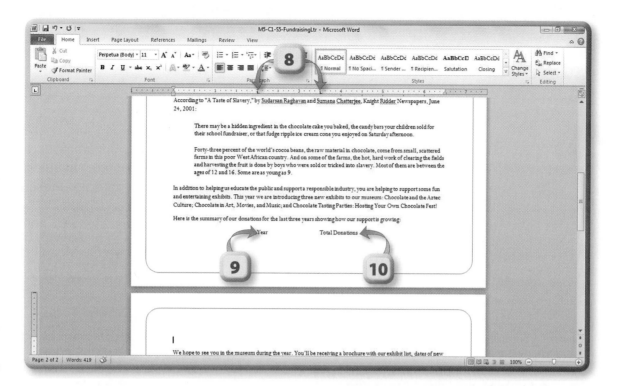

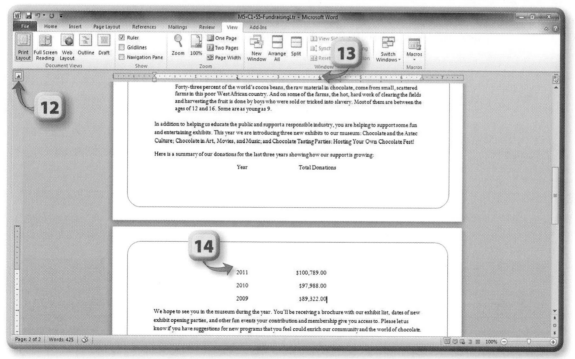

Taking It Further

Adding Tabs to Existing Text If you have already typed a list using existing tabs and decide you would like to change those tabs—for example, because your columns of text seem too close together to be easily read—you can. Select all the text whose tab settings you wish to change. To move the tab, drag the tab symbol to the new location on the Ruler. To remove a tab, drag the tab marker off the Ruler. To insert a new tab for the selected text, follow the method outlined in this skill.

Word

Skill 6

Video M5_C1_S06

Set Margins

Margins are the areas of white space that surround the text on your page. The four margins in any document are: top, bottom, left, and right. The preset margins for Word documents work in most cases, but you might choose to use narrower margins to fit more text on a page or use a wider top margin to accommodate a pre-printed corporate heading on stationery, for example. Preset margin settings are available, and you can easily apply them to any document.

Steps

1 If it is not already open, open **M5-C1-S5-FundraisingLtr.docx**, the file you saved in the previous skill, and save the file as **M5-C1-S6-FundraisingLtr**.

2 Click the Page Layout tab.

3 Click the Margins button in the Page Setup group.

4 In the drop-down gallery that appears, click the *Moderate* option. This action creates narrower margins on the left and right of the letter.

4 *Another Way*
You can also adjust the top, bottom, and side margins in your document by using the vertical or horizontal ruler. Hover your mouse over the area of the Ruler where the dark gray and light gray areas meet, until the margin label appears. Drag to the right or left to adjust the margin size on the Ruler across the top of the page. Drag up or down to adjust margins on the Ruler along the left side of the page.

5 Save the file.

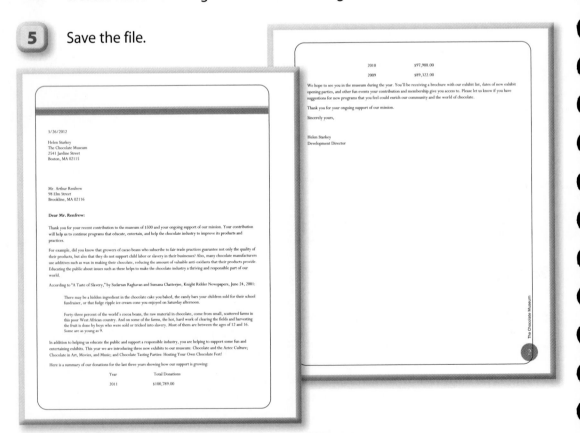

Completed Skill 6

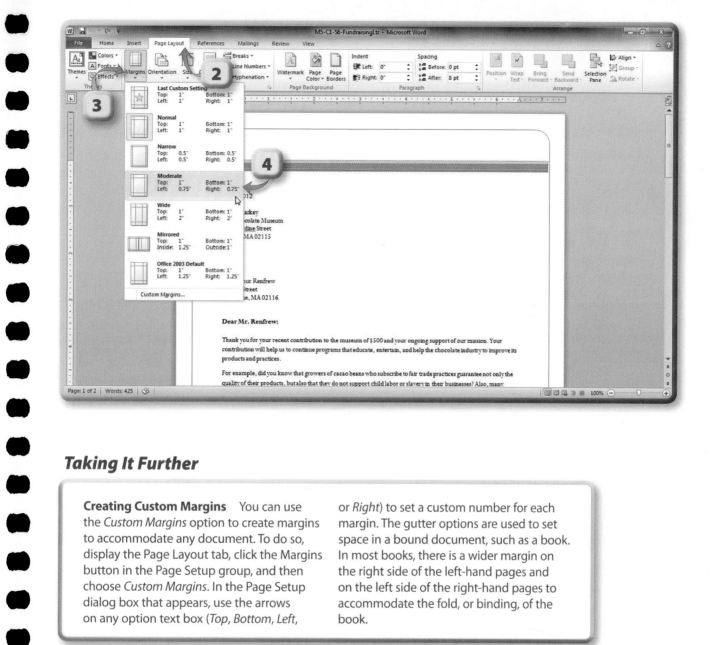

Taking It Further

Creating Custom Margins You can use the *Custom Margins* option to create margins to accommodate any document. To do so, display the Page Layout tab, click the Margins button in the Page Setup group, and then choose *Custom Margins*. In the Page Setup dialog box that appears, use the arrows on any option text box (*Top*, *Bottom*, *Left*, or *Right*) to set a custom number for each margin. The gutter options are used to set space in a bound document, such as a book. In most books, there is a wider margin on the right side of the left-hand pages and on the left side of the right-hand pages to accommodate the fold, or binding, of the book.

Word

Word

Insert a Page Break

Video M5_C1_S07

When you are working on a document, you may find that the automatic page breaks that Word inserts do not work for you. For example, you might find that a paragraph breaks across a page so that a single line of text or a single row in a list is left dangling. Or you might want a new section of a report or new chapter of a book to start on a new page. In your fundraising letter, for example, the page breaks in the middle of the short tabbed list, making it hard to follow. The solution is simple: insert a manual page break.

Steps

1 If it is not already open, open **M5-C1-S6-FundraisingLtr.docx**, the file you saved in the previous skill, and save the file as **Lastname-M5-C1-S7-FundraisingLtr**, but replace *Lastname* with your last name. Be sure to save the file in your Module 5 working folder on your storage medium.

2 Click at the start of the paragraph that begins with the text *Here is a summary of our donations….*

3 Click the Insert tab.

4 **Shortcut**
Insert Page Break
Ctrl + Enter

4 Click the Page Break button in the Pages group to insert a page break.

▶**Tip** If you insert a page break in the wrong place, you may delete it by using either the backspace key (placed just after the page break) or the delete key (placed just before the page break).

5 Save the file.

6 Print a hard copy or submit the file as directed by your instructor.

7 Close the file.

Completed Skill 7

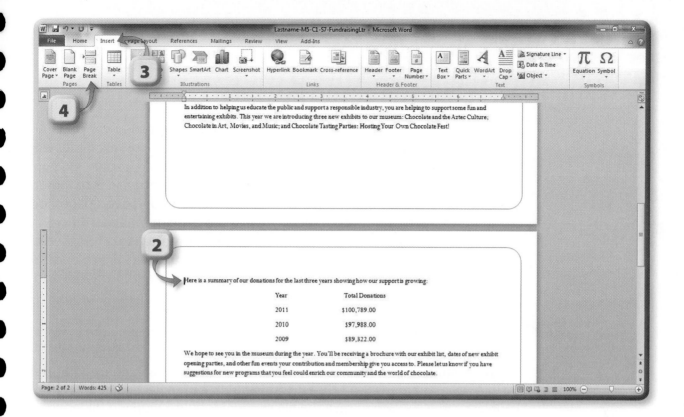

Taking It Further

Using Page Breaks Effectively Page breaks should be used sparingly. If you place breaks throughout a long document, and then edit it by deleting or adding text, the page breaks may not make sense anymore. For example, say you were working on a 20-page report instead of the 2-page letter in this skill. If you had placed a page break at the end of each page, you would have to go through the report and adjust several page breaks if you added or deleted text. Instead, only use page breaks in situations where you truly have to start a new page—for example, to separate the cover page of a report from the first page, the end of a chapter from the start of the next chapter, or the last page of your report from the first page of its index. If you know your document is essentially final, you might also use page breaks as you did in this skill to adjust awkward breaks between pages, or remove breaks that split tables or lists.

Word

Word

Skill 8

Insert Headers and Footers

Video M5_C1_S08

If you want text or graphics to appear at the top or bottom of most of the pages in a document, you can add them in either the header (top) or footer (bottom) areas. Word makes it easy to add text, such as your company name or logo, document identifier, page number, or date, to a document. You can also choose not to have your header or footer appear on the first page of your document—for example, on the cover sheet of a report. Or, you can place different header or footer content on odd and even pages, or place the page numbers in different locations, as is often true for a book, where page numbers are to appear opposite each other in the left and right corners.

Steps

1   Open the student data file named **M5-C1-S8-FundraisingLtr.docx** and save the file as **Lastname-M5-C1-S8-FundraisingLtr**, but replace *Lastname* with your last name. Be sure to save the file in your Module 5 working folder on your storage medium.

2   Click the Insert tab.

3   Click the Footer button in the Header & Footer group and then click the *Blank (Three Columns)* option.

▶ **Tip** The advantage of using buttons like Page Number and Date & Time to insert text in your header or footer is that they automatically update. So whenever you print the letter, the current date appears, and however many pages you add to your document, each is numbered correctly.

4   Click the Page Number button in the Header & Footer group on the Header & Footer Tools tab. From the drop-down list, click the *Bottom of Page* option and then *Plain Number 1*. A page number is inserted on the left side of the footer.

5   Click to the right of the inserted page number and press Tab to place the cursor at the center of the footer.

6   Click the Date & Time button in the Insert group on the Header & Footer Tools tab.

7   Choose the first available format from the list in the dialog box that appears and then click OK.

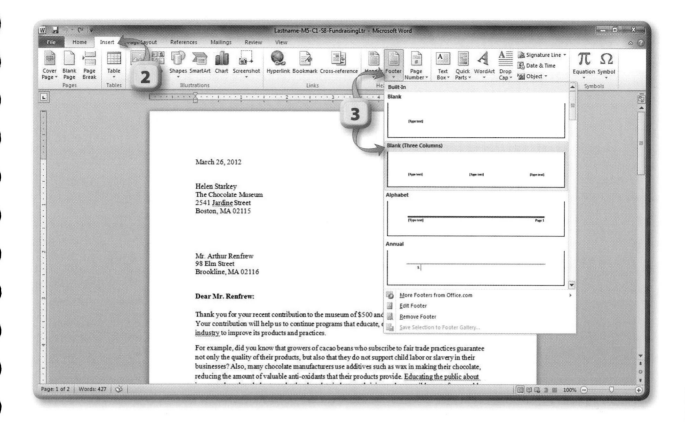

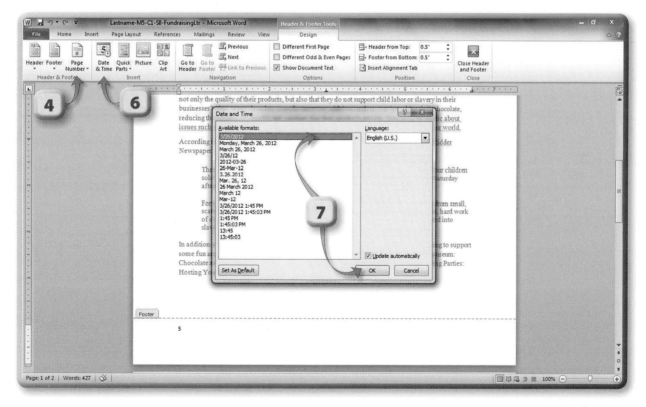

More

Tip You can quickly open a header or footer for editing by double-clicking in the top or bottom margin of a page.

8 Press Tab and then type your name in the right portion of the footer.

9 Click in the header area of the page (you may need to scroll up or down to locate it) and type 2012 Fund Drive.

10 Click the *Different First Page* check box in the Options group on the Header & Footer Tools tab to insert a check mark. The text is removed from the first page header and footer.

11 Save the file.

12 Print a hard copy or submit the file as directed by your instructor.

13 Close the file.

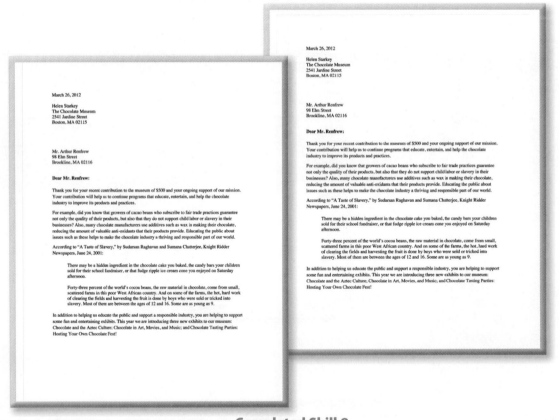

Completed Skill 8

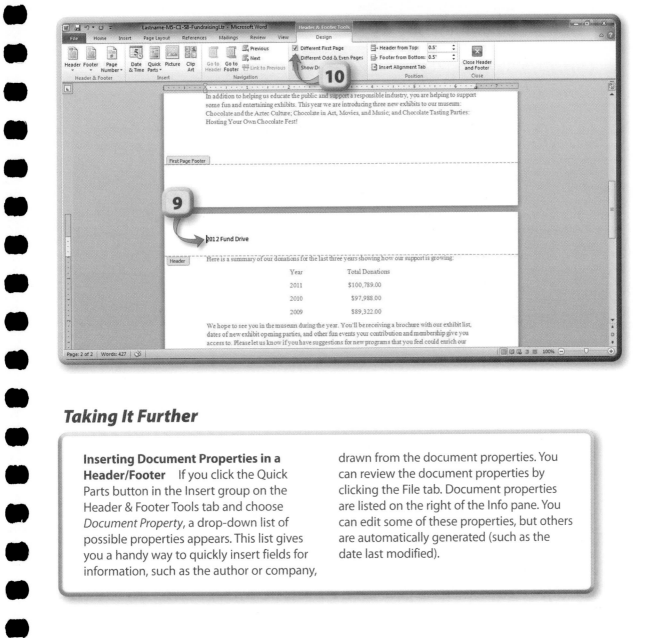

Taking It Further

Inserting Document Properties in a Header/Footer If you click the Quick Parts button in the Insert group on the Header & Footer Tools tab and choose *Document Property*, a drop-down list of possible properties appears. This list gives you a handy way to quickly insert fields for information, such as the author or company, drawn from the document properties. You can review the document properties by clicking the File tab. Document properties are listed on the right of the Info pane. You can edit some of these properties, but others are automatically generated (such as the date last modified).

Word
Chapter 1 Assessments

Tasks Summary

Task	Ribbon Tab, Group	Button, Option	Shortcut, Alternative
Delete text			Backspace or Delete
Select a word			Double-click
Select a paragraph			Triple-click
Cut text	Home, Clipboard	✂	Ctrl + X
Copy text	Home, Clipboard	📋	Ctrl + C
Paste text	Home, Clipboard	📋	Ctrl + V
Perform a spell check	Review, Proofing	ABC✓	F7
Create a new document	File, New	📄	Ctrl + N
Display the ruler	View, Show	*Ruler* checkbox	
Indent a block of text	Home, Paragraph	▦	Ruler
Set tabs	Home, Paragraph	Paragraph dialog box	Ruler
Set margins	Page Layout, Page Setup	▦	Ruler
Insert page break	Insert, Pages	▤	Ctrl + Enter
Insert Headers and footers	Insert, Header & Footer	📄 📄	Double-click top or bottom margin
Edit headers and footers	Insert, Header & Footer	📄 📄	Double-click top or bottom margin
Insert fields in headers and footers	Header & Footer Tools, Header & Footer	📄 📄 📄	

Features Review

Select the best answer from the choices given.

1. When you open Word, it displays
   a. the last document you worked on.
   b. a list of available templates.
   c. a blank document.
   d. the Open dialog box.

2. The Save command is accessed via which tab?
   a. Home
   b. View
   c. Page Layout
   d. File

3. Pressing the Delete key deletes what text?
   a. to the right of the insertion point
   b. to the left of the insertion point
   c. the last word you entered
   d. None of the above

4. When you cut text, what happens to it?
   a. It is placed on the Windows clipboard.
   b. It is deleted and irretrievable.
   c. It is placed on the Word clipboard.
   d. It is placed in the Recycle Bin.

5. The Spell Check feature
   a. is not infallible.
   b. doesn't flag correctly spelled words that may not have been the correct word choice for your sentence.
   c. checks both grammar and spelling.
   d. All of the above

6. You initiate a spell check from which tab?
   a. Home
   b. References
   c. Review
   d. None of the above

7. Templates may contain settings for
   a. the buttons available on the ribbon.
   b. text formatting and graphics.
   c. the location for storing the file.
   d. the maximum number of pages in the document.

8. You can set tabs in your document using which Word feature?
   a. the View tab
   b. options accessed through the File menu
   c. Word Styles
   d. the Ruler

9. Margins are
   a. the area of white space that surrounds text on your page.
   b. set on the Page Layout tab.
   c. adjustable so you can fit more or less text on a page.
   d. All of the above

10. Headers and footers provide a way for you to
    a. add a footnote to a page.
    b. insert text you'd like to appear on every page in the document.
    c. set tabs.
    d. add white space to the edges of your document.

Hands-On Skills Review

Exercise **A** **Check Spelling/Grammar and Proofread an Instruction Guide**

Skills   Enter and edit text, and perform a spell check

Scenario Update a Word document to be used as part of an instruction guide for purchasing a computer. Use the spelling and grammar checker to correct the paragraph and then proofread for errors that are not caught by the spelling and grammar check feature.

Steps

1 Open the student data file named **M5-C1-ExA-ComputerPurchase.docx** and save the file as **Lastname-M5M5-C1-ExA-ComputerPurchase**, but replace *Lastname* with your last name.

2 Type your name, a comma, and the current date on the first line of the document and then press Enter.

3 Use the spelling and grammar checker to correct the errors in the text.

4 Proofread the document to be sure it is correct.

5 Make any additional corrections to errors that you find.

6 Save and close the file.

7 Print a hard copy or submit the file as directed by your instructor.

Student Name, Current Date

Before purchasing a computer, take some time to consider how you wish to use your computer. This will help you decide if a portable computer is needed. Then investigate the various types of software that can be used for your purposes. Check the specification for the software and make a list of minimum and recommended hardware. Then it's time to consider your computer choices. Visit some online sites and review their computer sales. Compare the processor type and speed, the amount of RAM, and the size of the hard drive, as well as additional features you might find useful. Check the hardware specifications against the list for the software you plan to use. When you are comfortable that you are looking at computers that meet your needs, you will be able to make an informed purchase decision.

Completed Exercise A

Exercise **B** Download and Modify a Memo Template

Skills Enter and edit text, perform a spell check, and open a document based on a template

Scenario Jane Doe, your supervisor at Premiere Cell Phones, Inc., has asked you to send a memo to John Smith and Sasha Jenish requesting a meeting to discuss the pricing of cell phones manufactured by your company. Ms. Doe would like you to copy her supervisor, Pamen Loosh. Download a memo template and modify it with the necessary information.

Steps

1 Download the Memo (Professional design) template. You may need to search for the appropriate memo style at the office.microsoft. com website. (Click *templates* near the top of the page.)

2 Replace *Company Name Here* with *Premiere Cell Phones*.

3 Enter the appropriate text for *To, From* (your name), and *CC*. The *Date* will automatically show the current date. For *Re*, type Pricing of Phones.

4 Replace the text in bold, *How to Use This Memo Template*, with Meeting called by Jane Doe, CFO.

5 Enter the paragraph below, which is also shown in the finished sample.
Please mark your schedule to attend a meeting on Wed March 17 at 2:00 PM in Conference Room

A to discuss the selling price of our cell phones. The cost of our materials has risen dramatically over the past three months, necessitating a price increase to our vendors. It is imperative that we find ways to hold the increase to a minimum. Please respond with your intention to attend.

6 Use the spelling and grammar checker to correct errors. Proofread the document to be sure it is correct.

7 Use Save As to save the file with the name **Lastname-M5-C1-ExB-Memo**, but replace *Lastname* with your last name.

8 Print a hard copy or submit the file as directed by your instructor.

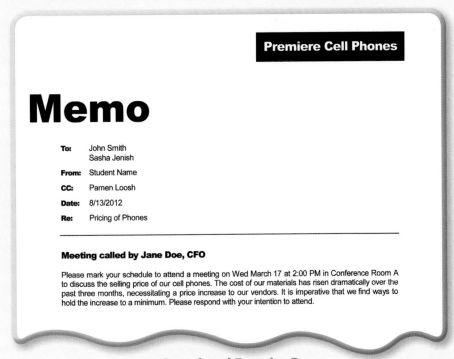

Completed Exercise B

Exercise **C** **Change Document Properties and Insert Elements into a Story**

Skills Enter and edit text; use cut, copy, and paste; perform a spell check; indent and add tabs using the Ruler; set margins; insert a page break; and add headers and footers

Scenario Your friend told you a story about her missing chocolate bars. You write the story and decide to submit it to a local publication that prints amusing tales. You have reviewed the submission guidelines and need to make some changes to your document for it to be acceptable for submission.

Steps

1 Open the student data file named **M5-C1-ExC-Chocolate.docx** and save the file as **Lastname-M5-C1-ExC-Chocolate**, but replace *Lastname* with your last name.

2 Insert a page break at the end of the document.

3 Select the text on the first page of the document, copy it, and then paste it on the empty second page. You should now have two identical pages in this document. **NOTE:** *If you have a third, blank page, you may have copied the page break. Position the insertion point at the end of the document and backspace until you have only two pages.*

4 Add a header to the document, including your name in the left margin and the current date in the right margin. **HINT:** *Insert tab, Header button, Blank Three Columns option. Use the left and right placeholders and delete the one in the center.*

5 Add a footer that places the page number in the center of the document.

6 Change the margins to 1" on the top and bottom and 2" on the left and right.

NOTE: *Perform all editing in Steps 7, 8, and 9 on Page 2 of the document.*

7 Replace the words *My brother* and *My sister* with the names of your brother and sister. If you do not have a brother or sister, use the names of friends.

8 Select those lines in the middle of the document that represent the responses of your family members to your questioning (the lines beginning with *Mom* and ending with *Who me?*) and set a left tab at 1.5 inches.

9 Indent the first line of the two paragraphs by one-half inch. **HINT:** *See* Taking It Further *in Skill 5.*

10 Save and close the file.

11 Print a hard copy or submit the file as directed by your instructor.

Student Name   Current Date

I Want Chocolate!

Last night after dinner I decided to enjoy a piece of chocolate. But when
I went to my secret chocolate hiding place, I found out it was empty! I
was sure I had at least 3 candy bars hidden away. Someone had found
my stash. I asked each member of my family if they had eaten my
chocolate bars. Here are the answers they provided:

Mom   No.

Dad   No.

My brother   Why would I have your chocolate?

My sister   No, but can I have a candy bar if you find them?

Grandmother   No, but here's $5.00 so you can buy more.

Grandfather   Who me?

I thanked my Grandmother and went to the store to purchase more
candy bars. I ate one on the way home and hid the others in a new
secret hiding place. Later than night, the mystery of the disappearing
chocolate was solved. I found the wrappers from one of my candy bars.
It was hiding under my Grandfather's pillow!

1

Completed Exercise C

Student Name   Current Date

I Want Chocolate!

Last night after dinner I decided to enjoy a piece of chocolate.
But when I went to my secret chocolate hiding place, I found out it was
empty! I was sure I had at least 3 candy bars hidden away. Someone had
found my stash. I asked each member of my family if they had eaten my
chocolate bars. Here are the answers they provided:

Mom   No.

Dad   No.

Brother Name   Why would I have your chocolate?

Sister Name   No, but can I have a candy bar if you find them?

Grandmother   No, but here's $5.00 so you can buy more.

Grandfather   Who me?

I thanked my Grandmother and went to the store to purchase
more candy bars. I ate one on the way home and hid the others in a
new secret hiding place. Later than night, the mystery of the
disappearing chocolate was solved. I found the wrappers from one of
my candy bars. It was hiding under my Grandfather's pillow!

2

Chapter 2

Formatting Documents

In Chapter 1 you learned about creating documents, entering and editing text, and working with the page layout in Word. Now you learn how to format that text so that it is attractive and easy to read. Formatting involves working with fonts and effects, such as bold, italic, and underlining. Word offers some nice shortcuts in the form of styles, which are formatting settings grouped together so that you can apply the group of settings with a single step. World also includes the Format Painter, which allows you to copy formats from one section of text to another. The ability to consistently apply formatting settings is convenient and gives your documents a cohesive look.

Formatting tools enable you to organize text by aligning it on the page or putting it into bulleted or numbered lists. You can call attention to the elements of your text and help your readers find their way through the document when you organize and arrange your text and add useful spaces within it.

When writing reports or research papers, it is important that you include the appropriate citations for the sources you have used to create your document. Word offers tools to help you cite sources properly, using accepted, professional styles for endnotes, citations, and Works Cited pages.

Skills You Learn

1   Change font and font size
2   Use formatting tools
3   Apply styles
4   Align text
5   Format paragraph and line spacing
6   Create bulleted or numbered lists
7   Copy formatting with Format Painter
8   Insert a footnote
9   Insert citations using professional styles
10 Create a Works Cited page
11 Format text in columns

Files You Need
In this chapter, you need the following student data files.

M5-C2-S1-MayanCulture.docx

M5-C2-S8-MayanCulture.docx

What You Create

A large part of The Chocolate Museum's mission is to educate the public about the role of chocolate in societies throughout recorded history. You have been asked to write a short report on chocolate's role in the Mayan society, a group of sovereign states with a common culture, which was located primarily in southern Mexico and on the Yucatan Peninsula. Chocolate had a role in the economy, mythology, and religious rites of this society. Your report will be available to visitors in a special display in the lobby of the Museum, so you want to make it both informative and attractive.

In this chapter, you work with Word formatting tools to refine the report's appearance and with references tools to make sure that all sources are accurately credited.

Report on Mayan Culture

Origins of Chocolate in Mayan Culture

Report from The Chocolate Museum, Posted February 24, 2012

Introduction

Key Points

* Cacao was an important crop and cultural influence in the Mayan culture
* The Mayan culture began cultivating cocoa over 2,500 years ago
* Chocolate became a major force in Mayan society
* In the heyday of Mayan society cacao beans were an important commodity

Cacao was an important crop and cultural influence in the Mayan culture, a Central American society with a rich heritage of early written language, art, architecture, and astronomical systems. This culture is thought to have peaked between 250 AD and 900 AD. Its demise was largely brought about by the arrival of Spanish explorers in the seventeenth century.

Cacao's popularity followed this timeline:

1. Traces of chocolate found in Mayan pots dating from 600 BC.
2. Cacao and hot water brewed by Mayans and Aztecs in Pre-Columbian era.
3. Cortez brings hot chocolate back to Spain in 1527.
4. European courts develop passion for chocolate drinks in seventeenth and eighteenth centuries.
5. 1825 Van Houten of Holland discovers how to degrease chocolate, spreading its popularity.

Cacao Varieties

The Mayan culture began cultivating cocoa over 2,500 years ago. Criollo cacao came from Central America, and evolved separately from the cacao in the Amazon River basin that belong to the Forastero variety. Criollo cacao trees are still found in the Lacadonia rainforest.[1]

Criollo cacao is a wild variety that is genetically distinct from the other varieties of cacao found throughout Central and South America.

---
[1] The Lacadonia rainforest is located in the eastern part of the state of Chiapas, Mexico.

Chocolate through History

One of the Mayan myths of creation tells of a woman who stroked a head impaled on a cacao tree and then magically became impregnated. She escaped to earth to avoid her father's wrath and gave birth to twins, the ancestors of the Mayan culture.

Chocolate was a major force in Mayan society. Pottery cups unearthed in the nineteenth century are called *chocolateros* by local Indians and were possibly used in ceremonial events. These cups include hollow handles, which were used to blow into a chocolate drink to create foam, a practice especially associated with Mayans *(see Figure 1.1)*.

Figure 1.1: A Mayan pottery cup known as a "chocolatero."

Traces of chocolate drinks found on Mayan pottery were analyzed and the contents suggest that Mayans also added honey and pepper to their drinks. (Trivedi)

Chocolate and the Mayan Economy

In the heyday of Mayan society, cacao beans were an important commodity used in trade among the Mayans and with other societies. For example, a record from 1530 notes the purchase of a rabbit and some turkey eggs for 10 cacao beans. However, the value of cacao declined over the years, according to the Museum of San Cristobal. In 1535, 200 beans were worth one real (a unit of currency). By 1720, according to Robert Miller, "one real would be worth only 15 beans." (Miller)

Works Cited

Miller, Robert J. The Mayan Empire. New York: Cultural Exchange, 1998.

Trivedi, Bijal P. "Ancient Chocolate Found in a Mayan Teapot." National Geographic Today (2009): 24-30.

Word

Chapter 2

Skill 1

Video M5_C2_S01

Change Font and Font Size

Fonts are character sets for the text you type and can add tremendous visual appeal to your documents. Word comes with many built-in fonts that you can apply to some or to all of the text in your document. Some font families, such as Arial, come in several variations—in this case, Arial, Arial Bold, and Arial Narrow. You can also modify the font size to add emphasis or increase readability.

Steps

1 Open the student data file named **M5-C2-S1-MayanCulture.docx**, and if you have not already done so, save the file in your Module 5 working folder on your storage medium.

2 Select the words *The Chocolate Museum* on the second line. (Do not select the comma.)

3 In the Font group on the Home tab, click the down-pointing arrow next to the *Font* text box and then click *Arial* from the *All Fonts* category of the drop-down list.

4 *Another Way*
You can also click in the *Font Size* text box and type the number of the font size you want.

4 With *The Chocolate Museum* still selected, click the down-pointing arrow next to the *Font Size* text box and click *14* from the drop-down list.

▶ ***Tip*** From the Font dialog box, you can make multiple changes to font formatting (including font style, font size, and font effects). Open the Font dialog box by clicking the dialog box launcher in the bottom right corner of the Font group on the Home tab.

5 Scroll down to the second page of the document and highlight the words *Figure 1.1*, which appear below the photo.

6 In the Font group, click the down-pointing arrow next to the *Font* text box and click *Arial* from the *Recently Used Fonts* section of the drop-down list.

7 Save the file.

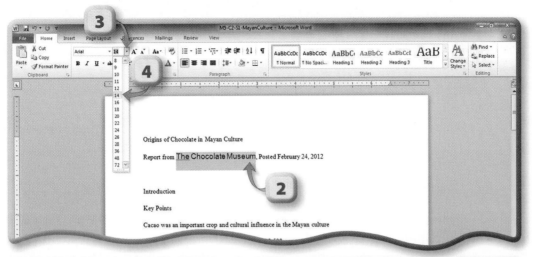

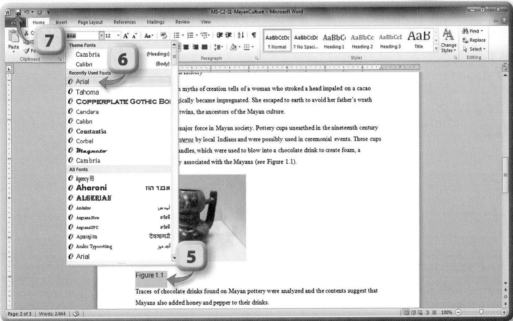

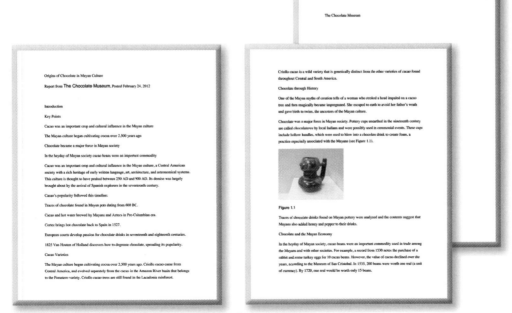

Completed Skill 1

Word

Video M5_C2_S02

Use Formatting Tools

There are several ways you can format text beyond the font and font size. You can apply effects such as bold, italic, underlining, and color. Bold and italic add emphasis. Italics and underlining are used for widely accepted styles, such as for book and movie titles. You can also change the font color to add visual interest and affect the tone of your document. Choose only a few font colors and select them to blend or contrast with each other. Keep in mind how your document will be viewed. If it will be viewed on-screen or printed on a color printer, emphasizing with color will work well. If it will be printed in black and white, using font colors will not help the look of your document.

Steps

1 If it is not already open, open **M5-C2-S1-MayanCulture.docx**, the file you saved in the previous skill, and save the file as **M5-C2-S2-MayanCulture**.

2 Select the fourth line of text, *Key Points*.

3 Click the Underline button in the Font group on the Home tab.

> **3** *Shortcut*
> Underline Text
> Ctrl + U

4 Select the text in the second line, *The Chocolate Museum*. (Do not select the comma after *Museum*.)

> ▶**Tip** More color options are available by clicking *More Colors* under the color palette. You can choose a color from the options on either the Standard tab or the Custom tab.

5 Click the down-pointing arrow on the Font Color button in the Font group and select *Tan, Background 2, Darker 50%* from the color palette that appears.

6 Scroll down to the second page of the document and highlight the words *Figure 1.1*, which appear below the photo.

> **7** *Shortcut*
> Bold Text
> Ctrl + B

7 Click the Bold button in the Font group.

8 Select *(see Figure 1.1)* at the end of the paragraph just above the photo. (Do not select the final period.)

9 Click the Italic button in the Font group.

10 Save the file.

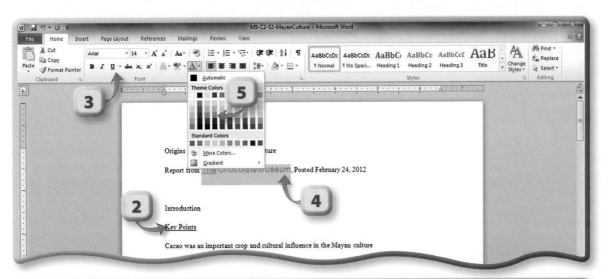

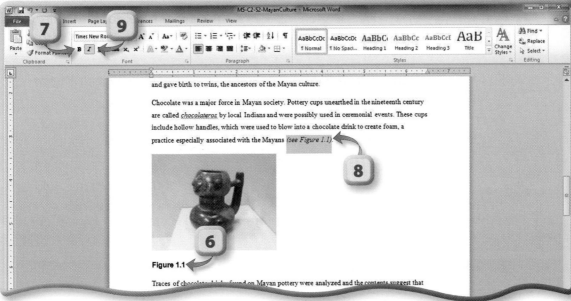

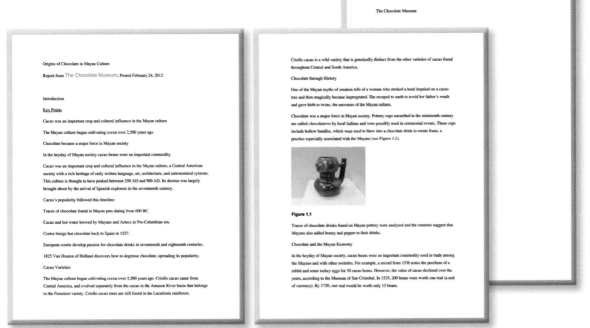

Completed Skill 2

Word

Word

Apply Styles

Video M5_C2_S03

Styles are built-in groups of formatting settings that you can apply to text with one action rather than having to perform multiple, separate formatting actions. Styles are useful for creating headings in your documents or for formatting your company name in a unique way. You can even create and save your own styles for use in all documents.

Steps

1 If it is not already open, open **M5-C2-S2-MayanCulture.docx**, the file you saved in the previous skill, and save the file as **M5-C2-S3-MayanCulture**.

2 Click anywhere in the document heading *Origins of Chocolate in Mayan Culture*.

▶**Tip** If you don't see the style you want, you can click the More button in the bottom right corner of the Styles gallery to display all styles.

3 Click *Heading 1* in the Styles group on the Home tab to apply the style.

4 Select the words *Report from* on the second line of the document, hold down the Ctrl key, and then select the comma and *Posted February 24, 2012*. (Be sure to include the comma before the word *Posted*.)

▶**Tip** To quickly apply a style to several areas of the document, select the first area of text, press and hold down Ctrl and select the others, and then apply the style to all selected text with one click.

5 Click *Heading 2* in the Styles gallery.

6 Apply the Heading 1 style to the following lines of text: *Introduction*, *Cacao Varieties*, *Chocolate through History*, and *Chocolate and the Mayan Economy*.

7 Save the file.

Taking It Further

Saving Formats as a Style   To save a set of applied formats as a style, select the formatted text and click the More button on the Styles gallery. In the list of links at the bottom, click *Save Selection as a New Quick Style*, give the style a name, and then click the OK button.

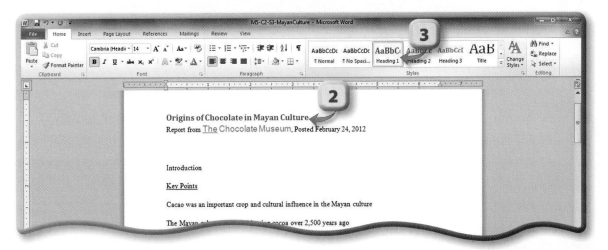

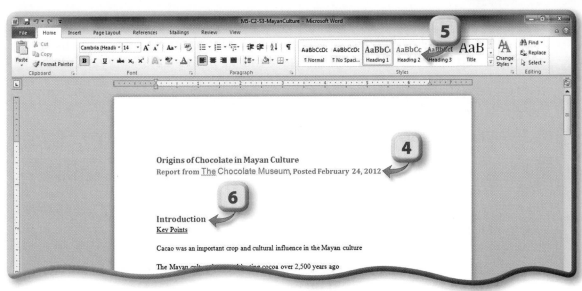

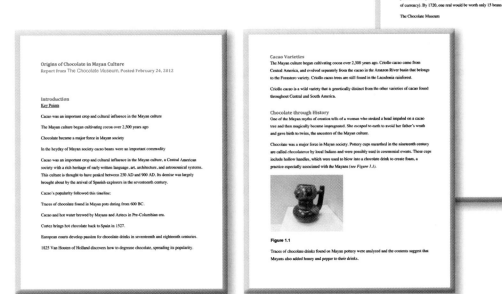

Completed Skill 3

Word

Word

Video M5_C2_S04

Align Text

Word allows you to align text in your document in four ways relative to the margins that are set: at the left, at the right, in the center, or justified. A document's default alignment is at the left margin. Document titles are often centered. Justified alignment spreads the text out between the two margins, which some people prefer for giving their text the look of a published book or magazine.

Steps

1 If it is not already open, open **M5-C2-S3-MayanCulture.docx**, the file you saved in the previous skill, and save the file as **M5-C2-S4-MayanCulture**.

2 Select the first two lines of text in the document.

3 Shortcut
Center Text
Ctrl + E

3 Click the Center button in the Paragraph group on the Home tab.

4 Scroll to the end of the document and click anywhere in the final line of text, *The Chocolate Museum*.

5 Click the Center button.

▶**Tip** Use the single down arrow near the bottom of the scroll bar to navigate through the document.

6 On the first page of the document, select the paragraph that begins *Cacao was an important crop…* (not the first line after *Key Points*), press and hold down the Ctrl key, and then select the text paragraphs that start with the following phrases:

> *The Mayan culture began cultivating cocoa*
> *Criollo cacao is a wild variety*
> *One of the Mayan myths of creation*
> *Chocolate was a major force in Mayan*
> *Traces of chocolate drinks found on Mayan pottery*
> *In the heyday of Mayan society*

7 Shortcut
Justify Text
Ctrl + J.

7 Click the Justify button in the Paragraph group on the Home tab.

8 Save the file.

Taking It Further

Formatting with Tabs You can only apply one alignment setting to a paragraph. For example, you cannot align your address at the left and your phone number at the right on the same line at the top of your resume. Instead, left align the text and set a right tab at the right margin. Enter the address, press the Tab key, and then enter the phone number.

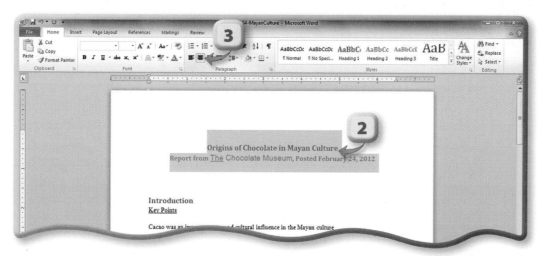

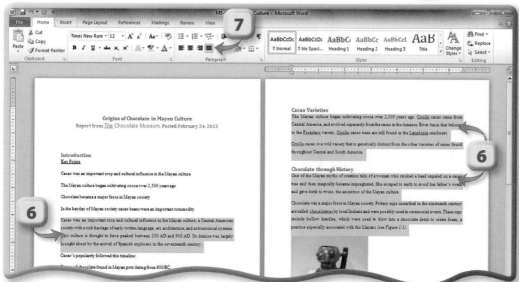

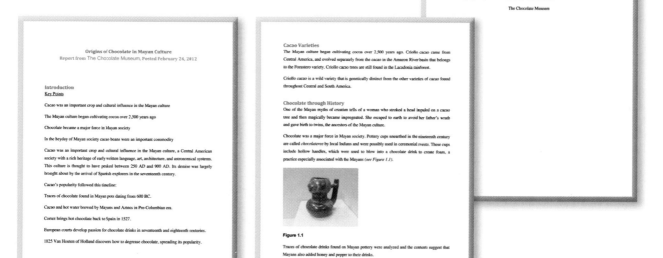

Completed Skill 4

Word

Skill 5

Format Paragraph and Line Spacing

Video M5_C2_S05

Word enables you to adjust spacing between the lines of a paragraph. The amount of white space you provide between lines can affect the readability of your document. It can also provide a visual break between the paragraphs in your text. You can apply preset spacing settings to selected text using tools in the Paragraph group on the Home tab.

Steps

1 If it is not already open, open **M5-C2-S4-MayanCulture.docx**, the file you saved in the previous skill, and save the file as **M5-C2-S5-MayanCulture**.

2 On the first page of the document, select the paragraph that begins *Cacao was an important crop…* (not the first line after *Key Points*), press and hold down the Ctrl key, and then select the text paragraphs that start with the following phrases:

> *The Mayan culture began cultivating cocoa*
>
> *Criollo cacao is a wild variety*
>
> *One of the Mayan myths of creation*
>
> *Chocolate was a major force in Mayan*
>
> *Traces of chocolate drinks found on Mayan pottery*
>
> *In the heyday of Mayan society*

3 *Another Way*
Open the Paragraph dialog box by clicking the dialog box launcher in the Paragraph group in the Home tab. In the *Spacing* section, click the arrow next to the *At* text box and select *1.15* from the drop-down list. Click OK.

3 Click the Line and Paragraph Spacing button in the Paragraph group on the Home tab and click *1.15* from the drop-down list.

4 Select the first two lines of the document (the title and subtitle).

5 Click the dialog box launcher in the bottom right corner of the Paragraph group.

6 In the Paragraph dialog box that appears, click the up-pointing arrow on the *After* field in the *Spacing* section three times to set the value at *12 pt*.

7 Click OK to close the dialog box. Extra space has been added after the selected lines of text.

8 Save the file.

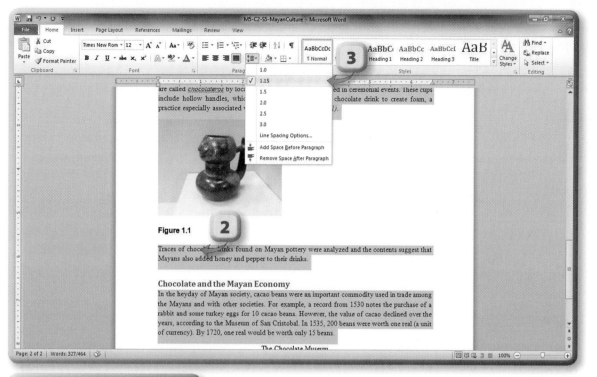

Figure 1.1

Traces of chocolate drinks found on Mayan pottery were analyzed and the contents suggest that Mayans also added honey and pepper to their drinks.

Chocolate and the Mayan Economy

In the heyday of Mayan society, cacao beans were an important commodity used in trade among the Mayans and with other societies. For example, a record from 1530 notes the purchase of a rabbit and some turkey eggs for 10 cacao beans. However, the value of cacao declined over the years, according to the Museum of San Cristobal. In 1535, 200 beans were worth one real (a unit of currency). By 1720, one real would be worth only 15 beans.

The Chocolate Museum

Completed Skill 5

Taking It Further

Formatting Line Spacing You can further customize line spacing by using the *Before* field in the *Spacing* section in the Paragraph dialog box. By choosing a value in this field, you can set how much space appears before a paragraph rather than within or after a paragraph.

Word

Skill 6 · **Create Bulleted or Numbered Lists**

Video M5_C2_S06

We all make lists that help us organize the information in our lives. In documents, lists help to set off similar items such as product parts, indicate steps in a procedure, or draw the reader's attention to your listed items. Bulleted lists and numbered lists are two common types of lists that are easy to set up in Word. Bulleted lists are used for items that have no particular sequence, such as the books or magazines on your bookshelf or a list of movies. Numbered lists suggest an order to the items within them, as with the sequential steps in a process, such as the steps in filling out a form.

Steps

Apply a Bulleted Style

1 If it is not already open, open **M5-C2-S5-MayanCulture.docx**, the file you saved in the previous skill, and save the file as **M5-C2-S6-MayanCulture**.

2 Select the four lines under the underlined heading *Key Points* on the first page.

3 On the Home tab, click the Bullets button in the Paragraph group.

Apply a Numbered Style

4 Select the five lines after the paragraph that reads *Cacao's popularity followed this timeline*.

5 Click the Numbering button in the Paragraph group on the Home tab. The default numbered list style is applied to the selected steps.

6 Save the file.

2 *Another Way*
You can click at the beginning of the first line of text to be selected, press and hold the Shift key, and then click at the end of the last line to make the selection.

▶ *Tip* Clicking the Bullets button applies the default bullet style at the beginning of each selected paragraph. You can choose different bulleted list styles such as square or diamond shapes rather than circles, by clicking the arrow on the Bullets button.

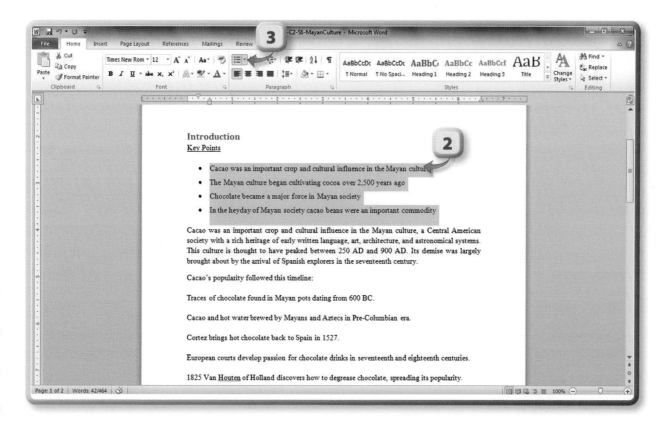

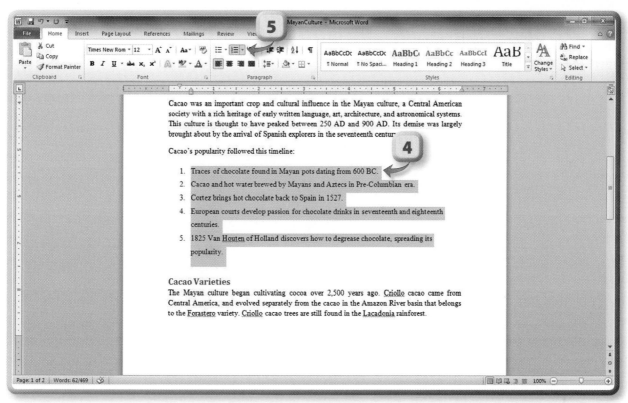

More

7 Select the bulleted text under the *Key Points* heading on the first page of the document.

8 Click the down-pointing arrow on the Bullets button.

9 In the gallery that appears, click *Define New Bullet*.

10 Click the Symbol button to open the Symbol dialog box.

11 Click the down-pointing arrow next to the *Font* field, scroll down the list, and select *Wingdings*.

12 In the *Character code* field, type 175.

13 Click OK to close the Symbol dialog box.

14 Click OK to close the Define New Bullet dialog box and apply the new bullet style.

15 Save the file.

Word

Origins of Chocolate in Mayan Culture

Report from The Chocolate Museum, Posted February 24, 2012

Introduction
Key Points

* Cacao was an important crop and cultural influence in the Mayan culture
* The Mayan culture began cultivating cocoa over 2,500 years ago
* Chocolate became a major force in Mayan society
* In the heyday of Mayan society cacao beans were an important commodity

Cacao was an important crop and cultural influence in the Mayan culture, a Central American society with a rich heritage of early written language, art, architecture, and astronomical systems. This culture is thought to have peaked between 250 AD and 900 AD. Its demise was largely brought about by the arrival of Spanish explorers in the seventeenth century.

Cacao's popularity followed this timeline:

1. Traces of chocolate found in Mayan pots dating from 600 BC.
2. Cacao and hot water brewed by Mayans and Aztecs in Pre-Columbian era.
3. Cortez brings hot chocolate back to Spain in 1527.
4. European courts develop passion for chocolate drinks in seventeenth and eighteenth centuries.
5. 1825 Van Houten of Holland discovers how to degrease chocolate, spreading its popularity.

Cacao Varieties
The Mayan culture began cultivating cocoa over 2,500 years ago. Criollo cacao came from Central America, and evolved separately from the cacao in the Amazon River basin that belongs to the Forastero variety. Criollo cacao trees are still found in the Lacandonia rainforest.

Criollo cacao is a wild variety that is genetically distinct from the other varieties of cacao found throughout Central and South America.

Chocolate through History
One of the Mayan myths of creation tells of a woman who stroked a head impaled on a cacao tree and then magically became impregnated. She escaped to earth to avoid her father's wrath and gave birth to twins, the ancestors of the Mayan culture.

Chocolate was a major force in Mayan society. Pottery cups unearthed in the nineteenth century are called *chocolateros* by local Indians and were possibly used in ceremonial events. These cups include hollow handles, which were used to blow into a chocolate drink to create foam, a practice especially associated with the Mayans *(see Figure 1.1)*.

Figure 1.1

Traces of chocolate drinks found on Mayan pottery were analyzed and the contents suggest that Mayans also added honey and pepper to their drinks.

Chocolate and the Mayan Economy
In the heyday of Mayan society, cacao beans were an important commodity used in trade among the Mayans and with other societies. For example, a record from 1530 notes the purchase of a rabbit and some turkey eggs for 10 cacao beans. However, the value of cacao declined over the years, according to the Museum of San Cristobal. In 1535, 200 beans were worth one real (a unit of currency). By 1720, one real would be worth only 15 beans.

The Chocolate Museum

Completed Skill 6

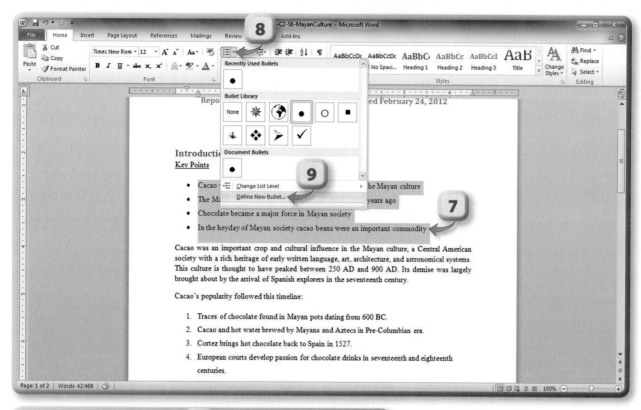

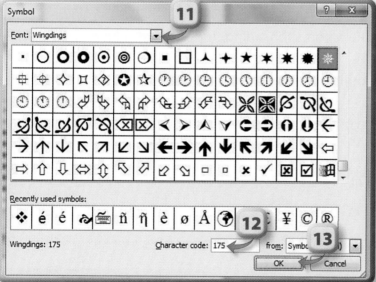

Taking It Further

Creating Lists with Multiple Levels To create a multilevel numbered or bulleted list, place your cursor just before the item you want to place at a new level. Use the Increase Indent and Decrease Indent buttons in the Paragraph group on the Home tab to move the item lower or higher in the outline. Another way to change levels is to press the Tab button, and the item indents one level. If you enter text and then press Enter, your cursor automatically moves to the start of a new line at the same indent level. Press Shift + Tab or the Decrease Indent button to move an item up by one level. Using these methods, you can modify any numbered or bulleted list to contain multiple levels.

Word

Copy Formatting with Format Painter

Video M5_C2_S07

When you have spent time formatting text in your document—for example, applying a font style, adding settings such as bold or italic, or modifying the text color—you can apply those same settings to other text using Format Painter. It also copies paragraph formatting, such as line spacing and paragraph indentation. Format Painter allows you to copy the format settings of selected text and apply them to another selection, which could be a single character, word, or entire pages of text. Format Painter saves you time and helps ensure that formatting settings are consistent throughout your document.

Steps

1 If it is not already open, open **M5-C2-S6-MayanCulture.docx**, the file you saved in the previous skill, and save the file as **Lastname-M5-C2-S7-MayanCulture**, but replace *Lastname* with your last name. Be sure to save the file in your Module 5 working folder on your storage medium.

2 Click anywhere in the report subheading, *The Chocolate Museum*, on page 1.

3 In the Clipboard group on the Home tab, click the Format Painter button.

3 *Shortcut*
Activate the Format Painter
Ctrl + Shift + C

▶ *Tip* Use Format Painter to copy formats from one drawn shape, such as a box or circle, to another.

4 Scroll to the bottom of the document and select the last line, *The Chocolate Museum*. Note that the formatting is copied to the destination text.

5 Save and close the file.

Completed Skill 7

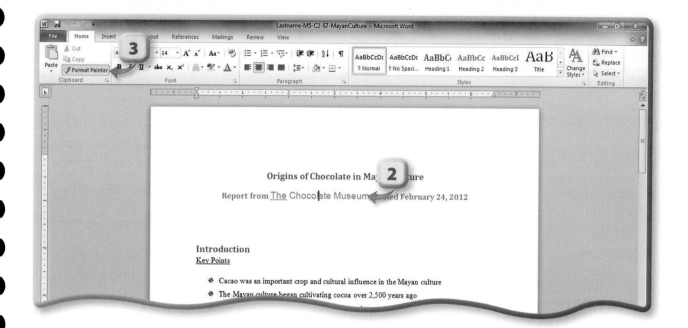

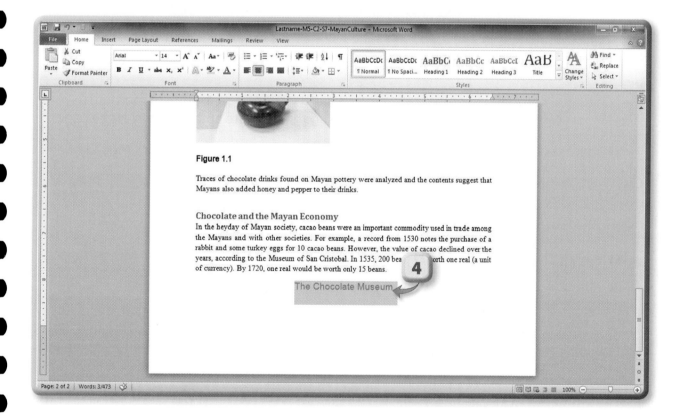

Taking It Further

Using Format Painter Multiple Times You can copy formatting to more than one place in your document. In Step 3 above, double-click the Format Painter button, and then apply the format to as many paragraphs, words, or phrases as you like. When you are done, click the Format Painter button again, or press the Esc key on your keyboard to deactivate Format Painter.

Word

Skill 8

Video ▸ M5_C2_S08

Insert a Footnote

Footnotes place information at the bottom of a page, in contrast with endnotes, which place them at the end of a document. You can use the References tab in the Ribbon to insert a footnote or an endnote reference wherever your cursor is placed in your document.

Steps

1 Open the student data file named **C1-S8-MayanCulture.docx** and, if you have not already done so, save the file in your Module 5 working folder on your storage medium.

2 Click after the period that follows the words *Lacadonia rainforest* at the end of the first paragraph under the heading *Cacao Varieties*.

3 Click the References tab.

4 **Shortcut**
Insert a Footnote
Alt + Ctrl + F

4 In the Footnotes group, click the Insert Footnote button. A footnote reference number is inserted and the footnote at the bottom of the page opens for editing.

5 Type the following footnote text: The Lacadonia rainforest is located in the eastern part of the state of Chiapas, Mexico.

▸**Tip** If you prefer to place your notes at the end of the document rather than at the bottom of each page, use an endnote. Insert an endnote by clicking the Insert Endnote button in the Footnotes group on the References tab, or press Alt + Ctrl + D.

6 Save the file.

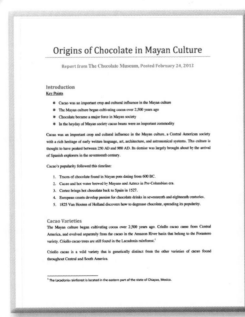

Completed Skill 8

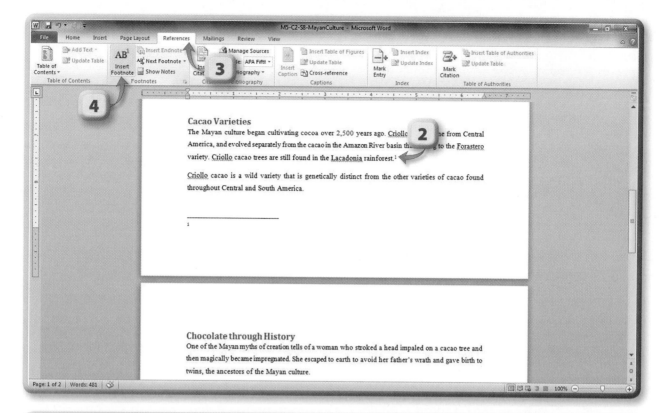

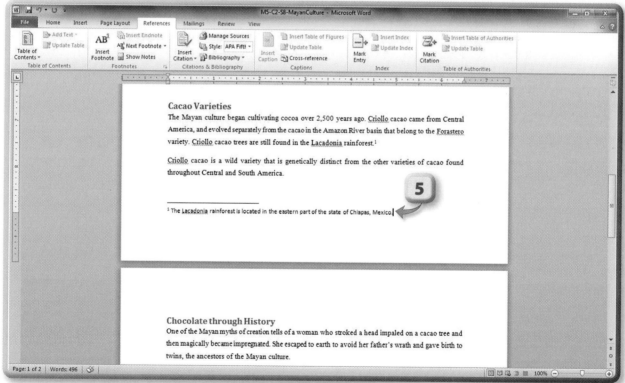

Taking It Further

Navigating Footnotes and Endnotes To locate footnotes or endnotes in a document, you can use the Next Footnote button on the References tab. When you click this button, you are given the options of going to the *Next Footnote, Previous Footnote, Next Endnote,* or *Previous Endnote.*

Word

Skill 9

Video M5_C2_S09

Insert Citations Using Professional Styles

Citations give appropriate credit to sources you have quoted or taken information from when creating your document. You can use Word's Citation feature to create sources and insert their information within your text according to one of several accepted professional styles, such as MLA or APA.

Steps

1 If it is not already open, open **M5-C2-S8-MayanCulture.docx**, the file you saved in the previous skill, and save the file as **M5-C2-S9-MayanCulture**.

2 Scroll to the second page, below the figure, and click after the period at the end of the sentence that begins *Traces of chocolate drinks found…*.

3 In the Citations & Bibliography group on the References tab, click the *Style* drop-down arrow and select *MLA Sixth Edition*. This option applies the Modern Languages Association professional style for citations.

4 Click the Insert Citation button in the Citations & Bibliography group.

5 From the drop-down list, click the *Add New Source* option.

▶ Tip Once you enter information about a resource, you can insert it again by choosing it from the list that appears when you click Insert Citation.

6 Make sure that *Journal Article* is selected for the *Type of Source* text box and then type the following information in the Create Source dialog box.

Author	Trivedi, Bijal P.
Title	Ancient Chocolate Found in a Mayan Teapot
Journal Name	National Geographic Today
Year	2009
Pages	24-30

7 Click OK to insert the citation.

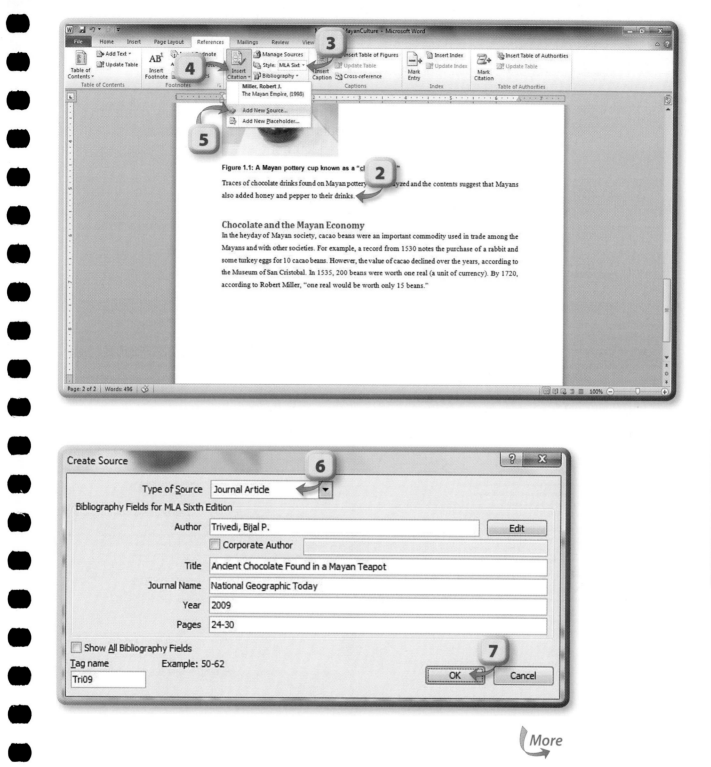

Figure 1.1: A Mayan pottery cup known as a "c[...]"

Traces of chocolate drinks found on Mayan pottery [...]yzed and the contents suggest that Mayans also added honey and pepper to their drinks.

Chocolate and the Mayan Economy

In the heyday of Mayan society, cacao beans were an important commodity used in trade among the Mayans and with other societies. For example, a record from 1530 notes the purchase of a rabbit and some turkey eggs for 10 cacao beans. However, the value of cacao declined over the years, according to the Museum of San Cristobal. In 1535, 200 beans were worth one real (a unit of currency). By 1720, according to Robert Miller, "one real would be worth only 15 beans."

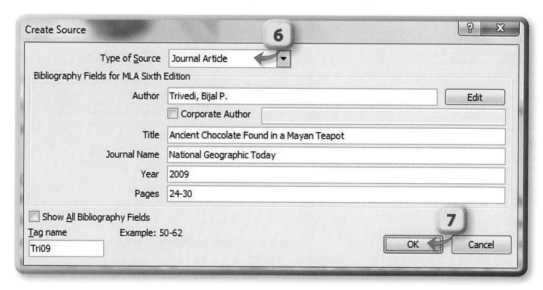

More

8 Click after the final closing quotation mark of the document, which is located at the end of the last sentence of the paragraph that begins *In the heyday of Mayan society*....

9 Click the Insert Citation button in the Citations & Bibliography group on the References tab and click *Miller, Robert J.*, a source that already exists. This action inserts the citation into the document.

10 Save the file.

Chocolate through History

One of the Mayan myths of creation tells of a woman who stroked a head impaled on a cacao tree and then magically became impregnated. She escaped to earth to avoid her father's wrath and gave birth to twins, the ancestors of the Mayan culture.

Chocolate was a major force in Mayan society. Pottery cups unearthed in the nineteenth century are called *chocolateros* by local Indians and were possibly used in ceremonial events. These cups include hollow handles, which were used to blow into a chocolate drink to create foam, a practice especially associated with Mayans *(see Figure 1.1)*.

Figure 1.1: A Mayan pottery cup known as a "chocolatero."

Traces of chocolate drinks found on Mayan pottery were analyzed and the contents suggest that Mayans also added honey and pepper to their drinks. (Trivedi)

Chocolate and the Mayan Economy

In the heyday of Mayan society, cacao beans were an important commodity used in trade among the Mayans and with other societies. For example, a record from 1530 notes the purchase of a rabbit and some turkey eggs for 10 cacao beans. However, the value of cacao declined over the years, according to the Museum of San Cristobal. In 1535, 200 beans were worth one real (a unit of currency). By 1720, according to Robert Miller, "one real would be worth only 15 beans." (Miller)

Origins of Chocolate in Mayan Culture

Report from The Chocolate Museum, Posted February 24, 2012

Introduction
Key Points

* Cacao was an important crop and cultural influence in the Mayan culture
* The Mayan culture began cultivating cocoa over 2,500 years ago
* Chocolate became a major force in Mayan society
* In the heyday of Mayan society cacao beans were an important commodity

Cacao was an important crop and cultural influence in the Mayan culture, a Central American society with a rich heritage of early written language, art, architecture, and astronomical systems. This culture is thought to have peaked between 250 AD and 900 AD. Its demise was largely brought about by the arrival of Spanish explorers in the seventeenth century.

Cacao's popularity followed this timeline:

1. Traces of chocolate found in Mayan pots dating from 600 BC.
2. Cacao and hot water brewed by Mayans and Aztecs in Pre-Columbian era.
3. Cortez brings hot chocolate back to Spain in 1527.
4. European courts develop passion for chocolate drinks in seventeenth and eighteenth centuries.
5. 1825 Van Houten of Holland discovers how to degrease chocolate, spreading its popularity.

Cacao Varieties
The Mayan culture began cultivating cocoa over 2,500 years ago. Criollo cacao came from Central America, and evolved separately from the cacao in the Amazon River basin that belong to the Forastero variety. Criollo cacao trees are still found in the Lacadonia rainforest.[1]

Criollo cacao is a wild variety that is genetically distinct from the other varieties of cacao found throughout Central and South America.

---
[1] The Lacadonia rainforest is located in the eastern part of the state of Chiapas, Mexico.

Completed Skill 9

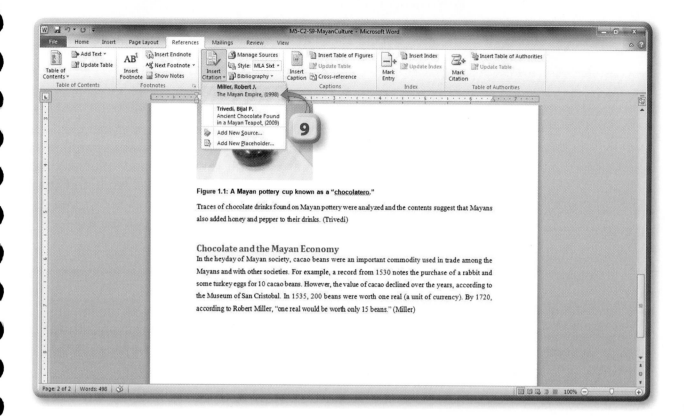

Figure 1.1: A Mayan pottery cup known as a "chocolatero."

Traces of chocolate drinks found on Mayan pottery were analyzed and the contents suggest that Mayans also added honey and pepper to their drinks. (Trivedi)

Chocolate and the Mayan Economy

In the heyday of Mayan society, cacao beans were an important commodity used in trade among the Mayans and with other societies. For example, a record from 1530 notes the purchase of a rabbit and some turkey eggs for 10 cacao beans. However, the value of cacao declined over the years, according to the Museum of San Cristobal. In 1535, 200 beans were worth one real (a unit of currency). By 1720, according to Robert Miller, "one real would be worth only 15 beans." (Miller)

Taking It Further

Editing Sources Once you have entered source information, you may change it, either by deleting sources or managing which sources are available to your current document. Click the Manage Sources button in the Citations & Bibliography group on the References tab. Clicking this button opens the Source Manager dialog box. In this dialog box you can browse for sources you have saved; preview the styles, such as MLA and APA; and add, edit, or delete sources.

Word

Skill 10

Create a Works Cited Page

Video M5_C2_S10

Once you have inserted citations in your document, you can create a Works Cited page, which appears at the end of your document and gives detailed information about your quoted sources. Adding citations and a Works Cited page ensures that you have given appropriate credit and avoided plagiarizing another individual's work and that your document can be viewed as authoritative and complete.

Steps

1 If it is not already open, open **M5-C2-S9-MayanCulture.docx**, the file you saved in the previous skill, and save the file as **M5-C2-S10-MayanCulture**.

2 Place your cursor at the end of your document, after *(Miller)*.

3 Press Enter.

▶ **Tip** Some instructors may prefer that you place the Works Cited on its own page. To do so, press Ctrl + Enter instead of Enter.

4 Type Works Cited.

5 Click the Home tab and apply the Heading 1 style to the title.

▶ **Tip** Traditionally, a bibliography lists all sources you used as research materials when creating your document, while a Works Cited page lists only those sources you quoted.

6 Click the References tab.

7 Click the Bibliography button in the Citations & Bibliography group and then click *Insert Bibliography* from the drop-down menu that appears. This action inserts the cited works under the *Works Cited* heading.

8 Save the file.

Taking It Further

Selecting Citation Styles   The format of citations vary based on the professional standard for publication. Three of the most commonly used standards are MLA (Modern Languages Association), most commonly used in English and humanities publications; APA (American Psychological Association), most commonly used in scientific publications; and Chicago, based on *The Chicago Manual of Style*. Ask your instructor which standard he or she prefers.

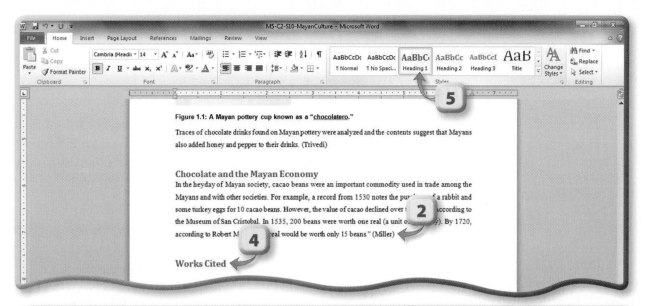

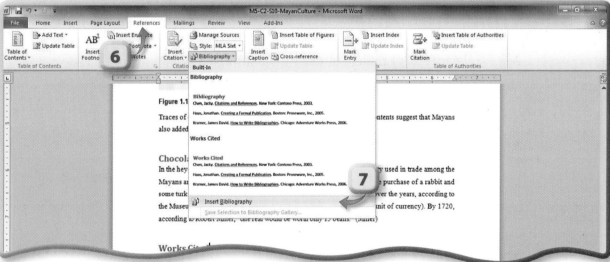

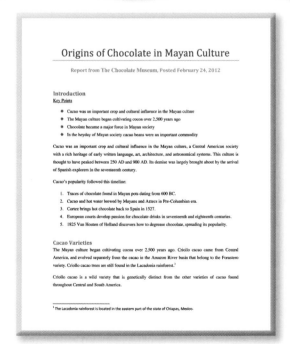

Origins of Chocolate in Mayan Culture

Report from The Chocolate Museum, Posted February 24, 2012

Introduction
Key Points

- Cacao was an important crop and cultural influence in the Mayan culture
- The Mayan culture began cultivating cocoa over 2,500 years ago
- Chocolate became a major force in Mayan society
- In the heyday of Mayan society cacao beans were an important commodity

Cacao was an important crop and cultural influence in the Mayan culture, a Central American society with a rich heritage of early written language, art, architecture, and astronomical systems. This culture is thought to have peaked between 250 AD and 900 AD. Its demise was largely brought about by the arrival of Spanish explorers in the seventeenth century.

Cacao's popularity followed this timeline:

1. Traces of chocolate found in Mayan pots dating from 600 BC.
2. Cacao and hot water brewed by Mayans and Aztecs in Pre-Columbian era.
3. Cortez brings hot chocolate back to Spain in 1527.
4. European courts develop passion for chocolate drinks in seventeenth and eighteenth centuries.
5. 1825 Van Houten of Holland discovers how to degrease chocolate, spreading its popularity.

Cacao Varieties
The Mayan culture began cultivating cocoa over 2,500 years ago. Criollo cacao came from Central America, and evolved separately from the cacao in the Amazon River basin that belong to the Forastero variety. Criollo cacao trees are still found in the Lacandonia rainforest.[1]

Criollo cacao is a wild variety that is genetically distinct from the other varieties of cacao found throughout Central and South America.

---
[1] The Lacadonia rainforest is located in the eastern part of the state of Chiapas, Mexico.

Chocolate through History
One of the Mayan myths of creation tells of a woman who stroked a head impaled on a cacao tree and then magically became impregnated. She escaped to earth to avoid her father's wrath and gave birth to twins, the ancestors of the Mayan culture.

Chocolate was a major force in Mayan society. Pottery cups unearthed in the nineteenth century are called *chocolateros* by local Indians and were possibly used in ceremonial events. These cups include hollow handles, which were used to blow into a chocolate drink to create foam, a practice especially associated with Mayans *(see Figure 1.1)*.

Figure 1.1: A Mayan pottery cup known as a "chocolatero."

Traces of chocolate drinks found on Mayan pottery were analyzed and the contents suggest that Mayans also added honey and pepper to their drinks. (Trivedi)

Chocolate and the Mayan Economy
In the heyday of Mayan society, cacao beans were an important commodity used in trade among the Mayans and with other societies. For example, a record from 1530 notes the purchase of a rabbit and some turkey eggs for 10 cacao beans. However, the value of cacao declined over the years, according to the Museum of San Cristobal. In 1535, 200 beans were worth one real (a unit of currency). By 1720, according to Robert Miller, "one real would be worth only 15 beans." (Miller)

Works Cited
Miller, Robert J. The Mayan Empire. New York: Cultural Exchange, 1998.

Trivedi, Bijal P. "Ancient Chocolate Found in a Mayan Teapot." National Geographic Today (2009): 24-30.

Word

Word

Chapter 2

Skill 11

Video M5_C2_S11

Format Text in Columns

Sometimes, you may want to use columns to save space or arrange text or lists in a more interesting or helpful pattern. To do this you simply select the text you want to arrange in columns and then specify how many columns you need by using the Columns feature in Word.

Steps

1. If it is not already open, open **M5-C2-S10-MayanCulture.docx**, the file you saved in the previous skill, and save the file as **Lastname-M5-C2-S11-MayanCulture**, but replace *Lastname* with your last name. Be sure to save the file in your Module 5 working folder on your storage medium.

2. Select the four bullets under the heading *Key Points*.

3. Click the Page Layout tab.

4. Click the Columns button in the Page Setup group.

5. Click *Two* from the drop-down list.

6. Save and close the file.

▶**Tip** If you need more than three columns, you can click the *More Columns* option in the drop-down menu and adjust the settings in the dialog box that appears.

Taking It Further

More Options for Formatting Columns
If you wish to have two columns of unequal width, you have two options for creating them. First, when selecting the style of column, you can choose the Left or Right style in the Columns dialog box. Left makes the left column smaller; right makes the right column smaller. If these options do not suit your needs, consider instead using a table to organize text. Tables give you great flexibility in making columns of varying widths. If you like, you can even remove the lines around the table, which results in a layout that looks more like columns than like a table. See Chapter 3 for more about creating tables.

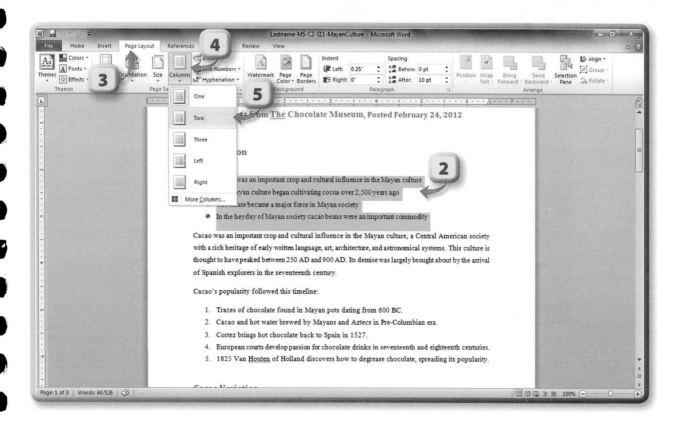

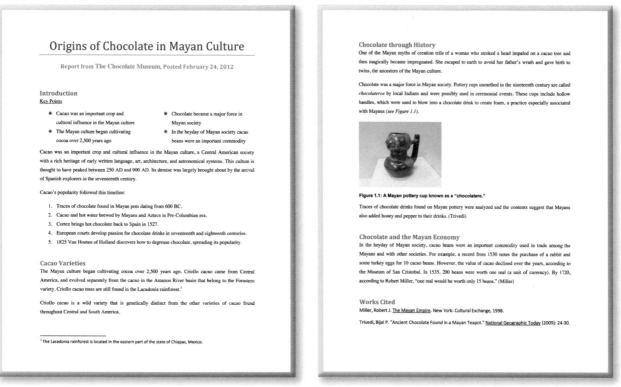

Report from The Chocolate Museum, Posted February 24, 2012

Origins of Chocolate in Mayan Culture

Report from The Chocolate Museum, Posted February 24, 2012

Introduction
Key Points

* Cacao was an important crop and cultural influence in the Mayan culture
* The Mayan culture began cultivating cocoa over 2,500 years ago
* Chocolate became a major force in Mayan society
* In the heyday of Mayan society cacao beans were an important commodity

Cacao was an important crop and cultural influence in the Mayan culture, a Central American society with a rich heritage of early written language, art, architecture, and astronomical systems. This culture is thought to have peaked between 250 AD and 900 AD. Its demise was largely brought about by the arrival of Spanish explorers in the seventeenth century.

Cacao's popularity followed this timeline:

1. Traces of chocolate found in Mayan pots dating from 600 BC.
2. Cacao and hot water brewed by Mayans and Aztecs in Pre-Columbian era.
3. Cortez brings hot chocolate back to Spain in 1527.
4. European courts develop passion for chocolate drinks in seventeenth and eighteenth centuries.
5. 1825 Van Houten of Holland discovers how to degrease chocolate, spreading its popularity.

Cacao Varieties
The Mayan culture began cultivating cocoa over 2,500 years ago. Criollo cacao came from Central America, and evolved separately from the cacao in the Amazon River basin that belong to the Forastero variety. Criollo cacao trees are still found in the Lacadonia rainforest.[1]

Criollo cacao is a wild variety that is genetically distinct from the other varieties of cacao found throughout Central and South America.

_____
[1] The Lacadonia rainforest is located in the eastern part of the state of Chiapas, Mexico.

Chocolate through History
One of the Mayan myths of creation tells of a woman who stroked a head impaled on a cacao tree and then magically became impregnated. She escaped to earth to avoid her father's wrath and gave birth to twins, the ancestors of the Mayan culture.

Chocolate was a major force in Mayan society. Pottery cups unearthed in the nineteenth century are called *chocolateros* by local Indians and were possibly used in ceremonial events. These cups include hollow handles, which were used to blow into a chocolate drink to create foam, a practice especially associated with Mayans *(see Figure 1.1)*.

Figure 1.1: A Mayan pottery cup known as a "chocolatero."

Traces of chocolate drinks found on Mayan pottery were analyzed and the contents suggest that Mayans also added honey and pepper to their drinks. (Trivedi)

Chocolate and the Mayan Economy
In the heyday of Mayan society, cacao beans were an important commodity used in trade among the Mayans and with other societies. For example, a record from 1530 notes the purchase of a rabbit and some turkey eggs for 10 cacao beans. However, the value of cacao declined over the years, according to the Museum of San Cristobal. In 1535, 200 beans were worth one real (a unit of currency). By 1720, according to Robert Miller, "one real would be worth only 15 beans." (Miller)

Works Cited
Miller, Robert J. The Mayan Empire. New York: Cultural Exchange, 1998.

Trivedi, Bijal P. "Ancient Chocolate Found in a Mayan Teapot." National Geographic Today (2009): 24-30.

Completed Skill 11

Word

Word
Chapter 2 Assessments

Tasks Summary

Task	Ribbon Tab, Group	Button, Option	Shortcut, Alternative
Select text	Home, Editing	*Select* drop-down list	Selection bar
Change font	Home, Font	*Font* drop-down list	Ctrl + Shift + F
Change font size	Home, Font	*Font size* drop-down list	Ctrl + Shift + P
Display Font dialog box	Home, Font	◰	Ctrl + D
Underline text	Home, Font	U ▾	Ctrl + U
Change font color	Home, Font	A ▾	
Bold text	Home, Font	B	Ctrl + B
Italicize text	Home, Font	I	Ctrl + I
Apply styles	Home, Styles	Styles Gallery	
Align text left	Home, Paragraph	▤	Ctrl + L
Align text right	Home, Paragraph	▤	Ctrl + R
Align text center	Home, Paragraph	▤	Ctrl + E
Align text justified	Home, Paragraph	▤	Ctrl + J
Change line spacing	Home, Paragraph	▤▾	
Format text as bulleted list	Home, Paragraph	▤ ▾	
Format text as numbered list	Home, Paragraph	▤ ▾	
Define custom bullet	Home, Paragraph	Bullet button arrow	
Copy formatting	Home, Clipboard	🖌	Ctrl + Shift + C
Insert endnote	References, Footnotes	📄	Alt + Ctrl + D
Choose citation style	References, Citations & Bibliography	*Style* drop-down list	
Insert citation	References, Citations & Bibliography	📄	
Create a works cited page	References, Citations & Bibliography	*Bibliography* drop-down list	
Format text in columns	Page Layout, Page Setup	📄	

Features Review

Select the best answer from the choices given.

1 Fonts are defined as
   a. effects such as bold and underline
   b. character sets for type.
   c. either italic or bold.
   d. the way Word formats text.

2 Heading 1 is a
   a. font.
   b. template.
   c. style.
   d. None of the above

3 Using alignment tools, text is aligned relative to
   a. tabs.
   b. the Ruler.
   c. left and right margins.
   d. headers and footers.

4 Paragraph settings are found on this tab.
   a. Page Layout
   b. Home
   c. File
   d. View

5 Bulleted lists are typically used for a list of items
   a. that has no sequence.
   b. that has a particular sequence.

6 Format Painter is used to
   a. copy text.
   b. format pictures.
   c. copy formatting from one piece of text to another.
   d. None of the above

7 Endnotes place information
   a. at the bottom of the page.
   b. at the end of the document.
   c. in a footer.
   d. in a header.

8 One common professional style used in documents is
   a. MLB.
   b. MLA.
   c. ABA.
   d. Illinois.

9 A Works Cited page helps to ensure that you
   a. provide appropriate credit to your sources.
   b. have plagiarized the cited work.
   c. have included endnotes in your document.
   d. All of the above

10 To create columns you must
   a. set tabs.
   b. click the Columns button and then select text.
   c. first select text and then click the Columns button.
   d. change margins.

Hands-On Skills Review

Exercise **A** **Format a Document about Formatting**

Skills   Change font and font size; use formatting tools: bold, italic, and underline text; align text; format paragraph and line spacing; format text in columns; and insert headers and footers

Scenario   Use various formatting tools to add emphasis and highlight important information in this document that describes Word formatting features.

Steps

1 Open the student file named **M5-C2-ExA-Formatting.docx** and save the file as **Lastname-M5-C2-ExA-Formatting**, but replace *Lastname* with your last name.

2 Add a header to the document that includes your name at the left margin and the current date at the right margin.

3 Add a footer to the document, placing the page number in the center.

4 Remove the first-line indentation from all paragraphs beginning with *Using Microsoft Word* and ending with *even more useful*. **HINT:** *Click the dialog box launcher in the Paragraph group on the Home tab. In the Indentation section, click the Special text box arrow and select (none). Click OK.*

5 Add 10-pt spacing after each paragraph.

6 Justify the document body.

7 Place the names of the tab on the Microsoft Word ribbon into four columns of equal size, from *File* to *View*.

8 Set the line spacing for all paragraphs beginning with *Using Microsoft Word* and ending with *even more useful* to 1.15.

9 Change the title (*Format It!*) to Script MT Bold and set the size to 22 pt.

10 Italicize all instances of *Microsoft Word, Word,* or *Word's.* **HINT:** *Italicize the first occurrence. Double-click the Format Painter and then double-click the next instance of Word. It automatically adopts the same formatting. Continue in this manner until you have italicized all occurrences of* Word. *Click the Format Painter again to turn it off.*

11 Bold the text that begins with *Term paper* and ends with *problem.*

12 Underline *spelling bee champ.*

13 Save and close the file.

14 Print or submit the completed document as directed by your instructor.

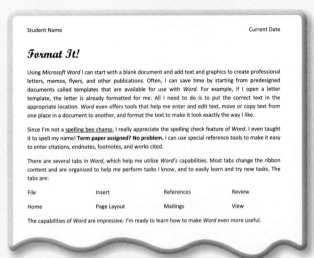

Completed Exercise A

Exercise **B** Format an Exercise List

Skills Change font and font size, italicize text, align text, create a bulleted or numbered list, and insert headers and footers

Scenario It is difficult to focus on the calories burned by each activity when the activities are presented in the paragraph format shown. Separate the activities and create a bulleted list for easier reading.

Steps

1 Open the student data file named **M5-C2-ExB-Calories.docx** and save the file as **Lastname-M5-C2-ExB-Calories**, but replace *Lastname* with your last name.

2 Add a header to the document that includes your name at the left margin and the current date at the right margin.

3 Add a footer to the document, placing the page number in the center.

4 Separate each statement into a list item and add bullets. *Hint: Press Ener between each statement to place each statement on its own line before changing to a bulletted list.*

5 Change the bullets to check marks and the font size for all bulleted items to Calibri 16 pt.

6 Change the font for the title *Burning Calories* to Lucinda Sans 28 pt and center the text.

7 Use Format Painter to apply the title's formatting to the final sentence of the document, which begins *Find something.* Italicize the last sentence.

8 Save and close the file.

9 Print or submit the completed document as directed by your instructor.

Completed Exercise B

Exercise C Format a Report

Skills   Change font and font size, use formatting tools, align text, format paragraph and line spacing, insert citations using professional styles, create a Works Cited page, add headers and footers, enter and edit text, indent and add tabs using the Ruler, and insert a page break

Scenario   Format a term paper so it is ready for submission. The research has already been done, but your instructor provided the following guidelines:

Font: Arial 12 pt
Spacing: double
Alignment: left
Paragraph Indent: 0.5"
Header: your initials and page number in upper right corner
References: MLA Sixth Edition parenthetical citations
Works Cited Page: required

Skills

1 Open the student data file **M5-C2-ExC-NativeLang.docx**, and save the file as **Lastname-M5-C2-ExC-NativeLang**, but replace *Lastname* with your last name.

2 Change the font for the entire document to Arial 12 pt.

3 Remove the blank lines between paragraphs, beginning with *In this essay* through the end of the document **HINT:** *Click the Show/Hide button, delete each extra paragraph mark, and click the Show/Hide button to turn it off.*

4 Highlight the body of the document, from *In the essay* to *approach to instruction*, and set paragraph indents, alignment, and spacing as directed.

5 Bold and center the title and the author lines of the document.

6 Enter your name on the title line in parentheses next to the author's name: *Nancy Robinson*

7 Add a one-field header that is your initials followed by a hyphen and the page number. **HINT:** *Enter your initials, a hyphen, and then the page number. Add a blank line as the second line of the header. Right-align the header. The header font and size should be the same as in the rest of the document (Arial 12 pt).*

8 Set the reference style to *MLA Sixth Edition*.

9 Add the following sources.

Type of Source	*Web site*
Author	Cummings, Jim
Name of Web Page	Bilingual Children's Mother Tongue: Why Is It Important for Education?

Year	2003
Year Accessed	2012
Month Accessed	May
Day Accessed	4
URL	http://www.emcp.net/iteachilearn/cummings/mother.html

Type of Source	*Journal Article*
Author	Dahlberg, Joan S.
Title	Pros and Cons of the English-Only (EO) Classroom
Journal Name	ESL Journal 29.2
Year	2006
Pages	10-15

Type of Source	*Journal Article*
Author	Leonard, Martin; Rivera, Hector
Title	Language Skills and Achievement in the Content Areas
Journal Name	English Teachers Journal 65
Year	2010
Pages	211-15

Type of Source	*Conference Proceedings*
Author	Tan, Amy
Title	Mother Tongue
Pages	1208-14
Year	2008

Conference	
Publication Name	Mirrors & Windows: Connecting with Literature, American Tradition
City	St. Paul, MN
Publisher	EMC Publishing
Type of Source	Web site
Name of Web Page	Teacher Talk
Year	2007
Year Accessed	2012
Month Accessed	May
Day Accessed	4
URL	http://www.emcp.net/ttalk

10 After entering the data shown above for the Teacher Talk website, insert a check mark in the *Show All Bibliography Fields* check box and enter the following additional information.

Editor   Walsh, Debbie

11 Enter the citations in the indicated locations using the Insert Citation tool. Be sure to delete the citation markers. Each citation marker begins and ends with **.

12 Position the cursor at the end of the document and add a page break. **HINT:** *Click the Page Break button in the Pages group in the Insert tab.*

13 Use the Bibliography tool to create a Works Cited page. Do not modify the format of the Works Cited page.

14 Save and close the file.

15 Print or submit the document as directed by your instructor.

SN-1

An Argument for Using Native Language in the Classroom
By Nancy Robinson (Student Name)

In the essay "Mother Tongue," Amy Tan describes the limited English skills of her mother, a Chinese immigrant, noting that "my mother had long realized the limitations of her English" (Tan). Tan goes on to describe how her mother had to compensate for these limitations throughout her life.

This is the experience of many immigrants to the United States, who struggle to learn a new language while adapting to life in a new country. Immigrant children have the opportunity to learn English in the public schools, but educators do not agree on the best approach to teaching them. Some advocate total immersion in an English-only classroom, while others contend that students should be allowed to use their native language at least while they develop English language skills. Using native language in the classroom is necessary for immigrant students' academic success.

Students who cannot speak English well enough to participate in the classroom will suffer academically. Teachers report that when students are not allowed to use their native language, they often repeat what they have heard without actually understanding the concepts (Dahlberg). Doing so affects their ability to learn not only English but content in other subject areas, as well.

Results from standardized tests demonstrate that many English language learners lag behind their peers in academic achievement (Leonard and Rivera).

Students who are allowed to use their native language in the classroom feel a greater sense of security, which enhances their ability to learn. Third grade teacher Debbie Walsh, who teaches in a bilingual program in Miami, Florida, strongly believes that "children need to know they can ask for help, explain problems, say how they feel,

SN-2

and so on" (Teacher Talk). For many children, doing so requires using their native language, at least early on.

Students who are discouraged from speaking their native language may feel personally rejected. According to Professor Jim Cummins, an expert on language acquisition, "When [students] feel this rejection, they are much less likely to participate actively and confidently in classroom instruction" (Cummins). It follows that students who do not or cannot participate in the classroom will lose their motivation for learning (Dahlberg).

Allowing students to use their native language also enhances their critical-thinking skills, further boosting their academic achievement. Again quoting Cummins, "Bilingual children may develop more flexibility in their thinking as a result of processing information through two different languages" (Cummins). Research involving elementary-age students has shown that when children continue to develop skills in two or more languages, they have broader language skills and a better understanding of how to use language effectively (Leonard and Rivera).

Conversely, children who do not have regular opportunities to use their native language can lose their ability to speak it within two or three years of starting school (Cummins).

Allowing immigrant students to use their native language in the classroom is key in their academic success. Not only does native language use support students in developing English language skills and learning academic content, but it also gives them the confidence and motivation to participate in the classroom community. The critical-thinking abilities that have been proven to result from speaking multiple

Completed Exercise C

SN-3

languages should encourage educators nationwide to adopt a bilingual model of education. Native and nonnative English speakers alike would benefit from that approach to instruction.

SN-4

Works Cited

Cummins, Jim. Bilingual Children's Mother tongue: Why Is It Important for Education? 2003. 4 May 2012 <http://www.emcp.net/iteachilearn.com/cummins/mother.html>.

Dahlberg, Joan S. "Pros and Cons of the English-Only (EO) Classroom." ESL Journal 29.2 (2006): 10-15.

Leonard, Martin and Hector Rivera. "Language Skills and Achievement in the Content Areas." English Teachers Journal 65 (2010): 211-15.

Tan, Amy. "Mother Tongue." Mirrors & Windows: Connecting with Literature, American Tradition. St. Paul, MN: EMC Publishing, 2008. 1208-14.

Teacher Talk. Ed. Debbie Walsh. 2007. 4 May 2012 <http://www.emcp.net/ttalk>.

Completed Exercise (continued)

Chapter 3

Working with Tables and Objects

There are several features in Word that help you organize information and add visual appeal to your documents. Tables organize information into rows and columns, allowing you to convey a great deal of data in a small, neat space. You can also insert visual objects, including photos, illustrations, and shapes to better illustrate a point or make your document more attractive. In this chapter you learn how to build tables and insert and manipulate objects.

Skills You Learn

1. Create tables
2. Convert text to tables
3. Change page orientation
4. Insert a row in a table
5. Merge rows or columns in a table
6. Format tables
7. Insert shapes
8. Insert clip art objects
9. Resize objects
10. Rotate objects

Files You Need

In this chapter, you need the following student data files.

M5-C3-S1-HCRecipe.docx

M5-C3-S3-HCRecipe.docx

M5-C3-S7-HCRecipe.docx

What You Create

You are helping to organize an open house to celebrate The Chocolate Museum's 10th year in operation. The Museum will give each guest a small tote bag containing a pad and pen stamped with the Museum's logo, a bar of chocolate from a local chocolate company, and a recipe for Mexican Hot Chocolate. Your boss has asked you to create the recipe document, including a table of ingredients, fun illustrations and pictures of hot chocolate, and recipe instructions.

In this chapter you build the recipe in Word using Word's table and column features to organize the recipe contents and then add a shape and a clip art object for visual interest.

Hot Chocolate Recipe

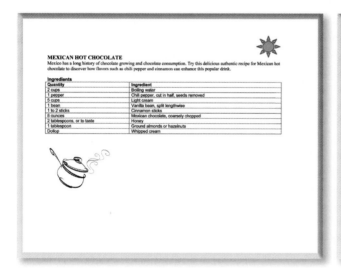

MEXICAN HOT CHOCOLATE

Mexico has a long history of chocolate growing and chocolate consumption. Try this delicious authentic recipe for Mexican hot chocolate to discover how flavors such as chili pepper and cinnamon can enhance this popular drink.

Ingredients

Quantity	Ingredient
2 cups	Boiling water
1 pepper	Chili pepper, cut in half, seeds removed
5 cups	Light cream
1 bean	Vanilla bean, split lengthwise
1 to 2 sticks	Cinnamon sticks
6 ounces	Mexican chocolate, coarsely chopped
2 tablespoons, or to taste	Honey
1 tablespoon	Ground almonds or hazelnuts
Dollop	Whipped cream

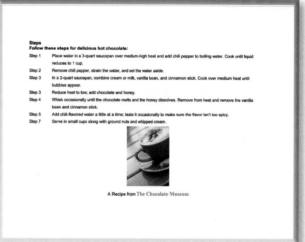

Steps

Follow these steps for delicious hot chocolate:

Step 1 — Place water in a 3-quart saucepan over medium-high heat and add chili pepper to boiling water. Cook until liquid reduces to 1 cup.

Step 2 — Remove chili pepper, strain the water, and set the water aside.

Step 3 — In a 2-quart saucepan, combine cream or milk, vanilla bean, and cinnamon stick. Cook over medium heat until bubbles appear.

Step 3 — Reduce heat to low; add chocolate and honey.

Step 4 — Whisk occasionally until the chocolate melts and the honey dissolves. Remove from heat and remove the vanilla bean and cinnamon stick.

Step 5 — Add chili-flavored water a little at a time; taste it occasionally to make sure the flavor isn't too spicy.

Step 7 — Serve in small cups along with ground nuts and whipped cream.

A Recipe from The Chocolate Museum

Word

Skill 1

Video M5_C3_S01

Create Tables

Tables use columns and rows to help organize sets of information and show relationships among separate pieces of information. For example, imagine a table used to compare the nutritional information for types of snacks. The first column of the table lists the name of each snack. The second column lists the quantity of calories in each snack. The third column lists the quantity of carbohydrates in each snack. The fourth column lists the quantity of fat in each snack. By reading down the table's columns you could compare the nutritional ingredients of each type of snack, and might use that information to help you select which snack to eat. In this skill, you create a table to list the amounts of each recipe ingredient in the first column and the type of ingredient in the second column.

Steps

1 Open the student data file named **M5-C3-S1-HCRecipe.docx**, and if you have not already done so, save the file in your Module 5 working folder on your storage medium.

2 Click in the blank line between the words *Ingredients* and *Steps*.

3 Click the Insert tab.

4 Click the Table button in the Tables group and then click *Insert Table*.

5 In the Insert Table dialog box that appears, type 2 in the *Number of columns* field and 9 in the *Number of rows* field.

6 Click OK.

4 *Another Way*
You can also click and drag to select the boxes that appear in order to insert a table containing up to eight rows and columns.

5 *Another Way*
Click the arrows on the right side of each of the number fields to change the number of rows and columns.

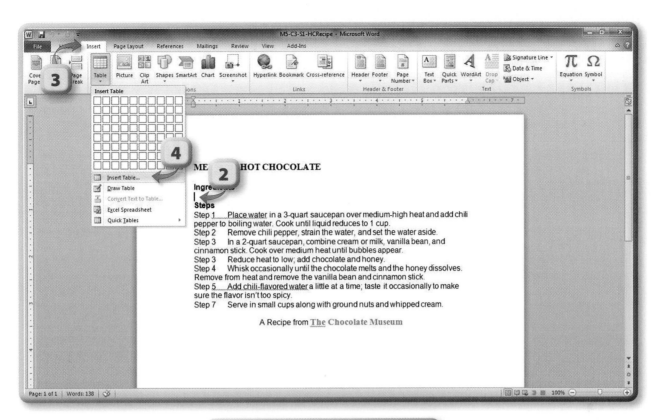

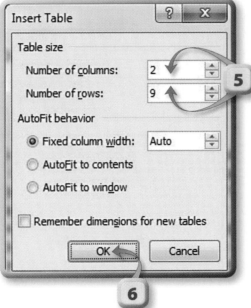

More

Word

7 Click in the cells of the table and enter the following text:

2 cups	Boiling water
1 pepper	Chili pepper, cut in half, seeds removed
5 cups	Light cream
1 bean	Vanilla bean, split lengthwise
1 to 2 sticks	Cinnamon sticks
8 ounces	Mexican chocolate, coarsely chopped
2 tablespoons, or to taste	Honey
1 tablespoon	Ground almonds or hazelnuts
Dollop	Whipped cream

8 Save the file.

MEXICAN HOT CHOCOLATE

Ingredients

2 cups	Boiling water
1 pepper	Chili pepper, cut in half, seeds removed
5 cups	Light cream
1 bean	Vanilla bean, split lengthwise
1 to 2 sticks	Cinnamon sticks
8 ounces	Mexican chocolate, coarsely chopped
2 tablespoons, or to taste	Honey
1 tablespoon	Ground almonds or hazelnuts
Dollop	Whipped cream

Steps
Step 1   Place water in a 3-quart saucepan over medium-high heat and add chili
pepper to boiling water. Cook until liquid reduces to 1 cup.
Step 2   Remove chili pepper, strain the water, and set the water aside.
Step 3   In a 2-quart saucepan, combine cream or milk, vanilla bean, and
cinnamon stick. Cook over medium heat until bubbles appear.
Step 3   Reduce heat to low; add chocolate and honey.
Step 4   Whisk occasionally until the chocolate melts and the honey dissolves.
Remove from heat and remove the vanilla bean and cinnamon stick.
Step 5   Add chili-flavored water a little at a time; taste it occasionally to make
sure the flavor isn't too spicy.
Step 7   Serve in small cups along with ground nuts and whipped cream.

A Recipe from The Chocolate Museum

Completed Skill 1

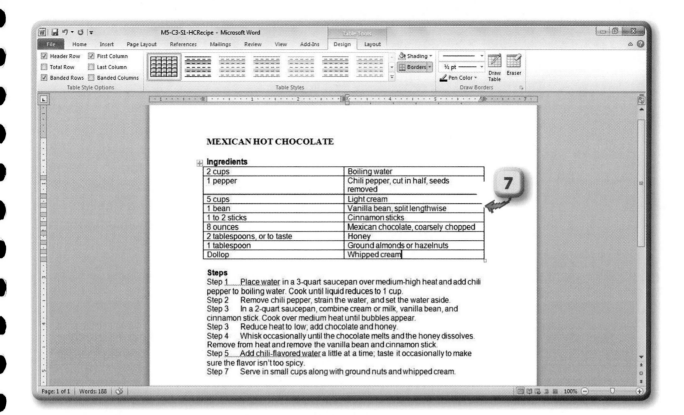

Taking It Further

Formatting Tables   To save yourself
some formatting time, try the Quick Tables
feature. You can access Quick Tables from
the Table button in the Insert tab. Quick
Tables includes common table styles that
you might find useful, such as two column
lists or calendars.

Word

Video M5_C3_S02

Convert Text to Tables

If you have entered text outside of a table, you can convert that information into table form. You must provide an indicator to mark where each new column begins. For these indicators, or separators, people often use tabs, but you can also use commas, paragraphs, or single characters such as hyphens. When you convert text to tables, separators break the text into columns and a hard return (pressing the Enter key) between lines separates your text into rows.

Steps

1 If it is not already open, open **M5-C3-S1-HCRecipe.docx**, the file you saved in the previous skill, and save the file as **Lastname-M5-C3-S2-HCRecipe**, but replace *Lastname* with your last name. Be sure to save the file in your Module 5 working folder on your storage medium.

▶*Tip* Before using the Convert Text to Table feature, verify that you have inserted column and row separators. Click the Show/Hide button in the Paragraph group in the Home tab to display the arrows that represent tabs and the paragraph symbols that indicate paragraph breaks.

2 Select the text under the heading *Steps*, from the start of *Step 1* through the end of *Step 7*. The step list includes tabs to separate the step numbers from the step descriptions.

3 Click the Insert tab and then click the Table button.

4 Click *Convert Text to Table*.

▶*Tip* Note that the *AutoFit behavior* section of the Convert Text to Table dialog box defaults to *Auto* in the *Fixed column width* option. The *Auto* setting adjusts column widths to fit the text in them, as shown in the images on the next page.

5 In the Convert Text to Table dialog box, be sure that the *Tabs* option is selected under the *Separate text at* section.

6 Click OK.

7 Save and close the file.

MEXICAN HOT CHOCOLATE

Ingredients

2 cups	Boiling water
1 pepper	Chili pepper, cut in half, seeds removed
5 cups	Light cream
1 bean	Vanilla bean, split lengthwise
1 to 2 sticks	Cinnamon sticks
8 ounces	Mexican chocolate, coarsely chopped
2 tablespoons, or to taste	Honey
1 tablespoon	Ground almonds or hazelnuts
Dollop	Whipped cream

Steps

Step 1	Place water in a 3-quart saucepan over medium-high heat and add chili pepper to boiling water. Cook until liquid reduces to 1 cup.
Step 2	Remove chili pepper, strain the water, and set the water aside.
Step 3	In a 2-quart saucepan, combine cream or milk, vanilla bean, and cinnamon stick. Cook over medium heat until bubbles appear.
Step 3	Reduce heat to low; add chocolate and honey.
Step 4	Whisk occasionally until the chocolate melts and the honey dissolves. Remove from heat and remove the vanilla bean and cinnamon stick.
Step 5	Add chili-flavored water a little at a time; taste it occasionally to make sure the flavor isn't too spicy.
Step 7	Serve in small cups along with ground nuts and whipped cream.

A Recipe from The Chocolate Museum

Completed Skill 2

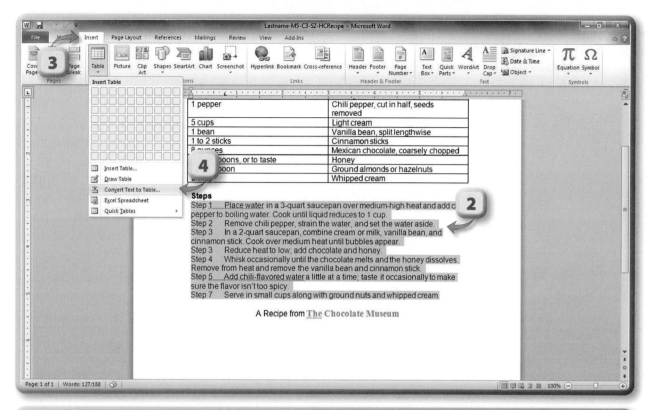

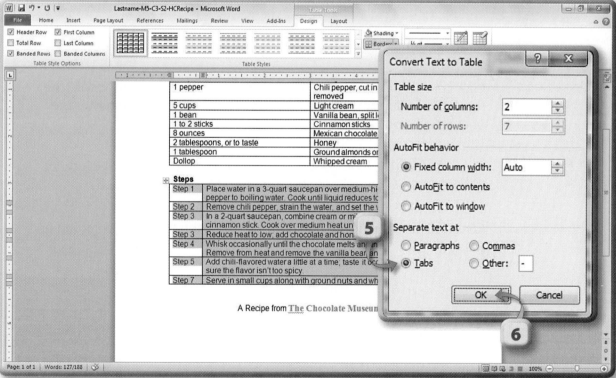

Taking It Further

Converting a Table to Text   You can also select the text in a table and convert it back to plain text. You do this by clicking the Convert to Text button in the Data group in the Table Tools Layout tab. You then get a choice of what to use as a separator in the text (tabs, paragraphs, commas, or another symbol you indicate).

Word

Chapter 3

Skill 3

Video M5_C3_S03

Change Page Orientation

Sometimes in order to fit more text on a page or improve the design, you may want to change the page orientation of a document. Word offers two types of document orientations. By default, Word documents are set up in portrait orientation, where the height of a page is greater than the width. You can change to landscape orientation, where the width of a page is greater than the height. Although you should try to set the page orientation before entering content, you may need to make a change once the content is entered.

Steps

1 Open **M5-C3-S3-HCRecipe.docx**, the student data file, and save the file as **M5-C3-S3-HCRecipe** in your Module 5 working folder.

2 Click the Page Layout tab.

3 Click the Orientation button in the Page Setup group.

4 Click *Landscape*. The text in the document shifts to accommodate the margins of a landscape orientation. To fill the space of the new page orientation, you can resize the table.

5 Hover over the right edge of the first table until the I-beam pointer changes to two vertical lines with arrows pointing to the right and left.

6 Click and drag the right edge of the table to the 8.5" margin setting on the Ruler.

7 Repeat Steps 5 and 6 with the edge of the second table.

8 Save the file.

▶**Tip** Apply the correct page orientation as early as you can while building a document so there are no surprises about how text or inserted objects, such as pictures, might shift on the page once the new margin settings are applied.

▶**Tip** If it is not already displayed, click the *Ruler* check box in the Show group on the View tab to turn on display of the Ruler.

Taking It Further

Fitting Text on a Page The standard page size for most documents is 8½" × 11". Sometimes you may have a landscape orientation document that runs slightly longer than a single page. To fit it on one page, consider printing to another paper size, such as 8½" × 14". You can also fit more text on a page by narrowing the margins in the document. See Module 5 Chapter 1 for more about adjusting margins in Word.

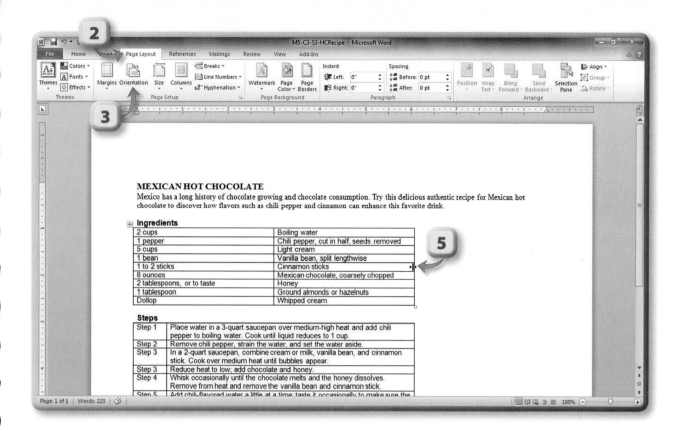

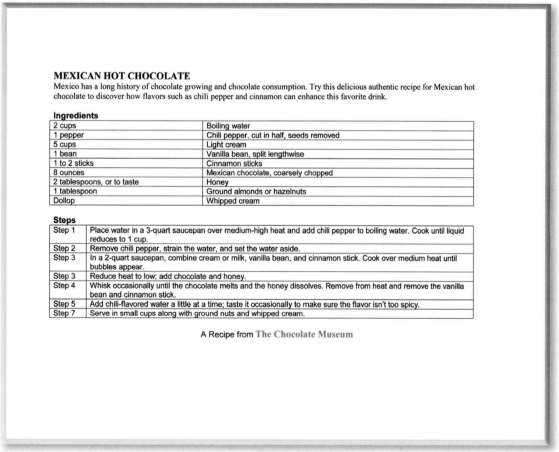

Completed Skill 3

Word

Skill 4 | **Insert a Row in a Table**

At times you will need to add more data to an already-created table. To accommodate the additional data, you can easily insert new columns or rows. In this skill, you insert a heading row in one of your tables.

Steps

1 If it is not already open, open **M5-C3-S3-HCRecipe.docx**, the file you saved in the previous skill, and save the file as **M5-C3-S4-HCRecipe**.

2 Click in the first row of the first table.

3 Click the Table Tools Layout tab.

4 Click the Insert Above button in the Rows & Columns group. A row is inserted above the selected row.

5 Type Quantity in the new top-left cell and Ingredient in the new top-right cell.

6 Select the new first row by dragging your mouse over the text you just typed.

7 Click the Home tab.

8 Click the Bold button in the Font group.

▶ **Tip** To insert a column rather than a row, simply select a column and then click the Insert Left or Insert Right button in the Table Tools Layout tab.

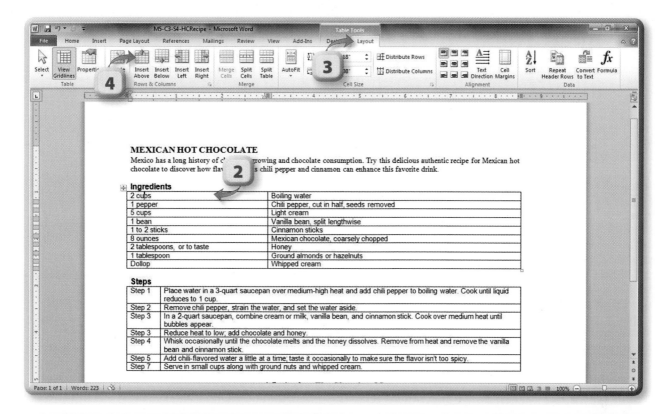

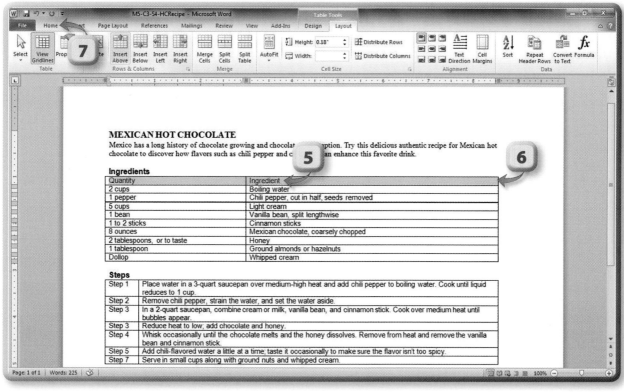

9 Click in the first cell of the second table.

10 Click the Table Tools Layout tab.

11 Click the Insert Above button in the Rows & Columns group.

12 Type Follow these steps for delicious hot chocolate: in the first cell of the new row.

13 Save the file.

Tip When you insert a new column, you may find that the column width does not accommodate the data within it very well. You can resize columns by placing your cursor over a column dividing line until the cursor turns into two vertical lines with arrows facing left and right. Click and drag the divider to the right or left to adjust column widths.

Completed Skill 4

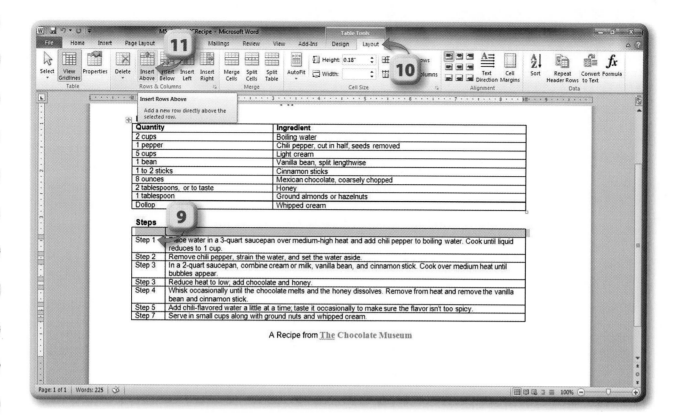

Taking It Further

Deleting Table Content   If you need to delete a row or column, there are a couple of ways to do so. To select a column you wish to delete, place your mouse pointer at the top of the column until the pointer turns into a solid black arrow, click to select the column, and then drag over any additional columns to be deleted. To select a row you wish to delete, place your mouse pointer to the left of a row, click to select the row, and then drag over any additional rows to be deleted. Once you have selected the appropriate rows or columns, right-click, and in the shortcut menu that appears, select either *Delete Rows* or *Delete Columns*. You can also use the Delete button in the Table Tools Layout tab to perform the same action.

Word

Skill 5

Video M5_C3_S05

Merge Rows or Columns in a Table

Not all tables are made up of consistent sets of rows and columns. Some may combine the top row into a single cell that contains a table title. In other cases, you may want to combine a set of cells so they create a larger block in a table-based form, just as a passport has a large square for the person's picture and other lines containing personal data. The process of combining rows or columns is called merging.

Steps

1 If it is not already open, open **M5-C3-S4-HCRecipe.docx**, the file you saved in the previous skill, and save the file as **M5-C3-S5-HCRecipe**.

2 Select the first row of the second table.

3 Click the Table Tools Layout tab.

▶**Tip** You can merge rows, columns, or rows and columns, based on the combination of rows and/or columns you select before clicking Merge Cells.

4 Click the Merge Cells button in the Merge group. Clicking this button merges the two selected cells.

5 With the first row still selected, click the Home tab.

6 **Shortcut**
Bold Text
Ctrl + B

6 Click the Bold button.

7 Save the file.

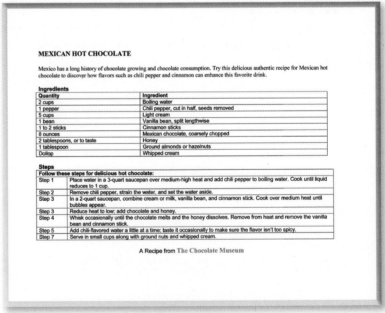

MEXICAN HOT CHOCOLATE

Mexico has a long history of chocolate growing and chocolate consumption. Try this delicious authentic recipe for Mexican hot chocolate to discover how flavors such as chili pepper and cinnamon can enhance this favorite drink.

Ingredients

Quantity	Ingredient
2 cups	Boiling water
1 pepper	Chili pepper, cut in half, seeds removed
5 cups	Light cream
1 bean	Vanilla bean, split lengthwise
1 to 2 sticks	Cinnamon sticks
8 ounces	Mexican chocolate, coarsely chopped
2 tablespoons, or to taste	Honey
1 tablespoon	Ground almonds or hazelnuts
Dollop	Whipped cream

Steps

Follow these steps for delicious hot chocolate:	
Step 1	Place water in a 3-quart saucepan over medium-high heat and add chili pepper to boiling water. Cook until liquid reduces to 1 cup.
Step 2	Remove chili pepper, strain the water, and set the water aside.
Step 3	In a 2-quart saucepan, combine cream or milk, vanilla bean, and cinnamon stick. Cook over medium heat until bubbles appear.
Step 3	Reduce heat to low; add chocolate and honey.
Step 4	Whisk occasionally until the chocolate melts and the honey dissolves. Remove from heat and remove the vanilla bean and cinnamon stick.
Step 5	Add chili-flavored water a little at a time; taste it occasionally to make sure the flavor isn't too spicy.
Step 7	Serve in small cups along with ground nuts and whipped cream.

A Recipe from The Chocolate Museum

Completed Skill 5

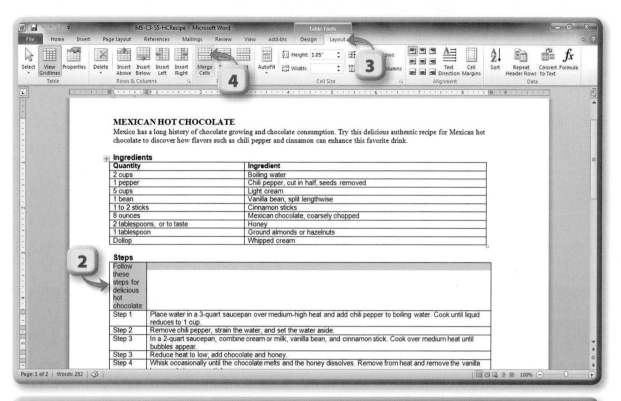

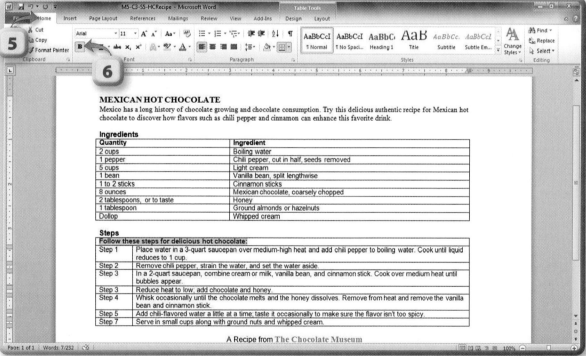

Taking It Further

Formatting with Tables   Use a table and the merge function to build forms or documents such as resumes. The following table is an example of a portion of a resume. Once the information is organized, you can hide the borders, if you wish.

Languages spoken	English	French
	Spanish	Italian
References	John Cartwright, Acme Products. Additional references provided upon request.	

Word

Skill 6

Format Tables

There are a variety of ways you can format a table. You can add shading or modify the thickness or color of the lines that define the table cells. You can also specify which border lines should be displayed and which should not. In this skill you learn how to alter a table so that it has no borders showing at all.

Steps

1 If it is not already open, open **M5-C3-S5-HCRecipe.docx**, the file you saved in the previous skill, and save the file as **Lastname-M5-C3-S6-HCRecipe**, but replace *Lastname* with your last name. Be sure to save the file in your Module 5 working folder on your storage medium.

2 *Another Way*
Click and drag to select all the cells of the table.

2 Right-click in the second table to open a shortcut menu, point to *Select*, and then click *Table*.

3 Click the Table Tools Design tab.

▶ **Tip** Instead of using borders, you can apply shading to individual cells of your table to visually separate cell contents.

4 Click the arrow on the Borders button in the Table Styles group and click *No Border*. Clicking this option removes borders from all of the cells in the table.

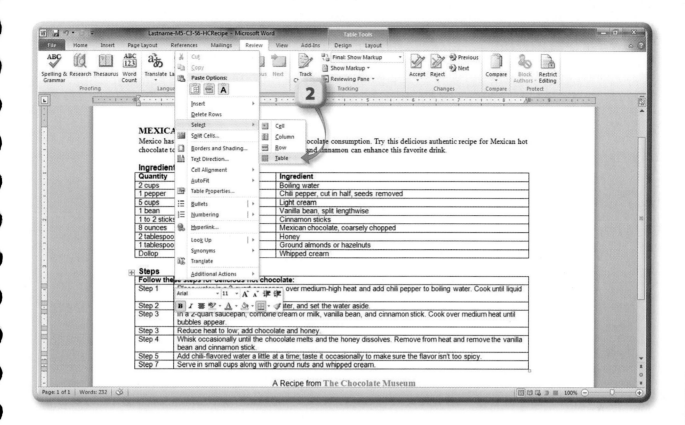

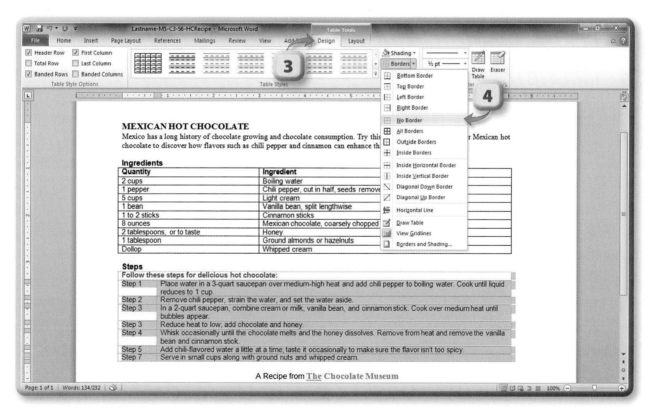

More

5 Click the Home tab.

6 With the table contents still selected, click the Line and Paragraph Spacing button in the Paragraph group and choose *1.15*.

7 Save and close the file.

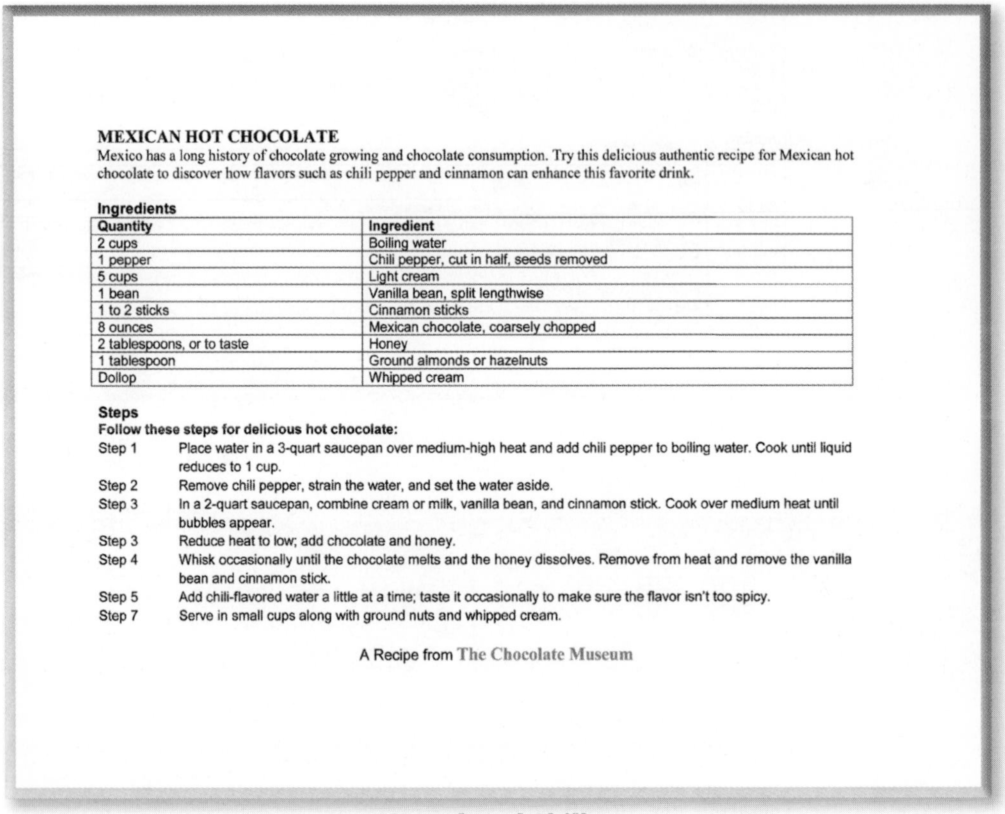

MEXICAN HOT CHOCOLATE
Mexico has a long history of chocolate growing and chocolate consumption. Try this delicious authentic recipe for Mexican hot chocolate to discover how flavors such as chili pepper and cinnamon can enhance this favorite drink.

Ingredients

Quantity	Ingredient
2 cups	Boiling water
1 pepper	Chili pepper, cut in half, seeds removed
5 cups	Light cream
1 bean	Vanilla bean, split lengthwise
1 to 2 sticks	Cinnamon sticks
8 ounces	Mexican chocolate, coarsely chopped
2 tablespoons, or to taste	Honey
1 tablespoon	Ground almonds or hazelnuts
Dollop	Whipped cream

Steps
Follow these steps for delicious hot chocolate:

Step 1   Place water in a 3-quart saucepan over medium-high heat and add chili pepper to boiling water. Cook until liquid reduces to 1 cup.
Step 2   Remove chili pepper, strain the water, and set the water aside.
Step 3   In a 2-quart saucepan, combine cream or milk, vanilla bean, and cinnamon stick. Cook over medium heat until bubbles appear.
Step 3   Reduce heat to low; add chocolate and honey.
Step 4   Whisk occasionally until the chocolate melts and the honey dissolves. Remove from heat and remove the vanilla bean and cinnamon stick.
Step 5   Add chili-flavored water a little at a time; taste it occasionally to make sure the flavor isn't too spicy.
Step 7   Serve in small cups along with ground nuts and whipped cream.

A Recipe from The Chocolate Museum

Completed Skill 6

Word

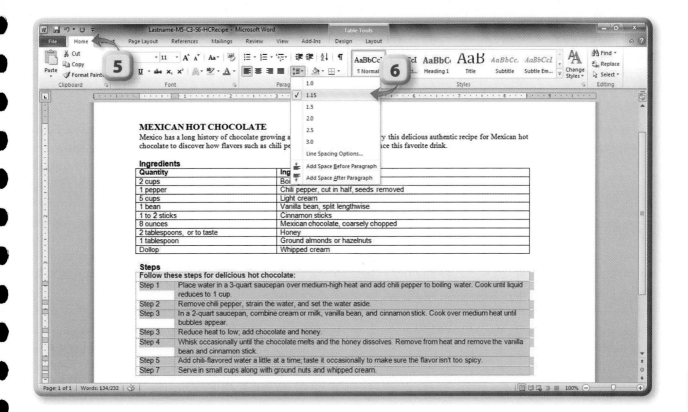

Taking It Further

Previewing the Table Styles Table styles offer a great way to add formatting pizzazz to tables with just a click. The gallery of table styles is found on the Table Tools Design tab. Just click in a table and move your pointing device over the various style options in the gallery, which are simultaneously previewed on your table. When you see one that you like, click on it and the style is applied to your table, instantly!

Word

Word

Chapter 3

Skill 7

Video M5_C3_S07

Insert Shapes

Word includes a feature called Shapes that lets you easily draw a variety of shapes in your documents, from lines to stars and arrows. You can use these shapes to build flow charts or simple illustrations to help you make a point or add visual appeal.

Steps

1 Open the student data file named **M5-C3-S7-HCRecipe.docx**, and if you have not already done so, save the file in your Module 5 working folder on your storage medium.

2 Click the Insert tab.

3 Click the Shapes button in the Illustrations group.

4 Click the *Sun* shape in the *Basic Shapes* section.

5 Click and drag on the page above the recipe title to draw a sun, about the size of the one in the completed Skill 7 document shown on this page.

6 *Another Way*
Right-click an object and choose *Format AutoShape* to choose a fill color from the Format AutoShape dialog box.

▶ *Tip* You can determine a color's name, which is a three-part color description, by hovering your mouse pointer above any color square in the Shape Fill color palette.

6 In the Drawing Tools Format tab, click the Shape Fill button in the Shape Styles group.

7 Click the *Orange, Accent 6, Darker 25%* option from the color palette.

8 Drag the sun object to the top-right corner of the page.

9 Save the file.

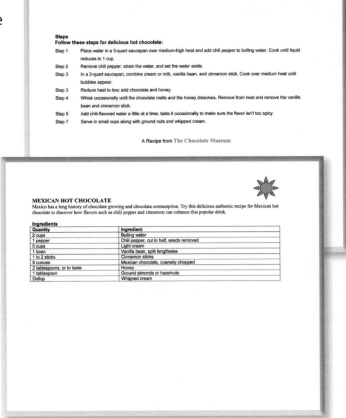

Completed Skill 7

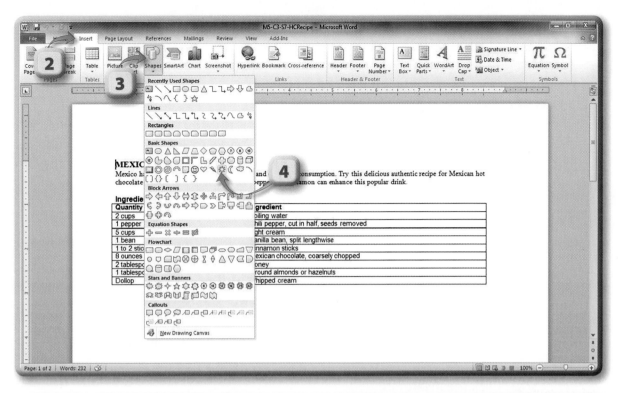

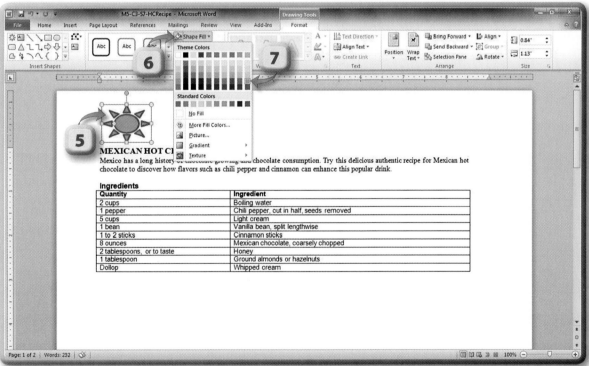

Taking It Further

Creating a Diagram If you want to draw a diagram, you can use a shortcut rather than drawing individual shapes. Use the SmartArt feature in the Illustrations group in the Insert tab to insert certain types of diagrams, such as an organizational chart or pyramid diagram. Once you have drawn a SmartArt object, you can click in individual elements of the diagram and enter text labels.

Word

Skill 8

Video M5_C3_S08

Insert Clip Art Objects

Microsoft provides a rich repository of illustrations, photos, and audio and video clips for use in your documents. These items can help you pack a design punch with very little effort. You use the Clip Art task pane to locate and insert objects installed with the Office program and from Office.com.

Steps

1 If it is not already open, open **M5-C3-S7-HCRecipe.docx**, the file you saved in the previous skill, and save the file as **M5-C3-S8-HCRecipe**.

2 Click in the blank line below the first table in the document.

3 Click the Insert tab.

4 Click the Clip Art button in the Illustrations group.

5 Type saucepan in the *Search for* field in the Clip Art task pane.

6 Make sure there is a check mark in the *Include Office.com content* check box.

7 Click the Go button.

8 Scroll down the previews of clip art images until you find the one shown selected on the opposite page. Click the image to insert it in your document.

▶**Tip** Because online clip art offerings sometimes change, you may be unable to find that exact image. Instead, simply locate and click on a similar image.

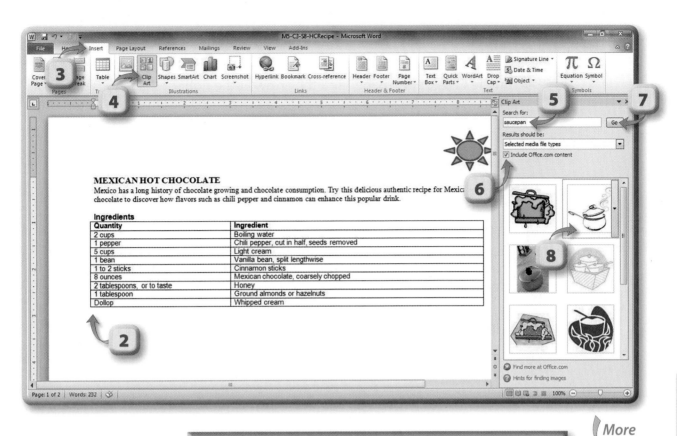

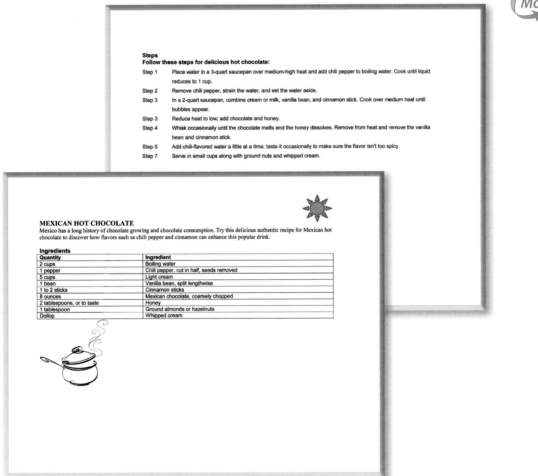

Completed Skill 8, Pages 1 and 2

Word

9 Click in the blank line below the second table in the document.

10 In the Clip Art task pane, click the arrow at the right of the *Results should be* field and click in the check boxes to remove the check marks in all but the *Photographs* media type.

11 Type chocolate in the *Search for* field.

13 *Another Way*
If you have a saved photo stored on your computer you can click the Picture button in the Illustrations group in the Insert tab. The Insert Picture dialog box appears, allowing you to locate the picture. Click the Insert button to insert it.

12 Click Go.

13 Scroll down to find the image shown in the screen capture on the opposite page (or one that is similar) and click the image to insert it into the document.

14 Click the Close button (x) in the Clip Art task pane to close it.

15 Save the file.

Taking It Further

Inserting Audio and Video Clips The Clip Art task pane also contains video and audio clips. Your documents can benefit from these clips if they are published online where viewers can click on links to play audio and video content.

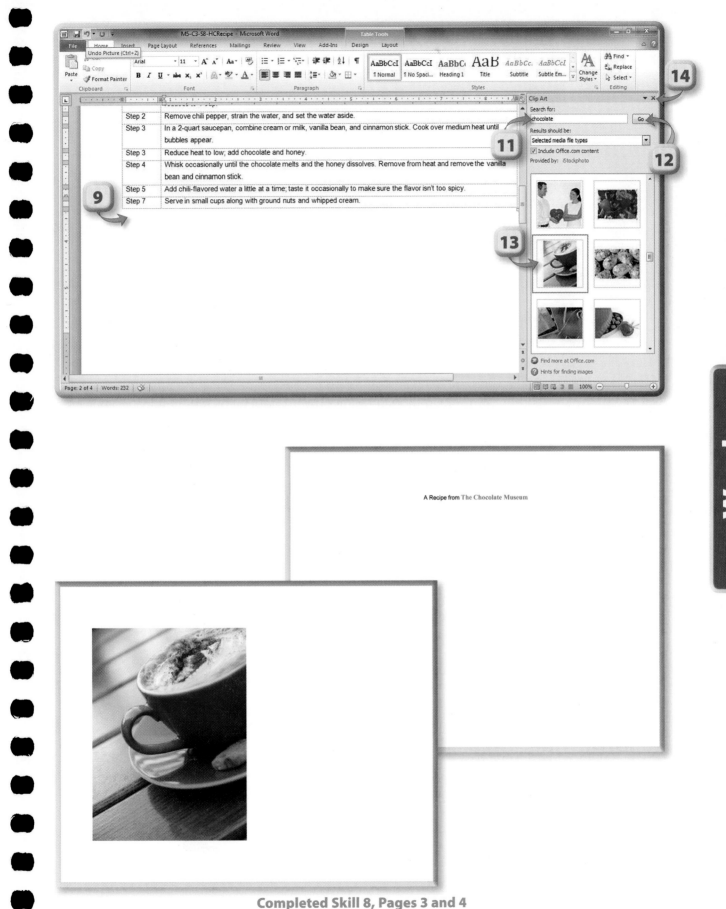

Step 2	Remove chili pepper, strain the water, and set the water aside.
Step 3	In a 2-quart saucepan, combine cream or milk, vanilla bean, and cinnamon stick. Cook over medium heat until bubbles appear.
Step 3	Reduce heat to low; add chocolate and honey.
Step 4	Whisk occasionally until the chocolate melts and the honey dissolves. Remove from heat and remove the vanilla bean and cinnamon stick.
Step 5	Add chili-flavored water a little at a time; taste it occasionally to make sure the flavor isn't too spicy.
Step 7	Serve in small cups along with ground nuts and whipped cream.

A Recipe from The Chocolate Museum

Completed Skill 8, Pages 3 and 4

Word

Word

Skill 9

Video M5_C3_S09

Resize Objects

You can see from the size of the inserted objects in the previous skill that they do not always appear in a size that suits your document. You can easily resize graphic objects by using the handles located in each corner or along the sides of the selected object. If you need to maintain the object's original proportions, resize by dragging a corner handle. If you don't want to retain the object's original proportions, resize the image by dragging a side handle.

Steps

1   If it is not already open, open **M5-C3-S8-HCRecipe.docx**, the file you saved in the previous skill, and save the file as **M5-C3-S9-HCRecipe**.

2 Another Way
Click the object and then the Picture Tools Format tab. Adjust the settings for height and width in the Size group.

2   Select the saucepan illustration on the first page. Click the bottom-right corner of the illustration and drag inward until it is about half its original size.

3   Scroll to the third page of the file and click the photograph you inserted.

4   Click and drag the bottom-right corner handle until the image appears at about the size shown. The instruction steps, the image, and the last line of the document, *A Recipe from The Chocolate Museum*, should now fit on the second page.

5   With the picture selected, click the Center button in the Paragraph group in the Home tab to center the picture on the page.

6   Save the file.

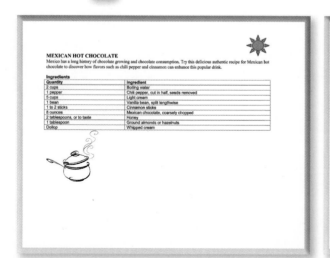

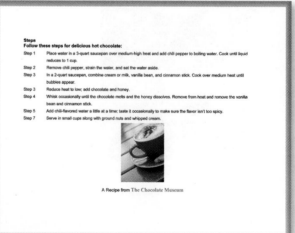

Completed Skill 9

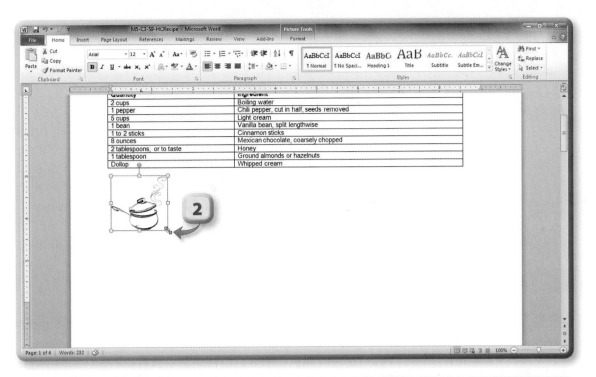

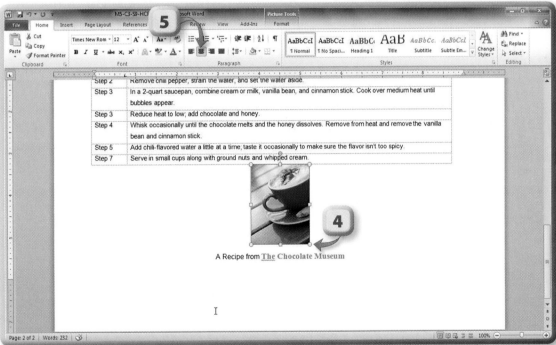

Taking It Further

Wrapping Styles When you place an object in a document, the object is by default set off, or separated, from the text. Thus, you may have text above and below the object, but not next to or behind it. To adjust how the object and text are arranged select the picture, then select the Wrap Text button in the Arrange group in the Picture Tools Format tab. In this drop-down menu you have many arrangement options such as placing the picture behind the text, in front of the text, or in line with the text. Play with these settings to learn about their different effects in your documents.

Word

Skill 10

Video M5_C3_S10

Rotate Objects

Some objects contribute more clearly to your document's message if they are rotated from their original orientation, either to fit with your page design and with other objects or to suggest a relationship between objects. You can also rotate an object to suggest movement. In this recipe, for example, the saucepan is inserted as if it's sitting flat on a stove. However, rotating it to bring the handle upward suggests that you are pouring the contents into cups, which is the result described in the recipe text. It is easy to rotate objects by using the rotation handle, which displays as a green circle above a selected object.

Steps

1. If it is not already open, open **M5-C3-S9-HCRecipe.docx**, the file you saved in the previous skill, and save the file as **Lastname-M5-C3-S10-HCRecipe**, but replace *Lastname* with your last name. Be sure to save the file in your Module 5 working folder on your storage medium.

2. Click the saucepan illustration. A green rotation handle appears at the top of the object.

3 *Another Way*
Select an object and click the Rotate button in the Arrange group in the Picture Tools Format tab.

▶ **Tip** Rotating the object in this way may cause it to jump to the next page. You can fix or prevent this by either deleting any extra spacing before the object or resizing the object to be smaller.

3. Click the rotation handle and drag it to the right to rotate the illustration at an angle.

4. Save and close the file.

Taking It Further

Creating Word Art   You can further enhance Word documents by using WordArt. Click the WordArt button in the Text group of the Home tab and select a WordArt style to insert a text box that reads *Your text here*. Select the placeholder text and type to customize the text. Make further formatting changes to the WordArt text by clicking options in the Drawing Tools Format tab, which is available when the WordArt object is active.

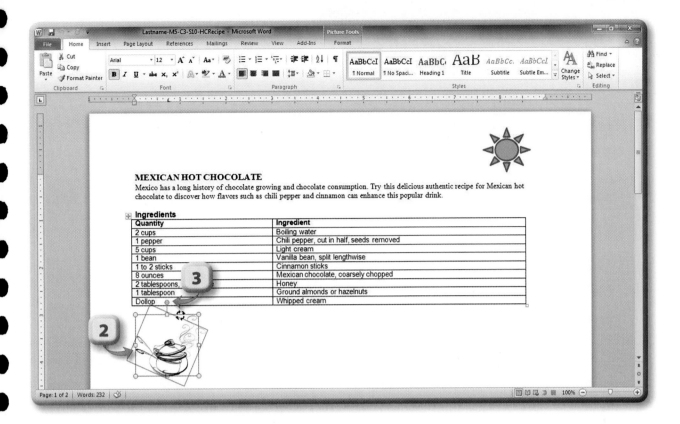

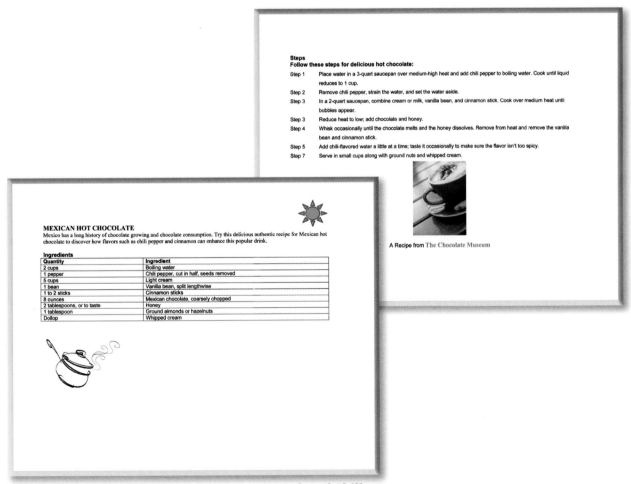

Completed Skill 10

Word

Chapter 3
Assessments

Tasks Summary

Task	Ribbon Tab, Group	Button, Option	Shortcut, Alternative
Insert table	Insert, Tables		
Move to next cell			Tab
Convert selected text to table	Insert, Tables		
Change document orientation	Page Layout, Page Setup		
Insert rows	Table Tools/Layout, Rows & Columns		
Insert columns	Table Tools/Layout, Rows & Columns		
Merge cells	Table Tools, Layout		
Format cell borders	Table Tools/Design, Table Styles		
Insert shapes	Insert, Illustrations		
Change shape fill	Drawing Tools/Format, Shape Styles	*Shape Fill* drop down palette	
Display clip art pane	Insert, Illustrations		
Insert picture	Insert, Illustrations		
Resize objects	Drawing Tools/Format, Size	*Shape Height* and *Shape Width* text boxes	Click and drag on resizing handles
Rotate objects	Drawing Tools/Format, Arrange	*Rotate* drop down list	Rotation handle

Features Review

Select the best answer from the choices given.

1 Tables are made up of
   a. numbered lists.
   b. bulleted lists.
   c. rows and columns.
   d. formulas.

2 The following can indicate where a new column begins when converting text to a table.
   a. tab
   b. comma
   c. hyphen
   d. All of the above

3 Which orientation has the shorter side of the document running across the top and bottom?
   a. landscape
   b. portrait
   c. horizontal
   d. None of the above

4 You can insert a new row above the selected row by
   a. displaying the Table Tools, Layout tab and clicking the Insert Above button.
   b. displaying the Table Tools, Layout tab and clicking the Insert Below button.
   c. pressing Ctrl + Alt + A.
   d. None of the above. You can't add rows to tables after you've created them.

5 The process of combining cells in a table is called
   a. combining.
   b. mail merge.
   c. merging.
   d. None of the above

6 A table can be made to look like columnar text by
   a. removing the cell borders.
   b. changing the font colors.
   c. modifying the line spacing.
   d. changing the paragraph spacing.

7 The Shapes feature in Word allows you to insert various shapes by
   a. choosing them from clip art.
   b. drawing them on your page.
   c. inserting pictures.
   d. All of the above

8 The Clip art task pane allows you to insert
   a. illustrations.
   b. photos.
   c. audio and video.
   d. All of the above

9 To resize a graphic object, you click and drag on
   a. handles.
   b. object borders.
   c. proportional handles.
   d. rotating handles.

10 To keep an object proportional while resizing it, click and drag
   a. a corner handle.
   b. a side handle.
   c. a proportional handle.
   d. the center of the object.

Hands-On Skills Review

Exercise **A** **Create a Party Invitation List**

Skills   Create tables; change page orientation; insert rows; format tables; insert a page break; add headers and footers; enter and edit text; and use cut, copy, and paste

Scenario   You are planning a birthday party for John and inviting your family and a few close friends. You expect to send out seven invitations. Create a table to assist with tracking the responses to your invitations.

The table will have the following columns:

Name—this may be one name (Jamal Sawatdee), a couple (Rose and Jimmy Redcedar), or a family (The Stone family)

Snail Mail Address—for paper invitations

Email Address—for "Hold the Date" notices

Invited Number—how many people are invited? Using the example above, 1 for Jamal Sawatdee, 2 for the Redcedars, and 3 or more for the Stone family

RSVP Date—date when a response is received

Number Attending—how many people are planning to come? This number may differ from the number invited

Steps

1 Open **M5-C3-ExA-PartyGuests.docx**, the student data file, and save the file as **Lastname-M5-C3-ExA-PartyGuests**, but replace *Lastname* with your last name.

2 Change the page orientation to *Landscape*.

3 Change the font of the title *John's Birthday Party* to Calibri 18 pt and center the title.

4 Insert a table that contains six columns and eight rows (one for the header information and seven for the invitee information.) The rows can be added when the table is created or as you enter data.

5 Enter the column header information given at the beginning of this exercise.

6 Enter the following data into the columns.
   Clinton, Hillary and Bill;
   864 Sunny Street,
   Chappaqua, NY 10514;
   theclintons@emcp.net;
   2 invited guests

   Franklin, Benjamin;
   56 Electric Way,
   Philadelphia, PA 19102;
   benji@emcp.net;
   1 invited guest

   Hopper, Grace and Alvin;
   12 Technology Drive,
   Richmond, VA 23219;
   debug@emcp.net;
   2 invited guests

   Maher, Bill;
   27 Hollywood Bowl,
   Los Angeles, CA 90005;
   comicbill@emcp.net;
   1 invited guest

   Nguyen, Lily;
   89 Broadway,
   Montana City, MT 59634;
   lily@emcp.net;
   1 invited guest

   Obama, Barack, Michelle, and family;
   1600 Pennsylvania Ave NW,
   Washington, DC 20500;
   firstlady@emcp.net;
   4 invited guests

   Washington, George;
   1222 Cherry Tree Lane,
   Washington, DC 20374;
   george@emcp.net;
   1 invited guest

7 Size the columns to fit the data. **HINT:** *Use the AutoFit button in the Table Tools Layout tab, then adjust the columns, if needed, to ensure the* Snail Mail Address *column uses only two lines for each invitee and all other columns use only one line per invitee.*

8 Bold all column headings.

9 Center the headings both vertically and horizontally. **HINT:** *Use the appropriate Alignment button in the Table Tools Layout tab.*

10 Center the data in the *Invited Number* column.

11 Insert a page break at the end of the document.

12 Highlight the content of the title and the entire table and copy and paste the selected content below the page break. **HINT:** *You may want to turn on Show/Hide to ensure you are pasting the content just below the page break.*

13 Make the following changes to page 2 of the document. Do not modify page 1.
   a. You had an argument with Benjamin Franklin and decided he should not be invited. Delete that row from the table.
   b. Recently you became friends with the Jones family. You have decided to invite the entire family. Your invitees are arranged in alphabetical order by last name. Insert a row at the correct location and add the data for the Jones family:
      Jones Family; 1999 Pine Road, Dallas, TX 75203; momtheresa@emcp.net; 5 invited guests

14 Adjust the columns in the table on page 2 if needed to ensure that the *Snail Mail Address* column uses only two lines per invitee and all other columns use only one line per invitee.

15 Insert a header with your name on the left and the current date on the right.

16 Insert a footer that displays the page number centered.

17 Save and close the file.

18 Print or submit the document as specified by your instructor.

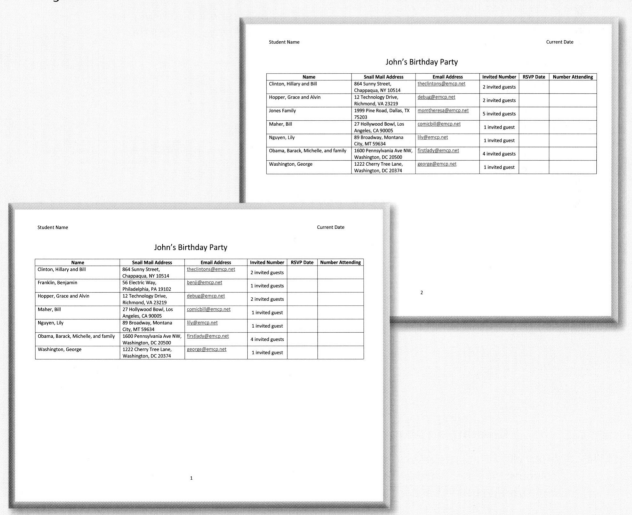

Completed Exercise A

Exercise **B** Creating a New Kind of "Dear John Letter"

Skills Enter and edit text; perform a spell check; add headers and footers; change font and font size; use formatting tools; apply styles; convert text to tables; and insert a row in a table

Scenario Jane has been offered a new position with additional responsibilities, and a large salary increase. She had interviewed for the position several months ago, but just got the offer this morning. And the new position begins tonight! The only bad news with this job is the rather complex work schedule. Format the note she is leaving for John to make it easy for him to follow her new daily work schedule.

Steps

1 Open **M5-C3-ExB-JobNote.docx**, the student data file, and save the file as **Lastname-M5-C3-ExB-JobNote**, but replace *Lastname* with your last name.

2 Add a header to the document that includes your name at the left margin.

3 Check the spelling in the document and fix all errors.

4 Replace the words *Current Date* with the date for today and format the date using the *Intense Emphasis* style.

5 Bold the text *My new work schedule will be:*

6 Convert the schedule (the lines beginning with the days of the week, from Sunday through Saturday) into a table format. The file contains tabs separating the day of the week and the work hours. The table should appear as shown in the image of the completed exercise document.

7 There should be one blank line between the table and the final paragraph that begins *It will take….*

8 Apply the *Intense Emphasis* style to the closing, *Love,* and *Jane.*

9 Change the font of all text in the document to Calibri, 14 pt.

10 Draw a red heart (in the *Basic Shapes* section of the Shapes button drop-down list) that is 1.23" in height and 2.15" in width. Place the heart to the right of the closing. **HINT:** *Select the heart and use the Drawing Tools Format tab to adjust the size. Select Wrap Text, Square, in the Arrange group on the Drawing Tools Format tab. For more information, see the Taking It Further in Skill 9 of this chapter.*

11 Save and close the file.

12 Print or submit the completed document as directed by your instructor.

Completed Exercise B

Exercise **C** Creating an Attractive Newsletter

Skills Insert clip art objects; resize objects; rotate objects; change page orientation; format text in columns; format paragraph and line spacing; align text; use formatting tools; change font and font size; add headers and footers; set margins; use cut, copy, and paste; and enter and edit text

Scenario Open the text for the first page of a newsletter. Reformat the text so it looks similar to the final four-column newsletter shown at the end of the exercise.

Steps

1. Open **M5-C3-ExC-Newsletter.docx**, the student data file, and save the file as **Lastname-M5-C3-ExC-Newsletter**, but replace *Lastname* with your last name.

2. Change to landscape orientation.

3. Set margins to *Narrow* (0.5" on each side).

4. Add a three-part header:
   - Left: Your name
   - Center: Newsletter (Change font to Copperplate Gothic Bold, 22 pt.)
   - Right: Winter Edition, December 28, 2012

   Press enter after typing the date to add a blank line in the header.

5. Highlight the body of the newsletter and create four columns of equal width.

6. Single space the body text and change the after paragraph spacing to 6 pt.

7. Bold the four headings in the newsletter and change them to Small caps. **HINT:** *Use the dialog box launcher in the Font group on the Home tab to open the Font dialog box. Click the* Small caps *check box to insert a check mark and then click* OK.

8. Insert a column page break to force the heading *Discounts and More Discounts* to appear at the top of the second column. **HINT:** *Position the mouse pointer in front of the heading, click the Page Layout tab, click the Breaks button in the Page Setup group, and then click the* Column *option.*

9. Move the *Red Cross Blood Drive* heading and the related text to the second column following the *Discounts and More Discounts* section.

10. Insert a column break to force the heading *On This Day:* to appear at the top of the third column.

11. Place a column page break before *1945* so that the balance of this section moves to the fourth column.

12. Enter the following text at the bottom of the fourth column: "My New Year's resolution is to stop feeling guilty about last year's resolution." Change the font to Calibri, 14 pt and bold and italicize the text.

13. Insert a hard return after the 2008 entry at the end of the *On This Day* section and insert a Happy New Year clip art image like the one shown in the image of the completed exercise document.

14. Insert a text box at the bottom of the third column. **HINT:** *In the Text group on the Insert tab, click the Text Box button and then click Simple Text Box.* Enter the text "If you really put a small value upon yourself, rest assured that the world will not raise your price." (Anonymous). Change the font to Calibri, 16 pt and italicize and center the text. Size the text box height and width to *2.42".* **EXPERIMENT:** *Click the Shape Effects button in the Shape Styles group on the Drawing Tools Format tab. Select* 3-D Rotation *in the drop-down menu and then click the* Off Axis 2 Left *option in the* Parallel *section.*

15. Enter "Blessed are we who can laugh at ourselves for we shall never cease to be amused." (Anonymous) at the bottom of column 1. Change the font to Calibri, 14 pt and bold and italicize the text.

16. Justify the entire document.

17. Add an underline to each year in the section *On This Day*.

18. Save and close the file.

19. Print or submit the completed document as directed by your instructor.

Completed Exercise C

Chapter 4

Finalizing and Sharing Documents

Some documents require the input of several people in addition to their author. People at work might have to give feedback on a report or project schedule prepared by another employee; your family might add names to a holiday card list generated by one member, and so on. Word makes it easy to provide that input through the tools on the Review tab. These tools allow others to make changes that can be tracked and to insert comments with suggestions or questions. You can then review their suggested changes and choose which ones to accept or reject. You can also review their comments and questions and decide whether to act on them. When you're done reviewing comments, simply delete all comments and accept or reject changes and your document is final.

So how do you get your document into the hands of other people so they can begin providing you with feedback, and how do you later distribute the final version to them? Word allows you to share documents in two ways: by sending them as email attachments or by posting them to the Web in PDF format (a format that doesn't require you to have the originating software). The free, easy-to-use Adobe Reader software enables widespread use of PDF documents.

Skills You Learn

1   Turn on Review features
2   Send a document via email
3   Make changes and add comments
4   Accept or reject changes and review comments
5   Create a PDF document
6   Publish to the Web

What You Need
In this chapter, you need the following student data files.

M5-C4-S1-WorkSchedule.docx

M5-C4-S5-WorkScheduleFinal.docx

What You Create
Today you're focusing on coordinating several volunteers who will work in a new exhibit, Chocolate in the Media, during its opening weekend at The Chocolate Museum. The exhibit presents photos and movies that feature chocolate as a major theme, such as the movie *Willy Wonka and the Chocolate Factory*. The volunteers will help make sure all the media are working correctly on this first weekend of the Museum's new exhibit.

You need to create a memo to the volunteers that includes a work schedule. To first make sure that the schedule is acceptable to all the volunteers, you send it to each of them to review, suggest changes and make comments, and return. To get the draft schedule out, you send the memo in an email and then review changes and comments that others have made so you can decide how to revise and finalize the schedule. Once you have a final schedule, you learn how to save it as a PDF file so you can publish it to the Web and share it with anybody, whether or not they have Word on their computer.

Work Schedule Memo

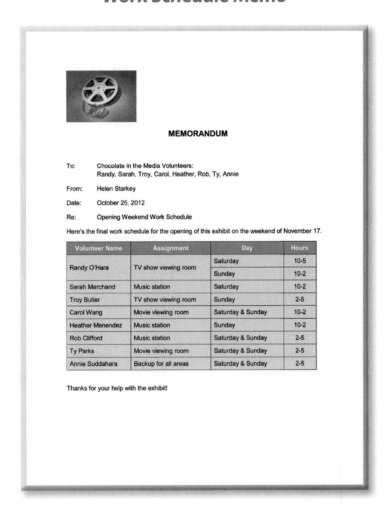

MEMORANDUM

To: Chocolate in the Media Volunteers:
Randy, Sarah, Troy, Carol, Heather, Rob, Ty, Annie

From: Helen Starkey

Date: October 25, 2012

Re: Opening Weekend Work Schedule

Here's the final work schedule for the opening of this exhibit on the weekend of November 17.

Volunteer Name	Assignment	Day	Hours
Randy O'Hara	TV show viewing room	Saturday	10-5
		Sunday	10-2
Sarah Marchand	Music station	Saturday	10-2
Troy Butler	TV show viewing room	Sunday	2-5
Carol Wang	Movie viewing room	Saturday & Sunday	10-2
Heather Menendez	Music station	Sunday	10-2
Rob Clifford	Music station	Saturday & Sunday	2-5
Ty Parks	Movie viewing room	Saturday & Sunday	2-5
Annie Suddahara	Backup for all areas	Saturday & Sunday	2-5

Thanks for your help with the exhibit!

Word

Skill 1

Video M5_C4_S01

Turn on Review Features

When you are almost done with your document, you may want to ask others to review it. To ensure that their changes are highlighted for you, you can turn on Word's Track Changes feature before you send it out. This feature keeps a record of all changes made by reviewers, striking a line through deleted text and applying a font color to added text so you can see what changes each person has suggested. In addition, the tools on the Review tab allow you to display various versions of the document—versions with certain types of changes displayed and also as a final document with no revision marks included.

Steps

1 Open the student data file named **M5-C4-S1-WorkSchedule.docx** and if you not already done so, save the file in your Module 5 working folder on your storage medium.

2 Click the Review tab.

3 Click the Track Changes button in the Tracking group.

3 Shortcut
Track Changes,
Ctrl + Shift + E

▶Tip Selecting *Final* displays the document with all changes accepted. *Original* shows the original document with no changes. The *Final: Show Markup* option shows all changes to formatting, as well as all deletions and additions.

4 Confirm that the *Final: Show Markup* option is active in the *Display for Review* option box in the Tracking group. If not, click the arrow at the right of the option box and select *Final: Show Markup* from the drop-down list.

5 Save the file.

6 Test the Track Changes feature. Select and delete the word *Memorandum*. Note that the deleted text changes color and has a strikethrough mark.

7 Click the Undo button in the Quick Access toolbar to undo the deletion.

7 Shortcut
Undo, Ctrl + Z

8 Close the file without saving.

Taking It Further

Comparing Documents The Compare feature on the Review tab is useful if you want to compare two versions of a document but have not turned on Track Changes. To view the changes made to the original document, click the Compare button. You can then select two documents to compare, review the differences between them, and incorporate or reject those changes. You can also merge multiple documents into a single document using the Compare feature.

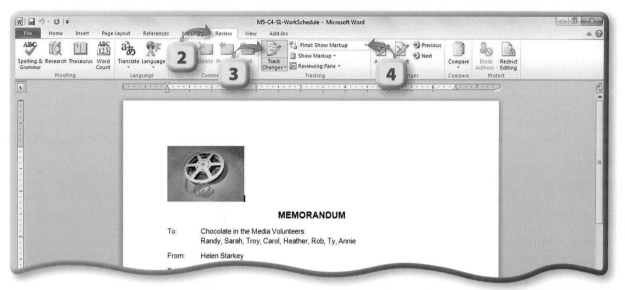

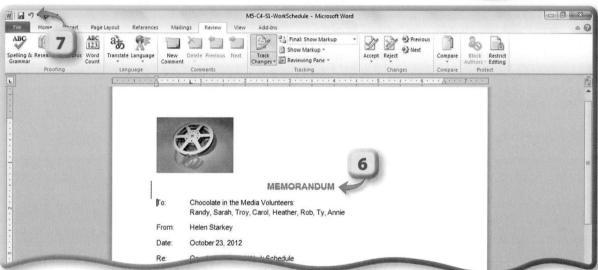

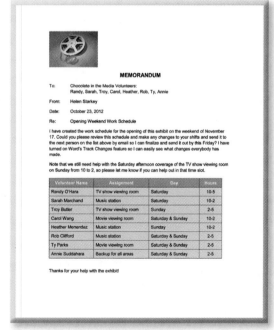

Completed Skill 1

Word

Word

Chapter 4

Skill 2 **Send a Document via Email**

Video M5_C4_S02

To get people's input on your document, you have to get it into their hands. A quick and easy route is to email a copy of the Word file to others and ask them to review and return the marked-up file via email. You can then compile their feedback to create a final document.

In this skill, you use Word's simple *Send Using E-mail* option to send the file as an attachment in Outlook. If you are unable to use Outlook for this purpose, skip this skill and check with your instructor for alternate tasks.

Steps

1 If it is not already open, open **M5-C4-S1-WorkSchedule.docx**, the file you saved in the previous skill.

2 Click the File tab.

3 Click the Save & Send tab.

4 Click the *Send Using E-mail* option in the Save & Send category.

5 Click the *Send as Attachment* option in the Send Using E-mail category. An email form appears.

6 Enter your own email address in the *To* field.

7 Type the following message in the body of the email: Randy, [Press Enter.] Please review this work schedule and let me know if any of the times assigned to you will cause problems. [Press Enter.] Helen

8 Click the Send button.

▶**Tip** You can also send a document as a link contained within your email message. The recipient clicks on the link to go to the document. Using this method requires that you post the document on a publicly accessible online site or company network.

▶**Tip** The file name is automatically placed in the *Subject* field. Take a moment to modify the *Subject* field if the file name is not very descriptive.

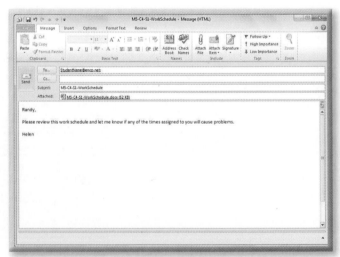

Completed Skill 2

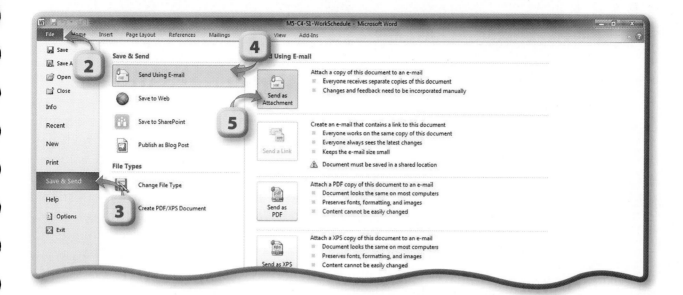

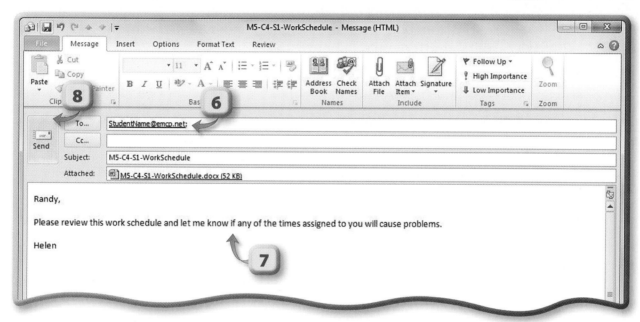

Taking It Further

Controlling the Review of the Files

If you email multiple copies of a document to different people for review, you may find yourself with a "version control" issue when the many responses arrive. You may have to place each copy on your local storage medium, separately review each person's changes, and then be careful to integrate all desired changes into a single, master copy of the document. With a short document, such as our work schedule, where each person is likely to change only the small bits of content that refer to him- or herself, you may not have a major problem. However, with large documents, such as a 20-page report, filtering through several commented documents to decide upon changes and then implementing those decisions from multiple documents into the master can be a version-management headache. In such cases, consider routing a single version of the document from person to person with direction to have the last person in the chain return the document to you. Or post one version on an online document-sharing space, such as Google docs, OfficeLive.com, or KeepandShare.com. Many sites are free and control access to avoid version-management problems.

Word

Word

Video M5_C4_S03

Make Changes and Add Comments

When you work in a document that has Track Changes turned on, any changes you make to it are automatically recorded. You can perform standard editing tasks, such as adding, deleting, or editing text, and those changes are indicated in colored text and by strikethroughs. In addition, the Review tab offers a display setting that shows markups, which places small callout bubbles in the margin containing details about the formatting changes made.

As an alternative to directly changing the document text, you can add comments to suggest changes, explain your edits, or ask the document author questions. In this skill, you make direct changes and add comments to the document. Note that Word tracks the changes from different responders in different colors. Comments are numbered and are indentified with the responders initials.

Steps

1 If it is not already open, open **M5-C4-S1-WorkSchedule.docx**, the file you saved in Skill 1, and save the file as **M5-C4-S3-WorkSchedule**.

2 Confirm that the Track Changes button in the Tracking group in the Review tab is active.

3 Select the last paragraph before the table, the one that begins *Note that we still…*, and then press the Delete key.

4 Select *Randy O'Hara* in the *Volunteer Name* column of the table.

5 Change the font to Comic Sans MS.

6 In the *Randy O'Hara* row, click to the right of the word *Saturday* in the *Day* column.

7 Insert a space and type & Sunday 10-2.

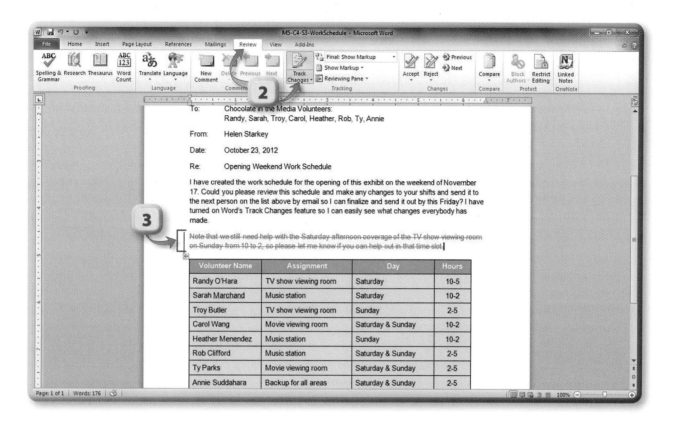

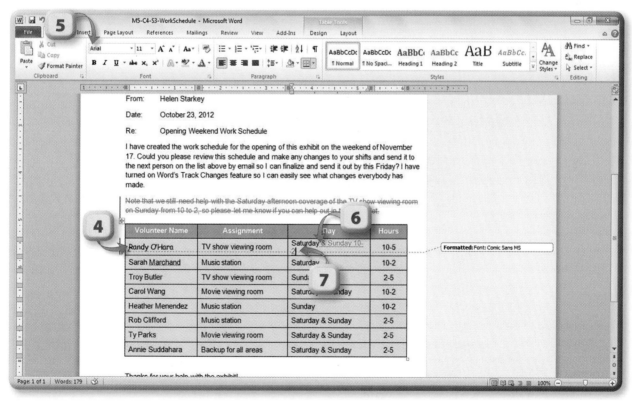

More

8 Click the Review tab.

9 Click the New Comment button in the Comments group on the Review tab.

10 In the comment balloon that appears, type I can cover the Sunday 10-2 slot so I've added that here. Randy

11 Save the file.

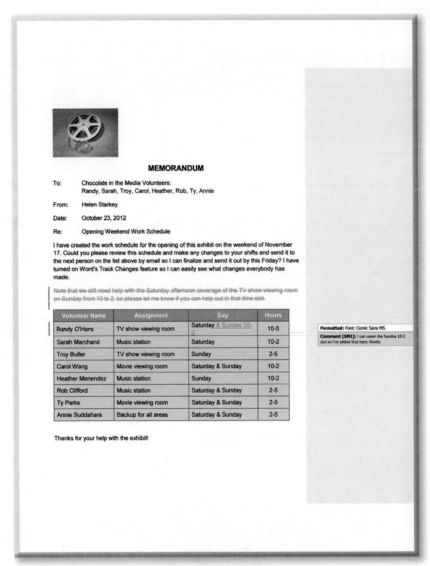

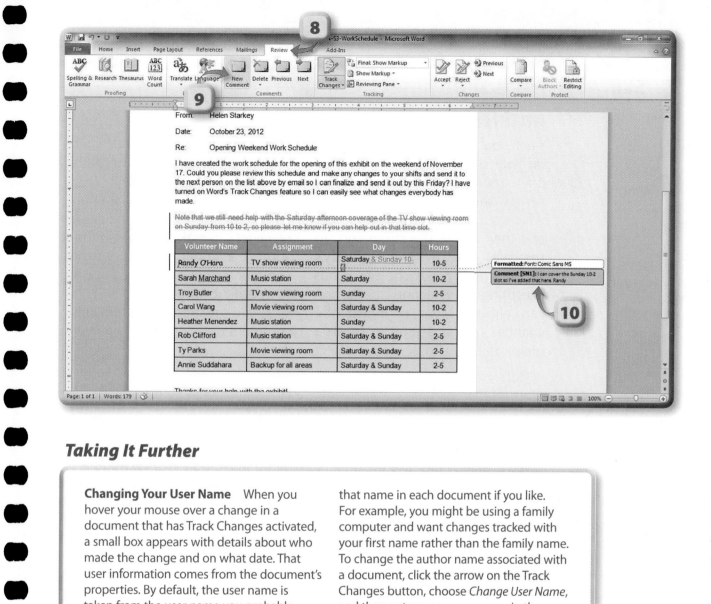

Taking It Further

Changing Your User Name When you hover your mouse over a change in a document that has Track Changes activated, a small box appears with details about who made the change and on what date. That user information comes from the document's properties. By default, the user name is taken from the user name you probably entered for your computer when you first set up Windows. However, you can change that name in each document if you like. For example, you might be using a family computer and want changes tracked with your first name rather than the family name. To change the author name associated with a document, click the arrow on the Track Changes button, choose *Change User Name*, and then enter a new user name in the dialog box that appears.

Word

Skill 4

Video M5_C4_S04

Accept or Reject Changes and Review Comments

After you have gathered feedback on your document, you must take a few more steps to finalize it. You review the feedback and decide which suggestions to incorporate and then delete the comments. In this skill, you review everybody's changes and make choices about accepting or rejecting them. You can either accept or reject the changes one at a time or make a global decision to accept or reject *all* document changes at once. After you have acted on the suggested changes within the text body, you may have some comments remaining in the margin, because a reviewer can make changes without adding a comment and provide comments that are not connected to specific changes. Thus, as a last step, you must delete all remaining comments.

Steps

1 If it is not already open, open **M5-C4-S3-WorkSchedule.docx**, the file you saved in Skill 3, and save the file as **Lastname-M5-C4-S4-WorkSchedule**, replacing *Lastname* with your name. Be sure to save the file in your Module 5 working folder on your storage medium.

2 If it is not already active, click the Review tab.

3 Click the Reviewing Pane button in the Tracking group. This opens the Reviewing pane.

4 Click *Deleted* in the Reviewing pane.

5 *Another Way*
You can also right-click on the change in the Reviewing pane and choose *Accept Deletion* from the menu that appears.

5 Click the Accept button in the Changes group. This accepts the change in the file and removes *Deleted* from the Reviewing pane.

6 Click *Formatted* in the Reviewing pane.

7 Click the Reject button in the Changes group to reject the change.

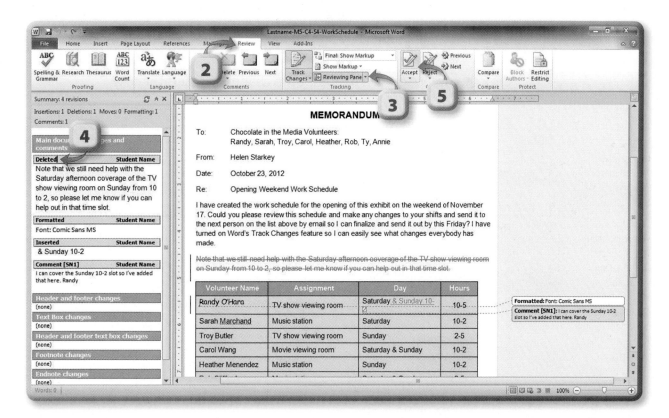

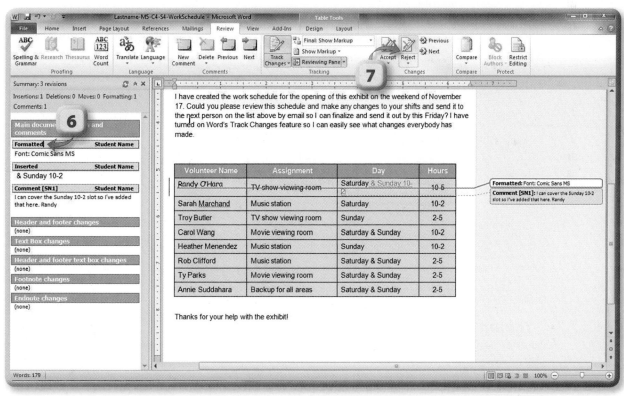

8 Click *Inserted* in the Reviewing pane.

9 Click the Accept button to accept the change to insert the text.

10 Click *Comment* in the Reviewing pane.

11 Click the Delete button in the Comments group.

12 Click the Reviewing pane button in the Tracking group to close the Reviewing pane.

13 Save and close the file.

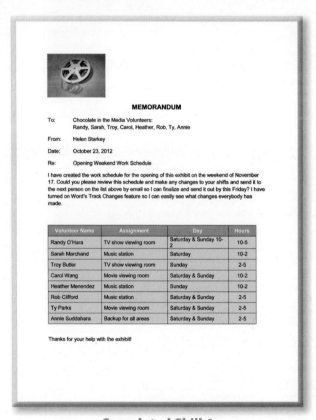

Completed Skill 4

Taking It Further

Protecting Files If you find that some of the changes made by your document reviewers are not useful, the Protect group in the Review tab provides two tools for limiting what reviewers can do when looking over your future documents: Restrict Editing and Block Authors. For example, in cases where you do not want people to directly change your text, only make comments on it so you can decide what to do, you would click the Restrict Editing button and choose *Comments* from the four Editing restrictions offered. The Block Authors button allows you to prevent certain people (whether a family member or a co-worker) from making any changes at all.

Word

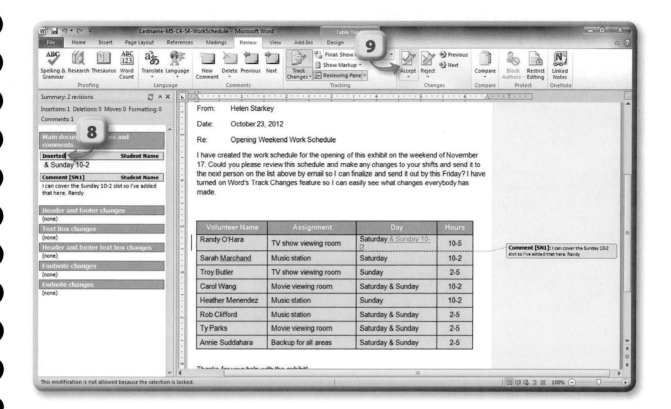

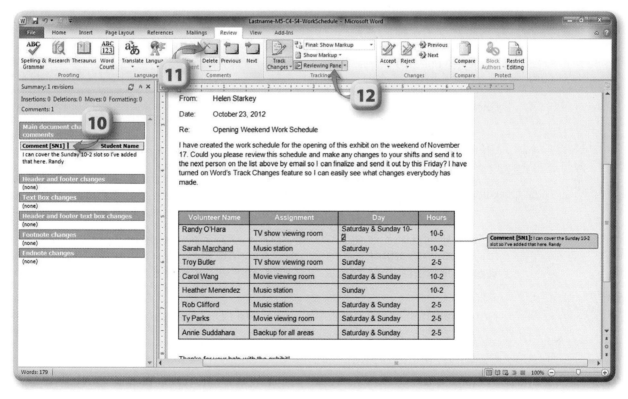

Word

Skill 5

Video ▶ M5_C4_S05

Create a PDF Document

You are ready to share a copy of your final work schedule with others. It may be useful to save the file as a PDF file. PDF is a file format created by Adobe and is the standard for document sharing. Using the free Adobe Reader program, anybody can view a PDF file, whether or not they have Word installed on their computer. A PDF version of your document is in some ways like a picture, because what people see is an accurate image of what you created at the moment of capture. Thus, the file, or image, won't be compromised by being opened in different versions of Word, some of which may not support the fonts and features you used to create your document. In addition, PDF files are smaller in size than Word files, so they may be easier to send as attachments.

Steps

1 Open the student data file **M5-C4-S5-WorkScheduleFinal.docx**.

2 Click the File tab.

3 Click the Save & Send tab.

4 Click the *Create PDF/XPS Document* option in the File Types category.

5 Click *Create PDF/XPS*.

5 Another Way
Another way to save to the PDF format is to simply use the Save As button on the File tab. In the Save As dialog box that opens, select *PDF (*.pdf)* in the *Save as type* option box and then click the Save button.

6 In the Publish as PDF or XPS dialog box, locate your Module 5 working folder on your storage medium and save the file as **Lastname-M5-C4-S5-WorkScheduleFinal**, replacing *Lastname* with your last name.

7 Note that the *Save as type* option is set to *PDF (*.pdf)*.

▶**Tip** To get the free Adobe Reader software used to view PDF files, go to www.adobe.com.

8 Click the Publish button. You can now share the file as an email attachment or using any of the methods described in the next skill.

9 Close the PDF file.

10 Close **M5-C4-S5-WorkScheduleFinal.docx**.

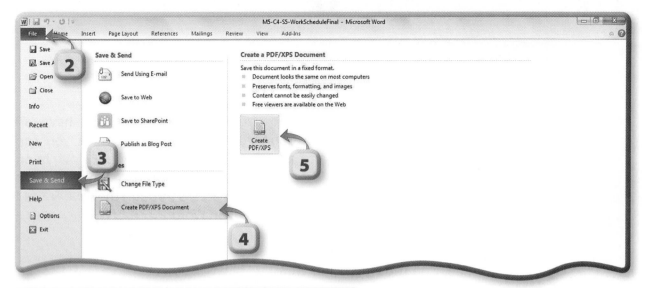

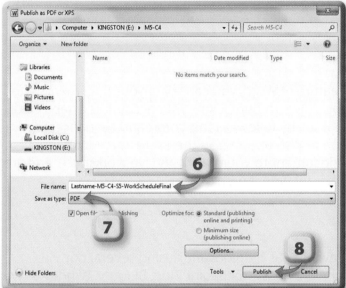

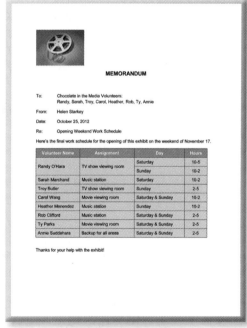

Completed Skill 5

Taking It Further

Viewing PDFs Adobe Acrobat offers both the free Adobe Reader software and a more robust software program for purchase. The Reader version allows you to read a document in PDF format, while the full Adobe Acrobat program allows you to edit PDF files, add comments to them, and more. For many people, the Reader version is sufficient, but if you do a lot of collaboration on files with people who don't have Office 2010 (for example, with people working with another word processor or on a Mac computer), you might want to consider purchasing the full Adobe Acrobat program.

Word

Skill 6

Video   M5_C4_S06

Publish to the Web

Sharing documents on the Web is a great way to get information out to others, educate them, and receive feedback. Today it is easy to post your files, and all Microsoft Office products make posting files easy.

There are three ways to post a document on the Web using Word.

Each requires that you have an online location to which you can save the document. Below is an overview of the three methods you can access through the Save & Send tab in Word.

Steps

Save to the Web

Using the Save to Web feature of Word, you can share your documents after you have set up a Windows Live account. Once your account is established, you upload the document file by following this command sequence: File tab, Save & Send tab, *Save to Web* option. You then sign into your Windows Live account, save your document to your Windows Live workspace, and are ready to share a link to the document with others.

Publish as a Blog Post

Word 2010 is set up to save files as blog postings using several popular blogging sites, including WordPress, SharePoint Blog, Blogger, Windows Live spaces, Community Server, and TypePad, as of this textbook's publication. Because the Web is ever-changing, additional blog sites may now be available. After you establish an account on one of these (or similar) services, you simply use the File tab, Save & Send tab, *Publish as Blog Post* option sequence to post your document to a blogging site.

Save to SharePoint

SharePoint is a software tool typically used by companies to set up online file sharing sites. If your company or organization has set up a SharePoint site, you can use the File tab, Save & Send tab, *Save to SharePoint* option sequence to save a file to the site.

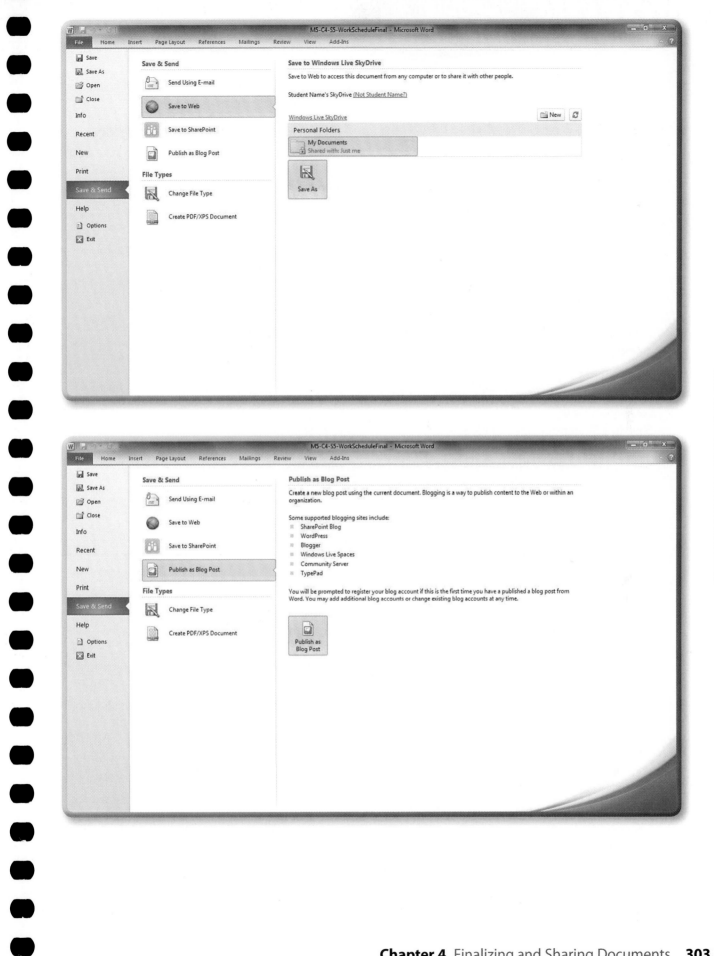

Word

Chapter 4 Assessments

Tasks Summary

Task	Ribbon Tab, Group	Button, Option	Shortcut, Alternative
Turn on Track Changes	Review, Tracking		Ctrl + Shift + E
Send a document via email	File, Save & Send	*Send Using Email* option	
Add comments	Review, Comments		
Display Reviewing pane	Review, Tracking		
Accept individual or all changes	Review, Changes		
Reject individual or all changes	Review, Changes		
Publish to the Web	File, Save & Send	*Save to Web* option	
Publish to a blog	File, Save & Send	*Publish as Blog Post* option	
Save to a Sharepoint Site	File, Save & Send	*Save to Sharepoint* option	
Save in PDF format	File, Save & Send	*Create PDF/XPS Document* option	

Features Review

Select the best answer from the choices given.

1 To turn on Review features in Word, click this button on the Review tab.
   a. Show Markup
   b. Reviewing Pane
   c. Track Changes
   d. Review

2 Word's *Send as E-mail* option is set up to send an attachment via email using
   a. Internet Explorer.
   b. Yahoo! Mail.
   c. Outlook.
   d. All of the above

3 If several people add comments to a Word document, Word indicates this by
   a. using different colors and commenter initials.
   b. saving the comments in separate files.
   c. using different colors and shading.
   d. None of the above

4 When you review comments in a document you can accept them, or
   a. highlight them.
   b. turn off Track Changes.
   c. reject them.
   d. refuse them.

5 The three methods you can access for sharing documents on the Web using Microsoft Word can be accessed through this tab.
   a. Print
   b. Home
   c. Save & Send
   d. Share

6 The company that provides software for reading PDF files is
   a. Microsoft.
   b. Adobe.
   c. Apple.
   d. Acrobat.

7 Saving a document to the Web uses
   a. Yahoo! Workspaces.
   b. Windows Live workspaces.
   c. Outlook.
   d. Google Docs.

8 The Restrict Editing button on the Review tab allows you to
   a. turn off the Track Changes feature.
   b. prevent people from adding pictures to documents.
   c. limit changes that reviewers can make.
   d. None of the above

9 You can choose to reject a single change or:
   a. all changes.
   b. changes by a certain reviewer.
   c. no changes.
   d. changes made past a certain date.

10 Which of the following is *not* a benefit of a PDF file created from a Word document?
   a. The program needed to view the PDF file is free.
   b. The PDF file is smaller in size than the original Word document.
   c. The PDF file is compromised by being opened and viewed by different computers.
   d. The PDF file can be opened in Word.

Hands-On Skills Review

Exercise **A** **Have the Courage to Edit Shakespeare**

Skills   Turn on Review features, make changes and add comments, add headers and footers, and enter and edit text

Scenario   Shakespeare's *Macbeth* is one of the great plays of all time. In this exercise you help correct mistakes in the script. Use Track Changes on the Review tab to correct the original document. Add the comments where indicated to help the average reader better understand an older version of the English language

Steps

1 Open the student data file named **M5-C4-ExA-Tragedy.docx** and save the file as **Lastname-M5-C4-ExA-Tragedy**, replacing *Lastname* with your last name.

2 Turn on Track Changes on the Review tab.

3 Change the font for the first two lines of text in the document, *The Tragedy of Marybeth* and *By Shakespeare* to Calibri, 14 pt.

4 Insert a header that contains your name on the left side and the current date on the right side.

5 Insert a footer that displays a centered page number.

6 While tracking changes, implement the following corrections to the file.
   a. In the first line, change *Marybeth* to *Macbeth*.
   b. In the second Gentlewoman line (begins *it is an…*), change *15 minutes* to *a quarter of an hour*.
   c. In the third Doctor line (begins *Hark!*), change *memory* to *remembrance*.
   d. In the second Lady Macbeth line (begins *Out, damn'd spot!…*), change *do it* to *do't*.
   e. In the same Lady Macbeth line, change *Fe Fie Fo Fum* to *Fie*.
   f. In the same Lady Macbeth line, insert *none can call our pow'r to* after *knows it, when*.
   g. In the third Lady Macbeth line (begins *The thane of Fife…*), delete *I guess I need more soap!*
   h. In the third Gentlewoman line (begins *She has spoke…*), select the word *spoke* and insert a comment that reads *Incorrect tense based on our current standards of English.*
   i. In the eighth Doctor line (begins *This disease is…*), select the word *practise* and insert a comment that reads *Old English spelling of practice.*

7 Save the document.

8 Print or submit the completed document as directed by your instructor.

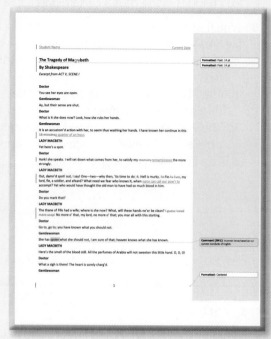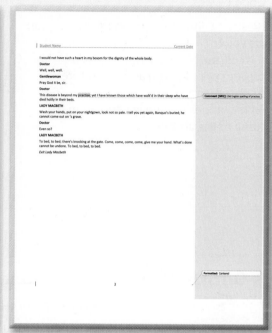

Completed Exercise A

Exercise **B** Revise a Poorly Edited Nursery Rhyme

Skills Insert headers and footers, change font and font size, turn on Review features, accept or reject changes, and review comments.

Scenario "Four and Twenty Blackbirds" is a nursery rhyme that is a favorite among children. They recite the words and wait for someone to pretend to "snip off" their nose.

This version of "Four and Twenty Blackbirds" has been reviewed and changes are provided that are meant to correct the errors. Unfortunately, the editor's suggestions are not all correct. Locate the real version of the nursery rhyme on the Web or use the version shown in Completed Exercise B. Compare the words in this version with the correct words. Accept or reject the editor's modifications accordingly. After acting upon the comments as needed, delete them. Do not make any other changes to the text.

Steps

1 Open the student data file named **M5-C4-ExB-NRhyme.docx** and save the file as **Lastname-M5-C4-ExB-NRhyme**, but replace *Lastname* with your last name.

2 Turn off the Track Changes feature.

3 Change the title *Four and Twenty Blackbirds* to Calibri, 14 pt, Bold.

4 Add a header with your name on the left side and the current date on the right side.

5 Accept or reject the changes in the student data file so that the final file matches the displayed file.
  a. Accept the change of *six cents* to *sixpence*.
  b. Reject the change of *sing* to *fly*.
  c. Read the comment related to the *king* to *queen* change and delete it.
  d. Reject the change of *king* to *queen*.
  e. Reject the change of *parlour* to *parlor*.
  f. Accept the change of *steak* to *bread*.
  g. Accept the change of *wash* to *clothes*.
  h. Read and delete the comment related to the last line.

6 Save the document.

7 Print or submit the completed document as directed by your instructor.

Completed Exercise B

Exercise **C** Finalize a Letter and Email It as a PDF Attachment

Skills   Enter and edit text, use formatting tools, align text, change font and font size, create a PDF document, send a document via email

Scenario   Edit the letter to include the current date. Place your signature at the bottom. Then send the document to your instructor as an attachment to an email or as otherwise instructed for submission.

Steps

1 Open the student data file named **M5-C4-ExC-Email.docx** and save the file as **Lastname-M5-C4-ExC-Email**, but replace *Lastname* with your last name.

2 Replace *March 12, 2012* with the current date.

3 Format the date so it is right-aligned and italicized.

4 Replace *Glenda Romero* in the closing with your name.

5 Change the font style of your name to Script MT Bold and the size to 14 pt.

6 Save the document.

7 Save the document as a PDF file. Use the same name as your Word document: Lastname-M5-C4-ExC-Email. This file will have a .pdf extension rather than a .docx extension.

8 Share the PDF file with your instructor by sending it as an email attachment. ***NOTE:*** *Your instructor may provide different instructions for submission.*

Completed Exercise C

Module 5 Projects

Project 1

Skills Enter and edit text, add headers and footers, apply styles, format text in columns, create bulleted or numbered list, change font and font size, use formatting tools, insert clip art and shape objects, and resize objects

Scenario You would like to send your favorite recipe to the local cooks' competition. You decide that the recipe might be better received if the page looks inviting. Add formatting to your recipe so that the judges can't help but give it serious consideration.

Steps

1 Open the student data file named **EOM-P1-TunaSalad.docx** and save the file on your student media as **Lastname-EOM-P1-TunaSalad**, replacing *Lastname* with your last name.

2 Insert a header as follows: your name on the left, the current date on the right.

3 Apply Title style to *World's Best Tuna Salad*.

4 Change the layout for the ingredients list (not the subheading, Ingredients) to 2-column, single-spaced, with solid bullets. **HINT:** *Before selecting the text, turn on Show/Hide to be sure you do not include the paragraph mark before or after the ingredient list.*

5 The directions list should be displayed in an outline-level numbered list. Indent the content to create a sub-list as shown in the completed project image.

6 Add a section after the *Directions* section. Press the Enter key to insert a blank line before you enter the following content:

   To Serve
   Line a platter with lettuce.
   Place tuna in center.
   Place tomato slices around the tuna.
   Serve with rolls, bread, or crackers.

7 Format the list under *To Serve* as a bulleted list using check marks.

8 Search in clip art for an image of someone mixing ingredients by entering *mix* in the *Search for* field of the Clip Art pane. Select the graphic of the female chef that is shown in the completed project image. If you cannot find the exact clip art item shown, select another, appropriate graphic.

9 Size the image to a height of 2" and a width of 2".

10 Change the Wrap Text setting to *Square* and move the image to the right of the *Directions* section. Using the Ruler, position the upper-left corner of the clip art chef horizontally at 4.5" and vertically at 3.5".

11 Insert a 16-Point Star shape (*Stars and Banners* section on the Shapes button drop-down list) under the clip art image. Adjust the size to a height and width of 1". Change the Shape Fill to *Orange* (in the *Standard Colors* section) and the Shape Outline to *Black, Text 1* (second option in the first row of the *Theme Colors* section). Position the shape horizontally centered under the clip art image and bottom-aligned with the last line of text.

12 Change the section subheadings (*Ingredients*, *Directions*, and *To Serve*) to Calibri, bold, small caps, 14 pt.

13 Save the document.

14 Print or submit the file as instructed.

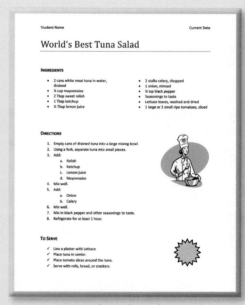

Completed Project 1

Project 2

Skills   Enter and edit text; use cut, copy, and paste; add headers and footers; change font and font size; use formatting tools; apply styles; align text; format paragraph and line spacing; create tables; and format tables

Scenario   You are the sales manager for a company that sells video games. You have good news to report to the president of the company. Create and format a memo that advises the president that sales are increasing and more inventory is needed.

Steps

1 Open the student data file named **EOM-P2-SalesReportLtr.docx** and save the file as **Lastname-EOM-P2-SalesReportLtr**, replacing *Lastname* with your last name.

2 Insert a Blank (Three columns) header with: your name on the left, *Project 2* in the center, and the current date on the right.

3 Insert a footer that includes the file's name flush left. ***EXTENSION ACTIVITY:*** *Rather than type the file name, double click the footer to make it active and then click the Quick Parts button in Insert group on the Header & Footer Tools Design tab. From the drop-down list, click* Field, *select* FileName *from the options in the* Field names *list box, and then click OK.*

4 Select the first line, *Best Games, Inc.* and apply the Heading 1 style.

5 Modify the three lines containing the Best Games contact information (address and phone number) as follows:
   a. Place the street address on the same line as the city, state and zip code, separated by a comma and a single space. You now have two lines with company contact information, with the second line containing just the phone number.
   b. Apply the Subtitle style the two lines of contact information
   c. Single-space these lines and set the paragraph format, *Spacing After* to *0*.

6 Center the company name and contact information.

7 Create the memo heading as follows:
   a. Cut and paste the lines so that they appear in the correct order: *To:, From:, Date:, Subject:*.
   b. Set a left-tab at 1".
   c. Bold each of the key words: *To:, From:, Date:, Subject:*.

   d. Insert the current date in the *Date:* section of the memo heading.
   e. Insert your name in the *From:* section of the memo heading.

8 Remove the extra blank line between the two paragraphs of the memo body.

9 Format *Summary of Top Sales* with the following:
   a. Cambria, bold, 14 pt
   b. Center alignment
   c. Font color: Blue, Accent 1

10 Insert a table on the line below *Summary of Top Sales* as follows:
   a. Insert a table that has 2 columns and 11 rows.
   b. Column headings:
      Left column: *Name,* bold, left-aligned
      Right column: *Release Year,* bold, centered
   c. Table Data
      i. Enter the game names and years:
         The Sims, 2000
         Big Shock, 2007
         Grand Theft Auto III, 2001
         Halo, 2001
         Resident Evil 4, 2005
         God of War, 2005
         Guitar Hero, 2005
         The Elder Scrolls IV: Oblivion, 2006
         Shadow of the Colossus, 2005
         World of Warcraft, 2004
      ii. Left-align the data in the *Name* column.
      iii. Center the data in the *Release Year* column.
   d. Size the columns to fit the contents using the AutoFit button in the Table Tools Layout tab.
   e. Center the table using the Center button on the Home tab.

11 Save the document.

12 Print or submit the file as instructed.

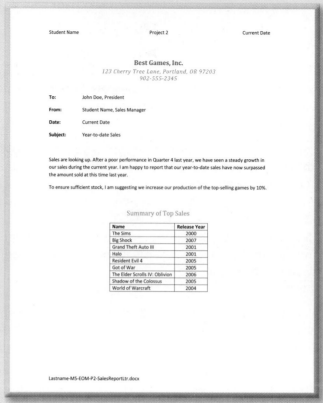

Completed Project 2

Project 3

Skills   Enter and edit text, perform a spell check, add headers and footers, insert clip art objects, resize objects, send a document via email, turn on Review features, make changes and comments, track changes, add comments, accept or reject changes, and review comments

Scenario   Prepare a flyer about a classmate that introduces the classmate to the members of the class. To ensure the introductory content is correct, the subject of the flyer will have the opportunity to review, edit, and comment on the content of the flyer, which will be returned to you for final editing prior to submitting and sharing with your classmates.

Use at least five formatting features of Word to complete the project such as change the font and font size, use formatting tools, apply styles, align text, format paragraph spacing, create a bulleted or numbered list, format text in columns, create tables, change document orientation, insert shapes

Part A: It is time to learn more about your classmates. Your instructor will pair you (Student 1) with another student (Student 2). Interview one another and prepare an introductory flyer that can be shared with your instructor and classmates. Student 1 interviews and creates an informative flyer about Student 2. Likewise, Student 2 interviews and creates an informative flyer about Student 1.

The flyer must include, text and a clip art image. Use at least five different formatting techniques and fill one page completely, without going over onto a second page. The flyer is to be informative and attractive. It should be ready for printing and posting of the printed copy or for electronic posting.

Some questions you may want to ask your partner to help develop content for the flyer include:
- Where were you born?
- Where do you live now?
- What are your favorite activities?
- Where do you work and what do you do at work?
- Why are you taking this class?
- What are your career goals?

When you complete the flyer, save it as **Lastname-EOM-P3A-Flyer**, replacing *Lastname* with your last name. Send it as an email attachment to your partner and to your instructor.

Part B: Your partner has sent you the introductory flyer that he or she prepared. You have the opportunity to review and edit your own introduction before it is shared with the class. All changes you make in the document are to be tracked using Track Changes. You can also add comments that you believe will be helpful to your partner as your partner makes the final modifications to the flyer. The reviewed document must contain at least two modifications to text, at least one modification to format, and at least three comments.

Save your reviewed document with the same name that your partner used to create the file in Part A, but change P3A to P3B, so the file name will be **Lastname-EOM-P3B-Flyer**.

When your review is complete, send it back to your partner and your instructor as an email attachment.

Part C: The edited introductory flyer has been reviewed by its subject, Student 2, and returned to you, its creator, Student 1. Read the review comments and look over the changes suggested. Make decisions about the suggested changes by using the Accept or Reject buttons on the Review tab. After you complete the review, check the document for any spelling errors. Ensure that the formatting makes the appropriate sections stand out and that the content fits on one page only. Save the completed document using the same name that your partner used when saving the edited file in Part B, but change P3B to P3C, so the file name will be **Lastname-EOM-P3C-Flyer**.

Share the file with your classmates via email, by posting to a course website, or as instructed.

MODULE 6

Microsoft® Excel 2010

Before beginning the module skills, copy the Module6–Excel folder from the Student Resources CD to your storage medium. The copied folder will become the working folder for this module.

Guidelines to Planning and

When you create a workbook file in Excel, you should take the time to plan how you will organize the data on the worksheets. To do so, consider the source data you will use and the results you want to produce. Your plan will guide you as you enter the data on the worksheets.

For example, say you are creating a workbook of annual sales data. You have a list of four quarters of sales data and you also have a long list of products sold. You might see two arrangement options that make sense. One option is to place the data for each quarter on a separate worksheet. The other option is to

create a different worksheet for each product and display each product's sales by quarter. In this example, the choice you make may depend on whether you want to emphasize the total sales of all your products for each quarter (the first option), or focus on the total sales by product (the second option).

Once you have entered and organized data on the worksheets, you can make any necessary calculations. For example, for each column of data you can create a formula that sums the values to give you a quarterly total. And for each data row, you can create a formula that sums the results for the product in each row.

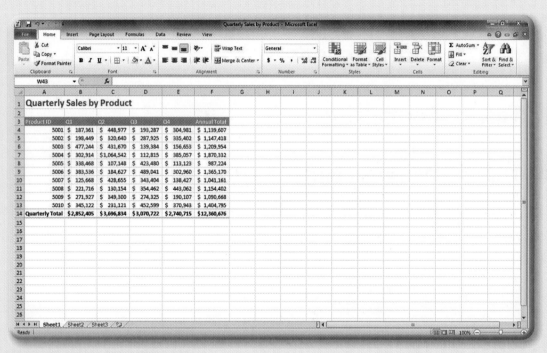

The data should guide your decisions about
the best way to lay out a workbook.

Creating a Worksheet in Excel

If your worksheet includes an area where the user enters values to be calculated by Excel, position those input cells in a prominent location—usually near the top of the worksheet. Apply formatting that prompts the user for entries.

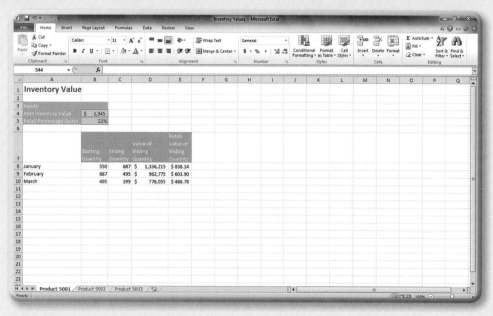

If a worksheet includes an input area, position those cells near the top of the worksheet or on a separate sheet.

In Excel, you can use clip art, shapes, and other graphics to enhance the appearance of your worksheets. Excel can also convey your worksheet data graphically in a chart. Charted data helps you to spot trends and abnormalities, which can help you make better business decisions. For example, if sales for a particular product lag far behind other products' sales, a chart can help you quickly identify the trend.

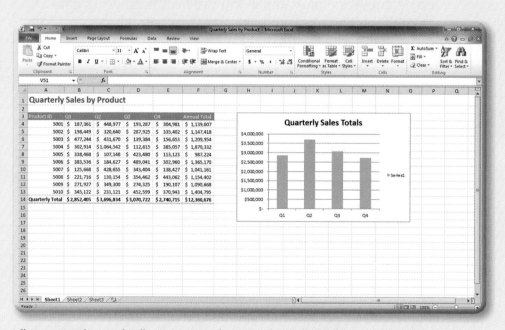

Charts convey data graphically, so you can easily spot trends and abnormalities.

When planning a worksheet, keep in mind your audience's expectations as well as industry standards. For example, in the financial industry, professionals follow accepted conventions and, in some cases, legal requirements when they design reports such as profit & loss statements, balance sheets, and loan payment tables.

Chapter 1

Creating an Excel Workbook

Excel is a spreadsheet program. Each Excel file is called a workbook. A workbook is divided into worksheets and each worksheet is divided into cells so that you can organize data in a table-like format and perform calculations on that data. In this chapter, you learn how to enter data and navigate in Excel.

Excel arranges data in cells. To move from one piece of data to another you move from cell to cell. Because you will be dealing with different types of data—numbers, text, and dates—you will learn how to enter each type of data to ensure that your calculations work. There are tools and tricks to help you out, such as automatically filling entries, quickly adding rows or columns, or checking the spelling of cell contents.

Rather than setting up each Excel spreadsheet as a single and lengthy page of data, you learn how to organize data on multiple pages, called worksheets, to help you group like kinds of data on their own sheets and make navigating your data easier. If you have sales data for different years, for example, you can track each year's data on a separate sheet in a single workbook. You can add sheets to a file, or workbook, and name and rename sheets as needed so that the data is easy to find and work with. Finally, you will learn how to set up and print a worksheet.

Skills You Learn

1 Understand worksheet and workbook structure
2 Use cell references
3 Enter text, values, and dates
4 Use the Auto Fill feature
5 Use Spell Check
6 Insert and delete columns and rows
7 Create a new worksheet
8 Name and rename worksheets
9 Explore options for printing

Files You Need
In this chapter, you do not need any student data files.

What You Create

You are continuing your work for The Chocolate Museum, a nonprofit organization that provides educational exhibits and information on the history of chocolate and its role in world cultures. The Museum must plan and budget for its exhibits and gift shop, and this planning requires tracking dates and calculating financial information. In this chapter, you produce an Excel workbook containing schedule and cost information for a new exhibit on chocolate in world cultures.

Schedule and Cost Information for the
New Chocolate Museum Exhibit

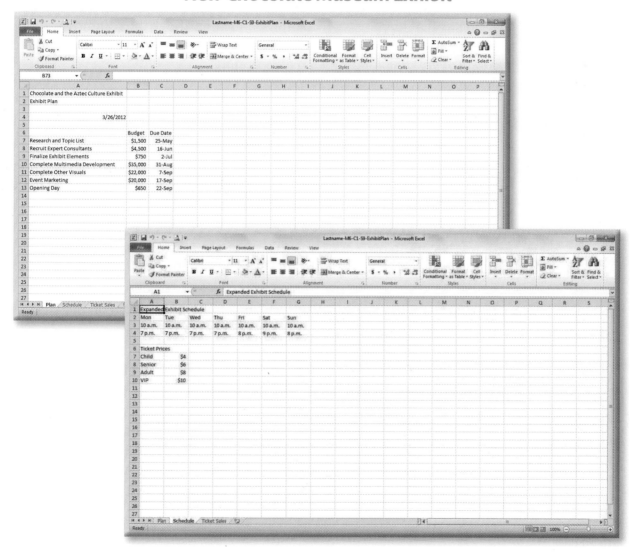

Excel

Skill 1

Understand Worksheet and Workbook Structure

Video ▶ M6_C1_S01

When you start Excel, a blank file opens, called a *workbook*. Each newly created workbook holds *three worksheets* of information. Worksheets are like pages in a notebook. To keep your materials well organized, you might enter different catagories of information onto separate worksheets.

The single, capital letters across the top of the worksheet are *column headings* that identify each column. The numbers down the left side are *row headings* that identify each row. The intersection of each row and column is a *cell*, into which you can type an entry. An entry can be a data value like a name, number, or date, or a formula that instructs Excel to perform a calculation. As you work, a heavy black border appears around the *active cell*. You can only make entries in the active cell. You also can select a *range* of cells.

After you have made cell entries, you can use the Formula bar that is located above the column headings to view and work with the entered data.

Steps

1 Open the Excel application on your computer and a new, blank workbook is displayed. Save the file as **M6-C1-S1-ExhibitPlan** in your Module 6 working folder on your storage medium.

2 Move the mouse pointer over the Formula bar. A ScreenTip that reads *Formula Bar* appears to identify that screen element.

3 Move your mouse pointer over the Sheet2 tab at the bottom of the screen but do not click on the tab.

▶ **Tip** The active cell is highlighted with a black border and the cell name appears in the Name box next to the Formula bar.

4 Click in the cell that is in row 3 of column B, known as cell B3, to make it the active cell. Notice that the Name box displays *B3*.

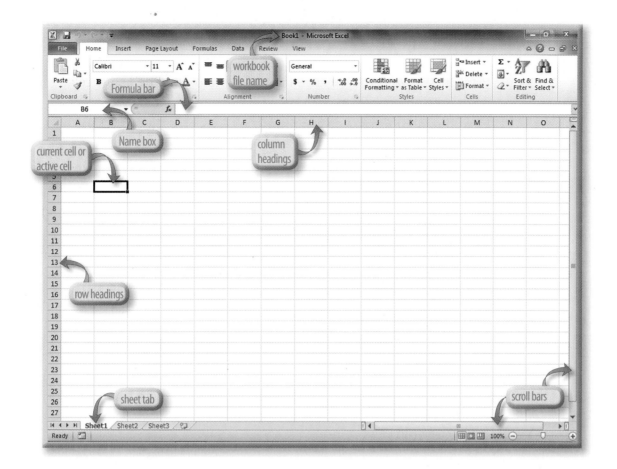

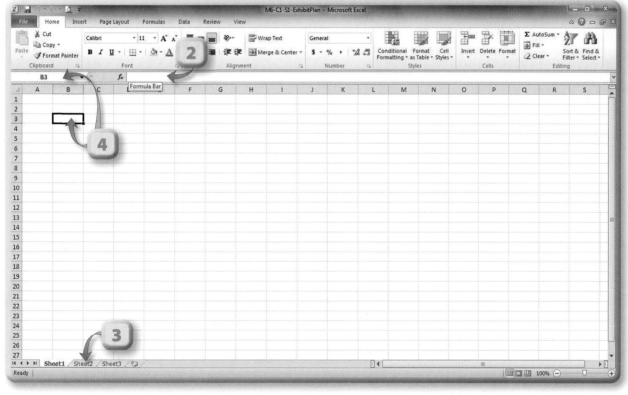

5 *Shortcut*
Make A1 the Active cell
Ctrl + Home

5 Click in cell A1 to make it the active cell.

6 Press the Down Arrow key five times. Cell A6 is now the active cell.

▶**Tip** Click any cell
that is visible on-screen
to select and make it the
active cell.

7 Press the Right Arrow key five times. Cell F6 is now the active cell.

8 Click below the scroll box on the vertical scroll bar to move down the page.

▶**Tip** Notice that
scrolling does not change
the selected cell.

9 Click above the scroll box on the vertical scroll bar to move up the page.

10 *Another Way*
To select a range, press
the left mouse button
and drag over the range
or click the upper left cell
and Shift + click the lower
right cell.

10 Press and hold down the Shift key, and press the Down Arrow three times and the Right Arrow two times to select a range.

11 Click in cell A1 to make it the active cell.

12 Save the file.

Taking It Further

Jumping to a Cell   You can jump directly to a cell by clicking the Find & Select button in the Editing group in the Home tab and then clicking *Go To* or by pressing F5. Either method opens the Go To dialog box, where you can enter a cell address in the *Reference* text box and then click OK to jump to that cell.

Excel

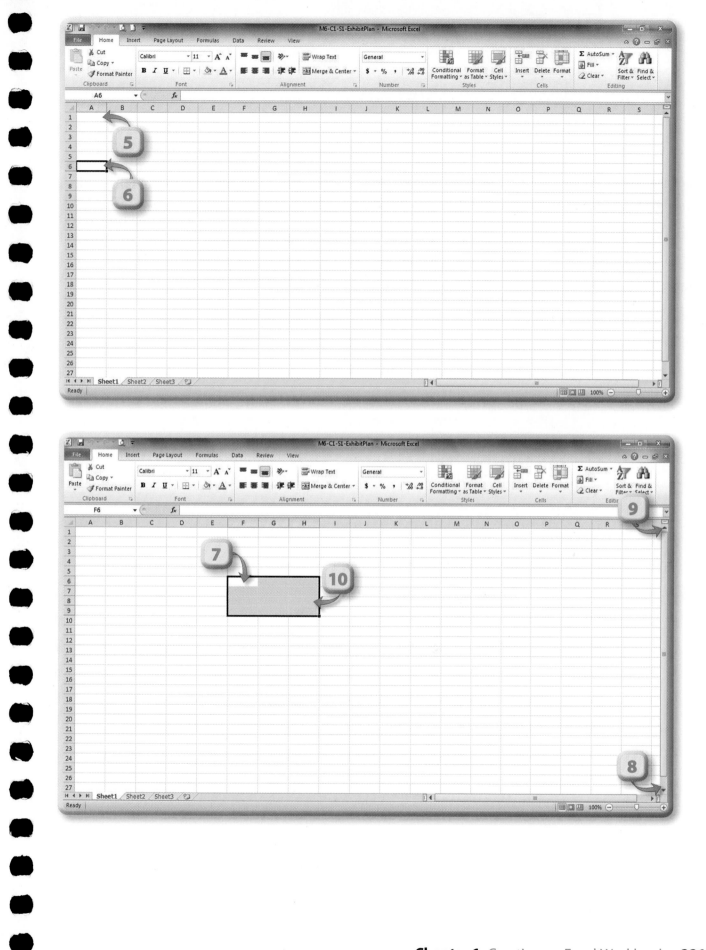

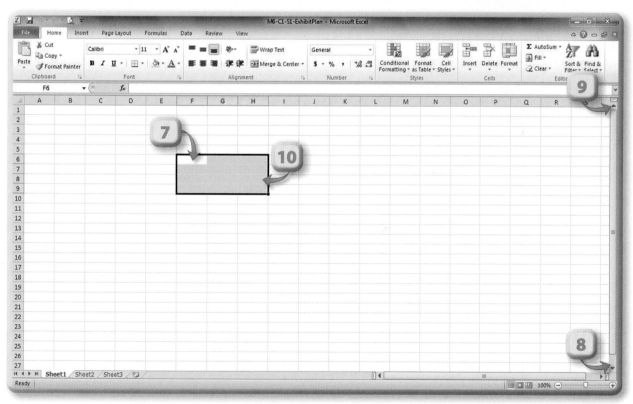

Excel

Skill 2

Use Cell References

You can identify each cell by its column letter and row number, called its *cell address*, *cell reference*, or *cell name*. For example, the cell in the first column of the first row is cell A1. The cell in the eighth column of tenth row the is cell H10.

A range of cells has an address, too. Identify a range by the addresses of its upper left and lower right cells, separating the addresses with a colon. For example, D5:J15 is the range that spans from cell D5 at the upper left to J15 at the lower right. A range can span a single row, such as when you select several column titles, perhaps A3:F3. A range also can fall within a single column, as in C3:C10.

You can use the Name box to the left of the Formula bar to go to a cell or range. Understanding cell and range addresses is also important when building formulas, a skill you will learn about in Module 6 Chapter 2.

Steps

1 If it is not already open, open **M6-C1-S1-ExhibitPlan.xlsx**, the file you saved in the previous skill, and save the file as **M6-C1-S2-ExhibitPlan**.

2 Click the Sheet3 sheet tab.

3 Type your name in cell A1 and press Enter.

4 Click in cell F6 to make it the active cell.

5 Type =A1. Press Ctrl + Enter. This action finishes entering the formula and it does not change the active cell.

6 Look in the Formula bar and verify that it displays the entry you made in cell F6, while the cell itself displays the result.

7 Click in the Name box to the left of the Formula bar, which currently displays *F6*.

▶**Tip** The entire content of a data cell will be displayed in the worksheet even if it is too long to fit in the cell, as long as the next cell is empty.

▶**Tip** When you are selecting cells, the mouse pointer is a thick white cross.

▶**Tip** All Excel formulas begin with an equals sign.

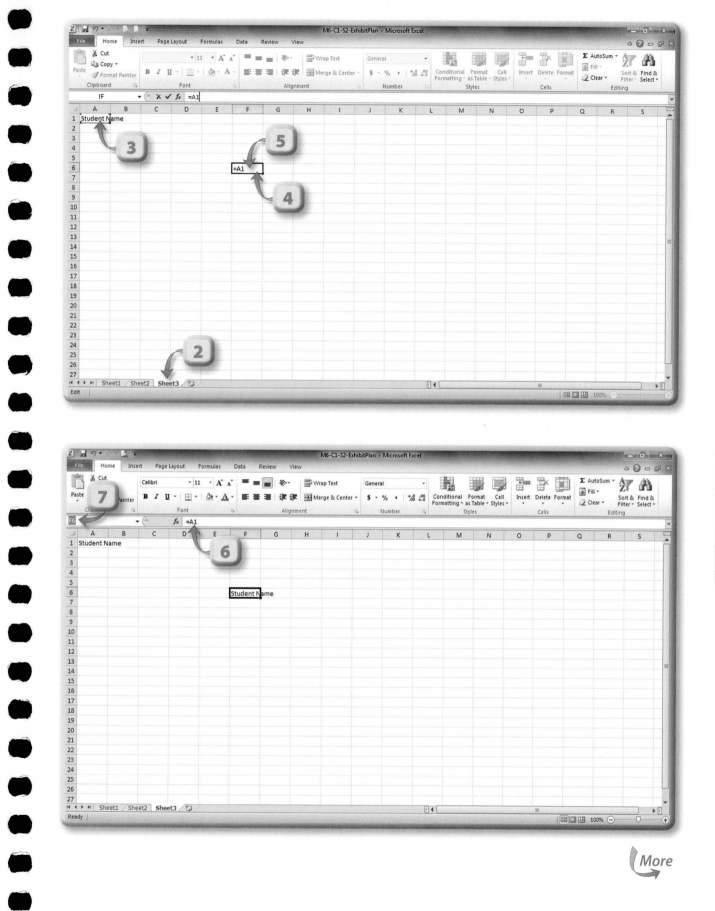

More

8 Type G7 and press Enter. Cell G7 is selected.

9 Click in the Name box to the left of the Formula bar, which currently displays *G7*.

10 Type E5:G7 and press Enter. The range of cells E5 through G7 is selected.

11 In the Font group in the Home tab, click the arrow to the right of the Fill Color button. Select *Yellow* from the *Standard Colors* section of the drop-down gallery.

12 Click in cell A1 to make it the active cell.

13 Save the file.

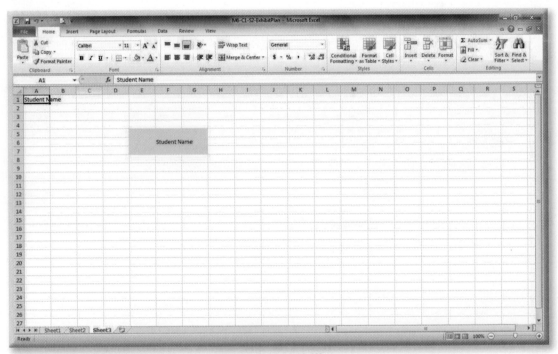

Completed Skill 2

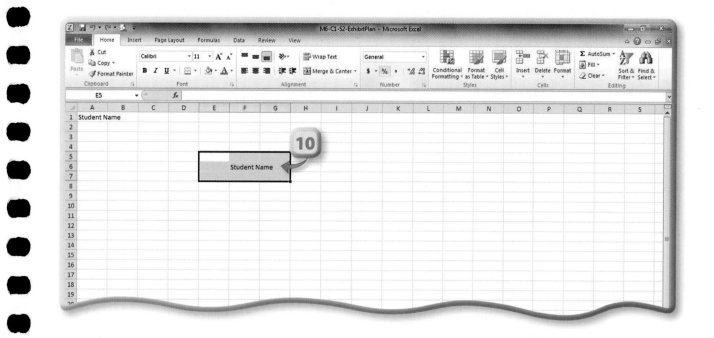

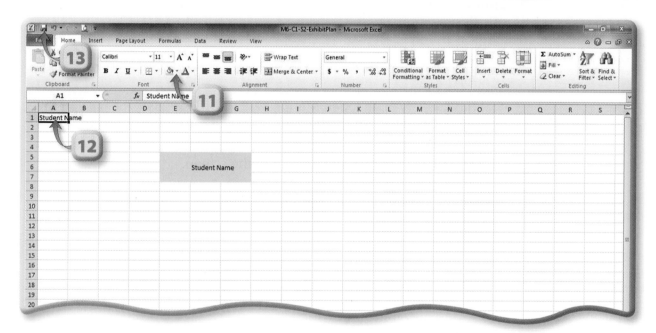

Taking It Further

Exploring a Worksheet   A worksheet contains a fixed number of columns and rows, the exact count depending upon the amount of RAM available to your computer. Cells within a worksheet can contain numbers and dates in various formats, text, and formulas using arithmetic operators or functions. Check to see how many rows and columns are in your Excel worksheet by opening a blank workbook and then pressing End + Right Arrow.

Excel

Chapter 1

Skill 3

Enter Text, Values, and Dates

Video M6_C1_S03

Each cell on an Excel worksheet can hold a single entry. That entry can be text, a date, a value, or a formula that calculates a result.

A text entry can contain any combination of letters, numbers, or symbols that you can type on your keyboard. *Qtr 1*, *Sales*, or *Region#* are examples of text entries. By default, Excel aligns text entries at the left side of the cell. This is true even of phone numbers because they usually are entered with hyphens or other characters and are treated as text. Numbers are numeric entries, including whole numbers (15) and decimal values(2.5). You can enter numbers that have certain characteristics, such as currency symbols or a number of decimal places. Number entries are right-aligned. Last, you enter dates in typical date formats, with hyphens (4-1-13) or slashes (4/1/13). By default, you enter 4/1/13 or 4-1-13, Excel displays 4/1/13 in the cell.

Steps

1 If it is not already open, open **M6-C1-S2-ExhibitPlan.xlsx**, the file you saved in the previous skill, and save the file as **M6-C1-S3-ExhibitPlan**.

2 Click the Sheet1 tab near the bottom of the screen.

3 Make cell A1 the active cell, type Chocolate and the Aztec Culture Exhibit, and then press Enter.

4 *Another Way*
Press the Down Arrow to finish a cell entry and move one cell down, the Right or Left Arrow to move one column to the right or left, or the Up Arrow to move up one row.

4 Type Exhibit Plan in cell A2 and then press Enter twice.

5 Type 3-26-12 in cell A4 and then press Enter.

▶ *Tip* Excel automatically reformats the date.

6 Make cell B6 the active cell, type Due Date, and then press Enter.

7 Make cell A7 the active cell and type the following entries exactly as shown into the range A7:A12. You will correct mistakes later!

Research [**Press Enter**]
Topic List [**Press Enter**]
Recriut Espert Consultatnts [**Press Enter**]
Finalize Exhibit Elements [**Press Enter**]
Complete Multimedia Development [**Press Enter**]
Complete Other Visuals [**Press Enter**]
Opening Day [**Press Enter**]

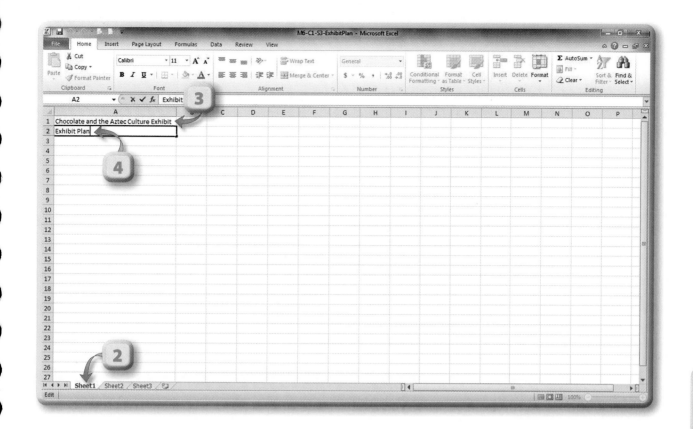

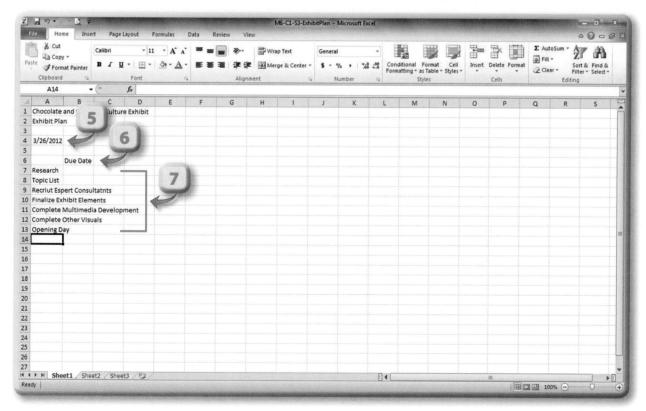

Excel

8 Make cell B7 the active cell and type the following entries into the range B7:B12.
5/18 [Press Enter]
5/25 [Press Enter]
6/16 [Press Enter]
7/2 [Press Enter]
8/31 [Press Enter]
9/7 [Press Enter]
9/22 [Press Enter]

▶**Tip** The entire content of a data cell will be displayed in the worksheet even if it is too long to fit in the cell, as long as the next cell is empty.

▶**Tip** Click a cell and look at the Formula bar to confirm that the entire entry is retained in a cell even when it is only partially displayed.

9 Notice that the date entries in column B appear to have cut off the entries in column A. The length of your entries requires that you resize the column to accommodate them. Move the mouse pointer up over the divider line to the right of the column A header and double-click to resize the column.

10 Save the file.

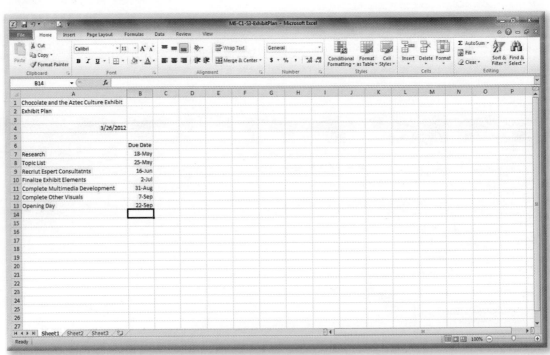

Completed Skill 3

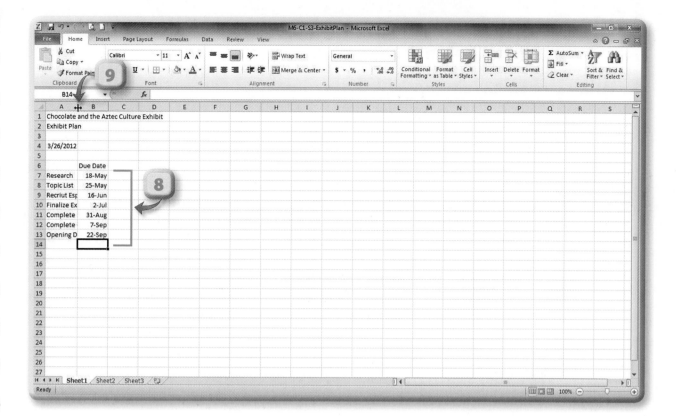

Taking It Further

Removing ### from a Cell In certain situations, such as if you enter a very large number in a cell, Excel displays a series of pound signs (######) rather than the entry itself. These signs indicate that the numeric entry is too wide to display in the cell. This feature is designed to keep readers of the data from being mislead seeing only a portion of a number. Increase the column width for the cell contents to display properly.

Excel

Skill 4

Use the Auto Fill Feature

Video ▶ M6_C1_S04

Excel 2010 can help you save time when entering data into a worksheet. Excel includes a feature called *Auto Fill* that enables you to either copy an entry across a row or down a column or create a *series* of entries across a row or down a column. In addition, some types of entries that you might fill often are built into Excel. For example, if you enter *Jan* in a cell and use the Auto Fill feature, Excel enters the following months: *Feb*, *Mar*, *Apr*, and so on. Excel can fill the days of the week or common business entries such as Qtr 1, Qtr 2, and so on.

If you Auto Fill a number or other entry that Excel does not recognize as part of a series, Excel simply copies the entry to the area you are filling. You can create your own series by entering the first two or three values in the series and then using Auto Fill from there.

Steps

1. If it is not already open, open **M6-C1-S3-ExhibitPlan.xlsx**, the file you saved in the previous skill, and save the file as **M6-C1-S4-ExhibitPlan**.

2. Make cell D16 the active cell, type Expanded Exhibit Schedule, and then press Enter.

3. Type Mon and press Ctrl + Enter.

> **Tip** Ctrl + Enter finishes an entry without moving your cursor to another cell.

4. Move the mouse pointer over the black fill handle in the lower right corner of the cell D17. When the mouse pointer changes to a black crosshair, press and hold down the left mouse button and then drag to the right until you see a ScreenTip that reads *Sun*.

> **Tip** Click the Auto Fill Options button that appears after a fill if you want to change the fill, for example, if you want to fill formatting only or if you want to copy cells rather than fill a series.

5. Release the mouse button to finish filling the days of the week.

6. Make cell D18 the active cell, type 10 a.m., and then press Enter.

7. Drag over the range D18:J18 to select it. (Do not use the Auto Fill feature.)

8. In the Editing group in the Home tab, click the Fill button.

9. Click the *Right* option. Excel copies the *10 a.m.* entry across the selected range.

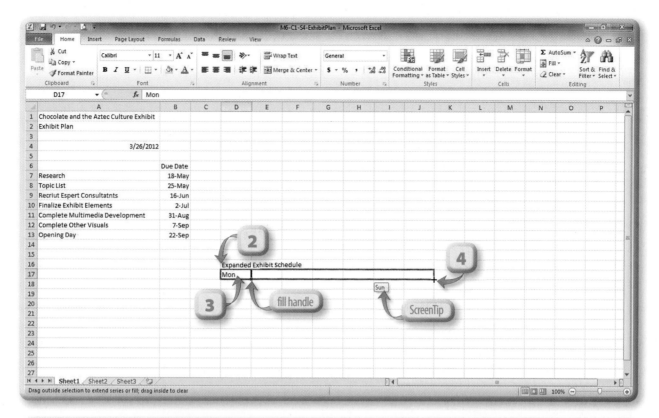

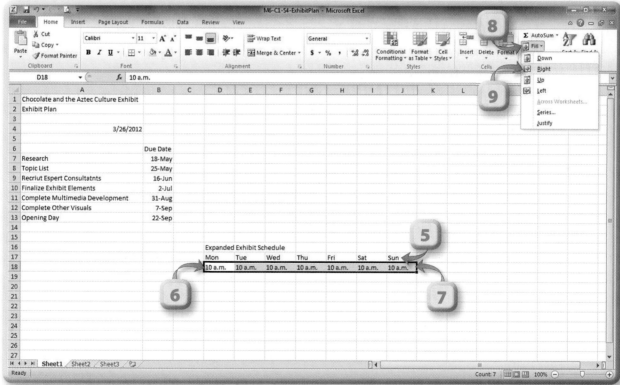

10 Make cell D19 the active cell, type 7 p.m., and then press Enter.

11 Drag over the range D19:G19 to select it.

12 In the Editing group of the Home tab, click the Fill button and then click *Right*. Excel copies the *7 p.m.* entry across the selected range.

13 Make cell G19 the active cell. Drag the fill handle to the right until cell I19 is selected.

> **▶Tip** Excel will not fill all times correctly. It fills *12 p.m.* and then *13 p.m.*, an obvious error.

14 Release the mouse button to finish filling the series from *7 p.m.* to *9 p.m.*

15 Make cell J19 the active cell, type 8 p.m., and then press Enter.

16 Make cell D21 the active cell and then type the following entries:

Ticket Prices [Press Enter]
Child [Press Enter]
Senior [Press Enter]
Adult [Press Enter]
VIP [Press Enter]

> **▶Tip** You can type some number formats, such as dollar signs and percent signs, when entering the numbers, or you can apply number formatting later.

17 Make cell E22 the active cell and then type the following entries:

$4 [Press Enter]
$6 [Press Enter]

18 Drag over the range E22:E23 to select it.

19 Drag the fill handle down until cell E25 is selected.

20 Release the mouse button to finish filling the custom series from *$4* to *$10*.

21 Save the file.

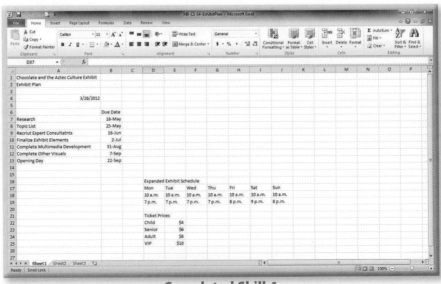

Completed Skill 4

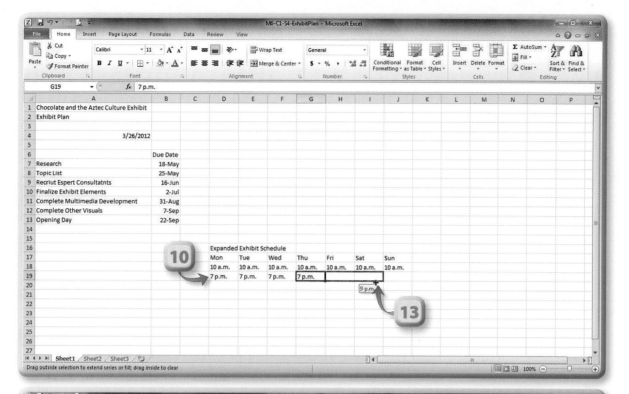

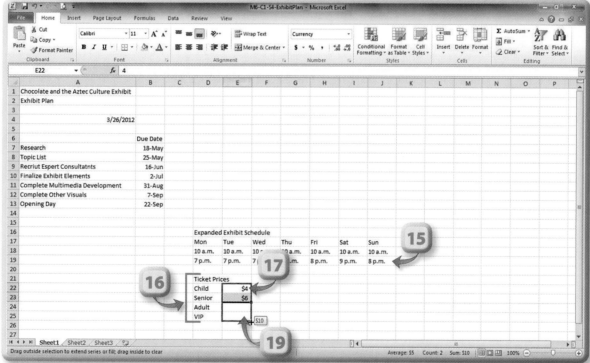

Excel

Skill 5

Use Spell Check

Video ▶ M6_C1_S05

Spreadsheets can be filled with typos, requiring an eagle-eyed person to read closely to find and eliminate those pesky misspellings. Excel includes a feature to help you ensure that your worksheets are free of typos. The Spell Check feature in Excel works just as it does in Word. There is one important caution, however. A spell check only reviews text entries. It cannot ensure that you have entered numbers and dates correctly, so double-check your data thoroughly!

Steps

1. If it is not already open, open **M6-C1-S4-ExhibitPlan.xlsx**, the file you saved in the previous skill, and save the file as **M6-C1-S5-ExhibitPlan**.

2. Make cell A1 the active cell.

▶**Tip** The spelling check starts from the current cell, and Excel displays a message when it needs to return to the beginning of the sheet.

3. Click the Review tab.

4. Click the Spelling button in the Proofing group.

4 Shortcut
Spell Check
F7

5. The Spelling dialog box displays the first typing mistake, *Recriut*. The correct spelling is already selected in the *Suggestions* list box, so click the Change button to replace the misspelled word.

6. Click the Change button twice more to correct the next two misspellings, *Espert* and *Consultatnts*.

7. In the message box that informs you that the spelling check is complete, click OK.

8. Save the file.

Taking It Further

Using Auto Correct   Excel can correct some misspellings for you as you type. Each of us has our own unique tendency to mistype certain words. For example, say your last name is *Smith*, but you often mistype it as *Simth*. Excel cannot, by default, correct that mistake. However, you can customize the AutoCorrect feature so that the correction will be made. To do so, click the File tab and then click the Options button. Click *Proofing* at the left side of the Excel Options dialog box, and then click the AutoCorrect Options button in the right-hand panel. In the AutoCorrect tab of the AutoCorrect dialog box, type your frequent typo (such as *Simth*) in the *Replace* text box and type the correction (*Smith* in this instance) in the *With* text box. Click Add and then click OK twice.

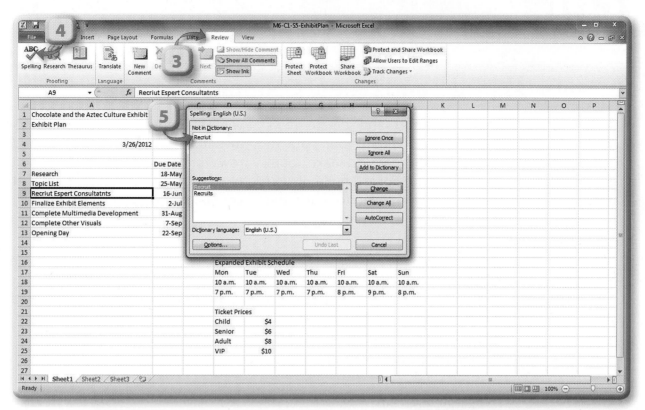

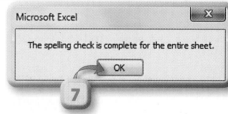

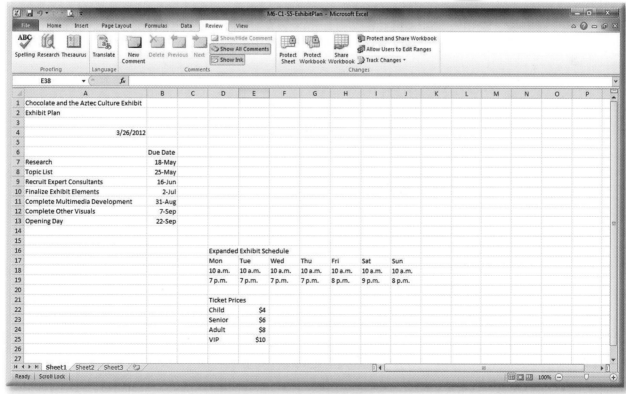

Completed Skill 5

Excel

Skill 6

Video M6_C1_S06

Insert and Delete Columns and Rows

You can insert and delete rows and columns within your data to rearrange the data or make room for new data. For example, if you created a worksheet to track the value of products in your company's inventory, you might need to add rows for new products that you add to your catalog or remove rows that contain products you discontinue.

Steps

1 If it is not already open, open **M6-C1-S5-ExhibitPlan.xlsx**, the file you saved in the previous skill, and save the file as **M6-C1-S6-ExhibitPlan**.

2 On Sheet1, make cell A7 the active cell.

3 Click the Home tab.

4 In the Cells group, click the Delete button arrow.

5 Click *Delete Sheet Rows*. Excel removes the row immediately and does not display a warning that you will be deleting the contents of the row.

6 With cell A7 still selected but now reading *Topic List*, type Research and Topic List and then press Enter to update the contents of the cell.

7 Make cell A12 the active cell.

8 In the Cells group of the Home tab, click the Insert button arrow.

9 Click *Insert Sheet Rows*.

▶ **Tip** Before deleting rows and columns, save your worksheet. Make sure to check the rows and columns before you delete them to be sure you will not be losing important data.

▶ **Tip** If you accidentally delete the wrong row or column, immediately click the Undo button on the Quick Access toolbar to restore the deleted content.

5 *Another Way*
Right-click a column or row heading and use the Insert or Delete commands.

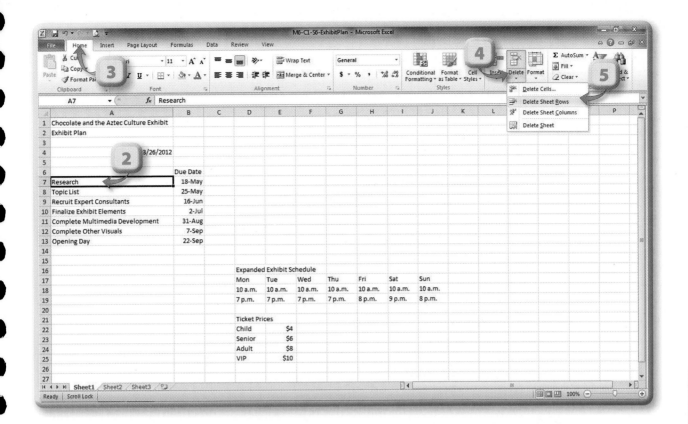

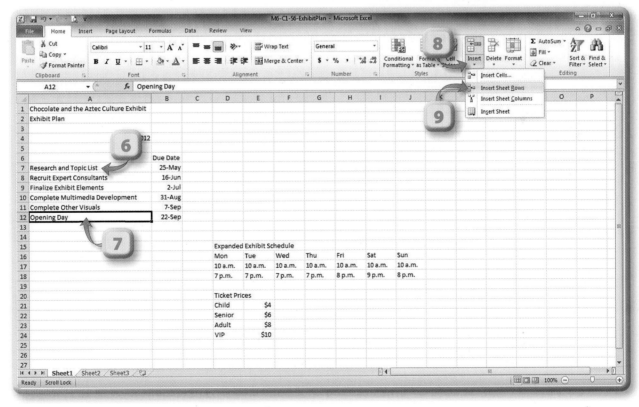

More

10 In cell A12, type Event Marketing and then press the Right Arrow key.

11 In cell B12, type 9/17 and then press Enter.

12 Right-click the column B column heading to display a shortcut menu.

13 Click *Insert*. A new column appears.

▶Tip Each Excel worksheet always has the same number of rows and columns. When you insert and delete rows and columns, you are simply changing where the blank rows and columns appear in the sheet.

14 Make cell B6 the active cell, and then type the following entries down the column:

Budget [Press Enter]
$1,500 [Press Enter]
$4,500 [Press Enter]
$750 [Press Enter]
$35,000 [Press Enter]
$22,000 [Press Enter]
$20,000 [Press Enter]
$650 [Press Enter]

15 Move the mouse pointer to the right border of the column B heading and double-click to resize the column.

16 Right-click the column D heading to display a shortcut menu.

17 Click *Delete*. The *Expanded Exhibit Schedule* and *Ticket Prices* tables shift to the left.

18 Save the file.

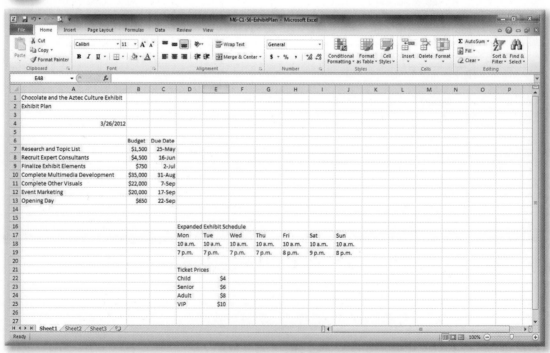

Completed Skill 6

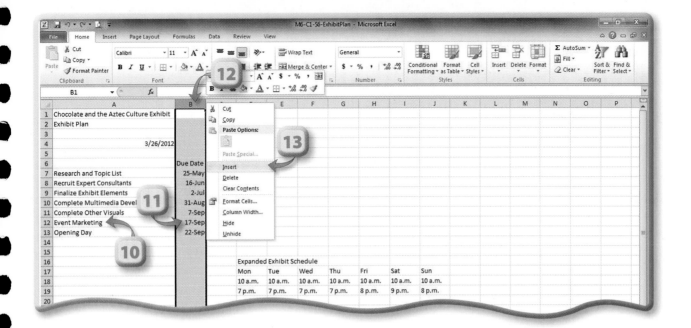

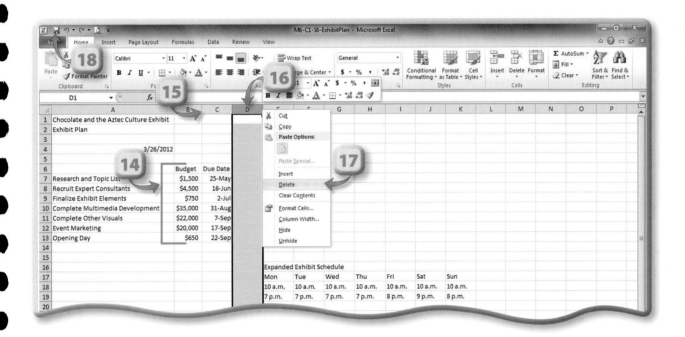

Taking It Further

Designing Worksheets Using Rows and Columns Rows and columns can play both functional and design roles in your worksheet. For example, when you perform calculations and certain other activities such as charting, you will find the actions easiest to perform when all the data is located in adjoining rows and columns.

Excel

Skill 7

Video M6_C1_S07

Create a New Worksheet

Given the size of each worksheet, it would be possible to arrange a wide variety of different sets of data in ranges spread throughout a single sheet. However, you then would have to spend a lot of time scrolling and otherwise navigating to find the section of the sheet containing the data you want to view and use. Dividing data into multiple worksheets can be more efficient for reading the data.

Each Excel workbook enables you to have dozens of sheets. If you have to track data for many stores, no problem! You can create a sheet for each one or copy an existing sheet to a new sheet for editing. You also can delete sheets with old data you no longer need.

Steps

1 If it is not already open, open **M6-C1-S6-ExhibitPlan.xlsx**, the file you saved in the previous skill, and save the file as **M6-C1-S7-ExhibitPlan**.

2 Make cell A1 the active cell on Sheet1.

3 Click the Sheet2 tab, press and hold down the Ctrl key, and click the Sheet3 tab.

Tip The Ctrl key allows you to select multiple items.

4 In the Home tab, click the Delete button arrow in the Cells group.

4 *Another Way* You can right-click a sheet tab and click *Delete* in the pop-up menu.

5 Click *Delete Sheet*.

6 In the message box that warns you that sheets may contain data that will be deleted, click Delete.

7 Right-click the Sheet1 sheet tab and click *Move or Copy*.

8 In the Move or Copy dialog box, click *(move to end)* in the *Before sheet* list box.

9 Click the *Create a copy* check box to insert a check mark.

10 Click OK. The new sheet, named *Sheet1 (2)*, appears and is the active sheet.

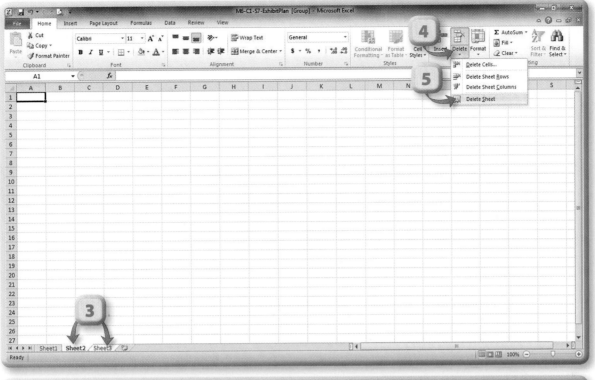

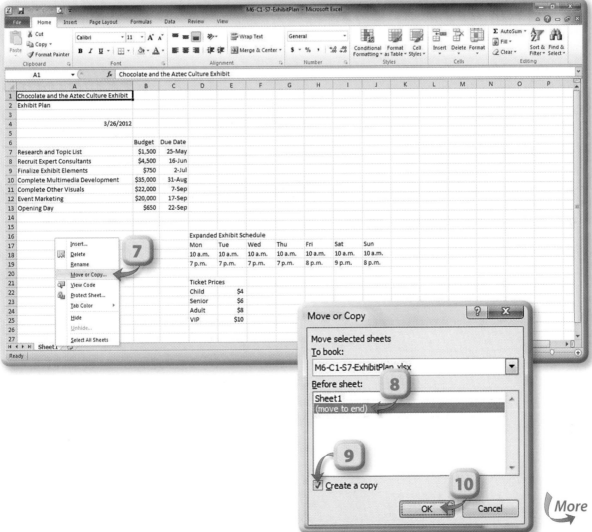

More

11 On the new sheet, drag your mouse over the column headings for columns A through C to select them, right-click the column headings, and then click *Delete*.

12 Drag over the row headings for rows 1 through 15 to select those rows, right-click the row headings, and then click *Delete*.

13 Click the Sheet1 sheet tab. Drag over the column headings for columns D through J to select those columns, right-click the column heading, and then click *Delete*. You have separated the data you created onto two sheets.

14 Click the Sheet1 (2) sheet tab.

15 Make cell A1 the active cell.

16 *Shortcut*
Add a New Sheet
Shift + F11

16 Click the Insert Worksheet tab to the right of the Sheet1 (2) tab. The new sheet, named *Sheet3*, appears.

17 Save the file.

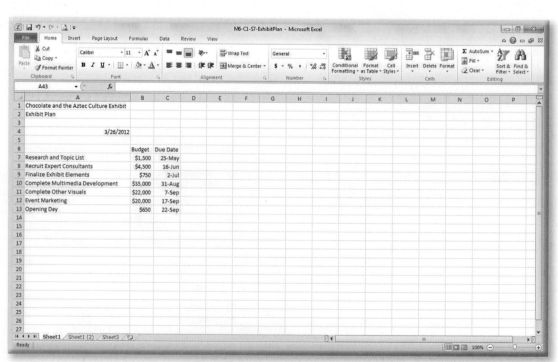

Completed Skill 7, Sheet 1

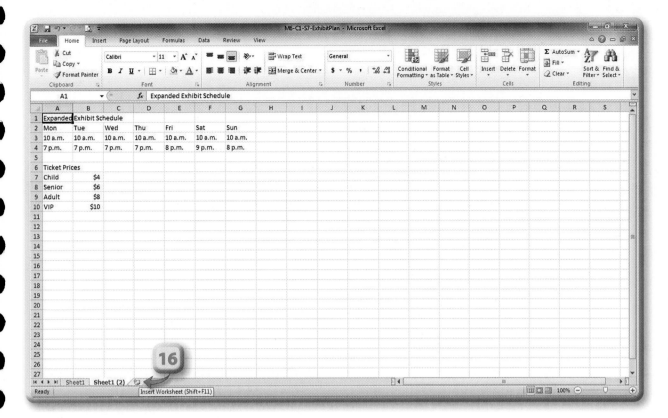

Taking It Further

Copying Data to Another Workbook You may have noticed that the Move or Copy dialog box includes a *To book* drop-down list at the top. If you have another workbook open, you can select it from this list to move or copy the specified worksheet to that workbook rather than within the current workbook. This action enables you to reuse data in other workbook files using a method that is faster than copying and pasting.

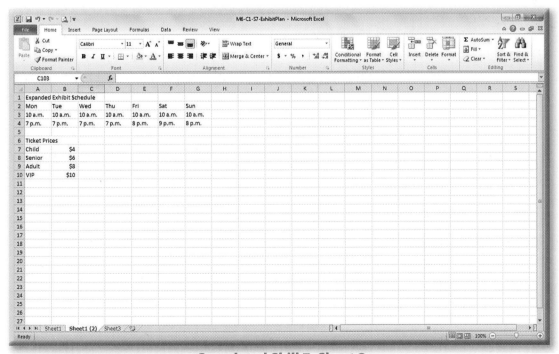

Completed Skill 7, Sheet 2

Excel

Name and Rename Worksheets

Video ▶ M6_C1_S08

If the goal of adding worksheets is to make information easier to find and identify, then "mystery names," such as Sheet1 and Sheet2 for worksheets, certainly do not help. If instead you give each worksheet a unique name that identifies its contents, you will know which tab to click to find the data you need.

Use the worksheet tab to rename the worksheet. A sheet name can be up to 31 characters and can contain most characters on the keyboard, including spaces. Only a handful of characters, such as / (slash), \ (backslash), * (asterisk), ' (apostrophe), and : (colon) are not allowed in worksheet names.

Steps

1 If it is not already open, open **M6-C1-S7-ExhibitPlan.xlsx**, the file you saved in the previous skill, and save the file as **M6-C1-S8-ExhibitPlan**.

2 Click the Sheet1 worksheet tab.

3 Make cell A1 the active cell.

3 Another Way
You also can double-click the sheet tab to start the renaming process.

4 Right-click the Sheet1 tab.

5 Click *Rename*.

6 Type Plan and press Enter.

7 Double-click the Sheet1 (2) tab, type Schedule, and then press Enter.

8 Double-click the Sheet3 tab, type Ticket Sales, and then press Enter.

9 Click the Plan tab.

10 Save the file.

Taking It Further

Color Coding Sheet Tabs You also can color-code your worksheets. Right-click the sheet tab, point to *Tab Color*, and click the color you want from the palette. For example, if you are tracking store profitability, you could make green tabs for all the stores making a profit and red tabs for all the stores losing money.

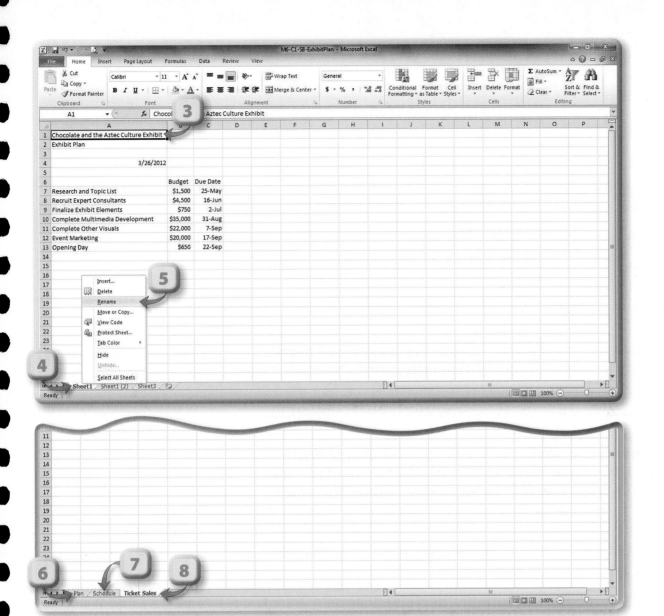

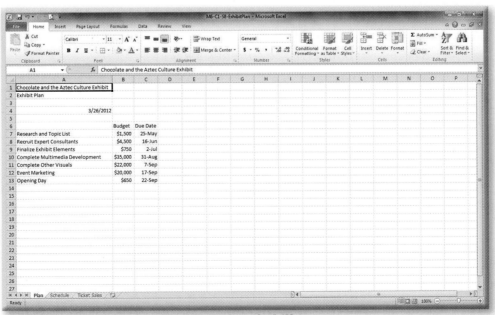

Completed Skill 8

Excel

Skill 9

Video ▶ M6_C1_S09

Explore Options for Printing

Handing out printouts is sometimes the most convenient way to collectively review information in a meeting and other situations. When each person has a copy of the item being discussed, individuals can freely jump from page to page and zero in on the data they find important.

Excel offers numerous options for setting up and printing a worksheet. This skill will give you a preview of the most useful print settings.

Steps

1 If it is not already open, open **M6-C1-S8-ExhibitPlan.xlsx**, the file you saved in the previous skill, and save the file as **Lastname-M6-C1-S9-ExhibitPlan**, but replace *Lastname* with your last name. Be sure to save the file in your Module 6 working folder on your storage medium.

▶**Tip** You should select a range of cells when you want to print only a portion of data that is on the worksheet.

2 In the Plan tab, drag over the range A1:C13.

3 Click the File tab.

4 Click Print. The Backstage view presents print settings and a preview of the printout.

5 Verify that the correct printer is selected from the *Printer* drop-down list. Ask your instructor if more than one printer is available and you are not sure which one to choose.

▶**Tip** You could instead click other options to print only the active sheets or the entire workbook.

6 Open the first drop-down list in the Settings category and click *Print Selection* to print only the current selection.

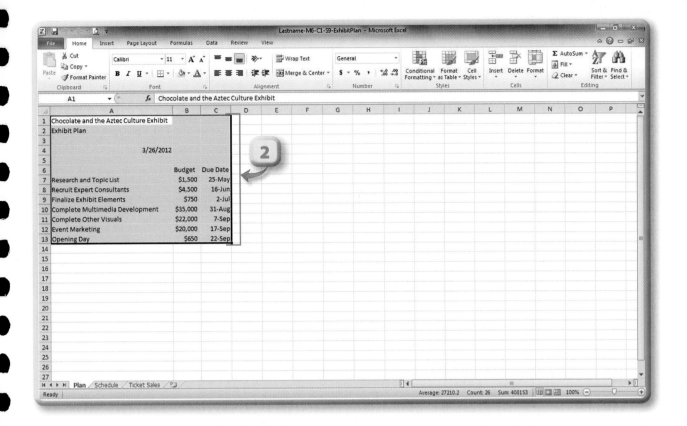

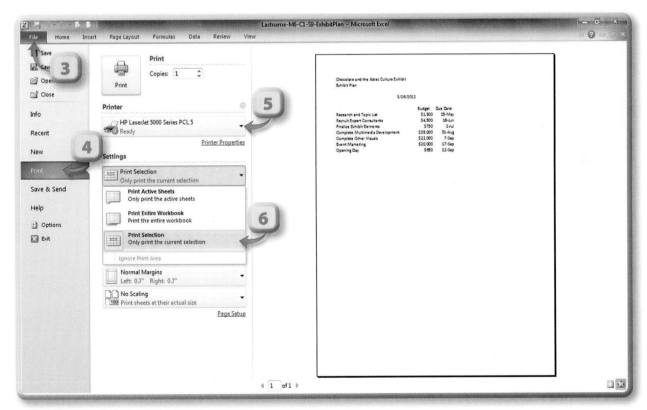

More

Excel

Tip The Page Layout tab also offers settings for orientation and margins. Click the Page Setup dialog box launcher to open the Page Setup dialog box, where you can work with additional settings, such as page scaling.

7 In the third drop-down list in the Settings category, change to *Landscape Orientation*.

8 If your instructor asks you to print the document, click Print. Otherwise, click the Home tab.

9 Save and close the file.

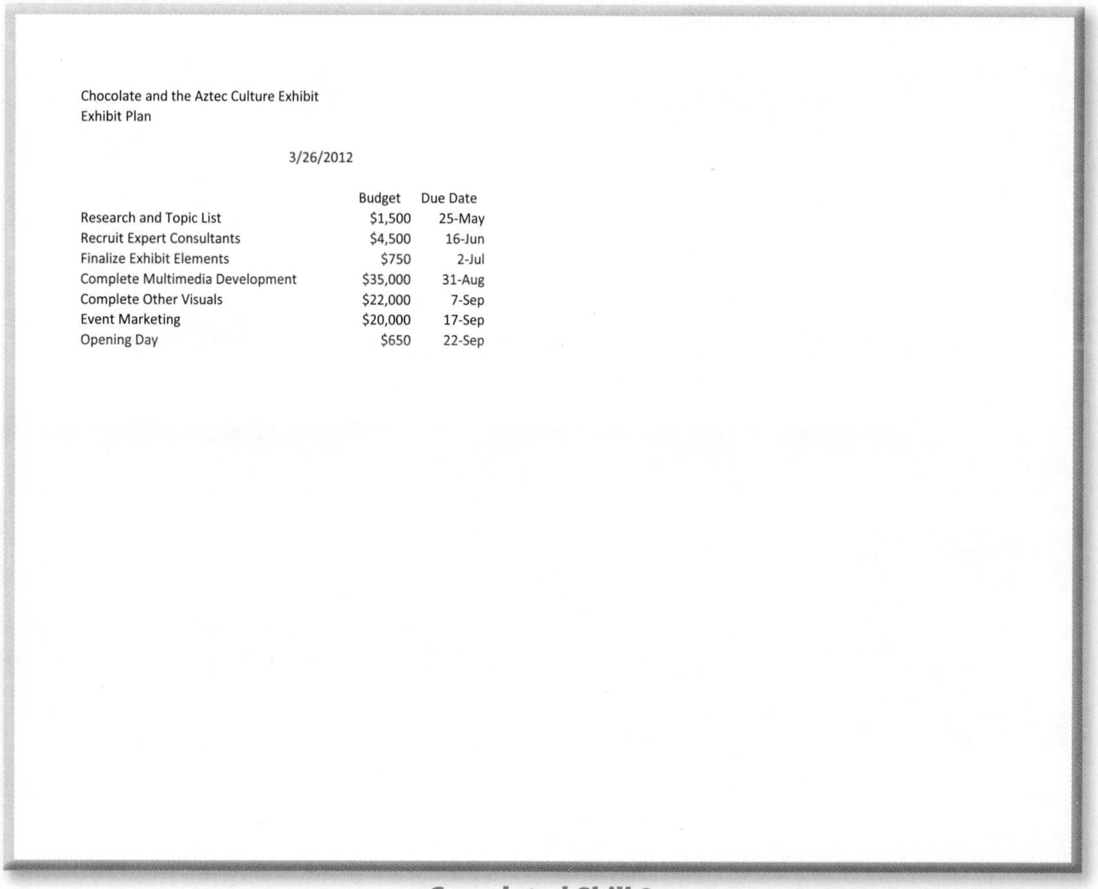

Chocolate and the Aztec Culture Exhibit
Exhibit Plan

3/26/2012

	Budget	Due Date
Research and Topic List	$1,500	25-May
Recruit Expert Consultants	$4,500	16-Jun
Finalize Exhibit Elements	$750	2-Jul
Complete Multimedia Development	$35,000	31-Aug
Complete Other Visuals	$22,000	7-Sep
Event Marketing	$20,000	17-Sep
Opening Day	$650	22-Sep

Completed Skill 9

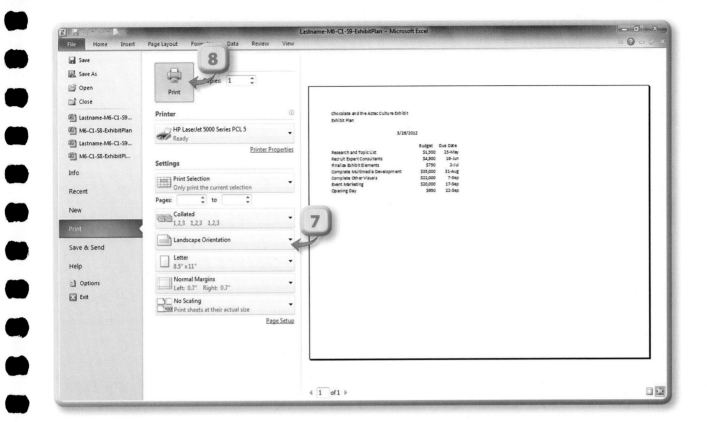

Taking It Further

You can add a header and a footer to an Excel worksheet to include identifying information such as the file name, your name, your company name, or page numbers on a printout. Click the Insert tab and then click the Header & Footer button in the Text group. Type information in the placeholders that appear on the worksheet for the header or footer, or use the choices in the Header & Footer Tools Design tab to insert elements such as page numbers and the file name. You also can use the Header button and Footer button drop-down lists in the Header & Footer group to add predefined text to the selected header or footer area. Note that adding a header or a footer switches the workbook to Page Layout view, so click the View tab and click Normal in the Workbook Views group to return to the Normal view.

Chapter 1
Assessments

Tasks Summary

Task	Ribbon Tab, Group	Button, Option	Shortcut, Alternative
Navigate			Arrow keys, Ctrl + Home
Select sheet tab			Click tab
Enter text			Enter, Ctrl + Enter, Tab, or arrow key to finish entry
Select a range	Name box		Drag, click upper left cell and then Shift + click lower right cell, click upper left cell and then use arrow keys to extend the selection
Select an entire sheet			Ctrl + A
Fill a series or values	Home, Editing	Fill ▾	Drag fill handle
Perform a spelling check	Review, Proofing	ABC ✓	F7
Insert a row	Home, Cells		Right-click selected rows and click *Insert*
Insert a column	Home, Cells		Right-click selected columns and click *Insert*
Delete a row	Home, Cells		Right-click selected rows and click *Delete*
Delete a column	Home, Cells		Right-click selected columns and click *Delete*
Copy a worksheet			Right-click sheet tab and click *Move or Copy*
Insert a blank worksheet	Home, Cells		Click Insert Worksheet tab or click Shift + F11
Delete a worksheet	Home, Cells		Right-click sheet tab and click *Delete*
Rename a worksheet			Double-click sheet name and type new name
Print	File, Print		

Features Review

Select the best answer from the choices given.

1. Finish a cell entry by doing this.
   a. pressing Enter
   b. pressing Ctrl + Enter
   c. pressing the Right Arrow key
   d. All of the above

2. Use these to move around on a worksheet without changing the active cell.
   a. Ribbon tabs
   b. scroll bars
   c. arrow keys
   d. All of the above

3. The column letter and row number make up the cell reference or
   a. value.
   b. range name.
   c. cell address.
   d. formula.

4. Name a way to select a range of cells.
   a. Drag over it.
   b. Search for it.
   c. Type it in a cell.
   d. Insert dashes.

5. The _____ feature enables you to create a series of entries down a column or across a row.
   a. Copy
   b. Auto Fill
   c. Templates
   d. Clear

6. The Spell Check feature can find errors in these types of entries.
   a. text
   b. values
   c. dates
   d. All of the above

7. Doing this to a row or column removes it and its contents.
   a. inserting
   b. copying
   c. deleting
   d. summing

8. An equals sign is the first item entered in a
   a. numeric entry.
   b. text entry.
   c. date entry.
   d. formula.

9. Change the _____ for a worksheet on the sheet tab to describe its contents.
   a. theme
   b. color
   c. value
   d. name

10. Click Print on the File tab to display printing choices in
    a. Backstage view.
    b. Print Preview view.
    c. the Print dialog box.
    d. the Page Layout tab.

Hands-On Skills Review

Exercise **A** Tracking Song Purchases

Skills Understand worksheet and workbook structure; use cell references; enter text, dates, and values; use the Auto Fill feature; insert and delete columns and rows; and explore options for printing

Scenario You have recently begun purchasing digital songs online, and you want to create a list of your purchases. Create a new workbook and enter the initial data about your collection now.

Steps

1. Create a new, blank workbook file.

2. Save the file as **Lastname-M6-C1-ExA-Songs**, but replace *Lastname* with your last name.

3. In cell A1, type My Digital Songs.

4. In cell A2, type your name.

5. Type the following entries in cells A3:F3.
   Title
   Artist
   Format
   Price
   Date Purchased

6 Type the following entries in cells A4:F4.

California Gurls
Katy Perry
MP3
$1.29
3/12/2012

7 Use Auto Fill to fill the first Artist entry and Format entry.

8 Add these entries where appropriate on rows 5 and 6:

Hot 'N Cold $.99   3/12/2012
Waking Up in Vegas $.99   3/14/2012

9 Insert a new column C.

10 Type Rating as the column title.

11 Type 5, 3, and 4 in the new column as shown in the completed worksheet.

12 Change the width of columns A and B to fit the contents.

13 Click File and then Print to see how the file will look when printed.

14 Save the workbook file.

15 Print or submit the completed workbook file as directed by your instructor.

	A	B	C	D	E	F	G
1	My Digital Songs						
2	Student Name						
3	Title	Artist	Rating	Format	Price	Date Purchased	
4	California Gurls	Katy Perry	5	MP3	$1.29	3/12/2012	
5	Hot 'N Cold	Katy Perry	3	MP3	$0.99	3/12/2012	
6	Waking Up in Vegas	Katy Perry	4	MP3	$0.99	3/14/2012	

Completed Exercise A

Exercise **B** Creating a Meal Budget

Skills   Understand worksheet and workbook structure; use cell references; enter text, values, and dates; use the Auto Fill feature; insert and delete columns and rows; and explore options for printing

Scenario   You sell security products for Endpoint, Inc. You will be taking a sales trip soon and need to create a report of projected expenses for your food. You have researched the cost of meals in restaurants in the area you will be visiting. Create an Excel worksheet that displays the daily cost for food while traveling.

Steps

1 Create a new, blank workbook file.

2 Save the file as **Lastname-M6-C1-ExB-FoodExpense**, but replace *Lastname* with your last name.

3 In cell A1, type Trip Meal Expenses.

4 In cell A2, type your name.

5 Type Mon for Monday in cell B3.

6 Auto Fill the entry in B3 across the row, through the *Sat* value.

7 Make the following entries in cells A4:A8.

Breakfast
Snack
Lunch
Dinner
Snack

8 Make the following entries in cells B4:B8.

$20.00
$1.25
$25.00
$45.00
$2.50

9 Select the range B4:B8 and copy the values across the rows through column G.

10 Delete row 5, the first *Snack* row.

11 Replace the entry in cell F6 with $75.00.

12 Delete the entries in cells G5:G7.

13 Change the print orientation to *Landscape Orientation*.

14 Save the workbook file.

15 Print or submit the completed workbook file as directed by your instructor.

	A	B	C	D	E	F	G
1	Trip Meal Expenses						
2	Student Name						
3		Mon	Tue	Wed	Thu	Fri	Sat
4	Breakfast	$20.00	$20.00	$20.00	$20.00	$20.00	$20.00
5	Lunch	$25.00	$25.00	$25.00	$25.00	$25.00	
6	Dinner	$45.00	$45.00	$45.00	$45.00	$75.00	
7	Snack	$2.50	$2.50	$2.50	$2.50	$2.50	
8							

Completed Exercise B

Exercise Listing Birthdays

Skills Understand worksheet and workbook structure; use cell references; enter text, values, and dates; use the Auto Fill feature; use Spell Check; name and rename worksheets; and explore options for printing

Scenario Your company sends clients birthday cards on their birthdays. Create a workbook file for tracking each client's birthday by month.

Steps

1 Create a new, blank workbook file.

2 Save the file as **Lastname-M6-C1-ExC-BDays**, but replace *Lastname* with your last name.

3 Enter Birfhdays in cell A1. (Type exactly as written here. You will correct typos later.)

4 In cell A2, type your name.

5 Enter Janary in cell A3 and Name in cell B3.

6 Enter the date 1/1 in cell A4.

7 Use Auto Fill to fill the dates in cells A5 through A34 (*31-Jan*).

8 Type the following entries in the specified cells.

B5	June Holloway
B7	Jim Levinson
B10	Linda Lemur
B16	Rolanda James
B24	Butch Wilson
B34	Carson Myers

9 Check spelling in the worksheet, fixing only obvious type errors and not names.

10 Rename the current sheet as *January*.

11 Change the size of column B so that the names fit in the column.

12 Print preview the worksheet to ensure it looks like the completed worksheet shown.

13 Save the workbook file.

14 Print or submit the completed workbook file as directed by your instructor.

⊿	A	B
1	Birthdays	
2	Student Name	
3	January	Name
4	1-Jan	
5	2-Jan	June Holloway
6	3-Jan	
7	4-Jan	Jim Levinson
8	5-Jan	
9	6-Jan	
10	7-Jan	Linda Lemur
11	8-Jan	
12	9-Jan	
13	10-Jan	
14	11-Jan	
15	12-Jan	
16	13-Jan	Rolanda James
17	14-Jan	
18	15-Jan	
19	16-Jan	
20	17-Jan	
21	18-Jan	
22	19-Jan	
23	20-Jan	
24	21-Jan	Butch Wilson
25	22-Jan	
26	23-Jan	
27	24-Jan	
28	25-Jan	
29	26-Jan	
30	27-Jan	
31	28-Jan	
32	29-Jan	
33	30-Jan	
34	31-Jan	Carson Myers

Completed Exercise C

Chapter 2

Working with Formulas and Functions

Excel offers more than the ability to simply organize data in neat rows and columns; it can also perform calculations using that data. You can use calculations to determine the payments on a new car, to decide which home would be a better buy, or to budget for your next family vacation. In business, Excel can be used for financial tracking, business decision making, trend analysis, and more. Excel recalculates formulas when you change the data in your worksheet. This makes it easier for you to repurpose worksheets you have created for new projects.

With Excel's help, you can quickly create complicated calculations, even if you are not a math lover. Use simple mathematical operators, like + for addition, – for subtraction, * for multiplication, and / for division, to create formulas and use parentheses () to ensure that Excel performs calculations in the correct order. Excel also offers a number of shortcuts for quickly building formulas and for creating complex formulas using a calculation feature called functions.

Formulas can be copied from cell to cell and they will automatically adjust relative to the cell they are copied to. When you make a cell containing a formula the active cell, you see the result of the formula in the cell but see the formula in the Formula bar.

Skills You Learn

1   Enter a formula
2   Enter a function
3   Insert a function
4   Use AutoSum
5   Use absolute and relative cell references
6   Copy and paste cell contents
7   Edit cell contents
8   Use Show Formulas

Files You Need
In this chapter, you need the following student data file.

M6-C2-S1-DailySales.xlsx

What You Create

The Chocolate Museum operates a small gift shop to raise money to support the annual operating budget. The gift shop sells a variety of items, including gourmet chocolates and other chocolate foods, cooking utensils for preparing various types of chocolate dishes, chocolate recipe books, books about the history of chocolate, and other keepsake and novelty items. The museum totals the daily sales for the gift shop on a worksheet and uses that information to double-check against the cash, check, and charge amounts collected for the day. The museum also uses the daily data to calculate weekly totals.

In this chapter, you work on the daily sales worksheet to add the formulas and functions needed to calculate the desired results.

The Chocolate Museum Gift Shop's Daily Sales Worksheets

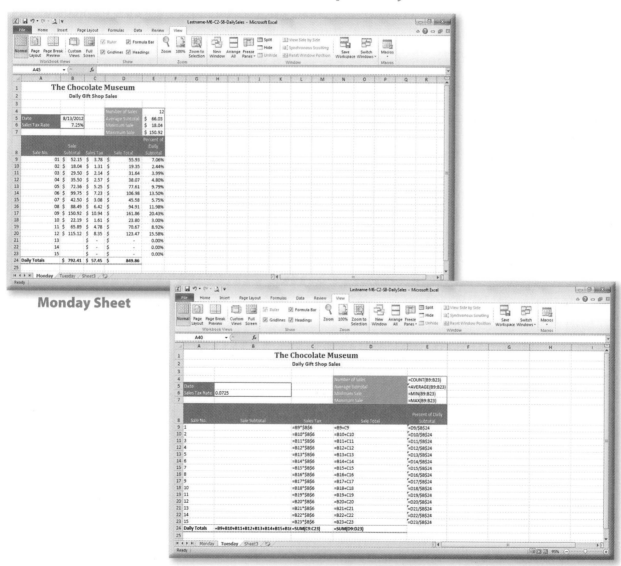

Monday Sheet

Tuesday Sheet

Excel

Enter a Formula

Video M6_C2_S01

In Excel, you can enter formulas directly in cells or use the Formula bar. Formulas perform calculations, the most important capability offered by Excel. There are rules for creating formulas. If you don't follow the rules, Excel indicates an error.

When you enter a formula, always type an = (equals) sign first, and then enter the rest of the formula. You can enter a number or a cell reference in a formula. For example, if you want to add the gift shop sales and the ticket sales together, you would enter the formula =C1+D1, where C1 and D1 are the cells that contain those values. When you finish entering the formula, the cell displays the calculated result. If you later update the data in any cells referenced in the formula, Excel will automatically recalculate and display the updated result.

After you have entered a formula in a cell, you can edit it.

Steps

1 Open the student data file named **M6-C2-S1-DailySales.xlsx**, and if you have not already done so, save the file in your Module 6 working folder on your storage medium.

2 Click in cell B23 to make it the active cell. You will enter a formula to total the daily sale subtotals here.

> **Tip** The formula appears in both the Formula bar and the cell as you type it or when you later select the cell.

3 Type =B8+B9+B10+B11+B12+B13+B14+B15+B16+B17+B18+B19+B20+ B21+B22.

4 Press Ctrl + Enter. The calculated value *$792.41* displays in cell B23 and the formula you entered in Step 3 displays in the Formula bar.

> **Tip** You learn to use a function to simplify this formula in Skill2.

5 Click in cell D8 to make it the active cell.

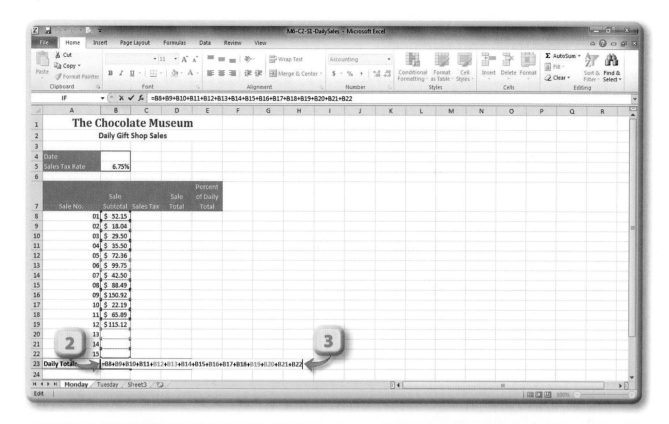

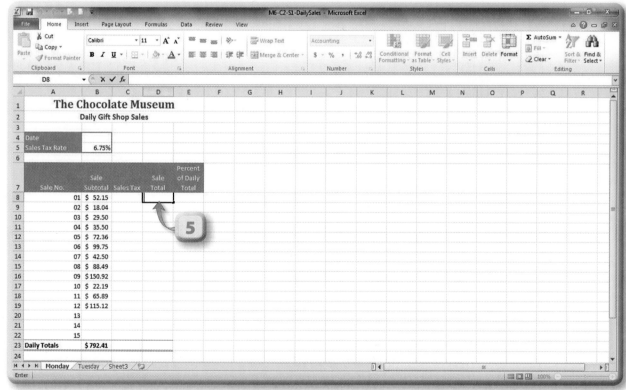

More

8 Another Way
Rather than typing a cell reference into a formula, click the cell on the worksheet to add it to the formula.

▶ **Tip** Click the Formula bar Cancel button (looks like an x) to cancel the cell entry.

6   Type =B8+C8, which calculates the total for the first sale.

7   Press the Right Arrow key to enter the formula and make cell E8 the active cell.

8   Click in the Formula bar and type =D8/B23.

9   Click the Formula bar Enter button (looks like a check mark) to the left of the formula to finish entering the formula in the cell.

10   Save the file.

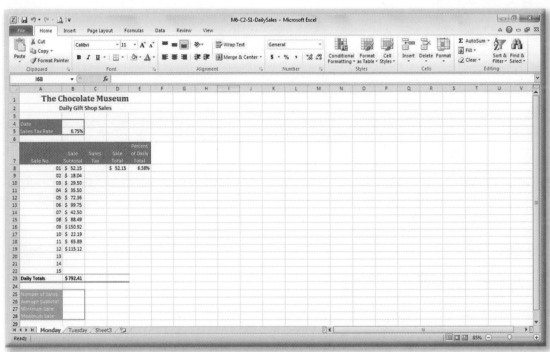

Completed Skill 1

Taking It Further

Calculating in Excel   Excel follows the standard mathematical order of operations when evaluating formulas. This means that Excel performs multiplication (*) and division (/) before performing addition (+) and subtraction (-). If the operator precedence is the same, Excel calculates from left to right. Adding parentheses enables you to control the calculation order. Parentheses must be used in pairs, and you can use multiple pairs. Excel calculates from the innermost set of parentheses outwards. For example, the formula =5+6*3 calculates to 23, because Excel multiplies first. In contrast, =(5+6)*3 calculates to 33, because Excel adds the values in parentheses first.

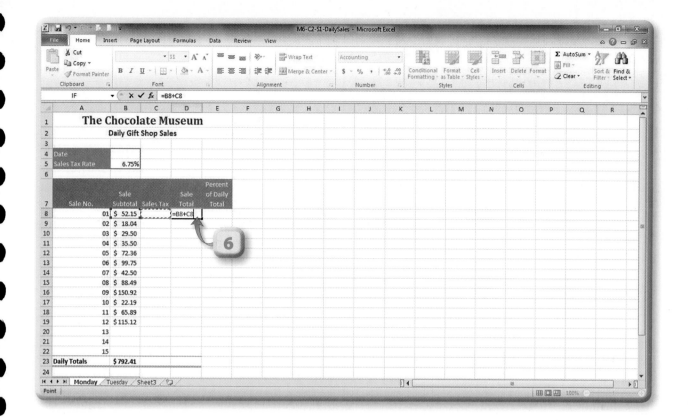

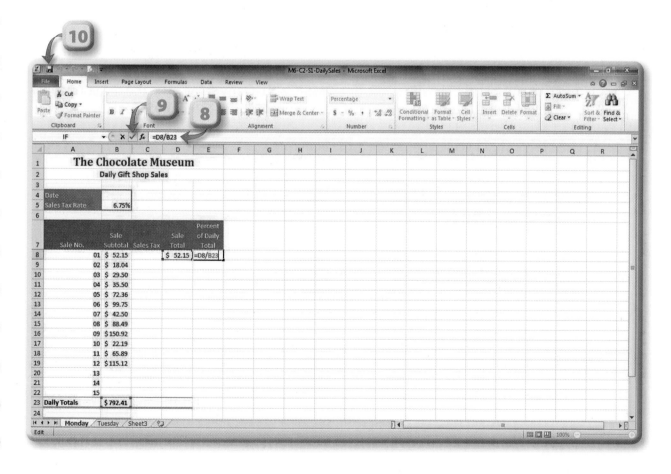

Excel

Enter a Function

Video **M6_C2_S02**

Excel functions simplify entry of lengthy and complicated formulas. Each function has a name and performs a predefined calculation when you include it in a formula. Excel offers dozens of functions in several different categories, such as Math & Trig, Financial, Logical, Statistical, Lookup, and more.

The function name typically indicates what type of calculation the function performs. For example, the SUM function sums a range of values, the AVERAGE function finds the average of a range of values, and the COUNT function counts the number of cells in a specified range. You can use the MAX and MIN functions to find the maximum or minimum value in a range. Use the TODAY function to enter the current date, which will update each time you open the workbook.

Most functions require one or more arguments surrounded by parentheses. The arguments are the values on which the function performs its calculations. For example, the SUM function needs to know which numbers to add.

Steps

3 *Another Way*
Functions are not case-sensitive, so typing them in all lowercase letters also works.

▶ **Tip** When you are typing in a function, a ScreenTip appears to help you type the proper arguments.

1 If it is not already open, open **M6-C2-S1-DailySales.xlsx**, the file you saved in the previous skill, and save the file as **M6-C2-S2-DailySales**.

2 Click in cell B4 to make it the active cell.

3 In the Formula bar, type =TODAY(. (Do not type the period.)

4 Press Enter to finish the formula. The current date appears in cell B4.

5 Click in cell C23 to make it the active cell.

6 Type =SUM(. (Do not type the period.)

7 *Another Way*
Type the range address.

7 Drag to select the range C8:C22 to enter it in the formula.

8 *Another Way*
Press Enter.

8 Click the Formula bar Enter button (looks like a check mark) to the left of the formula to finish entering the formula that sums the sales tax for all the sales in the cell. (You create the sales tax formulas in a later skill.)

9 Save the file.

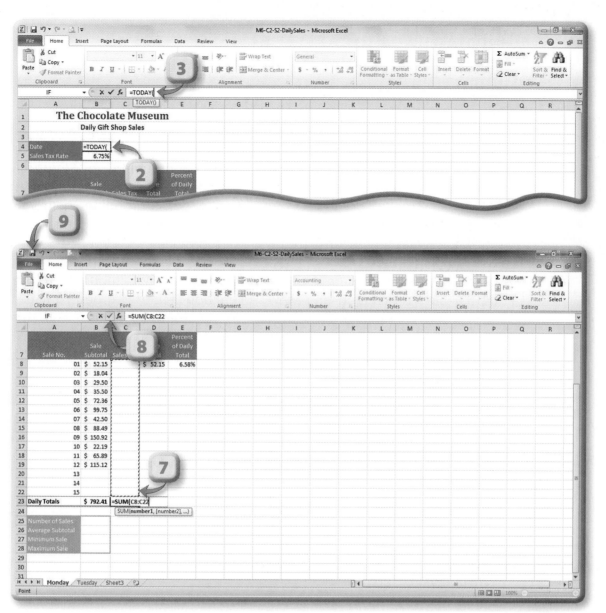

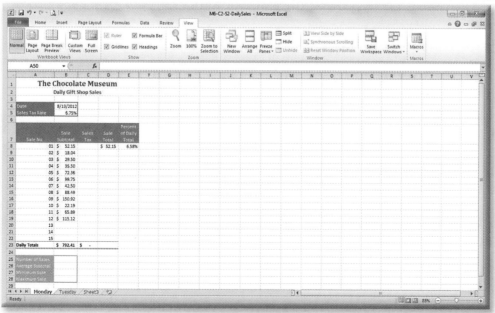

Completed Skill 2

Excel

Excel

Skill 3 | **Insert a Function**

Video M6_C2_S03

You can insert a function using buttons in the Function Library group on the Formulas tab. Function buttons include Financial, Logical, and Math & Trig. If you don't know the name of the function you need but know what you want it to do, you can find the function in the Function dialog box. Here you can type a brief description and view a list of possible matches. Click an item in the list to view its arguments and a description of what it does.

Functions can be viewed by category, such as *Math & Trig* or *Lookup & Reference*. There are additional groupings for *Statistical*, *Engineering*, and *Compatibility* functions. The groupings help you locate the function you need for your formula.

You can also choose a function from a list of categories in the Function Library group on the ribbon's Formula tab. You begin this skill by entering a function in cell B25 to count the day's total number of sales.

Steps

1 If it is not already open, open **M6-C2-S2-DailySales.xlsx**, the file you saved in the previous skill, and save the file as **M6-C2-S3-DailySales**.

2 Scroll down if necessary and make cell B25 the active cell.

3 Click the Insert Function button on the Formula bar to open the Insert Function dialog box.

3 Another Way
Click the Formulas tab and click Insert Function in the Function Library group.

▶**Tip** Rather than searching, you could select a category from the *Or select a category* drop-down list.

▶**Tip** Drag the dialog box to move it out of the way if it is covering the cell ranges.

▶**Tip** The dialog box collapses automatically, but you also could use the Collapse Dialog button at the right end of the text box to collapse and expand the dialog box.

4 Type count to replace the contents of the *Search for a function* text box.

5 Click the Go button.

6 Confirm that *COUNT* is selected in the *Select a function* list box.

7 Click OK to close the Insert Function dialog box. The Function Arguments dialog box appears, with the contents of the *Value1* text box selected. (Each text box represents an argument.)

8 Drag over the range B8:B22 on the Monday worksheet to enter it in the *Value1* text box.

9 Click OK. The counted result *12* appears in cell B25.

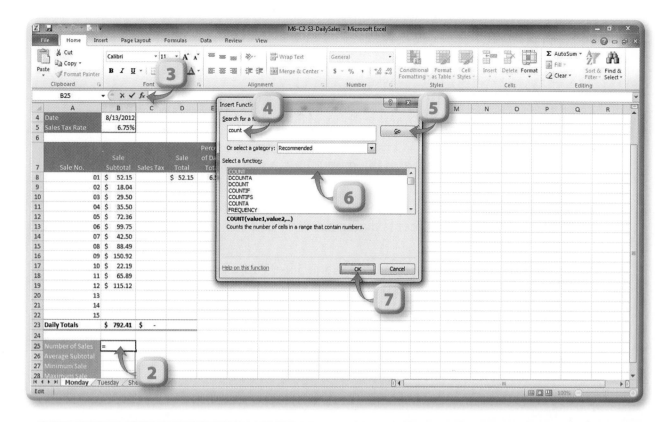

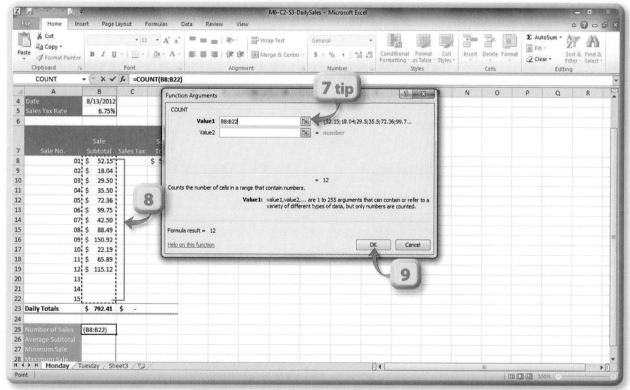

More

Excel

10 Press Down Arrow to make B26 the active cell.

11 Click the Formulas tab.

12 Click the More Functions button in the Function Library group.

13 Point to *Statistical* in the menu that appears and then click *AVERAGE*.

14 Drag over the range B8:B22 to enter it in the *Number1* text box in the Function Arguments dialog box.

15 Click OK. The calculated average *$66.03* appears in cell B26.

16 Press Down Arrow to make cell B27 the active cell.

17 Type =M. (Do not type the period.)

18 Double-click *MIN* in the *Formula AutoComplete* list.

19 Drag over the range B8:B22 to enter it into the formula.

20 Press Enter. Cell B27 displays *$18.04*, the minimum value found in the range B8:B22.

21 Save the file.

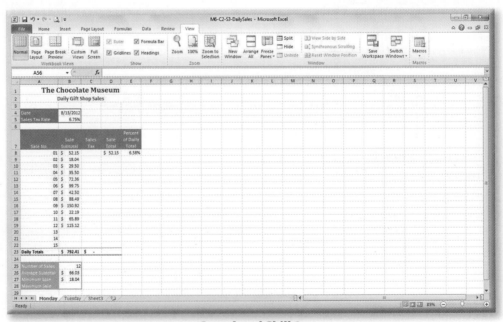

Completed Skill 3

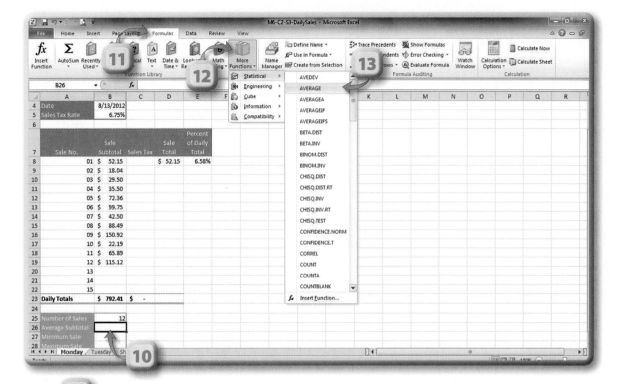

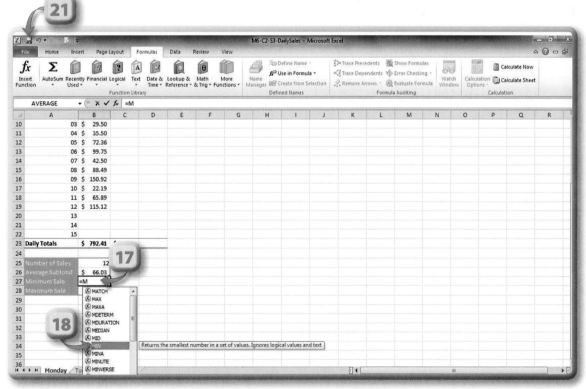

Taking It Further

Inserting Multiple Arguments More complex functions require multiple arguments. When you are typing in a function and need to include multiple arguments—such as multiple cell or range addresses or other values—add a comma between arguments. For example, the IF function is used to display one value if a condition is true and another value if false and requires multiple arguments, such as = if (A5> 100,1,0).

Excel

Skill 4

Use AutoSum

Video M6_C2_S04

The AutoSum feature provides a quick way to enter commonly used functions into a formula. These functions include SUM, AVERAGE, COUNT, MIN, and MAX.

To see the result of an AutoSum function without actually entering the formula into a cell, drag over a range of cells and then check the Status bar.

Steps

1 If it is not already open, open **M6-C2-S3-DailySales.xlsx**, the file you saved in the previous skill, and save the file as **M6-C2-S4-DailySales**.

2 Click the Home tab.

3 Drag over the range B8:B22.

4 Observe the *Average*, *Count*, and *Sum* values that appear in the Status bar.

5 Make cell D23 the active cell.

6 In the Editing group on the Home tab, click the AutoSum button.

7 Press Enter to accept the suggested range and insert the formula in cell D23.

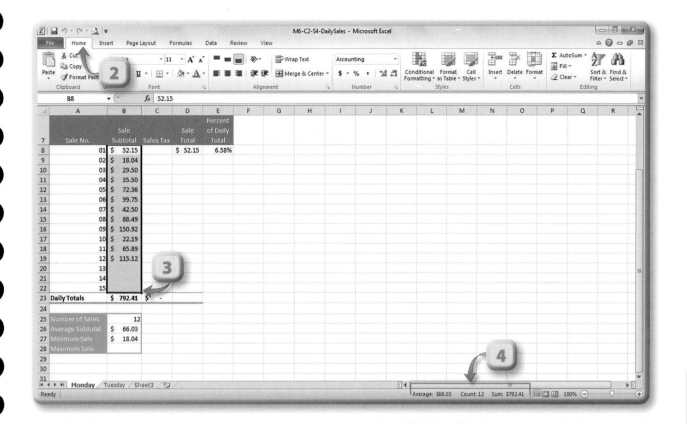

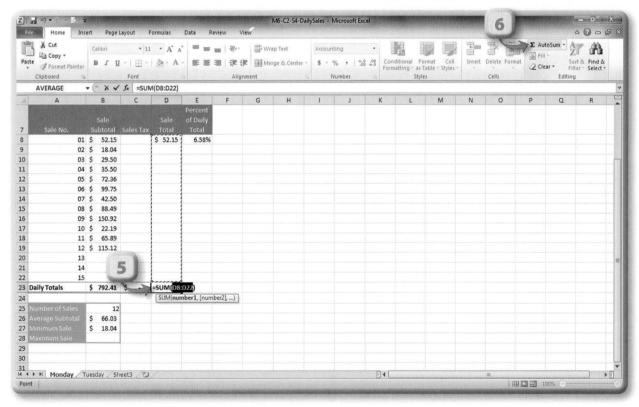

More

8   Scroll down, if necessary, and make cell B28 the active cell.

9   Click the AutoSum button arrow.

10   Click *Max*.

11   Drag over the range B8:B22 to enter it into the formula.

12   Press Enter. Cell B28 displays *$150.92,* the maximum value found in the specified range.

13   Save the file.

Taking It Further

Using Additional Functions   In addition to MIN, MAX, AVERAGE, SUM, COUNT, and TODAY, there are several other functions that you will find valuable as you begin exploring Excel. The IF function permits you to test a condition and perform different computations based on the result. COUNTIF counts the number of cells that meet a specified condition. The PMT function calculates the payment amount of a loan. For example, you might use this function to determine the payments if you are planning on taking out a car loan.

Excel

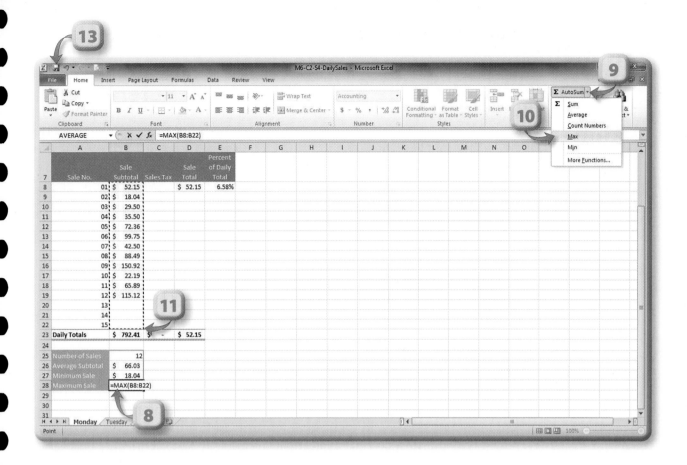

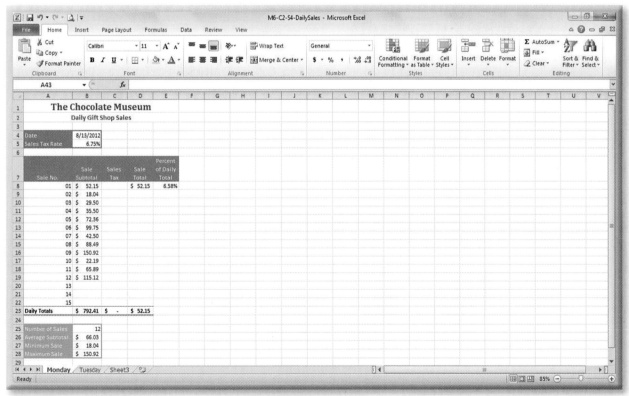

Completed Skill 4

Excel

Excel

Use Absolute and Relative Cell References

Cell references in formulas can be either relative or absolute. A relative cell reference will change if you copy or move the formula. For example, say you created a worksheet that tracks household expenses by month. In January, you entered the expenses for that month and entered a formula to total them at the bottom of column A. Now it is February. You enter the February expenses in column B, but rather than type the SUM formula again, you decide to copy it from column A. Even though the formula was originally written to reference the January expenses in column A, copying the formula one column to the right adjusts the column references in the formula by one column, causing it to reference the February expenses. For example, =SUM(A3:A10) would change to =SUM(B3:B10) if you copied it one column to the right.

If you don't want a cell reference to change when you are copying a formula, make it an absolute reference by placing a dollar sign before the column letter and row number, for example, A5. Use an absolute reference when a formula contains a key piece of data, such as tax rate or interest rate. To create an absolute reference, type dollar signs before the column letter and row number as you enter the cell reference into a formula.

Steps

1 If it is not already open, open **M6-C2-S4-DailySales.xlsx**, the file you saved in the previous skill, and save the file as **M6-C2-S5-DailySales**.

2 Make cell C8 the active cell.

3 Type =B8*B5.

Tip The reference to cell B5 is made to be an absolute cell reference because the same sales tax rate applies to all of the sold items.

4 Press F4. Excel changes the formula to =B8*B5, making the second cell reference an absolute reference.

4 *Another Way*
You also can type the dollar signs to create an absolute reference.

5 Press Ctrl + Enter to finish creating the formula with the absolute reference. Notice that the values in cells D8:E8 and C23:D23 recalculate automatically.

6 Save the file.

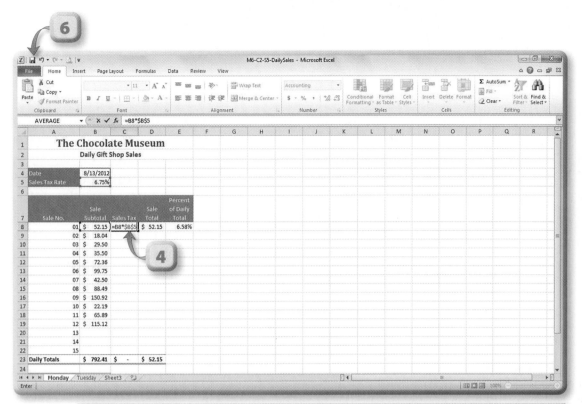

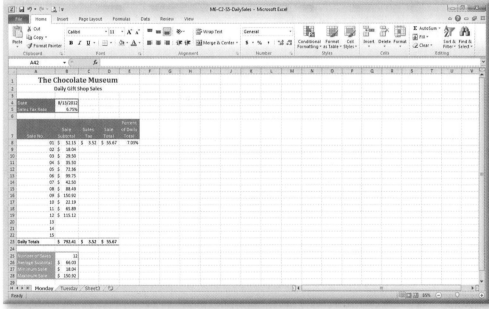

Completed Skill 5

Taking It Further

Placing Reference Data Choosing a good position for key data referenced by formulas on a worksheet can save you trouble later. If you need to change the value in a cell or cell(s) referenced in formulas throughout the worksheet, placing that information near the top of the worksheet makes it more accessible. Some worksheet designers set up an input range at the top of the worksheet to give the workbook user clear direction about where to enter values. For other types of workbooks, you might want the user to be able to see the results but not the data on which those results are based. In such a case, you would place the input data far down and to the right on the sheet, or even on another worksheet in the workbook file.

Copy and Paste Cell Contents

Often, a worksheet or workbook will contain cell content, such as data values and formulas, that repeats. For example, if a workbook contains budget information for two different chain store locations, the budget data for each store is likely to use the same column and row headings and the same formulas.

You can save time entering duplicate data by using the Copy and Paste buttons. You can also use the Cut and Paste buttons to move data or formulas from one location on a worksheet to another. When copying cells that contain formulas, the relative cell references will adjust when the formula is pasted. However, absolute cell references will not.

Steps

1 If it is not already open, open **M6-C2-S5-DailySales.xlsx**, the file you saved in the previous skill, and save the file as **M6-C2-S6-DailySales**.

2 Drag to select the range C8:D8.

3 On the Home tab, click the Copy button in the Clipboard group.

4 Make cell C9 the active cell.

5 Click the Paste button in the Clipboard group on the Home tab. The first relative reference in the pasted formula in cell C9 has been updated to refer to cell B9, but the absolute reference in the copied formula still refers to cell B5.

6 Make cell C10 the active cell.

7 Press Enter to paste the copied formula again.

8 With C10:D10 selected, double-click the fill handle at the lower right corner of cell D10 to use Auto Fill to copy the formulas down through cells C22:D22.

> **Tip** Excel pastes copied information to the Office Clipboard, a memory holding area for copied and cut information. The Clipboard can store up to 24 items. Click the dialog box launcher in the Clipboard group on the Home tab to open the Office Clipboard to choose a selection to paste.

> **Tip** Click Paste if you expect to paste copied cells into more than one location. Press Enter to paste the content for a single or the final time.

> **Tip** Pressing Esc clears the flashing marquee.

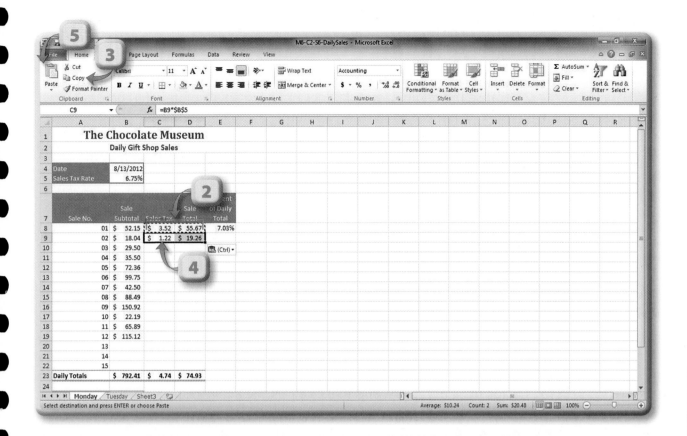

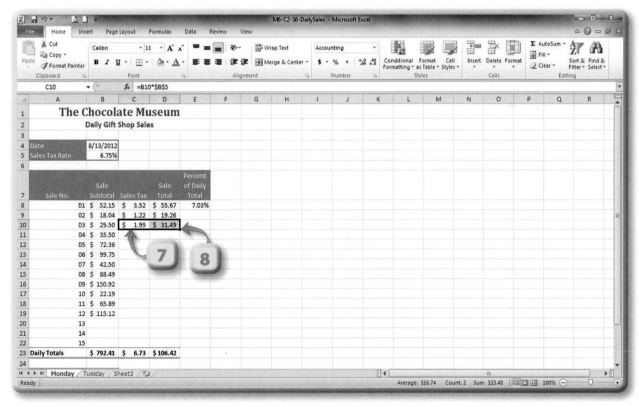

More

9   Make cell E8 the active cell.

10   Double-click the fill handle. A number of #DIV/0! errors appear in the range because the original formula does not have an absolute reference, but needs to. You will learn how to edit the cell to fix this issue in the next skill.

11 *Shortcut*
Undo
Ctrl+Z

11   Click the Undo button on the Quick Access tool bar.

▶ **Tip** Relative references also adjust when you insert or delete rows or columns.

12   Right-click the row 3 row heading.

13   Click *Insert* to insert a sheet row.

14   Scroll down, if necessary, and select the range A26:B29.

15 *Shortcut*
Cut
Ctrl+X

15   Click the Cut button in the Clipboard group to cut the range from that location. A scrolling marquee appears around the selected cells.

16   Scroll up, if necessary, and make cell D4 the active cell.

17 *Shortcut*
Paste
Ctrl+V

17   Click the Paste button in the Clipboard group on the Home tab. The moved selection appears in its new location. Notice that even though the formulas contain relative references to the range B9:B23, none of the results change when you move the formulas.

18   Double-click the border to the right of the column D column heading to correct the width of the column.

19   Save the file.

Taking It Further

Using Paste Button Options   Clicking the bottom half of the Paste button (with the down arrow on it) in the Clipboard group on the Home tab displays additional paste options, such as the Formulas button for pasting only formulas, the Transpose button for transposing (vertical to horizontal and vice versa) the location of the pasted cells, and the Values button for pasting data without underlying formulas or formatting. The numerous choices here enable you to achieve outcomes not possible without the Paste option. You also can access the Paste choices by clicking the Paste Options button that appears at the lower right corner of any pasted cell or range.

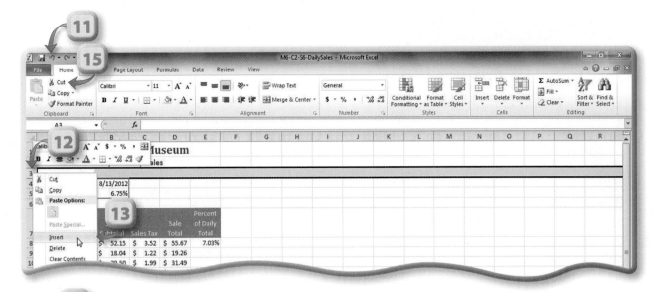

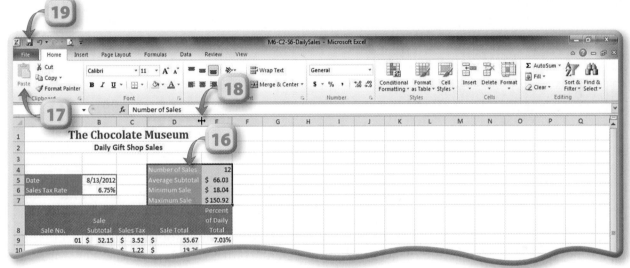

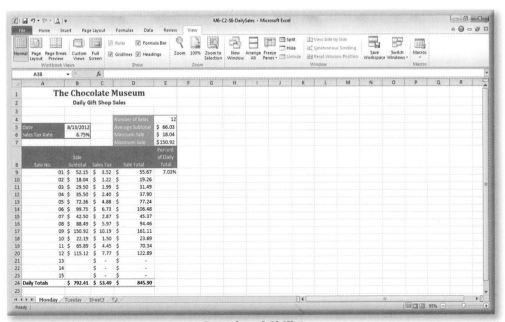

Completed Skill 6

Excel

Excel

Skill 7   Edit Cell Contents

When you want to use different labels for data, update the data to reflect new information, or make corrections to formulas, you have to edit a cell's contents. Excel offers a number of methods for removing or changing cell contents. You can edit a cell's content directly in the cell or in the Formula bar. You can also use the Clear button in the Editing group on the Home tab to edit a cell's contents.

Steps

1 If it is not already open, open **M6-C2-S6-DailySales.xlsx**, the file you saved in the previous skill, and save the file as **M6-C2-S7-DailySales**.

2 Make cell B6 the active cell.

3 Type 7.25 and press Enter. This number is a new sales tax rate.

4 Double-click cell E8.

5 Change the last word in the cell from *Total* to *Subtotal* and press Enter.

6 Click in the Formula bar, which shows the formula for the active cell, E9. The D9 reference is correct, but the reference to cell B24 needs to be an absolute reference. Click in the B24 cell reference, press F4, and then press Ctrl + Enter.

7 Double-click the fill handle at the lower right corner of cell E9 to copy the formula down the column through cell E23.

8 Select the range A1:E24.

9 Click the Copy button in the Clipboard group on the Home tab.

Shortcut
Open a Cell for Editing
F2

▶**Tip** Changing cell contents does not change the formatting. To remove formatting, click the Clear button and then select *Clear Formats*.

▶**Tip** Pressing F2 or double-clicking in a cell to edit it puts Excel in Edit mode, and the left end of the Status bar displays *Edit*.

Shortcut
Copy
Ctrl+C

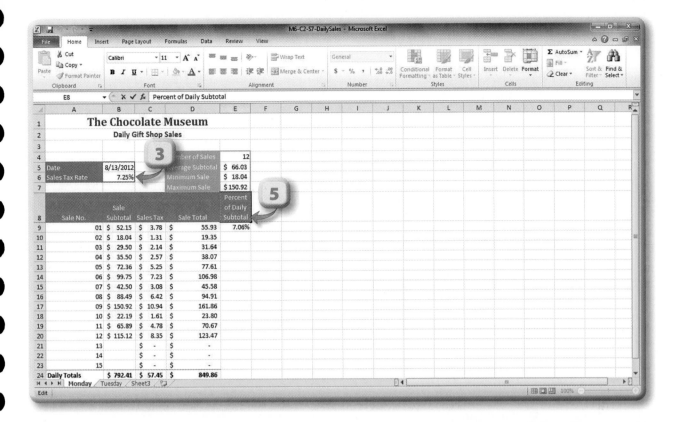

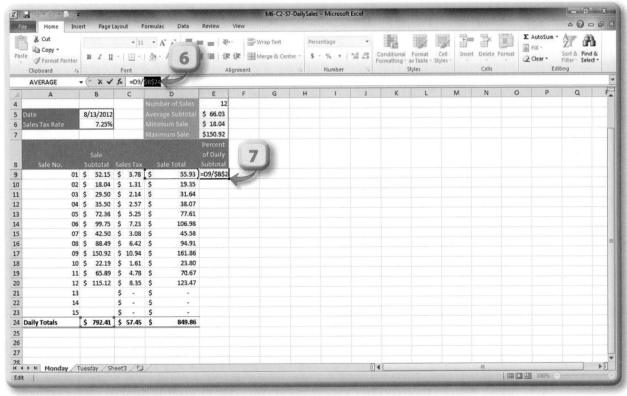

More

Excel

10 Click the Tuesday sheet tab.

11 Shortcut
Paste
Ctrl+V

11 Click the Paste button in the Clipboard group to paste the data on a new sheet.

12 Click the Paste Options button that appears at the lower-right corner of the pasted range.

13 Click the Keep Source Column Widths button.

14 Make cell B5 the active cell and then press Delete.

15 Select the range B9:B20.

16, 17 *Another Way*
You also can right-click the selection and click *Clear Contents* in the shortcut menu.

16 Click the Clear button in the Editing group on the Home tab.

17 Click *Clear Contents*.

18 Save the file.

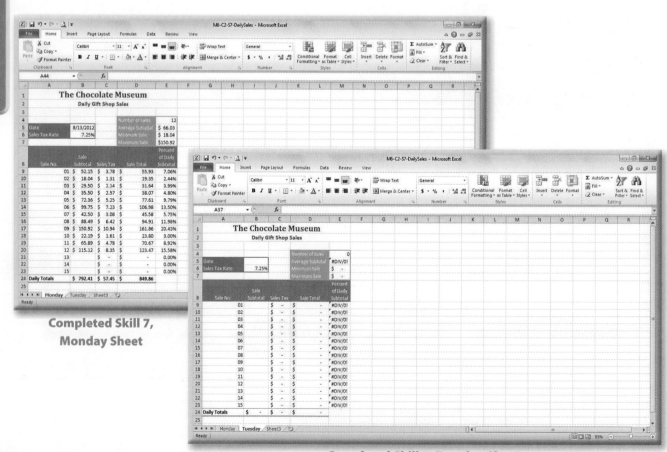

Completed Skill 7, Monday Sheet

Completed Skill 7, Tuesday Sheet

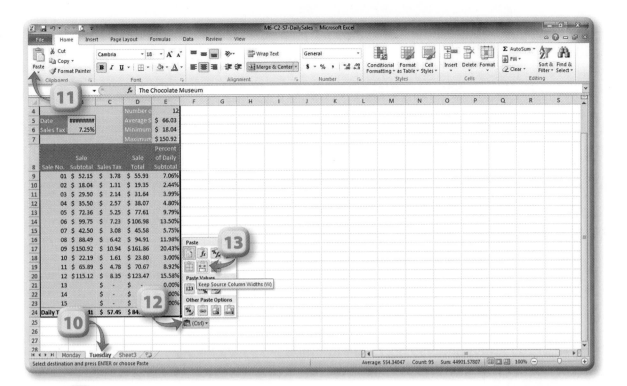

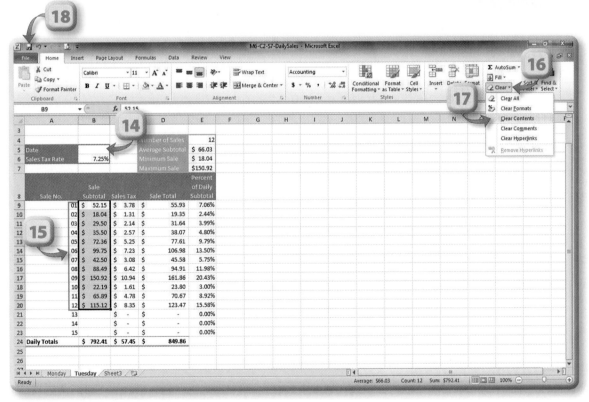

Taking It Further

Using the Clear Button Options The menu for the Clear button in the Editing group on the Home tab offers additional choices so you can specify exactly what to clear from the selected cell or range. For example, you can take separate actions by selecting only *Clear Formats*, *Clear Comments*, or *Clear Hyperlinks*, or you can use *Clear All* to clear both the cell contents and any formatting and comments.

Excel

Excel

Skill 8

Use Show Formulas

Excel displays an error code in a cell if you have made an error when entering a formula. For example, #DIV/0 means the formula is trying to divide by 0 and #VALUE means the formula is using the wrong type of argument. However, there are errors Excel will not catch. For example, if you reference the wrong column of numbers in a SUM function, Excel adds the wrong numbers. Because of this, you should always double-check your formulas.

Rather than clicking cells one by one to review their formulas in the Formula bar, you can use the Show Formulas feature to display all the formulas on the worksheet at once. This makes it easy for you to thoroughly review all cell references and formula structures so that you can ensure that the worksheet calculations are correct.

Steps

1 If it is not already open, open **M6-C2-S7-DailySales.xlsx**, the file you saved in the previous skill, and save the file as **Lastname-M6-C2-S8-DailySales**, but replace *Lastname* with your last name. Be sure to save the file in your Module 6 working folder on your storage medium.

2 Click the Tuesday sheet tab, if it isn't already selected.

3 Make cell A1 the active cell.

4 Click the Formulas tab.

5 Click the Show Formulas button in the Formula Auditing group.

6 Save and close the file.

5 *Shortcut*
Show Formulas
Ctrl+`

▶**Tip** Click the Show Formulas button again to hide the formulas.

Taking It Further

Printing a Worksheet with Formulas Shown   If you print while formulas are displayed, the formulas print but the cell contents do not. This type of printout can provide a handy reference to how the data in the sheet is constructed. In this situation, review the print preview carefully. You may need to adjust print settings, such as orientation and margins.

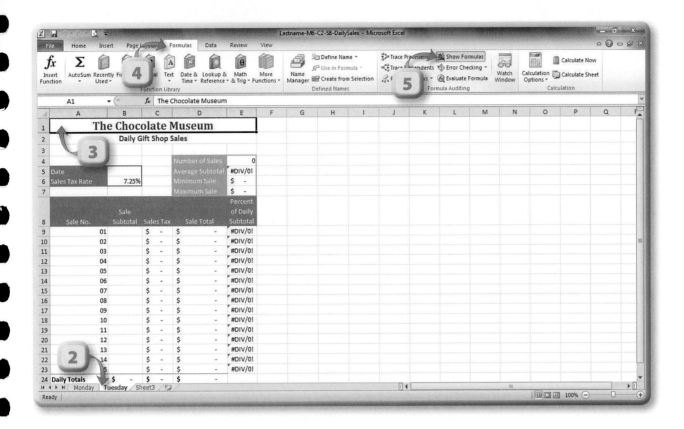

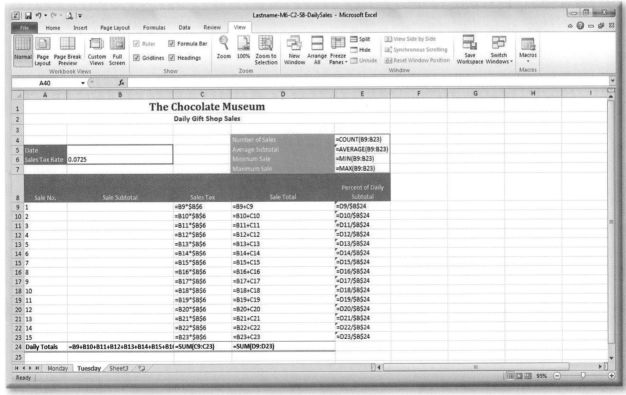

Completed Skill 8

Excel

Tasks Summary

Task	Ribbon Tab, Group	Button, Option	Shortcut, Alternative
Enter formulas			= key, other keyboard keys
Insert a function with the Insert Function dialog box	Formulas, Function Library		
Insert a function with Function AutoComplete			=key, type first few letters, click item, press Tab
Use AutoSum	Home, Editing or Formulas, Function Library	Σ	Enter, Ctrl + Enter, Tab, or arrow key to finish entry
Copy a cell or selection	Home, Clipboard		Ctrl + C
Cut a cell or selection	Home, Clipboard		Ctrl + X
Paste a cell or selection	Home, Clipboard		Ctrl + V
Toggle absolute reference when entering or editing a cell reference			F4
Delete cell contents	Home, Editing	, Clear Contents	Delete
Enter Edit mode			F2, or double-click cell
Show formulas	Formulas, Formula Auditing	Show Formulas	Ctrl + `

Features Review

Select the best answer from the choices given.

1 Start every formula by typing this.
   a. +
   b. @
   c. =
   d. -

2 The order in which Excel calculates operators is called
   a. order of priority.
   b. order of hierarchy.
   c. operator processing.
   d. order of operations.

3 You can enter _____ in a formula to tell Excel what to calculate.
   a. numbers
   b. cell references
   c. range references
   d. All of the above

4 C27 contains the value 10. What is the result when Excel evaluates the formula =2*3+C27/5?
   a. 8
   b. 5.2
   c. 10
   d. More information is needed to determine the formula result.

5 Functions
   a. are grouped by category.
   b. can be entered directly into a cell.
   c. can be entered as the result of a search.
   d. All of the above

6 Which formula will add the values in cells B3, C3, and D3?
   a. =B3+C3+D3
   b. =SUM(B3,C3,D3)
   c. =SUM(B3:D3)
   d. All of the above

7 Most functions require one or more _____ that specify what to calculate.
   a. lists
   b. rows
   c. arguments
   d. All of the above

8 The _____ group on the Home tab contains the tools for copying and pasting.
   a. Clipboard
   b. Font
   c. Number
   d. Editing

9 When you want to have a reference remain unchanged when you copy a formula, use this type of reference.
   a. fixed
   b. absolute
   c. relative
   d. circular

10 Press _____ to remove the contents of the selected cells.
   a. Backspace
   b. Tab
   c. Spacebar
   d. Delete

Hands-On Skills Review

Exercise **A** **Splitting the Bill**

Skills Use cell references; enter text, values, and dates; use the AutoFill feature; explore options for printing; enter a formula; enter a function; insert a function; use AutoSum; use absolute and relative cell references; copy and paste cell contents; and edit cell contents

Scenario You often meet with a large group of friends for lunch. One person picks up the bill and the tip at the restaurant, and then the others reimburse that person later on. You need a worksheet to calculate the correct amount for each person.

Steps

1. Open the student data file named **M6-C2-ExA-Tip.xlsx**. Save the file as **Lastname-M6-C2-ExA-Tip**, but replace *Lastname* with your last name.

2. Type your name in cell A2.

3. In cell B14, enter a formula that totals the meal costs.

4. Copy the formula so that totals display in the *TipDue* and *Totals* columns.

5. In cell C6, enter a formula that calculates the percentage of the first diner's meal out of the total meal, using an absolute reference in the appropriate place. The percentage for each person is the cost of his or her meal divided by the cost of all the meals.

6. Copy the formula from cell C6 down the column.

7. In cell D6, enter a formula that calculates the first diner's share of the tip, using the *Gratuity*

Percentage in cell B3 and an absolute reference where appropriate.

8. Copy the formula from cell D6 down the column.

9. In cell E6, enter a formula that adds the *Cost of Meal* and *Tip Due* for the first diner.

10. Copy the formula from cell E6 down the column.

11. Cell E14 displays pound signs because the number is too long to fit in the cell.

12. You realize that the gratuity paid was 20%. Change the entry in cell B3 to *20%*. The other values recalculate accordingly.

13. Save the workbook file.

14. Print or submit the completed workbook as directed by your instructor.

	A	B	C	D	E
1	**Tip Share Calculator**				
2	Student Name				
3	Gratuity Percentage	20%			
4					
5		Cost of Meal	Percentage of Total	Tip Due	Total
6	Jane	$ 21.50	19.47%	$ 4.30	$ 25.80
7	Allen	$ 17.12	15.50%	$ 3.42	$ 20.54
8	Tina	$ 9.95	9.01%	$ 1.99	$ 11.94
9	Tom	$ 7.95	7.20%	$ 1.59	$ 9.54
10	Fred	$ 4.50	4.07%	$ 0.90	$ 5.40
11	Kendall	$ 16.24	14.70%	$ 3.25	$ 19.49
12	Sasha	$ 18.19	16.47%	$ 3.64	$ 21.83
13	Kiki	$ 14.99	13.57%	$ 3.00	$ 17.99
14	**Total**	$ 110.44		$ 22.09	$ 132.53

Completed Exercise A

Exercise B Completing an Invoice

Skills   Use cell references; enter text, values, and dates; use the AutoFill feature; create a new worksheet; name and rename worksheets; explore options for printing; enter a formula; enter a function; insert a function; use absolute and relative cell references; copy and paste cell contents; and edit cell contents

Scenario   You sell security products for Endpoint, Inc. You create an invoice that totals the amount due for each item purchased based on the quantity, that calculates and adds tax, and that adds the amount of tax and invoice totals. Then you create a blank version of the worksheet that you can use as a starting point for additional invoices.

Steps

1 Open the student data file named **M6-C2-ExB-Invoice.xlsx**. Save the file as **Lastname-M6-C2-ExB-Invoice**, but replace *Lastname* with your last name.

2 Type your name in cell A3.

3 Change the entry for *Invoice Number* to *1010*.

4 Insert a function to change the entry for *Date* to the current date.

5 In cell D9, enter a formula that calculates the cost amount for the quantity purchased and then copy it through row 15.

6 In cell E9, enter a formula that calculates the tax due and then copy it through row 15. You will need to use an absolute reference.

7 In cell F9, enter a formula that adds the amount and tax for the first item and copy it through row 15.

8 Create a formula for *Tax Total* that totals the amount of tax for this order.

9 Create a formula that provides the invoice total in cell F18.

10 Adjust the width of column A so the contents of all cells are completely visible.

11 Select the range A1:F18, copy it, and then paste it to the Sheet2 sheet, using Paste options to keep the original column widths.

12 On Sheet2, clear the contents from cells B4:B5 and A9:C12 to prepare a blank invoice.

13 Rename Sheet2 Blank Invoice and Sheet1 Invoice 1010.

14 Save the workbook file.

15 Print or submit the completed workbook as directed by your instructor.

Completed Exercise B, Invoice 1010 + Blank Invoice

Exercise C Calculating Your Utility Budget

Skills Enter formulas, use Formula AutoComplete, use AutoSum, copy formulas, copy a range, edit a cell, use absolute references, and show formulas

Scenario You keep track of your monthly utility bills and want to use that data to create a budget for next year. You expect your utility bill will be higher based on modifications to your purchase plans as well as a projected percentage increase from all suppliers. Complete the budget and review its formulas.

Steps

1 Open the student data file named **M6-C2-ExC-UtilBudget.xlsx**. Save the file as **Lastname-M6-C2-ExC-UtilBudget**, but replace *Lastname* with your last name.

2 Type your name in cell A2.

3 Calculate the monthly totals in row 9.

4 Calculate the monthly averages in row 10.

5 In the range N5:P10, use functions to find the annual *Total*, *Average*, and *Max* values.

6 Copy the range A3:P10 and paste it at cell A14 to use the current year data as the base data for next year.

7 Change the entry in cell A14 to *Projected*.

8 Change the Water/Sewer values in the range B19:M19 to *$23.99*.

9 In cell A23, type Total Plus Increase.

10 In cell B23, enter a formula that multiplies the total from B20 by the *Increase Percentage* in cell B12. Do not use an absolute reference.

11 When you finish the entry, you can see that the amount calculated is below the total, which means the formula is incorrect. The amount shown is the increase, not the new total including the increase.

12 Edit the formula in cell B23, changing it so the formula adds the total to the increase, displaying a new total. Since you plan to copy this formula, you will need to use an absolute reference.

13 Copy the formula in cell B23 to the appropriate cells in row 23.

14 Apply Accounting format to B23:N23.

15 Save the workbook file.

16 Print or submit the completed workbook as directed by your instructor.

▲	A	B	C	D	E	F	G	H	I	J	K	L	M	N	O	P
1	**Utility Budget**															
2	Student Name															
3	**Current Year**															
4	Utility	Jan	Feb	Mar	Apr	May	Jun	Jul	Aug	Sep	Oct	Nov	Dec	Total	Average	Max
5	Mobile Phone	$ 75.50	$ 65.97	$ 72.93	$ 76.77	$ 75.50	$ 75.50	$ 98.22	$ 75.50	$ 93.09	$ 88.24	$101.99	$ 75.50	$ 974.71	$ 81.23	$ 101.99
6	Electricity	$ 78.22	$ 65.21	$ 56.12	$ 44.09	$ 65.09	$101.99	$121.99	$ 92.80	$ 88.55	$ 99.04	$115.15	$ 99.99	$ 1,028.24	$ 85.69	$ 121.99
7	Natural Gas	$215.09	$180.99	$176.77	$ 39.99	$ 14.90	$ 12.50	$ 10.50	$ 10.50	$ 67.04	$ 88.50	$ 97.65	$201.98	$ 1,116.41	$ 93.03	$ 215.09
8	Water/Sewer	$ 22.50	$ 22.50	$ 22.50	$ 22.50	$ 22.50	$ 22.50	$ 22.50	$ 22.50	$ 22.50	$ 22.50	$ 22.50	$ 22.50	$ 270.00	$ 22.50	$ 22.50
9	Total	$391.31	$334.67	$328.32	$183.35	$177.99	$212.49	$253.21	$201.30	$271.18	$298.28	$337.29	$399.97	$ 3,389.36	$ 282.45	$ 399.97
10	Average	$ 97.83	$ 83.67	$ 82.08	$ 45.84	$ 44.50	$ 53.12	$ 63.30	$ 50.33	$ 67.80	$ 74.57	$ 84.32	$ 99.99	$ 847.34	$ 70.61	$ 99.99
11																
12	Increase Percentage	5.90%														
13																
14	**Projected**															
15	Utility	Jan	Feb	Mar	Apr	May	Jun	Jul	Aug	Sep	Oct	Nov	Dec	Total	Average	Max
16	Mobile Phone	$ 75.50	$ 65.97	$ 72.93	$ 76.77	$ 75.50	$ 75.50	$ 98.22	$ 75.50	$ 93.09	$ 88.24	$101.99	$ 75.50	$ 974.71	$ 81.23	$ 101.99
17	Electricity	$ 78.22	$ 65.21	$ 56.12	$ 44.09	$ 65.09	$101.99	$121.99	$ 92.80	$ 88.55	$ 99.04	$115.15	$ 99.99	$ 1,028.24	$ 85.69	$ 121.99
18	Natural Gas	$215.09	$180.99	$176.77	$ 39.99	$ 14.90	$ 12.50	$ 10.50	$ 10.50	$ 67.04	$ 88.50	$ 97.65	$201.98	$ 1,116.41	$ 93.03	$ 215.09
19	Water/Sewer	$ 23.99	$ 23.99	$ 23.99	$ 23.99	$ 23.99	$ 23.99	$ 23.99	$ 23.99	$ 23.99	$ 23.99	$ 23.99	$ 23.99	$ 287.88	$ 23.99	$ 23.99
20	Total	$392.80	$336.16	$329.81	$184.84	$179.48	$213.98	$254.70	$202.79	$272.67	$299.77	$338.78	$401.46	$ 3,407.24	$ 283.94	$ 401.46
21	Average	$ 98.20	$ 84.04	$ 82.45	$ 46.21	$ 44.87	$ 53.50	$ 63.68	$ 50.70	$ 68.17	$ 74.94	$ 84.70	$100.37	$ 851.81	$ 70.98	$ 100.37
22																
23	Total Plus Increase	$415.98	$355.99	$349.27	$195.75	$190.07	$226.60	$269.73	$214.75	$288.76	$317.46	$358.77	$425.15	$ 3,608.27		

Completed Exercise C

Chapter 3

Formatting Cells

Applying formatting to worksheet cells provides organization and context. Formatting also clarifies the meaning of the data. For example, to specify whether Excel should format a cell value as a date, currency amount, or percentage, you would apply a number format. Other formatting tools, such as those that control font and size, determine how labels and values look and align within cells. You can also change the column width and row height to ensure entries display completely and correctly.

You can use other tools to group data visually. For example, you can apply a new fill color to cells that contain the column labels in a worksheet, or add a border around a range, or even merge cells together. You learn how to use formatting to enhance a worksheet in this chapter.

Skills You Learn

1 Apply number formats
2 Work with other formatting tools
3 Adjust column width and row height
4 Fill cells with a color
5 Add borders
6 Merge cells

Files You Need

In this chapter, you need the following student data file.

M6-C3-S1-MajorDonors.xlsx

As a non-profit organization, The Chocolate Museum accepts donations to help support their operating costs, exhibits, and educational programs. A staff member has created a worksheet to track donations made over the last few years. It's up to you to apply formatting to the worksheet.

Worksheet for Tracking Major Donors

	A	B	C	D	E	F	G
1		The Chocolate Museum					
2		Major Donors					
3	Updated:	Friday, March 23, 2012					
4							
5			Donation				
6	Donor ID	Donor/Organization Name	This Year	Last Year	Change in Dollars	Change in Percentage	Action Required
7	001	Mr. and Mrs. Jeff Butler	$ 1,500	$ 1,250	$250	20.0%	Donation receipt
8	002	Krell Foundation	$ 1,250	$ 1,500	($250)	-16.7%	Donation challenge
9	003	Ms. Wanda Matheson	$ 1,250	$ 1,250	$0	0.0%	Donation receipt
10	004	Carson Partners	$ 1,750	$ 1,850	($100)	-5.4%	Donation challenge
11	005	Dr. Peter Winter	$ -	$ 1,500	($1,500)	-100.0%	Reminder letter
12	006	Mr. and Mrs. Carl Thomas	$ 1,600	$ 1,460	$140	9.6%	Donation receipt
13	007	Peterson Family Foundation	$ 10,000	$ 7,500	$2,500	33.3%	Donation receipt
14	008	Miss Sylvia Phillips	$ 1,150	$ 1,150	$0	0.0%	Donation receipt
15	009	The Chocolatier, LLC	$ 1,750	$ 1,600	$150	9.4%	Donation receipt
16	010	Positivity Center	$ 2,500	$ 1,500	$1,000	66.7%	Donation receipt
17	011	Mr. and Mrs. James Lyon	$ 1,000	$ 500	$500	100.0%	Donation receipt
18	012	Mr. Fred Morgan	$ 1,250	$ 3,250	($2,000)	-61.5%	Donation receipt
19	Totals		$ 25,000	$ 24,310	$690	2.8%	

Excel

Skill 1

Apply Number Formats

Video M6_C3_S01

When you type an entry into a cell, it is automatically formatted according to the General format. When you type a date in a cell, Excel recognizes it and formats it automatically as a date. You can apply formats to add dollar signs, commas, and other characters to the cells. Applying a new format changes the display of an entry.

The number format applied to a cell holding numerical data determines how Excel displays the number. For example, applying the Accounting number format to a cell places, by default, a dollar symbol ($) to the left of the value, adds a thousands separator, adds two decimal places for the "cents," and aligns the amount in the cell according to the decimal point. You can apply other formats, such as date, currency, or percentage, and change number formats as needed.

Steps

1 Open the student data file named **M6-C3-S1-MajorDonors.xlsx** and, if you have not already done so, save the file in your Module 6 working folder on your storage medium.

2 Make cell B3 the active cell.

3 Enter the date 3/23 and then press Ctrl + Enter.

▶**Tip** When you do not include the year, Excel assumes you want the current year. Dates are stored as sequential serial numbers so they can be used in calculations.

4 Click the *Number Format* list box arrow in the Number group on the Home tab.

5 Click *Long Date*. The width of column B increases automatically to accommodate the longer number format.

6 Drag to select the range C7:D19.

7 *Another Way*
Click the *Number Format* list box arrow, and click *Accounting*.

7 Click the Accounting Number Format button in the Number group on the Home tab.

▶**Tip** Excel will recognize some number formats when you type special symbols, such as dollar signs and percent signs.

8 Click the Decrease Decimal button in the Number group on the Home tab two times.

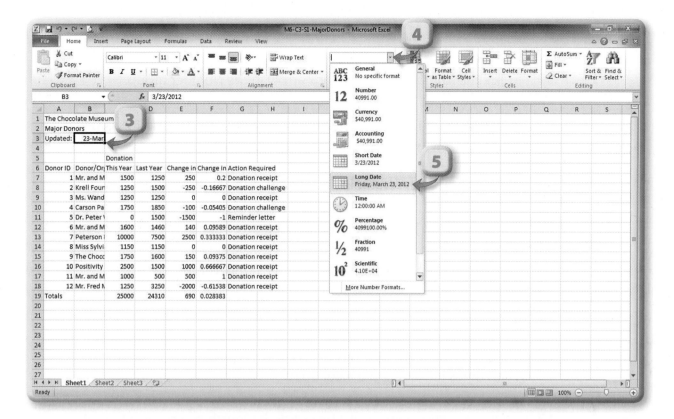

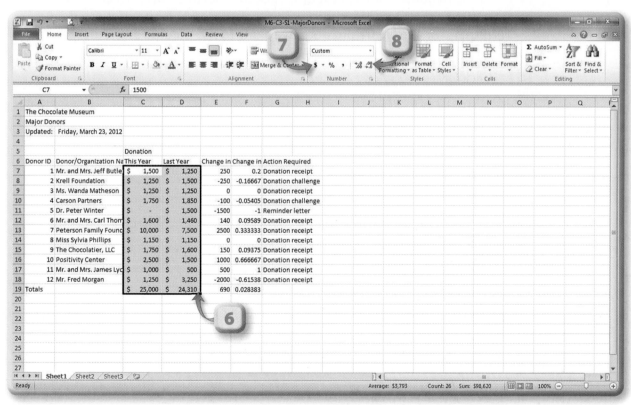

Excel

9 Drag to select the range E7:E19.

10 Click the *Number Format* list box arrow in the Number group.

11 Click *Accounting* from the drop-down list. This format displays negative values in parentheses.

12 Click the *Number Format* list box arrow in the Number group.

13 Click *Currency*. This format displays negative values with a minus sign (-).

14 Click the *Number Format* list box arrow in the Number group.

15 Click *More Number Formats*. This opens the Format Cells dialog box.

16 *Another Way*
Highlight the number and type in the decimal places box.

16 In the Format Cells dialog box, click the *Decimal places* down-pointing arrow two times to change the value to *0*.

17 In the *Negative numbers* list box, click the fourth choice, which displays negative numbers in red and with parentheses. This changes the default display for currency from negative signs to red parentheses.

18 Click OK.

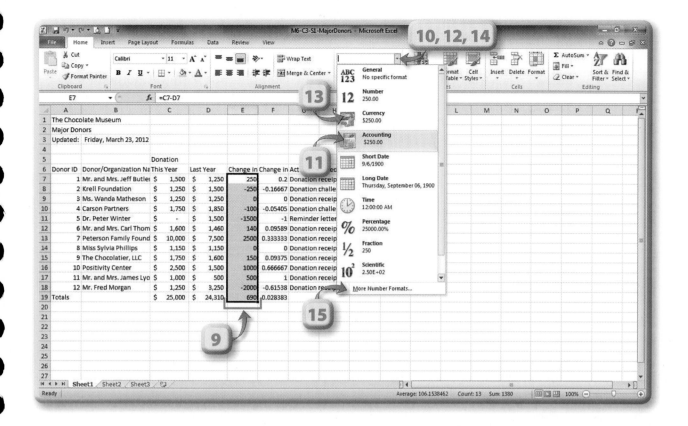

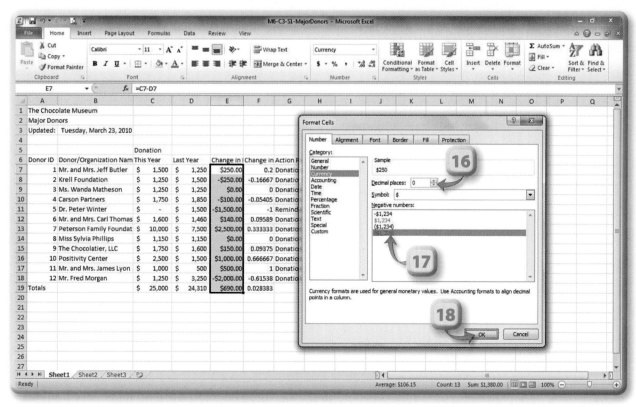

More

19 Drag to select the range F7:F19.

20 Click the Percent Style button in the Number group on the Home tab.

21 Click the Increase Decimal button in the Number group on the Home tab.

22 Drag to select the range A7:A18.

23 Click the Number group dialog box launcher button on the Home tab.

24 In the Format Cells dialog box with the Number tab selected, click *Custom* in the *Category* list.

25 Double-click *General* in the *Type* text box, and type 00#.

26 Click OK.

27 Save the file.

> ▶ **Tip** Steps 24–26 create and apply a custom style, something you can do if none of the existing styles and options displays a number the way you prefer.

◢	A	B	C	D	E	F	G	H	I
1	The Chocolate Museum								
2	Major Donors								
3	Updated:	Tuesday, March 23, 2010							
4									
5			Donation						
6	Donor ID	Donor/Organization Nam	This Year	Last Year	Change in I	Change in	Action Required		
7	001	Mr. and Mrs. Jeff Butler	$ 1,500	$ 1,250	$250	20.0%	Donation receipt		
8	002	Krell Foundation	$ 1,250	$ 1,500	($250)	-16.7%	Donation challenge		
9	003	Ms. Wanda Matheson	$ 1,250	$ 1,250	$0	0.0%	Donation receipt		
10	004	Carson Partners	$ 1,750	$ 1,850	($100)	-5.4%	Donation challenge		
11	005	Dr. Peter Winter	$ -	$ 1,500	($1,500)	-100.0%	Reminder letter		
12	006	Mr. and Mrs. Carl Thomas	$ 1,600	$ 1,460	$140	9.6%	Donation receipt		
13	007	Peterson Family Foundat	$ 10,000	$ 7,500	$2,500	33.3%	Donation receipt		
14	008	Miss Sylvia Phillips	$ 1,150	$ 1,150	$0	0.0%	Donation receipt		
15	009	The Chocolatier, LLC	$ 1,750	$ 1,600	$150	9.4%	Donation receipt		
16	010	Positivity Center	$ 2,500	$ 1,500	$1,000	66.7%	Donation receipt		
17	011	Mr. and Mrs. James Lyon	$ 1,000	$ 500	$500	100.0%	Donation receipt		
18	012	Mr. Fred Morgan	$ 1,250	$ 3,250	($2,000)	-61.5%	Donation receipt		
19	Totals		$ 25,000	$ 24,310	$690	2.8%			
20									

Completed Skill 1

Taking It Further

More Choices for Number Formatting
Some variations of the number formats are available as styles in the Cell Styles gallery. Click the Home tab and then click the Cell Styles button in the Styles group to access the gallery. The *Number Format* section of the gallery lists the number styles you can apply. You also can click *New Cell Style* to create a custom cell style to apply to the selected cell or range.

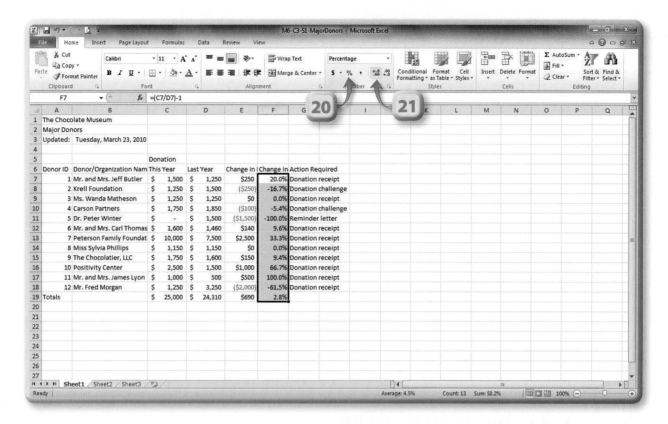

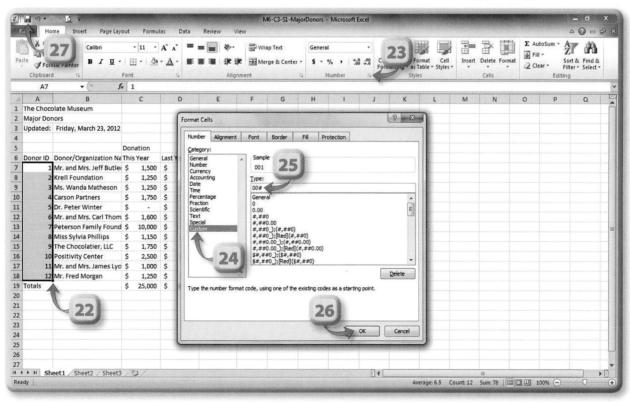

Excel

Excel

Skill 2

Work with Other Formatting Tools

Video M6_C3_S02

Excel lets you apply a variety of formats to cells to change the basic look of a worksheet. You also can use the Increase Font Size and Decrease Font Size buttons to adjust the size of the contents of selected cells.

You can also apply bold, italic, and underlining, as well as change the color of the text and the cell background. Use the alignment tools to change the vertical and horizontal alignment of cell entries. The Cell Styles button in the styles group of the Home tab lets you apply several formatting settings at once.

Steps

1 If it is not already open, open **M6-C3-S1-MajorDonors.xlsx**, the file you saved in the previous skill, and save the file as **M6-C3-S2-MajorDonors**.

2 Make cell A1 the active cell.

3 Click the Cell Styles button in the Styles group on the Home tab.

4 Click *Title* in the *Titles and Headings* section to apply the Title style to the selected cell.

5 Drag to select the range A2:B3.

6 Click the *Font* list box arrow in the Font group.

7 Click *Cambria* under *Theme Fonts*.

Tip Font size is measured in points (pt), with each point equal to 1/72nd of an inch.

8 Click the Increase Font Size button twice.

9 Drag to select the range A5:G6.

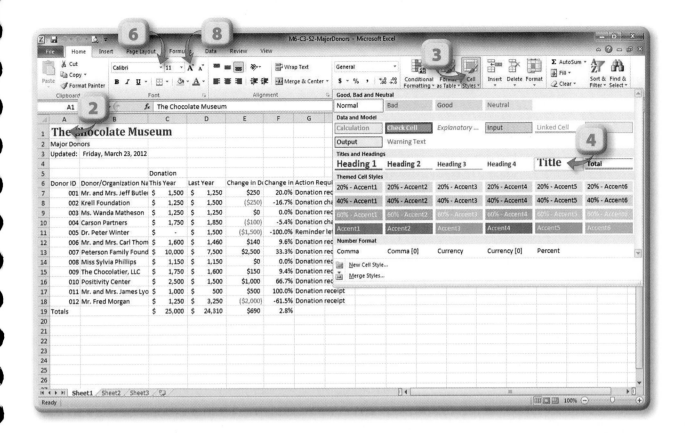

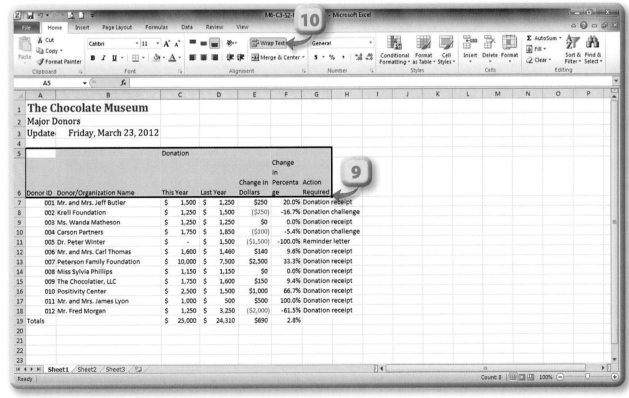

More

10 Click the Wrap Text button in the Alignment group on the Home tab.

11 Click the Cell Styles button in the Styles group on the Home tab.

13 *Shortcut*
Bold
Ctrl + B

▶**Tip** If you want to combine a cell style with other Font group formatting, apply the style first.

12 Click *Accent2* in the *Themed Cells Styles* section.

13 Click the Bold button in the Font group on the Home tab.

14 Drag to select the range A19:F19.

15 *Shortcut*
Italic
Ctrl + I

15 Click the Italic button in the Font group on the Home tab.

▶**Tip** To apply underlining to text, use the keyboard shortcut Ctrl + U or the Underline button in the Font group on the Home tab.

16 Make cell G11 the active cell.

17 Click the Font Color button arrow in the Font group on the Home tab.

18 Click *Orange, Accent 6* (the rightmost color in the top row of the *Theme Colors* section).

19 Save the file.

	A	B	C	D	E	F	G	H
1	**The Chocolate Museum**							
2	Major Donors							
3	Update Friday, March 23, 2012							
4								
5			Donation			Change in		
6	Donor ID	Donor/Organization Name	This Year	Last Year	Change in Dollars	Percentage	Action Required	
7	001	Mr. and Mrs. Jeff Butler	$ 1,500	$ 1,250	$250	20.0%	Donation receipt	
8	002	Krell Foundation	$ 1,250	$ 1,500	($250)	-16.7%	Donation challenge	
9	003	Ms. Wanda Matheson	$ 1,250	$ 1,250	$0	0.0%	Donation receipt	
10	004	Carson Partners	$ 1,750	$ 1,850	($100)	-5.4%	Donation challenge	
11	005	Dr. Peter Winter	$ -	$ 1,500	($1,500)	-100.0%	Reminder letter	
12	006	Mr. and Mrs. Carl Thomas	$ 1,600	$ 1,460	$140	9.6%	Donation receipt	
13	007	Peterson Family Foundation	$ 10,000	$ 7,500	$2,500	33.3%	Donation receipt	
14	008	Miss Sylvia Phillips	$ 1,150	$ 1,150	$0	0.0%	Donation receipt	
15	009	The Chocolatier, LLC	$ 1,750	$ 1,600	$150	9.4%	Donation receipt	
16	010	Positivity Center	$ 2,500	$ 1,500	$1,000	66.7%	Donation receipt	
17	011	Mr. and Mrs. James Lyon	$ 1,000	$ 500	$500	100.0%	Donation receipt	
18	012	Mr. Fred Morgan	$ 1,250	$ 3,250	($2,000)	-61.5%	Donation receipt	
19	Totals		$ 25,000	$ 24,310	$690	2.8%		
20								

Completed Skill 2

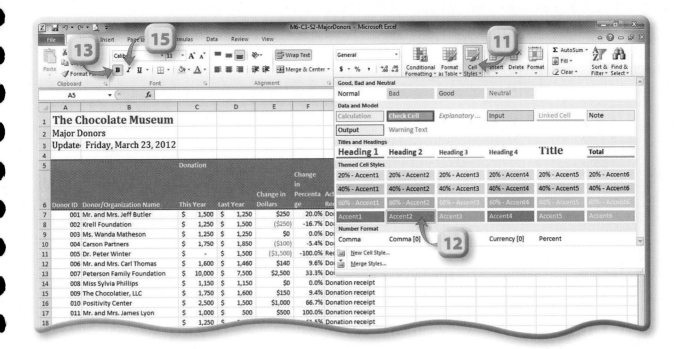

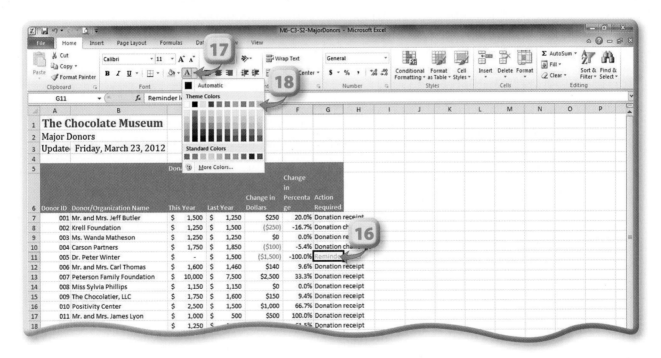

Taking It Further

Changing the Theme You can change the overall look of the worksheets in a workbook simply by changing the theme. The theme supplies the overall formatting settings for the workbook file, including the theme fonts (those used by default for that specific theme), theme colors, theme effects, and cell styles. If you have applied your own cell styles or if you have chosen a theme and decide you do not like it, you can choose another. You can do so by clicking the Themes button in the Themes group on the Page Layout tab and then clicking the theme you want. Pointing to any theme displays a Live Preview of the changes it applies.

Excel

Skill 3   Adjust Column Width and Row Height

Video M6_C3_S03

When you perform some actions, such as when you change the cell format, Excel automatically widens a column or increases the height of a row. If you make a change and Excel doesn't automatically widen the column or increase the height of the row to accomodate the changed entry, you could find that some entries don't fit into their cells. If the cell to the right is empty, the long entry simply runs over, into the cell(s) to the right. But if the cell to the right is not empty and the entry is text, Excel only displays as much of the entry that fits in the cell, hiding the rest. If the entry is a number that is too large to display in the cell width, Excel displays a string of pound signs (######) to cue you that the numeric cell entry does not fit. You need to resize the column.

You may need to adjust the row height when you wrap text or increase font size. Modifying row height and column width can also help make the worksheet more readable.

Steps

1. If it is not already open, open **M6-C3-S2-MajorDonors.xlsx**, the file you saved in the previous skill, and save the file as **M6-C3-S3-MajorDonors**.

2. Make cell A1 the active cell.

3. Click the Format button in the Cells group on the Home tab.

4. Click *Row Height* in the *Cell Size* section of the drop-down list.

5. Type 35 in the *Row height* text box.

6. Click OK to close the dialog box.

7. Click the Middle Align button in the Alignment group on the Home tab.

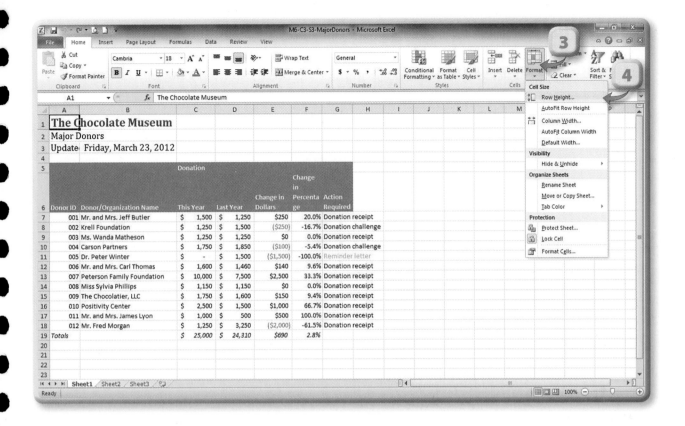

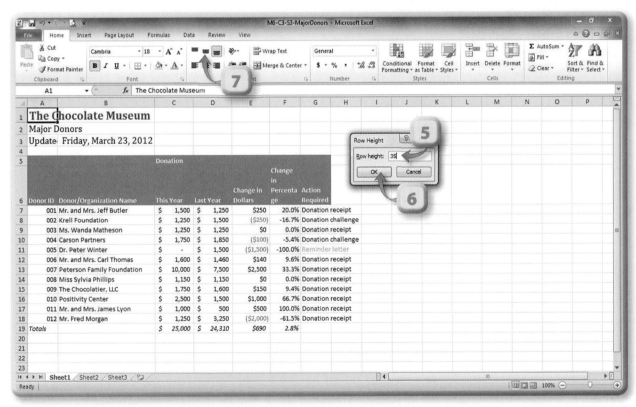

More

8   Make a cell in column F the active cell.

9   Click the Format button in the Cells group on the Home tab.

10 **Another Way**
Click the AutoFit Column Width button in the *Cell Size* section to AutoFit the column to its widest entry.

10   Click *Column Width* in the *Cell Size* section of the drop-down list.

11   Type 12 in the *Column width* text box.

12   Click OK to close the dialog box.

13   Move the mouse pointer over the right border of the column G column heading until the mouse pointer becomes a vertical line with a left- and right-pointing arrow, and double-click to allow Excel to AutoFit the column size.

14   Move the mouse pointer over the right border of the column A column heading until the mouse pointer becomes a vertical line with a left- and right-pointing arrow, drag right until the ScreenTip reads *Width: 11.00 (82 pixels)*, and then release the mouse button.

Tip When text wrapping is applied to cells in a row, the row height does not decrease automatically to fit the text. You have to manually reduce the row height to fit the text.

15   Move the mouse pointer over the bottom border of the row 6 row heading until the mouse pointer becomes a horizontal line with an up- and down-pointing arrow, and double-click.

16   Save the file.

	A	B	C	D	E	F	G
1	**The Chocolate Museum**						
2	Major Donors						
3	Updated:	Friday, March 23, 2012					
4							
5			Donation				
6	Donor ID	Donor/Organization Name	This Year	Last Year	Change in Dollars	Change in Percentage	Action Required
7	001	Mr. and Mrs. Jeff Butler	$ 1,500	$ 1,250	$250	20.0%	Donation receipt
8	002	Krell Foundation	$ 1,250	$ 1,500	($250)	-16.7%	Donation challenge
9	003	Ms. Wanda Matheson	$ 1,250	$ 1,250	$0	0.0%	Donation receipt
10	004	Carson Partners	$ 1,750	$ 1,850	($100)	-5.4%	Donation challenge
11	005	Dr. Peter Winter	$ -	$ 1,500	($1,500)	-100.0%	Reminder letter
12	006	Mr. and Mrs. Carl Thomas	$ 1,600	$ 1,460	$140	9.6%	Donation receipt
13	007	Peterson Family Foundation	$ 10,000	$ 7,500	$2,500	33.3%	Donation receipt
14	008	Miss Sylvia Phillips	$ 1,150	$ 1,150	$0	0.0%	Donation receipt
15	009	The Chocolatier, LLC	$ 1,750	$ 1,600	$150	9.4%	Donation receipt
16	010	Positivity Center	$ 2,500	$ 1,500	$1,000	66.7%	Donation receipt
17	011	Mr. and Mrs. James Lyon	$ 1,000	$ 500	$500	100.0%	Donation receipt
18	012	Mr. Fred Morgan	$ 1,250	$ 3,250	($2,000)	-61.5%	Donation receipt
19	*Totals*		$ 25,000	$ 24,310	$690	2.8%	
20							

Completed Skill 3

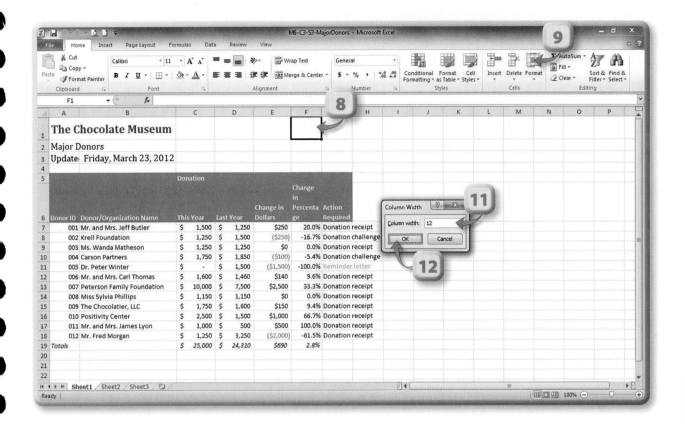

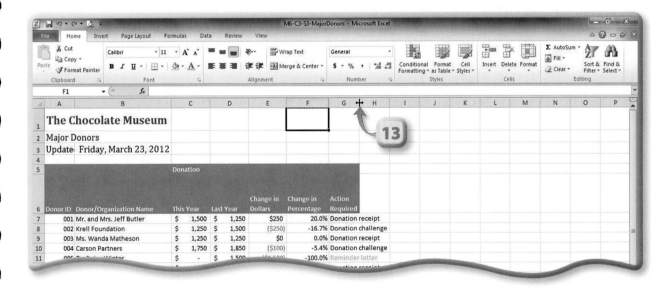

Taking It Further

Changing Column Width Default Settings
With the default Office Theme applied, the default column width is 8.43 characters and the default row height is 15 points. Changing the theme applied to the workbook may change these defaults. You can adjust the

default column setting by clicking *Default Width* on the Format menu in the Cells group on the Home tab. A dialog box then displays for you to enter a new *Standard column width* for the workbook.

Excel

Video | M6_C3_S04

Fill Cells with a Color

You can color fill a selected cell or cell range independent of other settings. Click the drop-down arrow for the Fill Color tool in the Font group on the Home tab to display a gallery of colors. You can then click a color to apply it to the selection. Conveniently, the color you applied most recently appears on the button itself. You can simply click the button to apply that same color to other selections.

Another way to apply formatting is by using the Format Painter button in the Clipboard group of the Home tab. Make the cell with the formatting you wish to apply the active cell, click the Format Painter button, and then click the cell you wish to format.

Steps

1. If it is not already open, open **M6-C3-S3-MajorDonors.xlsx**, the file you saved in the previous skill, and save the file as **M6-C3-S4-MajorDonors**.

2. Make cell A1 the active cell.

3. Click the Fill Color button arrow in the Font group on the Home tab.

4. Click *Olive Green, Accent 3, Lighter 40%* (the fourth color down in the seventh column) in the *Theme Colors* section of the palette. The title is not completely shaded, but you fix this in the final skill in this chapter.

5. Drag to select the range A19:G19.

6. Click the Fill Color button in the Font group on the Home tab. Excel fills the selection with the color you clicked in Step 4.

7. Make cell G8 the active cell.

8. Click the Fill Color button arrow in the Font group on the Home tab.

9. Click *Yellow* (the fourth option) in the *Standard Colors* section.

10. Click cell G10.

11. Click the Fill Color button in the Font group on the Home tab. Excel fills the selection with the color you used in Step 9.

12. Save the file.

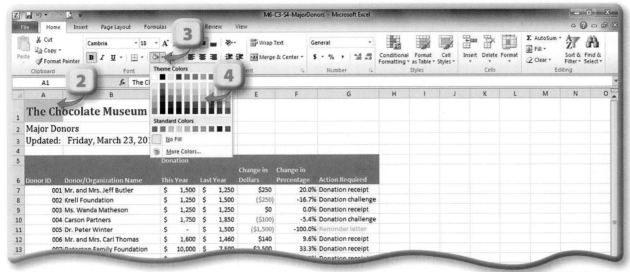

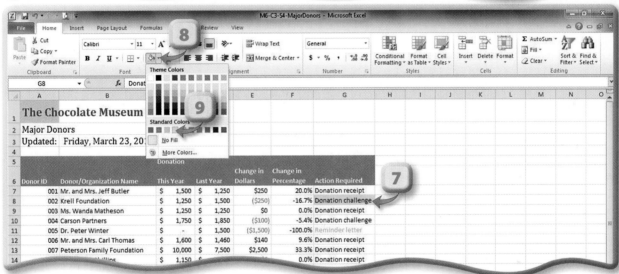

	A	B	C	D	E	F	G
1	**The Chocolate Museum**						
2	Major Donors						
3	Updated: Friday, March 23, 2012						
4							
5			Donation				
6	Donor ID	Donor/Organization Name	This Year	Last Year	Change in Dollars	Change in Percentage	Action Required
7	001	Mr. and Mrs. Jeff Butler	$ 1,500	$ 1,250	$250	20.0%	Donation receipt
8	002	Krell Foundation	$ 1,250	$ 1,500	($250)	-16.7%	Donation challenge
9	003	Ms. Wanda Matheson	$ 1,250	$ 1,250	$0	0.0%	Donation receipt
10	004	Carson Partners	$ 1,750	$ 1,850	($100)	-5.4%	Donation challenge
11	005	Dr. Peter Winter	$ -	$ 1,500	($1,500)	-100.0%	Reminder letter
12	006	Mr. and Mrs. Carl Thomas	$ 1,600	$ 1,460	$140	9.6%	Donation receipt
13	007	Peterson Family Foundation	$ 10,000	$ 7,500	$2,500	33.3%	Donation receipt
14	008	Miss Sylvia Phillips	$ 1,150	$ 1,150	$0	0.0%	Donation receipt
15	009	The Chocolatier, LLC	$ 1,750	$ 1,600	$150	9.4%	Donation receipt
16	010	Positivity Center	$ 2,500	$ 1,500	$1,000	66.7%	Donation receipt
17	011	Mr. and Mrs. James Lyon	$ 1,000	$ 500	$500	100.0%	Donation receipt
18	012	Mr. Fred Morgan	$ 1,250	$ 3,250	($2,000)	-61.5%	Donation receipt
19	Totals		$ 25,000	$ 24,310	$690	2.8%	
20							

Completed Skill 4

Excel

Excel

Add Borders

Video M6_C3_S05

Applying a border around a cell or cell range in a worksheet provides another way to group or emphasize the data visually. Borders can be especially useful when you use the default print setting and print a worksheet without cell gridlines. For example, accountants often place a single border at the top and a double border at the bottom of a row presenting data totals. You also can use a border to set off a range where the user should type in data for calculations or to highlight important data or formula results. Lastly, you can add borders as purely decorative elements—but make sure the border appearance fits with the other formatting that you have applied.

Steps

1 If it is not already open, open **M6-C3-S4-MajorDonors.xlsx**, the file you saved in the previous skill, and save the file as **M6-C3-S5-MajorDonors**.

2 Make cell A2 the active cell.

▶ **Tip** In Step 3, you should not worry that the border does not underline all of the text in cell A2. The next skill teaches you how to address that issue.

3 Click the Borders button in the Font group on the Home tab. Excel applies a single border to the bottom of the cell.

4 Drag to select the range A19:G19.

▶ **Tip** In Step 3, if a border other than a bottom border appears, open the Borders button drop-down list and click *Bottom Border*.

5 Click the Borders button arrow in the Font group on the Home tab.

6 Click *Top and Double Bottom Border* in the *Borders* section of the drop-down list.

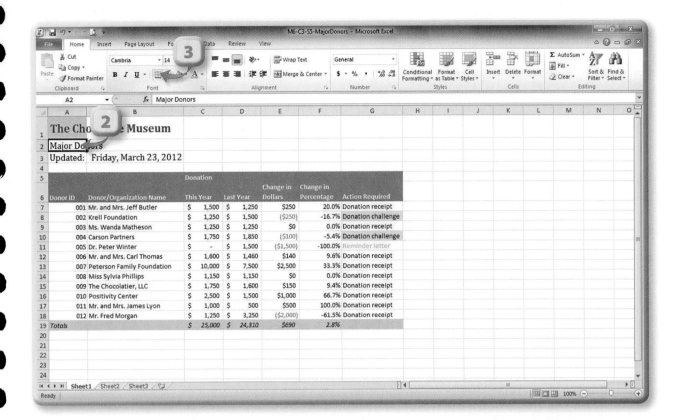

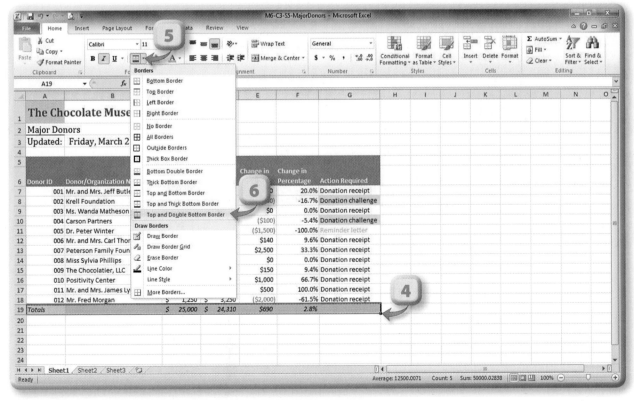

More

7   Drag to select the range A11:G11.

8   Hold down the Ctrl key, drag to select the range A17:G17, and then release the Ctrl key.

9   Click the Borders button arrow in the Font group on the Home tab.

10   Click *More Borders* from the drop-down list.

11   On the Border tab of the Format Cells dialog box, click the *Color* arrow.

12   Click *Purple, Accent 4* (the first color in the eighth column) in the *Theme Colors* section of the palette.

▶**Tip** The Outline preset places the border around the entire range, not around each individual cell in the range.

13   Click the Outline button under the *Presets* section.

14   Click OK.

15   Save the file.

◢	A	B	C	D	E	F	G
1	**The Chocolate Museum**						
2	Major Donors						
3	Updated: Friday, March 23, 2012						
4							
5			Donation				
6	Donor ID	Donor/Organization Name	This Year	Last Year	Change in Dollars	Change in Percentage	Action Required
7	001	Mr. and Mrs. Jeff Butler	$ 1,500	$ 1,250	$250	20.0%	Donation receipt
8	002	Krell Foundation	$ 1,250	$ 1,500	($250)	-16.7%	Donation challenge
9	003	Ms. Wanda Matheson	$ 1,250	$ 1,250	$0	0.0%	Donation receipt
10	004	Carson Partners	$ 1,750	$ 1,850	($100)	-5.4%	Donation challenge
11	005	Dr. Peter Winter	$ -	$ 1,500	($1,500)	-100.0%	Reminder letter
12	006	Mr. and Mrs. Carl Thomas	$ 1,600	$ 1,460	$140	9.6%	Donation receipt
13	007	Peterson Family Foundation	$ 10,000	$ 7,500	$2,500	33.3%	Donation receipt
14	008	Miss Sylvia Phillips	$ 1,150	$ 1,150	$0	0.0%	Donation receipt
15	009	The Chocolatier, LLC	$ 1,750	$ 1,600	$150	9.4%	Donation receipt
16	010	Positivity Center	$ 2,500	$ 1,500	$1,000	66.7%	Donation receipt
17	011	Mr. and Mrs. James Lyon	$ 1,000	$ 500	$500	100.0%	Donation receipt
18	012	Mr. Fred Morgan	$ 1,250	$ 3,250	($2,000)	-61.5%	Donation receipt
19	*Totals*		$ 25,000	$ 24,310	$690	2.8%	
20							

Completed Skill 5

Excel

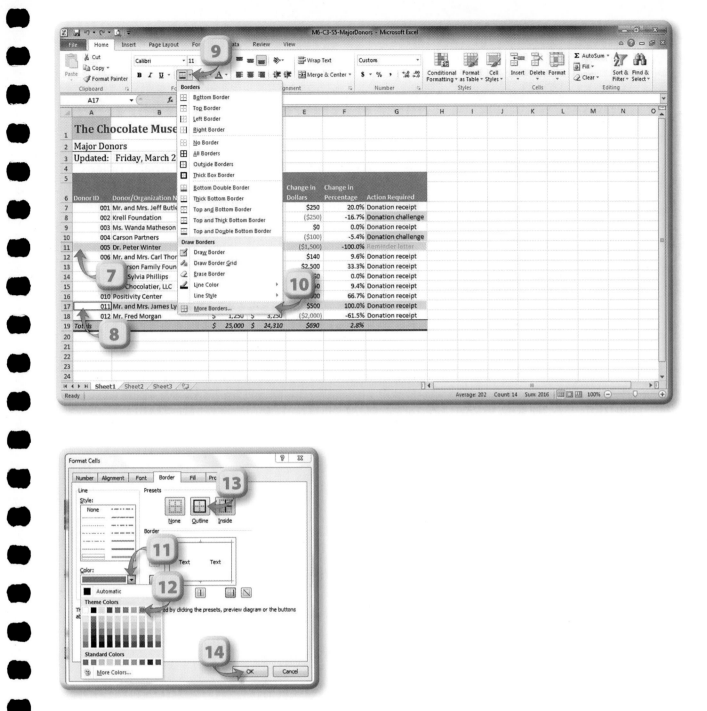

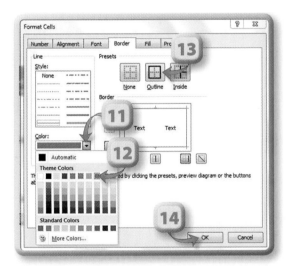

Taking It Further

More Border Options   When you click *More Borders* to display the Format Cells dialog box, you can see a Style list that enables you to choose another border weight or a different border appearance, such as dashed or dotted. Because these border styles are a bit less formal than a plain cell border or outline, you should use them sparingly, especially in business documents.

Excel

Skill 6

Video M6_C3_S06

Merge Cells

To enhance the readability of a worksheet, you might choose to center the sheet title across all the columns of data in the sheet. In Excel you can use the Merge & Center button in the Alignment group on the Home tab to combine selected cells into a single cell. The combined text is centered in the single cell.

The Merge & Center button also includes a drop-down list arrow. The three additional choices on this list enable you to merge the columns across each selected row without merging the rows themselves (Merge Across), as well as merging a range into a single cell (Merge Cells) and unmerging a merged cell (Unmerge Cells).

Steps

1. If it is not already open, open **M6-C3-S5-MajorDonors.xlsx**, the file you saved in the previous skill, and save the file as **Lastname-M6-C3-S6-MajorDonors**, but replace *Lastname* with your last name. Be sure to save the file in your Module 6 working folder on your storage medium.

2. Drag to select the range C5:D5.

3. On the Home tab, click the Merge & Center button in the Alignment group. This action merges and centers a title that is common to the two columns of data.

4. Click the Cell Styles button in the Styles group on the Home tab.

5. Click *60% - Accent 3* from the *Themed Cell Styles* section of the gallery.

6. Drag to select the range A1:G2.

7. Click the Merge & Center button arrow in the Alignment group on the Home tab.

8. Click *Merge Across* from the drop-down list.

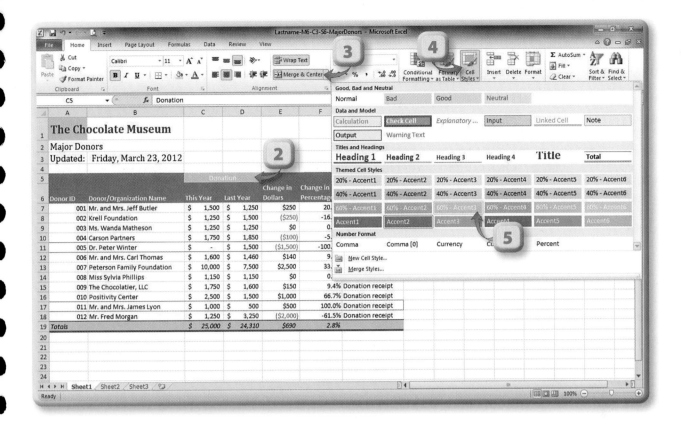

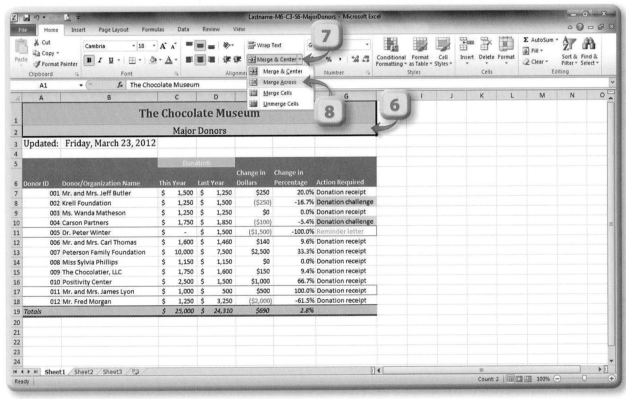

More

9 Click the Center button in the Alignment group on the Home tab.

Tip The cell address listed in the Name box in the top-left corner is the address for the far left cell in the merged range.

10 Make cell A2 the active cell.

11 Click the Borders button arrow in the Font group on the Home tab.

12 Click *Bottom Border* in the *Borders* section of the drop-down list.

Tip Be sure to check all formatting when merging and centering. In this case, merging removed the previously applied bottom border, so you must reapply the border.

13 Save and close the file.

	A	B	C	D	E	F	G
1				**The Chocolate Museum**			
2				Major Donors			
3	Updated:	Friday, March 23, 2012					
4							
5			Donation				
6	Donor ID	Donor/Organization Name	This Year	Last Year	Change in Dollars	Change in Percentage	Action Required
7	001	Mr. and Mrs. Jeff Butler	$ 1,500	$ 1,250	$250	20.0%	Donation receipt
8	002	Krell Foundation	$ 1,250	$ 1,500	($250)	-16.7%	Donation challenge
9	003	Ms. Wanda Matheson	$ 1,250	$ 1,250	$0	0.0%	Donation receipt
10	004	Carson Partners	$ 1,750	$ 1,850	($100)	-5.4%	Donation challenge
11	005	Dr. Peter Winter	$ -	$ 1,500	($1,500)	-100.0%	Reminder letter
12	006	Mr. and Mrs. Carl Thomas	$ 1,600	$ 1,460	$140	9.6%	Donation receipt
13	007	Peterson Family Foundation	$ 10,000	$ 7,500	$2,500	33.3%	Donation receipt
14	008	Miss Sylvia Phillips	$ 1,150	$ 1,150	$0	0.0%	Donation receipt
15	009	The Chocolatier, LLC	$ 1,750	$ 1,600	$150	9.4%	Donation receipt
16	010	Positivity Center	$ 2,500	$ 1,500	$1,000	66.7%	Donation receipt
17	011	Mr. and Mrs. James Lyon	$ 1,000	$ 500	$500	100.0%	Donation receipt
18	012	Mr. Fred Morgan	$ 1,250	$ 3,250	($2,000)	-61.5%	Donation receipt
19	Totals		$ 25,000	$ 24,310	$690	2.8%	
20							

Completed Skill 6

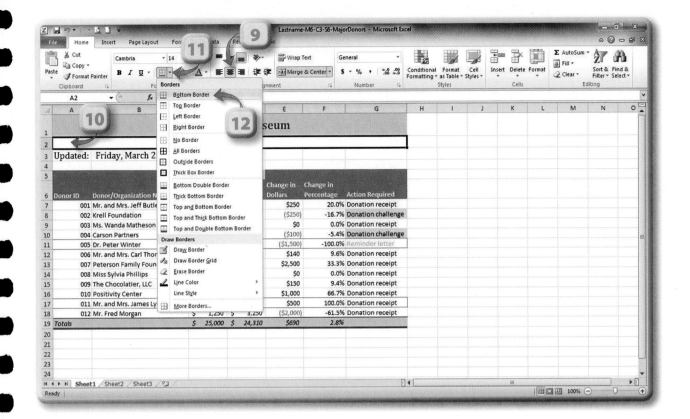

Taking It Further

Designing Worksheets In this skill you created a balanced appearance in the completed worksheet by using the same fill color for the top and bottom rows and limiting the number of formats applied.

Keeping your design simple and taking advantage of the color palette supplied by the theme helps you to design professional workbooks and worksheets that highlight the most important data for decision making.

Tasks Summary

Task	Ribbon Tab, Group	Button, Option	Shortcut, Alternative
Choose a number format	Home, Number	General	
Apply Accounting Number format	Home, Number	$	
Apply Percent Style format	Home, Number	%	
Apply Comma Style format	Home, Number	,	
Increase or decrease decimal places	Home, Number	←.0 .00 / .00 →.0	
Apply a cell style	Home, Styles		
Copy a cell style	Home, Clipboard		
Change the font	Home, Font	Calibri	
Change the font size	Home, Font	11	
Increase or decrease the font size	Home, Font	A^ A^	
Apply bold	Home, Font	B	Ctrl + B
Apply italics	Home, Font	I	Ctrl + I
Apply underline	Home, Font	U	Ctrl + U
Change character color	Home, Font	A	
Wrap cell entries	Home, Alignment		Press Alt + Enter when making a cell entry to wrap lines manually
Change vertical or horizontal cell alignments	Home, Alignment	☰ ☰ ☰ / ☰ ☰ ☰	
Change column width or row height	Home, Cells	Column Width or Row Height	Drag or double-click the right column border or bottom row border

Task	Ribbon Tab, Group	Button, Option	Shortcut, Alternative
Fill a cell with color	Home, Font		F2, or double-click cell
Add borders to a cell or selection	Home, Font		
Merge cells	Home, Alignment		

Features Review

Select the best answer from the choices given.

1 This number format applies a currency symbol, adds two decimal places, and changes the cell's alignment.
a. Accounting
b. Number
c. Percent
d. General

2 Use the Format Painter to
a. choose a background color for a cell.
b. shrink the width of the text in a cell.
c. copy formatting from one cell to another cell.
d. copy a formula from one cell to another cell.

3 When creating a worksheet, it is good professional style to
a. make each column a different color.
b. use borders to help organize the worksheet into sections.
c. select the Accounting number style for entries that represent money.
d. Both b and c are correct.

4 If you do not modify the display of a cell, the cell entry displays using which format?
a. Accounting
b. Number
c. Currency
d. General

5 Excel stores dates as
a. labels.
b. cell references.
c. sequential serial numbers.
d. All of the above

6 Use the _____ feature to display a cell's entry on multiple lines within the cell.
a. wrap text
b. Merge & Center
c. borders
d. cell styles

7 Use the _____ feature to combine multiple cells into a single cell.
a. wrap text
b. Merge & Center
c. borders
d. cell styles

8 These may include font, border, fill, and other formatting settings.
a. wrap text
b. Merge & Center
c. borders
d. cell styles

9 Applying _____ helps set off data, which especially helps the reader if you do not print gridlines.
a. wrap text
b. Merge & Center
c. formulas
d. cell styles

10 The _____ feature helps you size a row or column automatically.
a. Format Painter
b. wrap text
c. Format Cells
d. AutoFit

Exercise **Formatting a Tip Shares Worksheet**

Skills Use a cell style, apply number formats, work with other formatting tools, adjust column width and row height, fill cells with color, and merge cells

Scenario You are working with another tip calculation worksheet. This time, you apply formatting to make the worksheet more attractive.

Steps

1 Open the student data file named **M6-C3-ExA-Tip.xlsx** and save the file as **Lastname-M6-C3-ExA-Tip**, but replace *Lastname* with your last name.

2 Type your name in cell A2.

3 Apply the Title cell style to cell A1 and change the font color to Olive Green, Accent 4, Lighter 40%.

4 Merge and center cells A1:E1.

5 Increase the font size for cells A3:B3 to 14, and apply bold.

6 Format the entry in cell B3 to use the Percent Style with zero decimal places.

7 Format the ranges B6:B12 and D6:D12 to use Accounting number format with two decimal places.

8 Format the range C6:C11 to use Percent Style with two decimal places.

9 Fill the range A5:E5 with Blue-Gray, Accent 6, Lighter 40%.

10 Change the font color for A5:E5 to white, apply bold, and center and wrap the text.

11 Autofit the columns as needed.

12 Autofit the height of row 5.

13 Select the range A12:E12, and apply the Total cell style and format with two decimal places.

14 Apply the Blue-Gray, Accent 6, Lighter 40% fill to A12:E12.

15 Save the file.

16 Print or submit the completed worksheet as directed by your instructor.

	A	B	C	D	E	F
1			Tip Share Calculator			
2	Student Name					
3	Gratuity	18%				
4						
5		Cost of Meal	Percentage of Total	Tip Due	Total	
6	Robert	$ 21.50	21.94%	$ 3.87	$ 25.37	
7	Allen	$ 17.12	17.47%	$ 3.08	$ 20.20	
8	Tina	$ 9.95	10.15%	$ 1.79	$ 11.74	
9	Kendall	$ 16.24	16.57%	$ 2.92	$ 19.16	
10	Sasha	$ 18.19	18.56%	$ 3.27	$ 21.46	
11	Kiki	$ 14.99	15.30%	$ 2.70	$ 17.69	
12	Total	$ 97.99		$ 17.64	$115.63	
13						

Completed Exercise A

Exercise B Formatting Stock Portfolio Information

Skills Insert and delete columns and rows, explore options for printing, apply number formats, work with other formatting tools, adjust column width and row height, fill cells with a color, add borders, and merge cells

Scenario You track a portfolio of stocks and other securities using an online service such as Yahoo! Finance. You are able to download daily quote data, but it downloads in a raw, unformatted version that makes it difficult to review. Apply formatting to make the downloaded data more attractive and useful.

Steps

1 Open the student data file named **M6-C3-ExB-Quotes.xlsx** and save the file as **Lastname-M6-C3-ExB-Quotes**, but replace *Lastname* with your last name.

2 Type your name in cell A28.

3 Delete column D, which holds time information.

4 Insert two new rows at the top of the sheet, and then type Quotes in cell A1.

5 Format the cell A1 text to be 24 pt. size in Aqua, Accent 5 color.

6 Use Merge & Center to combine cells A1:G1.

7 Select the cells in the *Closing Price* and *Change* columns and apply the Currency number format with two decimal places while displaying negative values in red with parentheses.

8 Apply a date format to the cells in the *Date* column that displays the dates in 3/14 format. **HINT:** *Use the* More Number Formats *option on the* Number Format *drop-down list to display the Format cells dialog box. With the* Date *selected in the* Catagory *list box, select* 3/14 *in the* Type *list box.*

9 Apply the Number format with the thousands separator and zero decimal places to the cells in the *Volume* column. **HINT:** *Use the* More Numbers Formats *option on the* Number Format *drop-down list to display the Format Cells dialog box. Select* Number *in the* Category *list box and adjust the number of decimals and separator values as needed.*

10 Apply the Accent5 cell style to the range A3:G3, and bold, center, and wrap the text.

11 Select the range A4:G4, choose the *Aqua, Accent 5* border color, and add a bottom border only.

12 Use the Format Painter to copy the formatting from A4:G4 to A5:G28. **HINT:** *In this case Excel copies the border formatting without changing any of the formatting you have previously applied.*

13 Change the height for row 2 to 6.00, and fill cells A2:G2 with the Olive Green, Accent 3 theme color.

14 Save the workbook file.

15 Print or submit the completed workbook as directed by your instructor.

	A	B	C	D	E	F	G
1				Quotes			
2							
3	Ticker	Closing Price	Date	Change	Low	High	Volume
4	AAPL	$249.64	8/20	($0.24)	$249.38	$253.92	12,819,960
5	AFL	$46.63	8/20	$0.07	$46.27	$46.82	3,538,567
6	AIBDX	$14.31	8/19	($0.03)	N/A	N/A	N/A
7	CREE	$57.93	8/20	($0.30)	$58.50	$58.99	2,817,486
8	CSCO	$22.23	8/20	$0.01	$22.19	$22.41	50,631,176
9	CSX	$49.79	8/20	($0.50)	$49.75	$50.14	2,570,915
10	DNDN	$38.22	8/20	$0.81	$37.31	$38.42	2,776,871
11	F	$11.77	8/20	($0.12)	$11.85	$11.90	48,953,016
12	GE	$15.03	8/20	($0.22)	$15.18	$15.18	62,621,528
13	GOOG	$462.02	8/20	($5.95)	$467.26	$471.59	3,746,910
14	HGT	$19.97	8/20	($0.21)	$20.22	$20.27	123,582
15	HI	$20.09	8/20	($0.05)	$20.21	$20.21	223,294
16	HRC	$33.47	8/20	($0.55)	$33.86	$33.92	492,225
17	JNK	$39.10	8/20	$0.12	$38.98	$39.10	2,469,011
18	PAYX	$25.38	8/20	$0.12	$25.23	$25.44	2,842,257
19	PFF	$39.86	8/20	($0.01)	$39.90	$39.91	889,101
20	QCOM	$38.91	8/20	$0.80	$38.24	$39.09	17,744,644
21	RMBS	$19.38	8/20	$0.63	$18.95	$19.53	1,960,981
22	SNDK	$41.50	8/20	($0.40)	$41.61	$41.85	19,264,916
23	SPH	$48.29	8/20	($0.06)	$48.59	$48.59	56,686
24	SWK	$55.05	8/20	($0.14)	$54.64	$55.22	934,075
25	TBT	$31.69	8/20	$0.07	$31.49	$31.81	10,221,104
26	TIVO	$8.69	8/20	$0.21	$8.40	$8.70	1,029,798
27	TLT	$106.04	8/20	($0.12)	$106.42	$106.83	6,652,347
28	WFC	$24.60	8/20	$0.17	$24.43	$24.71	37,754,832
29							
30	Student Name						

Completed Exercise B

Exercise C Reviewing Sales Bonus Eligibility

Skills   Use the Auto Fit feature, explore options for printing, apply number formats, work with other formatting tools, adjust column width, fill cells with a color, add borders, and merge cells

Scenario   You track a small sales force and are reviewing quarterly sales for the prior year. Each salesperson receives a base salary and commission. To keep the team members motivated and competitive, you offer an additional bonus based on the percentage that each sales person achieves relative to total sales. Finish your tracking worksheet by formatting it now.

Steps

1 Open the student data file named **M6-C3- ExC-Sales.xlsx** and save the file as **Lastname-M6-C3-ExC-Sales**, but replace *Lastname* with your last name.

2 Type your name in cell A3.

3 Use the Page Layout tab to apply the Grid theme to the workbook. ***HINT:*** *Use the Themes button in the Themes group on the Page Layout tab.*

4 Apply the Title cell style to cell A1.

5 Use *Merge Across* to merge A1:G1 and A2:G2. Do not change the new alignments.

6 Change cell A2 to the Long Date format.

7 Select the range A4:B5, and add a Thick Box border around it using the Tan, Accent 1 theme color.

8 Fill cell B4 with the Tan, Accent 1, Lighter 80% theme color, and cell B5 with the Tan, Accent 1, Lighter 60%.

9 Format the range A7:G7 with the Accent2 cell style, and center and wrap the entries.

10 Apply the Accounting number format with zero decimal places to the values for each quarter and the totals.

11 Apply the Percent Style number format with zero decimal places to cells B4:B5.

12 Apply the Percent Style number format with two decimal places to the *Production Percentage* column.

13 AutoFit all columns to display all entries without being too wide.

14 Format the *Productions Percentage* column entries that meet or exceed the Level 1 Bonus (cell B4) but are less than the Level 2 Bonus (cell B5) with the same fill color as the Level 1 (Tan, Accent 1, Lighter 80%).

15 Save the file.

16 Print or submit the completed file as directed by your instructor.

	A	B	C	D	E	F	G	H
1	**Sales Review**							
2						Tuesday, January 01, 2013		
3	Student Nane							
4	Bonus Level 1	20%						
5	Bonus Level 2	25%						
6								
7	Salesperson	Q1	Q2	Q3	Q4	Total	Production Percentage	
8	Jameson	$ 440,220	$ 355,907	$ 672,001	$ 109,554	$1,577,682	17.24%	
9	Parker	$ 598,033	$ 409,556	$ 342,999	$ 667,884	$2,018,472	22.06%	
10	Khalil	$ 129,999	$ 794,202	$ 882,001	$ 203,229	$2,009,431	21.96%	
11	Carter	$ 357,899	$ 594,009	$ 204,506	$ 662,087	$1,818,501	19.87%	
12	West	$ 202,455	$ 611,770	$ 400,229	$ 511,887	$1,726,341	18.87%	
13	Total	$1,728,606	$2,765,444	$2,501,736	$2,154,641	$9,150,427		
14								

Completed Exercise C

Working with Charts

If you have a lot of numbers in a worksheet, a chart can simplify your understanding of the data by showing it in a visual arrangement. When you represent the data in a chart, you can easily show patterns or trends in the data. You can create a variety of chart types in Excel, including pie, bar, and line:

- A *pie chart* is a circular chart that is divided into parts. Each part represents a piece of the whole pie, or a percentage of the total. The example of a pie chart, *Visitors*, illustrates that out of all the visitors to The Chocolate Museum, 18% are from the local area, 64% are out-of-town visitors, and 18% are international visitors.

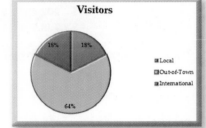

- You can use a *bar chart* or a *column chart* to compare differences between values. A bar chart has horizontal bars and a column chart has vertical bars. These examples of bar and column charts compare the total number of Chocolate Museum visitors by calendar year.

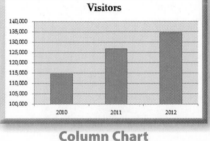

Bar Chart　　　　**Column Chart**

- *Line charts* illustrate changes, or trends, over time. The example of a line chart, *Visitors by Month*, shows how the number of monthly visitors to The Chocolate Museum varied through the years 2011 and 2012.

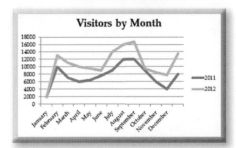

This chapter helps you to understand the parts of a chart, including the parts labeled here:

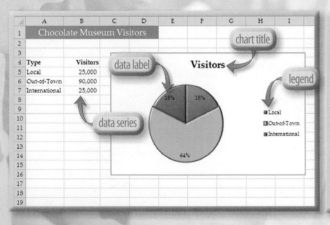

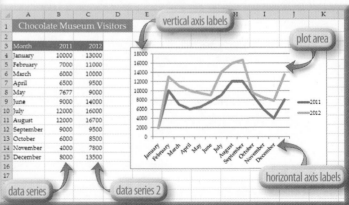

Skills You Learn

1. Create a line chart
2. Modify chart data
3. Create a column chart
4. Add chart labels
5. Create a pie chart
6. Modify a pie chart

Files You Need

In this chapter, you need the following student data files.

M6-C4-S1-CocoaProduction.xlsx

M6-C4-S3-CocoaProduction.xlsx

What You Create

The Chocolate Museum has a number of exhibits, including one that shows how much cocoa is produced in various countries. You prepare a pie chart and a column chart to illustrate these production levels by country. You apply a theme, add a style, and change the formatting to enhance the appearance of the charts. You also add descriptive titles so that the reader can easily understand the data represented in the charts.

Cocoa Bean Production by Country Line Chart

Cocoa Bean Production by Country Bar Chart

Cocoa Bean Production by Region Pie Chart

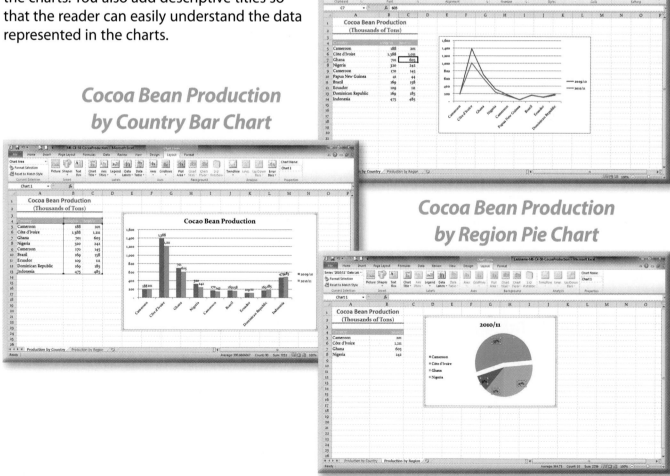

Excel

Chapter 4

> **Skill 1**

Create a Line Chart

Video M6_C4_S01

In this skill, you create a line chart. The line chart uses two series of data from the worksheet. One data series charts the cocoa bean production for several cocoa-producing countries for the fiscal year 2009/10 and the other data series charts that production for the fiscal year 2010/11. Once you create the line chart, you move and size the chart.

Steps

1 Open the student data file named **M6-C4-S1-CocoaProduction.xlsx** and, if you have not already done so, save the file in your Module 6 working folder on your storage medium.

2 On the Production by Country worksheet, select cells A4:C13.

3 Click the Insert tab.

4 Click the Line button in the Charts group to display a gallery of line charts.

5 Click the *Line* chart subtype (the first option in the *2-D Line* section) to insert a line chart in the worksheet.

6 Move the mouse pointer over the chart border so it changes to a four-headed arrow and then drag the chart so that its upper-left corner is positioned over cell E3.

7 Position the mouse pointer over the lower-right corner of the chart border so that the mouse pointer changes to a two-headed diagonal arrow. Drag down and to the right so that the bottom-right corner of the chart covers cell L19.

8 Save the workbook.

▶**Tip** Rest the mouse pointer on a chart subtype to display the name of the chart.

▶**Tip** The names of the countries that produce the cocoa are listed along the horizontal axis. Cocoa bean production amounts are listed along the vertical axis.

▶**Tip** In a line chart, the chart legend tells you which line belongs to which category of data. In this case, the legend tells you, by color, which line belongs to which fiscal year.

Taking It Further

Moving the Chart Location By default, a chart is placed in the existing worksheet. You can move the chart to a new worksheet by first selecting the chart. When you select a chart, the Chart Tools Design tab becomes the active tab. To move the chart, click the Move Chart button in the Location group and then select the *New sheet* option in the Move Chart dialog box. When you click OK, the chart moves to a new worksheet named *Chart1*. This option automatically changes the chart to a full-screen size.

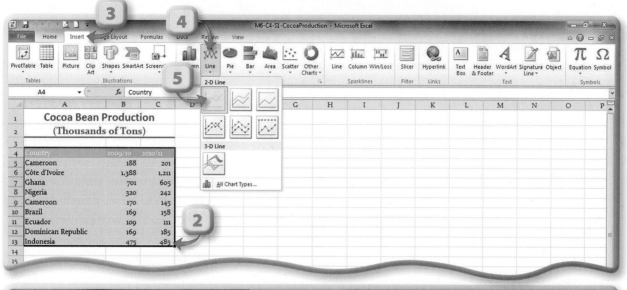

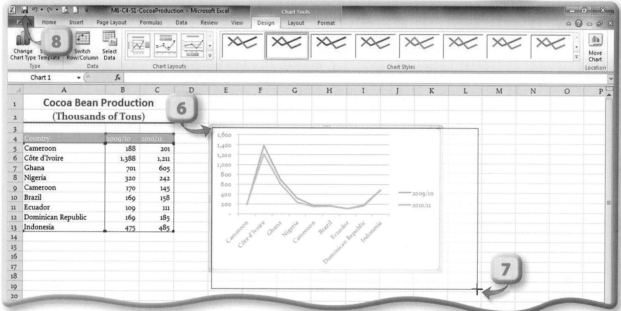

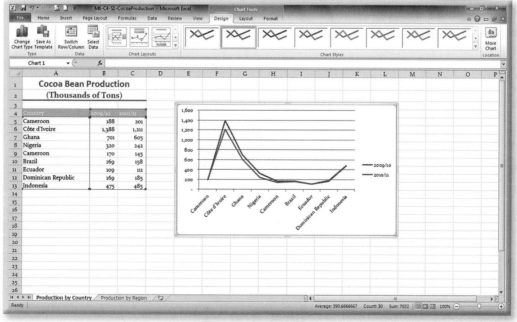

Completed Skill 1

Excel

Skill 2

Modify Chart Data

Video M6_C4_S02

When you select a chart, colored boxes appear around the data that you used to create the chart. Different colored boxes appear around the different parts of the chart. For example, the *data series* used to create the chart has a blue box around it. If you change a number in the data series or add another row to the data series, the chart automatically updates because it is linked to the worksheet data.

Steps

1. If it is not already open, open **M6-C4-S1-CocoaProduction.xlsx**, the file you saved in the previous skill, and save the file as **Lastname-M6-C4-S2-Cocoa Production**, but replace *Lastname* with your last name. Save the file in your Module 6 working folder on your storage medium.

2. With the chart selected on the Production by Country worksheet, drag the lower-right selection handle for the blue selection box (located in the bottom right corner of cell C13) up until you have changed the range to B5:C12. The chart updates automatically and the Indonesia data is no longer included on the chart.

3. Right-click the row 10 heading,

4. Click *Insert* to insert a new row.

5. Type the following entries in cells A10:C10 to add the data for that category to the chart, pressing Tab after each entry.

A10	Papua New Guinea
B10	41
C10	44

   > **Tip** The line chart automatically updates to show the data you have entered in row 10 of the table.

6. Type 1011 in cell C6 and press Enter. The line chart updates automatically.

7. Save and close the workbook.

Taking It Further

Editing Chart Data   Sometimes when you create a chart, the labels along an axis or in the legend do not appear just the way you would like. You can use the Select Data button in the Data group on the Chart Tools Design tab to edit this chart data. Clicking the Select Data button displays a dialog box that shows the current axis labels and legend data. You can click the Edit button and then select the correct cells in the worksheet to change the labels or the information in the legend.

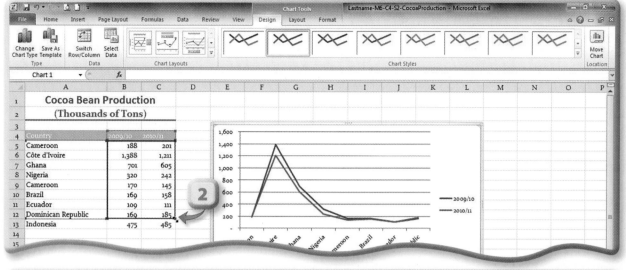

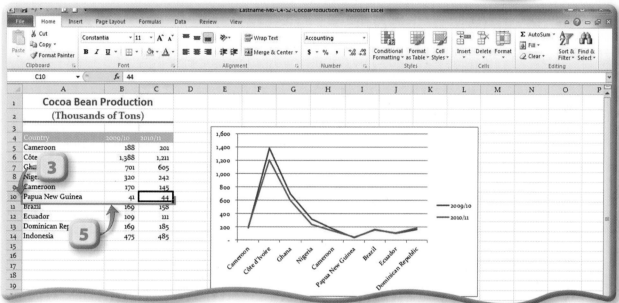

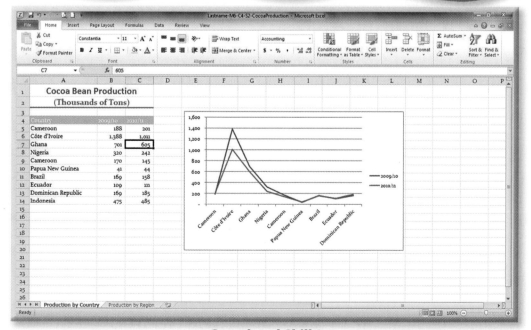

Completed Skill 2

Excel

Skill 3

Create a Column Chart

Video M6_C4_S03

In this skill, you create a column chart. Column charts compare differences between values over time. The column chart you create shows how the cocoa production in each country increased or decreased between the 2009/10 and the 2010/11 fiscal years.

Steps

1 Open the student data file named **M6-C4-S3-CocoaProduction.xlsx** and, if you have not already done so, save the file in your Module 6 working folder on your storage medium.

2 On the Production by Country worksheet, select cells A4:C13.

3 Click the Insert tab.

4 Click the Column button in the Charts group to display a gallery of column chart subtypes.

▶ **Tip** Rest the mouse pointer on a chart subtype to display the name of the chart.

5 Click the *Clustered Column* subchart type in the *2-D Column* section to insert the column chart in the worksheet.

6 Move the mouse pointer over the chart border so it changes to a four-headed arrow. Drag the chart so that its upper-left corner is positioned over cell E3.

7 Position the mouse over the lower-right corner of the chart border so that the mouse pointer changes to a two-headed diagonal arrow. Drag down and to the right so that the bottom right corner of the chart covers cell L18.

8 Save the workbook.

Taking It Further

Changing the Chart Type Bar charts, like column charts, can clearly show differences in charted values, and you can easily change a column chart into a bar chart. To do so, select the chart and click the Chart Tools Design tab. Then click the Change Chart Type button in the Type group and then click *Bar* in the left pane. Select a bar chart subtype in the right pane and then click OK.

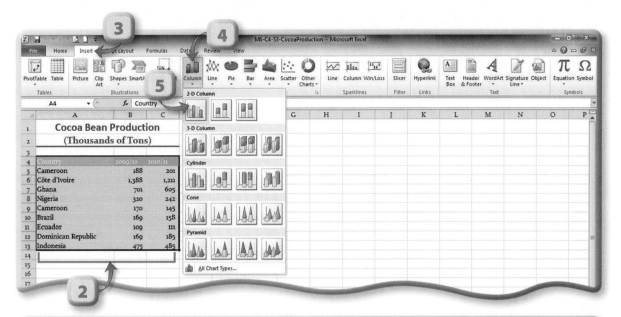

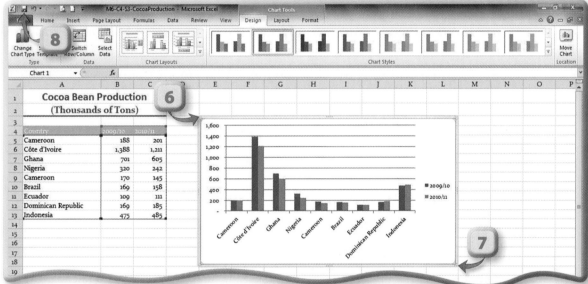

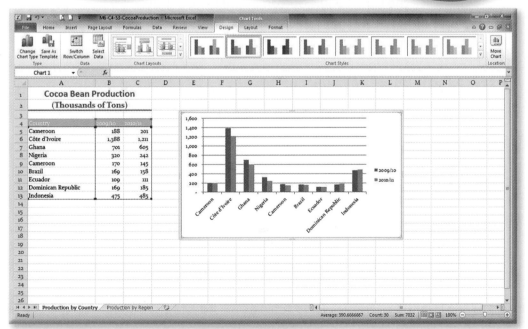

Completed Skill 3

Excel

Excel

Skill 4

Video M6_C4_S04

Add Chart Labels

You can add labels to a chart to make its elements easier to understand. For example, you can add a chart title such as *Cocoa Bean Production* to describe the data in the chart. You can also add individual data labels to show the quantity that a single column or pie slice represents. When you create a chart, Excel adds some labels automatically, based on the data you selected to create the chart. You can add other labels using options on the Chart Tools Layout tab.

Steps

1 If it is not already open, open **M6-C4-S3-CocoaProduction.xlsx**, the file you saved in the previous skill, and save the file as **M6-C4-S4-CocoaProduction**.

2 Click the border of the chart on the Production by Country worksheet.

3 Click the Chart Tools Layout tab.

4 Click the Chart Title button in the Labels group.

5 Click the *Above Chart* option.

6 Type Cocoa Bean Production and then press Enter to add the title to the chart.

7 Click the Data Labels button in the Labels group.

8 Click the *Outside End* option.

9 Enlarge the chart by dragging the lower-right corner of the chart border down and to the right so that it covers cell N23.

10 Save the workbook.

Tip You can place data labels in various places, such as at the *Outside End* of the data point, the *Inside End* of the data point, and *Center* on the data point. For some chart types, you can also select a *Best Fit* option that places the data labels where Excel determines they fit best in the chart.

Taking It Further

Adding Axis Titles Along with a chart title, you may want to add titles to the vertical and horizontal axes to describe what the numbers or labels along each axis represent. For example, the numbers along the vertical axis in the Cocoa Bean Production column chart represent production in thousands of tons. You could add a title *Production (in thousands of tons)* to the vertical axis so the reader can better understand your chart. You can use the Axis Titles button in the Labels group on the Chart Tools Layout tab to add titles to the horizontal and vertical axes.

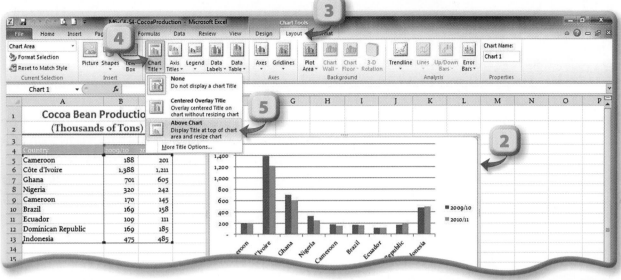

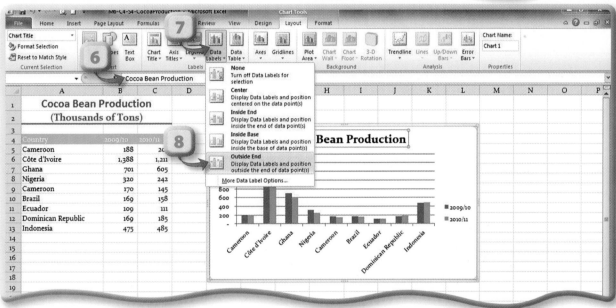

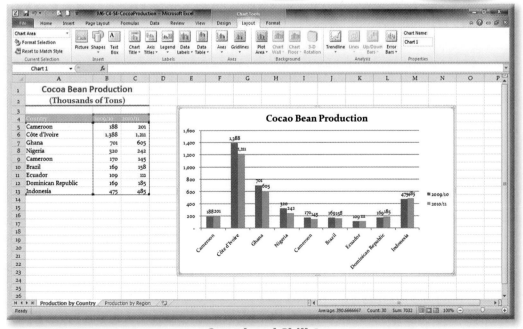

Completed Skill 4

Excel

Excel

Chapter 4

Skill 5

Video   M6_C4_S05

Create a Pie Chart

In this skill, you create a pie chart. A *pie chart* is a circular chart that is divided into parts. Each part represents a percentage of the total quantity. The pie chart you create represents the total amount of cocoa production for four countries. The pie is divided into four parts, one for each country's cocoa production. The size of each piece represents how much of the total cocoa output comes from that country.

Steps

1. If it is not already open, open **M6-C4-S4-CocoaProduction.xlsx**, the file you saved in the previous skill, and save the file as **M6-C4-S5-CocoaProduction**.

2. Click the Production by Region worksheet tab.

▶**Tip** A pie chart can contain only one data series.

3. In the Production by Region worksheet, select cells A4:B8.

4. Click the Insert tab.

5. Click the Pie button in the Charts group to display a gallery of pie chart subtypes.

6. Click the *Pie* chart subtype in the *2-D Pie* section to insert the pie chart into the worksheet.

7. Move the mouse pointer over the chart border so it changes to a four-headed arrow. Drag the chart so that its upper-left corner is positioned over cell D2.

8. Position the mouse pointer over the lower-right corner of the chart border so that the mouse pointer changes to a two-headed diagonal arrow. Drag down and to the right so that the lower-right corner of the chart covers cell J17.

9. Save the workbook.

Taking It Further

Changing the Chart Legend   When the slices in a pie chart or the lines in a line chart have different colors, how do you know what the colors represent? You look at the chart legend. The chart legend tells you which piece of data each colored slice or line represents. By default, Excel places the legend at the right side of the chart. You can change the position of the legend by clicking the Legend button in the Chart Tools Layout tab and selecting an option from the drop-down list. You can even remove the legend if you think the reader can easily understand the chart without it.

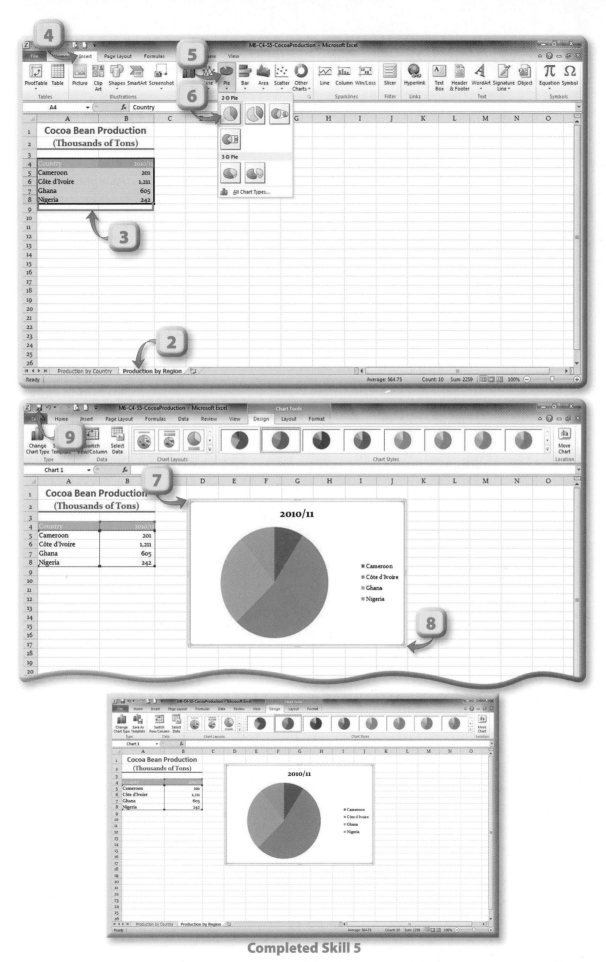

Completed Skill 5

Excel

Excel

Skill 6

Video M6_C4_S06

Modify a Pie Chart

You can rotate the pie chart and you can *explode* a slice away from the rest of the pie chart. An exploded slice sits outside the circle of the pie, to call attention to the content or data it represents. Also, by default, data labels display as numbers or figures, such as 1011. However, the data labels in pie charts typically display as a percentage, such as 80%. In this skill, you learn to display data labels as percentages.

Steps

1. If it is not already open, open **M6-C4-S5-CocoaProduction.xlsx**, the file you saved in the previous skill, and save the file as **Lastname-M6-C4-S6-CocoaProduction**, but replace *Lastname* with your last name. Be sure to save the file in your Module 6 working folder on your storage medium.

2. In the pie chart on the Production by Region worksheet, double-click the largest slice, the slice that represents *Côte d'Ivoire* cocoa bean production. This action opens the Format Data Series dialog box.

3. Drag the *Angle of first slice* slider to the right until the value in the text box below it reads *220*.

4. Click Close.

5. Drag the *Côte d'Ivoire* pie slice up and away from the rest of the pie.

6. Click a blank area of the chart to deselect the pie piece.

7. Click the Chart Tools Layout tab.

8. Click the Data Labels button in the Labels group.

9. Click *More Data Label Options* to display the Format Data Label dialog box.

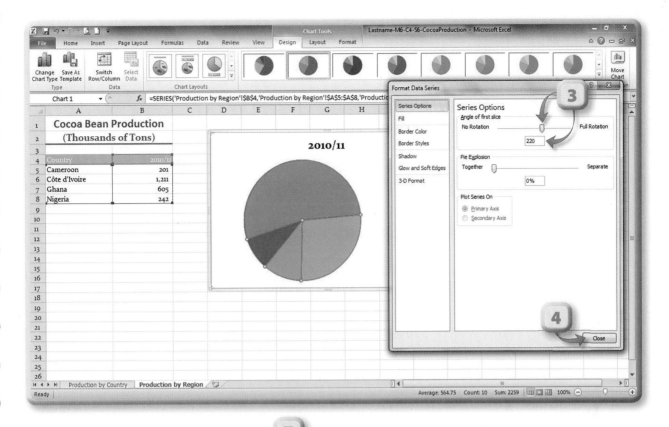

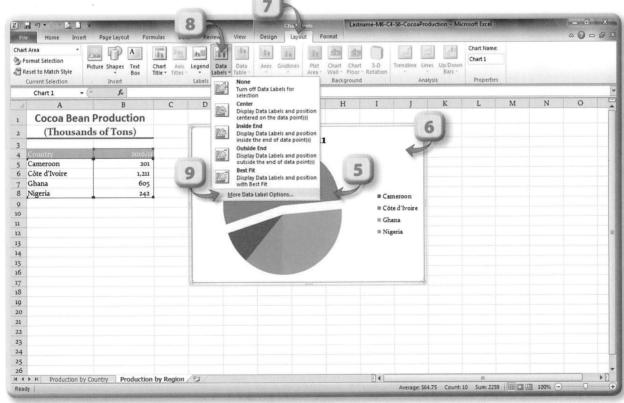

More

10 Click the *Value* check box in the *Label Contains* section to remove the check mark.

11 Click the *Percentage* check box in the *Label Contains* section to insert a check mark.

12 Click Close.

13 Click the Data Labels button in the Labels group.

14 Click the *Inside End* option to place the data labels on the slices at that location.

15 Click the Legend button in the Labels group.

16 Click *Show Legend at Left*.

17 Save and close the workbook.

Taking It Further

Changing Pie Chart Themes and Styles
When you create a chart, the theme applied to the workbook file determines the chart colors. If you apply a different theme to the file, using the Theme button in the Page Layout tab, the colors in the chart update automatically. Another way to modify the chart colors is to apply a chart style. Chart styles change the chart color, and they may also change the chart background color and apply other effects. You can change the chart style by clicking the More button to the right of the Chart Styles group on the Chart Tools Design tab and then clicking a different chart style.

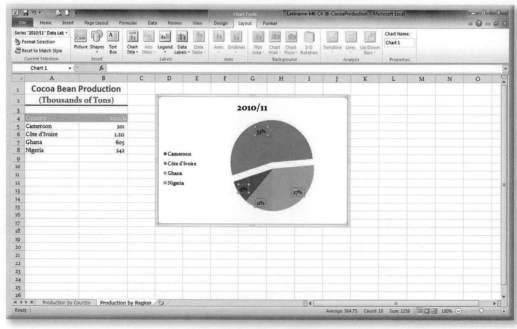

Completed Skill 6

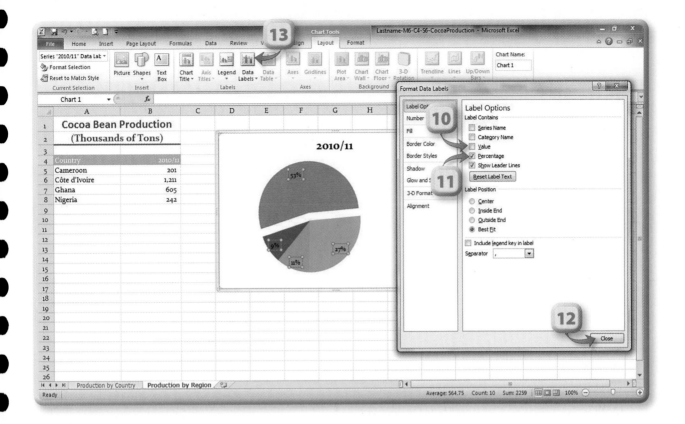

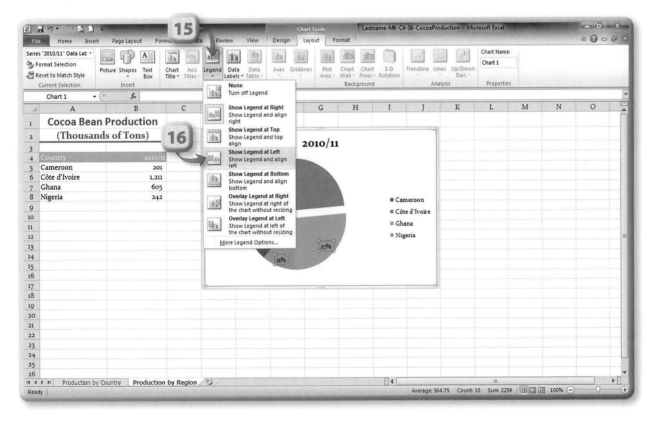

Excel

Tasks Summary

Task	Ribbon Tab, Group	Button, Option	Shortcut, Alternative
Insert a default column chart on the current worksheet	Insert, Charts		Alt + F1
Insert a default column chart on a chart worksheet			F11
Insert another chart type on the current worksheet	Insert, Charts		
Move a chart to a chart worksheet	Chart Tools Design, Location		
Modify chart data	Chart Tools Design, Data		Change values in charted range with keyboard
Add chart labels	Chart Tools Layout, Labels		
Change the chart legend	Chart Tools Layout, Labels		Move or remove legend
Modify chart style	Chart Tools Design, Chart Styles		
Change pie chart rotation			Double-click pie, use *Angle of first slice setting*
Explode a pie slice			Drag slice away from pie

Features Review

Select the best answer from the choices given.

1. Which chart type would best compare the attendance at an annual meeting for the past four years?
   a. column
   b. line
   c. pie
   d. All of the above

2. Which chart type would best show the average monthly rainfall for a year?
   a. bar
   b. column
   c. line
   d. pie

3. Which chart type would best show how much of a company's total salary budget was spent on each department in the company?
   a. bar
   b. column
   c. line
   d. pie

4. To select a chart,
   a. use Find.
   b. click near the border or edge within the chart.
   c. click the worksheet tab that contains the chart.
   d. scroll.

5. Name one way you can modify charted data.
   a. Change an entry in the charted range.
   b. Click the chart and then click Bold.
   c. Change the text color of the charted range.
   d. All of the above

6. A descriptive heading for a chart is a chart
   a. layout.
   b. label.
   c. legend.
   d. title.

7. You can remove a legend from a chart.
   a. True
   b. False

8. This can be added to a chart to display the value or percent for the data points.
   a. data labels
   b. a chart style
   c. a theme
   d. All of the above

9. You can move a chart to a new worksheet in the workbook.
   a. True
   b. False

10. To explode a pie slice,
   a. select it and then drag it away from the other slices.
   b. double-click it.
   c. rotate it 220 degrees.
   d. None of the above

Hands-On Skills Review

Exercise **Charting Budget Data**

Skills Create a pie chart, add chart labels, and modify a pie chart

Scenario You have created a monthly budget to manage your finances. You have organized your spending into the categories rent, entertainment, food, car, and savings. Create a pie chart to show how much you are spending on each budget category.

Steps

1. Open the student data file named **M6-C4-ExA-Budget.xlsx** and save the file as **Lastname-M6-C4-ExA-Budget**, but replace *Lastname* with your last name.

2. Type your name in cell A10.

3. Create a 2-D pie chart from the cells in A3:B7.

4. Add the chart title *Monthly Budget* above the chart.

5. Explode the *Car* slice.

6. Move the chart so that its top-left corner covers cell D2.

7. Add data labels and display the data labels as percentages.

8 Add category labels to each slice. **HINT:** *Click the Data Labels button in the Labels group on the Chart Tools Layout tab and then click More Data Label Options. Click the check box* Category Name *so it contains a check mark and then click Close.*

9 Remove the legend. **HINT:** *On the Chart Tools Layout tab, click Legend and then* None.

10 Save the workbook file.

11 Print or submit the completed workbook file as directed by your instructor.

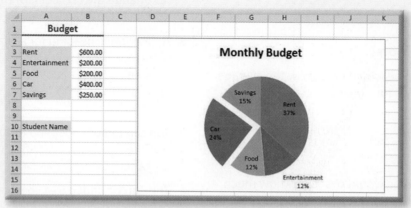

Completed Exercise A

Exercise B Comparing Temperatures

Skills Create a line chart, modify chart data, and add chart labels

Scenario You are deciding where and when to go on your next vacation. You have charted the average monthly temperature in two cities to help you make your decision. You create a line chart to illustrate the differences in temperature.

Steps

1 Open the student data file named **M6-C4-ExB-Temperatures.xlsx** and save the file as **Lastname-M6-C4-ExB-Temperatures**, but replace *Lastname* with your last name.

2 Insert a 2-D line chart using the data in A3:C15.

3 Move the line chart to a new sheet.

4 Add the chart title *Average Monthly Temperatures* above the chart.

5 Add an *x*-axis title *Months*. **HINT:** *Use the Axis Titles button in the Labels group on the Chart Tools Layout tab.*

6 Add a *y*-axis title *Temperature in Degrees F.*

7 Use the Chart Tools Design tab to change to the Style 45 chart style. **HINT:** *Chart styles are listed in numeric order in the Chart Styles group on the Chart Tools Design tab.*

8 Save the workbook file.

9 Print or submit the completed workbook file as directed by your instructor.

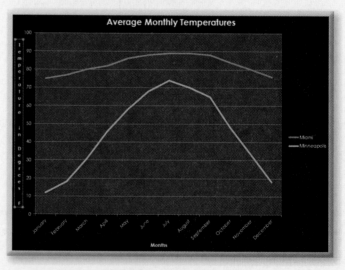

Completed Exercise B

Exercise C Charting Sales

Skills   Create a column chart, add chart labels, and modify chart data

Scenario   You manage a sales team. You have sales numbers, by employee, for the 1st Quarter and the 2nd Quarter of this year. You create a column chart to compare sales levels among your employees.

Instructions

1 Open the student data file named **M6-C4-ExC-Sales.xlsx** and save the file as **Lastname-M6-C4-ExC-Sales**, but replace *Lastname* with your last name.

2 Select the quarterly sales data for all four salespeople along with the column titles.

3 Insert a column chart using the 3-D Clustered Column subtype under 3-D Column section from the gallery that appears when you insert a column chart.

4 Add *Sales Performance* as the chart title above the chart. If requested by your instructor, save the file at this point and submit it.

5 Andre Perez has left the company. Remove his sales data from the chart and the worksheet.

6 Change the chart type to a *Clustered Bar* in the *Bar* section.

7 Move the chart to a new sheet.

8 Save the workbook file.

9 Print or submit the completed workbook file as directed by your instructor.

Completed Exercise C

Module 6 Projects

Project ①

Skills Enter text, values, and dates; name and rename worksheets; explore options for printing; work with other formatting tools; adjust column width and row height; merge cells and create a column chart

Scenario You are working in a marketing department. You company is looking at marketing a new product internationally and you have been asked to do prepare a spreadsheet and chart that show the population in various countries.

Steps

1 Open the student data file named **M6-EOM-P1-Population.xlsx** and save the file as **Lastname-M6-EOM-P1-Population.xlsx**, but replace *Lastname* with your last name.

2 Type Population in cell A1.

3 Merge and center cells A1:B1.

4 Format cell A1 with the Heading 1 cell style.

5 Enter the following data in cells A4:B9.

Japan	126,804,433
United States	310,232,863
Mexico	112,468,855
Canada	33,759,742
France	64,057,792
Germany	82,282,988

6 In cell A11, type the label Total.

7 In cell A12, type the label Minimum.

8 In cell A13, type the label Maximum.

9 Right-align and bold the labels in A11:A13.

10 Use the appropriate function to insert the total population for the listed countries in cell B11.

11 Use the appropriate function to insert the lowest population in cell B12.

12 Use the appropriate function to insert the highest population in cell B13.

13 Widen both column A and column B so that they are just wide enough to display the data in the column.

14 Select cells A3:B3 and then format the cells with the Accent 1 cell style.

15 Select cells A3:B9 and then insert a Clustered Column chart.

16 Change the Chart Style to Style 44. **HINT:** *Chart Styles are listed in numeric order in the Chart Styles group on the Chart Tools Design tab. Click the More button to see a gallery of chart styles.*

17 Move the chart so that the top left corner of the chart is in cell D2.

18 Change the name of Sheet 1 to *Population*.

19 Save the workbook file.

20 Print a copy of the worksheet or submit the completed workbook as directed by your instructor.

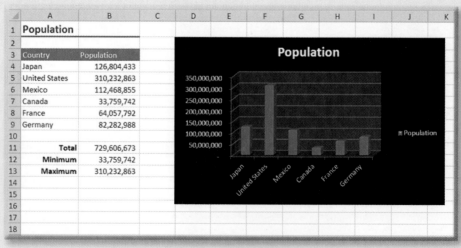

Completed Project 1

Project

Skills   Create a new worksheet; enter text values, and dates; merge cells; insert and delete columns and rows; use spell check; explore options for printing; apply number formats; work with other formatting tools; adjust column width and row height; format cell backgrounds; create a pie chart; and modify a pie chart

Scenario   You manage a restaurant. You want to try and cut some of your monthly expenses. To do this you create a worksheet that displays your expenses. You then chart the information.

Steps

1 Open a blank workbook in Excel and name it **Lastname-M6-EOM-P3-RestarantExpenses**, but replace *Lastname* with your last name.

2 Type Restaurant Expenses in cell A1.

3 Merge and center cells A1:D1.

4 Format cell A1 with the Heading 1 cell style.

5 Enter the following data in cells A3:B7.

Expense	Cost
Food	14500
Building	3500
Taxes	1890
Advertising	1450

6 You forgot to add an expense. Insert a row between row 4 and row 5 and enter the following data.

Staff	16000

7 Spell check the worksheet.

8 Format cells B4:B8 with Currency format.

9 Widen column A and column B so the columns are just wide enough to display the data in the columns.

10 Select cells A3:B3 and then format the cells with the Heading 3 cell style.

11 Right-align cell B3.

12 Select cells A3:B8 and then insert a Pie in 3-D chart.

13 Change the chart title from *Costs* to *Restaurant Expenses*. **HINT:** *Click in the chart title in order to edit it.*

14 Move the chart so that the top left corner of the chart is in cell E2.

15 Add data labels to the inside end of the chart. Display the data labels as percentages.

16 Print a copy of the worksheet or submit the completed file as directed by your instructor.

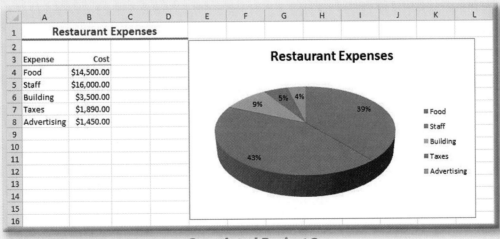

Completed Project 2

Project 3

Skills   Use cell references, enter and edit text, name and rename worksheets, explore options for printing, insert a function, use AutoSum, copy and paste cell contents, use absolute and relative cell references, apply number formats, adjust column widths and row heights, add borders, merge cells, insert a pie chart, and modify a pie chart

Scenario   You are in charge of calculating the payroll for the employees at Paradigm Steel. The employees receive a base salary plus commission. You need to calculate a new salary figure for all of the employees because all employees will receive a 5.25% raise.

Steps

1   Open the student data file named **M6-EOM-P3-Steel.xlsx** and save the file as **Lastname-M6-EOM-P3-Steel**, but replace *Lastname* with your last name.

2   Change the width of columns A and B to *18*.

3   Change the width of columns C through G to *14* and format the values as Currency with 0 decimals.

4   Type the title Commission in cell E2.

5   In cell E3, calculate the commission using a formula that multiplies projected sales by the commission rate. **HINT:** *Use an absolute reference for cell B18.* Copy the formula in cell E3 to cells E4:E12.

6   Type the title Salary in cell F2.

7   In cell F3, calculate the salary by adding the base salary and the commission. Copy the formula in cell F3 to cells F4:F12.

8   Type the title New Salary in cell G2.

9   Employees will all receive a 5.25% raise. In cell G3, calculate the new salary using the formula Salary + (Salary * 5.25%). Copy the formula in cell G3 to cells G4:G12.

10   Set the row height of rows 13 to 16 to *22*.

11   Right align the *Total*, *Average*, *Lowest*, and *Highest* labels and format the labels as bold.

12   Use the appropriate function to calculate the *Total*, *Average*, *Highest*, and *Lowest* values for all columns except column B.

13   Merge and center cells A1:G1 and set the row height of row 1 to *48*.

14   Format the font and font size of cell A1 as Cooper Black, size 28.

15   Set the row height of row 2 to *20*.

16   Center the column headings in row 2 and format the font as Cambria, size 12, bold.

17   Create a thick box border around the column headings in row 2.

18   Create a 3-D pie chart of the new salary for all employees. **HINT:** *Use the Ctrl key to highlight A2:A12 and G2:G12 before creating the chart.*

19   Add data labels that are formatted as percentages on the outside end of the pie pieces.

20   Modify the chart title so that it reads *Employee 2012 Salaries*.

21   Rename Sheet1 as *Data*.

22   Move the location of the chart to a new sheet and name the sheet *Salary Chart*.

23   Save the workbook.

24   Print a copy of both worksheets in landscape orientation or submit the completed workbook as directed by your instructor.

Paradigm Steel Company

Employee	Hire Date	Base Salary	Projected Sales	Commission	Salary	New Salary
Chronowski, John	10/12/2004	$46,950	$422,165	$13,720	$60,670	$63,856
Mandinka Al-Jab Bar	12/14/2009	$30,250	$323,912	$10,527	$40,777	$42,918
McDonald Jack	10/25/2008	$29,581	$238,584	$7,754	$37,335	$39,295
Meeks Tyrone	6/13/2002	$42,500	$342,413	$11,128	$53,628	$56,444
Putin, Nikita	5/24/1997	$39,500	$750,450	$24,390	$63,890	$67,244
Adley, Martha	4/11/2011	$36,253	$384,616	$12,500	$48,753	$51,313
Damato, Michelle	5/13/2010	$37,157	$489,401	$15,906	$53,063	$55,848
DeJesus, Gino	2/10/2004	$44,219	$599,689	$19,490	$63,709	$67,054
Flynn, Georgeana	3/20/2007	$41,821	$619,984	$20,149	$61,970	$65,224
Frost, Leonard	11/19/2006	$41,272	$338,914	$11,015	$52,287	$55,032
Total		$389,503	$4,510,128	$146,579	$536,082	$564,226
Average		$38,950	$451,013	$14,658	$53,608	$56,423
Lowest		$29,581	$238,584	$7,754	$37,335	$39,295
Highest		$46,950	$750,450	$24,390	$63,890	$67,244
Commission Rate	3.25%					

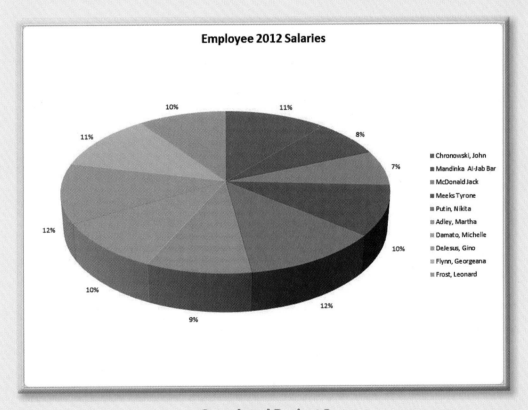

Completed Project 3

MODULE 7

Microsoft® Access 2010

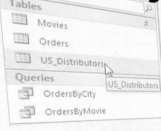

Before beginning the module skills, copy the Module7–Access folder from the Student Resources CD to your storage medium. The copied folder will become the working folder for this module.

Guidelines for Understanding Relational

You may have heard our present time referred to as the *Information Age*. Businesses, schools, and individuals rely on instant access to information and expect to have that information at their fingertips. Computers today enable you to store large amounts of data and to quickly retrieve and organize that data. Much of the information you retrieve from a computer or from a website is stored in a database.

A database is an organized collection of related data. A business's employee data, a store's inventory, and an airline's flight listing are all examples of data that is typically stored in a database.

To understand how databases work, you need to learn some database terminology.

- Databases such as Access use an object called a *table* to enter and organize data. When you open a table in Access, the table displays in a datasheet. For example, this Products table is part of a computer store database for tracking the store's inventory and sales.

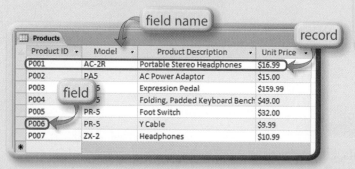

- A field is a set of information that is stored in the database.

- Each field has a field name, such as *Product ID*, *Model*, *Product Description*, or *Unit Price*.

- A collection of related fields is called a *record*. In the Products table example, all of the information supplied for one product (ID, model, description, and unit price) makes up a single record.

Access is a relational database, meaning that Access uses a series of related tables to organize the database. Each table is usually related to at least one other table by sharing a column of data. For example, the Products table and the Inventory table are part of the same Access database. The Products table contains a *Product ID* field but no *Product Name* field. The *Product Name* field is stored in another table, the Inventory table. But the tables are related because both contain the *Product ID* column of data. This relationship allows you to access all the information for each product, regardless of where it is stored.

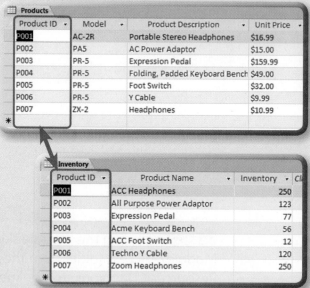

Databases and the Best Uses of Access

To enter records into a database, you can either enter the data directly into the table or fill in user-friendly forms that are designed for data entry. When you enter data in a form, that information is also entered into the corresponding table. A form for entering information about products is shown below.

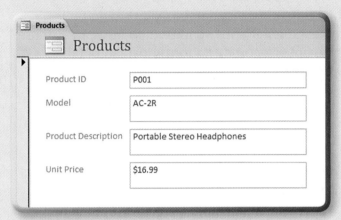

Once you have entered records into a database, you can use Access to answer queries or questions about the data. For example, you could query a computer store's database to find out which customers have ordered ACC headphones. The results of this query are shown below.

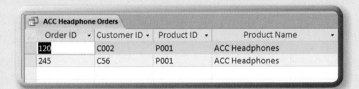

Or you could query the database to find out which products have an inventory of 100 items or fewer and may need to be reordered. The results of this query are shown below.

You can also generate printed reports about the stored data. You may want to put query results information in a professional-looking report, like the one shown below, that you can pass along to the supervisor who makes reordering decisions.

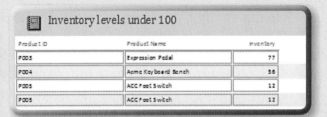

Use Access when you need to organize and store large amounts of data, such as employee or inventory records. By organizing that information in a database, you are able to quickly find the data and answers you need.

Chapter 1

Working with Databases

The Access database application is used to manage large amounts of data, such as the contact information for all the members of The Chocolate Museum.

In this chapter, you learn to work with the objects in an Access database, including tables, forms, queries, and reports. You use Access tables to enter and organize data. You can also use Access *forms* to enter data. Some users prefer to enter records into forms instead of tables, because forms allow them to enter and view one record at a time.

Once you have entered data in a database, you can then organize the data by sorting or filtering it. Filtering temporarily displays only those records meeting a certain condition or conditions, such as just those members of The Chocolate Museum who live in Boston, Massachusetts. You can also run a *query* (ask a question) to locate specific information in a database. For example, you could query the database to find all Chocolate Museum members whose last name is Brown. Also, queries can be saved and run at a later time. If you need to print information from a database, you can create a *report* to present the information in a professional-looking format.

In this chapter, you learn how to enter data in a table and in a form. You edit, sort, and filter data and format a datasheet. You also run a query and display a report.

Skills You Learn

1 Open and navigate a database
2 Enter data
3 Edit data
4 Sort data
5 Filter data
6 Format a datasheet
7 Use existing queries and reports

Files You Need
In this chapter, you need the following student data file.

M7-C1-Members.accdb

Note: *Before you begin working with student data files for this chapter, make sure you have copied your Module7-Access folder from the Student Resources CD to your storage medium. Access database files opened directly from the Student Resources CD are read-only. You need to open all database files from your working folder on your storage medium. Steps for copying a folder from the CD are provided on the inside front cover of this textbook.*

What You Create

The Chocolate Museum has a membership program that people can join to receive admission discounts and the monthly newsletter and be among the first invited to preview new exhibits. All of the information about the Museum's membership program is stored in a database. In this chapter, you explore the objects in this database. You also add records, sort and filter data, run a query, and display a report.

Membership Program Database

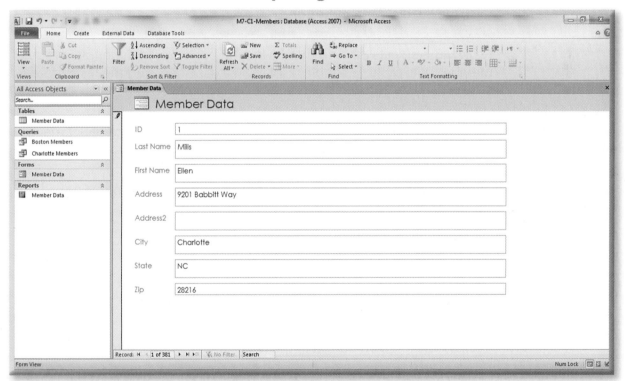

Access

Skill 1

Open and Navigate a Database

Video M7_C1_S01

When a database opens, you do not see a document as you do in Word or a workbook as you do in Excel. Instead, you see a Navigation pane on the left side of the window that lists the names of the objects that make up the database. This list of objects includes all tables, forms, queries, and reports that are part of the database. To open an object, you double-click the object in the Navigation pane.

Steps

Tip Be sure to open all database files from your working folder on your storage medium. Access database files opened directly from the Student Resources CD are read-only. Steps on how to copy a folder from the CD are presented on the inside front cover of this textbook.

1. Open the student data file named **M7-C1-Members.accdb** from your Module 7 working folder on your storage medium.

2. Click the Enable Content button.

3. Review the objects listed in the Navigation pane and then double-click the Member Data table. The table displays in a datasheet and the first record is selected.

Tip If the Navigation pane is not open, click the Shutter Bar Open/Close button at the top of the Navigation pane.

4. Click the Next record button in the Record Navigation bar to select the second record.

5. Click the Last record button in the Record Navigation bar to select the last record in this table, record 379.

6. Click the Close button to close the table.

Tip You can use the Member Data form to enter records in the Member Data table. The form contains the same fields found in the table.

7. In the Navigation pane, double-click the Member Data form. The form displays only one record.

8. Click the Next record button in the Record Navigation bar to display the next record.

9. Click the New (blank) record button in the Record Navigation bar to display a new blank record. However, do not enter any new data at this time.

10. Click the Close button to close the form.

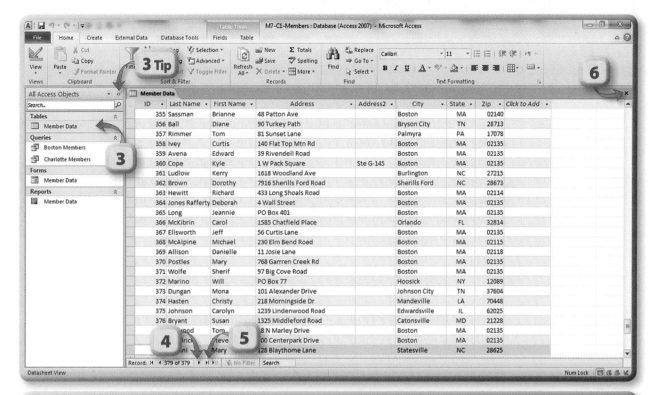

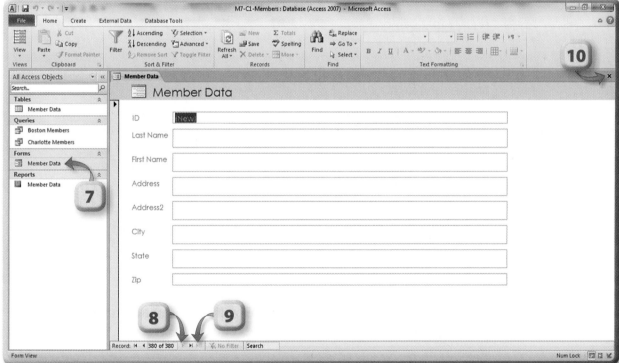

Completed Skill 1

Taking It Further

Opening More Objects You can have more than one object open at a time in Access. For example, you can open a table and then open a second table or a form.

Switch between open objects by clicking the tab at the top of the object. Each tab contains the name of the object and an icon that indicates the object type.

Access

Skill 2

Video M7_C1_S02

Enter Data

You can enter data in a table or in a form. Entering data in a table is useful for comparing records because you can see multiple records at once. However, this method can be confusing if you are entering a record with a lot of fields and you have to scroll through the fields. A form only displays one record at a time, and you usually do not have to scroll to enter the data for a record. Entering data into a form can also help you to avoid data entry errors.

Steps

Tip A database file may contain a huge amount of data. Instead of continually duplicating the database by saving it with a new name, users schedule regular Access file backups. Thus, you can use the same database file throughout each chapter of this module without saving it with a different file name.

Tip The *ID* field is an AutoNumber field. For such fields, the new record will automatically be assigned the next number, which is Member ID 380 in this case. Pressing the Tab key moves you from field to field.

Tip Access automatically saves records that you enter in a table or a form. So you do not have to save your file before closing the table.

Tip The data value for a field is called an *entry*.

1 With the **M7-C1-Members.accdb** database open, double-click the Member Data table in the Navigation pane.

2 Click the New (blank) record button in the Record Navigation bar.

3 Press Tab.

4 Add the following information to create a new record, pressing Tab to move to the next field:

Last Name	First Name	Address	Address2	City	State	Zip
Marks	Carol	3015 Mossdale Ave	(blank; press Tab)	Durham	NC	27707

5 Close the Member Data table.

6 In the Navigation pane, double-click the Member Data form.

7 Click the New (blank) record button in the Record Navigation bar.

8 Press the Tab key and then add the following information to create a new record, pressing Tab to move to the next field:

Last Name	First Name	Address	Address2	City	State	Zip
Conway	Philip	12 Church Street	Apt A	Boston	MA	02135

9 Close the form.

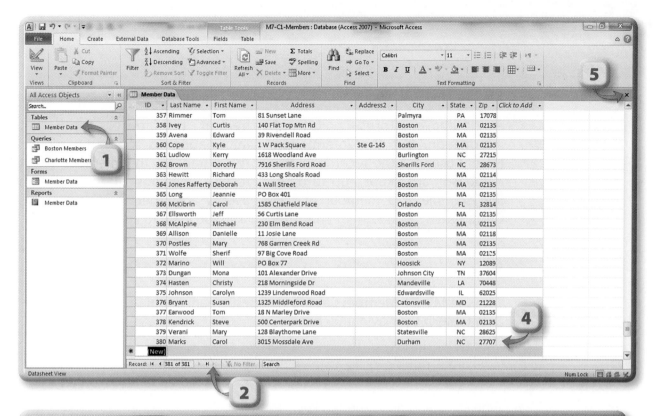

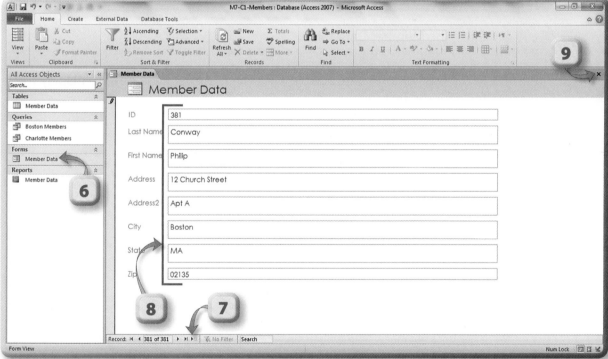

Completed Skill 2

Taking It Further

Checking Spelling The information that you enter into a database must be correct so that you can run queries and reports successfully and avoid problems down the road. In addition to proofreading your formulas and cell references, use spell check to check the correctness of your data. To do so, click the Spelling button on the Home tab. If Access finds any spelling errors, it displays a dialog box you can use to correct errors.

Access

Skill 3 Edit Data

Video M7_C1_S03

A database stores a lot of information, but the information is only useful if the records in the database are kept up-to-date. For example, if a member of The Chocolate Museum changes her or his address and that information is not updated in the database, the member won't receive mailings about museum events and special offers. In this skill, you learn to edit data in a table.

Steps

1 With the **M7-C1-Members.accdb** database open, double-click the Member Data table in the Navigation pane.

2 In record 2, double-click *Dasha* in the *First Name* column.

3 Type Darla and press the Tab key.

4 Close the Member Data table.

5 In the Navigation pane, double-click the Member Data form to display the form for the first record.

6 Double-click *Allen* in the *First Name* field.

7 Type Ellen and press the Tab key.

8 Close the Member Data form.

Taking It Further

Deleting a Record If a member, such as Mr. Saake, does not renew his membership, you need to delete the record. In such cases, locate the specific record in the table. Then click the record selection area, which is the gray box to the left of the record's first field. Next, click the Home tab and click the Delete button arrow. In the drop-down menu, click *Delete Record* and then click Yes to confirm the deletion.

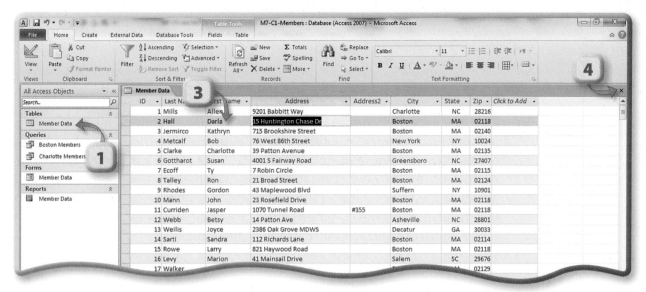

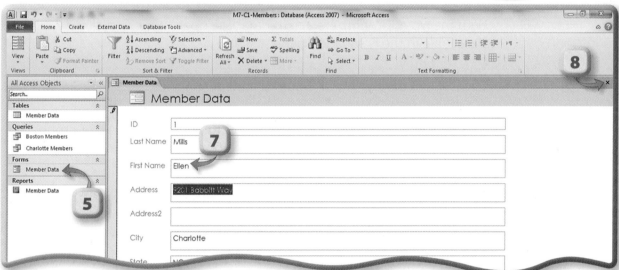

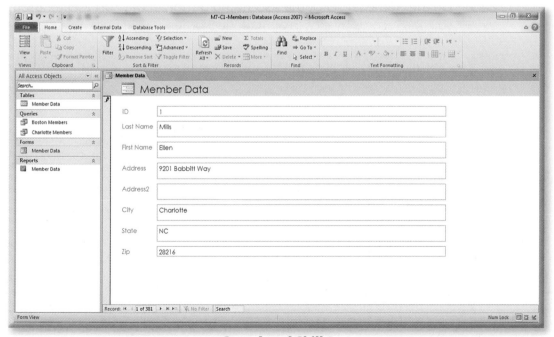

Completed Skill 3

Access

Access

Skill 4

Sort Data

Video M7_C1_S04

It is good practice to enter database records in the order in which you receive them. For example, you might enter a new Chocolate Museum member's data on the day you receive it. However, when you are looking for specific information, you may find it helpful to sort a table by a particular column, such as *Last Name* rather than by date entered, so that you can easily find the member you are looking for. In this skill, you learn to sort the data in a table.

Steps

1 With the **M7-C1-Members.accdb** database open, double-click the Member Data table in the Navigation pane.

2 Click *Mills* in the *Last Name* column in the first record.

▶ **Tip** *Ascending* means to sort alphabetically from A to Z.

3 On the Home tab, click the Ascending button in the Sort & Filter group. The records are now sorted by last name, in alphabetical order.

3 *Another Way*
Click the drop-down arrow in the *Last Name* column heading and then click *Sort A to Z.*

4 On the Home tab, click the Remove Sort button. The records are no longer sorted by the *Last Name* column.

5 Click *Charlotte* in the *City* column in the first record.

6 On the Home tab, click the Ascending button in the Sort & Filter group to sort the records by city, in alphabetical order.

7 On the Home tab, click the Remove Sort button.

8 Close the Member Data table.

9 Select No in the dialog box that appears. You have not made any permanent changes to the design and do not need to save the table.

Taking It Further

Sorting a Form   When you sort records in a table, the sort affects only that table. It does not affect the order of records displayed in the related form. For example, if you sort the Member Data table by the *Last Name* column and then open the Member Data form, the records in the Member Data form will not be sorted by last name. However, you can sort the data in a single field in a form by clicking a field entry box and then clicking either the Ascending button or the Descending button in the Sort & Filter group on the Home tab.

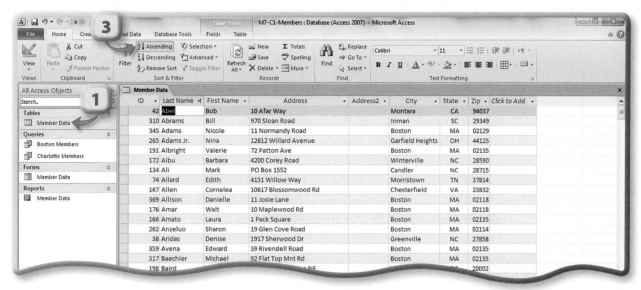

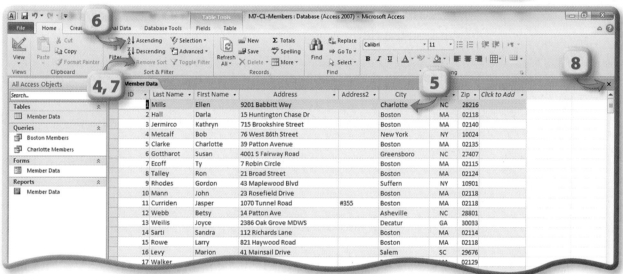

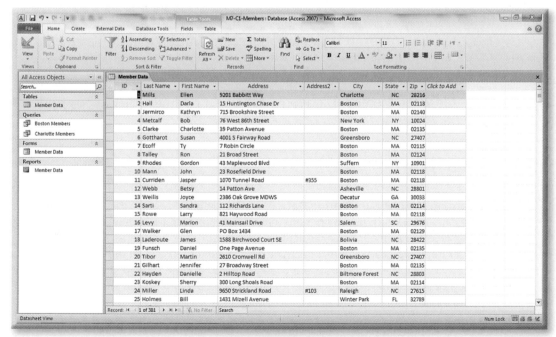

Completed Skill 4

Access

Skill 5

Video M7_C1_S05

Filter Data

If you are looking for specific records, such as the records of all members who live in the city of Charlotte, North Carolina, you can filter the records based on data in a specific field. When you apply a filter, records that do not meet the condition you specify are temporarily hidden from view. But when you remove the filter, those records that have been "hidden" in the table redisplay.

Steps

1 With the **M7-C1-Members.accdb** database open, double-click the Member Data table in the Navigation pane.

2 Click *Charlotte* in the *City* column in the first record.

3 Another Way
Click the drop-down arrow in the *City* column heading.

3 On the Home tab, click the Filter button in the Sort & Filter group.

4 Click the *(Select All)* check box. All of the check marks are cleared from the check boxes in the drop-down filter list.

5 Scroll down the list and click *Charlotte*.

6 Click OK. Only three records are displayed and all of the displayed records have the entry *Charlotte* in the *City* column.

7 On the Home tab, click the Toggle Filter button to redisplay the other records in the table.

8 Close the Member Data form and select No in the dialog box that appears.

Taking It Further

Learning More about Filtering Data

You can filter records based on more than one piece of information in a particular field. For example, you can filter records to find members who live in Charlotte and those who live in Boston. To do so, click both city names in the drop-down filter list. You can also filter by more than one column. For example, if you apply a filter that displays just those members living in Charlotte, you could then click in the *Last Name* column and apply a second filter to display only those members having the last name *Mills* who also live in Charlotte.

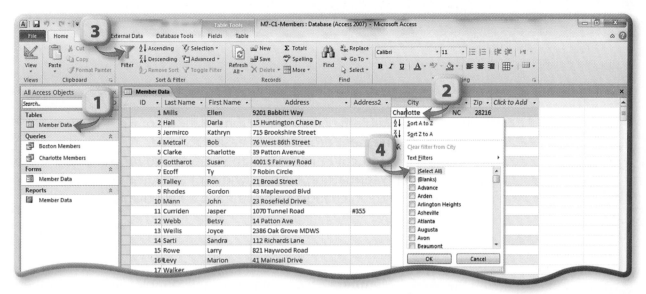

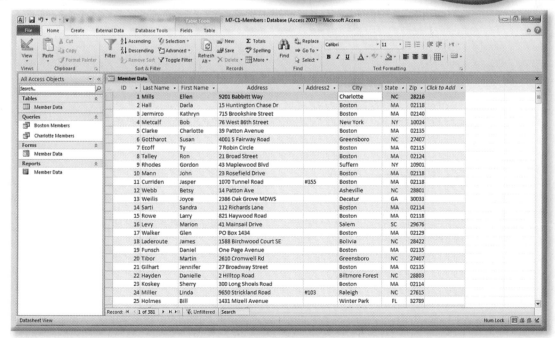

Completed Skill 5

Access

Skill 6

Format a Datasheet

When you open a table, it displays in a datasheet. A datasheet organizes the data in rows and columns. You may want to apply formatting, such as bold and italic, or change the font size to make the datasheet easier to read. You can also align the data in a column and adjust the width of a column so that all of the data in a field displays.

Steps

1. With the **M7-C1-Members.accdb** database open, double-click the Member Data table in the Navigation pane.

2. Click the first record in the *State* column.

3. On the Home tab, click the Align Text Left button in the Text Formatting group. The formatting is applied to all of the records in the *State* column.

4. Click the *Font Size* list arrow in the Text Formatting group.

▶**Tip** ### indicates that the column is not wide enough to display all of the data for the data contained in that column.

5. Click *14*. The font size changes for the entire table and the *Zip* column now displays #####.

6. Move the mouse pointer over the right border of the *Zip* column heading. When the pointer changes to ✛, double-click. The column widens to display all the data in the column.

7. Move the mouse pointer over the right border of the first *Address* column heading. When the pointer changes to ✛, double-click.

8. Close the Member Data table and click Yes to save the changes to the table.

Taking It Further

Learning More about Formatting a Datasheet By default, every other row in a datasheet has a different background color. You can change the background color of every second row by clicking the Alternate Row Color button in the Text Formatting group on the Home tab and selecting a different color. Also by default, the horizontal and vertical gridlines display. Visible gridlines help you to clearly see the borders of each cell in the datasheet. You can change the gridlines that are displayed by clicking the Gridlines button in the Text Formatting group on the Home tab.

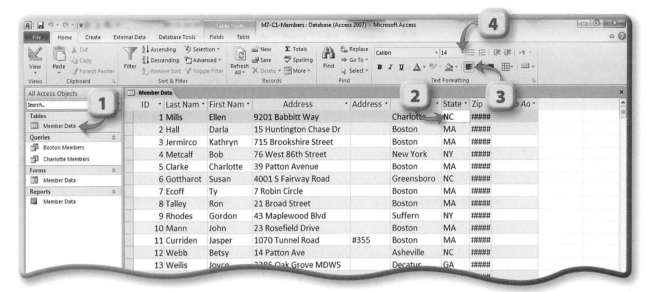

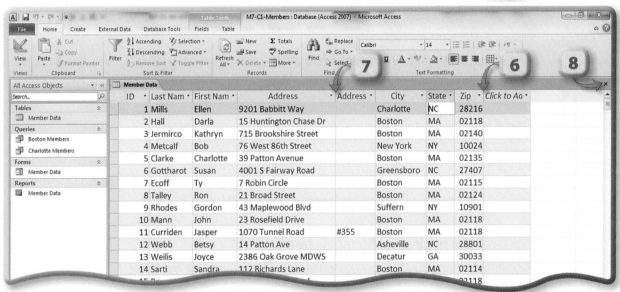

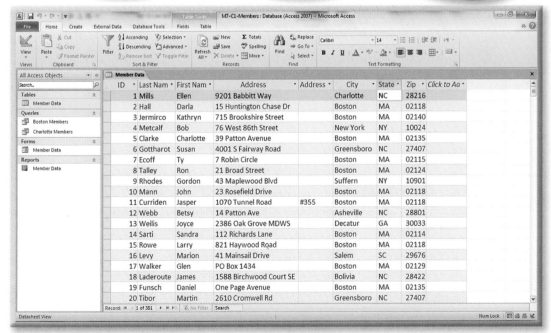

Completed Skill 6

Access

Access

Skill 7 — Use Existing Queries and Reports

Video M7_C1_S07

In previous skills in this chapter, you learned to use existing tables and forms to enter and edit data. In this skill, you work with two other objects: queries and reports. You create a query to find records that meet a certain condition. The records are pulled from one or more tables, in a process called *extracting*. You also run two queries that have been created for you. Lastly, you display a report that has been saved in the database. A report presents data from a combination of one or more tables and queries.

Steps

1 With the **M7-C1-Members.accdb** database open, double-click the Charlotte Members query in the Navigation pane to display records of all members living in Charlotte, North Carolina.

2 Close the Charlotte Members query.

3 In the Navigation pane, double-click the Boston Members query to display records of all members living in Boston, Massachusetts.

4 Close the Boston Members query.

▶ **Tip** Creating a query differs from simply filtering records. Because a query is an Access object, it is saved with the database. As a result, once you create a query, you can run it over and over again.

5 In the Navigation pane, double-click the Member Data report. The report displays records of The Chocolate Museum members.

6 Close the Boston Members report.

Taking It Further

Printing an Object You can print any open objects, including tables, forms, queries, and reports. To print an active object, click the File tab and then click the Print tab. You then have three print options to choose from. Click *Quick Print* to print the object when you are sure you don't need to change any print settings. Or, click *Print* to display the Print dialog box, where you can change print settings, such as the number of copies. You should always click *Print Preview*, the third option, to view the object before you print it.

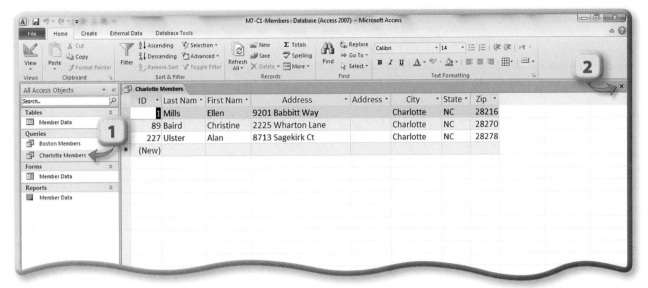

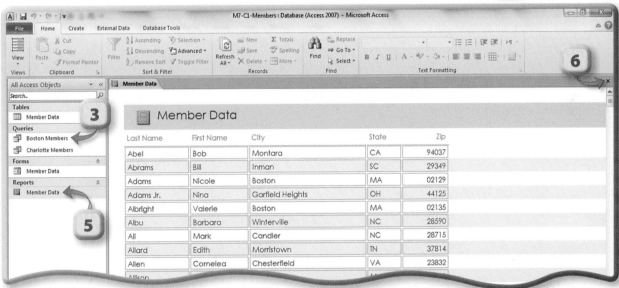

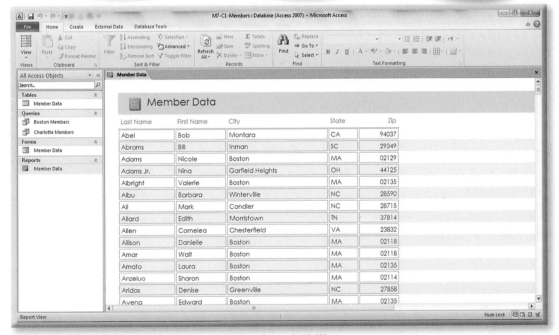

Completed Skill 7

Access

Tasks Summary

Task	Ribbon Tab, Group	Button , Option	Shortcut, Alternative
Collapse or expand the Navigation pane		«	
Open an object			Double-click object in Navigation pane; select object in Navigation pane and press Enter
Navigate in a datasheet			Tab, Arrow Keys
Display the next record		▶	
Display the last record		▶|	
Close the table/form		✕	
New (blank) record		▶✳	
Check spelling	Home, Records	ᴬᴮꞆ Spelling	
Delete a record	Home, Records	✕ Delete ▾	
Sort data	Home, Sort & Filter	ᴬꜱₑ Ascending	
Remove sort	Home, Sort & Filter	ᴬꜱₒ Remove Sort	
Filter data	Home, Sort & Filter	▽	
Remove a filter	Home, Sort & Filter	▽ Toggle Filter	
Left align a field	Home, Text Formatting	☰	
Change the font size	Home, Text Formatting	14 ▾	
Widen a column			Double-click a column border
Format the background color of every second row	Home, Text Formatting	▦ ▾	

Features Review

Select the best answer from the choices given.

1. The Navigation pane lists all _____ in the database.
   a. records
   b. worksheets
   c. objects
   d. macros

2. You can enter data in a
   a. table.
   b. form.
   c. All of the above
   d. None of the above

3. A piece of information, such as a first name or city, that is entered in a database is called a
   a. field.
   b. column.
   c. record.
   d. row.

4. A group of related fields, such as all the information about one employee, is stored in a
   a. field.
   b. column.
   c. record.
   d. row.

5. In a form, you usually see
   a. one field.
   b. one record.
   c. one table.
   d. the entire database.

6. Which of the following is a valid method for moving between cells in a table?
   a. Press Tab.
   b. Press the right arrow key.
   c. Click a cell.
   d. All of the above

7. Which sort order arranges data alphabetically from *A* to *Z*?
   a. ascending
   b. descending
   c. reverse
   d. None of the above

8. Which action temporarily displays records matching the criteria you specify for one or more fields?
   a. sort
   b. hide
   c. filter
   d. parse

9. The _____ group on the Home tab has choices for formatting the datasheet.
   a. Sort & Filter
   b. Records
   c. Find
   d. Text Formatting

10. Which action closes an open object?
    a. Double-click it in the Navigation pane.
    b. Click its Close button.
    c. Click the Last record button.
    d. Click its tab and then press Enter.

Hands-On Skills Review

Exercise **A** **Updating a Jewelry Store Database**

Skills   Open and navigate a database, enter data, edit data, and sort data

Scenario   You are in charge of updating the records in a jewelry store database. You add some new items to the database and make an edit to an existing record. You also sort a datasheet to make it easier to find information in the table.

Steps

1. Open the student data file named **M7-C1-ExA-Jewelry.accdb** and save the file as **Lastname-M7-C1-ExA-Jewelry**, but replace *Lastname* with your last name.

2. Open the Customers table.

3. In record 3, edit the *Last Name* field to be *Katz* instead of *Kati*.

4. Close the Customers table.

5. Double-click the Products form.

6. Click the New (blank) record button in the Record Navigation bar.

7 Add the following information to create three new records:

Item Number	Item Description	Price
A682	Emerald Earrings	1795.00
D328	Diamond Necklace	2845.00
K325	Diamond Bracelet	1550.00

8 Close the Products form.

9 In the Navigation pane, double-click the Orders table.

10 Sort the Orders table by the *Customer ID* field in ascending order.

11 Print the Orders table or submit the completed database as directed by your instructor.

12 Close the Orders table.

Products Form

Orders Table

Exercise B Sorting and Filtering a Bookstore Database

Skills   Open and navigate a database, filter data, and use existing queries and reports

Scenario You are the manager of a bookstore. You order books for your store from several suppliers. You have some questions about the orders you have made and so you filter the records and run existing queries to find the information that you need.

Steps

1 Open the student data file named **M7-C1-ExB-Books.accdb** and save the file as **Lastname-M7-C1-ExB-Books**, but replace *Lastname* with your last name.

2 The Tons of Books Orders query displays all of the orders from the Tons of Books supplier. Open this query.

3 Close the Tons of Books Orders query.

4 The Book Depot Orders query displays all of the orders from the Book Depot supplier. Open this query.

5 Close the Book Depot Orders query.

6 You now need to check the orders from the Books Unlimited supplier. Open the Orders table.

7 Filter the *Supplier Name* column so that only the *Books Unlimited* records are displayed.

8 Print the Orders table or submit the completed database as directed by your instructor.

9 Remove the filter.

10 Close the Orders table.

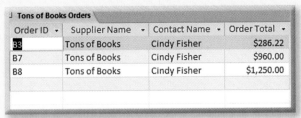

Tons of Books Orders Query

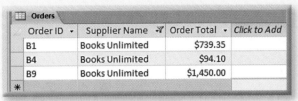

Orders Table

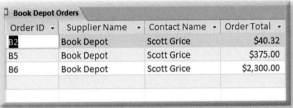

Book Depot Orders Query

Exercise C Tracking Community Volunteers

Skills   Open and navigate a database, format a datasheet, sort data, and use existing queries and reports

Scenario   You have set up a database to track student community service hours. This data is important because many students volunteer to meet graduation or financial aid requirements. You sort the data in this database, format a datasheet, and display a report.

Instructions

1   Open the student data file named **M7-C1-ExC-CommunityService. accdb** and save the file as **Lastname-M7-C1-ExC-CommunityService**, but replace *Lastname* with your last name.

2   The Organizations report displays information about the community agencies at which students can volunteer. Display the Organizations report.

3   Close the Organizations report.

4   Display the Volunteer Hours table.

5   Change the font size to 12.

6   Center the fields in the *Service Date* column.

7   Sort the table by the *Organization Name* column in ascending order.

8   Print the Volunteer Hours table or submit the completed document as directed by your instructor.

9   Save the changes to the Volunteer Hours table.

10   Close the Volunteer Hours table.

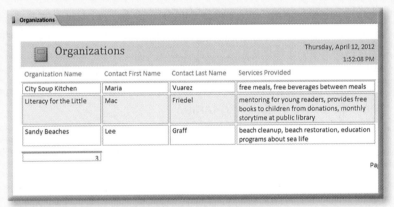

Organizations Report

Volunteer Hours Table

Chapter 2

Using Forms and Tables

In this chapter, you learn to create a table and a form. When you create a table, you need to give each field a name and also assign a field type. The field type tells Access which type of data you will be storing in that field. There are a number of field types you can use, including:

- AutoNumber field— automatically stores a number that is one greater than the last number used

- Text field—stores characters and numbers that do not require calculations, such as names and zip codes

- Number field—stores numbers only

- Date/Time field—stores dates and times

- Currency field—stores dollar amounts

Access has several views that you use to perform different tasks. When you enter records in a table, you do so in Datasheet view. When you create a table in this chapter, you create it in Design view. To switch views, you use the View button arrow on the Home tab.

You can enter data in a table or form. A form provides a user-friendly interface to enter data to be stored in a table. When you enter a record using a form, that record is added to the corresponding table just as if you added the record directly into the table in Datasheet view. When you use the Form button to create a form, the form initially displays in Layout view. You can edit the form in either Design or Layout view. You then must switch to Form view to add records to the underlying table.

In this chapter, you learn how to create a table and a form and you also enter data in a table and a form.

Skills You Learn

1 Create a table
2 Enter data in a table
3 Create a form
4 Enter data in a form

Files You Need
In this chapter, you need the following student data file.

M7-C2-Members.accdb

What You Create

The Chocolate Museum charges an annual fee for its membership program. The standard fee is $120. Many members choose to donate additional funds to support the Museum. In this chapter, you create a table that stores data on the annual fee payments and additional donation amounts that members make to The Chocolate Museum. You also create a form so that you can easily enter records in this table.

Membership Fee and Donations Table

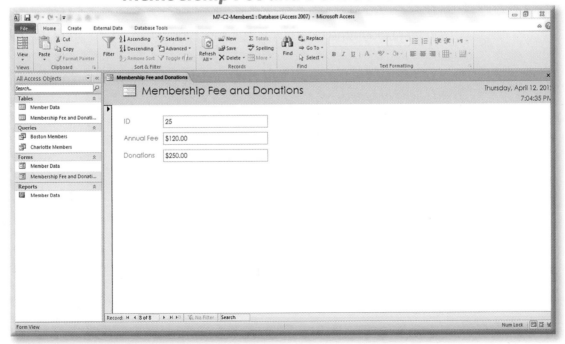

Membership Fee and Donations Form

Access

Video   M7_C2_S01

Create a Table

In Chapter 1, you opened a table, added a record to the table, and edited data in the table. In this skill, you add a new table to the database. This new table will store membership fee and donations data for each member of The Chocolate Museum. You create the table in Design view. You need to name each field and select a data type for each field in the table. When you save the table, Access asks you if you want to make one of the fields a primary key. You won't assign a primary key to the table you create in this skill, but you should know that a primary key can be assigned to one of the fields in a table, such as a member ID number, to make sure no two records in a table are the same. The primary key column cannot contain duplicate entries.

Tip Be sure to open all database files from your working folder on your storage medium. Access database files opened directly from the Student Resources CD are read-only. Steps on how to copy a folder from the CD are located on the inside front cover of this textbook.

Tip The field in the *Description* column, to the right of the *Data Type* column, is optional. You can use it to describe the contents of the field.

Steps

1 Open the student data file named **M7-C2-Members.accdb** from your storage medium.

2 If a security warning appears immediately below the ribbon, click the Enable Content button.

3 Click the Create tab.

4 Click the Table Design button in the Tables group so that you can create the table in Design view.

5 In the first field in the *Field Name* column, type ID and then press the Tab key.

6 In the first field in the *Data Type* column, click the drop-down arrow and then click *Number*.

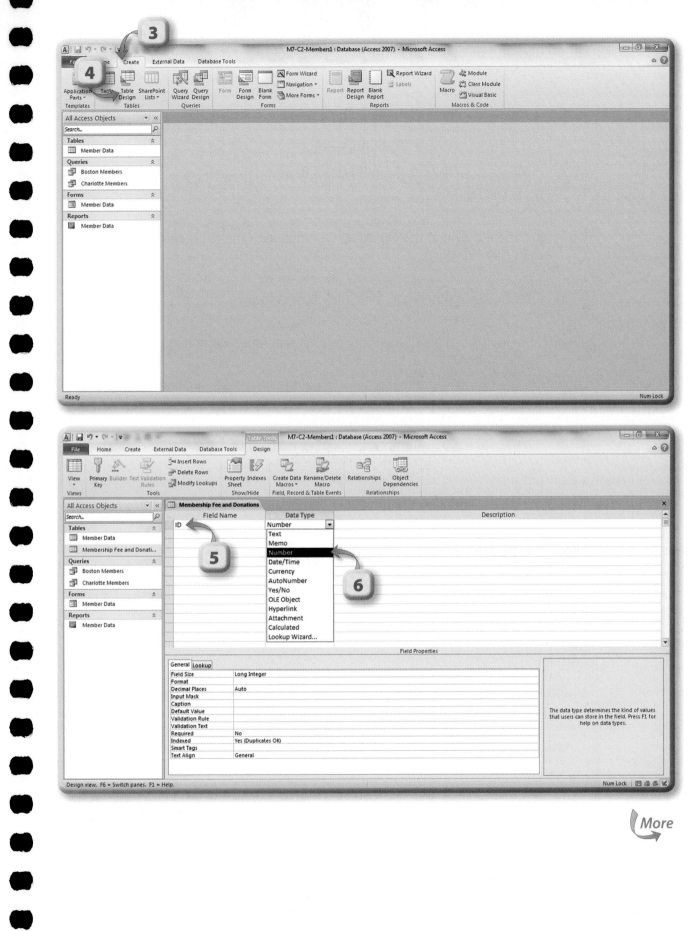

More

7 Click the second field in the *Field Name* column, type Annual Fee, and then press the Tab key.

8 In the second field in the *Data Type* column, click the drop-down arrow and then click *Currency*.

9 Click the third field in the *Field Name* column, type Donations, and then press the Tab key.

10 In the third field in the *Data Type* column, click the drop-down arrow and then click *Currency*.

11 Click the Save button on the Quick Access toolbar.

12 Type Membership Fee and Donations in the *Table Name* text box in the Save As dialog box.

13 Click OK.

14 Click No in the warning box indicating that a primary key is not selected.

15 Click Close to close the table.

> ▶ *Tip* You can assign a primary key to a field in a table to make sure no two records in a table are the same.

Taking It Further

Changing Field Size Some field types have a specified or a maximum field size. For example, Text fields can store up to 255 characters. If you want to limit a Text field to fewer characters (such as limiting fields for phone numbers or zip codes to help reduce data entry errors), replace the *Field Size* value of *255* with another value. Change this setting in the *Field Properties* section of the Design view window. A field size cannot be set for date/time, currency, or hyperlink fields.

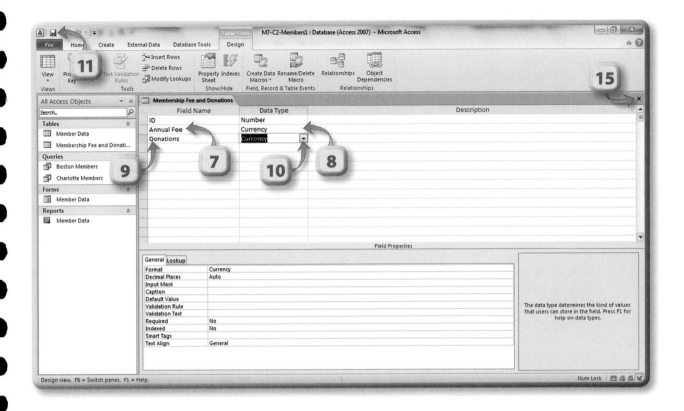

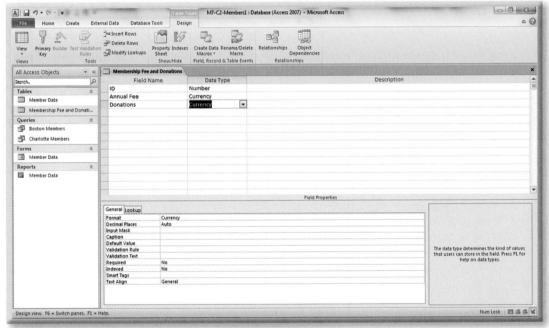

Completed Skill 1

Access

Skill 2

Video M7_C2_S02

Enter Data in a Table

In the previous skill, you created a new table. The new table is an object in the database. In this skill, you add records to the table. Typing records is one way to enter data in a table. You can also copy and paste data from other programs or databases, which saves time and also helps to prevent data entry errors. Adding records is sometimes referred to as *populating* the database.

Steps

1 With the **M7-C2-Members.accdb** database open, double-click the Membership Fee and Donations table in the Navigation pane.

▶**Tip** When you enter numbers in the fields in the *Annual Fee* and *Donations* columns, they are automatically formatted as currency to match the field type.

2 Add the following information to create a new record, using the Tab key to move between fields:

ID	Annual Fee	Donations
8	120	2000

▶**Tip** The ID number matches the member *ID* field assigned to the member in the Member Data table.

3 Click the record selection area to the left of record 1 to select all of the fields in record 1.

4 Click the Copy button in the Clipboard group on the Home tab.

▶**Tip** You can use copy and paste to save time when a new record is almost identical to an existing record. After pasting, you change only the part of the record that differs. In this case, all of the record data is the same except the *ID* field.

5 Click the record selection area to the left of record 2.

6 Click the Paste button in the Clipboard group on the Home tab.

7 Double-click record 2 the *ID* field and type 10.

8 Click Close to close the table.

Taking It Further

Copying and Pasting Data Another way to populate a table is to copy existing data from a Word or Excel file into an Access table. To copy all of the data from a Word source, first separate the data by tabs or copy it from a table. Whether you copy the data from Word or Excel, the data has to match the fields in the Access table. Click the record selection area for the next blank record before pasting the data. Note that you may copy and paste multiple records.

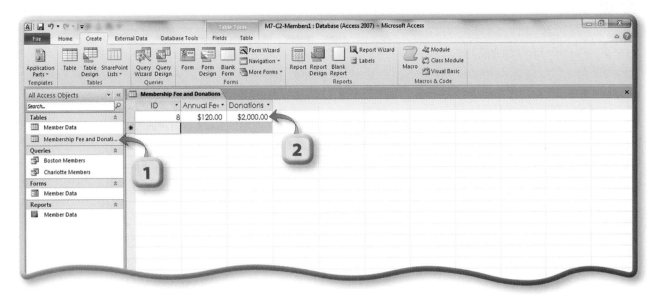

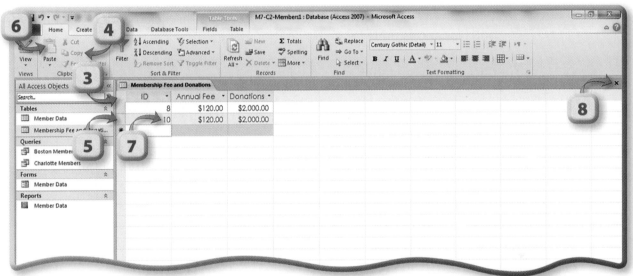

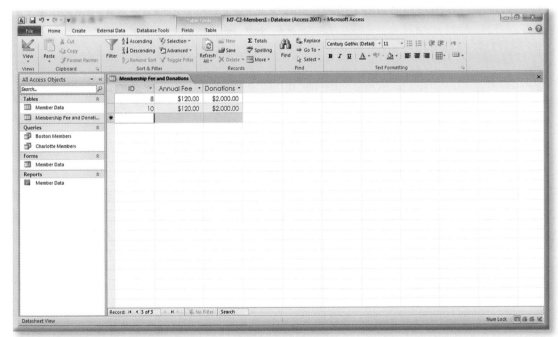

Completed Skill 2

Access

Access

Skill 3

Video M7_C2_S03

Create a Form

A form is a database object used for entering records in a table. You can also use a form to view existing records. Most forms show only one record at a time, which provides a simple interface for entering data and helps you to avoid data entry mistakes. A new form can be based on one or more database objects. The form you create in this skill is based on a table. When you first create a new form, it displays in Layout view, where you can format it.

Steps

1 With the **M7-C2-Members.accdb** database open, click the Membership Fee and Donations table in the Navigation pane.

2 Click the Create tab.

3 Click the Form button in the Forms group to display a form.

> **3** *Another Way*
> You can also use the Form Design button to create a form. In that case, the form displays in Design view, instead of in Layout view.

4 Hover the mouse over the right border of the *ID* field until it becomes a two-headed arrow, press and drag the right border to the left until the box is about half of its original size, and then release the mouse button. This action adjusts the size of all of the fields.

5 On the Form Layout Tools Design tab, in the Header/Footer group, click the Date and Time button.

6 In the Date and Time dialog box, click OK to add the date and time.

7 Click the Save button on the Quick Access toolbar.

8 Click OK to accept the form name *Membership Fee and Donations*. The form object is added to the Navigation pane.

9 Click Close to close the form.

Taking It Further

Changing Form Formatting and Views
When you create a form, the Form Layout Tools tabs for Design, Arrange, and Format are displayed on the ribbon. You can use options on the Form Layout Tools Format tab to change the font, font size, and font style. You can use the options on the Form Layout Tools Arrange tab to insert fields or alter the order of the fields. You can use options on the Form Layout Tools Design tab to add an image to the form or to change the form's theme. However, you cannot enter records in the form until you switch to Form view. To do so, click the View button arrow and select *Form view*.

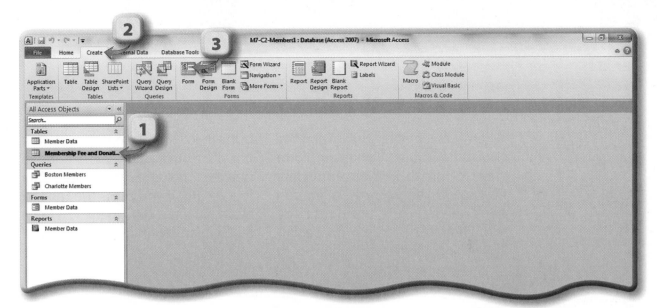

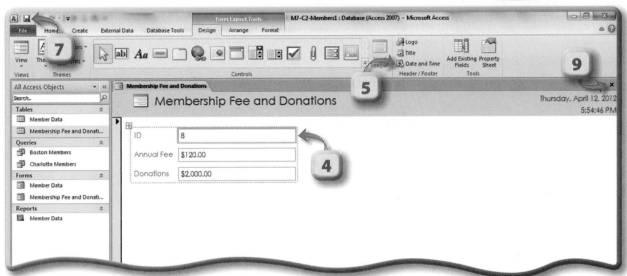

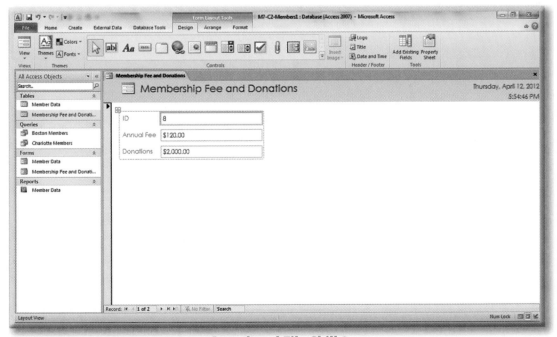

Completed File Skill 3

Access

Access

Skill 4

Video M7_C2_S04

Enter Data in a Form

When you open a form from the Navigation pane, it opens in Form view. You use this view to enter data in a form. The Record Navigation bar displays at the bottom of the form. You can add a new record by clicking the New (blank) record button in the Record Navigation bar. Use the Tab key to move between fields as you enter data in a record. If you press the Tab key after you enter data in the last field, a new blank form displays.

Steps

Tip If the form does not display in the Navigation pane, click the down-pointing arrow in the Navigation pane header and click *All Access Objects*.

1 With the **M7-C2-Members.accdb** database open, double-click the Membership Fee and Donations form in the Navigation pane.

2 In the Record Navigation bar, click the New (blank) record button.

3 Type 12 and press the Tab key.

4 Type 120 and press the Tab key.

5 Type 600 and press the Tab key. A new blank form displays.

6 Add these five additional records:

ID	Annual Fee	Donations
48	120	1000
17	120	2000
5	120	5000
37	120	0
25	120	250

Tip When you enter data in a form, Access saves the data automatically.

7 Click Close to close the form.

8 Close Access.

Taking It Further

Using Record Controls The Record Navigation bar indicates which record is currently displayed and how many records the table contains. For example, *1 of 4* indicates that record 1 is displayed and the table has 4 records. You can use record controls to scroll through the records. Record controls display at the bottom of an open form and include arrow buttons for moving directly to the First record, Previous record, Next record, and Last record.

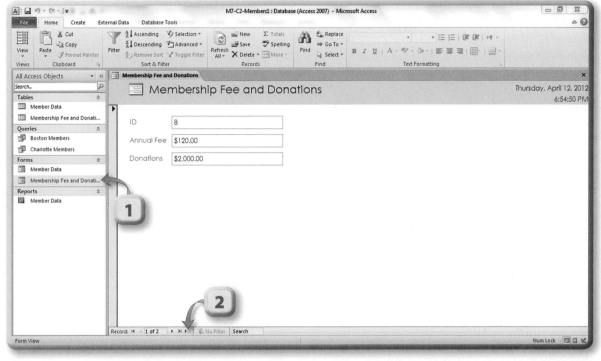

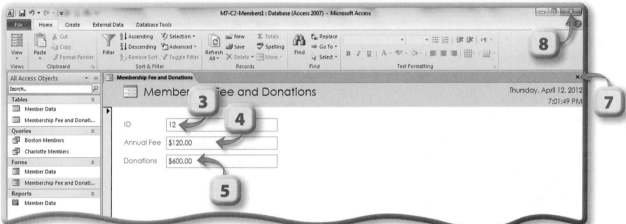

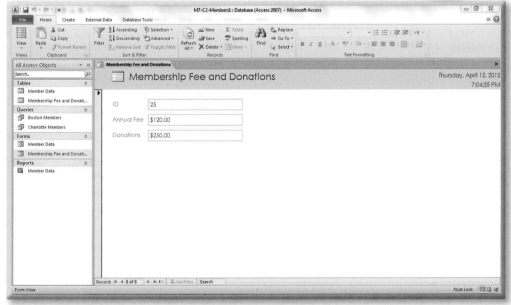

Completed File Skill 4

Access

Tasks Summary

Task	Ribbon Tab, Group	Button, Option	Shortcut, Alternative
Create a table	Create, Table		
Save a table			Ctrl + S
Select a record			Click the record selection area.
Copy a record	Home, Clipboard		Ctrl + C
Paste a record	Home, Clipboard		Ctrl + V
Create a form	Create, Form		
Add the date and time to a form	Form Layout Tools Design, Header/Footer	Date and Time	
Change views	Form Layout Tools Design, Views		Home, View

Features Review

Select the best answer from the choices given.

1 Which button do you use to create a table in Design view?
   a. Table Design
   b. Table
   c. Report
   d. Form Design

2 Which field type would you use to store a number that is one greater than the last number used?
   a. Text
   b. Number
   c. AutoNumber
   d. Currency

3 Which field type would you use to store dollar amounts?
   a. Text
   b. Number
   c. AutoNumber
   d. Currency

4 Which field type would you use to store characters and numbers that do not require calculations, such as zip codes?
   a. Text
   b. Number
   c. AutoNumber
   d. Currency

5 Which view do you use to enter records in a table?
   a. Design view
   b. Datasheet view
   c. Print Preview
   d. Layout view

6 Which action selects an entire record?
   a. Press the Tab key.
   b. Click the Record button.
   c. Click the first field in the record.
   d. Click the record selection area.

7 Which button creates a form and displays it in Layout view?
   a. Form
   b. Design
   c. Report
   d. Layout

8 Adding records is referred to as _____ the database.
   a. sorting
   b. populating
   c. filtering
   d. parsing

9 You can save a form by clicking the Save button on the
   a. Home tab.
   b. Create tab.
   c. Quick Access toolbar.
   d. All of the above

10 Which action copies a selected record?
   a. Click the record selection area.
   b. Click the Copy button.
   c. Click the Paste button.
   d. Click the Next record button.

Hands-On Skills Review

Exercise **A** **Adding to a Jewelry Store Database**

Skills   Create a table, enter data, edit data, format a datasheet, and enter data in a table

Scenario   You are in charge of updating a jewelry store database. You need to add a new table to the existing database. The table will store information about upcoming sales events. You also need to add some data to the new table.

Steps

1 Open the student data file named **M7-C2-ExA-Jewelry.accdb** and save the file as **Lastname-M7-C2-ExA-Jewelry**, but replace *Lastname* with your last name.

2 Create a new table in Design view.

3 Add three fields to the table.

Field Name	Data Type
Event	Text
Sale Item	Text
Discount	Currency

4 Save the table, naming it *Events*. If a warning box displays, indicating a primary key is not selected, click No.

5 Close the Events table.

6 Open the Events table in Datasheet view.

7 Add the following information to create three new records.

Event	Sale Item	Discount
Fall Celebration	Diamond Bracelet	100
Winter Sale	Emerald Earrings	200
Wedding Sale	Diamond Rings	200

8 Copy record 2.

9 Paste the copied data as record 4.

10 Edit the *Event* field in record 4 to read *Spring Sale* instead of *Winter Sale*.

11 Adjust the column widths in the datasheet so that all of the data in every column is visible.

12 Print the Events table or submit the completed database as directed by your instructor.

13 Close the Events table.

Events Table

Exercise B Making a Bookstore Database Easier to Use

Skills Create a form and enter data in a form

Scenario You are the manager of a bookstore. One of your responsibilities is to keep the bookstore's database up to date. To make data entry easier, you create a form to enter records.

Steps

1 Open the student data file named **M7-C2-ExB-Books.accdb** and save the file as **Lastname-M7-C2-ExB-Books**, but replace *Lastname* with your last name.

2 In the Navigation pane, click the Orders table.

3 Create a form based on the Orders table.

4 Modify the form to include the date and time.

5 Narrow the width of the fields in the form to about half of their original size.

6 Save the form, naming it *Orders*.

7 Close the form.

8 Open the Orders form and add five records to those that already exist in the table.

Order ID	Supplier Name	Order Total
B10	Books Unlimited	$560.00
B11	Tons of Books	$1350.00
B12	Books Unlimited	$765.00
B13	Book Depot	$250.00
B14	Book Depot	$375.00

9 Print the Orders table or submit the completed database as directed by your instructor.

10 Close the Orders table.

Order Form

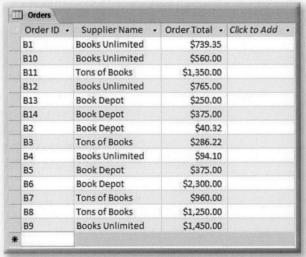

Orders Table

Exercise C Entering Information into the Community Volunteers Database

Skills   Create a form

Scenario   You have created a database to track student community service hours. In this exercise you create forms to make entering data in two of the tables in the database easier.

Steps

1 Open the student data file named **M7-C2-ExC-CommunityService.accdb** and save the file as **Lastname-M7-C2-ExC-CommunityService**, but replace *Lastname* with your last name.

2 Create a form based on the Volunteer Hours table.

3 Modify the form to include the date and time.

4 Narrow the width of the fields in the form to about half of their original size.

5 Change the form theme to Austin.

6 Save the form, naming it *Volunteer Hours*.

7 Create a form based on the Students table.

8 Change the form theme to Austin.

9 Save the form, naming it *Students*.

10 Print the Volunteer Hours and Students forms or submit the completed database as directed by your instructor.

11 Close both forms.

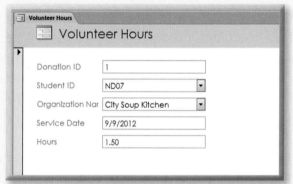

Volunteer Hours Form

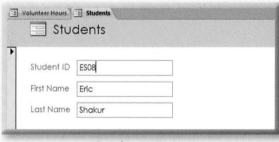

Students Form

Chapter 3

Working with Queries and Reports

A database may contain hundreds of records that are divided among many related tables. An easy way to find the information you are looking for is to create and run a query.

A query asks a question of the database, such as "How many members of The Chocolate Museum paid their annual fee?" or "How many members of The Chocolate Museum live in Boston?" A query shows only the data that you want to view at any given time. You can look at a limited number of fields from a single table or draw fields from multiple tables to view that data together. You can even sort or filter the query results to display only a subset of the results data, arranged in the order you prefer.

You can use the information in a table or in a query to create a professional-looking report. Then you can distribute the report in printed or electronic form. When preparing a report, you have several options. You might sort or group the report or format it using font options or by applying a theme.

In this chapter, you learn how to create queries to find the information you are looking for within an Access database. You also learn how to create, preview, and print a report.

Skills You Learn

1   Use the Query Wizard
2   Create a query in Design view
3   Use more than one table in a query
4   Create a report
5   Preview a report

Files You Need
In this chapter, you need the following student data file.

M7-C3-Members.accdb

What You Create
You create two queries in this chapter. One query displays only certain fields from the Member Data table. Another query finds all members of The Chocolate Museum who have donated more than $500 to the Museum. You then use the second query, focused on Museum members donating over $500, to create a report that is sorted and grouped. Lastly, you preview and then print the report.

Member Last Name and Zip Query

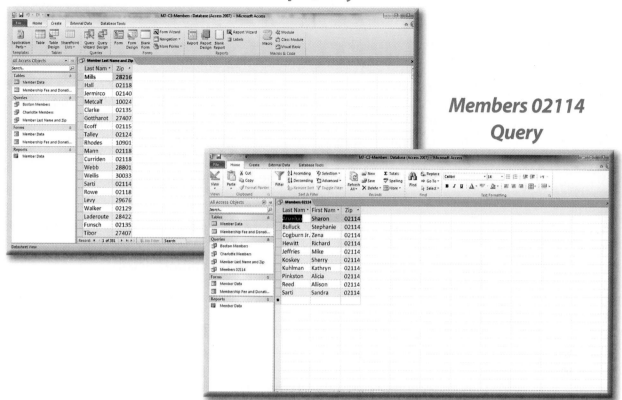

Members 02114 Query

Donations > $ 500 Query

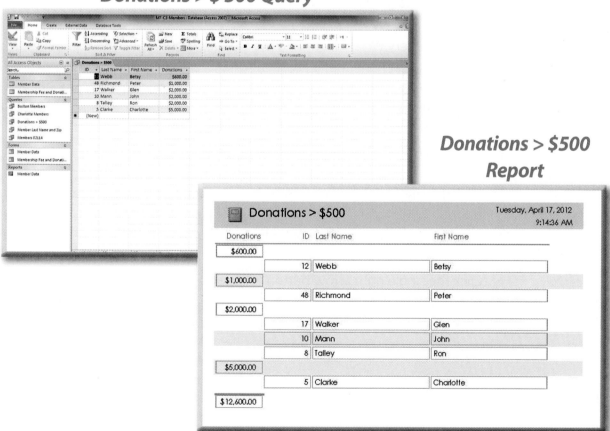

Donations > $500 Report

Access

Skill 1   Use the Query Wizard

Video   M7_C3_S01

Once you have entered information into a database, you can query the database to find records that meet certain criteria. A query pulls, or *extracts*, data from one or more tables. In this skill, you use the Query Wizard to create a simple query, which displays data from fields that you pick. Your simple query in this skill displays the *Last Name* and *Zip* fields from the Member Data table.

Steps

Tip Be sure to open all database files from your working folder on your storage medium. Access database files opened directly from the Student Resources CD are read-only. Steps on how to copy a folder from the CD are provided on the inside front cover of this textbook.

1 Open the student data file named **M7-C3-Members.accdb** from your storage medium.

2 If a security warning appears immediately below the ribbon, click the Enable Content button.

3 Click the Member Data table in the Navigation pane.

4 Click the Create tab.

5 Click the Query Wizard button in the Queries group.

6 In the New Query dialog box, select *Simple Query Wizard*, if it is not already highlighted, and then click OK.

Tip If you need to select all available fields, click the double right arrow button (>>).

7 Click *Last Name* in the *Available Fields* list box.

8 Click the single right arrow button (>) to add the field to the query.

9 Click *Zip* in the *Available Fields* list box.

10 Click the single right arrow button (>) to add the field to the query.

11 Click Next.

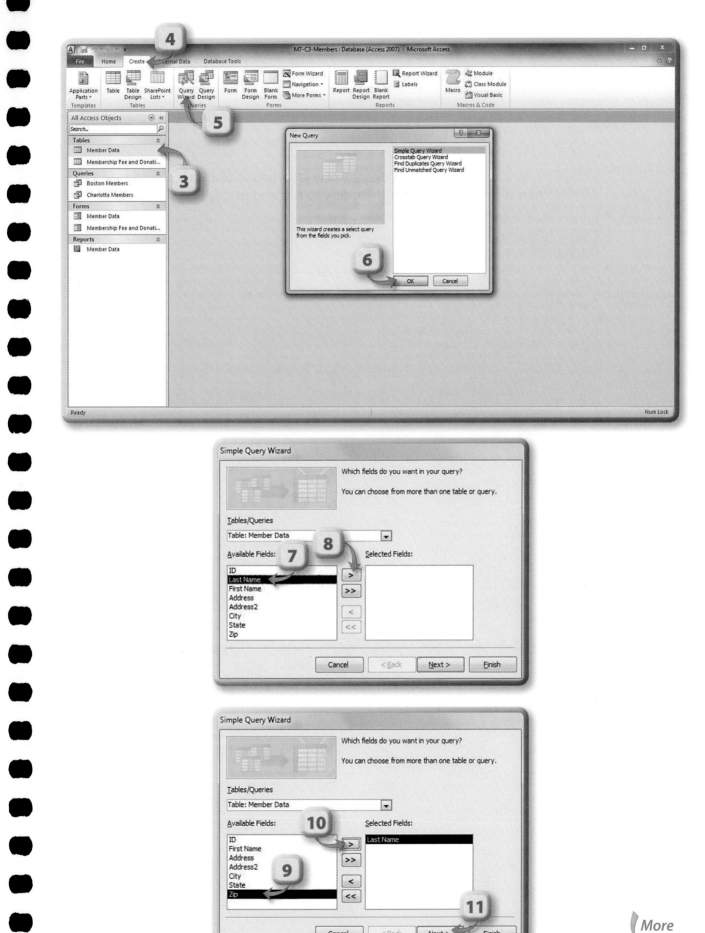

12 Select *Detail (shows every field of every record)*, if it is not already highlighted, and then click Next.

13 Select the text in the *What title do you want for your query?* text box and then type Member Last Name and Zip.

▶**Tip** The new query now appears in the *Queries* list in the Navigation pane.

14 Make sure the *Open the query to view information* option is selected and then click Finish to direct the query to run and to display the results.

15 Close the query.

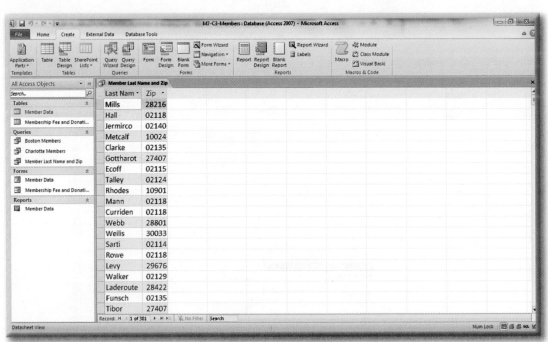

Completed Skill 1

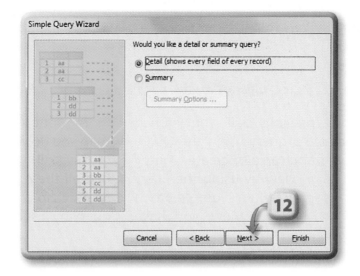

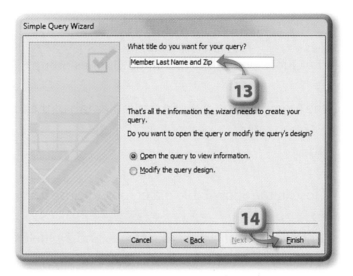

Taking It Further

Deciding to Query or to Filter There are important differences between running a query and simply filtering data. When you create a query, Access saves the query as an object in the database. Because the query is saved, you can run it again at a later time without having to recreate the query.

In contrast, filtering displays the results temporarily. Another advantage of running a query is that you can easily create a report from a query, giving you the option of presenting the query results in a professional format.

Access

Skill 2

Video ▶ M7_C3_S02

Create a Query in Design View

In the previous skill, you learned to create a query using the Query Wizard. You can also create a query in Design view by using the *query design grid*. When you create a query in Design view, you have more options and more control than you do with the Query Wizard. In this skill, you create a query to find all the members who live in a specific zip code. You then sort the query by last name.

Steps

1 With the **M7-C3-Members.accdb** database open, click the Create tab.

2 Click the Query Design button in the Queries group.

3 Click the Member Data table in the Tables tab of the Show Table dialog box.

4 Click Add.

5 Click Close in the Show Table dialog box to close it.

> ▶ **Tip** Double-click carefully, choosing only those fields that you need for the query. You may need to scroll to see the *Zip* field.

6 Double-click the *Last Name*, *First Name*, and *Zip* fields in the *Member Data* table field list box. The fields are added to the query design grid at the bottom of the window.

7 Click the *Sort* cell for the *Last Name* field in the query design grid.

8 Click the down arrow that appears and then click *Ascending* in the drop-down list.

9 Click in the *Criteria* cell for the *Zip* field in the query design grid and type 02114.

> **10** *Another Way*
> You can also run the query by clicking the View button. When you click the View button, you switch from Design view to Datasheet view and the query results display.

10 On the Query Tools Design tab, click the Run button in the Results group to display the query results in a datasheet.

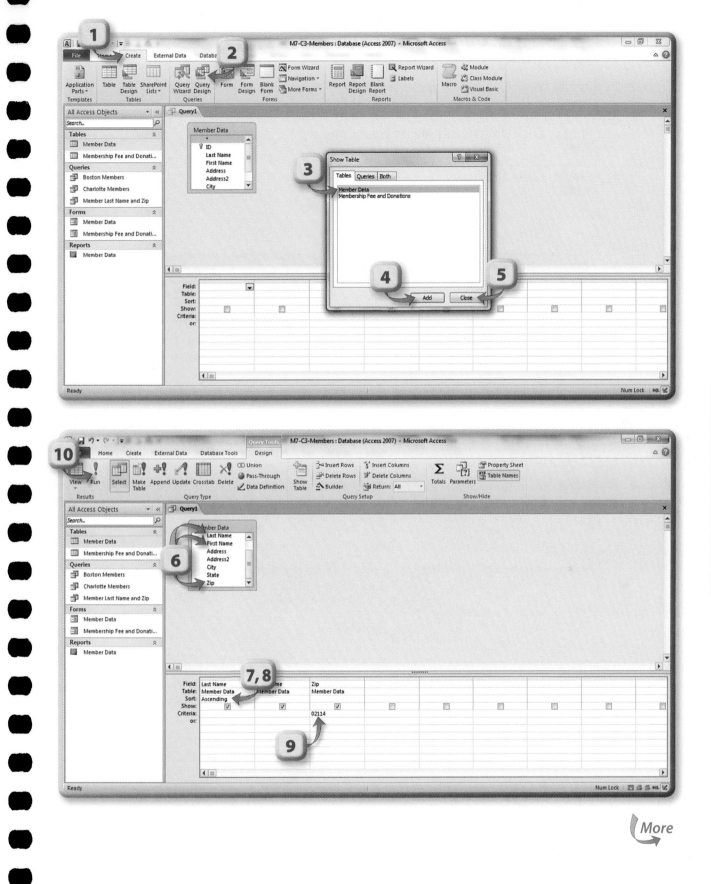

More

Access

11 Click the Save button on the Quick Access toolbar.

12 Type Members 02114 in the *Query Name* text box of the Save As dialog box.

▶ **Tip** The new query now appears in the Queries list in the Navigation pane.

13 Click OK to finish saving the query.

14 Close the query.

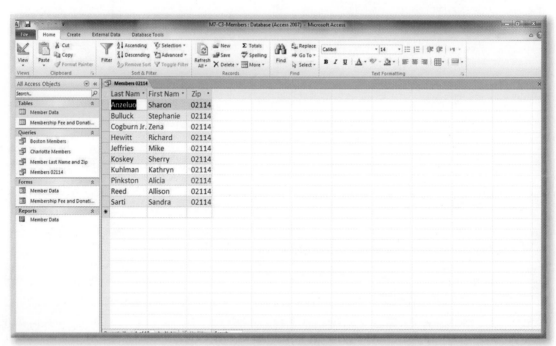

Completed Skill 2

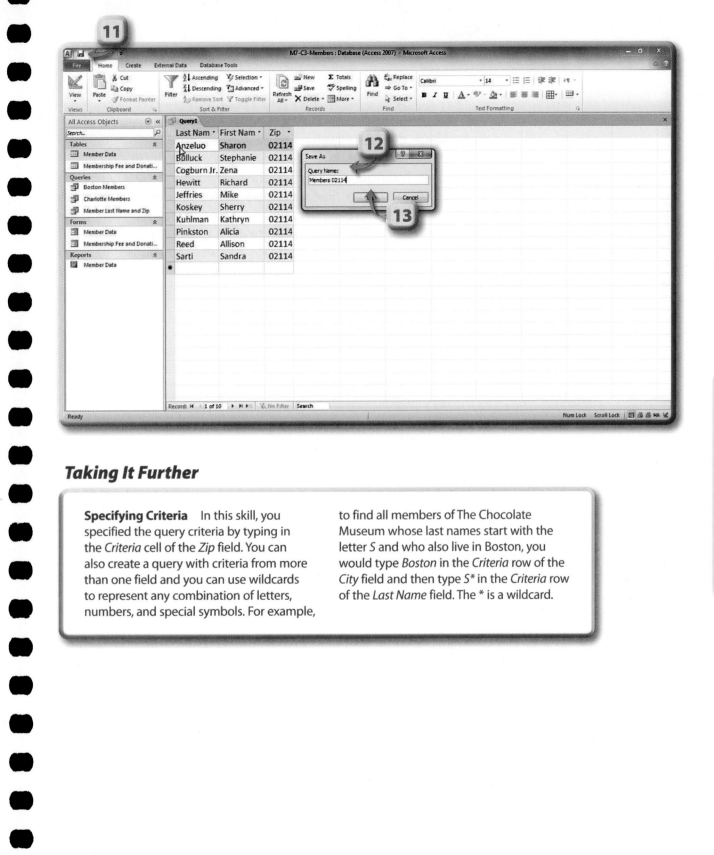

Taking It Further

Specifying Criteria   In this skill, you specified the query criteria by typing in the *Criteria* cell of the *Zip* field. You can also create a query with criteria from more than one field and you can use wildcards to represent any combination of letters, numbers, and special symbols. For example, to find all members of The Chocolate Museum whose last names start with the letter *S* and who also live in Boston, you would type *Boston* in the *Criteria* row of the *City* field and then type *S** in the *Criteria* row of the *Last Name* field. The * is a wildcard.

Skill 3

Use More Than One Table in a Query

Video M7_C3_S03

Tables in a database can be related through a common column of data. For example, the Member Data table and the Membership Fee and Donations table are related through the *ID* column. The field in this column assigns a unique number to each Museum member. Such database design features are helpful because the tables do not need to contain a lot of duplicate data and, as a result, the database operates more efficiently. When Access tables are related, you can pull data from more than one table to create a query. In this skill, you create a query that pulls data from both the Member Data table and the Membership Fee and Donations table.

Steps

1. With the **M7-C3-Members.accdb** database open, click the Create tab.

2. Click the Query Design button in the Queries group.

3. Make sure that *Member Data* is selected on the Tables tab of the Show Table dialog box and then click Add.

4. Click *Membership Fee and Donations* on the Tables tab in the Show Table dialog box and then click Add.

Tip A relationship line appears between the *ID* fields.

5. Click Close in the Show Table dialog box to close it.

Tip Double-click carefully, choosing only those fields specifically needed for the query.

6. Double-click *ID*, *Last Name*, and *First Name* in the *Member Data* table field list box.

7. Double-click *Donations* in the *Membership Fee and Donations* table field list box.

8. Click the *Sort* cell for the *Donations* field in the query design grid.

9. Click the down arrow that appears and then click *Ascending* in the drop-down list.

Tip In addition to > (greater than), you can use other relational operators including > = (greater than or equal to), < (less than), < = (less than or equal to), = (equal to), and < > (not equal to) as search criteria.

10. Click in the *Criteria* cell for the *Donations* field and then type >500.

11. On the Query Tools Design tab, click the Run button in the Results group. The query results appear in a datasheet.

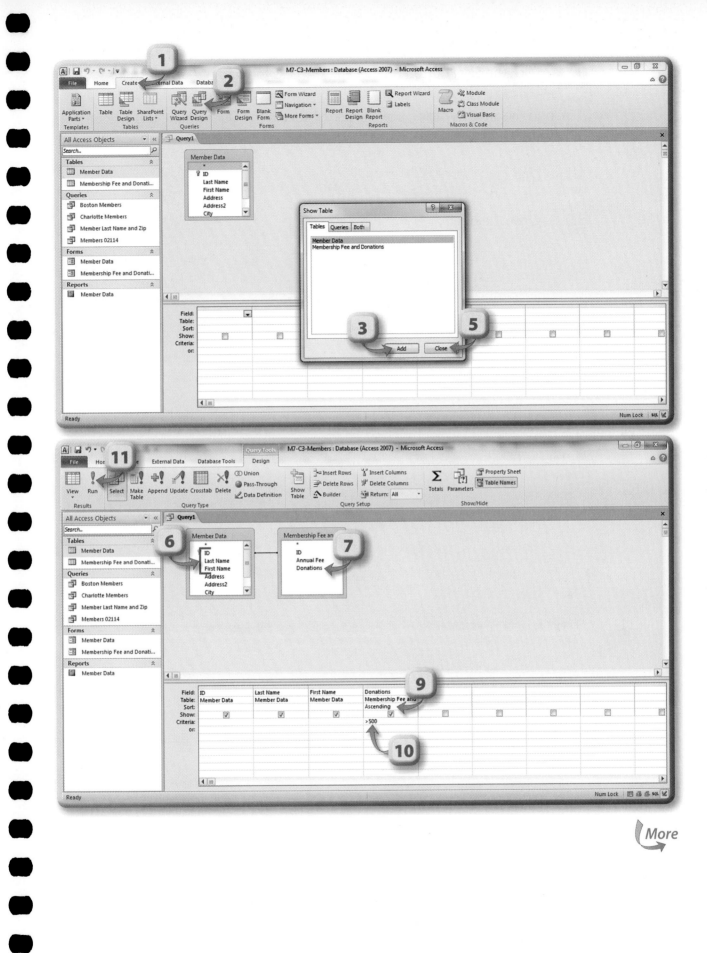

More

12 Click the Save button on the Quick Access toolbar.

13 In the Save As dialog box, select the text in the *Query Name* text box and then type Donations > $500.

14 Click OK.

15 Close the query.

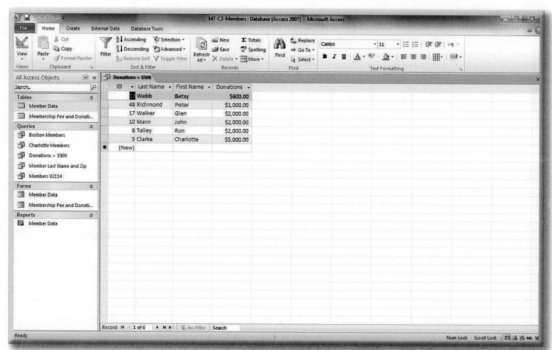

Completed Skill 3

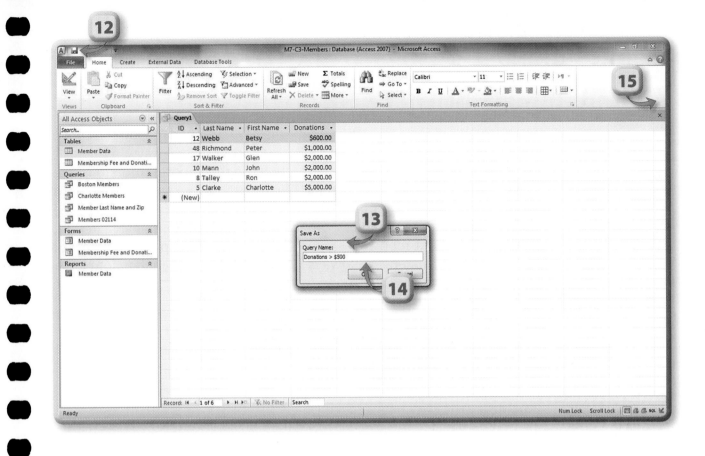

Taking It Further

Reviewing Relationships In most cases, an Access table is related to at least one other table in the database. You can view the existing table relationships by clicking the Relationships button in the Relationships group on the Database Tools tab. Then click the All Relationships button to display all existing relationships.

Access

Skill 4

Create a Report

Video ► M7_C3_S04

Reports present Access data in an attractive, easy-to-print format. A report is based on multiple, related tables or queries. When you create a report, Access links the report to the objects (query and/or tables) you used to create that report. Because the report is linked, it always displays current data. You can create a report in several ways. In this skill, you use the Report button to create a report based on the Donations > $500 query. When you use the Report button to create a report, the report is displayed in Layout view, where you can then format it.

Steps

1 With the **M7-C3-Members.accdb** database open, click the Donations > $500 query in the Navigation pane.

2 Click the Create tab.

▶**Tip** The Report Layout Tools Design tab is now the active tab.

3 Click the Report button in the Reports group to display the report in Layout view.

4 Click the Themes button in the Themes group.

5 Click *Austin* (the third theme in the second row) under the *Built-In* section to apply the Austin theme to the report.

6 Click the Group & Sort button in the Grouping & Totals group to display the Group, Sort, and Total pane.

7 Click the Add a sort button in the Group, Sort, and Total pane.

8 Select the *Donations* option to sort the report by the *Donations* column.

9 Click the *Donations Total* cell to make it active.

10 Hover the mouse pointer over the border of the cell until the pointer becomes a double-headed arrow and then double-click the cell border to AutoFit the cell.

11 Click the Add a group button in the Group, Sort, and Total pane.

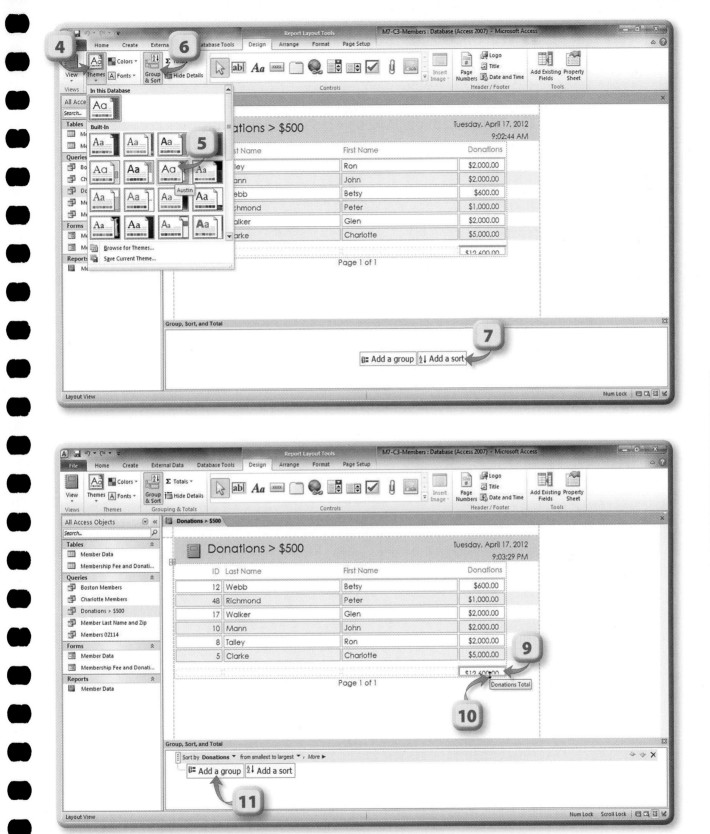

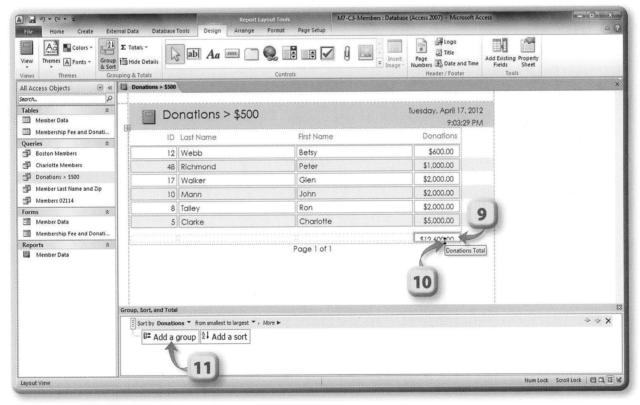

More

12 Select the *Donations* option to group the report by donation amount.

13 Click the Save button on the Quick Access toolbar.

14 Click OK to accept the *Donations > $500* report name.

15 Close the report.

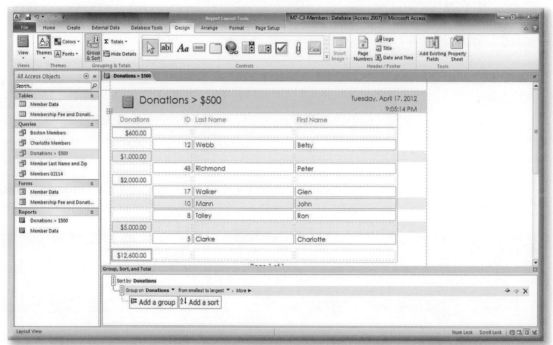

Completed Skill 4

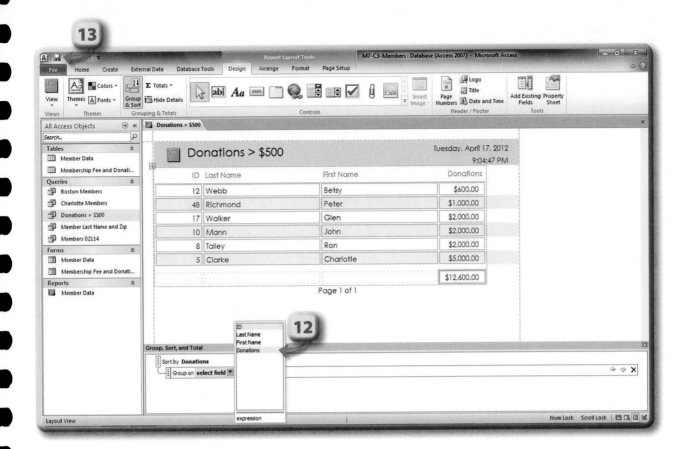

Taking It Further

Formatting a Report The Report Layout Tools Design tab contains options for formatting a report. For example, you can click the Logo button to add a business logo to the report. You can also modify the title and the date and time that are displayed by default in the report. Double-click the title to modify it or click the Date and Time button to display the date and time format options. The Report Layout Tools Format tab also contains options for formatting a report. You can click a cell in the report and then change options, such as the font, font size, text color, or fill color. You can also add a background image to the report. The Report Layout Tools Arrange tab contains options for inserting rows and columns and altering the layout of the report. The Report Layout Tools Page Setup tab contains options for formatting the page size and the page layout.

Video ▶ M7_C3_S05

Preview a Report

Before printing a report, it is good practice to use the Print Preview feature to view what the printed copy will look like and adjust the print settings, if necessary. The Print Preview tab in Access contains print and page layout options as well as options for exporting the report to another format, such as PDF. When you preview the report, you need to check the presentation of the data and the page setup.

Steps

1 With the **M7-C3-Members.accdb** database open, double-click the Donations > $500 report in the Navigation pane.

2 Click the down arrow on the View button in the Views group on the Home tab.

3 Select *Print Preview* from the drop-down list.

> **3 Another Way**
> Right-click a report object in the Navigation Pane and then select *Print Preview*.

4 On the Print Preview tab, click the Landscape button in the Page Layout group to change the print orientation to landscape.

5 Click the Print button.

6 Click OK if your instructor asks you to print the report, but if not, click Cancel.

7 Close the report.

8 Exit Access.

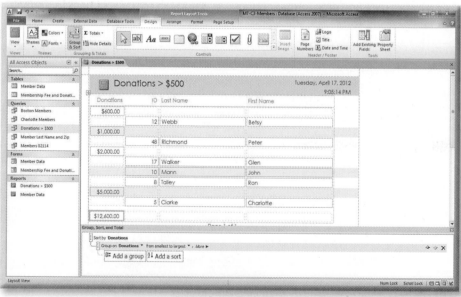

Completed Skill 5

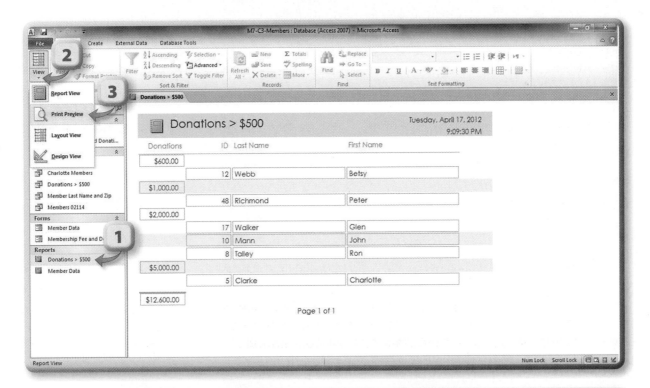

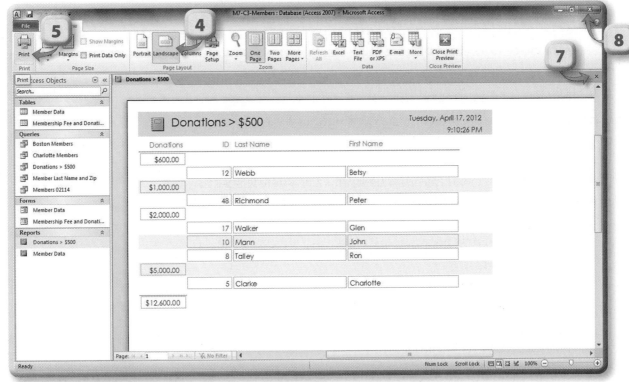

Taking It Further

Saving a Report as a PDF File   You can save an Access report in other formats. For example, you may want to save a report as a PDF file. PDF allows anybody to use a free reader program to view the report with its formatting intact, so the report looks the same on every computer. To save a report as a PDF file, click the PDF or XPS button in the Print Preview tab, type a file name, and then click the Publish button in the Publish as PDF or XPS dialog box.

Access

Access

Chapter 3 Assessments

Tasks Summary

Task	Ribbon Tab, Group	Button, Option	Shortcut, Alternative
Create a query using the Query Wizard	Create, Queries		
Create a query in Design view	Create, Queries		
Add a table from the Show Table dialog box		Add	
Close the Show Table dialog box		Close	
Run a query	Query Tools Design, Results	!	Click the View button to switch from Design view to Datasheet view.
Create a report	Create, Reports		
Apply a theme to a report	Report Layout Tools Design, Themes	Aa	
Display the Group, Sort, and Total pane	Report Layout Tools Design, Grouping & Totals		
Add a sort	Group, Sort, and Total pane	Add a sort	
Add a group	Group, Sort, and Total pane	Add a group	
Print Preview a report	Home, Views		
Change the print orientation to landscape	Print Preview, Page Layout		
Print a report	Print Preview, Print		
Create a PDF copy of the report	Print Preview, Data		

Features Review

Select the best answer from the choices given.

1 Which asks a question of the database?
   a. table
   b. form
   c. query
   d. report

2 When a query pulls data from one or more tables, the process that occurs is referred to as
   a. extracting data.
   b. importing data.
   c. sorting data.
   d. grouping data.

3 You can distribute a database report
   a. in printed format.
   b. in electronic format.
   c. as a PDF file.
   d. All of the above

4 When you create a query using the _____ button, you select query options from a series of dialog boxes.
   a. Query Design
   b. Query Wizard
   c. Query Report
   d. Report Wizard

5 When you create a query in Design view, you use the _____ to create the query.
   a. Query Wizard dialog boxes
   b. query design grid
   c. layout design grid
   d. Print Preview window

6 When creating a query, you can only select fields from one table.
   a. true
   b. false

7 To find all records where the *Amount* field was less than $1000, enter _____ in the *Criteria* cell for the *Amount* field.
   a. 1000
   b. >1000
   c. <1000
   d. <>1000

8 Which is a theme that you can apply to a report?
   a. XPS or PDF
   b. Austin
   c. alternate row colors
   d. Group & Sort

9 Which button changes the print orientation from the default setting of *Portrait*?
   a. Group & Sort
   b. Themes
   c. Landscape
   d. Print

10 Which view do you use to change the print orientation?
   a. Form view
   b. Datasheet view
   c. Print Preview
   d. Design view

Hands-On Skills Review

Exercise **A** **Summarizing Store Events—Jewelry Store Database**

Skills   Use the Query Wizard, create a report, and preview a report.

Scenario   You need to find out about all upcoming sale events and review the featured sale item for each event. You query the jewelry store database to find this information.

Steps

1 Open the student data file named **M7-C3-ExA-Jewelry.accdb** and save the file as **Lastname-M7-C3-ExA-Jewelry**, but replace *Lastname* with your last name.

2 Click the Events table in the Navigation pane.

3 Use the Query Wizard to create a simple query that lists the *Event* and the *Sale Item* fields.

4 Name the query *Events Query*.

5 Close the Events Query query.

6 Create a report based on the Events Query.

7 Save the report, naming it *Events Query*.

8 Print the Events Query report or submit the completed database as directed by your instructor.

9 Close the Events Query report.

Events Query

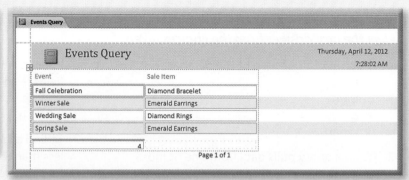

Events Query Report

Exercise B Finding Information in a Bookstore Database

Skills Create a query in Design view, use more than one table in a query, create a report, and preview a report

Scenario You are the manager of a bookstore. You need to query the database to find all orders over $500. You then create a report based on the query.

Steps

1 Open the student data file named **M7-C3-ExB-Books.accdb** and save the file as **Lastname-M7-C3-ExB-Books**, but replace *Lastname* with your last name.

2 Query the database to find all orders over $500. Use both the Orders and Suppliers tables to create your query in Design view. The query should display the *Order ID*, *Contact Name*, *Supplier Name*, and *Order Total* fields.

3 Save the query, naming it *Orders over $500*.

4 Create a report based on the Orders over $500 query.

5 Sort the report by the *Order Total* field.

6 Save the report, naming it *Orders over $500*.

7 Print Preview the report.

8 Print the Orders over $500 report or submit the completed database as directed by your instructor.

9 Close the Orders over $500 report.

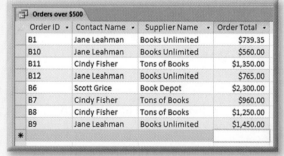

Orders over $500 Query

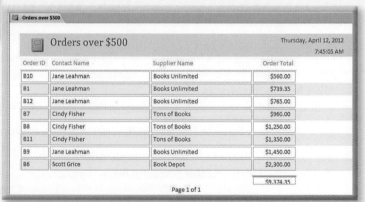

Orders over $500 Report

Exercise C Finding and Reporting Information from the Community Volunteers Database

Skills   Create a query in Design view, use more than one table in a query, create a report, and preview a report

Scenario   You have set up a database to track student community service hours. You first find out how many hours students are volunteering at the various organizations and then present this information in a report.

Steps

1 Open the student data file named **M7-C3-ExC-CommunityService.accdb** and save the file as **Lastname-M7-C3-ExC-CommunityService**, but replace *Lastname* with your last name.

2 Query the database to find out how many student hours are being spent at each organization. Use both the Organizations and Volunteer Hours tables to create your query in Design view. The query should display the *Organization Name* (from the Organizations table), *Student ID*, and *Hours* fields.

3 Save the query, naming it *Volunteer Hours by Organization*.

4 Create a report based on the Volunteer Hours by Organization query.

5 Group the report by the *Organization Name* field.

6 Sort the report by the *Hours* field.

7 Save the report, naming it *Volunteer Hours by Organization*.

8 Print Preview the report.

9 Print the Volunteer Hours by Organization report or submit the completed document as directed by your instructor.

10 Close the Volunteer Hours by Organization report.

Volunteer Hours by Organization Query

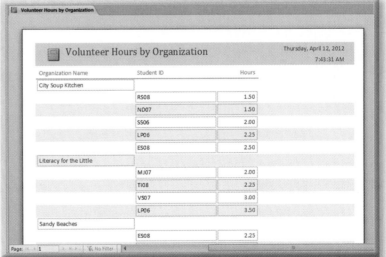

Volunteer Hours by Organization Report

Module 7 Projects

Project 1

Skills   Open and navigate a database, create a table, create a form, enter data in a form, enter data in a table, create a query in Design view, create a report, and preview a report

Scenario   You manage a movie rental store. You have created a database to store data on each of the store's movies. You now need to create a table to store the information about each movie and then create a form to enter records in the database.

Steps

1 Open the student data file named **M7-EOM-P1-Movie.accdb** and save the file as **Lastname-M7-EOM-P1-Movie**, but replace *Lastname* with your last name.

2 Create a new table in Design view.

3 Define the table to have the following fields and data types:

ID	Number
Title	Text
Rating	Text

4 Save and close the table, naming it *Movies*. Do not add a primary key.

5 Create a form based on the Movies table.

6 Add the date and time to the form.

7 Save the form, naming it *Movies*.

8 Use the Movies form in Form view to enter the following records in the database.

ID	Title	Rating
3155	Unstoppable	PG-13
3479	Morning Glory	PG-13

9 The movie rental store stocks many duplicate copies of the same movie. Enter the rest of the records using either the Movies Form view or the Movies Datasheet view. Use copy and paste where possible to save time and avoid data entry errors.

ID	Title	Rating
3480	Morning Glory	PG-13
3455	Skyline	PG-13
3466	Skyline	PG-13
3467	Skyline	PG-13
3877	Cool It	PG
3878	Cool It	PG
3901	The Next 3 Days	PG-13
3902	The Next 3 Days	PG-13

ID	Title	Rating
4011	Red	PG-13
4012	Red	PG-13
4015	Toy Story 3	G
4016	Toy Story 3	G
4017	Toy Story 3	G

10 Create a query to find all movies that are rated PG-13. Display the fields *Title* and *Rating* in your query.

11 Save the query, naming it *PG-13 Movies*.

12 Ask your instructor if you should print a copy of the query.

13 Create a report based on the PG-13 Movies query.

14 Sort the report in ascending order by the *Title* field.

15 Group the report by the *Title* field.

16 Save the report, naming it *PG-13 Movies*.

17 Ask your instructor if you should print a copy of the report.

18 Submit the completed file as directed by your instructor.

PG-13 Movies Query

PG-13 Movies

Wednesday, March 21, 2012
5:03:26 PM

Title	Rating
Morning Glory	
	PG-13
	PG-13
Red	
	PG-13
	PG-13
Skyline	
	PG-13
	PG-13
	PG-13
The Next 3 Days	
	PG-13
	PG-13
Unstoppable	
	PG-13
10	

PG-13 Movies Report

Project 2

Skills   Open and navigate a database, create a table, create a form, enter data in a form, create a query in Design view, create a report, and preview a report

Scenario   You run a web-based computer-support site. Users pay either a 6-month fee of $60.00 or an annual fee of $120.00 to have access to online computer help. You need to create a table in your database to store information about your subscribers.

Steps

1 Open the student data file named **M7-EOM-P2-ComputerSupport.accdb** and save the file as **Lastname-M7-EOM-P2-ComputerSupport**, but replace *Lastname* with your last name.

2 Create a new table in Design view.

3 Define the table to have the following fields and data types.

ID	*Number*
Last Name	Text
First Name	Text
Join_Month	Text
Fee	Currency

4 Save the table, naming it *Customers*. Do not define a primary key.

5 Create a form based on the Customers table.

6 Add the date and time to the form.

7 In Form Layout view press and drag the right border of the entry boxes to the right until the boxes are about half of their original size.

8 Save the form, naming it Customers.

9 Use the Customers form in Form view to enter the following records in the database.

ID	Last Name	First	Join_Month	Fee
5155	Mitchell	Paul	September	120.00
5167	Ableson	Michelle	October	60.00
5169	Quinn	Terry	October	60.00
5170	Samuels	Jennifer	November	60.00
5180	Watson	Robert	November	120.00
5290	Simpson	Ann	December	120.00
5400	Gregory	Michaela	December	60.00

10 Create a query of all customers that have paid a fee of $60.00. Display the *Last Name*, *First Name*, and *Fee* fields in the query.

11 Save the query, naming it *$60 Customers*.

12 Ask your instructor if you should print a copy of the query.

13 Create a report based on the $60 Customers query.

14 Sort the report based on the *Last Name* field.

15 Save the report, naming it *$60 Customers*.

16 Ask your instructor if you should print a copy of the query.

17 Submit the completed file as directed by your instructor.

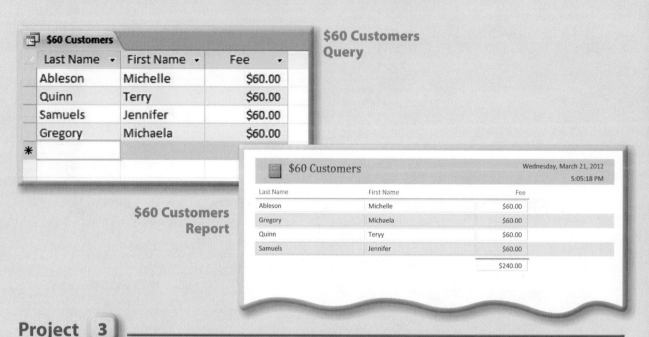

$60 Customers Query

$60 Customers Report

Project 3

Skills Open and navigate a database, create a table, create a form, enter data in a form, create a query in Design view, create a report, and preview a report

Scenario You run a car rental company. You need to add a table to the database to store information about your car inventory. You then add records to the table.

Steps

1 Open the student data file named **M7-EOM-P3-Cars.accdb** and save the file as **Lastname-M7-EOM-P3-Cars**, but replace *Lastname* with your last name.

2 Create a new table in Design view.

3 Define the table to have the following fields and data types.

Car_Year	Number
Model	Text
Make	Text
Color	Text
Mileage	Number

4 Save the table, naming it *Cars*. Do not define a primary key for the table.

5 Create a form based on the Cars table.

6 Add the date and time to the form.

7 In Form Layout view press and drag the right border of the entry boxes to the right until the boxes are about half of their original size.

8 Save the form, naming it *Cars*.

9 Use the Cars form in Form view to enter the following records in the database.

Car_Year	Model	Make	Color	Mileage
2010	Ford	Escape	Red	15000
2010	Ford	Escape	Blue	12000
2011	Honda	Civic	Brown	10000
2011	Honda	Civic	Black	12000
2011	Mazda	626	Black	20000
2011	Mazda	626	White	22000

10. Create a query of all 2011 cars. Display the *Car_Year*, *Model*, *Make*, and *Mileage* fields in the query.

11. Save the query, naming it *2011 Cars*.

12. Ask your instructor if you should print a copy of the query.

13. Create a report based on the Cars table.

14. Change the report title to *Car Inventory*. **HINT:** Click the title, Cars, to edit the report title.

15. Sort the report based on the *Mileage* field.

16. Change the page orientation to landscape.

17. Save the report, naming it *Car Inventory*.

18. Ask your instructor if you should print a copy of the report.

19. Submit the completed file as directed by your instructor.

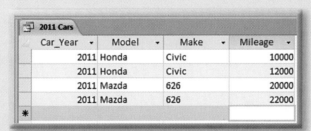

2011 Cars Query

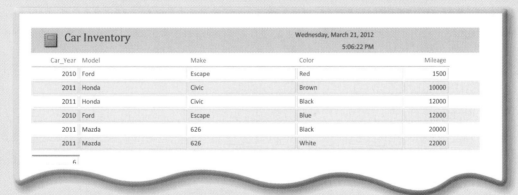

Car Inventory Report

MODULE 8

Microsoft® PowerPoint 2010

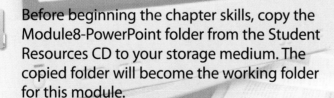

Before beginning the chapter skills, copy the Module8-PowerPoint folder from the Student Resources CD to your storage medium. The copied folder will become the working folder for this module.

Guidelines for Creating a

Before you begin to create a PowerPoint presentation, you should have a focused topic, a clear purpose, and know who your audience will be. Ask yourself how much your audience members are likely to know about your topic, what they might do with the information, and whether they would appreciate humor, for example.

A well-organized slide show helps you lead your audience to your presentation's goal. That goal may be to get them to take an action, such as joining a group or buying something. Or it may be to give them the information they need to get their jobs done, and so on.

Hand-drawn Storyboard

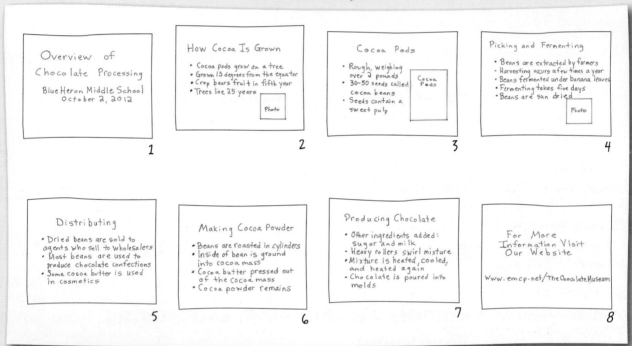

You should have a basic idea of how to organize the information in your presentation. To work out the best flow for the information, you might draw a quick storyboard (a tool used by many filmmakers), making brief notes and sketches on paper, by hand. Or you might even use PowerPoint itself to create the storyboard on slides, later refining those storyboard slides into polished content.

PowerPoint provides different layouts that you can use for different purposes. For example, use a Title Slide layout for the first slide in your show.

Title Slide Layout

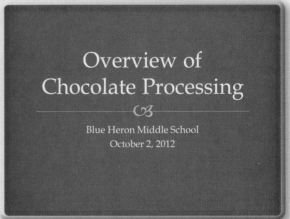

PowerPoint Presentation

Use Content layouts to provide concise bullet points or to insert graphics, videos, or photos for visual interest and richer communication.

Content Layout

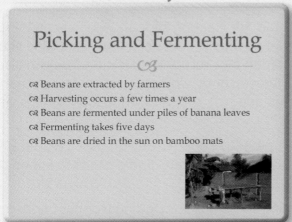

Include no more than six bullet points per slide, and keep them brief—fitting on a single line when possible. Bullet points guide the audience through the presentation and don't need to spell out every detail. The speaker's words are the focus and should provide the full story.

While you don't want to crowd your slides with information, you also don't want to overuse graphic elements and animations. These features, used sparingly, can provide interest and entertain. But if overdone, they can distract viewers from the speaker's message (and greatly increase file size).

You can keep the look of your slides consistent by using a built-in design. If you modify the design, a good tip is to avoid using more than two fonts on a single slide and two or three fonts in the entire presentation.

Set up your slide show either to be given in person and navigated manually (reflected by the options chosen in the screen capture below), or to run automatically with saved timings and a recorded narration when there is no speaker present.

When running a show in Slide Show view, take advantage of tools that enable you to easily navigate your slide show. Always rehearse your show several times, well ahead of time. Such preparation helps you find and eliminate technical problems. You can then be confident that the show runs within your allotted time slot, always allowing some time for audience questions.

Slide Show View

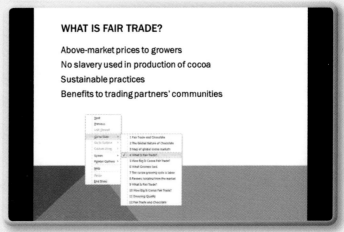

Creating a Presentation

PowerPoint is an easy-to-use presentation program for creating slide shows that can be run in front of an audience to reinforce a speaker's key points. Viewers can also run a slide show themselves and be guided through the presentation by a recorded narration. You can also publish a PowerPoint slide show to the Web where anybody who accesses it can run the presentation at their convenience. Slides may include text, graphics, animation, videos, and sound.

In this chapter, you begin to build and run a simple slide show. Once you have created slide content, you can reorganize the slides and apply different layouts and designs to enhance their visual impact.

PowerPoint offers several views for accomplishing these tasks, including Normal, Slide Sorter, and Reading. Most of your work building a slide show is done using the Normal view, which splits the screen into three main sections, or panes. The Slide pane includes a large view of an individual slide, the smaller Notes pane is below the Slide pane and provides an area for entering speaker notes, and the left side panel is called the Slides/Outline pane.

You probably use both tabs in the Slides/Outline pane on a regular basis. When you select the Slides tab, the Slides/Outline pane displays small, thumbnail views of the presentation slides. You can click a slide thumbnail and view the corresponding slide in the larger Slide pane. When you instead select the Outline tab, the Slides/Outline pane displays the text contained on each slide in an outline format.

In this chapter, you also work with the Slide Sorter view, which is the best view to use for organizing your presentation, and the Reading view, which you can use to preview slides in a window.

Skills You Learn

1 Open PowerPoint and insert a slide
2 Enter text on slides
3 Use the Outline feature
4 Add notes
5 Apply a layout
6 Apply a theme
7 Change the color scheme
8 Organize slides using Slide Sorter

Files You Need

In this chapter, you need the following student data files.

> M8-C1-S4-FairTrade.pptx
>
> M8-C1-S8-FairTrade.pptx

What You Create

The cocoa-growing industry is spread throughout several countries around the world. Because of its geographical range, the industry has varying standards for how growers get paid and how workers are treated. "Fair trade" is a term for an industry standard that requires that growers be paid fairly for what they grow and that workers are treated well.

In this chapter, you create a simple PowerPoint presentation on fair trade in the chocolate industry. Your presentation will be used to inform the public and gain funding for The Chocolate Museum. You create slides; enter text; organize the presentation; and use layouts, designs, and color schemes to add visual appeal.

Fair Trade Presentation

PowerPoint

Skill 1 Open PowerPoint and Insert a Slide

Video M8_C1_S01

When you open PowerPoint, a blank presentation with a single title slide appears in the Normal view. Most slides use placeholders into which you can enter text. A title slide contains a title placeholder, with the text *Click to add title*, and a subtitle placeholder, with the text *Click to add subtitle*. When you insert a new slide, by default it has a Title and Content layout, which includes a title placeholder and a content placeholder. The content placeholder contains a bullet symbol and the words *Click to add text*.

Steps

1 Click the Start button on the Windows taskbar.

2 Point to *All Programs*.

3 Click *Microsoft Office* and then click *Microsoft PowerPoint 2010* on the list of applications that appears in the menu. A blank presentation opens in Normal view with the Home tab displayed.

4 *Shortcut*
Insert new slide
Ctrl + M

4 Click the New Slide button in the Slides group on the Home tab. The new slide appears with a title placeholder on top and a content placeholder below.

4 *Another Way*
Right-click in the Slides/Outline pane on the left side of the Normal view and choose *New Slide* from the menu that appears.

5 Click the File tab, click the Save As button, type M8-C1-S1-FairTrade in the *File name* text box, and then click Save.

Taking It Further

Opening an Existing File To open an existing presentation, open PowerPoint, click the File tab, and then click the Open button. In the Open dialog box that appears, navigate to the file you wish to open. Click the file name so that it appears in the *File name* text box and click Open. Alternatively, if you have recently used the file you wish to open, you can click the File tab, click Recent, and then click the file name from the list of files.

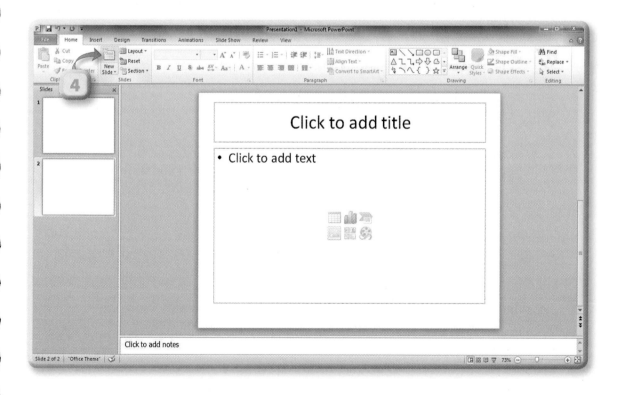

PowerPoint

Skill 2

Enter Text on Slides

Video M8_C1_S02

No matter how many graphics, videos, or animations you place on slides, the heart of any presentation is the text. Text that you enter on slides helps reinforce a speaker's ideas, helps viewers to focus on the key points of the presentation, and helps the speaker stay on track throughout the presentation. In this skill, you add text on slides using both the Slide pane and the Outline tab of the Slides/Outline pane.

Steps

1 If it is not already open, open **M8-C1-S1-FairTrade.pptx**, the file you saved in the previous skill, and save the file as **M8-C1-S2-FairTrade**. Be sure to save the file in your Module 8 working folder.

2 If the first slide does not already appear in the Slide pane, click Slide 1 in the Slides/Outline pane.

3 In the Slide pane, click anywhere on the title placeholder *Click to add title* and type Fair Trade and Chocolate.

4 In the Slide pane, click on the subtitle placeholder *Click to add subtitle* and type Promoting a Fair and Sustainable Industry.

5 Click Slide 2 in the Slides/Outline pane to display that slide.

6 In the Slide pane, click the title placeholder and type What Is Fair Trade?

7 Click the content placeholder (formatted as a bulleted list by default) and enter the following, pressing the Enter key after each line as indicated.

Above-market prices to growers [**Enter**]

No slavery used in production of cocoa [**Enter**]

Sustainable practices [**Enter**]

Benefits to trading partners' communities

▶ **Tip** If you accidently press Enter after the last bullet, click Ctrl + Z to undo the action.

▶ **Tip** You press Enter to start a new bullet point in a content placeholder, but there is no need to press Enter in other types of placeholders. PowerPoint automatically wraps text to fit within the placeholder width, expanding its height as needed.

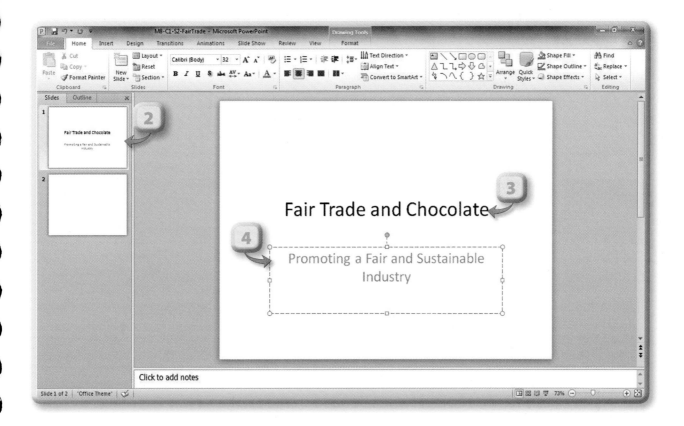

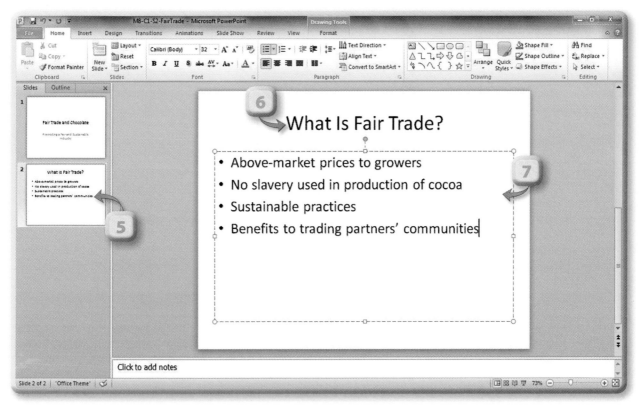

More

PowerPoint

8 Click the File tab.

9 Click Save.

10 Click the Slide Show tab.

11 Click the From Beginning button in the Start Slide Show group. This begins the slide show and the first slide fills your screen.

12 Click your mouse to advance to Slide 2.

13 At the screen that reads *End of slide show, click to exit*, click your mouse once to return to the Normal view.

Fair Trade and Chocolate

Promoting a Fair and Sustainable
Industry

What Is Fair Trade?

- Above-market prices to growers
- No slavery used in production of cocoa
- Sustainable practices
- Benefits to trading partners' communities

Completed Skill 2

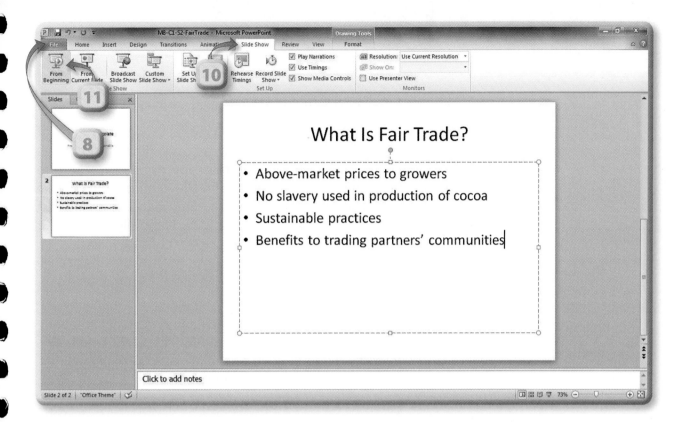

Taking It Further

Using Text Boxes   Another way to enter text in a presentation is to insert a text box by clicking the Text Box button in the Text group on the Insert tab. Be aware that the text within text boxes is not reflected in the presentation outline. Text boxes are essentially text objects, just as pictures or clip art are objects. You might use a text box to call attention to an item on a slide. For example, you might add the claim "FREE!" to a slide about a special product offer, dramatically reinforcing a point made within the regular text of the presentation.

PowerPoint

Use the Outline Feature

Video M8_C1_S03

When you are primarily focused on adding text rather than visual elements to your presentation, using the Outline tab in the Slides/Outline pane is helpful. This feature allows you to organize your ideas, enter text, promote lines of text to a higher level, demote lines of text to a lower level, and move content around a slide or among slides. In the Outline tab of the Slides/Outline pane, the highest level heading is the slide title and it marks the start of a new slide.

Steps

1. If it is not already open, open **M8-C1-S2-FairTrade.pptx**, the file you saved in the previous skill, and save the file as **Lastname-M8-C1-S3-FTTitleSlide**, but replace *Lastname* with your last name. Be sure to save the file in your Module 8 working folder on your storage medium.

2. Click the Outline tab in the Slides/Outline pane.

3. In Slide 2 in the Slides/Outline pane, click to the right of the last bullet point, *Benefits to trading partners' communities*.

4. Press Enter. The insert point moves to a new bullet on Slide 2.

5. Click the Home tab.

6. Click the Decrease List Level button in the Paragraph group. The line is promoted to the highest level, creating a new slide.

Another Way
Right-click and choose *Promote* from the shortcut menu.

Shortcut
Promote a line
Shift + Tab

7. Type The Global Nature of Chocolate Growing. The text appears in the title placeholder in the Slide pane.

8. Press Enter. The insert point moves to a new Slide 4.

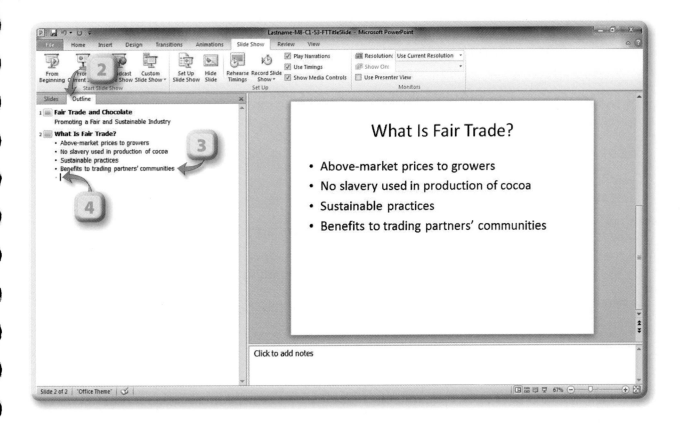

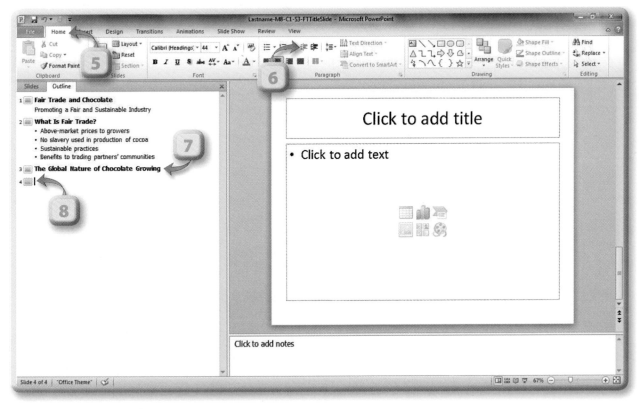

9 Click the Increase List Level button in the Paragraph group on the Home tab. The insert point is demoted to a bullet point on Slide 3.

▶ *Tip* PowerPoint automatically formats the subtopics within outlines as bulleted points.

10 Type the following text, pressing Enter as indicated to create new bullet points:

South America [**Enter**]

Africa [**Enter**]

Asia

▶ *Tip* You can use the slide icon in the Outline tab to move a slide.

11 On the Outline tab, click the slide icon to the left of the Slide 3 title.

12 Press the mouse button and, while holding it down, drag the slide 3 icon to just below the subtitle of Slide 1, *Promoting a Fair and Sustainable Industry*, and then release the mouse button. The slide moves to the second position in the outline.

13 Save and close the file.

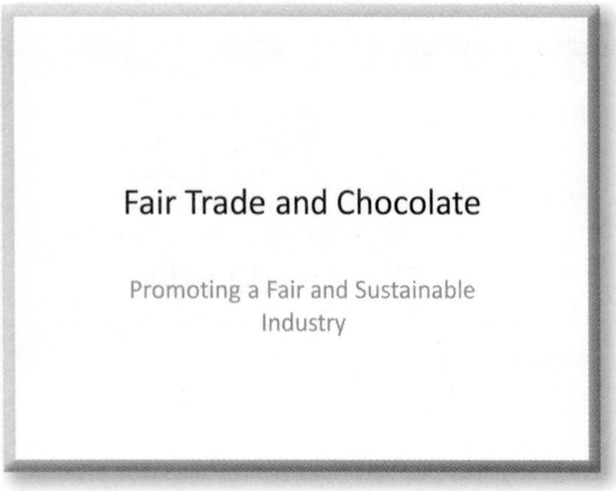

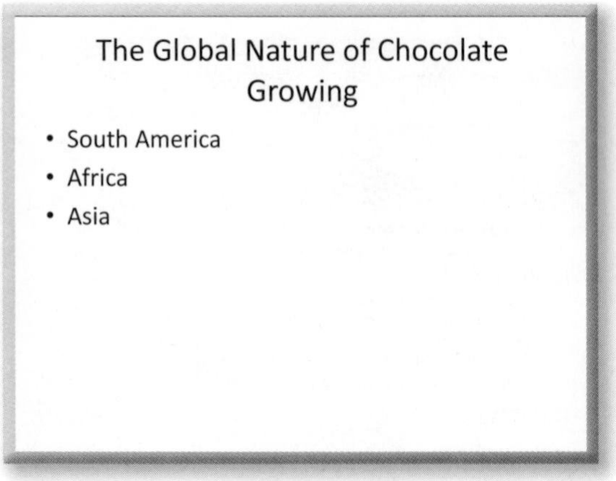

Fair Trade and Chocolate

Promoting a Fair and Sustainable Industry

The Global Nature of Chocolate Growing

- South America
- Africa
- Asia

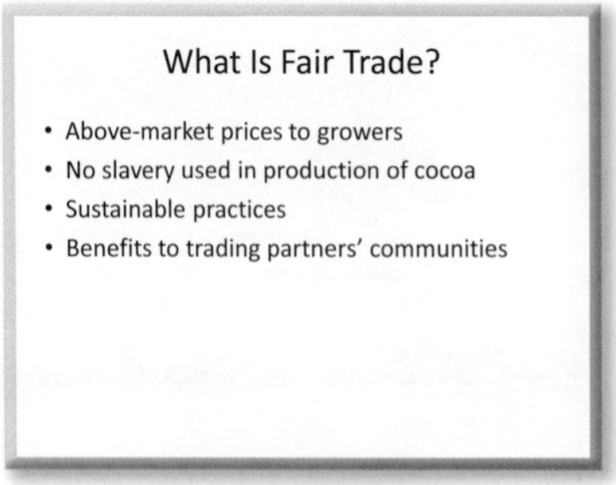

What Is Fair Trade?

- Above-market prices to growers
- No slavery used in production of cocoa
- Sustainable practices
- Benefits to trading partners' communities

Completed Skill 3

PowerPoint

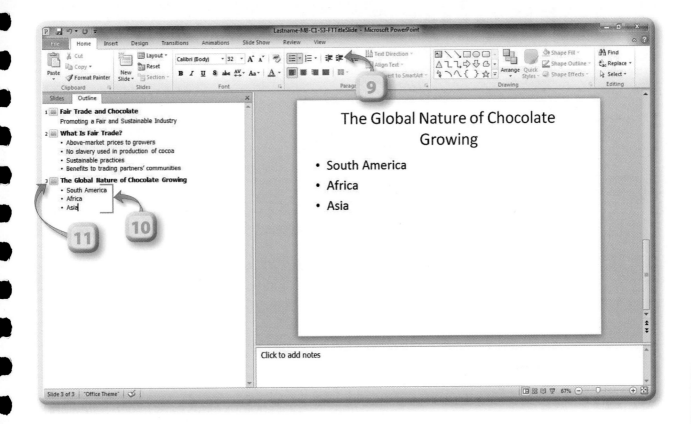

Taking It Further

Expanding and Collapsing Outlines   In cases where you have created a rather long presentation, the expand or collapse feature of the Outline tab in the Slides/Outline pane makes it easier to view the slide information. This feature collapses a slide, hiding its subtopics from view when you double-click a slide icon in the slide pane. To reverse the process, double-click again and the subtopics display. You can also right-click anywhere in the Slides/Outline pane with the Outline tab selected and choose *Collapse* or *Expand* from the submenu that appears. You can then choose either to expand or collapse only the currently selected slide contents or to *Expand All* or *Collapse All* slides.

PowerPoint

PowerPoint

Skill 4

Add Notes

Video ▶ M8_C1_S04

In the Notes pane of PowerPoint's Normal view, you can enter information that would be useful to a presenter but is not visible to the audience during a presentation. You can also view and print speaker notes from the Notes Page view.

Steps

1 Open the student data file named **M8-C1-S4-FairTrade.pptx** and, if you have not already done so, save the file in your Module 8 working folder on your storage medium.

2 Click on Slide 4, titled <u>How Big Is Cocoa Fair Trade?</u>, in the Slides/Outline pane.

3 Click in the Notes pane (where the placeholder reads *Click to add notes*) and type the text Ten origins for cocoa include Ghana, Ecuador, Bolivia, and the Dominican Republic.

▶ **Tip** Enlarge the Notes pane when in Normal view by clicking on the line dividing it from the Slide pane and dragging upward.

4 Scroll down the Slides/Outline pane and click on Slide 5.

5 Click in the Notes pane and type The ability to track beans to their origins ensures that chocolate flavors are pure and authentic.

6 *Another Way* You can change views by clicking the small icon at the lower right of the Status bar, to the left of the Zoom slider.

6 Click the View tab and click the Notes Page button in the Presentation Views group. This displays Slide 5, along with the associated note.

7 Click the Normal button in the Presentation Views group to return to Normal view.

8 Save the file.

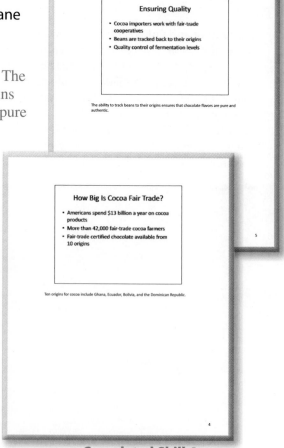

Completed Skill 4

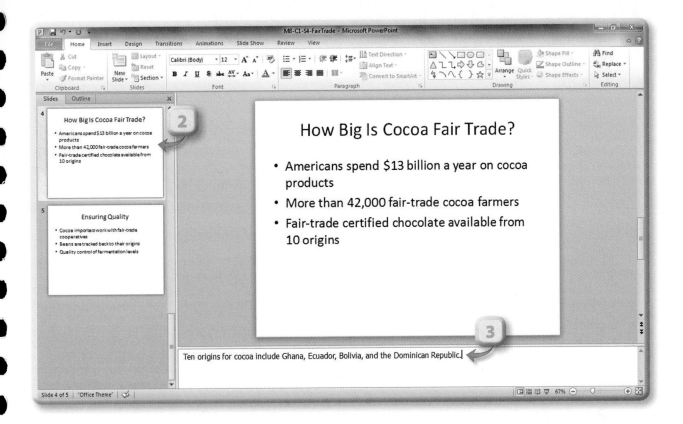

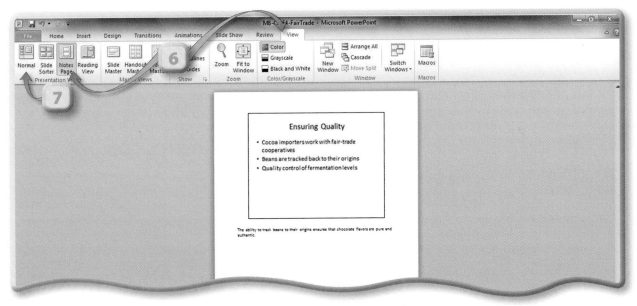

Taking It Further

Using Notes   What kind of information might you include in Notes? Back-up information like statistics or quotes can help you substantiate your points. Links to websites or articles you have used for research provide you with additional information in case your audience requests it or in case you need it later. You should include only key points on your slides and place supporting points or information in the Notes pane.

PowerPoint

Chapter 1

Skill 5

Video ▶ M8_C1_S05

Apply a Layout

You have seen how slides include placeholders for items such as titles, subtitles, and bullet points. You can apply these and other layouts to existing slides or create a new slide and design your own particular layout for the material. Layouts can include titles, subtitles, one or two content placeholders, or captions. They can even be blank—with no placeholders.

Steps

1 If it is not already open, open **M8-C1-S4-FairTrade.pptx**, the presentation you saved in the previous skill, and save it as **M8-C1-S5-FairTrade**.

2 In the Slides/Outline pane, click on Slide 2, titled *The Global Nature of Chocolate*.

3 Click the Home tab.

4 Click the Layout button in the Slides group.

5 Click the *Two Content* option from the drop-down gallery. This adds a right-hand content placeholder in Slide 2.

6 In the Slide pane, click the content placeholder on the right side and type
Europe is the largest cocoa-processing region [**Enter**]
Local markets dictate taxes and currency fluctuations.

7 In the Slides/Outline pane, click on Slide 5, titled <u>Ensuring Quality</u>.

8 In the Slides group on the Home tab, click the arrow on the New Slide button.

9 Click the *Picture with Caption* layout option to insert a new Slide 6 with that layout.

10 In the Slide pane, click the *Click to add title* placeholder and type Map of global cocoa markets.

11 Save the file.

> ▶ **Tip** If you click the New Slide button and not the arrow, a new slide is inserted with the same layout as the slide before it. Clicking the arrow on the New Slide button allows you to select from a gallery of slide layout options.

Completed Skill 5

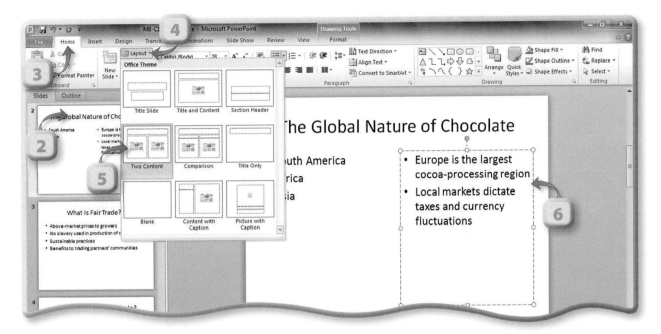

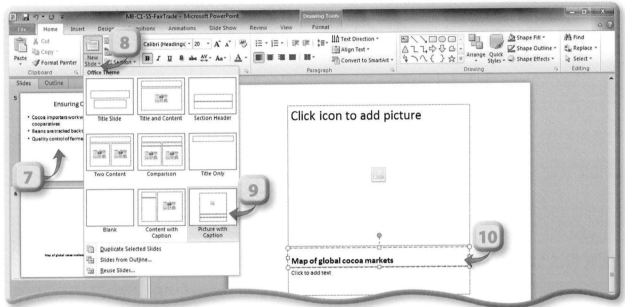

Taking It Further

Working with Placeholders The pre-defined layouts in PowerPoint do not cover every possible combination of placeholders. Therefore, you might want to insert a text box from the Text group in the Insert tab to add text. Remember, text in a text box is not included in the presentation outline. You can also delete a placeholder from a slide, which also deletes any text you have entered in that placeholder. Blank placeholders are not visible during the viewing of a presentation.

PowerPoint

Skill 6

Video M8_C1_S06

Apply a Theme

Just as the layout feature controls the type and number of placeholders on slides, the themes feature controls a slide's colors, fonts, and graphical elements. You can apply a theme to all slides or to individual slides in a presentation. You can also apply more than one theme in a presentation, but do so sparingly to avoid a disjointed look. Applying a theme creates a new slide master. (See Module 8, Chapter 2 for more about slide masters.)

Steps

1 If its not already open, open **M8-C1-S5-FairTrade.pptx**, the presentation you saved in the previous skill, and save the file as **M8-C1-S6-FairTrade**.

2 Click the Design tab.

3 Find the *Angles* design theme by hovering your mouse pointer over the themes in the Themes group. As the mouse pointer moves over a theme option, the theme's name displays and the theme is previewed on the current slide in the Slide pane.

4 Click on the *Angles* design theme option and the theme is applied to all slides in the presentation.

5 In the Slides/Outline pane, click on Slide 1.

6 Click the More arrow at the right side of the Theme gallery to display all built-in themes.

7 Right-click on the *Office Theme* design thumbnail (the first option in the *Built-In* section) and then click *Apply to Selected Slides*.

8 Save the presentation.

> ▶**Tip** After the first design theme (Office) the design themes are listed in alphabetical order.

> ▶**Tip** To create a custom theme, you can make individual settings for background and color using the Design tab tools and then click the More button on the Themes gallery and choose *Save Current Theme*.

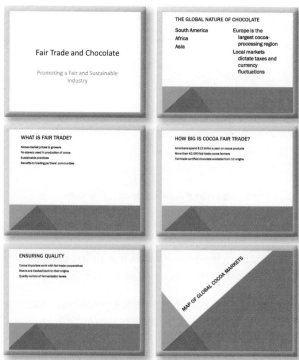

Completed Skill 6

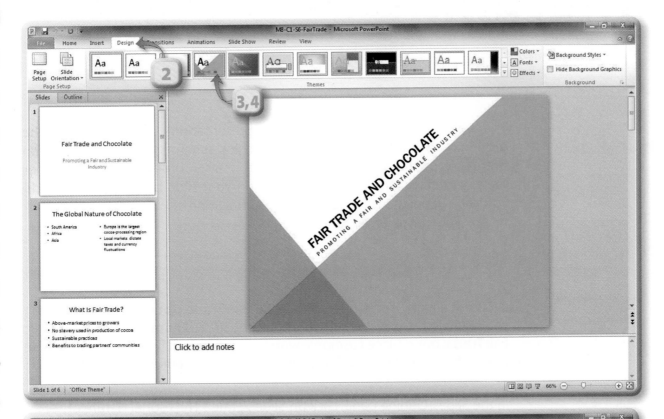

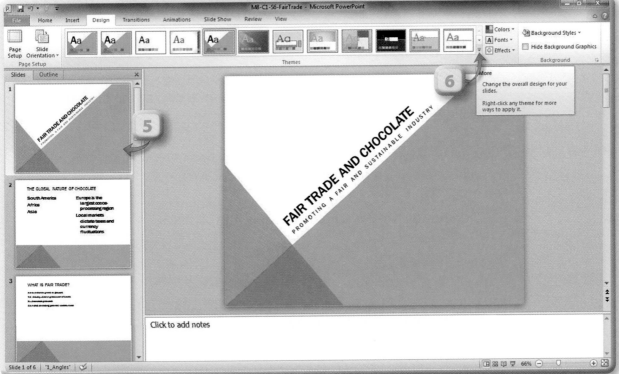

Taking It Further

Finding Themes Online There are several attractive built-in themes available to every PowerPoint user. To give your presentation a unique look, you might try to find additional themes online. Go to office.microsoft.com/en-us/templates and search for PowerPoint themes to explore more options for your presentations.

PowerPoint

Video ▶ M8_C1_S07

Change the Color Scheme

The colors used for slide backgrounds and graphical elements are preset by the theme you apply, but once you have applied a theme, you can change its color scheme to match your taste or enhance your presentation's tone or message. The color scheme gallery enables you to easily preview color schemes on your slide before you choose to apply one.

Steps

1 If it is not already open, open **M8-C1-S6-FairTrade.pptx**, the presentation you saved in the previous skill, and save the file as **Lastname-M8-C1-S7-FairTrade**, but replace *Lastname* with your last name. Be sure to save the file in your Module 8 working folder on your storage medium.

2 In the Slides/Outline pane, click on Slide 2, titled <u>The Global Nature of Chocolate</u>.

3 Click the Design tab.

4 Click the Colors button in the Themes group to display the drop-down gallery.

▶ **Tip** To view the name of the currently applied color scheme, move your mouse over the Colors button. The current theme name is listed in the *Theme Colors* information box that appears.

5 Move your cursor over the color schemes shown in the gallery and the colors are previewed on the slide in the Slide pane.

6 Click the *Equity* color scheme to apply it to all slides.

▶ **Tip** To apply a color scheme to the currently selected slide, right-click the color scheme in the gallery and choose *Apply to Selected Slides*.

7 Save the file.

8 View the presentation by clicking the From Beginning button in the Slide Show tab. When the show is over, press Esc to return to Normal view and then close the file.

Taking It Further

Creating a Custom Color Scheme You can customize a color scheme to create your own. In the Colors button drop-down gallery, click *Create New Theme Colors*. In the dialog box that appears, click the color button for each individual item you want to change and choose a different color from the palette that appears. Enter a name for the custom color scheme in the *Name* text box and then click Save to save it for future use.

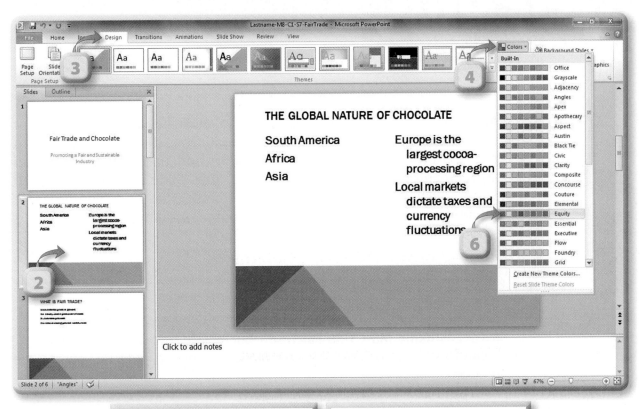

Completed Skill 7

PowerPoint

Organize Slides Using Slide Sorter

Video M8_C1_S08

Although you can move slides around using the Outline or Slides pane in Normal view, the best view for reorganizing slides is the Slide Sorter view. This view presents thumbnail images of your slides so you can view several at once and think about your options for organizing them. You can drag slides from one position to another in the Slide Sorter view and determine the best slide order for your presentation.

Steps

1 Open the student data file named **M8-C1-S8-FairTrade.pptx** and save the file as **Lastname-M8-C1-S8-FairTrade**, but replace *Lastname* with your last name. Be sure to save the file in your Module 8 working folder on your storage medium.

2 Click the View tab.

3 Click the Slide Sorter button in the Presentation Views group.

4 Press and hold down the mouse button on Slide 9 (when selected, the slide appears with a gold border) and then drag the slide to the space between Slide 2 and Slide 3. (The slide position is indicated with a thin, vertical line.)

5 Release the mouse button to place the slide in the new position.

> **Tip** Use the Shift key to select multiple, contiguous slides. Use the Ctrl key to select noncontiguous slides.

6 Click Slide 7, press and hold down the Shift key, and then click Slide 8. Both Slides 7 and 8 are now selected.

7 Press and drag one of the selected slides to the space between Slide 3 and Slide 4 and then release the mouse button.

8 Click Slide 1 to select it.

9 Click the Home tab.

> **10 Shortcut**
> Duplicate slide
> Ctrl + D

10 Click the arrow on the Copy button and then click *Duplicate*.

> **Tip** You can also delete a slide or add a new one while in Slide Sorter view. Right-click a slide and select *Delete Slide* or *New Slide*.

11 Press and drag the new Slide 2 to the end of the presentation and then release the mouse button.

12 Save and close the file.

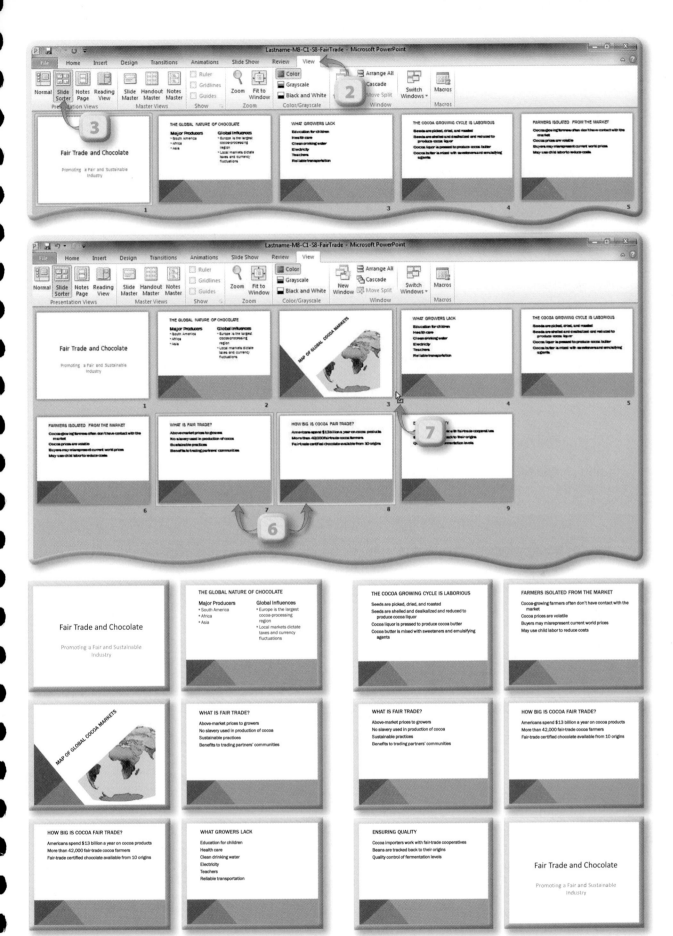

Completed Skill 8

PowerPoint

PowerPoint

Tasks Summary

Task	Ribbon Tab, Group	Button, Option	Shortcut, Alternative
Insert a new slide	Home, Slides		Ctrl + M
Save a presentation	Quick Access Toolbar		Ctrl + S
Display Slides/Outline pane	View, Presentation Views		
Demote a heading	Home, Paragraph		Tab
Promote a heading	Home, Paragraph		Shift + Tab
Enter notes	View, Presentation Views		
Display Notes page	View, Presentation Views		
Apply a Layout	Home, Slides		
Apply a design theme	Design, Themes		
Apply a color theme	Design, Themes		
Create a custom color theme	Design, Themes		
Display Slide Sorter view	View, Presentation Views		
Duplicate slides	Home, Clipboard		Ctrl + D

Features Review

Select the best answer from the choices given.

1 To access the New Slide button, display this tab.
   a. Insert
   b. Page Layout
   c. Home
   d. Slide Show

2 Clicking the File menu and clicking the Open button has this effect.
   a. The Open dialog box appears.
   b. The last viewed file appears.
   c. A new blank presentation appears.
   d. None of the above

3 A content placeholder is formatted to contain this by default.
   a. a numbered list
   b. clip art
   c. a slide title
   d. a bulleted list

4 The main difference between text entered in a placeholder and a text box is that text in a
   a. text box does not appear in the outline.
   b. placeholder does not appear in the outline.
   c. text box is not automatically formatted with a font.
   d. There is no difference.

5 To enter text in a presentation you can use the
  a. Notes pane.
  b. Slide Sorter view.
  c. Outline pane.
  d. All of the above

6 To demote a heading in the outline, press
  a. Home.
  b. Ctrl + D.
  c. Tab.
  d. Enter.

7 The Notes pane appears in
  a. the Slide Show view.
  b. Normal view.
  c. Slide Sorter view.
  d. all views.

8 Layouts can include
  a. content placeholders.
  b. title placeholders.
  c. subtitle placeholders.
  d. All of the above

9 Which is *not* true of themes?
  a. Themes provide colors, fonts, and graphical elements.
  b. Themes can be applied to all slides in a presentation.
  c. Only one theme can be applied to a presentation.
  d. None of the above

10 The best view to use to reorganize slides is the
  a. Reorganize Slides view.
  b. Normal view.
  c. Slide Sorter view.
  d. Slide Show view.

Hands-On Skills Review

Exercise **Prepare a Presentation about PowerPoint 2010**

Skills   Open PowerPoint and insert a slide, enter text on slides, add slides, apply a layout, and organize slides using the slide sorter

Scenario   You want to revise a presentation so that it provides a few key points about PowerPoint 2010. Edit the file provided to improve the presentation.

Steps

1 Open the student data file named **M8-C1-ExA-AboutPowerPoint.pptx** and save the file as **Lastname-M8-C1-ExA-AboutPowerPoint**, but replace *Lastname* with your last name.

2 Enter your name and the current date on the first slide in the subtitle placeholder so the information appears on two separate lines.

3 At the end of the presentation, insert a new slide with a two-column format for the text.
  a. Insert a title that reads *Features*.
  b. In the left column insert a first-level bullet that reads *Objects*. Under that bullet, type the following sub-bullets:
    Text
    Graphics
    Animation
    Videos
    Sound

  c. In the right column insert a first-level bullet that reads *Views*. Under that bullet, type the following sub-bullets:
    Normal
    Slide Sorter
    Notes Page
    Reading

4 Review the slide order and place the slides so they appear in the following sequence:
    Slide 1 *Title*
    Slide 2 *Uses*
    Slide 3 *Features*
    Slide 4 *Text Is Important*.

5 Save the file.

6 Preview the presentation. **HINT:** *Click the Slide Show tab and then click the From the Beginning button.*

7 Submit the completed presentation to your instructor.

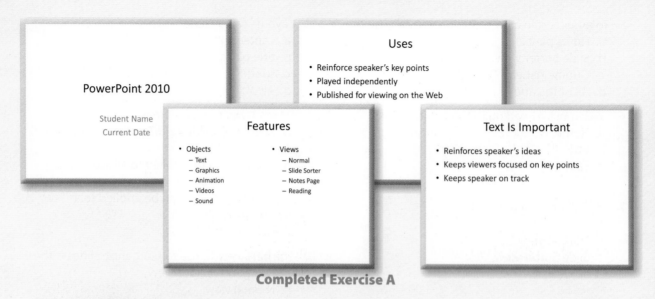

Completed Exercise A

Exercise B Prepare a Slide Show about Effective Presentations

Skills Enter text on slides, apply a theme, change the color scheme, and use the Outline feature

Scenario You are working on a presentation that will be delivered to your company's sales reps at the national sales meeting. This presentation will remind the reps how to make interesting and engaging presentations.

Steps

1 Open the student data file named **M8-C1-ExB-EffectivePresentations.pptx** and save the file as **Lastname-M8-C1-ExB-EffectivePresentations**, but replace *Lastname* with your last name.

2 Enter your name and the current date on the first slide in the subtitle placeholder so the information appears on separate lines.

3 Correct Slide 2 to demote (increase the list level) the four bullets that follow the *Order the slides* bullet point.

4 Apply the Trek presentation theme.

5 Apply the Office color scheme.

6 Save the presentation.

7 Preview the presentation.

8 Submit the completed presentation to your instructor.

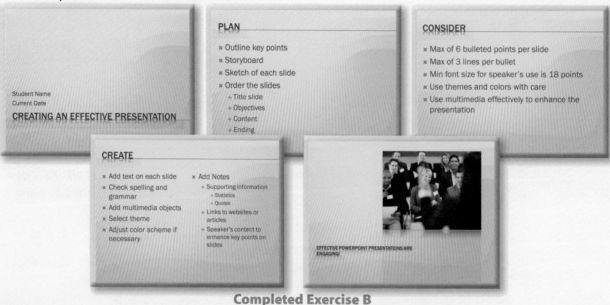

Completed Exercise B

Exercise **C** **Prepare a Slide Show about the Evolution of Phone Technology**

Skills   Enter text on slides, add notes, organize slides using the slide sorter, and apply a theme

Scenario   You recently found an old rotary-style phone in your attic. This discovery prompted you to look at the changes in phone communications over the past years. You documented what you learned in a presentation. Finish the presentation by making it more eye-catching. Add the remaining speaker notes so you have discussion points.

Steps

1 Open the student data file named **M8-C1-ExC-PhoneChanges.pptx** and save the file as **Lastname-M8-C1-ExC-PhoneChanges**, but replace *Lastname* with your last name.

2 Enter your name and the current date on the first slide in the subtitle placeholder so the information appears on two separate lines.

3 On Slide 1, format *Phones through the Ages* to Calibri 32 pt italic. **HINT:** *Select the text and use the Decrease Font Size button and the Italic button in the Font group on the Home tab.*

4 Place the slides into the correct sequence: (1) Title, (2) *Topics*, (3) *Dark Ages of Phones*, (4) *Dark Ages Start to Recede*, (5) *Heading Toward Enlightenment*, (6) *Current Age of Phones*, (7) *Phones of the Future*

5 Add the following bullet points to Slide 5, *Heading Toward Enlightenment:*
    Improving networks
    Smaller
    Lightweight
    One per person
    Replace land line?

6 Add the following speaker notes to Slide 3, *Dark Ages of Phones:*
    In the beginning, phones were installed in hallways in residential buildings. The phone and phone line were shared by all. Later, individual apartments and homes had a phone installed, but the phone number and the line were shared. This was called a party line. As additional phone service became available, each household had one or more individual phone lines and phone numbers.

7 Add a sentence to the end of the speaker notes for Slide 7, *Phones of the Future:*
    Let's ask the crystal ball!

8 Change the presentation design theme to Module.

9 Save the file.

10 Preview the presentation.

11 Submit the completed presentation to your instructor.

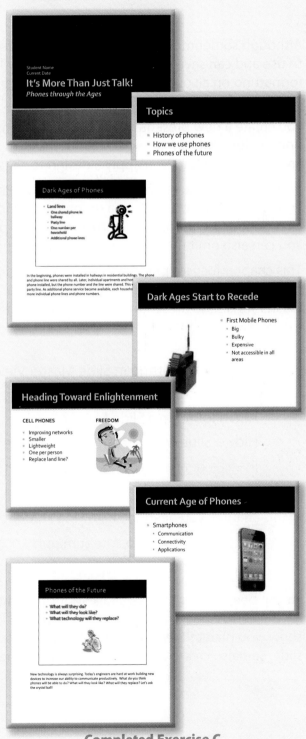

Completed Exercise C

Working with Slide Masters and Handouts

Although sometimes viewed as an advanced feature, PowerPoint Slide Masters are in fact easy to use and can save you a great deal of work when you want to add or remove graphics or formatting on all or most of the slides in your presentation.

The default Slide Master uses the Office Theme—the blank slide design that appears when you create a new presentation. The Office Theme contains no background or graphics but does assign font formatting to all placeholders in the slide presentation. Additional masters are created any time you apply a design to slides.

In this chapter, you learn about the power of PowerPoint Slide Masters, a feature that enables you to insert objects, such as a graphic or company logo, text, and slide numbers, or to change the formatting for a particular type of placeholder on all slides with a single action. You can also omit master elements on individual slides, as needed.

This chapter focuses primarily on formatting slides using the Slide Master, but features of the Handout Master and Notes Master work similarly. In the last skill, you work with a Handout Master for a slide presentation and print a handout of the presentation.

Skills You Learn

1. Change formatting in Slide Master View
2. Insert a graphic in Slide Master View
3. Add a footer in a Slide Master
4. Hide a Slide Master element on a slide
5. Insert a header in the Handout Master and print a handout

Files You Need

In this chapter, you need the following student data file.

M8-C2-S1-AboutChocMuseum.pptx

What You Create

You've been invited to give a talk about The Chocolate Museum at a prestigious trade show for the confection industry. Because your goal is to build awareness of your brand at the trade show, you plan to create a PowerPoint presentation including the Museum logo on every slide. You also create handouts of your presentation.

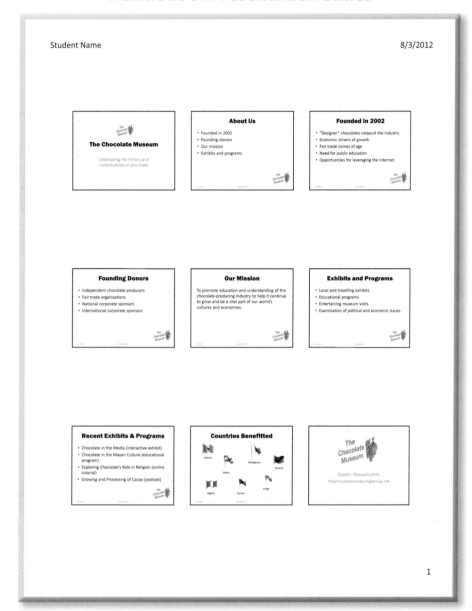

PowerPoint

Skill 1

Change Formatting in Slide Master View

Video M8_C2_S01

If your organization uses the COPPERPLATE GOTHIC BOLD font on all titles in company PowerPoint presentations, it would be time-consuming to format every slide title individually. You can easily format the slide title placeholder, just one time, in the Slide Master and every slide title placeholder in the entire presentation is formatted the same way. Also, if you later need to change slide titles to another font (perhaps someone decides the company font must be Tunga), you can use the Slide Master to change all title formatting with a single action.

Steps

1 Open the student data file named **M8-C2-S1-AboutChocMuseum.pptx** and, if you have not already done so, save the file in your Module 8 working folder on your storage medium.

▶**Tip** Be sure to make Slide Master settings first; be aware that all changes on individual slides override Slide Master settings.

2 Click the View tab.

3 Click the Slide Master button in the Master Views group.

▶**Tip** Hover your mouse over the layouts and the name of each layout displays.

4 Click the top (and largest) slide layout thumbnail (*Office Theme Slide Master*) in the slide layout thumbnail pane. This action displays the slide master layout in the Slide pane.

5 Click on the title placeholder and select the placeholder text *Click to edit Master title style*.

6,7,8 *Another Way*
Right-click the selected text and choose *Font* from the shortcut menu. Make changes to the font in the Font dialog box.

6 Click the Home tab.

7 Click the arrow in the *Font* option box in the Font group.

8 Click *Franklin Gothic Heavy* in the drop-down gallery.

9,10 *Another Way*
Click the Normal button in the View pane to close the Slide Master view and return to Normal view.

9 Click the Slide Master tab.

10 Click the Close Master View button to return to Normal view.

11 Save the file.

Completed Skill 1

PowerPoint

Insert a Graphic in Slide Master View

Video M8_C2_S02

Modifying global formatting is a great way to use Slide Masters. They can also be a useful tool when you want to insert a graphic on all or most slides in your presentation. For example, many companies place their logo on every slide.

Rather than inserting the logo on each slide individually, you can place it once in the Slide Master. In this skill, you place a logo on all slides that use the Title and Content layout.

Steps

Tip Chapter 3 includes skills about using graphics in PowerPoint presentations.

1 If if is not already open, open the student data file named **M8-C2-S1-AboutChocMuseum.pptx**, the file you saved in the previous skill, and save the file as **M8-C2-S2-AboutChocMuseum**.

2 Click the Museum logo in Slide 1 in the Slide pane.

3 **Shortcut**
Copy
Ctrl + C

3 Click the Copy button in the Clipboard group in the Home tab.

Tip If you want a graphic to appear on every slide in the presentation, you should place it on the uppermost slide in a Slide Master set, rather than on only one layout in the set.

4 Click the View tab.

5 Click the Slide Master button in the Master Views group.

6 Click the third slide layout thumbnail (*Title and Content Layout*) in the Slide Layout Thumbnail pane.

7 Click the Home tab.

8 **Shortcut**
Paste
Ctrl + V

8 Click the Paste button in the Clipboard group to paste the copied logo into the Slide Master.

9 **Another Way**
Use the arrow key to move the active logo on the slide.

9 Hover your mouse pointer over the logo until it becomes a four-headed arrow and then drag the pasted logo to the bottom-right corner of the content placeholder of the slide in the Slide pane.

Tip If the graphic is too close to the contents on any individual slide, reposition it on the Slide Master. You cannot access the graphic from the individual slides.

10 Click the View tab and then click the Normal button in the Presentation Views group. The logo is present in the bottom-right corner of all of the slides with the Title and Content Layout, Slides 2–8.

11 Save the file.

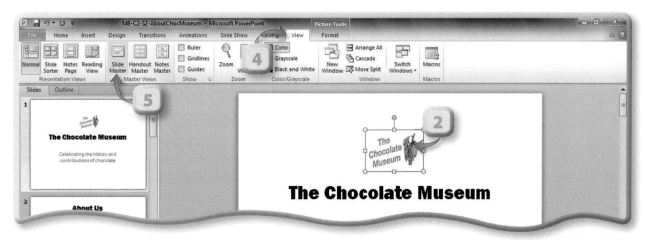

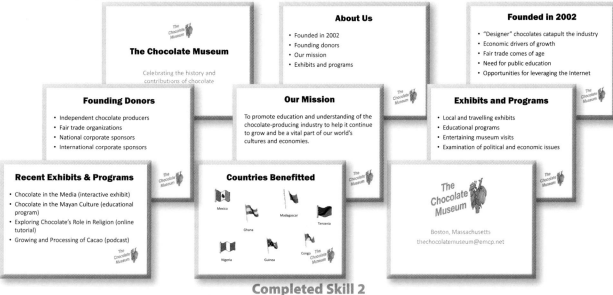

Completed Skill 2

PowerPoint

PowerPoint

> **Skill 3**

Add a Footer in a Slide Master

Video M8_C2_S03

Another item that you might want to place on every slide is a footer containing text. Footer placeholders in the Slide Master can accommodate information such as your company name, the presenter's name, slide numbers, and key words such as "Confidential" or "Copyrighted." The Slide Master offers three footer placeholders by default.

Steps

1 If it is not already open, open **M8-C2-S2-AboutChocMuseum.pptx**, the file you saved in the previous skill, and save the file as **M8-C2-S3-AboutChocMuseum**.

2 Click the Insert tab.

3 Click the Header & Footer button in the Text group.

4 In the Header and Footer dialog box with the Slide tab selected, click the *Date and time* check box to insert a check mark.

> ▶ **Tip** Header and footer formatting that is done on the Slide tab of the Header and Footer dialog box is applied to the Slide Master.

5 Confirm that the *Update automatically* option is selected.

> ▶ **Tip** If you want a specific date on your slides instead of the current date, click the *Fixed* option instead of *Update automatically*.

6 Click the *Slide number* check box to insert a check mark.

7 Click the *Footer* check box to insert a check mark.

8 Type Copyright 2012 in the *Footer* text box.

> ▶ **Tip** Step 9 removes the footer from all slides that use the Title layout.

9 Click the *Don't show on title slide* check box.

10 Click the Apply to All button.

11 Save the file.

Taking It Further

Customizing Slide Footers   You can apply a footer to individual slides using the same process described in this skill. However, remember that one of the benefits of inserting a footer on the Slide Master is that you do not have to create or change each footer individually. If only a few slides require a different footer, apply the global footer to all slides, and then make footer changes on the few individual slides one by one.

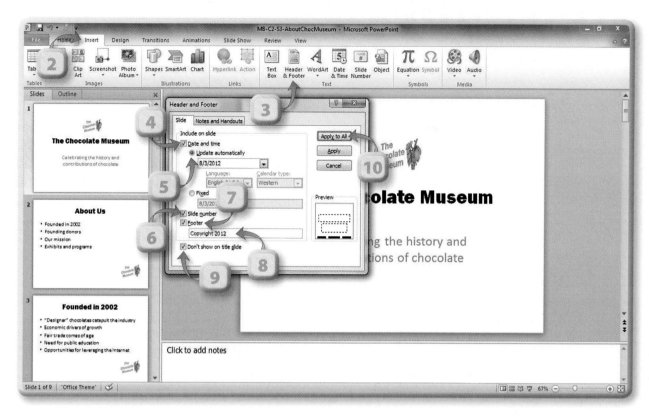

The Chocolate Museum

Celebrating the history and contributions of chocolate

About Us

- Founded in 2002
- Founding donors
- Our mission
- Exhibits and programs

Founded in 2002

- "Designer" chocolates catapult the industry
- Economic drivers of growth
- Fair trade comes of age
- Need for public education
- Opportunities for leveraging the Internet

Founding Donors

- Independent chocolate producers
- Fair trade organizations
- National corporate sponsors
- International corporate sponsors

Our Mission

To promote education and understanding of the chocolate-producing industry to help it continue to grow and be a vital part of our world's cultures and economies.

Exhibits and Programs

- Local and travelling exhibits
- Educational programs
- Entertaining museum visits
- Examination of political and economic issues

Recent Exhibits & Programs

- Chocolate in the Media (interactive exhibit)
- Chocolate in the Mayan Culture (educational program)
- Exploring Chocolate's Role in Religion (online tutorial)
- Growing and Processing of Cacao (podcast)

Countries Benefitted

Mexico
Madagascar
Tanzania
Ghana
Nigeria
Guinea
Congo

The Chocolate Museum

Boston, Massachusetts
thechocolatemuseum@emcp.net

Completed Skill 3

PowerPoint

Skill 4

Hide a Slide Master Element on a Slide

Video M8_C2_S04

A graphic placed on a master cannot be moved or resized on individual slides—it takes its size and position from the master slide. Sometimes you may need to hide a Slide Master graphic on a few individual slides. Hiding might be necessary if a slide starts to look too crowded or confusing once you apply other required graphics or if you need the space to accommodate a large graph or object that would overlap the master graphic. In such cases, you may want to hide master graphics on individual slides.

Steps

1. If it is not already open, open **M8-C2-S3-AboutChocMuseum.pptx**, the file you saved in the previous skill, and save the file as **M8-C2-S4-AboutChocMuseum**.

② Another Way
Navigate to specific slides by using the scrollbar at the right edge of the Slide pane. Click on the slide you want to be active.

2. Display Slide 8 in the Slide pane.

3. Click the Design tab.

▶Tip Hiding background graphics hides all graphics on the Slide Master; if you place more than one graphic there, you cannot hide each individually.

4. In the Background group, click the *Hide Background Graphics* check box to insert a check mark. The graphic from the Slide Master disappears.

5. Save the file.

Taking It Further

Inserting Graphics on Individual Slides
What if you hide the master graphic because the placement does not suit a particular slide, but you would still like to include some form of the graphic on that slide? You can insert the same graphic on the slide after hiding the master graphic. You can then move it around the slide, resize it, or even rotate it to make it work with the other slide elements.

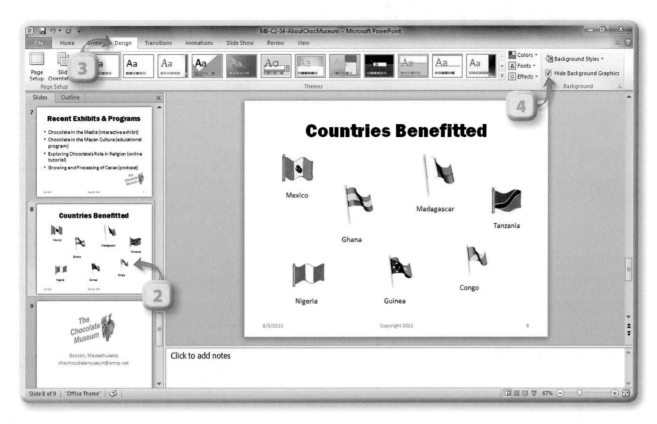

Completed Skill 4

PowerPoint

PowerPoint

Skill 5 Insert a Header on the Handout Master and Print a Handout

Video M8_C2_S05

The Handout Master and Notes Master have features similar to those of the Slide Master. The steps for adding text in these layouts are similar to those for adding text to slides. In this skill, you add a header to the Handouts Master and print a handout of the presentation you created in Skill 4.

Steps

1. If it is not already open, open **M8-C2-S4-AboutChocMuseum.pptx**, the file you saved in the previous skill, and save the file as **Lastname-M8-C2-S5-AboutChocMuseum**, but replace *Lastname* with your last name. Be sure to save the file in your Module 8 working folder on your storage medium.

2. Click the Insert tab.

3. Click the Header & Footer button in the Text group.

4. Click the Notes and Handouts tab in the Header and Footer dialog box.

5. Click the *Header* check box to insert a check mark.

6. Type your first and last names in the *Header* text box.

7. Click the Apply to All button.

8. Save the file.

9. Click the File tab.

10. Click the Print tab.

11. In the Settings category, click the *Full Page Slides* option and then click *9 Slides Horizontal* in the *Handouts* section.

12. Click the Print button if you would like handouts of the presentation.

13. Close the file.

> **Tip** Header and footer formatting that is done on the Handouts tab of the Header and Footer dialog box is applied to the Handouts Master.

> **Tip** Chapter 4 covers other printing options.

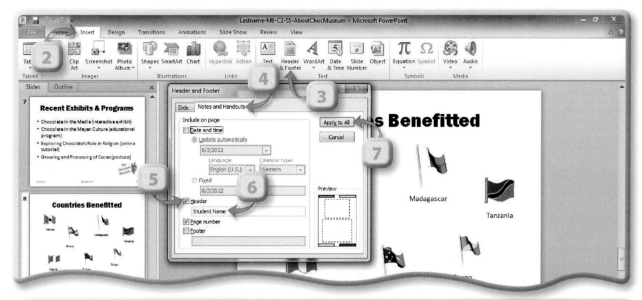

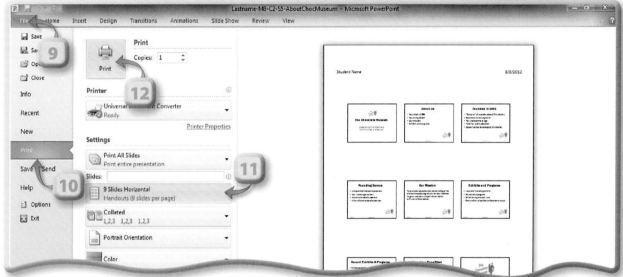

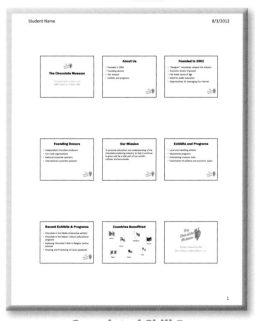

Completed Skill 5

Tasks Summary

Task	Ribbon Tab, Group	Button, Option	Shortcut, Alternative
Display Slide Master	View, Master Views		
Display Handout Master	View, Master Views		
Display Notes Master	View, Master Views		
Insert header and footer	Insert, Text		
Hide Master Graphic	Design, Background	*Hide Background Graphics*	
Print handouts	File	Print	Ctrl + P

Features Review

Select the best answer from the choices given.

1 Using Slide Masters you can
   a. insert text or graphics once and have them appear on every slide.
   b. apply a design template to every slide.
   c. create notes for every slide in the presentation.
   d. All of the above

2 The following applies to Slide Masters.
   a. Changes on individual slides override changes on masters.
   b. Changes on masters override changes made on individual slides.
   c. All of the above
   d. None of the above

3 The default Slide Master is
   a. the first theme you create.
   b. created by the first theme you apply.
   c. the Office theme.
   d. None of the above

4 To have a graphic appear on every slide in the presentation, place it on
   a. every slide.
   b. the uppermost slide in a Slide Master set.
   c. every slide in a Slide Master set.
   d. the first slide in your presentation.

5 Typical information placed in the footer includes
   a. slide numbers.
   b. slide titles.
   c. bullet points.
   d. clip art.

6 Footers on slides have this many placeholders by default.
   a. two
   b. five
   c. three
   d. none

7 The *Hide Background Graphics* check box is located on the
   a. View tab.
   b. Insert tab.
   c. Slide Show tab.
   d. Design tab.

8 Additional masters are created any time you
   a. apply a design to slides.
   b. insert a graphic on a slide.
   c. format text on a slide.
   d. All of the above

9 The Slide Master has features similar to the
   a. Notes Master.
   b. Handout Master.
   c. Both a and b
   d. Neither a nor b

10 If you want a specific date placed on your slides rather than the current date, use the
   a. *Fixed* option.
   b. *Date* option.
   c. *Current* option.
   d. Slide Show view.

Hands-On Skills Review

Exercise A Promote a School's Music Program

Skills   Open PowerPoint and insert a slide, enter text on slides, organize slides using the slide sorter, apply a theme, change the color scheme, change formatting in Slide Master view, and add a footer in a Slide Master

Scenario   It is the end of the school year. You are meeting with parents and students who are interested in joining the school's instrumental music program for the next academic year. Update the presentation to ensure it delivers the appropriate information.

Steps

1   Open the student data file named **M8-C2-ExA-GWHSMusicProg.pptx** and save the file as **Lastname-M8-C2-ExA-GWHSMusicProg**, but replace *Lastname* with your last name.

2   Enter your name and the current date in the subtitle placeholder on two separate lines on Slide 1.

3   Insert a new Slide 3 *Topics* slide that explains what you will discuss. The slide should look like the *Topics* slide in the final PowerPoint presentation provided. In addition to the title, include four bulleted points on the slide:

    Musical opportunities
    School commitment
    Student commitment
    Parent commitment

4   Review the slide order to be sure the slides are in the correct sequence: (1) *Title*, (2) *Topics*, (3) *Opportunities*, (4) *School Commitment*, (5) *Student Commitment*, (6) *Parent Commitment*, (7) *Parent Commitment (Continued)*, (8) *Looking forward to a wonderfully musical year!*

5   Apply the Grid theme to all slides and the Waveform color scheme.

6   Modify the Slide Master.
    a. Change the format for all text in the title placeholder to *Arial Narrow* and apply bold.
    b. Add a three-part footer—date, George Washington High School Music Program, slide number. Do not show the footer on the title slide.
    c. Close Slide Master view.

7   Make the following changes to Slide 1 and Slide 8:
    a. Modify the theme. Apply the default Office theme to these two slides.
    b. Apply the Style 3 background style to these two slides. **HINT:** *Click the Design tab, Background Styles, Style 3.*

8   Select the final slide (Slide 8) and modify the font of the title placeholder to All Caps. **HINT:** *Home tab, Font dialog box launcher, click All Caps to add the check mark to the check box, and then click OK.*

9   Save the presentation.

10   Preview the presentation.

11   Submit the completed presentation to your instructor.

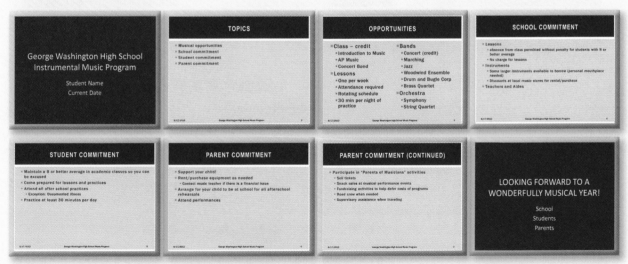

Completed Exercise A

Exercise B Enhance a Presentation

NOTE: This assignment can be done immediately if you are comfortable inserting clip art as directed in Word Chapter 3, Skills 8 and 9. As an alternative, return to this assignment after completing Skills 1 and 2 in PowerPoint Chapter 3.

Skills   Insert a graphic in Slide Master view, insert an object on a slide (a Module 8, Chapter 3 skill), and format a picture (a Module 8, Chapter 3 skill)

Scenario   The presentation you completed in Exercise A for the meeting with parents and students interested in joining next year's instrumental music program looks very plain. Add interest to the presentation by inserting a graphic in the master, so that the graphic appears on most slides.

Steps

1. Open **Lastname-M8-C2-ExA-GWHSMusicProg. pptx**, the file you saved in the previous exercise, and save the file as **Lastname-M8-C2-ExB-GWHSMusicProg**.

2. Modify the master slide to add Clip Art to all Title and Content Layout slides. **HINT:** *This is the third slide in the Master set.* Select the proper slide.

3. Using the Clip Art pane on the Insert tab, search for *school building* and scroll to select an image similar to the image shown in the final presentation.

4. Insert the clip art item in the lower right corner of the content box.

5. Resize the object if necessary.

6. Save the presentation.

7. Preview the presentation.

8. Submit the completed presentation to your instructor.

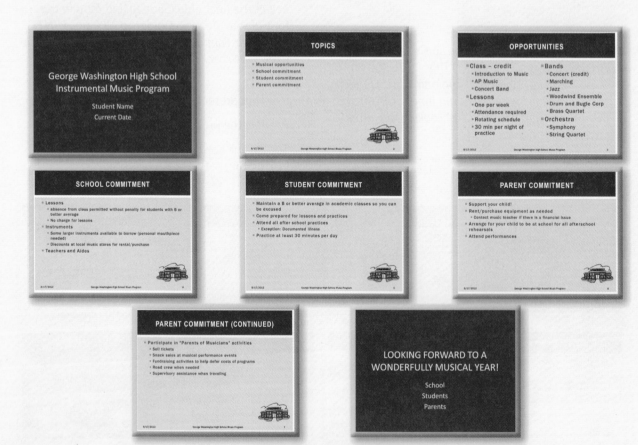

Completed Exercise B

Exercise C Format Handouts for a Presentation

Skills   Add a header and a footer to the Handout Master and print a handout

Scenario   The presentation you completed in Exercise B for the meeting with parents and students interested in joining next year's instrumental music program is ready to present, but you want to provide printed handouts to distribute at the meeting. Add a running header and footer to the Handout Master and print it so you can make copies.

Steps

1. Open **Lastname-M8-C2-ExB-GWHSMusicProg.pptx**, the file you saved in the previous exercise, and save the file as **Lastname-M8-C2-ExC-GWHSMusicProg** but replace *Lastname* with your last name.

2. Insert a header in the Handout Master that includes your first and last names and the current date.

3. Insert a footer in the Handout Master that includes your instructor's name and the page number.

4. Save the presentation.

5. Prepare the handouts to print horizontally with six slides per page.

6. Submit the completed presentation to your instructor. Submit the printed handout if required.

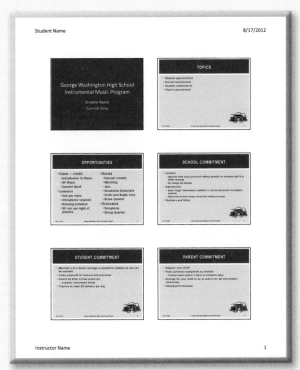 

Completed Exercise C

Adding Visual Elements and Sound

PowerPoint slides use words to communicate the ideas in your presentation, but visuals can help reinforce those ideas and make your slides more attractive. Visuals may include photos or illustrations, transition effects for moving from one slide to another, and animated sequences that can include sound. When you combine these elements in your presentation, you both get your message across and keep your audience engaged and entertained.

Skills You Learn

1 Insert an object on a slide
2 Format a picture
3 Add transitions
4 Add sound
5 Add animations
6 Choose animation effects

Files You Need

In this chapter, you need the following student data files.

M8-C3-S1-ChocProcessing.pptx

M8-C3-S1-CocoaGrowers.jpg

What You Create

Your local middle school has asked you to attend a career fair and give a presentation about how cocoa is grown and processed into chocolate. You want to create a PowerPoint presentation that uses visual and media elements, including photos, drawings, animations, and sounds, to tell the story of chocolate processing.

In this chapter, you learn how to work with visual objects in slides and perform basic formatting on those objects. You use effects to transition between slides, and add animations that put slide objects in motion. You also add sounds to the objects on your slides.

How Cocoa Is Grown

- Cocoa pods grow on a tree
- Grown 15 degrees north or south of equator
- A delicate crop, bears fruit in fifth year
- A tree can live 25 years or more

animation effect applied

illustration added and formatted

Overview of Chocolate Processing

Blue Heron Middle School
October 2, 2012

Cocoa Pods

- Rough, leather-like husk weighing over 2 pounds
- Filled with 30–50 seeds called cocoa beans
- Seeds contain a sweet pulp
- Pulp is half cocoa butter and half cocoa solids

Picking and Fermenting

- Beans are extracted by farmers
- Harvesting occurs a few times a year
- Beans are fermented under piles of banana leaves
- Fermenting takes five days
- Beans are dried in the sun on bamboo mats

photo added and positioned

Distributing

- Dried beans are sold to agents who sell to wholesalers
- Most are used to produce chocolate confections
- Some cocoa butter is used in cosmetics

Making Cocoa Powder

- Beans are roasted in cylinders
- Inside of bean (nib) ground into cocoa mass
- Cocoa butter pressed out of the cocoa mass
- Cocoa powder remains

Producing Chocolate

- Other ingredients are added: sugar, milk, etc.
- Heavy rollers swirl mixture (conching)
- Mixture is heated, cooled, and then heated (tempering)
- Chocolate is poured into molds
- Used to make candies such as chocolate surrounding caramel (enrobing)

sound and animation effect applied

For More Information Visit Our Website

www.emcp.net/TheChocolateMuseum

PowerPoint

Skill 1 Insert an Object on a Slide

Video M8_C3_S01

You can use the Clip Art feature of PowerPoint to search for and insert objects, including illustrations, photos, videos, and sounds. In any layout containing a Content placeholder, you can quickly access Clip Art by clicking one of the placeholder buttons. You can also insert a graphic file of your own or insert clip art on any slide by using the Insert menu.

Steps

Insert Clip Art

1 Open the student data file named **M8-C3-S1-ChocProcessing.pptx** and, if you have not already done so, save the file in your Module 8 working folder on your storage medium.

2 Click Slide 3 in the Slides/Outline pane to display it.

3 Click the Clip Art button to display the Clip Art task pane.

3 Another Way
On the Insert tab, click the Clip Art button in the Images group.

4 In the Clip Art task pane, click the *Search for* text box and type pods.

5 Click the down-pointing arrow at the right side of the *Results should be* option box and then click the *Photographs*, *Videos*, and *Audio* check boxes to remove the check marks. (The *Illustrations* check box should be the only one with a check mark.)

6 Click the Go button.

7 Click the cocoa pods clip art image.

▶ *Tip* To open your search to all types of images, click the arrow at the right of the *Results should be* field and insert a check mark in the *All media types* check box.

8 Click the Clip Art task pane Close button.

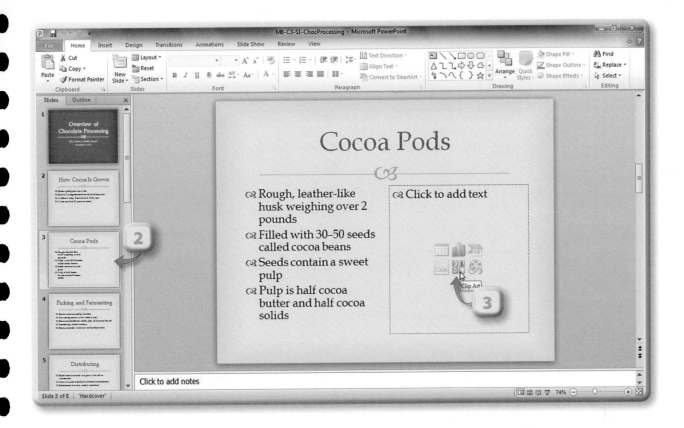

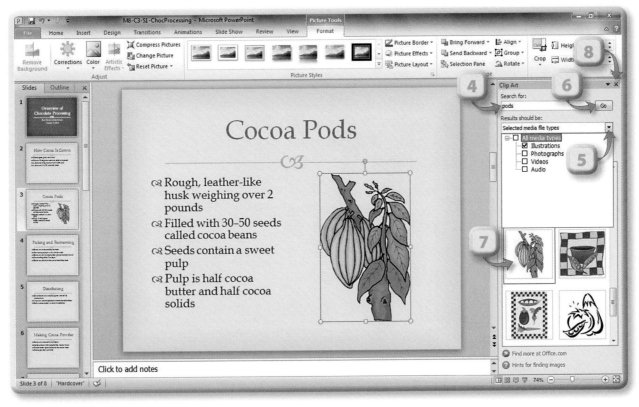

Insert a File

9 Click Slide 4 in the Slides/Outline pane.

10 Click the Insert tab.

11 *Another Way*
Display a layout with a content placeholder and click the Picture button.

11 Click the Picture button in the Images group.

12 In the Insert Picture dialog box that appears, navigate to and click the student data file named **M8-C3-S1-CocoaGrowers.jpg**.

13 Click the Insert button to place the picture on Slide 4.

14 Press and drag the picture to the bottom right corner of Slide 4 and then release the mouse button.

15 Save the file.

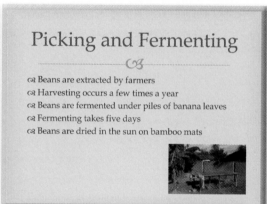

Completed Skill 1, Slides 3 and 4

Taking It Further

Insert Visuals in Masters   If you want to use a graphic on every slide or on most slides in a presentation, you should use the procedures in this skill to insert the image in the Slide Master view. With that method, you only have to insert the item once, and it appears on every slide. See the previous chapter for detailed information on using masters. Now that you know more about adding graphics, you may wish to repeat Skill 2 in Chapter 2.

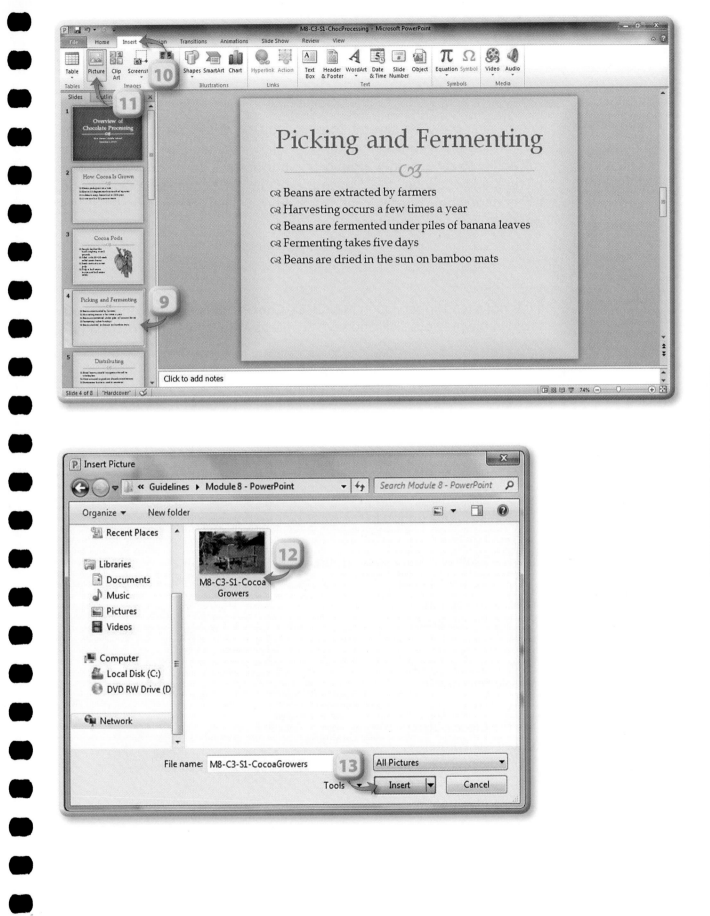

PowerPoint

PowerPoint

Skill 2

Video M8_C3_S02

Format a Picture

PowerPoint provides several tools for formatting pictures, including the ability to set a border around a picture, add shadows or a glowing effect to the border, modify photo colors and brightness, and crop or resize the image. You can take advantage of these tools to transform a commonly used piece of Clip Art, or even your own image, from ordinary to unique.

Steps

1. If it is not already open, open **M8-C3-S1-ChocProcessing.pptx**, the file you saved in the previous skill, and save the file as **M8-C3-S2-ChocProcessing**.

2. Click Slide 3 in the Slides/Outline pane.

3 *Another Way*
Click the Picture Tools Format tab and use the Picture Border and Picture Effects galleries in the Picture Styles group to make the changes listed in Steps 4–9.

3. In Slide 3 in the Slide pane, right-click the cocoa bean illustration and choose *Format Picture* in the shortcut menu.

4. In the Format Picture dialog box, click the *Line Color* option.

5. Click the *Solid Line* option in the *Line Color* section.

6. Click the *Glow and Soft Edges* option.

7. In the *Glow* section, click the *Presets* arrow.

▶**Tip** If you like the effect but not the color, select another color from the Color drop-down list.

8. Choose *Orange, 11 pt glow, Accent color 2*.

9. Click the Close button to close the Format Picture dialog box.

10. Save the file.

Completed Skill 2 (Slide 3)

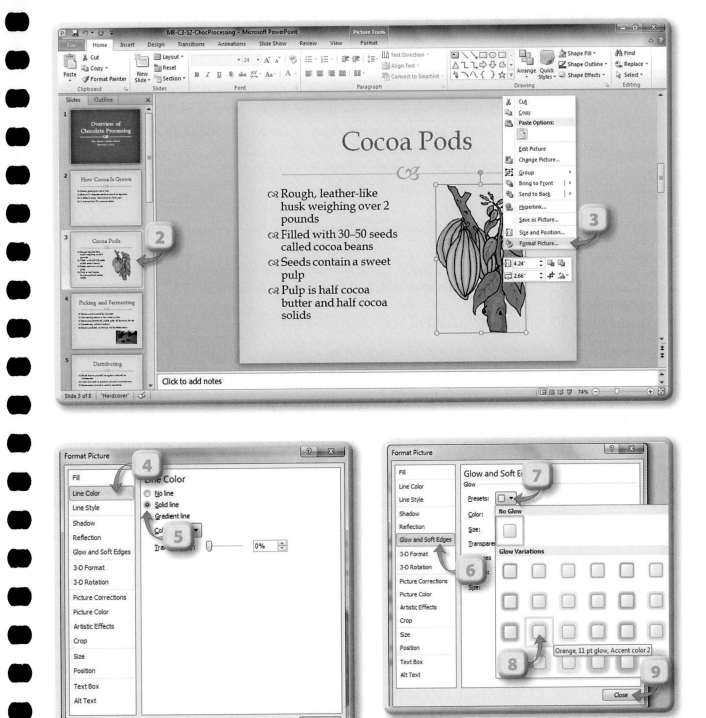

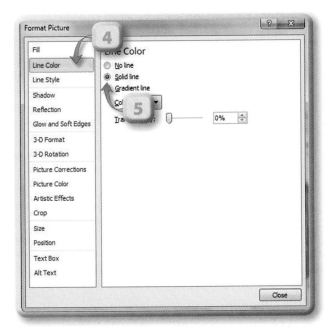

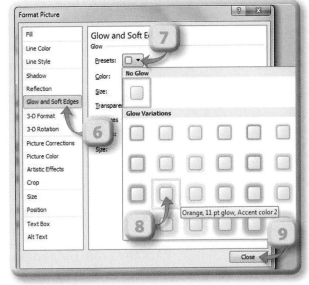

Taking It Further

Arranging Objects   If you place more than one image on a slide, you can arrange objects so that one appears to be in the front with the others tucked beneath. To create this effect, select one of the images to make it active, which displays the Picture Tools Format tab. In the Arrange group, use the *Bring Forward* and *Send Backward* options to change an object's position relative to the other images.

PowerPoint

PowerPoint

Add Transitions

Video M8_C3_S03

You can set up sounds to accompany transitions in your presentation. You can easily apply transition effects to a single slide, to multiple slides, or to all slides in a presentation. In addition, you can control the duration of the transition effect.

Steps

1 If it is not already open, open **M8-C3-S2-ChocProcessing.pptx**, the file you saved in the previous skill, and save the file as **M8-C3-S3-ChocProcessing**.

2 Click the Home tab.

3 Click Slide 1 the Slides/Outline pane to display it.

4 Click the Select button in the Editing group.

5 *Another Way*
Click Slide 1 in the Slides/Outline pane, press Shift, and then click the last slide.

5 Click *Select All* from the drop-down list. This action selects all of the slides in the Slides/Outline pane.

6 Click the Transitions tab.

7 In the Transition to This Slide group, click the Reveal button. A small transition icon (resembling a sliding star) appears below all slide numbers in the Slides/Outline pane, indicating that the transition is applied to each slide.

▶ *Tip* To view more effects in the Transitions to This Slide group, click the More button (marked by a down-pointing arrow with a dash above it and located at the right of the transitions options row).

8 Save the file.

9 Click the Slide Show tab.

10 Click the From Beginning button in the Start Slide Show group.

11 Navigate through the slide show to view the transition effects you applied. Click your mouse once at the end of the slide show to return to the Normal view.

Taking It Further

Removing Transitions Using too many transitions in a single presentation can be distracting for your audience. If you decide that you have too many transitions, you can remove one. Click the slide or slides where the transition is applied and click the Transitions tab. In the Transition to This Slide group, click the None button in the transitions gallery.

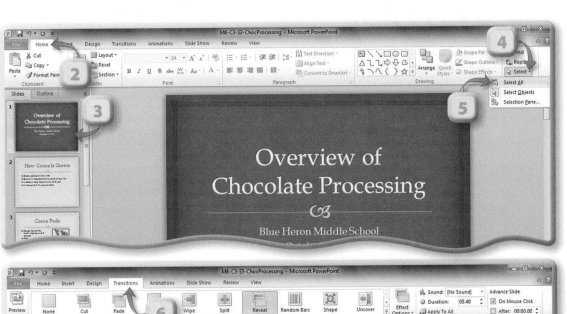

Reveal transition applied to all of the slides in this file.

Completed Skill 3 (All Slides)

PowerPoint

PowerPoint

Chapter 3

Skill 4

Add Sound

Video M8_C3_S04

Transitions can be accompanied by sounds. You may successfully use a carefully chosen sound for one or two transitions within the presentation. For example, if you displayed great sales numbers for the quarter, you might add the brief sound of applause, or if you display a slide containing a photo, you might add the camera click sound. But be careful that you do not overuse sounds. Playing a sound for every transition can annoy your audience and detract from your message. Use sounds rarely and strictly for emphasis or fun.

Steps

1. If it is not already open, open **M8-C3-S3-ChocProcessing.pptx**, the file you saved in the previous skill, and save the file as **M8-C3-S4-ChocProcessing**.

2. In the Slides/Outline pane, select the last slide in the presentation.

3. Click the Transitions tab.

4. In the Timing group, click the down arrow next to the *Sound* field to display a menu of sounds.

▶**Tip** Hover your mouse pointer over a sound option to preview the sound.

5. Click *Applause* in the drop-down list to apply this sound to the selected slide. Now, when the last slide appears during a slide show, this sound plays.

6 *Another Way*
Click in the *Duration* text box and type 3.00.

6. Click the down arrow next to the *Duration* field twice to change the time to *03.00*.

7. Save the file.

8. Preview the applied sound and animation for Slide 8 by clicking the Slide Show view button at the bottom of the screen.

9. After previewing the slide, press Escape to return to the Normal view.

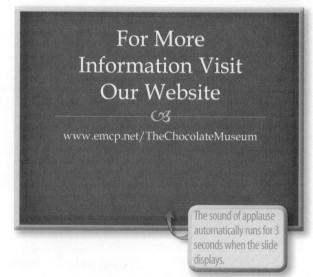

For More Information Visit Our Website

☙

www.emcp.net/TheChocolateMuseum

The sound of applause automatically runs for 3 seconds when the slide displays.

Completed Skill 4 (Slide 8)

570 Module 8 PowerPoint

Taking It Further

Using Your Own Audio in a Presentation
You can use any audio file that you have created or downloaded in your PowerPoint presentation. Simply click the Insert tab and click the Audio button. Browse to locate the audio file on your computer or storage medium and insert it. A small speaker icon appears on your slide with a play button during the slide show. Click the Play button to play the audio.

PowerPoint

Skill 5   Add Animations

Video   M8_C3_S05

Whereas transitions apply effects when a slide appears, animations apply effects to how the content on each slide appears. For example, you can have a heading zoom in or a picture fade in. You can use tools on the Animations tab or in the Animation pane to control what causes the effect to play—for example, when you click your mouse or when another animation starts. Animations can be applied to text or image objects.

Steps

1   If it is not already open, open **M8-C3-S4-ChocProcessing.pptx**, the file you saved in the previous skill, and save the file as **M8-C3-S5-ChocProcessing**.

2   Click Slide 1 in the Slides/Outline pane.

3   In Slide 1 in the Slide pane, click anywhere in the title placeholder.

4   Click the Animations tab.

5   In the Animation group, click the *Float In* option to apply the animation to the title. A *1* appears on the slide next to the title.

6   On Slide 1, click anywhere in the subtitle placeholder.

7   Click the Add Animation button in the Advanced Animation group.

8   In the *Entrance* section of the drop-down gallery, click *Random Bars*. A *2* appears next to the first line of the subtitle and a *3* appears next to the second line of the subtitle.

▶ **Tip** In a content placeholder with multiple entries of text, each bullet point is animated separately and in number order.

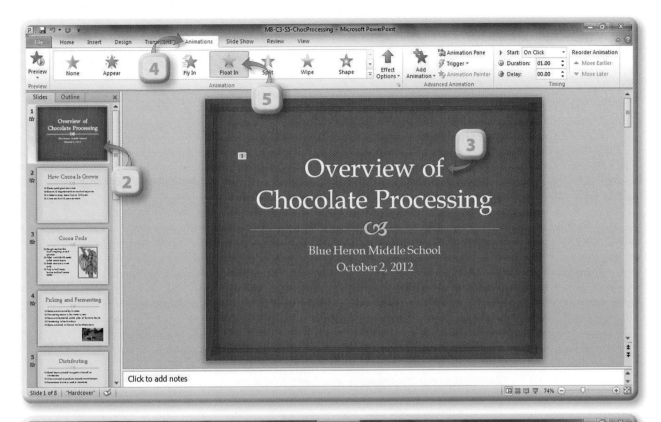

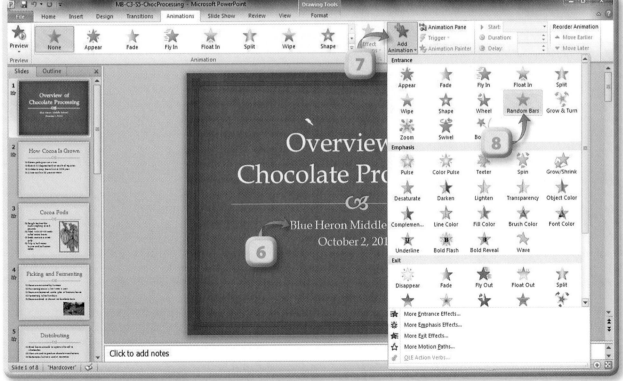

PowerPoint

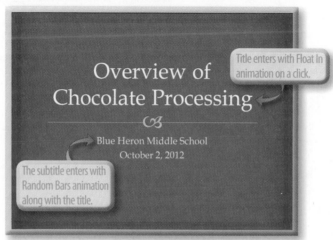
▶ **Tip** Items that are animated are numbered in order in the Animations pane. You can reorder the animations by selecting an animation and clicking the Reorder button in the Animation pane.

10 *Another Way*
Click the Preview button in the Animations tab.

9 Click the Animation Pane button in the Advanced Animation group to open the Animation pane.

10 Click the Play button to preview the animations applied to the current slide.

11 Click the arrow at the right of *Subtitle 2* in the Animation pane.

12 Click *Start With Previous* from the drop-down menu. This causes the animation of the subtitle to begin when the animation of the title begins.

13 Click the Play button in the Animation pane to preview timing.

14 Close the Animation pane.

15 Save the file.

Overview of
Chocolate Processing
ℭ

Title enters with Float In animation on a click.

Blue Heron Middle School
October 2, 2012

The subtitle enters with Random Bars animation along with the title.

Completed Skill 5 (Slide 1)

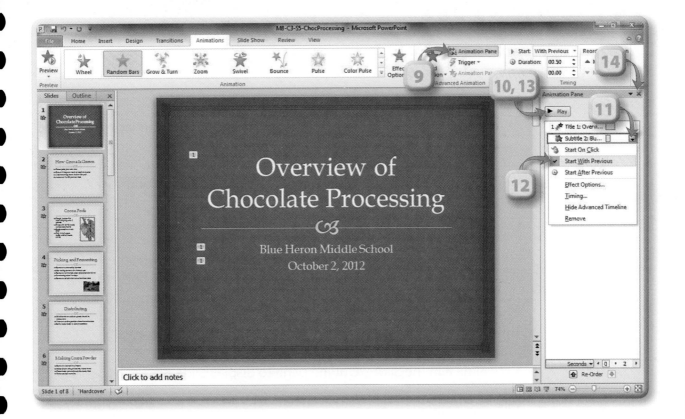

Taking It Further

More Animation Effects   If you don't like any of the effects shown in the Animation gallery, be sure to explore the options at the bottom of the expanded gallery. These offer additional entrance, emphasis, and exit effects, as well as motion paths. Motion path animations move the entire object along a path on your slide, such as around a circle or six-pointed star.

PowerPoint

PowerPoint

Chapter 3

Skill 6 | Choose Animation Effects

Video ▶ M8_C3_S06

You can refine animation styles in a variety of ways. For example, if you animate text so that it flies in, you can also choose the direction from which it enters. The ways in which you can refine an animation style depend on the style you choose. In this skill, you experiment with adding and refining a couple of animation styles.

Steps

1. If it is not already open, open **M8-C3-S5-ChocProcessing.pptx**, the file you saved in the previous skill, and save the file as **Lastname-M8-C3-S6-ChocProcessing**, but replace *Lastname* with your last name. Be sure to save the file in your Module 8 working folder on your storage medium.

2. Click Slide 8 in the Slides/Outline pane to display Slide 8.

3. Click the Animations tab.

4. Click the subtitle placeholder.

5. Click the *Float In* effect in the Animation group.

6. Click the Effect Options button in the Animation group.

7. Click *Float Down* in the *Direction* section.

8. Click the Preview button to view the Float Down animation.

9. Click the website address and then click the *Shape* option in the Animation group to apply a different animation style to the website address.

10. Click the Effect Options button.

▶ Tip Note that each effect you choose offers appropriate options for that effect.

11. Click *Out* in the *Direction* section.

12. Click the Preview button to view the animation in Slide 8.

13. Save and close the file.

For More Information Visit Our Website

ℭ

www.emcp.net/TheChocolateMuseum

The website address is animated to appear using the Shape animation and grows from the center out.

Completed Skill 6

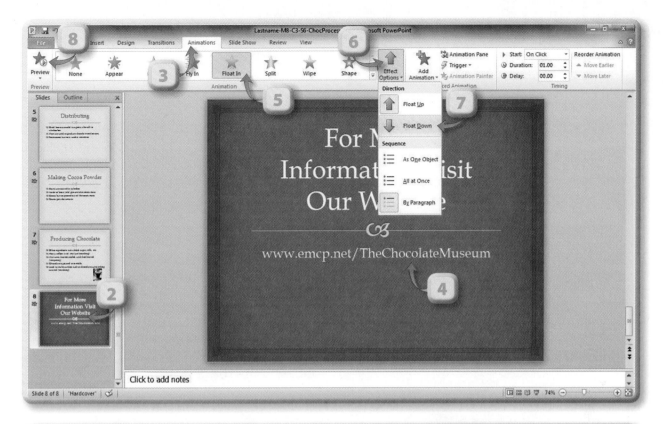

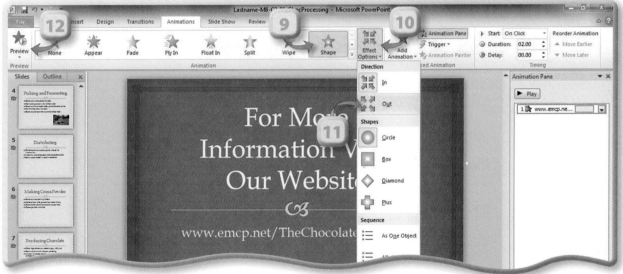

Taking It Further

Timing Animations You can change the timing of animations with the *Duration* and *Delay* fields in the Timing group in the Animations tab. Select an object with animation applied and use the *Duration* field to set the length of time the animation should play. Use the *Delay* field to set the length of delay between two animations.

While Skills 5 and 6 applied animation features to slides with the Title layout, you can also try applying animation to other slide layout types. You can animate the bullet points in your presentation by, for example, having them fade in or out or slide into place.

Tasks Summary

Task	Ribbon Tab, Group	Button, Option
Display Clip Art task pane	Insert, Images	
Insert a picture	Insert, Images	
Format a picture	Picture Tools, Format, Picture Styles	
Arrange objects	Picture Tools, Format, Arrange	
Apply a transition	Transitions, Transition to This Slide	
Add a sound	Transitions, Timing	
Set sound duration	Transitions, Timing	
Apply an animation	Animations, Animation	
Display Animation pane	Animations, Advanced Animation	
Choose animation effects	Animations, Animation	
Preview Animations	Animations, Preview	

Features Review

Select the best answer from the choices given.

1 To insert an object on a slide you can click icons in the
   a. content placeholder.
   b. Insert tab.
   c. Clip Art task pane.
   d. All of the above

2 To narrow results in clip art searches to only certain types of graphics, you can change the selection in the
   a. content placeholder.
   b. *Results should be* option in the Clip Art task pane.
   c. *Search for* option in the Clip Art task pane.
   d. *Include Office.com content* option.

3 To insert a picture that is located on a disc,
   a. click the Clip Art button in a content placeholder.
   b. click the Insert tab and then click the Clip Art button.
   c. click the Insert tab and then click the Picture button.
   d. None of the above

4 Formatting effects you can apply to pictures include
   a. borders.
   b. adjusting picture brightness.
   c. modifying picture colors.
   d. All of the above

5 One button you use to arrange objects on your slide is
   a. Group.
   b. Bring Forward.
   c. Picture Effects.
   d. Text Direction.

6 To enhance your slide presentation you should
   a. set the text color the same as the background color so the text is easy to read.
   b. add simple transitions and animations to help keep the audience engaged.
   c. add sounds that play repeatedly to every slide to be sure everyone is listening when you present.
   d. All of the above

7 Transitions are effects that occur
   a. when you move from one slide to another.
   b. when you click an animation button.
   c. when you display bullet points on a slide.
   d. if you play several animations on one slide.

8 Sounds can accompany
   a. animations.
   b. transitions.
   c. title slides.
   d. All of the above

9 Animations affect
   a. what appears when you move from one slide to another.
   b. transition sounds.
   c. how the content of each slide appears.
   d. videos inserted into your presentation.

10 You select animation effects to apply to objects on your slide using the
   a. Transitions gallery.
   b. Design gallery.
   c. Animations gallery.
   d. Effects Options button.

Hands-On Skills Review

Exercise **Promote the Music Industry**

Skills   Add notes, apply a theme, add a footer in the Slide Master, add transitions, add animations, and choose animation effects

Scenario   Format a presentation about a possible career in the music industry. The final presentation should be enhanced with appropriate transitions and animation effects.

Steps

1 Open the student data file named **M8-C3-ExA-MusicIndustry.pptx** and save the file as **Lastname-M8-C3-ExA-MusicIndustry.pptx**, but replace *Lastname* with your last name.

2 Enter your name and the current date on two separate lines in the subtitle placeholder of Slide 1.

3 Use the Header and Footer dialog box to insert a footer containing the current date, the slide number, and *The Music Industry* on all slides except the title slide.

4 Apply the Pushpin theme to all slides.

5 Animate the arrow shapes on Slide 6 (*Job Outlook*) as follows:
   a. To the arrow that points up apply the Wipe animation with the *From Bottom* effect option. Using the Animation Pane, set the transition to *Start After Previous*.

   b. To the arrow that points down apply the Wipe animation with the *From Top* effect option. Using the Animation Pane, set the transition to *Start After Previous*.

6 Insert animations that *Start With Previous* on all images as follows:
   a. Slide 2: Zoom, Effect Options: Object Center
   b. Slide 3: Fade
   c. Slide 4: Shape, Effect Options: Direction = In, Shape = Plus
   d. Slide 7: Teeter
   e. Slide 8: Grow/Shrink, Effect Options: Direction = Both, Amount = Larger

7 Add transitions as follows:
   a. Slide 1: Split, Effect Options: Vertical Out
   b. Slides 2–8: Push, Effect Options: From Right

8 Type the following speaker notes for Slide 2. Format the notes as a bulleted list.

- Musicians play musical instruments independently or in a group like a rock band, jazz band, or an orchestra.
- Singers may sing the part of a character, as in a musical.
- Directors and conductors lead instrumental and vocal groups.
- Composers create original music.
- Arrangers adapt existing music for use by specific performing groups.
- Repairers and tuners keep instruments in working order.

9 Save the presentation.

10 Preview the presentation.

11 Submit the completed presentation to your instructor.

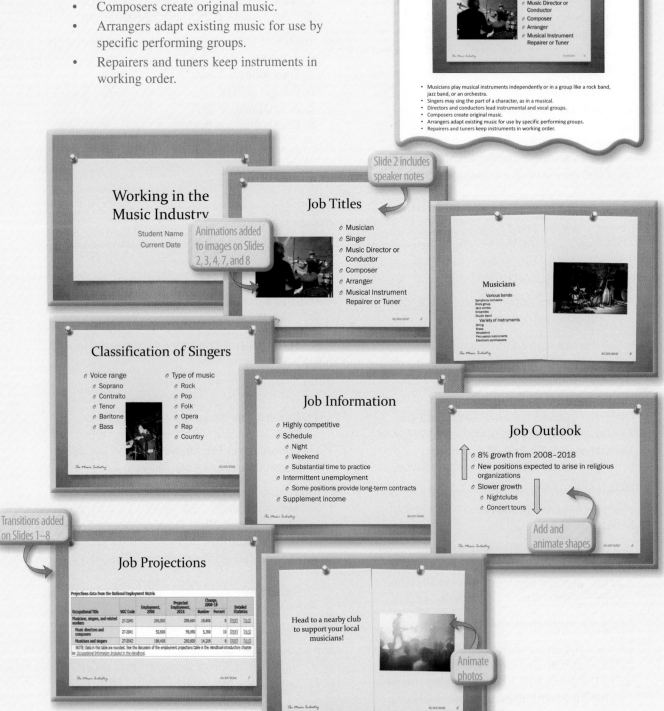

Completed Exercise A

Exercise B Enhance a Car Racing Presentation

Skills Insert a graphic in Slide Master view, add a footer in the Slide Master, hide a Slide Master element on a slide, insert an object on a slide, format a picture, add transitions, and add sound

Scenario Add interest to a presentation about race cars by adding images, a sound, and transitions.

Steps

1 Open the student data file named **M8-C3-ExB-CarRacing.pptx** and save the file as **Lastname-M8-C3-ExB-CarRacings**, but replace *Lastname* with your last name.

2 Enter your name and the current date on two separate lines in the subtitle placeholder of Slide 1.

3 Make the following modifications to the Slide Master:

   a. Insert the image of the race car from **M8-C3-ExB-RaceCar1.jpg**. The image should appear on all slides, regardless of the slide layout. Place the image of the race car in the lower right corner and size it as shown in the final presentation. **HINT:** *Use the Office Theme Slide Master layout (the top layout choice).*

   b. Add a footer to all slides that displays the date, *Car Racing*, and the slide number. Do not show the footer on the title slide.

4 Hide the **M8-C3-ExB-RaceCar1.jpg** image on Slide 6 and insert **M8-C3-ExB-RaceCar2.jpg** in the content placeholder on the right side.

5 Add Transitions:
   a. Slide 2: Doors
   b. Slides 3–5: Zoom
   c. Slide 6: Clock
   d. Slide 7: Vortex

6 Apply the camera sound to Slide 6.

7 Save the presentation.

8 Preview the presentation.

9 Submit the completed presentation to your instructor.

Completed Exercise B

Exercise C How I Found the Perfect Gift

Skills   Apply a theme, add a footer in the Slide Master, insert an object on a slide, format a picture, add transitions, add animations, choose animation effects, and add sounds

Scenario   You decide to tell your friends the story of your search for a perfect gift. Because you plan to show this presentation to your friends, you experiment to select some fun sounds and transitions, even though the combination you select might be considered "too much" for a business presentation.

Steps

1 Open the student data file named **M8-C3-ExC-BirthdayGift.pptx** and save the file as **Lastname-M8-C3-ExC-Perfume**, but replace *Lastname* with your last name.

2 Enter your name and the current date on two separate lines in the subtitle placeholder of Slide 1.

3 Using the Slide Master, insert the footer *Jane's Birthday Present* on all slides except the title slide.

4 Insert a clip art object on Slide 3 (*Idea*) that looks similar to the clip art on the final presentation. Position the clip art so it is approximately the same size and in the same location shown. **HINT:** *Search the clip art gallery for* cartoon idea.

5 On Slide 6 (*Perfect*) insert the picture of the sale bag, using the student data file named **M8-C3-ExC-Sale.jpg**, in the right column content placeholder.

6 Change the theme to Concourse for all slides.

7 Add transitions to slides as follows:
   a. Slide 1: Ripple
   b. Slide 7: Vortex

8 Add sounds that play during slide transitions as follows:
   a. Slide 2: Cash register
   b. Slide 3: Drum roll
   c. Slide 5: Wind
   d. Slide 7: Applause

9 Add animations to Slide 4 (*Look for the Perfect Scent*).
   a. Perfume bottle on left – Fly In animation and *From Left* effect option
   b. Perfume bottle on right – Fly In animation and *From Right* effect option
   c. Set the animations to *Start After Previous*.

10 Save the presentation.

11 Preview the presentation.

12 Submit the completed presentation to your instructor.

Completed Exercise C

Completing, Running, and Sharing Your Show

When you finish the contents of your presentation, you are not quite done. You should always perform a final spelling check to make sure that no embarrassing errors lurk in your text. You also have to specify settings for how your slide show should run. The settings control how your show moves forward from slide to slide, either manually with a click or key press, or automatically using recorded slide timings. You can also set up a show to loop continuously so that it plays over and over again.

You might want to print a copy of your slides for your own reference, print handouts for your audience, or print speaker notes that you would use while presenting or for studying the topic later. You can also use the powerful tools in PowerPoint to broadcast your presentation online where it can be viewed by others as you navigate through the slides.

Skills You Learn

1 Check spelling
2 Run a show
3 Rehearse timings
4 Set up the show
5 Print presentation notes
6 Broadcast a presentation to the Web

Files You Need

In this chapter, you use the following student data file.

M8-C4-S1-ChocolateInMovies.pptx

What You Create

A fun new exhibit is opening at the Museum. It focuses on the role of chocolate in the world of entertainment: movies, TV shows, and songs. You have been asked to create a short, self-running slide show highlighting the uses of chocolate in movies. The presentation is a teaser to encourage Museum visitors to step into the exhibit. Visitors can run the show at a kiosk set up in the lobby, so you need to prepare a few things ahead of time. You specify the slide show's playback settings, and set timings for how long each slide is displayed.

In this chapter, you master all of these tasks, print a copy of the presentation for the exhibit director, and broadcast the presentation online.

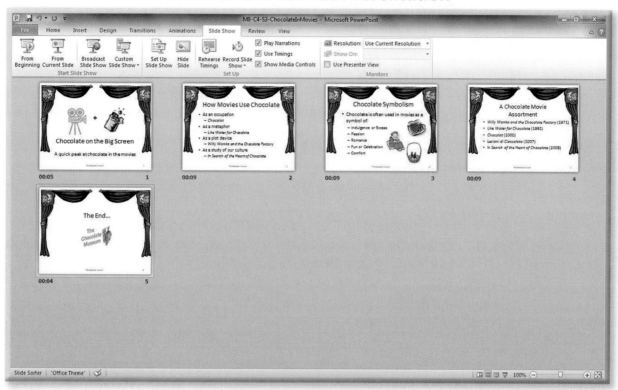

PowerPoint

Skill 1 | Check Spelling

Video M8_C4_S01

It is very important that your spelling be correct so your audience takes your message seriously. PowerPoint's built-in spelling check feature handles most of this for you, but you need to make a few decisions along the way.

Steps

1. Open the student data file named **M8-C4-S1-ChocolateInMovies.pptx** and, if you have not already done so, save the file in your Module 8 working folder on your storage medium.

2. Click the Review tab.

③ **Shortcut**
Spelling Check
F7

▶**Tip** If you are certain that a word only appears once, it is okay to click Ignore. But if it is possible that a word appears more than once, choose Ignore All.

3. Click the Spelling button in the Proofing group. This opens the Spelling dialog box.

4. In the Spelling dialog box, note the word *Chocolat* in the *Not in Dictionary* text box. Click the Ignore All button so PowerPoint doesn't flag any more instances of this correctly spelled French word.

5. When *metafor* appears in the *Not in Dictionary* text box, click the Change button to correct the spelling of the word to *metaphor*.

6. When *Wonka* appears in the *Not in Dictionary* text box, click the Ignore All button.

7. When *Lezioni* appears in the *Not in Dictionary* text box, click the Ignore button.

8. When *Cioccolato* appears in the *Not in Dictionary* text box, click the Ignore button.

9. When the message appears saying the spelling check is complete, click OK.

10. Save the file.

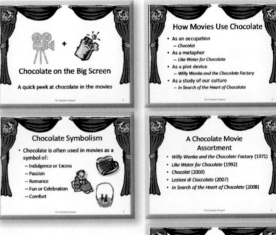

Completed Skill 1

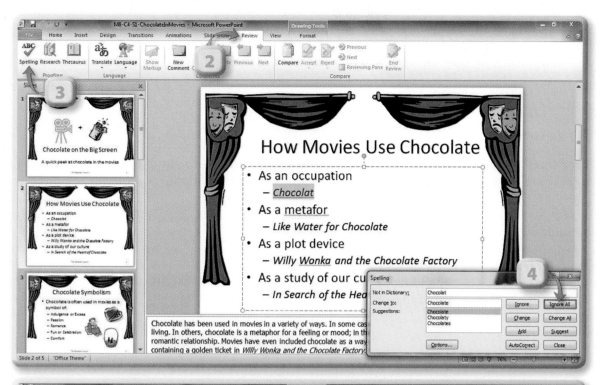

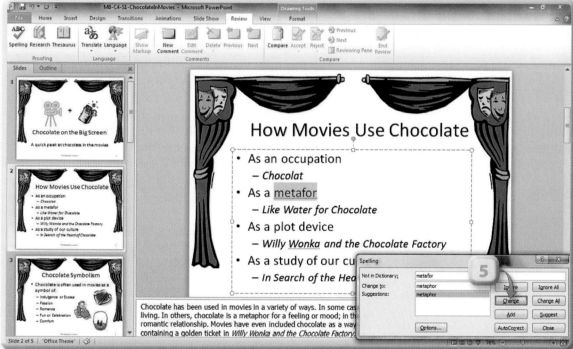

Taking It Further

Add Words to the Spelling Check Dictionary Any word not found in the dictionary is questioned during the spelling check. If you often use a word that the spelling check questions, such as your company name or your last name, you can add that word to the spelling check dictionary. Just click the Add button when that word is questioned as you run the spelling check. Once you add a word to the dictionary, it no longer appears in the *Not in Dictionary* text box.

PowerPoint

Skill 2 Run a Show

 Video M8_C4_S02

You run a slide show by switching to Slide Show view. The tools available in that view help you to navigate through your slides. Depending on whether you have set up a show to advance manually or automatically, running a show works differently. In this skill, you work with a show set up to advance manually.

Steps

1 If it is not already open, open **M8-C4-S1-ChocolateInMovies.pptx**, the file you saved in the previous skill. You will not be making changes to this file in this skill.

2 Click the Slide Show tab.

3 Click the From Beginning button to display the slide show from the first slide.

4 Press the right arrow key one time to proceed from Slide 1 (*Chocolate on the Big Screen*) to Slide 2 (*How Movies Use Chocolate*).

5 Press the left arrow key one time to move from Slide 2 back to Slide 1 (*Chocolate on the Big Screen*).

6 Click your mouse to move from Slide 1 to Slide 2 (*How Movies Use Chocolate*).

7 Press the spacebar one time to move from Slide 2 to Slide 3 (*Chocolate Symbolism*).

8 Press the Backspace key one time to move from Slide 3 to Slide 2 (*How Movies Use Chocolate*).

9 Right-click the mouse, click *Go to Slide* in the pop-up menu, and then click *4 A Chocolate Movie Assortment.* This takes you to Slide 4.

Tip If you are using an LCD display or television to show your presentation, check the device's user manual to make sure you set up the display equipment properly.

4 *Shortcut*
Next Slide
N

5 *Shortcut*
Previous Slide
P

7 *Another Way*
Advance one slide by clicking the Page Down button.

8 *Another Way*
Go back one slide by clicking the Page Up button.

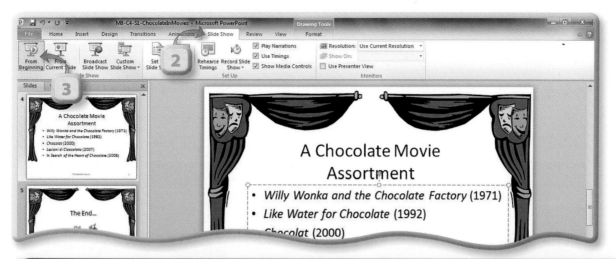

More

PowerPoint

10 Click the left arrow button in the Slide Show toolbar on the bottom-left corner of the screen to navigate from Slide 4 to Slide 3 (*Chocolate Symbolism*).

11 *Shortcut*
End Show
Esc

11 Right-click the current slide and click *End Show* in the pop-up menu. This returns you to the Normal view.

Taking It Further

Highlighting Slides During a Show   When running a slide show manually, a presenter can use the digital pen or a highlighter to draw viewers' attention to specific items on a slide. Access these tools from the Slide Show toolbar in the bottom-left corner of the slide. Click the Pen button and then click *Pen* in the pop-up menu to turn the mouse pointer into a small circle. Using the mouse, draw a circle around a key word on the slide. Erase the markings you made on the slide by clicking the Pen button and then clicking the *Erase All Ink on Slide* option. Note that you cannot access the Slide Show toolbar when you set up your show to run automatically.

PowerPoint

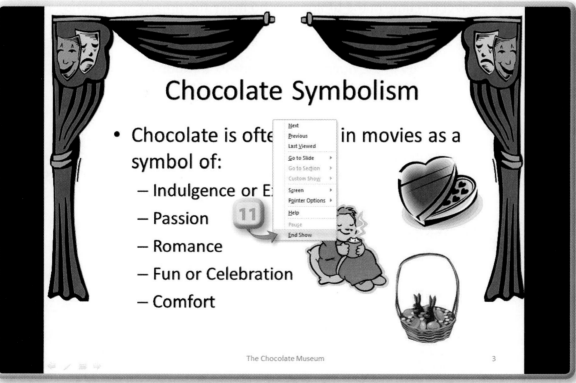

PowerPoint

Skill 3

Video ▶ M8_C4_S03

Rehearse Timings

If no speaker will be present to run the show, you need to record timings for how long each slide should display before advancing to the next slide. PowerPoint uses those timings to automatically advance the show. In this skill, you learn how to rehearse and save timings and you are given specific timings to use for each slide. In Skill 4 you make settings for your show to advance automatically.

Steps

1. If it is not already open, open **M8-C4-S1-ChocolateInMovies.pptx**, the file you saved in Skill 1, and save the file as **M8-C4-S3-ChocolateInMovies**.

2. Click the Slide Show tab.

3. Click the Rehearse Timings button in the Set Up group. Read the slide while the timer runs. Note how long it takes to read the slide content by noting the time in the Recording dialog box.

4 *Another Way*
You can allow the timer to run and then press Enter when you wish to stop the timer.

▶**Tip** The idea is to provide an appropriate amount of time for the slide to display, depending on the amount of information on the slide.

▶**Tip** If you are not happy with the timings you recorded, choose No in Step 7 so they are not saved.

4. Select the time in the timing box (to make the timer stop running), type 0:00:05, and then press Enter.

5. Type 0:00:09 in the timing box for Slides 2 through 4.

6. Type 0:00:04 in the timing box for Slide 5.

7. At the warning box indicating that the total time was 0:00:36, click Yes. This opens the presentation in Slide Sorter view. You can see the assigned times for each slide in the presentation.

8. Save the file.

Taking It Further

Recording a Narration   If you wish, you can record a narration to play along with your slide show. When you record a narration, you can save timings that match the length of each slide's narration. Use the Record Slide Show button in the Set Up group on the Slide Show tab to record a narration, such as the one contained in the Notes area of the movie slide show.

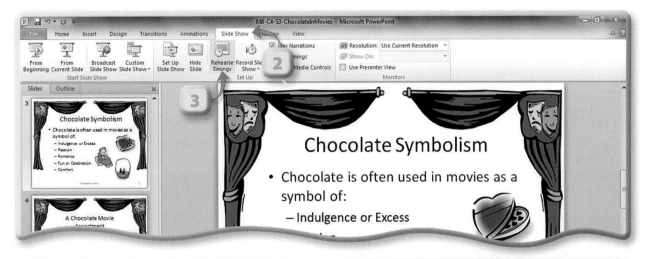

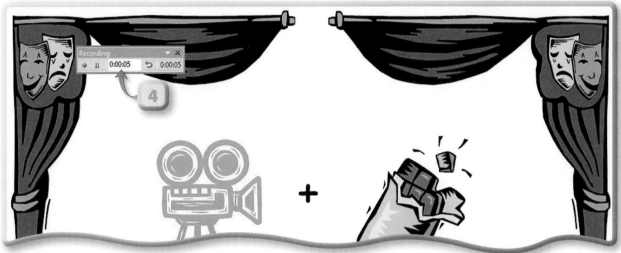

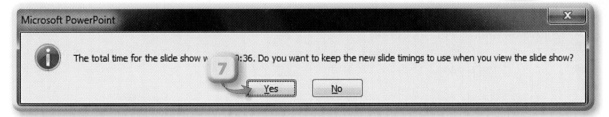

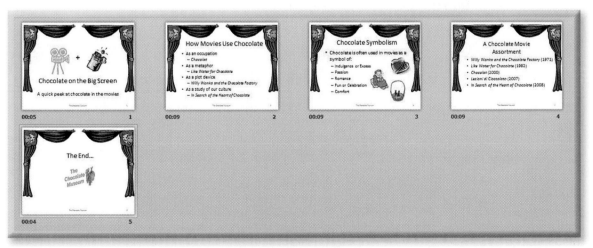

Completed Skill 3

PowerPoint

PowerPoint

Skill 4 — Set Up the Show

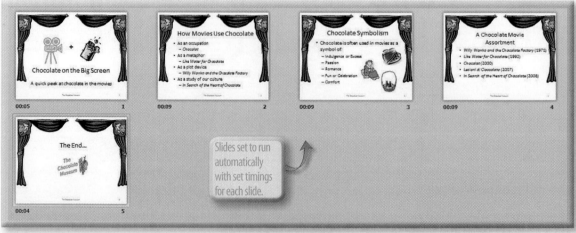

Video M8_C4_S04

The show type determines how a show is played back. There are three playback options. One option is to have the presentation given by a live speaker. With this choice, the speaker provides information and would typically forward each slide when he or she is ready to go to the next topic. Another option is to allow the show to be run by a viewer using onscreen controls. The final option is to have the show run on its own, continuously looping through the slide series over and over again. When you set up a show to run on its own, the timings you save determine when the show moves from one slide to another.

Steps

1. If it is not already open, open **M8-C4-S3-ChocolateInMovies.pptx**, the file you saved in the previous skill, and save the file as **M8-C4-S4-ChocolateInMovies**.

2. Click the Slide Show tab.

3. Click the Set Up Slide Show button in the Set Up group.

4. Click the *Browsed at a kiosk (full screen)* option in the *Show type* section.

Tip When you select the *Browsed at a kiosk (full screen)* setting, viewers cannot control the show.

5. Confirm that the *Using timings, if present* option is selected in the *Advance slides* section.

6. Click OK.

7. Save the file.

8 Shortcut
Run Show
F5

8. Run the show. Press Escape to close it when it's done.

Slides set to run automatically with set timings for each slide.

Completed Skill 4

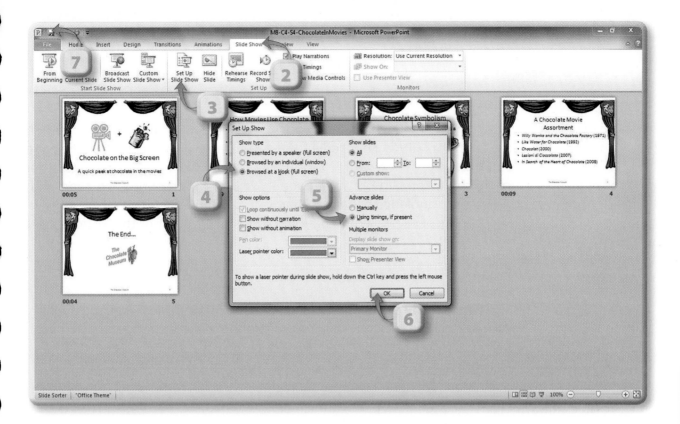

Taking It Further

Creating a Custom Show Creating a custom show allows you to select only certain slides from those in a larger presentation. For example, if you have a large presentation about student government, you might want to create a shorter version of only those slides specifically about school administration. To create a custom show, first click the Slide Show tab, click the Custom Slide Show button in the Start Slide Show group, and then click *Custom Shows* from the drop-down list to open the Custom Show dialog box. Click the New button to open the

Define Custom Show dialog box. Name the custom slide show by typing the name in the *Slide show name* text box. Choose a slide you wish to include in your show by clicking the slide number on the left. Click the Add button to move that slide to the *Slides in custom show* list. When you have added all the slides you want to include in your custom show, click OK and then click Close. Your custom show will then be available as a *Custom show* selection in the Set Up Show dialog box. Access that box by clicking the Set Up Slide Show button in the Set Up group.

PowerPoint

PowerPoint

Video ▶ M8_C4_S05

Print Presentation Notes

When you have finalized your presentation and checked your spelling, you may want to print copies of it. You can print full-page slides, print audience handouts that include any of several combinations of single or multiple slides oriented horizontally or vertically on the page (as you did in Module 8, Chapter 2, Skill 5), or print each slide with its accompanying speaker notes. In this skill, you print the Notes pages.

Steps

1 If it is not already open, open **M8-C4-S4-ChocolateInMovies.pptx**, the file you saved in the previous skill. You will not be making changes to this file.

2 Click the File tab.

3 Shortcut
Print Menu
Ctrl + P

3 Click the Print tab.

4 In the Settings category, click the *Full Page Slides* option.

5 In the *Print Layout* section of the drop-down list, click *Notes Pages*.

6 Click the Print button if your instructor would like a printout. The six slides in the presentation print as Notes pages on your default printer.

▶**Tip** If you want to print a subset of slides, click the first setting (by default, *Print All Slides*) and choose to print the currently active slide or click *Custom Range* and enter a range of slides to print.

▶**Tip** In the *Print Layout* section, you have two other options: *Full Page Slides* or *Outline*. The default option is *Full Page Slides*.

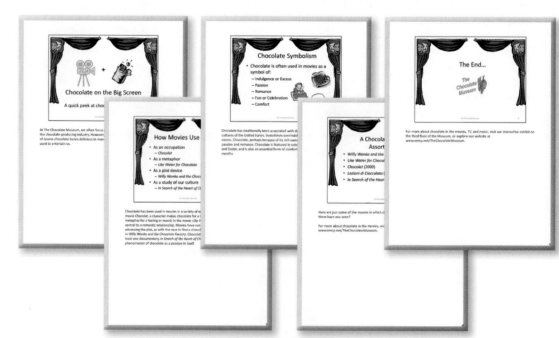

Completed Skill 5

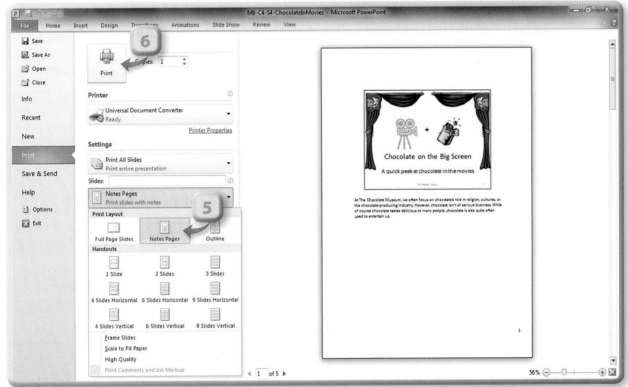

Taking It Further

Advanced Print Settings There are a few more settings you can select to affect how your document prints. You can choose to collate copies, so that multiple copies print as sets (rather than printing three page 1s in a stack, three page 2s in a stack, and so on).

You can also choose to print in color or on both sides of the paper (which may require that you turn over the paper in your printer after printing the first side). All these options are available in the Print menu.

PowerPoint

PowerPoint

Skill 6

Broadcast a Presentation to the Web

Video M8_C4_S06

PowerPoint provides a powerful feature for broadcasting your presentation online in real time. Broadcasting is completely free and uses the PowerPoint Broadcast Service, so you don't even need your own website to broadcast. However, you are required to first have a Windows Live account, which is also free and is easy to set up by visiting www.WindowsLive.com.

Steps

1 If it is not already open, open **M8-C4-S4-ChocolateInMovies.pptx**, the file you saved in Skill 4, and save the file as **Lastname-M8-C4-S6-ChocolateInMovies**, but replace *Lastname* with your last name. Be sure to save the file in your Module 8 working folder on your storage medium.

2 Click the File tab.

3 Click the Save & Send tab.

4 Click *Broadcast Slide Show* in the Save & Send category.

5 Click the *Broadcast Slide Show* option in the Broadcast Slide Show category.

6 In the Broadcast Slide Show dialog box, click the Start Broadcast button.

Tip If you do not have a Windows Live ID, click the Get a .NET Passport hyperlink to sign up.

7 Enter your email address and password in the text boxes provided in the Connecting to pptbroadcast.officeapps.live.com dialog box.

8 Click OK.

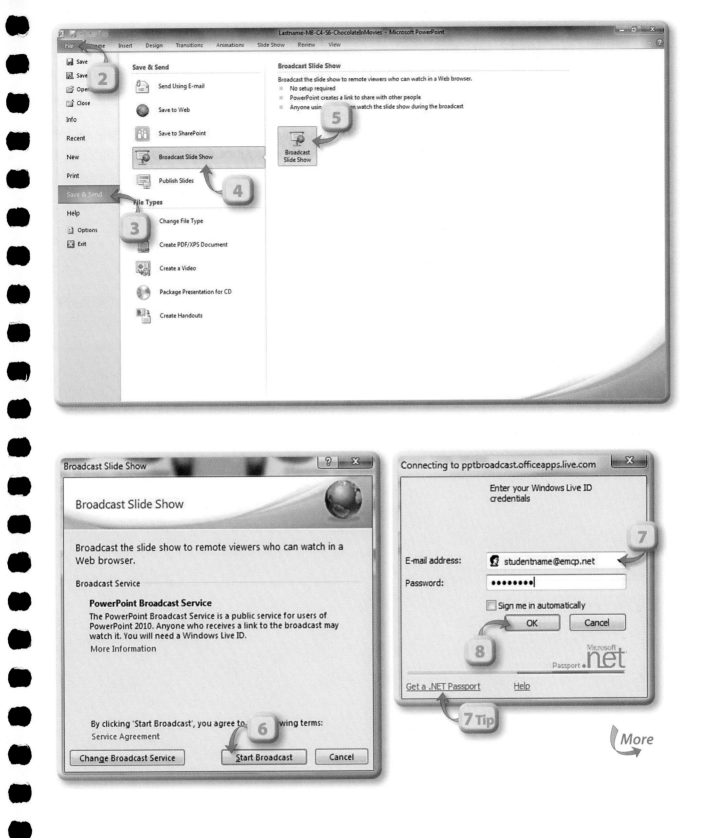

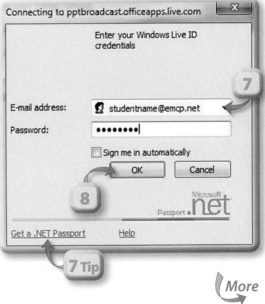

More

9 In the Broadcast Slide Show dialog box, click *Send in Email* and send the link to yourself.

10 Click the Start Slide Show button to begin the live presentation. Individuals who have followed the hyperlink provided in Step 9 can watch the presentation as you run it. The slides advance automatically according to the timings set in the slide show. The show continues to loop from Slide 6 back to Slide 1.

11 Press Esc when you are done watching the slide show.

12 Click the End Broadcast button.

13 At the warning box indicating that all remote viewers will be disconnected if you continue, click End Broadcast.

14 Close the file.

PowerPoint

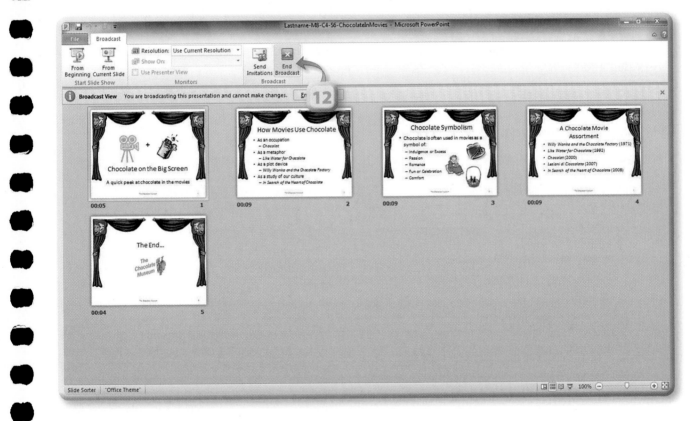

Taking It Further

Save a Presentation to the Web Using Sky Drive You can also save a presentation to the Web by clicking the File tab, clicking the Save & Send tab, and then clicking the *Save to Web* option in the Save & Send category.

Use the Windows Live account login and password you used in Skill 6. You can set the file to be shared and share the Windows Live SkyDrive link with others.

PowerPoint

Tasks Summary

Task	Ribbon Tab, Group	Button, Option	Shortcut, Alternative
Check spelling	Review, Proofing	ABC	F7
Set show type	Slide Show, Set Up		
Set how slides advance	Slide Show, Set Up		
Print a presentation	File, Print		Ctrl + P
Rehearse timings	Slide Show, Set Up		
Run a show	Slide Show, Start Slide Show		F5
Broadcast a presentation	File	Save & Send, *Broadcast Slide Show*	

Features Review

Select the best answer from the choices given.

1 If you want the spelling check feature to leave all instances of a spelling alone, choose this while running the spelling check:
   a. Ignore
   b. Ignore All
   c. Change All
   d. None of the above

2 The spelling check feature is based on
   a. an online dictionary.
   b. your past spelling choices.
   c. a built-in dictionary.
   d. Wikipedia.

3 Before you give an in-person presentation to a large group, you must
   a. obtain a copyright for the materials.
   b. connect display equipment to your computer.
   c. save a backup copy.
   d. add timings.

4 One way to manually advance from one slide to the next is to
   a. click your left mouse button.
   b. press Backspace.
   c. press Escape.
   d. All of the above

5 Pressing the P key while running a slide show
   a. ends the show.
   b. takes you to the next slide.
   c. takes you to the previous slide.
   d. restarts the show.

6 If you want your slide presentation to run continuously at a professional trade show, you must
   a. rehearse your presentation timings in advance.
   b. uncheck *Use timings if present*.
   c. log in to your Windows Live account.
   d. create a custom show.

7 The Slide Show type option that is typically used to advance manually from slide to slide is
   a. *Browsed by an individual (window)*.
   b. *Browsed at a kiosk (full screen)*.
   c. *Presented by a speaker (full screen)*.
   d. *Loop continuously until 'Esc'*.

8 In PowerPoint you can print
   a. full page slides.
   b. handouts.
   c. notes.
   d. All of the above

9 When you choose to print handouts, you can set
   a. how many slides to print on each page.
   b. whether to include icons for sounds.
   c. whether to include images on the printout.
   d. All of the above

10 Before you print a presentation, you should
   a. run the spelling check.
   b. change the design.
   c. back up the file.
   d. record a narration.

Hands-On Skills Review

Exercise **Complete an Animal Shelter Presentation**

Skills   Add a footer in a Slide Master, check spelling, and run a show

Scenario You are completing a presentation about pet adoption. As one of the final steps in your
          preparation, review the content for spelling errors.

Steps

1 Open the student data file named **M8-C4-ExA-Pets.pptx** and save the file as **Lastname-M8-C4-ExA-Pets**, but replace *Lastname* with your last name.

2 Enter your name and the current date in the subtitle placeholder on two separate lines on the title slide (Slide 1). If necessary, move an image so your entire name and the date are visible.

3 Use the Header and Footer dialog box to insert a footer on all of the slides, displaying *Helping Shelters* and the slide number. Do not show the footer on the title slide.

4 Check the spelling of the slide content and correct any errors you find. Check your corrections aginst the Completed Excercise A slides shown below.

5 Save the file.

6 Preview the presentation.

7 Submit the completed presentation to your instructor.

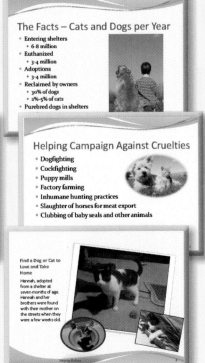

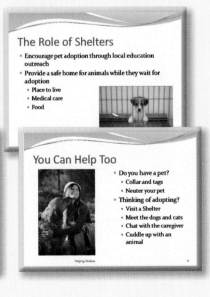

Completed Exercise A

Exercise B Print Animal Shelter Presentation Handouts and Notes Pages

Skills Add a header in the Handout Master and print a handout

Scenario You are preparing to deliver your presentation about pet adoption. Print handouts for the audience and print notes pages that you can use as a guide while presenting.

Steps

1 Open **Lastname-M8-C4-ExA-Pets.pptx**, the file you saved in the previous exercise, and save the file as **Lastname-M8-C4-ExB-Pets**, but replace *Lastname* with your last name.

2 Add a header and a footer to the notes and handouts pages. Insert your name and the date in the header and the page number in the footer.

3 Save the file.

4 Print one set of handouts of all of the slides in the presentation using three slides per page. **HINT:** *Select* 3 Slides *under* Handouts *in the Print menu.*

5 Print one set of the notes pages of all of the slides in the presentation to use as talking points during delivery of the presentation.

6 Submit both sets of printouts to your instructor.

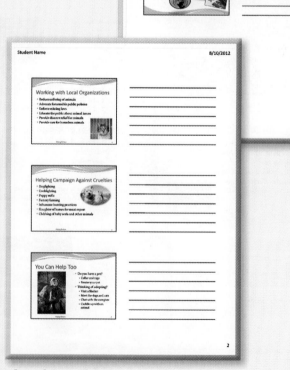

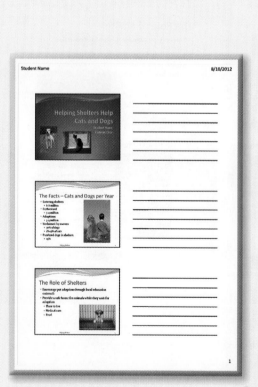

Completed Exercise B

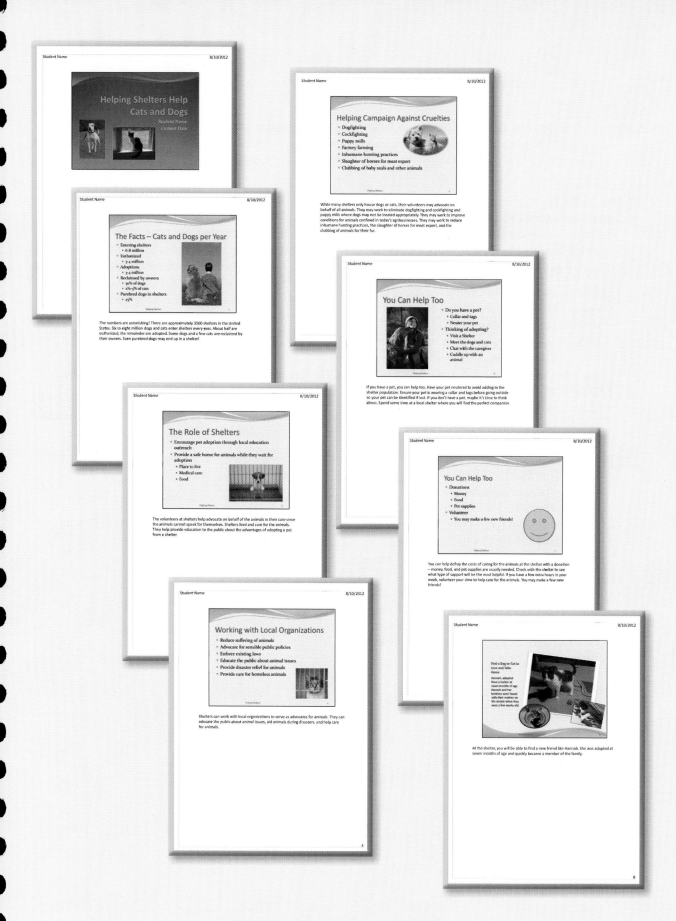

Completed Exercise B (continued)

Exercise C Broadcast an Animal Shelter Presentation

Skills Set up the show, rehearse timings, run a show, and broadcast a presentation to the Web
Extension activity: Record a narration and timings

Scenario Your presentation was popular and the audience enjoyed hearing about pets and adoption. A local shelter has asked if they can have a copy of the presentation to share with visitors. You decide to set timings so the slide show progresses without a speaker present.

Steps

1 Open **Lastname-M8-C4-ExB-Pets.pptx**, the file you saved in the previous exercise, and save the file as **Lastname-M8-C4-ExC-Pets**, but replace *Lastname* with your last name.

2 Complete one of the following:
   a. Set the timings for the slides in the presentation as follows:

Slide 1	*Helping Shelters Help Cats and Dogs*	0:00:03
Slide 2	*The Facts*	0:00:08
Slide 3	*The Role of Shelters*	0:00:07
Slide 4	*Working with Local Organizations*	0:00:07
Slide 5	*Helping Campaign Against Cruelties*	0:00:08
Slide 6	*You Can Help Too*	0:00:09
Slide 7	*You Can Help Too*	0:00:07
Slide 8	*Find a Dog or Cat*	0:00:15

   b. Add customized timings to all slides in the presentation using the Rehearse Timings button on the Slide Show tab. ***HINT:*** *It is difficult to determine how long each slide should appear. To achieve realistic timings, read every line on the slide slowly, as if you are seeing it for the first time, spend a moment looking at each of the images on the slide, and then move to the next slide.*

   c. ***Extension activity:*** Record a narration of the slide's notes and set the timing to match the length of the narration. ***HINT:*** *Review the Taking It Further: Recording a Narration in Skill 3. Find a quiet place to record the narration. Ask for a microphone if necessary. Speak slowly and give the viewer enough time to look at the slide images before moving to the next slide.*

3 Set up the slide show to play automatically.

4 If possible, broadcast the slide show to Windows Live. If a Windows Live account is not available, broadcast the slide show using the email selection.

5 Save the file.

6 Preview the presentation.

7 Submit the completed presentation to your instructor.

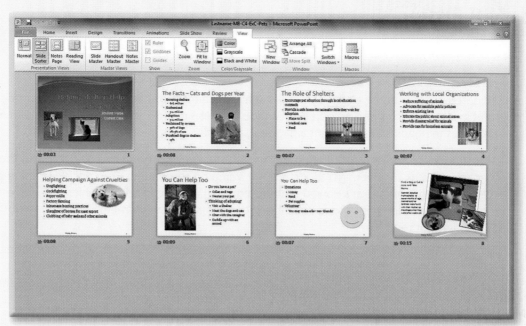

Completed Exercise C

Module 8 Projects

Project 1

Skills Add notes, apply a theme, change the color scheme, change formatting in Slide Master, add a footer in Slide Master, insert an object on a slide, format a picture, add transitions, run a show, add a header in the Handout Master, print a handout, and print presentation notes

Scenario You just returned from a great trip to New York City, where you visited many attractions. The school glee club is considering a trip to NYC for a singing competition. You decide to share your experience with them using a PowerPoint presentation. Be sure to add graphics and interest to the presentation and then print handouts, three slides per page, so club members can take notes while you discuss your trip.

Steps

1 Open the student data file named **M8-EOM-P1-NYC.pptx**, and save the file as **Lastname-M8-EOM-P1-NYC**, but replace *Lastname* with your last name.

2 Add four pictures to the slides as described below, using the image files provided:
   a. Add **M8-EOM-P1-img1.jpg** to the left content area of the Statue of Liberty slide (Slide 3).
   b. Add **M8-EOM-P1-img2.jpg** to the right content area of the Empire State Building slide (Slide 4).
   c. Add **M8-EOM-P1-img3.jpg** to the Central Park slide (Slide 5). Place the image in the lower-right corner of the content area and size the image to fit just under the text as shown in the Completed Project 1 image.
   d. Add **M8-EOM-P1-img4.jpg** to the content area of the final slide (Slide 6).

3 Center the caption "Lady Liberty" on Slide 3, just above the picture.

4 Open the Slide Master and change the font for the title on all slides to Broadway. **HINT:** *Select the top slide in the Slides pane and click in the title placeholder before changing the font.*

5 To all slides, add a footer that displays the current date on the left, *New York City* in the center, and the slide number on the right.

6 Add a header and a footer to Notes and Handouts pages. Enter your name and the date in the header. Enter *New York City* and the page number in the footer.

7 In Normal view, apply the Hardcover theme to Slide 6 and change the color to *Black Tie*.

8 Apply the Technic theme to Slide 1.

9 Apply the Checkerboard transition with the *From Left* effect option to Slide 2.

10 Apply the Blinds transition with the *Vertical* effect option to Slide 6.

11 Enter these speaker notes for Slide 2:

There is a lot to see and do when you visit NYC. Spend some time visiting the landmark buildings. Sit and relax in Central Park. See world-famous museums. Take in a Broadway show. The list is practically endless. A few landmarks are highlighted in this presentation.

12 Print handouts for your audience, three per page. **HINT:** *Select 3 Slides under Handouts from the Print menu.*

13 Print the Notes page for Slide 2.

14 Save the file.

15 Preview the presentation.

16 Submit the completed file, the handouts, and the Notes page to your instructor.

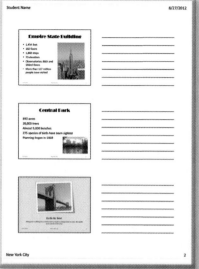

Completed Project 1

Project ②

Skills   Apply a theme, change formatting in Slide Master, add transitions, add animations, choose animation effects, run a show, and broadcast a presentation to the Web

Scenario   Your neighbor's son is learning arithmetic and needs some help. Create an arithmetic flash card tutorial using PowerPoint. Make it interesting and fun as well as educational so that he practices often.

Steps

1 Open the student data file named **M8-EOM-P2-FlashCards.pptx**, and save the file as **Lastname-M8-EOM-P2-FlashCards.pptx**, but replace *Lastname* with your last name.

2 Enter your name and the current date in the subtitle placeholder on two separate lines.

3 Display Slide Master view and click the Comparison layout.

4 Modify the Comparison layout by performing steps *a* through *d* (listed below) for both content placeholders. You can do so either by selecting the content placeholders in both the left and right columns of the slide and performing the steps just once or by selecting the content placeholders one at a time and performing steps *a* through *d* for each column separately. **HINT:** *To highlight both content placeholders, click one and then hold down the Shift key while you click the other, add then*

release the Shift key. This selects both content placeholders. Do not click anywhere else in the slide.

   a. Turn off bullets. **HINT:** *Home tab, Paragraph group, Bullets.*
   b. Center the text.
   c. Vertically center the text. **HINT:** *Home tab, Align Text button in the Paragraph group, Middle.*
   d. Change the font size to 40.

5 Select the caption placeholders above both the left and right columns of the slide. You can perform steps *a* and *b* (listed below) twice, once for each caption placeholder or, if you wish to perform the steps only once, click one placeholder, hold down the Shift key while you click the other, and then release the Shift key.
   a. Center the text.
   b. Change the text to All Caps. **HINT:** *Home tab, Font group dialog box launcher.*

6 Click the caption and content placeholders in the left column using Click, Shift + Click and then make the following changes:
   a. Set the shape outline to *Black, Text 1*.
   b. Set the shape fill to *Dark Blue, Text 2, Lighter 60%*.

7 Select the caption and content placeholders in the right column using Click, Shift + Click and make the following changes:
   a. Set the shape outline to *Black, Text 1*.
   b. Set the shape fill to *Olive Green, Accent 3, Darker 25%*.

8 Return to Normal view.

9 Add the Smiley Face shape to the final slide (Slide 7) and size and place the shape according to the location shown in the Completed Project 2 image. Fill the shape using *Red, Text 2*, and set the shape outline to *Indigo, Text 1*.

10 Add Transitions as follows:
   a. Slide 1: transition, *Fade*; effect option, *Smoothly*
   b. Slides 2–6: transition, *Push*; effect option, *From Right*
   c. Slide 7: transition, *Shape*; effect option, *Circle*

11 Add Animations as follows:
   a. Open Slide Master view.
   b. Select the Comparison layout. **HINT:** *This is the same layout that you modified in the first few steps of this assignment.*
   c. Select the caption and content text box in the right column using Click, Shift + Click.
   d. Apply the Appear animation and the *As One Object* effect option.
   e. Return to Normal view.

12 Apply the Clarity theme to the title slide and the final slide (Slides 1 and 7).

13 If possible, broadcast the slide show. If a Windows Live account is not available, broadcast the slide show using the email selection.

14 Save the file.

15 Preview the presentation.

16 Submit the completed file to your instructor.

Completed Project 2

Project 3

Skills Open PowerPoint and insert a slide, enter text on slides, apply a layout, add notes, apply a theme, change formatting in Slide Master view, add a footer in a Slide Master, insert an object on a slide, format a picture, add transitions, add sound, add animations, choose animation effects, check spelling, set up the show, rehearse timings (or *Extension activity: Record a narration and timings*), and run a show

Scenario Create an engaging and informative presentation about your home—real or imaginary. The presentation should provide detail about the place where you live or where you wish you lived.

Steps

1 Create a new PowerPoint file and save the file as **Lastname-M8-EOM-P3-Home.pptx**, but replace *Lastname* with your last name.

2 Create the presentation and include the following:
- At least five but not more than eight slides
- At least three slides should contain images from the Web, clip art, or your own photos. Include the source of each image in the Notes section of the slide it appears on.
- Title Slide layout used on Slide 1; two additional layouts used on other slides
- One or more design themes
- At least two different transitions should be applied to two or more slides
- One appropriate sound should play during a transition
- Animations of the images and/or text on two or more slides
- A footer that appears on all slides except the title slide and includes the date, your name, and the slide number
- A modification to the title font made on the Master Slide that affects all slides
- Speaker notes that can be used to deliver the presentation
- Timings that are appropriate for individuals viewing the slide show without a speaker (or *Extension activity: Narration and timings added*)

3 Ensure your slides are set to advance using the timings you have added.

4 Check your spelling on both the slides and in the notes.

5 Ask your instructor how you are to share the presentation: broadcast, email, or deliver in class. If you are to deliver the presentation in class, make any required adjustments so the slides advance manually.

6 Save the file.

7 Preview the presentation.

8 Submit the completed file to your instructor.

MODULE 9

Integrating Word, Excel, Access, and PowerPoint

Skills You Learn

1 Export a Word outline to PowerPoint
2 Insert an Excel chart in Word
3 Base an Access database on Excel data

Files You Need

In this module, you need the following student data files.

S1-BusinessPlan.docx

S2-Letter.docx

S2-Chart.xlsx

S3-Inventory.xlsx

S3-Chocolate.accdb

What You Create

In this module, you export a Word outline of a business plan into PowerPoint to create a new presentation. You then enhance a business letter by inserting an Excel chart into a Word document. You also copy Excel data into an Access table.

Business Plan Presentation

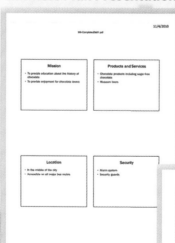

Fundraising Totals Letter

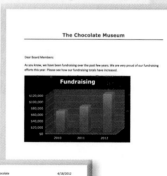

Chocolate Inventory Database

Before beginning the module skills, copy the Module9-Integrating folder from the Student Resources CD to your storage medium. The copied folder will become the working folder for this module.

Guidelines for Integrating

A key advantage in using the Office 2010 suite is that you can integrate data between the application programs. *Integrating* means that you bring together two or more different application files. First you create a document or file in the Office application that best suits the data. That application is called the *source* program. Then you copy or export that file or its data to one of the other applications, called the *destination* program. For example, if you needed to create an inventory chart, you would use Excel as shown in the screen at the right.

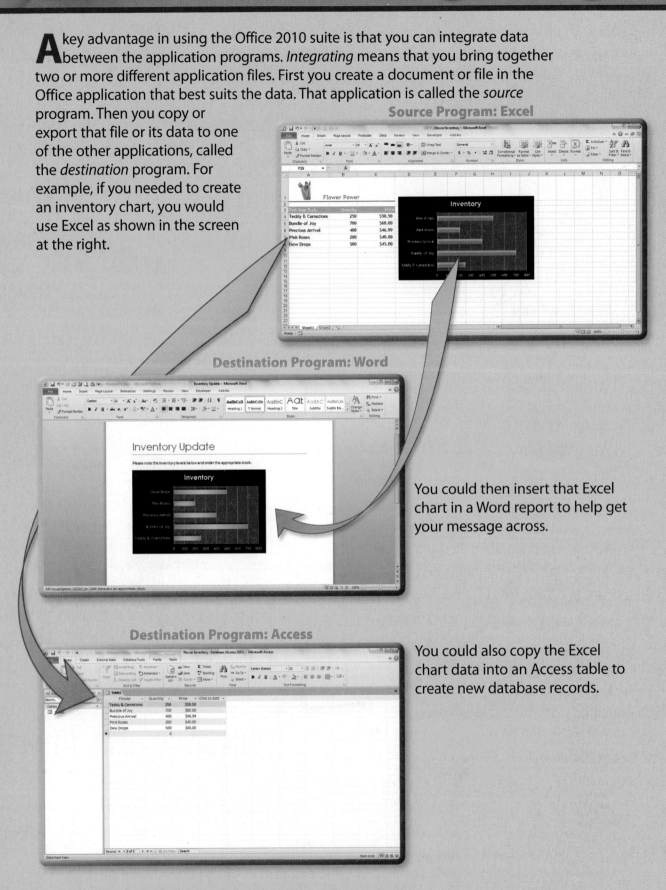

Source Program: Excel

Destination Program: Word

You could then insert that Excel chart in a Word report to help get your message across.

Destination Program: Access

You could also copy the Excel chart data into an Access table to create new database records.

Content between Programs

As another example, if you need to create a PowerPoint presentation and you already have the information for the slide show typed as an outline in a Word document, you don't need to retype the text into PowerPoint. Instead, you simply export, or copy, the Word outline into a blank PowerPoint presentation as shown below.

Source Program: Word

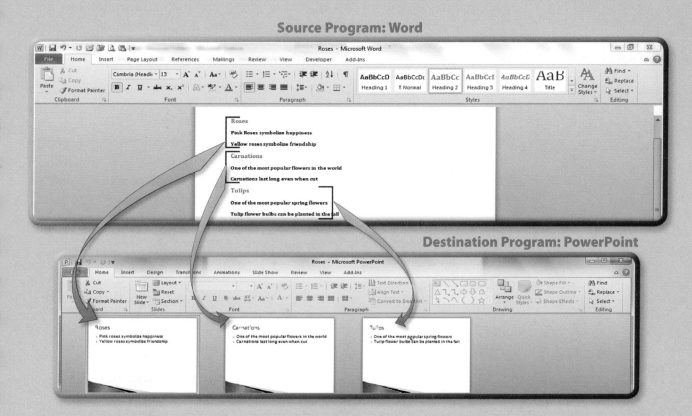

Destination Program: PowerPoint

When you integrate data or objects from one application into another, you can choose between two methods: 1) copying and pasting or 2) embedding or linking the data or object. Copying and pasting works well for single-use situations, such as the above example of copying the Word outline into PowerPoint. However, embedding or linking works well for situations in which you might continue to use the source and destination files separately as well as together.

Embedding and linking are notably different. When you *embed* an object, such as an Excel chart in a Word document, the chart becomes a separate object in the Word document. Any changes you make to the chart in the source Excel workbook will not affect the embedded chart in the Word document.

In contrast, if you *link* the chart, it then resides, or has its home, in the Excel workbook. Then, even though you can see that linked chart in the Word document, that chart is not a separate object. Because it is a linked object, when you change the chart in the Excel workbook, it will automatically be updated in the Word document. The embed option and the link option both have an advantage over copying and pasting, because you can edit an embedded or a linked object using the tools of the source program.

Integrating Word, Excel, Access, and PowerPoint

Module 9

Skill 1

Video M9_C0_S01

Export a Word Outline to PowerPoint

Some people prefer to plan their PowerPoint presentations by creating an outline in Word and then exporting that content to PowerPoint to work on slide design. PowerPoint creates new slides based on the heading styles that you used in the Word outline. PowerPoint creates slide titles from text that you formatted with the Heading 1 style. Paragraphs you formatted in the Heading 2 style become the first-level bulleted text. Paragraphs you formatted in the Heading 3 style become the second-level bulleted text, and so on.

Steps

1 Open the student data file named **M9-S1-BusinessPlan.docx**. This Word document has been formatted with the Heading 1 and Heading 2 styles.

2 Click the Customize Quick Access Toolbar button.

3 Click *More Commands* at the drop-down list.

4 Click the *Choose commands from* list box arrow.

5 Click *All Commands*.

▶**Tip** The commands are listed in alphabetical order.

6 Scroll through the list box and then double-click *Send to Microsoft PowerPoint*.

6 *Another Way*
Click the command and then click the Add button.

7 Click OK.

8 Click the Send to Microsoft PowerPoint button in the Quick Access toolbar. PowerPoint opens and the presentation displays on the screen.

▶**Tip** You are saving the file in PowerPoint and the file has a *.pptx* extension, even though you initially opened the file in Word, with a *.docx* extension.

9 Save the PowerPoint presentation as **Lastname-M9-S1-BusinessPlan**, but replace *Lastname* with your last name. Save the file in your Module 9 working folder on your storage medium.

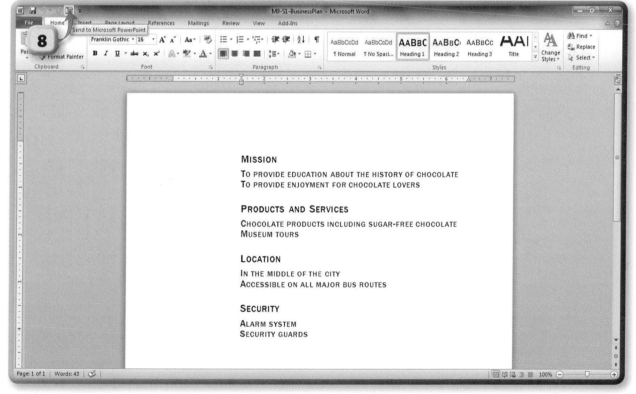

More

Integrating

10 Close PowerPoint.

11 In the Word window, right-click the Send to Microsoft PowerPoint button on the Quick Access toolbar.

12 Click *Remove from Quick Access Toolbar.*

13 Close Word without saving the document.

Taking It Further

Exporting a PowerPoint Presentation to Word You can also export a PowerPoint presentation to Word. You may want to do this so that you can use Word's features to customize your handout formatting. Another reason might be to use the contents of your presentation as the basis for a report or other document. To send presentation data to Word, click the File tab, click the Save & Send tab, click *Create Handouts,* and then click the Create Handouts button. In the Send To Microsoft Word dialog box that displays, click a layout option and then click OK.

Mission

- To provide education about the history of chocolate
- To provide enjoyment for chocolate lovers

Products and Services

- Chocolate products including sugar-free chocolate
- Museum tours

Completed Skill 1, Slides 1 and 2

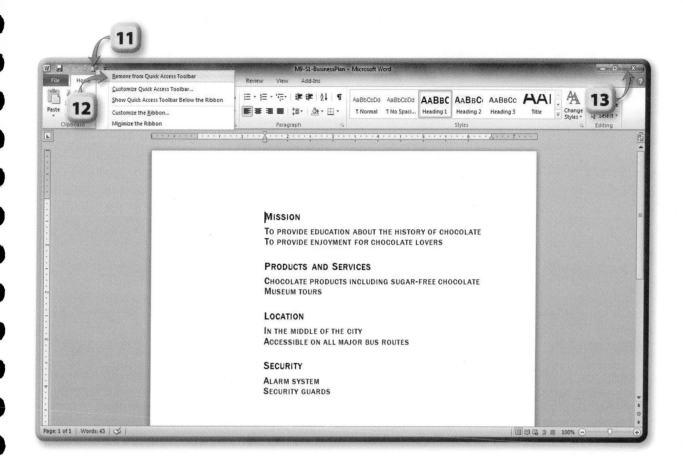

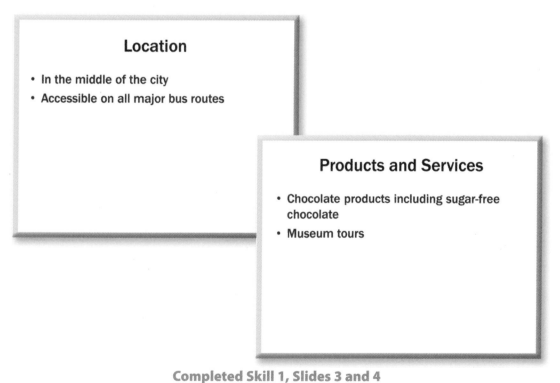

Completed Skill 1, Slides 3 and 4

Integrating

Module 9

Skill 2

Insert an Excel Chart in Word

Video M9_C0_S02

You can copy an Excel chart to a Word document. When you do so, you have the option to link the chart. When you link the chart, you will be able to edit the object in Excel (called the *source program*) even though the chart is in a Word document. Another advantage is that if you change the chart in Excel, the chart will also be updated in Word (called the *destination program*) if the destination file is open on the same computer when the source file is edited. Thus, you will always have an up-to-date chart.

Steps

1 Open the student data file named **M9-S2-Letter.docx** and save the file as **Lastname-M9-S2-Letter**, but replace *Lastname* with your last name. Be sure to save the file in your Module 9 working folder on your storage medium.

2 Press Ctrl + End to move the insertion point to the end of the document.

3 Open the student data file named **M9-S2-Chart.xlsx** and, if you have not already done so, save the file to your Module 9 working folder.

4 Click a blank area of the chart to select it.

5 Shortcut
Copy
Ctrl + C

5 Click the Copy button in the Clipboard group on the Home tab.

6 Click the Word button on the Taskbar.

▶ Tip You can see the linked object (chart) in the Word document but the object itself is located in its original Excel file.

7 Click the Paste button arrow in the Clipboard group on the Home tab.

▶ Tip Click Use Destination Theme & Link Data to link the chart and change the chart formatting to match the formatting in the document.

8 Click the Keep Source Formatting & Link Data button (the fourth button under *Paste Options*).

9 Save the Word document.

10 Close Word and Excel.

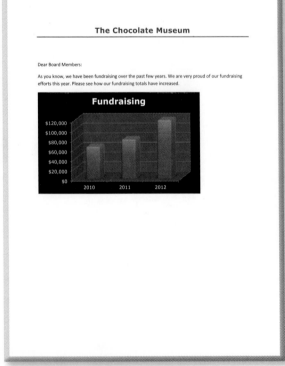

Completed Skill 2

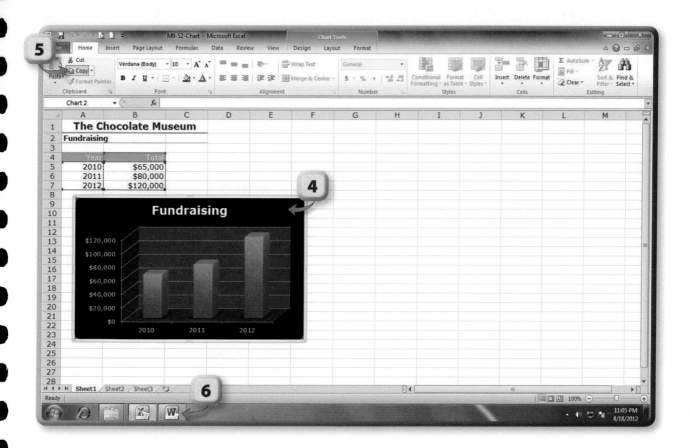

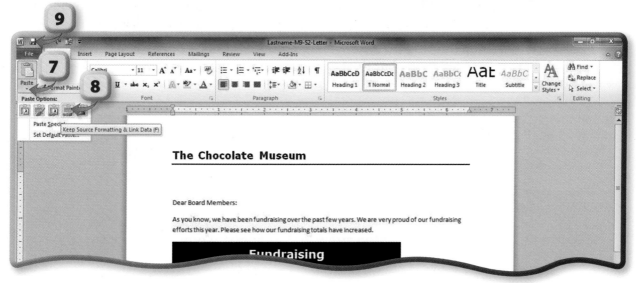

Taking It Further

Editing and Formatting a Linked Chart in Word In Word, click a linked chart to display the Chart Tools Design, Layout, and Format tabs. You can use options on these tabs to format and edit the linked chart without having to leave Word. For example, to change the chart style, click the Chart Tools Design tab and then select a chart style from the Chart Styles gallery. The Chart Tools Layout tab includes options for adding chart titles and data labels. This tab also includes options for changing shape styles and WordArt styles.

Integrating Word, Excel, Access, and PowerPoint

Module 9

Skill 3

Video ▶ M9_C0_S03

Base an Access Database on Excel Data

Add new records to an Access database by directly typing them in or by copying the information from a Word or Excel file. In this skill, you learn to add records to an Access database by copying them from an existing Excel file. Copying existing data can help you avoid mistakes that can sometimes occur when retyping data.

Steps

> **Tip** Be sure to open the database file from your working folder on your storage medium, not directly from the Student Resources CD.

1 Open the student data file named **M9-S3-Chocolate.accdb** and save the file as **Lastname-M9-S3-Chocolate**, but replace *Lastname* with your last name. Be sure to save the file in your Module 9 working folder on your storage medium.

2 If a security warning appears immediately below the ribbon, click the Enable Content button.

3 Open the Chocolate table. The table currently does not contain any records.

4 Open the student data file named **M9-S3-Inventory.xlsx**. The worksheet provides an inventory of chocolate products.

5 Select cells A2:C12.

6 *Shortcut*
Copy
Ctrl + C

6 Click the Copy button in the Clipboard group on the Home tab.

7 Click the Access button on the Taskbar.

8 Click the Paste button arrow in the Clipboard group on the Home tab.

> **Tip** You select the *Paste Append* command because you are adding records to an existing table.

9 Click *Paste Append*.

10 At the warning box asking if you are sure you want to paste the 11 records, click Yes.

11 Print the Chocolate table or submit the Access file as directed by your instructor.

12 Close Access and Excel.

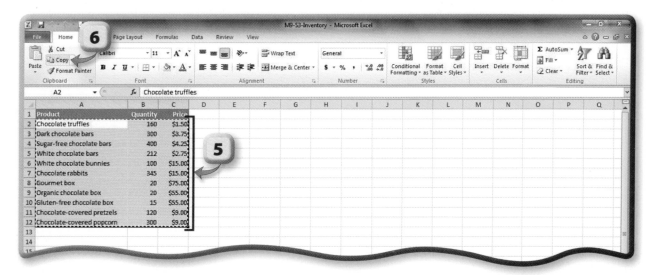

Completed Skill 3

Taking It Further

Importing Excel Data Another way to enter data into an Access table is to import the data from an existing Excel file. When you import data, the file is converted for use by the destination application. To import an Excel file, click the External Data tab in Access and then click the Excel button in the Import & Link group. You can then select the Excel file and specify other import options in the Import Spreadsheet Wizard dialog box.

Integrating

INDEX

AVERAGE function in, 362, 368, 370
COUNT function, 362, 368, 370
COUNTIF ( ) function in, 370
Lookup & Reference, 364
Math & Trig, 364
MAX function in, 362, 368, 370
MIN function in, 362, 368, 370
PMT() function in, 370
SUM function in, 362, 368, 370, 372
TODAY function in, 362, 370
general format in, 392
Go To dialog box, 320
Increase Font Size button, 398
Left Arrow, 326
Live Preview of changes in, 401
Merge & Center button in, 412
Move Chart dialog box, 424
Name box, 322
number entries, 326
    right alignment of, 326
number formats, 332
    accounting, 392
    applying, 392–397
Page Layout tab, 348
Page Setup dialog box, 348
pound sign display in, 402
printing in
    options for, 346–349
    worksheets, 382
reference data in, 373
Right Arrow, 326
rows in, 336
    deleting, 336–339
    inserting, 336–339
Spell Check, 334–335
text entries in, 326
    left alignment of, 326
    spell checking, 334
theme colors in, 401
theme effects in, 401
theme fonts in, 401
Undo button, 336
Up Arrow, 326
View tab in, 162
workbooks in, 316, 318
    cells in, 316
    copying data to another, 343
    creating, 316

worksheets in, 316, 318, 343
    adding headers and footers to, 349
    cells, 318
        active, 318
        range of, 318
    changing theme of, 401
    characters not allowed in name, 344
    color coding, 344
    column headings, 318
    creating new, 340–343
    designing, 415
        using rows and columns, 339
    enhancing readability, 412
    exploring, 325
    inserting and deleting columns and rows, 336–339
        naming and renaming, 344–345
        printing, 382
        row headings, 318
expansion slots, 43
exploded slice, 434
extracting, 464

F
Favorites Center, History tab in, 128
favorites in Internet Explorer, 130
    cleaning out, 132
file extensions
    displaying, 85
files, 75
    compressing and extracting, 84–85
    creating, 142–145
    deleting, 88–89
        multiple, 88
    downloading, 132
    names of, 75
    navigating within, 152–153
    opening and saving, 146–149
    printing, 168–171
    renaming, 82–83
        multiple, 83
    saving, in alternate formats, 148
    searching for, 86
    storage of, 75
filtering of data, 460–461, 491
find and replace, 154–157

Firefox, 174
firewall, 104
    reviewing settings, 104–105
F-1 key, 66
flash drives, 42
folders
    copying, 78–79
    creating, 80–81
    deleting, 88–89
    renaming, 82–83
Font color button, 166
font families, 218
font formatting, 68
footers, adding, to printed Web pages, 135
format, 166
Format button, 64
formatting, 70. See also specific programs
    font, 68
    tools for, 166–167
formulas. See under Excel 2010

G
gadgets, 110–111
GIF, 103
glass, 98
Google (www.google.com), 136, 137
Google docs, 291
grammar checking, 164–165
Grow Font button, 166

H
headers, adding, to printed Web pages, 135
Help window, 172–173
history, changing duration, 129
History Settings dialog box, 129
home pages, 60
    multiple, 126
    setting up, 126–127
Home tab, 166

I
icons
    in notification area, 57
    pinned, 56
Important updates section, 106
individual computing devices, 43